A History of Western Philosophy

The Twentieth Century to Quine and Derrida

Contents of *A History of Western Philosophy*

I. The Classical Mind, Second Edition

II. The Medieval Mind, Second Edition

III. Hobbes to Hume, Second Edition

IV. Kant and the Nineteenth Century, Second Edition, Revised

V. The Twentieth Century to Quine and Derrida, Third Edition

A History of Western Philosophy

The Twentieth Century to Quine and Derrida

THIRD EDITION

W. T. JONES
California Institute of Technology

ROBERT J. FOGELIN
Dartmouth College

Watkins College
of Art & Design

HARCOURT BRACE COLLEGE PUBLISHERS
Fort Worth • Philadelphia • San Diego • New York • Orlando • Austin • San Antonio
Toronto • Montreal • London • Sydney • Tokyo

Publisher	CHRISTOPHER P. KLEIN
Acquisitions Editor	DAVID TATOM
Developmental Editors	CLAIRE BRANTLEY, STEVE NORDER
Project Editor	AMY SCHMIDT
Production Manager	JANE TYNDALL PONCETI
Art Director	BURL SLOAN

ISBN: 0-15-500379-8

Library of Congress Catalog Card Number: 94-78916

Preface

Although this edition of the fifth volume of *A History of Western Philosophy* lists two authors, it remains both in content and in style predominantly the work of W. T. Jones. As second author, my charge was to extend the range of this work to include the writings of philosophers who came into prominence after World War II. To this end, I have added two chapters. Chapter 12 concerns ordinary-language philosophy and concentrates on the writings of J. L. Austin, P. F. Strawson, and Paul Grice. Chapter 13 examines the philosophy of W. V. O. Quine. I have selected these philosophers not only because they are important figures in the development of philosophy in the second half of this century but also because their positions stand in important relation to the philosophy of the first half of this century.

I have also made some additions to earlier chapters. To ensure that any mistakes I have made will not be attributed to W. T. Jones, let me indicate briefly what these additions are. In Chapter 3, on G. E. Moore, I have added a section on his "A Defense of Common Sense." I have also included a discussion of Moore's so-called open-question argument. In Chapter 4 I have presented a considerably more detailed account of Frege's discussion of sense and reference. There is only the most minor tinkering in Chapter 5, which considers Russell. In Chapter 6, which concerns Wittgenstein's *Tractatus*, I have added a section explaining what Wittgenstein meant when he said that a proposition is a truth function of elementary propositions. There are no changes to the discussion of logical positivism in Chapter 7; I think that Jones has it just right in giving prominence to Schlick, Neurath, and especially Carnap.

The only place where Jones's views and my views diverge is in Chapter 11 where he examines Wittgenstein's later thought. For the most part, however, our differences are matters of emphasis. I rarely disagree with what he does say; I simply would have given prominence to themes that are muted in his presentation: the notion of rule-following, for example. In the end—except for some minor changes—I decided to leave the chapter as he wrote it, since it represents a clear and insightful interpretation of very difficult texts where disagreements on the correct interpretation have been the norm.

In the process of rereading the second edition of this work, I was constantly struck by Jones's ability to provide not only clear but elegant readings of texts that are sometimes ferociously obscure. This gift is nowhere more apparent than in the chapter he has written on Derrida, which concludes this volume.

Robert J. Fogelin

Contents

3

4

12

13

14

Introduction

Studying the philosophy of the twentieth century is a matter of being surrounded by trees to such an extent that it is difficult to make out the shape of the woods as a whole. Nevertheless, despite all the diversity of movements and schools into which they are divided, we can still make out that philosophy in our times has a kind of unity. In the first place, since philosophy never develops in a vacuum but is part of the ongoing culture, all the various schools of twentieth-century philosophy have, as it were, a twentieth-century look. This distinctive look results from the fact that all twentieth-century philosophers, however much they differ philosophically, are resonating with and responding to the deep concerns of the society of which they are a part—its ambivalence toward science, its preoccupation with language, its worry over consciousness, and its loss of confidence. In the second place, almost all twentieth-century philosophers have been motivated by a desire to escape from the constructivism and relativism that was the nineteenth century's inheritance from Kant. Twentieth-century philosophers have wanted, above all, to reaffirm the possibility of knowledge—knowledge of an objectively existing universe, not merely of one that the mind constructs. Though the different schools of philosophy have taken different routes out of the Kantian paradigm (that, indeed, is why we can call them "schools") they are all characterized by a common aim: the recovery of objectivity (Chapter 1).

But these features that give philosophy in our time a kind of unity did not emerge full-blown as the century dawned. Bergson, Dewey, and Whitehead, whose theories dominated philosophy in the early decades of the century, were, in many respects, men of the nineteenth century, sharing its optimism, its belief in progress, and its vision of a universe that is in process, ever evolving new forms. Like Schopenhauer, Bergson held that reality is disclosed in intuition, but he believed reality to be a fruitful and productive *élan vital,* not a blind and insatiable will. Hence, his view of man and of man's relation to the universe was far more optimistic than Schopenhauer's. Dewey agreed with Bergson that intellect is instrumental to will and that "truth" is whatever satisfies the will, but he rejected both Bergson's intuition and his metaphysical tendencies. For Dewey, philosophy was not an inquiry into the nature of the universe; it was a way of making our traffic with nature and with other men and women more viable. In contrast to Bergson and Dewey, Whitehead was a rationalist. But his rationalism was very different from the traditional ideal of a complete deductive system. Rather, he worked out an open-ended "categorial scheme" that was designed to bridge the chasm between the world of ordinary experience and that of the physical and biological sciences (Chapter 2).

Though G. E. Moore was not much younger than the three process philosophers, his conception of philosophy was very different from theirs; he lived, in effect, in a different world—one that has become increasingly the world of twentieth-century philosophers. Whereas Bergson, Dewey, and Whitehead conceived of philosophy as a large-scale enterprise and deliberately addressed themselves to nonprofessional audiences, Moore deliberately tackled only small-scale problems of a very technical nature and addressed himself to a professional audience. In an attempt to introduce precision into philosophy, Moore made use of a method he called "analysis." Analysis, as Moore practiced it, exposed some of the muddles of idealist philosophers but did not altogether clear up all puzzles about the status of sense data and about the relation between sense data and material objects, as Moore had to confess. Nevertheless we may take Moore's realism as representative of one very frequently traveled path out of the Kantian paradigm (Chapter 3).

Frege's theories represent a second route out of constructivism and relativism. Although Frege was a mathematician and mathematical logician, his work in these technical fields—especially the distinction he drew between "sense" and "reference"—has had major repercussions on philosophical thinking. But Frege's main influence on philosophy was to give it a different orientation. Frege's basic assumption was, to realists, the seemingly simple claim that some assertions are true and others are false. This being the case, it seemed to Frege to follow that to analyze the logic of assertions is to expose the basic structure of the universe: Logical analysis discloses what must be the case about the world if any assertion whatever is true. Thus, for Frege and his followers, logic replaces epistemology as the way out of Kantianism: For them the old epistemological question, "What do we know?" is replaced by a new question, "What is the logic of 'know'?" (Chapter 4).

Like Moore, Russell had a strong realist bias; like Frege, he held that logical analysis would clear up most, if not all, philosophical problems by exposing the muddles of ordinary language, and his theories of types and of descriptions are brilliant examples of what logical analysis can do to resolve seemingly intractable puzzles. On the other hand, unlike Moore and Frege, he had deep metaphysical interests: He wanted to be another Descartes; that is, he hoped to put twentieth-century science on a secure basis. In an effort to do this he distinguished between what he called "hard" and "soft" data. Hard data are indubitable; we have a direct acquaintance with them. Soft data are anything but indubitable, but they can—at least in theory—be replaced by logical constructions in which only hard data occur. (We replace "dog" by a family of canoid color patches.) Obviously, if this program could be carried out, the sciences would indeed rest on a firm basis, on the basis of indubitable hard data. But during his long life Russell repeatedly changed his mind about the kinds of hard data that exist. He had to admit, regretfully, that much of what he believed could not be proved. Russell ended as an antimetaphysician, but he was an antimetaphysician in spite of himself (Chapter 5).

Wittgenstein's *Tractatus* was, in many respects, the culmination of the logical route out of the Kantian paradigm. Wittgenstein maintained that from an examination of the conditions that must hold if any proposition at all is meaningful, it is possible to conclude that the world must have certain features. It must, for instance, consist in a number of atomic facts or states of affairs, and "from the existence or nonexistence of one state of affairs, it is impossible to infer the existence or nonexistence of another." It follows that there is a chasm between the a priori and the empirical. The propositions of logic and mathematics are necessary, but they are not about the world; they are tautologies. On the other hand, propositions with sense, such as those that occur in the empirical sciences, are not necessary: "Outside logic, everything is accidental." These doctrines were congenial to Russell and to the Logical Positivists, but the *Tractatus* has another side that sets it apart from the mainstream of analytic thought. For Wittgenstein drew a distinction between what can be said and what cannot be said but only shown. About what can only be shown, we must remain silent. This is the domain of what Wittgenstein called the mystical; ethics and religion fall within this domain, and so does philosophy. Philosophy, properly understood, is not a kind of discourse, it is an activity—the activity of displaying the limits of what can be said. Hence, once the doctrine of the *Tractatus* is grasped, the book itself can be dispensed with: "The reader can throw away the ladder after he has climbed up it." (Chapter 6)

The Logical Positivists were the heirs of Russell. They undertook to carry out the program that he had only sketched. In this enterprise they used the *Tractatus,* or rather, those parts of the *Tractatus* that were devoted to what Wittgenstein held can be said, as a kind of handbook. If Russell's hard data could be identified with Wittgenstein's atomic states of affairs, it appeared to the early positivists that they need only formulate the sentences in which states of affairs are named (they called these "protocol sentences") in order to put the sciences on a firm basis. This line of reasoning underlay their Verifiability Principle, namely, the thesis that the meaning of a proposition is its method of verification. Sentences that are not verifiable, that is, which cannot be reduced to protocol sentences, are ruled out as meaningless. This includes the sentences of metaphysics and theology. These sentences may, some of the positivists allowed, have an emotional function (they may be bad poetry), but they are literally nonsense. Unfortunately it soon appeared that there were grave problems with the Verifiability Principle. Did the principle need to be verified? If not, why not? If so, how could one hope to verify it without becoming trapped in a vicious circle? Further, Carnap's Principle of Tolerance (the thesis that our criteria for distinguishing between what is real and what is unreal are related to language and that we can, and do, use different languages for different purposes) undermined the claim of the early Positivists that they provided *the* language for talking about the world. The Verifiability Principle now became merely a recommendation, thus taking the sting out of the Positivists' attack on metaphysics: Metaphysicians had only to reject the recommendation, and they were still in business (Chapter 7).

Chapters 3 through 7 have all been concerned with philosophers who, however much they may have differed among themselves, all belong to what in the text is called the analytic tradition. It had its roots in certain more or less implicit assumptions about the nature of the world that can be traced back to Hume and beyond Hume to Hobbes. Among these are the assumption that the universe is composed of a large number of very simple entities, that complex objects can be analyzed into the simple entities of which they are composed, and that these simple entities, being simple, are directly understandable whenever they are encountered. The next three chapters examine the second main movement that has dominated philosophical thinking in this century—what in the text is called the phenomenological tradition.

Husserl was the founder of phenomenology. Like many other post-Kantians, he held that reality consists in things-as-they-appear. But unlike the Hegelians and other objective idealists, he rejected the constructivist view of mind that Kant had introduced into philosophy. Like the realists, Husserl held that consciousness does not make a world; it merely displays the world. Accordingly, for him the task of philosophy is to describe the world that consciousness displays. But for this— and here he differed radically from the realists—a special method of "seeing," one that requires elaborate training, is necessary. This method of phenomenological seeing requires us to learn to "bracket" our experience, that is, neither to believe nor to disbelieve in the existence of what we experience, but to suspend belief and examine the experience itself. When we do this, according to Husserl, we discover much that completely eludes us in the "natural standpoint," that is, in ordinary experience. We discover not only "essences" and many other kinds of intentional objects but acts of consciousness as well. The advantage of phenomenological seeing, according to Husserl, is that what appears in our experience when we bracket is indubitable; being simply *there,* it cannot be doubted. Phenomenology thus seemed to provide the basis for the "rigorous science" that Husserl was seeking (Chapter 8).

Heidegger learned the phenomenological method from Husserl but put it to a very different use. He was not interested in rigorous science but in harkening to what he called "Being." Phenomenology, in Heidegger's view, can uncover Being, which, in the dark age in which we now live, hides itself from us. The first step toward uncovering Being is to make a phenomenological analysis of Dasein (Heidegger's technical term for human nature). Why Dasein? Because Dasein alone of all beings is interested in Being. Dasein alone asks, "Why is there anything at all, rather than nothing?" Heidegger's analysis of Dasein is often acute and sensitive (we experience things as ready-to-hand, he points out, not merely as present-at-hand), but it may be doubted whether he has uncovered the universal, a priori structure of human nature as he supposed, or merely given us an account of the experiential world of an anxious, concerned man. But in any event, even in Heidegger's own assessment, the road from Dasein's being to Being as such proved a dead end. He therefore shifted to poetry as a better clue to Being than ontological analysis. But even poetry proved inadequate, and in the end he decided that the ineffable nature of Being cannot be communicated in words. What is needed is "silence about silence." That would be "authentic saying" (Chapter 9).

Sartre is the third philosopher of the phenomenological tradition whose views are examined in this volume. Like Heidegger, he started from Husserlian phenomenology; like Heidegger, because he was less interested in rigorous science than in human ("existential") problems, he moved a very long way from Husserl. However, whereas Heidegger felt the presence of Being even when, as in the present age, it has withdrawn itself from us, Sartre is convinced that we live in a Godless world. The great question for him is not how to uncover Being and become open to it but how to live one's day-to-day life once one has purged oneself of all the illusions that make this life bearable. In Sartre's play *The Flies,* Orestes says, "Human life begins on the other side of despair." Sartre is far better at describing despair and the circumstances that lead to it than at dealing with life on the other side. The problem of how to live authentically would be difficult enough for a withdrawn individual like Heidegger, but for Sartre, who had been a political activist, it was particularly acute, and his writings suggest some relaxation of his earlier position. The difficulty of living authentically is no longer so much an existential problem, rooted in the nature of human nature, as it is a sociopolitical problem, a product of the "scarcity" that capitalism creates (Chapter 10).

When Wittgenstein finished writing the *Tractatus* he thought he had solved all the problems of philosophy. It was not long, however, before he concluded that the theory of meaning on which the whole analysis of the *Tractatus* had rested was an oversimplification. A picture, he said, had held him captive. This picture was the picture of language as a picture. Words, he had thought when he wrote the *Tractatus,* are essentially names, labels that we attach to objects. This picture of language, he now realized, was not *wholly* false: Some words do function as names. But if we want to understand language we must see that language functions in many different ways, depending on the "game" of which it is a part. Accordingly, we should look to the use not the meaning. But words do not have any specifically *philosophical* use. Philosophers ask, for instance, "What is time?" and become uneasy when they cannot answer. The cure for such philosophical disquietude is to put language back into use: Let us examine the circumstances in which people use the word "time." For instance, they say, "It's time for lunch," or ask, "What time is it?" There is no puzzle about what "time" means in these usages, and these usages are the only meanings that "time" has. Thus the age-old problem about the nature of time is dissolved—not solved, simply dissolved. The same is true for other philosophical problems. Philosophers, Wittgenstein thought, have been bewitched by language; *Philosophical Investigations* was intended as a kind of therapy to exorcise the psychological demons that bewitchment with language had generated. Though Wittgenstein's therapy was not quite as successful as he thought it would be (he did not put philosophy out of business) he did radically change the way in which most philosophers now do their business.

From the perspective of almost a half-century later, we now see that the circulation of Wittgenstein's ideas was a major turning point in the history of twentieth-century philosophy. Many philosophers fell completely under his spell, adopting not only his views but also his indirect and often challenging ways of expressing them. Others, most notably the so-called ordinary-language philosophers, who came to prominence at Oxford in the decades following World War II, though they took over many of Wittgenstein's ideas, developed them in a very different spirit. J. L. Austin, generally thought to be the central figure in this movement, had little patience with Wittgenstein's style of philosophizing. Austin and those who worked closely with him accepted Wittgenstein's leading idea that the meaning of an expression is its use in the language. They also agreed that philosophical problems often have their source in linguistic misunderstandings and thus can be resolved by removing these misunderstandings. Unlike Wittgenstein, however, they thought that this procedure could be carried out in a perfectly straightforward and systematic way. The various uses of language could be discovered and classified, much in the same way that entomologists have discovered and classified insects. This, for the ordinary-language philosophers, was not a matter of philosophical inspiration but of sustained hard work.

In their heyday, the philosophers of ordinary language thought that the fundamental nature of language could be charted and the philosophical problems based upon misunderstandings of language resolved in a relatively short period of time—perhaps in a few decades. This optimism faded as philosophical problems proved surprisingly resistant to linguistic cure. At the time the philosophers of ordinary language thought they had produced a revolution in philosophy. This now seems an overstatement. On the other hand, they did make important contributions to philosophy by pointing out cases where linguistic confusion did lead to philosophical muddles. Though not a cure-all, linguistic analysis was sometimes a cure. Furthermore, through their close examination of the ways in which language is actually used, they made substantial contributions to the empirical science of linguistics.

As this volume shows, the twentieth century began with a struggle between an entrenched idealism and an emerging reappearance of realism. The philosophical commitments of those on each side of the dispute came in two relatively well-defined packages. The idealists, inspired by Hegel, were holists, antiempiricists, and critics of formal (as opposed to dialectical) logic. They held that philosophical problems are resolved, to the extent that human beings are capable of resolving them, through understanding how mind or spirit unfolds or reveals itself in a dialectical process. The new realists, taking Bertrand Russell as our model, were, in contrast, atomists, empiricists, and champions of formal logic, in particular, in its new mathematical form that emerged at the turn of the century. For these new realists philosophical problems were resolved through analysis.

It might seem that the components in each of these clusters were made for each other. Holism, antiempiricism, and the rejection of formal logic sit comfortably together, as do atomism, empiricism, and a commitment to the methods of logical analysis. Yet as we approach the end of this century, we find a number of philosophers recombining these components in ways that were largely unthinkable at its beginning. Willard V. O. Quine is, perhaps, the most striking example of a philosopher producing such a realignment. Quine is a radical empiricist in epistemology, a physicalist in metaphysics, largely a behaviorist in philosophy of mind, and a leading figure in the development and application of methods of modern logic—all traits that suggest philosophical kinship with Bertrand Russell. At the same time Quine is a holist (or at least a strong contextualist) who, on this basis, argues for a wide range of indeterminacy. Instead of using the methods of logic to analyze the meanings of propositions, he maintains that the notion of propositions having meaning in isolation is a myth. For Quine there are no fully determinate answers to questions concerning what is meant, what there is, and what is the fact of the matter. All this is strikingly similar to holistic views accepted by Hegelian idealists. But Quine, as noted above, is not an idealist; he is an empiricist and a physicalist. It is this striking realignment of commitments, seemingly incompatible with one another, that gives Quine's position originality and strength.

The work ends with a chapter on Jacques Derrida. Derrida's writings present a radical critique of the central aspects of Western rationalism. In this respect they are part of the tradition that has Friedrich Nietzsche and Martin Heidegger as central figures. One of the targets of Derrida's critique is the concept of objective meaning. Thus, though it is hard to imagine two figures more different in philosophical temperament and outlook than Derrida and Quine, they are united in attitude toward the project of analyzing propositions in order to bring out their true or objective meaning. Both deny that this is possible.

Turning and turning in the widening gyre
The falcon cannot hear the falconer;
Things fall apart; the center cannot hold.

W. B. YEATS

Let's see the very thing and nothing else.
Let's see it with the hottest fire of sight.
Burn everything not part of it to ash.

WALLACE STEVENS

CHAPTER 1

The World We Live In

Four Ariadnean Threads through a Labyrinth

Now that we have reached the twentieth century in our discussion of the history of philosophy, terrain that is within, or at most just beyond, our own horizon, it might be supposed that things become easier: at least we know where we are. Surely we understand our own world better than Athens of the fourth century B.C. or Renaissance Europe. But the world we live in is so close to us, we are so much a part of it, that we do not know how to distinguish what is important in the history of philosophy from what is only trivial, a major trend from a passing fashion. Because it is hard to see the woods for the trees, a few clues may be helpful as we begin our study of twentieth-century philosophy, four Ariadnean threads to guide us through the labyrinth.

LOSS OF CONFIDENCE

Students of contemporary culture have characterized the twentieth century in various ways—for instance, as the age of anxiety, the aspirin age, the nuclear age, the age of one-dimensional humanity, the postindustrial age; but nobody, unless a candidate for office at some political convention, has called it a happy age. Most commentators, however differently they may diagnose the nature of the illness, agree that the twentieth century suffers from a serious malaise. The rise of dictatorships, two world wars, genocide, the deterioration of the environment, and the Vietnam War all had a share in undermining the old beliefs in progress, in rationality, and in people's capacity to control their destiny and improve their lot. Thus, our first Ariadnean threat is a collapse of confidence—a collapse that was already visible in the nineteenth century, but that has become much more noticeable in our own time. In fact, the underground man we saw emerging in the late nineteenth century—sick, spiteful, unsure of himself, lost—is now perhaps the representative and modern type.[1]

What is at the core of this collapse of confidence? It seems to be a growing feeling of the radical ambiguity of the human mode of being in the world. In the old days, when the religious worldview was still unquestioned, human beings lived in a world that was familiar and meaningful because it was, they believed, organized for them and around their values. Thus, though Dante might encounter bitter personal disasters, he was persuaded that they were all part of a divine plan and that, as a result of this plan, there would sooner or later be a balancing out. The opening lines of *The Inferno* express this conviction clearly: midway through his life, Dante says, he became lost in a dark wood, but, black as that wood was, he did not despair of finding his way out, because, looking up, he could see the light of the sun falling on the top of a hill. That his dark wood was only a small maze in a coherent, well-ordered world, he never doubted. In contrast there is William Butler Yeats's disoriented falcon:

> Turning and turning in the widening gyre
> The falcon cannot hear the falconer;
> Things fall apart; the center cannot hold;
> Mere anarchy is loosed upon the world.[a]

Yeats's falcon is not lost in a private wood of its own making and from which there is an exit. In a world that has no center—and no falconer—the disorientation is cosmic, not local.

Contemporary literature is filled with protagonists who find themselves in the falcon's world: a hostile—or, even worse, an indifferent—universe. For instance, at the climactic moment in Thomas Mann's *Magic Mountain,* Hans Castorp, "life's delicate child," pushes too far into the mountains and loses his way:

---

[1] See Vol. IV, pp. 10–11.

> He had just begun to mount again when the expected happened, and the storm burst, the storm that had threatened so long. Or may one say "threatened" of the action of blind, nonsentient forces, which have no purpose to destroy us—that would be comforting by comparison—but are merely horribly indifferent to our fate should we become involved with them?[b]

Again, in William Faulkner's short story "Old Man," a convict, who has been temporarily released from prison to help fight a flood, finds himself alone on the Mississippi in a small boat:

> He was being toyed with by a current of water going nowhere, beneath a day which would wane toward no evening. . . . The skiff ran in pitch streaming darkness upon a rolling expanse which . . . apparently had no boundaries. . . . Wild and invisible, it tossed and heaved about and beneath the boat, . . . objects nameless and enormous and invisible struck and slashed at the skiff and whirled on.[c]

In the falcon's world the notion of justice is irrelevant. If some balancing out happens to occur, as a result of which a wrong seems to be righted, this is but chance—the accidental coincidence of "senseless" forces. So, in Joyce Cary's *Horse's Mouth,* Gulley Jimson comments on his brother-in-law's misfortunes: "The trouble with Robert is he won't face facts, things if you like. He wants them to come and lick his feet. But they can't—they can't lick. They can only fall about like a lot of loose rocks in a runaway train."[d] In the dark wood of Robert's misfortune no hill and no sunlight are visible. Things, or facts, simply carry us with them, willy-nilly; what happens to us simply happens—it is no part of any "scheme of things."

This is what Günter Grass seems to be saying in *The Tin Drum.* At the end of the novel, Oskar is fleeing from the police, who are seeking to arrest him for a murder he did not commit. His flight leads him to a Paris metro station, where he gets on an escalator only to realize that the police are waiting for him at the top.

> Higher and higher it bore me. . . . Outside it was raining, and up on the top stood the detectives from the Interpol. . . . An escalator ride is a good time to reconsider, to reconsider everything: Where are you from? Where are you going? Who are you? What is your real name? What are you after?[e]

As Oskar himself remarks, an escalator "is high, steep, and symbolic enough" to represent life as twentieth-century humankind perceives it. During the ride one may have the impression of going somewhere, but that is an illusion. The escalator merely goes round and round mechanically, without regard to the passenger's desires. Thus what twentieth-century people acutely feel—if we are to believe the evidence of novelists and poets—is the absurdity of their situation, the "disproportion," as Albert Camus put it, between human hopes and fears and the silence of the universe.[f]

CONCERN WITH SCIENCE

Some people—including some philosophers—have been disposed to blame science for these feelings of disproportion and disorientation. Think, for instance, of the me that I experience in introspection and in ordinary perception (by means of the naked eye, as it were)—a rich, thick, fruity sort of plum pudding of odors, tastes, colors, likings and dislikings, prejudices and passions. And contrast this with the complex structure of animo acids and polypeptide chains that I am told I am. Which is the real me? Or if both are somehow real, how are they related? Or think of our conviction that our own acts and those of other people are praiseworthy or blameworthy, and that the moral quality they have depends on our having been free to do them or to abstain from doing them. And then contrast this with the scientific view that human behavior is, in principle, as predictable as a solar or lunar eclipse. If we are not free to choose one act in preference to another, but, instead, our behavior is wholly the outcome of antecedent events in time, including our heredity and past environment, then the consequences are that the notions of obligation and responsibility are as inapplicable to us as they are to automobiles, rockets, or computers. No wonder the falcon is disoriented.

But does science in fact entail these consequences? Some people—including some philosophers—argue that it does not. Indeed, quite the contrary. According to these people, science reorients the falcon by locating it once and for all in the real world instead of the various false worlds of myth, superstition, and fancy. Thus science, far from causing metaphysical anxiety by destroying the old orientation, provides a way of satisfying—and, for the first time in the history of culture, satisfying fully and securely—the ontological urge, the urge for objectivity. The falcon, then, has no reason to feel disoriented. It may indeed dislike the world in which science has disclosed that it is living. If so it must simply learn to put up with things as they are.

Twentieth-century reactions to science have thus been varied—some favorable, some hostile, some ambivalent. But everyone in this century has been affected by science—not merely by technology (against whose adverse effects it is now fashionable to complain) but also, and even more deeply if less obviously, by the repercussions of the scientific view of the world on people's perception of themselves. Here, then, is a second of those Ariadnean threads by which we hope to make our way through the maze of philosophical theories we will examine in this volume.

THE DISSOCIATED SENSIBILITY

A third thread is the theme of the divided self or, in T. S. Eliot's phrase, the "dissociated sensibility." Humankind has always agreed that it is distinguished from the rest of nature by its consciousness of what it does and what it experiences. But what was once regarded as a supremely valuable distinction—think of Socrates' "The unexamined life is not worth living"—has increasingly come to be regarded as a major misfortune. More and more people long to return to a simple unconscious mode of existence in which they are indistinguishable from the rest of nature instead of proudly separated from it. And since they realize that this mode of existence is impossible for them, they experience anguish and despair. So, in Jean-Paul Sartre's novel *The Reprieve* one of the characters, who is a homosexual, exclaims: "Why can't I *be* what I am, *be* a pederast? . . . Just *to be.* In the dark, at random! To be homosexual just as the oak is oak. To extinguish myself. To extinguish the inner eye."[g] The inner eye is self-consciousness. And to be self-conscious is not only to be separated from the rest of nature, it is also to be divided within oneself, for one is at once both subject and object—this is the new perception. The protagonist of Fyodor Dostoevsky's *Notes from Underground* was one of the first to make this discovery. "I am a sick man. . . . I am a spiteful man. No, I am not a pleasant man at all." And he then proceeded—by means, ironically, of a highly self-conscious analysis—to show that his self-consciousness was the cause of his spitefulness and his illness. "Any sort of consciousness is a disease. . . . For the direct, the inevitable, and the legitimate result of consciousness is to make all action impossible, or—to put it differently—consciousness leads to thumb-twiddling."[h]

But Dostoevsky's underground man was only the first of a long series of antiheroes in fiction. What these characters seek—what Mersault in Camus's *Stranger,* what Birkin in D. H. Lawrence's *Women in Love* are seeking—is to rid themselves of consciousness. If Birkin represents the kind of human being Lawrence admired, Hermione represents the kind he detested. "She was the most remarkable woman in the Midlands . . . a woman of the new school, full of intellectuality, and heavy, nerve-worn with consciousness." Birkin's condemnation of her—"Knowledge means everything to you. Even your animalism, you want it in your head. You don't want to *be* an animal, you want to observe your own animal functions"—is Lawrence's own. What Birkin wanted—that men and women "like the purely individual thing in themselves, which makes them act in singleness"—is what Lawrence wanted. But the tragedy of humanity is that men and women can never act in singleness, for consciousness divides them. Hence humanity must go.

> I abhor humanity, I wish it was swept away. It could go and there would be no *absolute* loss, if every human being perished tomorrow. The reality would be untouched. . . . You yourself, don't you find it a beautiful clean thought, a world empty of people, just uninterrupted grass, and a hare sitting up?[i]

And this search for immediacy, in contrast to acceptance of an experience mediated by consciousness, is by no means confined to fiction. Much of the appeal of New Age religions, of sensitivity training, of encounter groups, and of the drug culture can surely be traced to a similar distaste for the psychic distance that consciousness interposes between human beings and the world.

But not everyone condemns consciousness; as with science, old attitudes survive to produce another division within the culture, this time with respect to the varying assessments of the divisiveness of consciousness. Nevertheless, whether consciousness be evaluated favorably, hostilely, or ambivalently, it has become a central concern of the twentieth century, in that more than ever it is in the forefront of attention—no longer a phenomenon that is taken for granted but one we must take account of and toward which, therefore, it is important to adopt a stance. And this is evident not only in literature and the general culture but also, as we shall see, in philosophy.

THE LINGUISTIC TURN

A fourth thread is language. Those who derogate consciousness as creating a fatal gap between the knower and the world are likely to perceive language as a distorting lens through which the knower peers in vain. But do we peer wholly in vain? Some hold that by a special method or on special occasions we can experience pure reality, uncontaminated by language. Wallace Stevens described—perhaps "celebrated" is a better term—this kind of experience in many poems. For instance, in "Notes toward a Supreme Fiction":

> You must become an ignorant man again
> And see the sun again with an ignorant eye
> And see it clearly in the idea of it. . . .
>
> There is a project for the sun. The sun
> Must bear no name, gold-flourisher, but be
> In the difficulty of what it is to be.[j]

And again in "Credences of Summer":

> Let's see the very thing and nothing else.
> Let's see it with the hottest fire of sight.
> Burn everything not part of it to ash.
>
> Trace the gold sun about the whitened sky
> Without evasion by a single metaphor.
> Look at it in its essential barrenness
> And say this, this is the centre that I seek.[k]

But if there are those who hope to penetrate past language to the very thing itself, there are others who, like Eliot, hold that the use of language is a never-ending

> . . . raid on the inarticulate
> With shabby equipment always deteriorating
> In the general mess of imprecision of feeling,
> Undisciplined squads of emotion.[1]

Underlying this metaphor is a very different vision of the relation between language and reality from that expressed in Stevens's lines. For writers like Stevens, reality is essentially, intrinsically, independent of humankind. The problem of knowledge is the problem of finding, or framing, a language that is exactly isomorphic with this independent reality, language that has been purged of the distortions, the presuppositions, the built-in "evasions" of ordinary language. For writers like Eliot, the attempt to fashion a purified language fully adequate to reality is a hopeless quest. In the first place, reality and the would-be knower, these writers hold, are interinvolved. Knowers do not contemplate reality from outside; rather, they organize and articulate it (and themselves as well) from inside. In the second place, reality is too complex ever to be completely and finally articulated. Hence our attempt to understand the world and ourselves is an intolerable and never-ending "wrestle with words and meanings."[m]

These radically different visions of the relation between language and reality have not merely been expressed in verse; as we shall see, they also underlay and deeply influenced philosophical theory in the twentieth century. But the present point is simply that language—whether it be perceived as something to be got past, as something to be refined and purified, or as something to be put up with despite its limitations—can be seen as a central preoccupation of the twentieth century.

Freudian psychology probably had a good deal to do with this development. Dreams, jokes, slips of the tongue are held to be a veil that covers the reality of inner states, but a veil that can be penetrated by those who realize that dreams, slips, and jokes are in fact a special kind of language whose symbolism must be learned. But the shift of attention to language is by no means limited to those who share the assumptions of psychiatry. The so-called New Criticism in literature (now no longer very new), Content Analysis in political science and sociology, Marshall McLuhanism, and General Semantics are all manifestations of this trend. Indeed, since it is now widely held that problems of all kinds in large measure arise from either the deliberately (as in propaganda and advertising) or the unintentionally obfuscating influence of language, the current strategy for dealing with problems is to tackle them, at least initially, through the language in which they are formulated. A good example of this strategy is Bertrand Russell's reply to those who challenged him by asking what meaning life can have to an agnostic. "I feel inclined," he said, "to answer by another question: What is the meaning of 'the meaning of life'?"[n]

Here, then, are four themes that strongly marked twentieth-century culture— a concern with science, a worry over consciousness, a preoccupation with language, and an urge to recapture objectivity and so revive our belief in a universe that has purpose, direction, and proportion—one in which the falcon's flight is truly oriented. But even with these four threads to guide us, we shall find no easy path through the maze of twentieth-century philosophy, for the threads themselves crisscross in manifold and puzzling ways. For instance, among philosophers who have shared an interest in seeking clarity and have agreed that it can be attained by an "adequate" analysis, some have maintained that the language of science is our best—indeed, our only—resource, while others have preferred the ordinary language of ordinary people. Again, among philosophers who have agreed in assessing science favorably, some have emphasized its cognitive role and some its practical consequences for what John Dewey called our traffic with nature and with other people. And among philosophers who agree that scientific cognition is the ideal at which all cognitive enterprises should aim, there are further divisions regarding the role of philosophy: Is philosophy to be phased out and replaced by science? or is it to be reduced to tackling second-order problems regarding the methodology of science? or is there still a role for philosophy as *scientia generalis*, an inquiry that, starting from the basic concepts of physics (or biology or psychology), expands them into a universally applicable metaphysics of nature?

One reason for such diverse responses as these is obvious. Philosophers are no more disembodied cherubim than are other people. In their own way, and in their philosophical medium, philosophers articulate the hopes and fears of their times. Just as much as novelists or poets or painters, though perhaps less apparently, they resonate with the underlying—and often conflicting—themes of the culture.

The Kantian Paradigm

Yet, despite the influence on philosophical thinking of the diverse attitudes of society at large, philosophy in the twentieth century has had a kind of unity, inasmuch as all philosophical concerns cross, diverge, and cross again within the context of an attempt to escape from what we may call the Kantian paradigm. Despite a number of countermovements such as materialism, positivism, pragmatism, and existentialism, philosophy during the nineteenth century had moved largely within a Kantian framework, and moved there more or less contentedly.[2] Only near the end of that century did a strong attack on Kantian thought begin. Because almost all of twentieth-century philosophy can be viewed as one of a series of attempts to break out of the Kantian paradigm, it is essential if we are to understand philosophy in our own time to understand the model from which it has been seeking to escape. The next few pages will first summarize the main

[2]See Vol. IV, pp. 14–19.

features of Immanuel Kant's view and then sketch the line of development from him through Hegel to the end of the nineteenth century.[3]

Kant's *Critique of Pure Reason* (1781) was an attempt to avoid the formidable difficulties in which he saw that Cartesian dualism was enmeshed. René Descartes and his successors had held what seems at first a sensible and even self-evident view—that there are two fundamentally different entities in the universe: minds and material objects. A mind, according to the Cartesians, experiences only itself directly; it experiences objects (and other minds) only indirectly by means of mental states (variously called "ideas," "representations," or "impressions") that are caused in the mind by these objects acting on it via the sense organs and the nervous system. Knowledge of the external world depends on our ideas resembling the objects that cause them, and we can be confident that they do resemble their causes. God, Descartes maintained, would not allow us to believe in the resemblance of idea and object unless idea did in fact resemble object. That would be deception on such a grand scale that it is incompatible with God's goodness.

This line of reasoning, clearly, would appeal only to those willing to rest everything on divine intentions. David Hume was not and pointed out that if the mind knows only its own states, its own states are all that it knows. As a parallel case, consider the claim that some particular portrait is a good likeness of the sitter. If we have independent experience of the sitter, we can determine whether the portrait is a good or poor likeness. But if all we have is another portrait of the sitter, we can only compare portraits. Indeed, we cannot even be sure that the so-called portraits are what they claim to be—portraits. There may have been no sitter who was the subject of these pictures; they may be only figments of the artist's imagination. Similarly, if we have access only to ideas, we can never know that an external world, or that any other minds than our own, exist. Hume concluded that since the existence of other minds and of an external world are incapable of proof, our belief in them is wholly irrational.

It was at this point that Kant came on the scene. Hume's criticism of induction, he wrote, roused him from "dogmatic slumber." That is, Hume seemed to him to have shown that Cartesianism is incompatible with our having a knowledge of nature. Because Hume had demonstrated the breakdown of the hypothesis that minds and objects are independent of each other and that truth consists in the mind coming into agreement with objects, Kant proposed to try the opposite hypothesis that minds and objects are mutually involved in each other and that truth consists in the agreement of objects with minds.

> Hitherto it has been assumed that all our knowledge must conform to objects. But all attempts to extend our knowledge of objects . . . have, on this assumption, ended in failure. We must therefore make trial whether we may not have more success . . . if we suppose that objects must conform to our knowledge. . . . We should then be proceeding

---

[3] See Vol. IV, Chs. 2, 4, 6, and 9.

precisely on the lines of Copernicus' primary hypothesis. Failing of satisfactory progress in explaining the movements of the heavenly bodies on the supposition that they all revolved round the spectator, he tried whether he might not have better success if he made the spectator to revolve and the stars remain at rest. A similar experiment can be tried in metaphysics, as regards the experience[4] of objects. If experience must conform to the constitution of the objects, I do not see how we could know anything of the latter *a priori,* but if the object (as object of the senses) must conform to the constitution of our faculty . . . I have no difficulty in conceiving such a possibility.°

In saying that the object must conform to our minds, Kant did not mean that truth of particular judgments, such as "This rose is red," depends on the agreement of the object (in this case, the rose) with the mind's belief that the rose is red. Obviously the truth of "This rose is red" depends on the rose being in fact red. Rather, Kant held that all particular judgments of the *general* form "This rose is red" (judgments in which some quality or property is attributed to a substance) depend, not on the objective world consisting in substances that own properties, for this can never be known, but on minds organizing their experience in a substance-property sort of way. The same is true as regards a judgment of the general form "A is the cause of B." *Particular* causal judgments, such as "Friction is the cause of heat," are indeed inductive generalizations that depend on experience, both for their formulation and for their verification. But inductive generalizations are possible only because causality is a mode of the human understanding, that is, only because we have the sort of mind that organizes experiences into cause-effect patterns, or structures.

To put this differently, knowledge of nature is possible, but only because the mind does not—as philosophers from Descartes to Hume have assumed—merely react, or respond, to a completely independent external world, but constructs the form—the structure, not the details—of the world of its experience. As Kant wrote, "We can know *a priori* of things only what we ourselves put into them."ᴾ But knowledge of nature is possible precisely because we can know what we do put into nature, for example, the substance-property and the cause-effect ways of organizing experience.

It follows that, as regards whatever lies wholly outside our experience, we can know nothing, neither its structure nor the details. About things outside our experience (what Kant called "things-in-themselves") it is possible to say only that they exist; attempts to characterize reality-in-itself inevitably result in hopeless contradictions. Thus Kant's attack on "speculative metaphysics," which purports to assert necessary truths about ultimate reality, is even more devastating than Hume's. But where Hume went wrong, according to Kant, was in failing to

[4][The German term translated here as "experience" is a technical term used by Kant and is usually rendered as "intuition." But in the present context "intuition" would be badly misleading and "experience" is close enough to *Anschauung* for our purposes—AUTHORS.]

distinguish between what is wholly outside human experience and what is within human experience. Because Hume failed to draw this distinction it did not occur to him that we have good grounds for asserting that causality holds universally and necessarily within the domain of human experience, providing that causality is one of the organizing activities, or "categories," as Kant called them, by means of which the human mind structures its experience.

As we have seen, Kant likened this hypothesis about the knower and his or her relation to the objects of knowledge to Copernicus's revolution. Just as Copernicus had argued that motions attributed by the old astronomy to the sun and the other planets were better explained as being due to the motion of the earth, so Kant argued that features of experience (for instance, the substance-property relation), which dualism had attributed to the objects themselves and which it failed wholly to account for, could be satisfactorily explained by attributing them to the activity of mind. Copernicus's shift in perspective had momentous consequences; in calling his own hypothesis "Copernican," Kant claimed that it was an equally revolutionary shift in perspective. In this estimate he was correct, but paradoxically his hypothesis had an almost directly opposite effect. Whereas Copernicus's astronomical hypothesis had demoted the earth (and with it humankind) from the center to the periphery, Kant's epistemological hypothesis promoted humankind, as knower, into a place of prominence, as the constructor of experience. For Kant, the mind was no longer a Cartesian substance contemplating other Cartesian substances from outside and at a distance. It was not a "thing" at all but an activity, a number of "transcendental syntheses." And from this epistemological change there followed a profound metaphysical change. The so-called objective world (the objects of experience, not the world of things-in-themselves) is a construct, a product of the synthesizing activity of mind working on and organizing the materials of sense (what Kant called the "sensuous manifold").

Reactions to Kant's revolution were varied, but always strong. For some, it was liberating: in *The Prelude,* for instance, William Wordsworth emphasizes the active, synthesizing power of the mind in true Kantian fashion. What, Wordsworth asks, does a baby boy experience when he stretches out his hand toward a flower?[5] He does not merely contemplate a neutral physical object out there in space, for "already love . . . hath beautified that flower" for him. That is, the baby has fused together the physical flower and his response to his mother's loving, protective care. What Wordsworth saw in the Kantian revolution is that mind is active, not merely acted on. Mind does not merely receive impressions from outside; it organizes and synthesizes its experience to construct its own world. What is true of the "great Mind" that is the author of the whole universe is equally true of the baby boy and the tiny world of his experience:

> Emphatically such a Being lives,
> Frail creature as he is, helpless as frail,

[5] See Vol. IV, pp. 335–36.

> An inmate of this active universe.
> For feeling has to him imparted power
> That through the growing faculties of sense
> Doth like an agent of the one great Mind
> Create, creator and receiver both,
> Working but in alliance with the works
> Which it beholds.�q

It follows that in a profound sense all people are poets. It is true, of course, that most of us lose this "first poetic spirit of our human life"; as we grow older it is "abated or suppressed." But there is no fundamental difference between poets and ordinary people: the person we call a poet is only one who has managed to preserve this power "pre-eminent till death." Thus for Wordsworth—and for Samuel Taylor Coleridge—the Kantian revolution at once democratized the poetic spirit by extending it to all people and exalted it by likening it to God's creative power. Kantianism allowed them to assign a positive function to what Coleridge called "the primary Imagination," defined by him as "the living power and prime Agent of all human Perception, and as a repetition in the finite mind of the eternal act of creation in the infinite I AM."ʳ In a word, the poet is no longer merely a pleasing imitator of nature, but a creative god, albeit a minor one.

For others, however, the Kantian revolution was profoundly disturbing. For instance, Heinrich von Kleist wrote:

> Not long ago I became acquainted with Kant's philosophy; and now I must tell you of a thought in it, inasmuch as I cannot fear it will upset you as profoundly and painfully as me. We cannot decide whether that which we call truth is really truth or whether it merely appears that way to us. If the latter is right, then the truth we gather here comes to nothing after our death; and every aspiration to acquire a possession which will follow us even into the grave is futile. . . . My only, my highest aim has sunk, and I have none left.ˢ

These very different responses to Kantianism, representing very different temperaments, can be traced through the whole subsequent history of philosophy. To some, Kantian idealism and constructivism were exciting and liberating because they asserted that the world of our experience is in part our own creation. To others, as Friedrich Nietzsche noted, Kantianism led to "despair of truth," and "a gnawing and crumbling scepticism and relativism."ᵗ These latter saw in idealism and constructivism only the doctrine either that there is no objective reality at all or else that it is forever inaccessible to us, an unknowable thing-in-itself. It was this second response to Kantianism—the response that saw in Kantianism the defeat and frustration of the urge to objectivity—that emerged strongly at the beginning of this century. However, before this reaction occurred, idealism and constructivism had to run their course. This involved a steady expansion of the role mind plays.

Hegelianism was one of the first moves in this direction. Kant had conceived the role of mind in the construction of experience as limited to twelve "syntheses," which he held to be timeless and necessary features of all the mind's activities everywhere. G. W. F. Hegel, in contrast, maintained that mind has a history. It passes through a sequence of stages, to each of which there corresponds a particular pattern of experience—for instance, that of classical Greece, the Orient, and Renaissance Europe. It is true that Hegel held that these various patterns of experience succeed each other according to regular and necessary laws of logical development. Hence there was still something universal and objective about human experience, namely the sequential development that, he supposed, constitutes the history of culture. But this was much less than Kant had claimed and another big step on the path to relativism.

The next step, taken by Nietzsche, was even more relativistic: "We invent the largest part of the thing experienced," he wrote. "We are much greater artists than we know." That is, what each of us experiences (our world) is not merely a function of the social class of which we are members; it is a function of personal interests, and hence varies from individual to individual. "Most of the conscious thinking of a philosopher is secretly guided by his instincts and forced along certain lines. . . . Every great philosophy has been . . . a type of involuntary and unaware memoirs." Science, Nietzsche thought, is no better off than philosophy: "Physics, too, is only an interpretation of the universe, an arrangement of it (to suit us, if I may be so bold!), rather than a clarification."[u]

This, surely, was skepticism and relativism with a vengeance. But meanwhile, and independently of this process, other philosophers pointed out that if things-in-themselves are unknowable, there can be no evidence that they exist. F. H. Bradley expressed a commonly held opinion in his gibe at Herbert Spencer's "Unknowable":

> I do not wish to be irreverent, but Mr. Spencer's attitude towards his Unknowable strikes me as a pleasantry, the point of which lies in its unconsciousness. It seems a proposal to take something for God simply and solely because we do not know what the devil it can be.[v]

Bradley replaced the Unknowable with the "Absolute," but since this Absolute was supposed to transcend all finite (that is, human) experience, it is not easy to see in what way it was an improvement on unknown things-in-themselves. Bradley was obliged, for instance, to admit that "fully to realize the existence of the Absolute is for finite beings impossible. In order thus to know we should have to be, and then *we* should not exist. This result is certain, and all attempts to avoid it are illusory."[w]

Bradley's *Appearance and Reality* was published in 1893. What had begun in the *Critique of Pure Reason* as a confident rationalism, convinced that it had found a way of validating the natural sciences, had collapsed less than a hundred years later in what seemed to many critics a radical skepticism and to others an equally radical, and hardly distinguishable, mysticism, disguised from Bradley himself only by his refusal to draw the conclusion that followed logically from his premises. This result was very far indeed from satisfying what we have called the metaphysical urge—the urge experienced by Yeats's disoriented falcon as it turned in its ever-widening gyre. Some philosophers sought certainty. Others made a more modest demand—they would be content if they could establish no more than the possibility in principle of a knowledge of reality. Yet for there to be even a possibility of knowledge of reality there has to be a firm distinction between knowledge and belief, and in the Kantian paradigm this distinction was blurred, if not abolished. The first desideratum, then, was to escape from idealism and constructivism, to reassert the existence of an objective world independent of us and of our beliefs about it. As it turned out, this pursuit of objectivity took three main paths: one a revival of realism, one based on a revolution in logic, and one starting from what came to be called the phenomenological method— and all three were underway by the time *Appearance and Reality* was published.

Thus by the end of the nineteenth century the initial moves were already being made in what was to become increasingly the preoccupation of philosophers in our time—the quest for objectivity. But before we trace the course of these movements, we must, in the next chapter, consider the work of three philosophers who, though they continued to publish well into the new century and though they deeply influenced their contemporaries, are nevertheless more closely associated with earlier developments.

of reality, and in its assertion that reality can nonetheless be known—in intuition. In all these respects, Bergson was close to Arthur Schopenhauer, but because he took the theory of evolution seriously as a doctrine of progress, he had none of Schopenhauer's exaggerated pessimism.

If Bergson was close to Schopenhauer, Whitehead was in many ways close to Hegel. Whitehead reaffirmed the capacity of reason to know reality, and he sought to establish a new categorial scheme of metaphysically valid concepts. But whereas Hegel had derived his categorial scheme by reflecting on the meaning of an alleged identity-in-difference, Whitehead attempted to generalize the concepts underlying modern physics. Hence (and this is symptomatic of the change in nineteenth-century thought) Whitehead claimed to be empirical and scientific in a way Hegel had scorned.

Though Dewey as a young man was influenced by Hegel, he became skeptical of both the possibility and the desirability of building philosophical systems; like Nietzsche, he regarded the system-building urge as a reflection of our human sense of insecurity. But, unlike Nietzsche, Dewey believed that philosophy is useful—provided that it is modeled on the natural sciences and is content with probability, instead of absolute certainty. His emphasis on the instrumental and pragmatic character of knowledge was closely related to his deep interest in social problems. More than either Bergson or Whitehead, Dewey represented the great drive for social reform that had developed in the late nineteenth century.

Despite such differences, these three philosophers have a number of important characteristics in common. They were born within two years of each other, before the American Civil War. Yet Bergson lived until the Second World War had started; Whitehead, until after it had ended; and Dewey well into the nuclear age. To a large extent they had a common culture and a common outlook on life. Though they were younger than Søren Kierkegaard and Nietzsche, and though they were in their own ways innovators, their break with the past was less radical than that of Kierkegaard and Nietzsche, for all three were members of the philosophical establishment. These philosophers (especially Dewey) were critics of the status quo, but they were not alienated from it; temperamentally, each of them was well adapted (too well adapted, critics might say) to his social environment. They believed in the possibility of progress, which they thought could be promoted by intelligent action on the part of individuals. They were reformers, not rebels.

Again, though each of these philosophers presumably had to face his own existential problem, this problem did not fill his whole mental and emotional horizon. These philosophers regarded existence as essentially a matter to be dealt with in private; philosophy, as they conceived of it, was concerned with public problems. In this respect they were inheritors and continuators of the tradition of philosophizing in the grand manner; they believed that the business of philosophers was to tackle the classical questions about the nature of reality, of knowledge, and of value, and to produce well-rounded, articulated treatises on metaphysics, ethics, art, religion, and similar topics. This belief was true of

Three Philosophies

of Process:

Bergson, Dewey,

and Whitehead

The three philosophers whose views are examined in this chapter differ markedly among themselves. Henri Bergson and Alfred North Whitehead represent the metaphysical interest that survived Kant's "criticism" and continued to dominate much of nineteenth-century thought. John Dewey, however, represents the empirical, antimetaphysical trend that, since Hume, has been an increasingly powerful influence on Western thought.

Bergson's metaphysics, which grew directly out of the materialism versus vitalism controversy that was a major issue in the late nineteenth century,[1] was an attempt to use scientific findings to sustain an essentially antiscientific conception of reality. His metaphysics was "Romantic" in its emphasis on dynamism and continuity, in its denial of the capacity of reason to know the inner nature

[1] See Vol. IV, pp. 199–202.

Bergson and Dewey, both of whom attacked what they thought were the exaggerated claims of "reason," but it was especially true of Whitehead, whose philosophy of organism is the latest in a series of vast philosophical syntheses that began with Aristotle and continued with St. Thomas and Hegel.

More important, Bergson, Dewey, and Whitehead shared an interest in process. The two developments in nineteenth-century philosophy that most deeply influenced all three of these thinkers were the notion of a dynamic, changing reality, and the prestige accorded to the natural sciences. These two trends came together in the concept of evolution, and these three thinkers were all philosophers of evolution. They recognized that thought, as well as its objects, evolves, that ideas have a history relevant to their present status, and that philosophical theories are outgrowths of culture rather than eternal truths discovered by disembodied spirits.

Finally, and if only because their lives covered so great a span of years, they have shared a fate: neglect. They grew up in one period and lived into a very different one. The world of their youth was confident and serene; there was general agreement among philosophers about the nature and the role of philosophy and widespread acceptance of it as an important part of the culture. They lived into a period in which confidence seemed increasingly naïve and misplaced, and in which even philosophers had become divided and uncertain about the role of philosophy. Their theories, which had been in immense vogue in the early part of the twentieth century, therefore became increasingly outdated even while they still lived, and these three philosophers, who had once seemed bold innovators, looked more and more like conservatives, whose views were remote from contemporary issues. In sum, they were transitional figures between the late nineteenth and the early twentieth centuries, which explains why we begin this volume on twentieth-century philosophy with a study of their views.

Bergson

Bergson's[2] starting point was an attack on conceptual knowledge very similar to Schopenhauer's; it too was rooted in the conviction that concepts falsify a continuous real by dividing it. And, like Schopenhauer, Bergson believed that there is a superior kind of knowledge, which he called intuition, by means of which people have direct and immediate access to the nature of reality.

[2] Henri Bergson was born in France in 1859 and lived and taught there all his life. When, after the fall of France in 1940, the Vichy government introduced anti-Semitic measures based on the Nazi model, it was proposed, because of Bergson's international reputation, that he be exempted from them. He refused to be treated differently, resigned his various honors, and, although at that time an enfeebled old man who had to be supported while standing in line, registered with the other Jews. He died a few days later, in January 1941.

[There are] two profoundly different ways of knowing a thing. The first implies that we move round the object; the second that we enter into it. The first depends on the point of view at which we are placed and on the symbols by which we express ourselves. The second neither depends on a point of view nor relies on any symbol. The first kind of knowledge may be said to stop at the *relative;* the second, in those cases where it is possible, to attain the *absolute.*

Consider, for example, the movement of an object in space. My perception of the motion will vary with the point of view, moving or stationary, from which I observe it. My expression of it will vary with the system of axes, or points of reference, to which I relate it; that is, with the symbols by which I translate it. For this double reason I call such motion *relative:* in the one case, as in the other, I am placed outside the object itself. But when I speak of an *absolute* movement, I am attributing to the moving object an interior and, so to speak, states of mind; I also imply that I am in sympathy with those states, and that I insert myself in them by an effort of imagination. . . . I shall no longer grasp the movement from without, remaining where I am, but from where it is, from within, as it is itself. I shall possess an absolute.

Consider, again, a character whose adventures are related to me in a novel. The author may multiply the traits of his hero's character, may make him speak and act as much as he pleases, but all this can never be equivalent to the simple and indivisible feeling which I should experience if I were able for an instant to identify myself with the person of the hero himself. . . . Description, history, and analysis leave me here in the relative. Coincidence with the person himself would alone give me the absolute. . . .

It follows from this that an absolute could only be given in an *intuition,* whilst everything else falls within the province of *analysis.* By intuition is meant the kind of *intellectual sympathy* by which one places oneself within an object in order to coincide with what is unique in it and consequently inexpressible. Analysis, on the contrary, is the operation which reduces the object to elements already known, that is, to elements common both to it and other objects. To analyze, therefore, is to express a thing as a function of something other than itself. All analysis is thus a translation, a development into symbols, a representation taken from successive points of view. . . . In its eternally unsatisfied desire to embrace the object around which it is compelled to turn, analysis multiplies without end the number of its points of view . . . , and ceaselessly varies its symbols that it may perfect the always imperfect translation. It goes on, therefore, to infinity. But intuition, if intuition is possible, is a simple act. . . .

The inner life is all this at once: variety of qualities, continuity of progress, and unity of direction. It cannot be represented by . . . *concepts,* that is by abstract, general, or simple ideas. . . . Concepts . . . have the disadvantage of being in reality symbols substituted for the object they symbolize. . . . Just in so far as abstract ideas can render service to analysis, that is, to the scientific study of the object in its relations to other objects, so far are they incapable of replacing intuition, that is, the metaphysical investigation of what is essential and unique in the object. . . . Concepts, laid side by side, never actually give us more than an artificial reconstruction of the object. . . . Besides the illusion [that they give us the object instead of only its shadow] there is also a very serious danger. For the concept . . . can only symbolize a particular property by making it common to an infinity of things. It therefore always more or less deforms the property by the extension it gives to it.[a]

Limitations of Conceptual Knowledge

Kierkegaard would have felt considerable sympathy with much of this discussion. For instance, the distinction Bergson draws in this passage between reading about a character in a novel and *being* that character is close to Kierkegaard's distinction between objective and subjective truth. Both thinkers derogated whatever is indirect, impartial, and neutral. Further, like Kierkegaard, Bergson believed that the prime example of intuitive knowledge is the self—and not the abstract and impersonal self of traditional philosophy, but the individual self of the intuitive knower. However, though Bergson believed that intuitive knowledge starts with the self, he did not think it stops there. Whereas Kierkegaard was interested exclusively in his own existential problems and in how subjective knowledge could illumine them, Bergson was interested in what philosophy has traditionally been concerned with—the nature of reality. Hence, unlike Kierkegaard, he developed a metaphysics.

> Metaphysics . . . is only truly itself when it goes beyond the concept, or at least when it frees itself from rigid and ready-made concepts in order to create a kind very different from those we habitually use; I mean supple, mobile, and almost fluid representations, always ready to mould themselves on the fleeting forms of intuition. . . .
>
> Concepts . . . generally go together in couples and represent two contraries. There is hardly any concrete reality which cannot be observed from two opposing standpoints, which cannot consequently be subsumed under two antagonistic concepts [for example, the self is both a unity and a multiplicity]. Hence a thesis and an antithesis which we endeavor in vain to reconcile logically, for the very simple reason that it is impossible, with concepts and observations taken from outside points of view, to make a thing. But from the object, seized by intuition, we pass easily in many cases to the two contrary concepts; and as in that way thesis and antithesis can be seen to spring from reality, we grasp at

the same time how it is that the two are opposed and how they are reconciled.[b]

The last few sentences obviously refer to Hegel's account of thought as a triadic movement from thesis to antithesis to synthesis.[3] Bergson believed that Hegel was correct in aiming at unity, in not being content with plurality and diversity. But he thought Hegel was mistaken in holding that the same cognitive process that develops the contradictions can resolve them. To reconcile thesis and antithesis, a radically different kind of cognitive process is needed—intuition.

Hegel had already dealt with this argument—at least to his own satisfaction. Intuition is a lower, not a higher, level of cognition. To appeal to it is to return to the level of immediacy instead of rising to the level of self-mediation. In a word, Hegel took his stand on Kant's dictum that concepts without percepts are empty and percepts without concepts are blind. Intuitions are percepts without concepts—they are "the night in which all cows are black." Experience without the structure and organization that concepts supply is merely an undifferentiated "Aha!" The feeling may be powerful, moving, and exciting, but it does not *know* what it is or what it means.

Bergson was certainly not alone in rejecting this basically Kantian thesis. One of the central tenets of the Romantic movement was the belief that conceptual knowledge is distorting. But it is one thing for a Romantic poet to reject conceptual knowledge, or even for an existential thinker like Kierkegaard to do so, for the former is concerned chiefly with "expressing" feelings, and the latter focuses primarily on personal problems. It is another thing for a metaphysician to attack conceptual knowledge, for the metaphysician is committed to describing reality in general terms. To use a conceptual mode of discourse to argue that conceptual discourse is intrinsically distorting and inadequate is paradoxical. If reality is "unique," as Bergson claimed, this truth about it cannot be uttered. If reality is "inexpressible" by conceptual means, it is surely more appropriate to express its nature poetically than to expound a metaphysical and epistemological theory about its inexpressibility.

It is interesting in this connection to note that Bergson's writing is highly metaphorical. Though his reliance on metaphor is doubtless consistent with his derogation of analysis, Bergson did not recognize the limitations this imposed. It seemed to him that his metaphors functioned as a part of a reasoned argument— at least until they were challenged, at which point they became metaphors that were not to be taken literally. In his writings he gives the impression of having tried to make the best of both worlds. On the one hand, the reader is made to feel that what is presented is connected *theory*, not a poetic or mystic vision. On the other hand, as soon as the reader accepts it as a theory and looks for evidence, he or she is reminded that evidence is only a fiction created by intellect in its own image.

[3] See Vol. IV, pp. 124–26.

The Nature of Reality

But if we pass over this fundamental difficulty, the next question is, "What does intuition disclose the real to be?" The clue, as has already been seen, is the intuition one has—or is presumably capable of having—of one's own nature. We are, then, to look within. What we find when we do so Bergson variously called "duration," "mobility," and "life." It is an experience of change—not of states that change or of things with changing properties, but of change itself. It is an experience in which past infiltrates present through and through. This experience of duration, Bergson admitted, is very difficult to achieve. At best it is only momentary; furthermore, it is wholly private and incommunicable ("inexpressible" conceptually). Yet it is all the philosopher has to go on when setting out to construct a metaphysics.

INTUITION OF THE SELF AS DURATION

I find, first of all, that I pass from state to state. I am warm or cold, I am merry or sad, I work or I do nothing, I look at what is around me or I think of something else. . . . I change, then, without ceasing. But this is not saying enough. Change is far more radical than we are at first inclined to suppose.

For I speak of each of my states as if it formed a block and were a separate whole. . . . Of each state, taken separately, I am apt to think that it remains the same during all the time that it prevails. Nevertheless, a slight effort of attention would reveal to me that there is no feeling, no idea, no volition which is not undergoing change every moment: if a mental state ceased to vary, its duration would cease to flow. Let us take the most stable of internal states, the visual perception of a motionless external object. The object may remain the same, I may look at it from the same side, at the same angle, in the same light; nevertheless the vision I now have of it differs from that which I had just had, even if only because the one is an instant older than the other. My memory is there, which conveys something of the past into the present. My mental state, as it advances on the road of time, is continually swelling with the duration which it accumulates: it goes on increasing—rolling upon itself, as a snowball on the snow. . . .

Duration is the continuous progress of the past which gnaws into the future and which swells as it advances. And as the past grows without ceasing, so also there is no limit to its preservation. . . . In its entirety, probably, it follows us at every instant; all that we have felt, thought and willed from our earliest infancy is there, leaning over the present which is about to join it, pressing against the portals of consciousness that would fain leave it outside. The cerebral mechanism is arranged just so as to drive back into the unconscious almost the whole of this past, and to admit beyond the threshold only that which can cast light on the present situation or further the action now being prepared—in short, only that which can give *useful* work. At the most, a few superfluous recollections may succeed in smuggling themselves through the half-open door. These memories, messengers from the unconscious, remind us of what we are dragging behind us unawares. . . . Doubtless we think with only a small part of our past, but it is with our entire past, including the original bent of our soul, that we desire, will and act.[c]

To take knowledge of the self as the starting point for construction of a metaphysical theory has been a characteristic of philosophy since Descartes, and it is, of course, typical of post-Kantian views of the self to hold that self is activity and not a static, encapsulated substance. This view was as true of Hegel and Schopenhauer as it was of Kierkegaard and Nietzsche. There is thus nothing new in Bergson's basic thesis; it differs, however, in important ways from earlier versions, chiefly because it was deeply influenced by Bergson's understanding of the theory of evolution. What impressed Bergson about this theory was not the struggle for survival but the emergence of new forms of life; what caught his imagination was the vision of a great energy pouring itself forth in endless fecundity, instead of being confined to a few eternal archetypes. It was this cosmic vision that he transferred—in miniature, as it were—to the life experience of the individual; the self that is revealed in intuition, he maintained, is the continuous unfolding of new experiences that include and incorporate the past while moving steadily into the future.

In emphasizing the self as a continuous flow, Bergson differed sharply from psychologists of the then-dominant associationist school, who tended to think of the psychic life as consisting of a number of discrete blocks, or units, externally related to one another. He also differed from Kierkegaard and Nietzsche. They too rejected atomism in psychology and defined the self in terms of activity. But whereas Bergson viewed this activity as the continuous and relatively smooth unfolding of new experience, they viewed it as choosing and deciding. This divergence reflects the difference between an interest in the self that is primarily psychological and descriptive and one that is primarily concerned with existential problems. These differing views of the nature of the psychic life thus confirm Nietzsche's contention that our varied interpretations of the "original text" reveal our differing underlying values.

REALITY AS DURATION

But even if the self is correctly intuited to be duration, how do philosophers who have intuited this truth get outside themselves to a public reality? How can they know that the world is constituted of this same duration that they find in themselves? This is the problem Schopenhauer confronted and failed to solve when he maintained that the world is "really" will.[4] But in Bergson's case the problem is complicated by his claim that duration not only flows but is also creative and efficacious—that it is the underlying cause of the various visible and empirical transformations that are studied in the sciences. The following passage shows the inadequacy of the evidence by which Bergson moved from duration as a psychological characteristic of the self to duration as the metaphysical principle that explains all evolutionary change.

But if metaphysics is to proceed by intuition, if intuition has the mobility of duration as its object, and if duration is of a physical nature, shall we not be confining the philosopher to the exclusive contemplation of himself? . . . To talk in this way would be . . . to misconceive the singular nature of duration, and at the same time the essentially active, I might almost say violent, character of metaphysical intuition. It would be failing to see that the method we speak of alone permits us to go beyond idealism, as well as realism, to affirm the existence of objects inferior and superior (though in a certain sense interior) to us, to make them coexist together without difficulty, and to dissipate gradually the obscurities that analysis accumulates round these great problems. . . .

[Let us] place ourselves, by an effort of intuition, in the concrete flow of duration. . . . Strictly, there might well be no other duration than our own, as, for example, there might be no other color in the world but orange. But just as a consciousness based on color, which sympathized internally with orange, instead of perceiving it externally, would feel itself held between red and yellow, would even perhaps suspect beyond this last color a complete spectrum into which the continuity from red to yellow might expand naturally, so the intuition of our duration, far from leaving us suspended in the void as pure analysis would do, brings us into contact with a whole continuity of durations which we must try to follow, whether downwards or upwards; in both cases we can extend ourselves indefinitely by an increasingly violent effort, in both cases we transcend ourselves. In the first we advance towards a more and more attenuated duration, the pulsations of which, being rapider than ours, and dividing our simple sensation, dilute its quality into quantity; at the limit would be pure homogeneity, that pure *repetition* by which we define materiality. Advancing in the other direction, we approach a duration which *strains*, contracts, and intensifies itself more and more; at the limit would be eternity. No longer conceptual eternity, which is an eternity of death, but an eternity of life. A living, and therefore still moving eternity in which our own particular duration would be included as the vibrations are in light; an eternity which would be the

[4]See Vol. IV, p. 149.

concentration of all duration, as materiality is its dispersion. Between these two extreme limits intuition moves, and this movement is the very essence of metaphysics.[d]

Let us examine the difficulties with this view. This assertion that species evolve is an empirical hypothesis, subject to verification or disverification by biological and anatomical evidence. The assertion that duration is the force underlying all this evolutionary development is not an empirical hypothesis but a bald metaphysical statement, for there can be no evidence for or against it. Moreover, the assertion is highly ambiguous: Bergson became trapped in the old puzzle about the relation between reality and appearance—between the process (experienced in intuition) and the things processing (the material and bodily structures experienced in sense perception and studied in science). At times, as in the passage just quoted, Bergson wrote as if "matter" were one phase ("attenuated") of intuition; this suggests that Bergson's view was a form of monism. At other times, he assumed that matter is what the living force experienced in intuition works on. This suggests that matter has an independent existence of sorts and that Bergsonianism was a kind of dualism:

> We may compare the process by which nature constructs an eye to the simple act by which we raise the hand. . . . Let us now imagine that . . . the hand has to pass through iron filings which are compressed and offer resistance to it in proportion as it goes forward. At a certain moment the hand will have exhausted its effort, and, at this very moment, the filings will be massed and coordinated in a certain definite form, to wit, that of the hand that is stopped and of a part of the arm. Now, suppose that the hand and arm are invisible. Lookers-on will seek the reason of the arrangement in the filings themselves and in forces within the mass. Some will account for the position of each filing by the action exerted upon it by the neighboring filings: these are the mechanists. Others will prefer to think that a plan of the whole has presided over the detail of these elementary actions: they are the finalists. But the truth is that there has been merely one indivisible act, that of the hand passing through the filings. . . .
>
> The greater the effort of the hand, the farther it will go into the filings. But at whatever point it stops, instantaneously and automatically the filings coordinate and find their equilibrium. So with vision and its organ. According as the undivided act constituting vision advances more or less, the materiality of the organ is made of a more or less considerable number of mutually coordinated elements, but the order is necessarily complete and perfect.[e]

It is probably not possible to reconcile these different points of view. On the one hand Bergson spoke of "external resistances" to the living force; on the other, of "the materiality which it has had to assume."[f] Bergson wrote as if the evolutionary development he described was an objective fact. But the intellect that knows materiality has had a life history and has itself evolved. Hence the species and all their empirical unfoldings are merely appearances to intellects at a particular stage of their development. But this does not explain what is developing, and we are thrown back on our intuition of duration as the only real.

The Evolution of Intellect

Though this is a fundamental difficulty, it may nonetheless be useful to give a brief summary of Bergson's account of the course of evolution. The life force is "limited"; it "remains inadequate to the work it would fain produce" and operates on "inert matter." As a result evolutionary movement is not simple: "The resistance of inert matter was the obstacle that had first to be overcome. Life seems to have succeeded in this by dint of humility, by making itself very small and very insinuating, bending to physical and chemical forces . . . , [entering] into the habits of inert matter." In this way Bergson sought to account, in terms of his metaphysical scheme, for the evolutionary process beginning not from fully developed organisms but from "tiny masses of scarcely differentiated protoplasm." Despite their simplicity, these forms nevertheless possessed a "tremendous internal push."[g]

These most primitive forms cannot, properly speaking, be called either plants or animals, but they were more plantlike than animal-like. The first divergence occurred when differences in "alimentation" emerged. Plants derive their food directly from air, water, and soil; animals cannot assimilate their food unless it has already been transformed into organic substances by plants. This means that animals must be able to move about.

> Between mobility and consciousness there is an obvious relationship. No doubt, the consciousness of the higher organisms seems bound up with certain cerebral arrangements . . . , but . . . it would be as absurd to refuse consciousness to an animal because it has no brain as to declare it incapable of nourishing itself because it has no stomach. . . . [Even] the humblest organism is conscious in proportion to its power to move *freely*.[h]

Another divergence occurred when some animals "renounced" the protection of an "armor-plated sheath" and relied instead on "an agility that enabled them to escape their enemies, and also to assume the offensive, to choose the place and the moment of encounter. . . . It was to the animal's interest to make itself more mobile."[i] This naturally called for a correspondingly more complex nervous system. And the great mobility resulted, also naturally, in higher forms of consciousness.

The next divergence was the most important of all. It marked the different ways in which the nervous system developed to meet the needs of the new mobility. In one line of development, it was "distributed amongst a varying—sometimes a considerable—number of appendages, each of which has its special function." In the main line of development, it was "concentrated in two pairs of members only, and these organs perform functions which depend much less strictly on their form."[j]

Bergson was not interested in the actual evolution of the nervous system; nor did he know anything about these matters at first hand. All this descriptive detail was only a springboard to what *did* interest him—the "two powers immanent in life and originally intermingled," which (he was persuaded) have produced, respectively, the two types of nervous system just described. These powers, Bergson held, are "instinct" and "intelligence." But what, exactly, do these terms name? The two types of nervous system are observable facts, as are the specific behaviors associated with each. Unless "instinct" and "intelligence" are simply names for these behaviors, they do not name empirical facts. How, then, do these terms function in Bergson's writings? Bearing in mind Nietzsche's analysis of the meaning of "cause,"[5] we may suspect that instinct and intelligence are "fictions" ("myths" was another term Nietzsche used) in which "the personality betrays itself"—that is, these concepts enabled Bergson to express his preference for unmediated experience and his dislike for an objective, conceptual approach.

But as soon as he started talking about "powers" as distinct from nervous systems Bergson shifted from empirically grounded concepts to speculation. Because he did not notice this drift, however, he was able to assume that the metaphysical generalizations he was developing did not differ in kind from the scientific generalizations he had taken over from the biologists and anatomists. The former, he thought, were merely of much greater scope and hence more important. Accordingly, he proceeded to use the contrasting ideas of instinct and intelligence as if they were scientific concepts.

Instinct, as it has developed in insects such as ants and bees, makes use of "organized tools," that is, tools that are a part of the insect's body and that are each designed to perform a specific function necessary for the insect's survival. There is thus a wonderful certainty, precision, and inevitability about an insect's knowledge.

Intelligence, however, which has reached its highest development in human beings, operates by means of "unorganized tools." "Considered in what seems to be its original feature, [intelligence] is the faculty of manufacturing artificial objects, especially tools to make tools, and of indefinitely varying the manufacture." Thus, whereas the insect has a limited repertoire of actions, which it performs with great success, human beings have a much greater range of activities, but these are less certain and less effortless. "The advantages and drawbacks of these two modes of activity" are precisely complementary; indeed, they "balance so

5 See Vol. IV, pp. 242–43.

well" that "at the outset . . . it is hard to foretell which of the two will secure to the living being the greater empire over nature."[k]

Intellect and Action

Consciousness occurs in its most complete form in intelligent animals because intelligence presents the animal with options. Alternatives exist—the animal can use this tool or that one. The insect, on the other hand, does not have to worry about choices—its bodily organs are either adapted or not adapted to the situation. Consciousness in the full sense is always connected with "hesitation and choice":

> Consciousness is the light that plays around the zone of possible actions or potential activity which surrounds the action really performed by the living being. It signifies hesitation or choice. Where many equally possible actions are indicated without there being any real action (as in a deliberation that has not come to an end), consciousness is intense. Where the action performed is the only action possible (as in activity of the somnambulistic or more generally automatic kind), consciousness is reduced to nothing. . . . From this point of view, *the consciousness of a living being may be defined as an arithmetical difference between potential and real activity. It measures the interval between representation and action.*[1]

In a word, consciousness has a purely *practical* role. "Postulate action, and the very form of the intellect can be deduced from it." Because it is the function of intelligence (in contrast to instinct) to construct tools, intelligence must be especially competent to deal with matter.

> *Intelligence, as it leaves the hands of nature, has for its chief object the unorganized solid. . . .*
>
> The intellect is never quite at its ease, never entirely at home, except when it is working upon inert matter. [But] what is the most general property of the material world? It is extended: it presents to us objects external to other objects, and, in these objects, parts external to parts.[m]

In short, the primary function of intellect is to arrange and rearrange bits of solid matter in various spatial relations.

Now, because people live in communities, they must communicate with one another.[6] This requires language, and it is natural that language and the concepts employed in it should reflect the prime characteristic of intellect just described.

---

[6] Insects also live in societies, of course. But because instinct has already produced the co-operation required for communal living, it is not necessary that language evolve among them.

> Intelligence, even when it no longer operates upon its own object [that is, the unorganized solid], follows habits it has contracted in that operation. . . . Concepts, in fact, are outside each other, like objects in space; and they have the same stability as such objects, on which they have been modeled.[n]

It follows that "intellect is characterized by a natural inability to comprehend life"—that life and motion "escape it altogether."[o] Thus examination of evolutionary development has "confirmed"—at least in Bergson's view—the thesis of the *Introduction to Metaphysics;* by tracing the natural history of intellect, Bergson believed he had explained why conceptual thinking has those disabilities pointed out earlier. Because intellect is tied down to the useful, to the manipulation of solids, it never can comprehend the true, inner meaning of anything. If men and women had to depend on it, they would remain forever in outer darkness.

> The normal work of the intellect is far from being disinterested. We do not aim generally at knowledge for the sake of knowledge, but in order to take sides, to draw profit—in short, to satisfy an interest. . . . To try to fit a concept on an object is simply to ask what we can do with the object, and what it can do for us. To label an object with a certain concept is to mark in precise terms the kind of action or attitude the object should suggest to us. . . . But to carry this *modus operandi* into philosophy, . . . to use in order to obtain a disinterested knowledge of an object (that this time we desire to grasp as it is in itself) a manner of knowing inspired by a determinate interest, . . . is to go against the end we have chosen. . . . Either there is no philosophy possible, and all knowledge of things is practical knowledge aimed at the profit to be drawn from them, or else philosophy consists in placing oneself within the object itself by an effort of intuition.[p]

Bergson's attitude toward consciousness is thus different from Kierkegaard's and Nietzsche's. Whereas they derogated consciousness completely, Bergson held it to be useful at the level of action in the empirical world; it is seriously inadequate only when we mistakenly believe that it gives information about the inner nature of the things we encounter in our interactions with our environment. Given his presuppositions about evolution, Bergson was bound to assume that consciousness is useful: because it has survived, it must have some survival value. Doubtless this less critical evaluation of consciousness also reflects a temperament very different from Kierkegaard's and Nietzsche's. Whereas they were deeply alienated, Bergson was generally sunny and optimistic. In his view the universe is basically good, and despite its infinite variety it is unified, for it is the expression of a single life force.

These fundamental attitudes are also revealed in Bergson's insistence that, though intellect and instinct are divergent evolutionary paths, they are not completely sundered. "Everywhere we find them mingled; it is the proportion that differs. [Hence] there is no intelligence in which some traces of instinct are not to be discovered, . . . no instinct that is not surrounded with a fringe of intelligence." But instinct *is* sympathy; in contrast to intellect, which, as we have seen, "guides us into matter," instinct is "turned towards life" and thus gives us "the key to vital operations." It might be thought to follow that insects, in whom instinct predominates, are better metaphysicians than human beings and have a fuller understanding of duration. But this is not so. Though instinct is the *basic* element in intuition, it is not the only element. Intuition involves not just sympathy but "disinterested sympathy"; and to become disinterested, intelligence is required. Accordingly, intuition may be defined as "instinct that has become disinterested, self-conscious, capable of reflecting upon its object and of enlarging it indefinitely." Hence it turns out that people are better metaphysicians than the hymenoptera.[q]

Bergson has traced the evolutionary development as far as humankind, the highest stage yet reached. It is quite impossible, he thought, to predict what form duration will take in the future, or when it will make another evolutionary leap. Although it is possible, after an event occurs, to show why it came to be what it is, one can never say in advance what it is going to be.

The Two Sources of Morality and Religion

As has often been remarked, a metaphysical scheme provides an overarching set of concepts that gives the various domains of experience a unified interpretation. This function of metaphysics can be seen plainly in Bergson's account of morality and religion. Just as he used his basic distinction between the creative force and the "deposits" on which this force works to describe and evaluate two different kinds of cognitive process, so he used this distinction to describe and evaluate two different kinds of morality and two different kinds of religion. The creative force results in a "dynamic" religion and an "open" morality; the external forms result in a "static" religion and a "closed" morality. The former is a religion and morality of love and freedom; the latter is one of obligation and law. Once again, however, these two sources are divergent rather than sheerly distinct. Elements of both can be found in contemporary morals and religions.

CLOSED MORALITY AND STATIC RELIGION

According to Bergson, the whole apparatus of human obligations, ranging from moral duties such as keeping promises to social customs such as kissing, has its origin in those social pressures by which societies hold themselves together. Societies can survive only by organization, discipline, and division of labor. On the whole, social cohesion is provided far more adequately in insect societies than in human societies. The systems of law, duty, and custom that operate in human so-cieties are the rather inadequate reflections of the drives that operate instinctively in insects. Of course, human laws are more flexible and more diverse, precisely because the activities of human beings are more varied; but flexibility and variety are necessarily accompanied by a weakening of the drives for cohesion and by a strengthening of egocentric impulses. It follows from this view that philosophers such as Kant, who try to derive obligation from "reason," are talking nonsense. As a matter of fact, to the extent that reason and intelligence cause individuals to think of themselves as distinct from the community of which they are really an or-gan, they are disruptive of morality and order and must be counteracted by other forces. It is true that they have a positive (though subordinate) function in that they help to determine what particular, concrete forms the underlying impulse toward social cohesion will take. But the ultimate sanction, the ultimate "categor-ical imperative," is always this social impulse.

> The work done by intelligence in weighing reasons, comparing max-ims, going back to first principles, was to introduce more logical consis-tency into a line of conduct subordinated by its very nature to the claims of society; but this social claim was the real root of obligation. . . .
>
> [In civilized societies] social demands have . . . been co-ordinated with each other and subordinated to principles. But . . . the essence of obligation is a different thing from a requirement of reason. This is all we have tried to suggest so far. Our description would, we think, cor-respond more and more to reality as one came to deal with less devel-oped communities and more rudimentary stages of consciousness. . . . Conceive obligation as weighing on the will like a habit, each obliga-tion dragging behind it the accumulated mass of the others, and utilis-ing thus for the pressure it is exerting the weight of the whole: here you have the totality of obligation for a simple, elementary, moral con-science. That is the essential: that is what obligation could, if neces-sary, be reduced to, even in those cases where it attains its highest complexity.
>
> This shows when and in what sense (how slightly Kantian!) obligation in its elementary state takes the form of a "categorical imperative." We should find it very difficult to discover examples of such an imperative in everyday life. . . . So let us imagine an ant who is stirred by a gleam of reflexion and thereupon judges she has been wrong to work un-remittingly for others. Her inclination to laziness would indeed endure but a few moments, just as long as the ray of intelligence. In the last of these moments, when instinct regaining the mastery would drag her back by sheer force to her task, intelligence at the point of relapsing into instinct would say as its parting word: "You must because you must." This "must because you must" would only be the momentary

feeling of awareness of a tug which the ant experiences—the tug which the string, momentarily relaxed, exerts as it drags her back. . . . In a word, an absolutely categorical imperative is instinctive or somnam-bulistic, enacted as such in a normal state, represented as such if reflex-ion is roused long enough to take form, not long enough to seek for reasons. But, then, is it not evident that, in a reasonable being, an im-perative will tend to become categorical in proportion as the activity brought into play, although intelligent, will tend to become instinctive? But an activity which, starting as intelligent, progresses towards an im-itation of instinct is exactly what we call, in man, a habit. And the most powerful habit, the habit whose strength is made up of the accumulated force of all the elementary social habits, is necessarily the one which best imitates instinct. Is it then surprising that, in the short moment which separates obligation merely experienced as a living force from obligation fully realized and justified by all sorts of reasons, obligation should indeed take the form of the categorical imperative: "you must because you must"?[r]

There is, then, no *reason* for being moral—the basis for morality is merely a blind "you must because you must." And this imperative can never be "proved" by ar-gument or "justified" by logic; it simply expresses the elementary urge to self-preservation by which societies, like all other organisms, protect themselves from the "dissolvent power of intelligence."

This type of morality is accompanied by static religion, which functions to "re-inforce and sustain the claims of society." By means of its mythmaking power, static religion counteracts the dangerous inhibitions against effective, forceful ac-tion that intelligence creates by making known to us "the inevitability of death."[s]

OPEN MORALITY AND DYNAMIC RELIGION

Open morality and dynamic religion have a wholly different source. In this case the impulse is not social pressure but the sense of life and movement that rare individuals possess. Here is still another modulation of the Hegelian theme of the great man, the creative individual who breaks down old forms and fashions new ones. It is interesting to see this theme appearing again and again in nine-teenth-century thought and to see also how the paradigm of the great human being—whether it is Jesus, Socrates, Alcibiades, Napoleon, or Goethe—varies from one philosopher to another depending on that thinker's own creative individuality.

For Bergson the model of the great human being was not an artist or a war-rior but a moral and religious leader such as Jesus or Buddha. The saints of all the religions of the world are, as it were, orifices through which wells up the life force itself. A saint thus has an enormous drive and energy—is able to "move mountains," to inspire whole generations of lesser men and women to higher and nobler conceptions of morality. Such a saint is, in fact, just one of those creative leaps that the life force periodically makes and that is productive of a genuine novelty, like the leap by which animals developed out of plants. At such times the sense of obligation to some closed society is replaced by a morality of aspiration and love rooted in a feeling of our common unity.

> The great moral figures that have made their mark on history join hands across the centuries, above our human cities; they unite into a divine city which they bid us enter. We may not hear their voices distinctly, the call has none the less gone forth, and something answers from the depth of our soul. . . . It is these men who draw us towards an ideal society, while we yield to the pressure of the real one.[t]

After making such a leap into a saintly personality, the life force relaxes for a time; the great leader passes on and humankind relapses into static religion and closed social morality. But although most people are unable to live up to the ideals of the great personality who has departed from their midst, they remember the teachings and try to emulate them in their feeble way. Hence all actual moralities and religions are a blend of elements from these two sources. Thus, for instance, "justice [social morality] finds itself continually broadened by pity; 'charity' assumes more and more the shape of justice";[u] and so on.

Mysticism, Asceticism, and a Universal Society

According to Bergson, humankind was designed "for very small societies. . . . Yet nature, which ordained small societies, left them with an opening for expansion." This opening is the capacity for "the mystic life," which appears whenever "the fringe of intuition surrounding [human] intelligence is capable of expanding sufficiently to envelop its object," and which points in the direction of a truly democratic, free, and peaceful society that incorporates all humankind. Is this merely an ideal? Or can it be hoped that the deeply rooted instincts pulling men and women down into closed societies finally may be eradicated? It is possible, Bergson believed, that they may be. For centuries men and women have made a cult of comfort and luxury, but it is possible that they may be approaching a new period of asceticism and mysticism. There are two reasons, at any rate, to believe this may come about. First, there is a "possible link" between mysticism and industrialism. Second, a "law of twofold frenzy" seems to operate. As regards the role of industrialism, Bergson believed that mystic intuition is liable to relapse into ecstatic contemplation unless the mystic has a sense of power. Industrialism and the "advent of the machine" may give the mystic this necessary "faith in action." Hence, "instead of turning inwards and closing, the soul [can] open wide its gates to a universal love."ᵛ As regards the "law of twofold frenzy," Bergson held that periods of asceticism and of luxury seem not only to alternate but to produce each other by their own excesses. In medieval times, the "ascetic ideal" led to such "exaggerations" that people finally revolted against it. Thus, since "one frenzy brings on a counter-frenzy," "there is nothing improbable in the return to a simpler life."ʷ And this simple life may be productive of a new "mystic genius," who

> will draw after him a humanity already vastly grown in body, and whose soul he has transfigured. He will yearn to make of it a new species, or rather deliver it from the necessity of being a species; for every species means a collective halt. . . . Let once the summons of the hero come, we shall not all follow it, but we shall all feel that we ought to, and we shall see the path before us, which will become a highway if we pass along it. . . . It is always the stop which requires explanation, and not the movement.ˣ

Bergson and the Spirit of the Age

Nothing shows more strikingly Bergson's temperamental difference from Kierkegaard and Nietzsche than these points about industrialism and the return to a simpler and better life. Kierkegaard and Nietzsche had been deeply suspicious of the Enlightenment's idea of progress; Bergson was still committed to it, though not to the Enlightenment's belief in "reason." Whereas both Kierkegaard and Nietzsche had given up the masses and concentrated whatever hopes they had on a few rare individuals, and whereas Nietzsche had held that industrialism was producing a race of factory slaves and preparing the way for the rise of totalitarian dictatorships, Bergson believed that humanity might be on the verge of making a new creative advance.[7] Further, whereas Kierkegaard and Nietzsche were completely skeptical (though for different reasons) regarding the findings of science, Bergson believed that his views were as "scientific" as Charles Darwin's hypothesis about natural selection. Finally, Bergson was deeply committed to metaphysical inquiry, whereas Kierkegaard was indifferent to it and Nietzsche regarded it as phony.

Bergson, then, represented older, more traditional modes of thought that stem directly from the eighteenth century and ultimately from a tradition going back beyond the Renaissance to Plato and Aristotle. Yet, despite his differences from Kierkegaard and Nietzsche, he shared several fundamental attitudes with

[7] Nietzsche made his grimly prophetic observations in the 1880s; Bergson's optimistic views were published only a year before Hitler became the German chancellor.

them that show him to have been deeply affected by the antirationalistic "countermovement" in which they participated. Bergson thought that his discussions of instinct and intelligence were scientific, but they were actually highly speculative. Bergson was, in fact, as hostile to the positivism that characterizes the actual procedures of working scientists as any Romantic poet had been. "It is one thing," he said, "to recognize that outer circumstances [like natural selection] are forces evolution must reckon with, another to claim that they were the directing causes." And in another place he remarked that, although scientific theories of evolution are true in a "limited way," they take "a partial view."[y]

This commitment to metaphysical entities, which a Comtean empiricist would have regarded as redundant or worse, was thus all-important for Bergson. There is nothing unusual, of course, in demands for answers to the "why" questions; attempts to link these answers into a systematic worldview have recurred in the history of the Western mind since Plato's day. What was unusual about Bergson's position (and very suggestive of the new climate of opinion) was his denial that answers to the "why" questions could be found within any of the traditional frames of reference—within a rational or even a teleological order. Instead, he sought and found the answers in the life force, a process as irrational and purposeless as Schopenhauer's blind "will."

Like Goethe's Faust, Bergson wanted to probe deep below the surface to uncover those forces that bind the world together and that are the creative sources of all changes—forces of whose existence he was convinced on metaphysical grounds, not as a result of empirical observation. Like Faust, he was not content to be told *how* things evolve and change; he wanted to know *why* they do so. And, like Faust, he believed that it was possible to reach this deeper level of reality and of explanation in—but only in—intuition. As a result, Bergson's metaphysics took a nontraditional form. Explanation in terms of a systematic conceptual structure ("matter-form," "dialectic," or whatever) was replaced by a referral of all problems, all issues, and all questions to the same unintelligible source.

Further, Bergson's very quest for the nature of reality was undermined from the start by his attack on conceptual knowledge and his recognition that intelligence is always "interested." Bergson did not see and face up to the paradox that Nietzsche was delighted to accept;[8] this suggests the central tension in his position, as indeed in so much of the thought of our age. An antirationalistic metaphysics like Bergson's, in contrast both to the assured rationalism of the traditional metaphysics and to the confident antimetaphysical attitudes of positivism and pragmatism, is like the uneasy mixture of love and hatred that some people experience for their spouses or parents. It is one thing to throw out the "why" questions as phony; it is another thing to complain because intelligence cannot answer them. To complain that intelligence is inadequate suggests that it *ought* to be adequate; one then should look around for something better, or at least for a

---

[8] See Vol. IV, p. 248.

substitute. But once one begins the pursuit of substitutes there is no telling in what "leap of faith" or other "absolute" one is going to end.[9] However much the views of Kierkegaard and Nietzsche differ from those of Bergson, which reflect a more unified and confident personality, one is conscious of a very deep affinity among them. For all three philosophers gave expression to the deep irrationalism, or at least the antirationalism, that seems increasingly to characterize contemporary culture.

Dewey

PRAGMATISM, PRAGMATICISM, AND INSTRUMENTALISM

Dewey's theory is one version—the latest and the most systematically worked out—of a group of views loosely identified as "pragmatic." It is sometimes said that pragmatism is a "typical" expression of the American ethos. But there were many pragmatists who were not Americans and many Americans who were not pragmatists, and, in any case, it was not sui generis. Many different strands of influence—Hume's empirical analysis, Kant's phenomena (but not his noumena), Hegel's phenomenology, the social orientation of the Utilitarians, the positivism of Comte, and Bergson's activism—can be detected as having played a role in the development of pragmatism. For these reasons pragmatism was anything but a well-defined, uniform "school." The earliest version of pragmatism was put forward by C. S. Peirce in 1878.

Peirce was a rigorous thinker, a mathematician, a logician, and a metaphysician. What pragmatism (or "pragmaticism," a term he introduced after he concluded that William James had bowdlerized the original concept) meant to him was similar to what subsequently came to be called the operational criterion of meaning. As a result of reflecting on the actual procedure of the empirical sciences, which Peirce regarded as far and away the best examples available to us of what knowledge is, he concluded that the way to find out what any statement means is to list the operations that verify it. For instance, the statement "All

[9] It is interesting in this connection to note that Bergson himself ultimately turned to Catholicism. After the publication of *The Two Sources* (1932) his thoughts turned more and more to religious matters, and by 1937 he had reached the point where only the violent anti-Semitism of the age (which made him loath to give the appearance of abandoning his religious group) prevented his conversion and baptism. He asked, however, that a Catholic priest be permitted to pray at his funeral, and this was authorized. In view of his principal works having long been on the *Index,* and of the attack on conceptualism and dogmatism that was fundamental to his whole position, it might be supposed that his formal, official conversion would have occasioned some difficulties. But this is merely another episode in the old problem of reconciling mysticism and orthodoxy, in which the Church has had a rich experience.

bodies gravitate" is not about some force "gravity" that pulls, or attracts, bodies, for it is impossible to verify the existence of such a force. All that we actually find is that, as a matter of fact, bodies accelerate in such-and-such a uniform manner, and this is all that "All bodies gravitate" means. That is to say, a statement means what verifies it—nothing more, nothing less. It follows that any statement (for example, "The Absolute exists") that cannot be verified or falsified is literally meaningless. Though this rules out, at one blow, most of the traditional metaphysics, Peirce himself was far from being hostile to metaphysics. On the contrary, he was a realist of the strict medieval variety. He held that there is a real objective world, and that, though we can never know nature completely, we can, by means of the self-corrective method of science, approach it asymptotically.[10]

For James, who popularized pragmatism, what the pragmatic criterion meant was not that an assertion is true if it can be empirically verified but that it is true if it "works." The instrument that Peirce thought would lead us to an ever-expanding knowledge of the real world became a device for justifying one's believing whatever one is deeply committed to. James was, in fact, far less interested in ascertaining the truth about the universe than he was in helping people in quandaries make a successful adjustment. And this is what "working" really meant to him. The deepest quandary in which people of his generation were entangled, he thought, was the conflict between their religious instincts and their desire to accept the findings of science, which seemed opposed to their religious instincts. James sought to show that the conclusions of science are not so authoritative as they seem to be, and that science, like religion, is based ultimately on commitment rather than on evidence. In his hands, then, pragmatism was not an epistemological theory, as it was for Peirce, but a therapeutic device.[11]

Dewey's[12] version of pragmatism—which he called "instrumentalism," to distinguish it from both Peirce's and James's—was, like Peirce's and unlike James's, an attempt to deal with metaphysical and epistemological issues. But whereas Peirce was a medieval realist, Dewey had been brought up in the Hegelian tradition and was disposed to start with "experience," rather than with independently and objectively existing "reals." Like James and unlike Peirce, Dewey was deeply interested in "practical" problems, though the problems that chiefly concerned him were less those of the individual psyche than of society. Hence, instead of

---

[10] For a more detailed study of Peirce, see Vol. IV, Ch. 7.

[11] For a detailed examination of James's views, see Vol. IV, Ch. 8.

[12] John Dewey (1859–1952) was born in Vermont and grew up there. After graduating from the University of Vermont he went to Johns Hopkins University for his Ph.D. At the turn of the century he taught at the University of Chicago and directed the experimental school. From there his views on educational theory, with his emphasis on "learning by doing," spread across the country and had an immense influence on educational practice everywhere. In 1904 Dewey went to Columbia University, where he remained for the rest of his active life. He was one of the organizers of the American Civil Liberties Union and the American Association of University Professors, and he was active in many social causes, including the defense of Sacco and Vanzetti in the mid-1920s and of Trotsky after he had been denounced by the Soviet Union.

concentrating on personal adjustment, Dewey was concerned with the need for reorganizing the social and physical environment, and for this he held that sound empirical knowledge of the sort the sciences provide is indispensable.

Instrumentalism had both a negative thesis and a positive thesis. It was both an all-out attack on traditional philosophy and a vigorous "reconstruction" of philosophy on a new basis. The negative thesis can be stated in terms of the comment Dewey would have been disposed to make on Bergson. As has been seen, Bergson maintained that "the normal work of the intellect is far from being disinterested"; it follows, he held, that "either there is no philosophy possible, and all knowledge is practical, or else philosophy consists in intuition."[13] Bergson, of course, opted for the second alternative; Dewey, for the first. Because Dewey affirmed that all knowledge is "practical" and denied that intuition is knowledge, he concluded that "philosophy"—both in the traditional sense and in Bergson's sense—is impossible. Thus Dewey used the insight that intellect is "interested" in a negative way in destroying the old metaphysics. But he also used this insight in a positive way to rehabilitate empiricism by emphasizing the active, experimental, purposive elements in cognition.

In Dewey's view, intelligence cannot attain eternal truths; but, rightly understood and rightly applied, it is capable of dealing effectively with pressing social and political problems. Whereas Bergson had been interested in the esthetic enjoyment of "duration" as he experienced it in intuition, and whereas Kierkegaard and Nietzsche had been preoccupied with their personal existential problems, Dewey focused on the actual world and on what "interested" thought can do in it. He was concerned with our "traffic with nature," which he wanted to make "freer and more secure." Thus his motives were similar to those of such nineteenth-century social philosophers as Jeremy Bentham and John Stuart Mill, and he shared their generally optimistic outlook about our capacity to act intelligently. But to this undertaking he brought a much more sophisticated grasp of the nature of intelligence; indeed, it is characteristic of his concept of intelligence that he preferred the term "inquiry," which reflected his view that mind is directive and active, not merely an observer and recorder of information. In this respect he shared Kant's and, to a greater extent, Hegel's belief that experience is a product in which mind plays a decisive role. Kant and Hegel, however, emphasized the construction of a world to be known; Dewey emphasized the construction of a world to be lived in and acted on.

Concept of Human Nature

The center of interest in Dewey's thought was men and women and their practical problems. And since they are not only active but social animals, Dewey's starting

[13] See p. 28.

point was social psychology. Three factors in this connection require examination: habit, impulse, and intelligence.

HABIT

A habit is a "mechanism" for dealing with certain recurrent "classes of stimuli, standing predilections and aversions." But a habit is not necessarily a mere automatic mechanism, like the machine that prints, folds, conveys, and does everything but read, newspapers. It is necessary to distinguish between "two kinds of habit, intelligent and routine." And "the higher the form of life the more complex, sure and flexible" the habit. Furthermore, habits involve a functional relation between organism and environment, "in which the environment has its say as surely as the [organism]." A habit is a *function* between organism and environment by means of which life is furthered and maintained. It is possible, therefore, to look at habits as *arts.* "They involve skill of sensory and motor organs, cunning or craft, and objective materials. They assimilate objective energies, and eventuate in command of environment."[z]

IMPULSE

Habits are, of course, learned. What is original is impulse; habits are simply the shapings and canalizings of impulses. It is a mistake, according to Dewey, to suppose that any impulse has a specific character in itself. Impulses are indefinitely plastic and malleable. They acquire their meanings from the interaction of the organism with a "matured social medium." Under the influence of environment, that is, they develop into those relatively precise and specialized functions that Dewey called habits.

> In the case of the young it is patent that impulses are highly flexible starting points for activities which are diversified according to the ways in which they are used. Any impulse may become organized into almost any disposition according to the way it interacts with surroundings. Fear may become abject cowardice, prudent caution, reverence for superiors or respect for equals; an agency for credulous swallowing of absurd superstitions or for wary scepticism. . . . The actual outcome depends upon how the impulse of fear is interwoven with other impulses. This depends in turn upon the outlets and inhibitions supplied by the social environment.
>
> The traditional psychology of instincts obscures recognition of this fact. It sets up a hard-and-fast preordained class under which specific acts are subsumed, so that their own quality and originality are lost from view. This is why the novelist and dramatist are so much more illuminating as well as more interesting commentators on conduct than the schematizing psychologist. . . .

In the career of any impulse activity there are speaking generally three possibilities. It may find a surging, explosive discharge—blind, unintelligent. It may be sublimated—that is, become a factor coordinated intelligently with others in a continuing course of action. Thus a gust of anger may, because of its dynamic incorporation into disposition, be converted into an abiding conviction of social injustice to be remedied, and furnish the dynamic to carry the conviction into execution. . . . Such an outcome represents the normal or desirable functioning of impulse; in which, to use our previous language, the impulse operates as a pivot, or reorganization of habit. Or again a released impulsive activity may be neither immediately expressed in isolated spasmodic action, nor indirectly employed in an enduring interest. It may be "suppressed."

Suppression is not annihilation. "Psychic" energy is no more capable of being abolished than the forms we recognize as physical. If it is neither exploded nor converted, it is turned inwards, to lead a surreptitious, subterranean life. . . . A suppressed activity is the cause of all kinds of intellectual and moral pathology.[a]

INTELLIGENCE

Properly understood, intelligence is merely an unusually flexible and finely adjusted habit that functions to improve the organism's relation to its environment. Specifically, it is a habit that intervenes when other, more routine habits fail to perform efficiently. Human beings are not passive, inert spectators of a neutral world. They are organisms plunged into an environment that infiltrates at every point their own nature. Habits are the functions by which people normally make necessary adjustments. But since the environment is immensely complex and anything but static, these habitual adjustments constantly require modification. Their modification is the work of intelligence.

> *The function of reflective thought is to transform a situation in which there is experienced obscurity, doubt, conflict, disturbance of some sort, into a situation that is clear, coherent, settled, harmonious. . . .*

When a situation arises containing a difficulty or perplexity, the person who finds himself in it may take one of a number of courses. He may dodge it, dropping the activity that brought it about, turning to something else. He may indulge in a flight of fancy, imagining himself powerful or wealthy, or in some other way in possession of the means that would enable him to deal with the difficulty. Or, finally, he may face the situation. In this case, he begins to reflect.

The moment he begins to reflect, he begins of necessity to observe in order to take stock of conditions. . . . Some of the conditions are obstacles and others are aids, resources. No matter whether these conditions come to him by direct perception or by memory, they form the "*facts* of the case." They are the things that are *there,* that have to be reckoned with. . . . Until the habit of thinking is well formed, facing the situation to discover the facts requires an effort. For the mind tends to dislike what is unpleasant and so to sheer off from an adequate notice of that which is especially annoying.

Along with noting the conditions that constitute the facts to be dealt with, suggestions arise of possible courses of action. . . . [These lead] to new observations and recollections and to a reconsideration of observations already made in order to test the worth of the suggested way out. . . . The newly noted facts may (and in any complex situation surely will) cause new suggestions to spring up. . . . This continuous interaction of the facts disclosed by observation and of the suggested proposals of solution and the suggested methods of dealing with conditions goes on till some suggested solution meets all the conditions of the case and does not run counter to any discoverable feature of it. . . .

We shall illustrate what has been said by a simple case. Suppose you are walking where there is no regular path. As long as everything goes smoothly, you do not have to think about your walking; your already formed habit takes care of it. Suddenly you find a ditch in your way. You think you will jump it (supposition, plan); but to make sure, you survey it with your eyes (observation), and you find that it is pretty wide and that the bank on the other side is slippery (facts, data). You then wonder if the ditch may not be narrower somewhere else (idea), and you look up and down the stream (observation) to see how matters stand (test of idea by observation). You do not find any good place and so are thrown back upon forming a new plan. As you are casting about, you discover a log (fact again). You ask yourself whether you could not haul that to the ditch and get it across the ditch to use as a bridge (idea again). You judge that idea is worth trying, and so you get the log and manage to put it in place and walk across (test and confirmation by overt action). . . .

The two limits of every unit of thinking are a perplexed, troubled, or confused situation at the beginning and a cleared-up, unified, resolved situation at the close. . . .

In between, as states of thinking, are (1) *suggestions,* in which the mind leaps forward to a possible solution; (2) an intellectualization of the difficulty or perplexity that has been *felt* (directly experienced) into a *problem* to be solved, a question for which the answer must be sought; (3) the use of one suggestion after another as a leading idea, or *hypothesis,* to initiate and guide observation and other operations in collection of factual material; (4) the mental elaboration of the idea or supposition as an idea or supposition (*reasoning,* in the sense in which reasoning is a part, not the whole, of inference); and (5) testing the hypothesis by overt or imaginative action.[b]

Theory of Education

As has been said, all habits, including the habit called thinking, are learned. Unfortunately, most of them are learned unsystematically, with little care or forethought on the part of those who do the teaching. As a matter of fact, few people think of their behavior to others as being a form of teaching; fewer still understand the functional relationships, just described, that exist among habits, impulses, and intelligence. Even at the conscious, planned level, educational practice is often based on a mistaken conception of human nature. Is it surprising, therefore, that so many bad habits, so many maladjustments, and so many inefficient ways of functioning exist?

> Very early in life sets of mind are formed without attentive thought, and these sets persist and control the mature mind. The child learns to avoid the shock of unpleasant disagreement, to find the easy way out, to appear to conform to customs which are wholly mysterious to him in order to get his own way—that is to display some natural impulse without exciting the unfavorable notice of those in authority. Adults distrust the intelligence which a child has while making upon him demands for a kind of conduct that requires a high order of intelligence, if it is to be intelligent at all. The inconsistency is reconciled by instilling in him "moral" habits which have a maximum of emotional empressment and adamantine hold with a minimum of understanding. These habitudes . . . govern conscious later thought. They are usually deepest and most unget-at-able just where critical thought is most needed—in morals, religion and politics. These "infantilisms" account for the mass of irrationalities that prevail among men of otherwise rational tastes. . . . To list them would perhaps oust one from "respectable" society. . . .
>
> When we face this fact in its general significance, we confront one of the ominous aspects of the history of man. We realize how little the progress of man has been the product of intelligent guidance, how largely it has been a by-product of accidental upheavals.[c]

Accordingly, one of Dewey's primary interests was education—both in the narrow sense of curriculum reform and teacher training and in the more extended sense of the whole adjustment of the individual to the social and physical environment, including problems of sociology, politics, and international relations. In this respect Dewey belonged to the mainstream of social thought, along with the Utilitarians and the Comteans. But he tackled the problem of improving our traffic with nature in a radically different way. For one thing, he was far more aware than these earlier philosophers had been of the functional, organic relationships that exist between us and our environment. Further, although their view was relatively empirical, their conception of knowledge was what Dewey called the "spectator-type" of knowledge.[14] Differences about the nature of knowledge profoundly affect ideas of how knowledge should be put to work in the interests of reform. Thus Dewey agreed with Comte that the key to solving social problems lies in the application of the methods of natural science to those problems. And he was, if anything, even more optimistic than Comte had been about the possible fruits of such a social science. But his understanding of the nature of scientific method (and hence his conception of sociology) was more radically empirical than Comte's. Although Comte had reached the point of seeing that so-called natural laws are merely generalized descriptions of what happens, he held that it is possible to formulate general descriptions that are completely (and therefore permanently) adequate. He believed this to be possible because he took Newtonian physics as his model for social science. Just as the "law" of gravity is applicable to the universe at all times, so, Comte thought, the laws of sociology are applicable to human societies at all times. Hence he believed that once these laws are correctly formulated, they can be applied in a more or less mechanical manner.

Dewey rejected the idea of law even in this descriptive sense. He held that there are no final, or completely adequate, descriptions; there are merely more and more adequate instrumentalities for dealing with always changing and growing human situations. From this point of view there would be no danger of a doctrinaire application of oversimplified formulas to the solution of social problems. On the contrary, every application would be tentative, experimental, and hypothetical, capable of being adjusted in light of the new data that the preliminary solution generates.

Democracy

Dewey's assertion that there are no answers that are *the* answers had another important result. It led to his belief that social science is not the prerogative of a special elite who is to design the good life for the masses. In Dewey's view the good life is a matter of mutual makings. And precisely because human nature and human impulses are indefinitely malleable, it is possible to bring all citizens up to ever-higher levels of sensitive and responsible conduct. The problem of constructing the good life, therefore, is not the old Platonic problem of selection but the Christian problem of opportunity. Thus Dewey's conception of human nature was the basis for a fundamentally democratic political and social order rather than a humanely motivated authoritarianism. It might be said, indeed, that Dewey was trying to reinterpret, in a more empirical and practical spirit, the ideas of the founding fathers, which they had stated in the spirit of the rationalism of the Enlightenment.

[14]See p. 46.

The political and governmental phase of democracy is a means, the best means so far found, for realizing ends that lie in the wide domain of human relationships and the development of human personality. . . . The keynote of democracy as a way of life may be expressed, it seems to me, as the necessity for the participation of every mature human being in formation of the values that regulate the living of men together: which is necessary from the standpoint of both the general social welfare and the full development of human beings as individuals. . . .

The development of political democracy came about through substitution of the method of mutual consultation and voluntary agreement for the method of subordination of the many to the few enforced from above. . . . When [coercion] is habitual and embodied in social institutions, it seems the normal and natural state of affairs. The mass usually become unaware that they have a claim to a development of their own powers. Their experience is so restricted that they are not conscious of restriction. It is part of the democratic conception that they as individuals are not the only sufferers, but that the whole social body is deprived of the potential resources that should be at its service. . . .

The foundation of democracy is faith in the capacities of human nature; faith in human intelligence and in the power of pooled and coöperative experience. It is not belief that these things are complete but that if given a show they will grow and be able to generate progressively the knowledge and wisdom needed to guide collective action. Every autocratic and authoritarian scheme of social action rests on a belief that the needed intelligence is confined to a superior few, who because of inherent natural gifts are endowed with the ability and the right to control the conduct of others. . . .

While what we call intelligence may be distributed in unequal amounts, it is the democratic faith that it is sufficiently general so that each individual has something to contribute, and the value of each contribution can be assessed only as it enters into the final pooled intelligence constituted by the contributions of all. . . .

I have emphasized . . . the importance of the effective release of intelligence . . . because democracy is so often and so naturally associated in our minds with freedom of *action*, forgetting the importance of freed intelligence which is necessary to direct and to warrant freedom of action. Unless freedom of individual action has intelligence and informed conviction back of it, its manifestation is almost sure to result in confusion and disorder. The democratic idea of freedom is not the right of each individual to *do* as he pleases, even if it be qualified by adding "provided he does not interfere with the same freedom on the part of others." . . . The basic freedom is that of freedom of *mind* and of whatever degree of freedom of action and experience is necessary to produce freedom of intelligence.[d]

Attitude toward Metaphysics

Dewey thus had little interest in the traditional view of philosophical inquiry. In Dewey's view philosophical thinking, like all thinking, is "interested thinking." The problems metaphysics is concerned with are real problems, but the metaphysical solutions are fictitious and downright harmful. However much traditional philosophers differ among themselves, all of them—rationalists, empiricists, and intuitionists alike—believe they are exploring the nature of "reality." This whole enterprise, Dewey held, results from a maladjustment to environment. People have a fundamental urge to seek security. The pursuit of security is the real problem to which traditional philosophy provides only a pseudosolution. Instead of looking for security in the control of environment by scientific means, along the lines Dewey suggested, traditional philosophers flee to a dreamworld of their own creation, a never-never land of "absolutes" and "eternal verities." According to Dewey, philosophers of this type are unable to accept that security never is, and never can be, perfect—that even science never gives us *the* answers, and that life accordingly is a growing, living adventure. The traditional philosophers are simply individuals who are too weak to accept the world as it is, and their theories are nothing but a projection of their inner uneasiness, a flight from reality.

METAPHYSICS: A QUEST FOR CERTAINTY

Exaltation of pure intellect and its activity above practical affairs is fundamentally connected with the quest for a certainty which shall be absolute and unshakeable. . . .

Practical activity deals with individualized and unique situations which are never exactly duplicable and about which, accordingly, no complete assurance is possible. All activity, moreover, involves change. The intellect, however, according to the traditional doctrine, may grasp universal Being, and Being which is universal is fixed and immutable. . . . Man's distrust of himself has caused him to desire to get beyond and above himself; in pure knowledge he has thought he could attain this self-transcendence. . . .

Primitive [man] had none of the elaborate arts of protection and use which we now enjoy and no confidence in his own powers when they were reinforced by appliances of art. He lived under conditions in which he was extraordinarily exposed to peril. . . . Men faced the forces of nature in a state of nakedness which was more than physical. . . .

In such an atmosphere primitive religion was born and fostered. Rather this atmosphere *was* the religious disposition. . . .

The two dominant conceptions, cultural categories one might call them, which grew and flourished under such circumstances were those of the holy and the fortunate, with their opposites, the profane and the unlucky. . . . To secure the favor of the holy [was] to be on the road to success. . . . Because of its surcharge of power, ambivalent in quality, the holy has to be approached . . . with . . . rites of purification, humiliation, fasting and prayer. . . .

Prosaic beliefs about verifiable facts, beliefs backed up by evidence of the senses and by useful fruits, had little glamour and prestige compared with the vogue of objects of rite and ceremony. . . . Herein is the source of the fundamental dualism of human attention and regard. The distinction between the two attitudes of everyday control and dependence on something superior was finally generalized . . . in the conception of two distinct realms. The inferior was that in which man could foresee and in which he had instruments and arts by which he might expect a reasonable degree of control. The superior was that of occurrences so uncontrollable that they testified to the presence and operation of powers beyond the scope of everyday and mundane things.

The philosophical tradition regarding knowledge and practice, the immaterial or spiritual and the material . . . had for its background [this] state of culture. . . . Philosophy inherited the realm with which religion had been concerned. . . .

If one looks at the foundations of the philosophies of Plato and Aristotle as an anthropologist looks at his material, that is, as cultural subject-matter, it is clear that these philosophies were systematizations in rational form of the content of Greek religious and artistic beliefs. The systematization involved a purification. Logic provided the patterns to which ultimately real objects had to conform, while physical science was possible in the degree in which the natural world, even in its mutabilities, exhibited exemplification of ultimate immutable rational objects. Thus, along with the elimination of myths and grosser superstitions, there were set up the ideals of science and of a life of reason. Ends which could justify themselves to reason were to take the place of custom as the guide of conduct. These two ideals form a permanent contribution to western civilization.

But . . . they [also] brought with them the . . . notion, which has ruled philosophy ever since the time of the Greeks, that the office of knowledge is to uncover the antecedently real, rather than, as is the case with our practical judgments, to gain the kind of understanding which is necessary to deal with problems as they arise.

It thus diverted thought from inquiring into the purposes which experience of actual conditions suggest and from concrete means of their actualization. It translated into a rational form the doctrine of escape from the vicissitudes of existence by means of measures which do not demand an active coping with conditions. For deliverance by means of rites and cults, it substituted deliverance through reason. . . .

Although this Greek formulation was made long ago and much of it is now strange in its specific terms, . . . the main tradition of western culture has retained intact this framework of ideas. . . .

There is involved in these doctrines a whole system of philosophical conclusions. The first and foremost is that . . . what is known, what is true for cognition, is what is real in being. The objects of knowledge form the standards of measures of the reality of all other objects of experience. Are the objects of the affections, of desire, effort, choice, that is to say everything to which we attach value, real? Yes, if they can be warranted by knowledge; . . . as objects of desire and purpose they have no sure place in Being until they are approached and validated through knowledge. The idea is so familiar that we overlook the unexpressed premise upon which it rests, namely that only the completely fixed and unchanging can be real. The quest for certitude has determined our basic metaphysics.

Secondly, the theory of knowledge has its basic premises fixed by the same doctrine. . . .

The theory of knowing is modeled after what was supposed to take place in the act of vision. The object refracts light to the eye and is seen; it makes a difference to the eye and to the person having an optical apparatus, but none to the thing seen. . . . A spectator theory of knowledge is the inevitable outcome. There have been theories which hold that mental activity intervenes, but they have retained the old premise. They have therefore concluded that it is impossible to know reality. . . . It would be hard to find a more thoroughgoing confirmation than this conclusion provides of the complete hold possessed by the belief that the object of knowledge is a reality fixed and complete in itself. . . .

All of these notions about certainty and the fixed, about the nature of the real world, about the nature of the mind and its organs of knowing, . . . flow—such is my basic thesis—from the separation (set up in the interest of the quest for absolute certainty) between theory and practice, knowledge and actions.[e]

NIETZSCHE AND DEWEY CONTRASTED

Dewey's anthropological and psychological analysis of metaphysics is obviously very similar to Nietzsche's. Both philosophers agreed that the objects of metaphysical thinking are "fictions" that function to allay the insecurity people feel in the presence of change, decay, and death. But they differed sharply in their attitudes toward this discovery about the basic insecurity in human nature, as is shown not only by what they said but by the very styles in which they wrote. Nietzsche's writing was metaphorical, contentious, and highly personal. He shared the underlying insecurity that others experienced but differed from them in choosing to face it rather than flee from it. He felt, as they did, that humankind is hanging precariously on the edge of an abyss; his response was to affirm life despite its terror. In contrast, Dewey's exposition of the roots of metaphysics was calm, detailed, and scholarly. Since he did not experience an abyss within himself, since he did not feel divided and alienated, he was not *personally* involved in the discovery that most people experience deep insecurity. Rather, he looked at the situation from the outside, as a physician or psychiatrist might. He believed that the cure for insecurity was not (as Nietzsche had held) to bite the snake that had bitten one—to Dewey, this was a truly desperate remedy. The cure was to become involved in the day-to-day task of improving humankind's estate. Hence, though Dewey too affirmed life, he did not feel this affirmation to be particularly difficult or heroic. Further, the life that he affirmed did not involve a quantum jump to a level "beyond good and evil"; it consisted in a gradual, even "prosaic," advance to more-intelligent practice.

The Nature of Reality: "Experience"

Despite his "reduction" of metaphysics to the quest for certainty, and despite his belief that many of the traditional metaphysical problems are pseudoproblems, Dewey realized that instrumentalism could not escape dealing, at least in its own way, with some of the questions of "first philosophy." Here his position was much stronger than that of the earlier pragmatists, who were inclined to dispose of metaphysics by declaring that any metaphysics was true provided that it "worked."

Thus though Dewey did not ask, in the traditional way, "What is the real?" and "What are the ultimate values?" he nevertheless recognized that he had to ask and answer equivalent questions. So far it has been said that Dewey emphasized that people live in, and must adjust to, their social and physical environment. But what is this environment, and how are they to evaluate the values that their interested activity is constantly realizing in it?

One answer to the first question is "experience"; another is "nature." But what are experience and nature, and how are they related? To begin with, like the Kantians and the Hegelians, Dewey regarded reality as a whole within which distinctions are made and meanings develop. Our experience and the nature of which it is the experience—subject and object, knower and known—"are not enemies or alien." "Experience is *of* as well as *in* nature. . . . [It] reaches down into nature; it has depth. It also had breadth and to an indefinitely elastic extent. It stretches. That stretch constitutes inference."[f]

EVENTS AND OBJECTS

In ordinary everyday experience of objects, Dewey held that "events" (or "existences") are distinguished from meanings. An event is an "ongoing"; its "*intrinsic* nature is revealed in experience as the immediately felt qualities of things." And events are not just the ingredients of ordinary experience. Science, too, thinks in terms of events. "The tendency of modern science [is] to substitute qualitative events, marked by certain similar properties and by recurrences, for the older notion of fixed substances."[g] The concept of event may thus be said to have had the same pivotal importance and unifying function in Dewey's theory that substance had in the Cartesian metaphysics. This is an indication of the extent to which, as has already been suggested, process was becoming a fundamental modern idea.

"Event" seems a far more satisfactory metaphysical principle than "substance." Since a substance is by definition an independent, enclosed, and complete entity, any attempt to interpret reality substantively runs into hopeless dilemmas. For instance, is there one substance or are there several? Either answer is unsatisfactory. If there is but one substance, it is impossible to account for the experienced diversity. If there are many substances, it seems impossible that they can be related in any significant way. In contrast, the concept of event allows for the flexibility, multiple-relatedness, and change of state that Nietzsche's "will to power" as a cosmological principle was intended to achieve. Yet it does this without the danger of anthropomorphism that is inherent in that notion.

So much for event. According to Dewey, an object (whether a "gross, macroscopic" object of ordinary experience or a "refined, derived" object of scientific experience) can be defined as an "event with meaning." Consider any of the things ordinarily called objects: "Tables, the Milky Way, chairs, stars, cats, dogs, electrons, ghosts, centaurs, historic epochs"—these are all events with meanings. Take, for instance, the event that a writer would call "a piece of paper." This is but one meaning of the event in question; it merely happens to be foremost in the writer's mind because he or she is concerned about something to write on. This same event

> has as many other explicit meanings as it has important consequences recognised in the various connective interactions into which it enters. Since possibilities of conjunction are endless, and since the consequences of any of them may at some time be significant, its potential meanings are endless. It signifies something to start a fire with; something like snow; made of wood-pulp; manufactured for profit; property in the legal sense; a definite combination illustrative of certain principles of chemical science; an article the invention of which has made a tremendous difference in human history, and so on indefinitely. There is no conceivable universe of discourse in which the thing may not figure, having in each its own characteristic meaning. And if we say that after all it is "paper" which has all these different meanings, we are at bottom but asserting that . . . paper is its ordinary meaning for human intercourse.[h]

"ESSENCE": A PSEUDOPROBLEM

Dewey believed that the idea that an event can have many meanings provides a way of disposing of the traditional philosophical concern with "essence," which can now be seen to be a pseudoproblem. There is nothing unique, special, or privileged about essence; it is merely "a pronounced instance of meaning," hypostatized by our pursuit of certainty into an alleged eternal entity. "To be partial, and to assign *a* meaning to a thing as *the* meaning is but to evince human subjection to bias. . . . The very essence of a thing is identified with those consummatory consequences which the thing has when conditions are felicitous."[i] There is no more reason to say that the essence of an existent is "white surface for writing" than to say that its essence is "wood-pulp." Any such claim merely reflects the predominant interest that the definer happens to have in the existent in question.

This way of thinking also frees philosophy from the dualism of appearance and reality—another pseudoproblem. For instance, Galileo and the other early physicists held that the paper is "really" matter in motion and only "appears" to be a continuous, white surface. According to Dewey, they were simply giving preferred ontological status to one of two equally real meanings, which happened to be rooted in different frames of reference. Similarly, modern physicists might maintain that the paper is "really" electrons, but this merely reflects their preference for the electron frame of reference, possibly because of its practical significance or possibly because of its greater elegance.

STATUS OF UNIVERSALS

Universals, then, are not things but instruments; they are, specifically, the instruments by means of which problems are solved and meanings built up. The universal "piece of paper" is an instrument for solving the problem of taking notes at a lecture. The universal "wood-pulp" is an instrument for solving the problem of producing more paper. The universal "electron" is an instrument for solving the problem of relating many different existents by means of a single, generalized description. There is thus no intrinsic difference between ordinary commonsense thinking, as described by Dewey above, and scientific thinking. It is true that in their pursuit of certainty, philosophers and philosophically minded scientists sometimes suppose that they are exploring a realm of mathematico-material entities; but as a matter of fact "the history of the development of the physical sciences is [only] the story of the enlarging possession by mankind of more efficacious instrumentalities for dealing with the conditions of life and action."[j]

DEFECTS OF TRADITIONAL RATIONALISM AND EMPIRICISM

One of the test cases for Dewey's whole analysis is the nature and status of mathematical thinking. Is it, as the rationalists have always insisted, knowledge of an independent and intelligible order of eternal truths? Or are mathematical concepts simply instruments for implementing action, whose uniqueness lies in their very high degree of precision?

> Does the doctrine of the operational and experimentally empirical nature of conceptions break down when applied to "pure" mathematical

objects? The key to the answer is to be found in a distinction between operations overtly performed (or imagined to be performed) and operations *symbolically* executed. . . .

For long ages, symbols were . . . employed incidentally and for some fairly immediate end. . . . They carried all sorts of irrelevant associations that hampered their efficacy. . . . The loose and restricted character of popular thinking has its origin in these facts; its progress is encumbered by the vague and vacillating nature of ordinary words. Thus the second great step forward was made when special symbols were devised that were emancipated from the load of irrelevancy carried by words developed for social rather than for intellectual purposes. . . . Instead of being adapted to local and directly present situations, they were framed in detachment from direct overt use and *with respect to one another.* One has only to look at mathematical symbols to note that the operations they designate are others of the same kind as themselves, that is, symbolic not actual. . . .

Abstraction from use in special and direct situations . . . is a process, however, which is subject to interpretation by a fallacy. Independence from any specified application is readily taken to be equivalent to independence from application as such. . . . This fallacy . . . played its part in the generation of *a priori* rationalism. It is the origin of that idolatrous attitude toward universals so often recurring in the history of thought. Those who handle ideas through symbols as if they were things . . . are ready victims to thinking of these objects as if they had no sort of reference to things, to existence.

In fact, the distinction is one between operations to be actually performed and possible operations as such, as merely possible. Shift of reflection to development of possible operations in their logical relations *to one another* opens up opportunities for operations that would never be directly suggested. But its origin and eventual meaning lie in acts that deal with concrete situations. As to origin in overt operations there can be no doubt. Operations of keeping tally and scoring are found in both work and games. . . . These acts are the originals of number and of all developments of number. . . . If we generalize what happens in such instances, we see that the indispensable need is that of *adjusting things as means, as resources, to other things as ends.*

The origin of counting and measuring is in economy and efficiency of such adjustments. . . .

The failure of empiricism to account for mathematical ideas is due to its failure to connect them with acts performed. In accord with its sensationalistic character, traditional empiricism sought their origin in sensory impressions, or at most in supposed abstraction from properties antecedently characterizing physical things. Experimental empiricism has none of the difficulties of Hume and Mill in explaining the origin of mathematical truths. . . .

Once the idea of possible operations, indicated by symbols and performed *only* by means of symbols, is discovered, the road is opened to operations of ever increasing definiteness and comprehensiveness. Any group of symbolic operations suggests further operations that may be performed. *Technical* symbols [e.g., "H₂O"] are framed with precisely this end in view. . . . They are selected with a view to designating unambiguously one mode of interaction and one only. . . .

Mathematical conceptions [e.g., "3"], by means of symbols of operations that are irrespective of actual performance, carry abstraction much further. . . . [Each such symbol] designates an operative relation applic*able* to anything whatsoever, though not actually applied to any specified object. . . . The difficulties and paradoxes which have been found to attend the logic of number disappear when instead of their being treated as either essences or as properties of things in existence, they are viewed as designations of potential operations. Mathematical space is not a kind of space distinct from so-called physical and empirical space, but is a name given to operations ideally or formally possible with respect to things having spacious qualities: it is not a mode of Being, but a way of thinking things so that connections among them are liberated from fixity in experience and implication from one to another is made possible.ᵏ

Though Dewey believed that "traditional rationalism" has misread the nature of thought more seriously than has "traditional empiricism," he did not spare the latter. Dewey conceded that it has one great advantage in that it at least deals with the actual; but he held that it makes two serious mistakes. The first is that it conceives of the actual as a static world. The ideas of traditional empiricism are "dead" because "their value and function are essentially retrospective," not forward-looking. Like rationalism, traditional empiricism fails to see that all ideas and meanings are instruments for dealing with concrete problems. A good example of this is empiricism's attempt to derive mathematical ideas by "comparing particular objects" instead of recognizing their practical and operational origins.

In order to understand the second mistake Dewey attributed to the traditional empiricists, it is necessary to consider Dewey's criticism of "traditional nominalism." He held that it does not understand that meanings are shared, that "language is specifically a mode of interaction of at least two beings, a speaker and a hearer; it presupposes an organized group to which these creatures belong."ˡ When A requests B to bring A something, the stimulus activating B is not the sounds uttered by A. It is, rather, B's "anticipatory share in the consummation of a transaction in which both participate. The heart of language is . . . the establishment of cooperation in an activity in which there are partners, and in which the activity of each is modified and regulated by partnership." In Dewey's view, such facts as these reveal the defect of traditional nominalism: it fails to see that a word is "a mode of social action" and supposes it to be the "expression of a ready-made, exclusively individual, mental state. . . . Nominalism ignores organization and thus makes nonsense of meanings."ᵐ

DEFECTS OF IDEALISM

If these are the weaknesses of traditional rationalism and traditional empiricism, what about "idealism"?[15] The trouble with idealism, Dewey held, is, first, that it tries to do away with the existent. It tries to resolve existents into "combinations of meanings." But "to cause existences in their particularity to disappear into combinations of universals is at least an extreme measure." For his part, therefore, he preferred to "stick to the commonsense belief that universals, relations, meanings, are of and about existences, not their exhaustive ingredients."[n]

Dewey's criticism can be stated in another way. In his opinion idealism assumes that thought is more real than anything else and hence concludes that thought's products have a superior ontological status as compared with the feelings and the "gross macroscopic" objects that thought articulates. For example, Hegel set out a doctrine of degrees of reality—"Being" is barely real; "Absolute Spirit" is the most real of all. But in Dewey's view this metaphysical interpretation of thought's function is simply another aspect of philosophy's quest for certainty. Far from having such an exalted mission, thought simply serves as "an intermediary between some empirical objects and others." Hence thought's products are no more real than thought's starting points, just as the sculptor's figure is no more real (though it may be more beautiful or more useful) than the clay from which it is fashioned.

Thought's products are more useful than thought's starting points—that is why we think! But they have utility precisely because they refer back to the empirical needs that generated the thought. Idealism, because it regards the "refined products" as more real, is "arbitrary and aloof" and "occupies a realm of its own without contact with the things of ordinary experience."

> A first-rate test of the value of any philosophy which is offered us [is]: Does it end in conclusions which, when they are referred back to ordinary life-experiences and their predicaments, render them more significant, more luminous to us, and make our dealings with them more fruitful? Or does it terminate in rendering the things of ordinary experience more opaque than they were before, and in depriving them of having in "reality" even the significance they had previously seemed to have? . . . It is the fact . . . that so many philosophies terminate in conclusions that make it necessary to disparage and condemn primary experience, leading those who hold them to measure the sublimity of their "realities" as philosophically defined by remoteness from the concerns of daily life, which leads cultivated common-sense to look askance at philosophy.[o]

This sense of the actual and the active, which Descartes had faintly felt and which had made him unwilling to be a simon-pure rationalist, was thus one of the

---

[15] By this Dewey meant, of course, views of the Hegelian type.

cornerstones of Dewey's position. This is why he rejected Hegel's idealism as cloudy and unreal and insisted on the "irreducibility" of events. This is why he rejected Kant's compromise formula, according to which thought orders a sensuous manifold; in Dewey's view, the sensuous manifold is not sufficiently eventful. Although it doubtless saves meanings from dissolving into meanings of meanings of meanings, and so on, and thus performs a necessary *cognitive* function, it is hardly more than a limit. It is certainly not full-blooded, warm, and palpable. It fails to satisfy that aspect of reality that William James called its stubborn and irreducible factuality.

DEWEY ON REALISM AND LOGICAL ANALYSIS

Though Dewey rejected idealism, he had no sympathy with the ways in which the realists and the logical analysts went about reaffirming objectivity. It is easy to see, from the passage already quoted on the nature of thought,[16] how much Dewey differed from the logical analysts. Thought does not aim at truth but at the solution of some practical problem, such as the problem of getting across a stream, and thinking ceases when the present problem is solved. But new problems are bound to arise—that is what life is. We can hope, of course, by reflective self-criticism, to learn how to improve our problem-solving techniques and so solve our problems more efficiently. "Improving our problem-solving techniques" is advancing from commonsense, rule-of-thumb, trial-and-error methods to scientific methods (quantification, controlled experimentation, and so on); "learning how by reflective self-criticism to improve" is logic. That is, the norms in terms of which various human activities are assessed and evaluated are not abstract, ideal rules; on the contrary, they arise in critical reflection on these activities and what they accomplish. Logic, in a word, is a human activity, and like all other human activities it reflects human needs, and it changes in response to changes in them.

Thus Dewey's conception of logic differed radically from that of the Russellians. They thought that Dewey psychologized logic; he thought that, in a quest for certainty, they etherealized it. They held logic to be the analysis of propositions, an analysis that terminates in logical simples. Further, they held that "a proposition has one and only one complete analysis."[P] For Dewey, in contrast, far from there being only one complete analysis there are many "logics." Since logic is but the reflective criticism of actual problem-solving techniques, there are as many logics as there are different kinds of problems that need solving. There is, for instance, a logic of historical studies, which is the critical assessment, by historians, of their own methods of interpreting documents, and this logic is quite different from the logic of physics. And, far from logic terminating in logical simples, there are no such simples. Or rather, there are simples, but they are merely the end products of a particularly abstract and rarefied activity, the activity of logical analysis. They have no superior ontological status.

[16] See p. 39.

> Realism argues that we [must] admit that something eulogistically termed Reality . . . is but a complex made up of fixed, mutually independent simples. . . . For instrumentalism, the alleged results of abstraction and analysis are perfectly real; but they are real, like everything else, *where* they are real. . . . There is no reason for supposing that they exist *elsewhere* in the same manner.q

When, for instance, do we experience a blue sense datum? Typically, according to Dewey, when we are studying a cellular structure, and identify it by the blue color with which it has been stained. But recognition of a cellular structure is typical of those "units of thinking" that are intermediate between a confused and a cleared-up situation. Sense data "are not objects, but means, instrumentalities, of knowledge: things by which we know rather than things we know." The realists erect sense data into the ultimate constituents of the universe only because they "ignore the contextual situation." Their sense data "exist only within the procedure."r

Naturally, questions about where sense data are located and about how they are related to physical objects—questions that were central perplexities for the realists—hardly arose for Dewey. Such questions come to the fore only when experience is analyzed into an independent object on the one hand and a passive consciousness that contemplates this object on the other. But for Dewey experience is not a passing show at which we are merely spectators. We are primarily agents and doers—not simply observers of objects but manipulators, alterers, and makers of them. Still less are we observers of consciousness—except under very unusual circumstances. Consciousness is not a transparent element that *contains* experience and that is therefore always present and available for observation. It occurs from time to time *within* experience, and just at those points where problems arise that impede action.

> Consciousness is that phase of a system of meanings which at a given time is undergoing re-direction, transitive transformation. The current idealistic conception of consciousness as a power which modifies events, is . . . but another instance of the common philosophic fallacy of converting an eventful function into an antecedent force or cause. Consciousness *is* the meaning of events in the course of remaking. . . . Its causation is the need and demand for filling out what is indeterminate.s

Hence consciousness is "only a very small and shifting portion of experience."t

PUZZLES ABOUT RELATION OF THOUGHT TO EXPERIENCE

Thus Dewey completely rejected the epistemology of realism as such, as he rejected the epistemology of idealism. If the trouble with idealism was that it tried to do away with the existent, the trouble with realism, and even more obviously with Logical Positivism, was that it tended to identify the existent with sense data. To many people these criticisms will seem fair. But it remains to ask, What exactly *is* an existent? One can feel it or (as with Bergson) intuit it. But how is it to be incorporated in a philosophical theory except on thought's terms? Thought, as Dewey of course saw, has a special status, and this special status is what theories like Kant's and Hegel's attempted to recognize—the notion that, as Dewey put it, "any experienced subject-matter whatever may *become* an object of reflection and cognitive inspection." Even the actual, even the intuited, *insofar as it is known,* has been taken up and included in the "all-inclusiveness of cognitive experience." Must Dewey not admit with Hegel that only thought and its articulations are real? Or at least agree with Kant that the notion of an other-than-thought is simply the concept of a limit? On the contrary. According to Dewey,

> the emphasis [in the sentence just quoted] is upon "become"; the cognitive never *is* all-inclusive: that is, when the material of a prior noncognitive experience is the object of knowledge, it and the act of knowing are themselves included within a new and wider noncognitive experience—and *this* situation can never be transcended. It is only when the temporal character of experienced things is forgotten that the idea of the total "transcendence" of knowledge is asserted.[u]

But this view is hardly an improvement over Kant's. Insofar as the noncognitive experience is *in* thought, it is articulated *by* thought (that is, it becomes an object, an existent with meaning); insofar as it is *out* of thought, it is not known (that is, it reduces to a pure existent). And though perhaps otherwise experienced, it is incapable of being included in a philosophical theory.

This difficulty can be stated in another way. According to Dewey, objects are existents with meanings. But what are they *in themselves,* when not articulated by thought? Thought is a "latecomer" in the evolutionary process. Moreover, it "occurs only under highly specialized conditions, such as are found in a highly organized creature which in turn requires a specialized environment."[v] If it be admitted that galaxies, solar systems, and our own planet had an immensely long development before consciousness ever appeared, what kind of existence did they have during all those millennia? If they were not objects with meaning, what were they? This puzzle recalls Kant's difficulty with the status of phenomenal objects.[17] Phenomenal objects (planets, solar systems, galaxies) are needed to approximate anything like common sense and to escape a radically subjective view of experience. But how, according to Dewey's view of meaning, can there be phenomenal objects?

PUZZLES ABOUT NATURE OF TRUTH

Much the same sort of problem arises in connection with the nature of truth. It is clear that any view that, like Dewey's or Hegel's, denies the ultimacy of the distinction between experience and nature will have to abandon, or at least radically revise, the commonsense notion that truth consists in the correspondence of

[17] See Vol. IV, pp. 48–49.

ideas with external facts. For it is no longer possible to say, with common sense, that the judgment "There is a centaur in my office" is true if it agrees with the facts and false if it does not. In Dewey's view, what common sense calls the "facts" (office, centaur) are not pure existents but objects—existents with meaning. Truth, it would seem, lies in the expansion of meanings. Or to put it another way, truth consists in the degree to which one meaning coheres with others.

But now another difficulty arises. If truth is a matter of the coherence of a judgment with other judgments, rather than of the correspondence of judgments with "external" facts, what is the difference between a judgment about centaurs and a judgment about horses? Is a judgment about horses "truer" than a judgment about centaurs merely because, as it happens, the former coheres with the very large body of judgments called the science of zoology, whereas the latter coheres only with the much smaller body of judgments called Greek mythology? Is the difference between the reality of a horse and the fictionality of a centaur merely a difference in degree of meaning-expansion? Dewey wanted, of course, to eliminate the possibility that his doctrine of experience would collapse into a version of "idealism."

> The proposition that the perception of a horse is objectively valid and that of a centaur fanciful and mythical does not denote that one is a meaning of natural events and the other is not. It denotes that they are meanings referable to *different* natural events, and that confused and harmful consequences result from attributing them to the same events. . . .
>
> Genuinely to believe the centaur-meaning is to assert that events characterized by it interact in certain ways with other now unperceived events. Since belief that centaur has the same kind of objective meaning as has horse denotes expectation of like efficacies and consequences, the difference of validity between them is extrinsic. It is capable of being revealed only by the results of acting upon them. The awareness of centaur-meaning is fanciful not simply because part of its conditions lie within the organism; part of the conditions of *any* perception, valid as well as invalid, scientific as well as esthetic, lie within the organism. Nor is it fanciful, simply because it is supposed not to have adequate existential antecedents. Natural conditions, physiological, physical and social, may be specified in one case as in the other. But since the conditions in the two cases are different, consequences are bound to be different. Knowing, believing, involves something additive and extrinsic to having a meaning.
>
> No knowledge is ever merely immediate. The proposition that the perception of a horse is valid and that a centaur is fanciful or hallucinatory, does not denote that there are two modes of awareness, differing intrinsically from each other. It denotes something . . . with respect to consequences, namely, that action upon the respective meanings will bring to light (to apparency or awareness) such different kinds of consequences that we should use the two meanings in very different ways.[w]

Since Dewey refused to follow Hegel in identifying truth and reality—though he agreed with him that truth is a matter of degree—he had to find a place somehow for the difference (which is a difference in *kind*) between the actual and the nonactual.

This he did by shifting the focus of the problem of truth from the coherence of meanings with other meanings, in the purely cognitive sense, to the coherence of meanings with events, in the sense of behavioral consequences. Accordingly, he was able to hold that there is a difference (of kind, not merely of degree) between the real and the fictional. The difference between "horse" and "centaur" is thus not merely a difference in their meaning-expansion coefficients. There is also a difference in the way the meanings operate. According to Dewey, "this is the meaning of truth: processes of change so directed that they achieve an intended consummation." Consider any scientific hypothesis or theory. What makes it true? That it "modifies old beliefs," that it converts "actual immediate objects into *better*, into more secure and significant, objects."[x]

This definition of truth indicates where Dewey's interest lay—in social problems, and hence in truths and solutions that work. And this was not just a matter of a preference for one kind of philosophy over another. From his point of view, interest in truth in the traditional sense is merely a reflection of that quest for absolutes by which people seek to compensate for their sense of insecurity. But in what sense are Dewey's philosophical preferences better than those of more-traditional philosophers? Certainly, in the sense that they are more useful they are better, for this is the whole point of such preferences. But by the same logic traditional philosophers might claim that their view of truth is better in terms of *their* preferences. And is there not a sense in which one can ask whether it is *true* that such-and-such a view or solution is more useful than another—a sense, that is, in which "true" is not equivalent to "useful"?

The problem of escaping truth in the traditional sense parallels the problem, just discussed, of avoiding "the all-inclusiveness of cognitive experience," for truth (in the traditional sense) is a property of "cognitive experience." It would seem, then, that Dewey did not solve, except by shelving it, the problem of how the empirical and the rational elements in knowledge are related. If he seemed to many of his contemporaries to have done so, it was because they, too, were prepared to shelve it.[18]

The Nature of Value

Dewey's view of philosophical discussions about value parallels his view of philosophical discussions about metaphysics: though there are questions about value that have genuine importance, most of the questions that have been traditionally discussed by philosophers are only pseudoproblems.

[18] For the kind of reply Dewey might have made to this criticism, see p. 63.

Modern science, modern industry and politics, have presented us with an immense amount of material foreign to, often inconsistent with, the most prized intellectual and moral heritage of the western world. This is the cause of our modern intellectual perplexities and confusions. It sets the especial problem for philosophy to-day and for many days to come. Every significant philosophy is an attempt to deal with it. . . .

I believe that the method of empirical naturalism presented in this volume provides the way, and the only way—although of course no two thinkers will travel it in just the same fashion—by which one can freely accept the standpoint and conclusions of modern science: the way by which we can be genuinely naturalistic and yet maintain cherished values, provided they are critically clarified and reinforced. The naturalistic method, when it is consistently followed, destroys many things once cherished; but it destroys them by revealing their inconsistency with the nature of things—a flaw that always attended them and deprived them of efficacy for aught save emotional consolation. But its main purport is not destructive; empirical naturalism is rather a winnowing fan. Only chaff goes, though perhaps the chaff had once been treasured. An empirical method which remains true to nature does not "save"; it is not an insurance device nor a mechanical antiseptic. But it inspires the mind with courage and vitality to create new ideals and values in the face of the perplexities of a new world.y

VALUES ARE FACTS FOUND IN EXPERIENCE

Thus, according to Dewey, people discover values in nature just as they discover any other facts. "Experience actually presents esthetic and moral traits. . . . When found, their ideal qualities are as relevant to the philosophic theory of nature as are the traits found by physical inquiry." Such traits as poignancy, beauty, humor, annoyance, consolation, and splendor are as real as are colors, sounds, qualities of contact, taste, and smell. They all stand on "the same level"; indeed, in a way the former are prior: "Things are objects to be treated, used, acted upon and with, enjoyed and endured, even more than things to be known. They are things *had* before they are things cognized."z

This doctrine is obviously connected to Dewey's denial of the all-inclusiveness of thought and his assertion of the reality of the actual. What is relevant here is its bearing on his theory of value. So far facts have been defined as ongoings, or events. But events are not only ongoings. They have beginnings and proceed to "endings," to "consummations." "The presence of uncertain and precarious factors" makes these ends "unstable and evanescent," but because they are ends and hence fulfillments, "there is a tendency to perpetuate them, render them stable, and repeat them." The intervening stages in a process toward an end come to be thought of as means; when they are brought under control they become "tools, techniques, mechanisms." Hence, far from being the foes of values, facts are the means for realizing them; they are also the criteria for "differentiating genuine aims from merely emotional and fantastic ideals."[a]

VALUE: A PRACTICAL, NOT A METAPHYSICAL, PROBLEM

Thus, according to Dewey, the problem of value is not a metaphysical problem about the "status" of value or about the rank of values in some eternal hierarchy. These problems seemed real to the traditional philosophers because in their quest for certainty they first erected a "realm of values" and then proceeded to locate especially precious things in this realm. As soon as they did this, the problem of the "two worlds" naturally arose: How is this realm of absolute values related to the spatiotemporal world of actual decision making? "Is the world of value that of ultimate and transcendent Being from which the world of existence is a derivative or a fall? Or is it but a manifestation of human subjectivity, a factor somehow miraculously supervening upon an order complete and closed in physical structure?"[b]

Some philosophers adopt the first alternative; from this point of view values are the only realities, and attention becomes focused on questions about the order in which the precious things supposedly exist in the special realm of values, instead of on questions about current practice. Other philosophers adopt the second alternative; then only "facts" are real; values become subjective preferences and there is no basis for intelligent choice among current practices. Happily, a choice between these two alternatives "is arbitrary because the problem is arbitrary."

But if the problem of values is not a metaphysical question, what is it? According to Dewey, it is just the practical, social, and human problem of intelligent choice, and philosophy is nothing but the study of the methods of making intelligent choices.

> The important consideration and concern is not a theory of values but a theory of criticism; a method of discriminating among goods on the basis of the conditions of their appearance, and of their consequences. . . .
>
> Either . . . the difference between genuine, valid, good and a counterfeit, specious good is unreal, or it is a difference consequent upon reflection, or criticism, and the significant point is that this difference is equivalent to that made by discovery of relationships, of conditions and consequences. With this conclusion are bound up two other propositions: Of immediate values as such, values which occur and which are possessed and enjoyed, there is no theory at all; they just occur, are enjoyed, possessed; and that is all. The moment we begin to discourse about these values, to define and generalize, to make distinctions in kinds, we are passing beyond value-objects themselves; we are entering, even if only blindly, upon an inquiry into causal antecedents and

causative consequents, with a view to appraising the "real," that is the eventual, goodness of the thing in question. . . .

The other proposition is that philosophy is and can be nothing but this critical operation and function become aware of itself and its implications, pursued deliberately and systematically. It starts from actual situations of belief, conduct and appreciative perception which are characterized by immediate qualities of good and bad, and from the modes of critical judgment current at any given time in all the regions of value; these are its data, its subject-matter. . . . [Its] function is to regulate the further appreciation of goods and bads; to give greater freedom and security in those acts of direct selection, appropriation, identification and of rejection, elimination, destruction which enstate and which exclude objects of belief, conduct and contemplation.[c]

Dewey's approach to values was, then, empirical and antimetaphysical. What would Dewey have had to say about Kierkegaard's existentialist approach, which was also antimetaphysical? He would certainly have agreed that finding "a focus and a center" for one's life is a genuine problem, but he would have considered it an empirical problem—no different in kind from the problem of deciding how to vote in the next election or how to spend a summer vacation. Fortunately, some individuals can solve their existential problem by immersing themselves in action—for instance, in social reform and other "good causes." Clearly Kierkegaard was not of this type. His writings reveal that his situation was desperate, as he himself recognized. But in Dewey's view Kierkegaard misunderstood the nature of the help that he needed; he should have sought not God's help but that of a competent psychiatrist. The solution to the existential problem, like that of any other problem, requires intelligence, not a leap of faith.

COMMENT ON THIS VIEW OF VALUE

We may agree with Dewey that values are facts, in the sense that enjoyings stand on just as firm a footing as any other aspects of our experience. We may also agree with Dewey that intelligence is the faculty of choice and that one of the criteria for evaluating intelligence is its success in forging instruments for resolving choice situations. Obviously, as the Utilitarians had pointed out, knowledge of the causal context of our various options is relevant to intelligent choice.

For instance, to make an intelligent choice between going to a movie and staying home to study, a student would need to know the probable effects in *this* situation, at *this* time of the academic year, with his or her work in *this* stage of preparation, and so on, of going to a movie. The student must not only have a method that enables him or her to predict the probable effects of the various alternatives; he or she must also have one that provides a way of choosing intelligently between two rival enjoyings. This can be done only on the basis of a preference for some other good to which one or the other of these enjoyings is a means.

All of this, of course, was said long ago by Aristotle, and all of it was well said and useful. But though Aristotle was interested in the problems of intelligent choice, he was also interested in the metaphysical implications of the practical situation just described. People have to choose among values and can do so only on the basis of other values to which they are means; this led Aristotle to conclude that values form precisely that kind of hierarchy, or pyramid, whose existence Dewey denied.

The argument against Dewey runs roughly as follows. A person cannot choose intelligently between two rival enjoyments unless there is a basis for saying that one is better than the other. But Dewey's view allows for no such basis. How, in his view, can a person distinguish between what seems to be good now (because it is an enjoying) and what is *really* good? How is one to distinguish between what is desired and what is desirable? Between what is enjoyed and what is enjoyable (that is, worthy to be enjoyed)? Must there not be some criterion other than more (subsequent, later) enjoyings? Not all traditional philosophers based this criterion for choice, as Aristotle did, on a hierarchy of goods leading up to a supreme good-in-itself: Kant, for instance, derived it from a categorical imperative. But they all believed that some nonempirical standard was required. Dewey's naturalism, his critics maintained, committed him to a "fatal" relativism.

Dewey, of course, rejected this conclusion. It is possible, he thought, to maintain "a distinction between likings and that which is worth liking, between the desired and the desirable, between the is and the ought,"[d] without reference to any transcendental, or absolute, standards. The basis for making this distinction, he held, is exactly the same sort of operation as that by which we interrogate and establish "belief-judgments" about external events. No one proposes to use transcendental criteria to test a scientific hypothesis; everyone agrees that such belief-judgments are validated by means of empirical criteria. This is equally true, Dewey held, for belief-judgments about desirings, enjoyings, and (generally) values. Indeed, Dewey proposed to turn the tables on his critics by arguing that any appeal to standards that "descend from the blue," far from being the only basis for intelligent and reasonable choice, actually makes intelligent choice impossible.

> Operational thinking needs to be applied to the judgment of values just as it has now finally been applied in conceptions of physical objects. Experimental empiricism in the field of ideas of good and bad is demanded to meet the conditions of the present situation.
>
> The scientific revolution came about when material of direct and uncontrolled experience was taken as problematic; as supplying material to be transformed by reflective operations into known objects. The contrast between experienced and known objects was found to be a temporal one; namely, one between empirical subject-matters which were had or "given" prior to the acts of experimental variation and redisposition and those which succeeded these acts and issued from them. The notion of an act whether of sense or thought which supplied a valid

measure of thought in immediate knowledge was discredited. Consequences of operations became the important thing. . . .

Analogy suggests that we regard our direct and original experience of things liked and enjoyed as only *possibilities* of values to be achieved; that enjoyment becomes a value when we discover the relations upon which its presence depends. Such a causal and operational definition gives only a conception of a value, not a value itself. But the utilization of the conception in action results in an object having secure and significant value.

The formal statement may be given concrete content by pointing to the difference between the enjoyed and the enjoyable, the desired and the desirable, the satis*fying* and the satis*factory*. To say that something is enjoyed is to make a statement about a fact, something already in existence; it is not to judge the value of that fact. There is no difference between such a proposition and one which says that something is sweet or sour, red or black. It is just correct or incorrect and that is the end of the matter. But to call an object a value is to assert that it satisfies or fulfills certain conditions. Function and status in meeting conditions is a different matter from bare existence. The fact that something is desired only raises the *question* of its desirability; it does not settle it. Only a child in the degree of his immaturity thinks to settle the question of desirability by reiterated proclamation: "I want it, I want it, I want it." . . . Take for example the difference between the ideas of "satisfying" and "satisfactory." To say that something satisfies is to report something as an isolated finality. To assert that it is satis*factory* is to define it in its connections and interactions. The fact that it pleases or is immediately congenial poses a problem to judgment. How shall the satisfaction be rated? Is it a value or is it not? Is it something to be prized and cherished, *to be* enjoyed? Not stern moralists alone but everyday experience informs us that finding satisfaction in a thing may be a warning, a summons to be on the lookout for consequences. To declare something satis*factory* is to assert that it meets specifiable conditions. It is, in effect, a judgment that the thing "will do." It involves a prediction; it contemplates a future in which the thing will continue to serve. . . . It denotes an attitude *to be* taken, that of striving to perpetuate and to make secure.[e]

Thus, according to Dewey, the situation with respect to values is exactly the same as the situation with respect to physical objects. In our perceptual field there are all sorts of sensory experiences. Do we accept all of them at their face value? We do not; or at least if we begin by doing so, we are soon forced to become a bit more careful. For example, in my perceptual field at this moment there is a rowboat, with an oar bent in the water. Is the oar really bent? I run my hand along it to find out. This is a commonsense procedure for distinguishing between the seemingly true and the really true, between initial impressions of physical objects and the objects themselves. Such procedures have been greatly refined by the methods of scientific investigation and by the introduction of instruments such as telescopes, microscopes, and thermometers; all these procedures and instruments are capable of continuous refinement and improvement. A "fact" is simply an initial experience that has survived the tests available at any given time. For instance, a witness's initial impression may be that the person he or she now sees in the police lineup is the same one he or she saw leaving the scene of a crime; but fingerprints or tests of blood type may correct this impression and "establish" that it is not the same person.

As Dewey argued, values are not intrinsically different from other facts: there are initial enjoyings, just as there are initial impressions of the characteristics of physical objects. Insofar as and as long as the initial enjoyings are enjoyed, they are good. But experience shows that some of these initial enjoyings, like some initial sense experiences, are deceptive. Thus a bit of skepticism and a disposition to test enjoyings before we commit ourselves to them soon emerges. Just as the initial sense experiences that survive the tests of subsequent experience become "facts," so initial enjoyments that survive the tests of experience become values.

Although Dewey admitted—indeed, he insisted—that no belief-judgment (whether about physical objects or about values) can ever be absolutely true, he maintained that many such judgments are "reasonable." For instance, it is reasonable to conclude that the person in the police lineup is not the one who was seen leaving the crime if chemical tests show that the blood types are different. This is the reasonable conclusion to draw, even though the possibility cannot be excluded that further experimentation by chemists may someday throw doubt on the validity of currently accepted blood tests. To ask for more than this, to expect that people can ever be absolutely certain about a matter of fact such as the identity of the person in the lineup, is unreasonable. It is as unreasonable (quite literally) as it is for a child to demand to be in the front seat and in the back seat of the family car at the same time. In Dewey's view the notion that a belief-judgment can be absolutely true is a fiction, a product of human insecurity. We live in a world that will always be insecure, because it is living and changing. But by intelligent action we can make it progressively less insecure; we can make it into a world that "will do."

Similarly, as regards the problem of what is "good," we can never be absolutely sure that something we now assess as "desirable" will continue to be desirable. It may change, or we may change. Nonetheless, knowledge that a particular object or experience is desirable—that is, that it has survived the best available tests— "will do." This knowledge is a reasonably reliable rule for guiding conduct, and it is far better and far more reliable than a rule derived in any other way—say, a rule that tells us to obey strange voices that speak to us from the air, even though these voices order us to sacrifice our child.

Is Dewey's answer to the charge of relativism adequate? To begin with, it should be noted that Dewey did not deny that his view was relativistic; he claimed that relativism need not be "fatal" and that a relativism that makes available continuously improving criteria for choice is *not* fatal. Indeed, to ask for more than this—to look for an absolutely valid criterion—would probably be fatal, in the sense that such a demand would lead to poorer rather than better decisions in concrete situations.

Dewey recognized, of course, that this reply would not be acceptable to those who, like Kierkegaard, long for certainty. But then, in Dewey's estimation, such people are seriously disturbed. He did not expect his theory to satisfy neurotics, and he would not have regarded their rejection of it as relevant. He asked only that his theory be tried, that it be tested. That is, he applied to his own theory his general thesis about the nature of truth. He had defined truth as "processes of change so directed that they achieve an intended consummation"; the test of any theory, accordingly, is whether application of it leads to more-enlightened and more-effective practice in the domain of experience covered by the theory. The theory of empirical naturalism in the domain of decision making has not yet been tried. Dewey held that in ethics we are at the level we were in physics before the appearance of Galileo and the other early modern scientists. It was dogmatic to reject out of hand, as many people did in the seventeenth century, the proposal to apply empirical methods to the study of physical nature. It is equally dogmatic to reject out of hand, and prior to testing, the proposal to apply empirical methods to the problems of choice.

> What the method of intelligence, thoughtful valuation, will accomplish, if once it be tried, is for the result of trial to determine. Since it is relative to the intersection in existence of hazard and rule, of contingency and order, faith in a wholesale and final triumph is fantastic. But some procedure has to be tried; for life is itself a sequence of trials. Carelessness and routine, Olympian aloofness, secluded contemplation are themselves choices. To claim that intelligence is a better method than its alternatives, authority, imitation, caprice and ignorance, prejudice and passion, is hardly an excessive claim. These procedures have been tried and have worked their will. The result is not such as to make it clear that the method of intelligence, the use of science in criticizing and recreating the casual goods of nature into intentional and conclusive goods of art, the union of knowledge and values in production, is not worth trying.[f]

To many readers this passage will sound badly dated. In the first place, Dewey optimistically assumed that to a very great extent a consensus exists among people that "the positive concrete goods of science, art, and social companionship" *are* good, and further, that it is better for these goods to be widely, rather than narrowly, distributed. In this respect he shared the optimism of the Utilitarians and their eighteenth-century predecessors. Like them, he thought that the main problem of ethics was that of implementing agreed-on values, not that of reaching an agreement about values. The methods of empirical science are more obviously applicable to the former problem than to the latter.

In the years since Dewey wrote, people have become increasingly doubtful about whether the consensus Dewey described exists. He claimed to be able to "differentiate genuine aims from merely fantastic ideals" on the basis of future empirical consequences. The trouble is that a person who believes all Jews ought to be exterminated is as unlikely to be won over by a consideration of the deleterious consequences of this belief as a person who believes the world is flat is unlikely to be shaken by the accumulation of empirical evidence to the contrary. Dewey recognized this, of course, but he evidently did not consider the possibility that large numbers of people, for one reason or another, are deeply committed to such "fantastic ideals." Dewey's theory of value is workable only on the assumption that fanaticism, neurosis, and the "death wish" are minority phenomena. If the more pessimistic estimate of human nature proves to be correct, Dewey's theory may turn out to be untrue by its own criterion of truth.

In the second place, to many people Dewey's faith in the efficacy of "pooled intelligence" is likely to seem a bit naïve. Not everybody still shares Dewey's confidence that the problems created by technology can be solved by technology. And what about the alienation and dissociation of sensibility that so many people feel today? Here again Dewey's diagnosis may seem superficial. He thought there was nothing new in these anxieties. Indeed, since they stem from humankind's relative inability to control the environment, they are much more characteristic of primitive than of twentieth-century humanity. But, he said, wherever, whenever, and for whatever reason man has "distrusted himself," he has sought "to get beyond and above himself." This pathetic quest for certainty, this desire to escape from contingency, not only explains belief in gods, it also explains the philosopher's belief in a transcendent reality that is "universal, fixed and immutable," as well as the insistence on absolute truths, absolute values, absolutely reliable sense data, or an ideal language that is isomorphic with the world.

Moderate anxiety, Dewey would have said, is of course reasonable—after all, the world is an uncertain place—and it is also socially useful. In contrast to dogmatic assurance, it is a spur to improving our instruments of control. But extreme anxiety is unreasonable, since it ignores the empirical evidence that intelligent inquiry does indeed pay off.

But the acceptability of this account depends on men and women being content to live in the relativistic and uncertain world that Dewey's view allows them. It depends, that is, on anxiety not being existential, on its not being rooted in the divisiveness of consciousness or in our having been "thrown" into an indifferent and absurd universe. Dewey would have thought that belief in the absurdity of human existence is neurotic; existentialist critics can reply that Dewey was insensitive to our deepest needs and blind to our real nature. Who is correct? We can only say that, for the present at least, the culture as a whole seems to have moved away from Dewey's view of humankind.

Whitehead

The basic orientation of Whitehead's[19] mind was quite different from that of Dewey's. He had, for instance, a nostalgia for the past and a sense of tradition that Dewey lacked. Reminiscing about Sandwich, a town in the south of England near which he grew up, Whitehead remarked that the sleepy sixteenth- and seventeenth-century town he had known as a boy was no more. "In the last half century it has been revived by a golf-course, one of the best in England. I feel a sense of profanation amidst the relics of the Romans, of the Saxons, of Augustine, the medieval monks, and the ships of the Tudors and the Stuarts."[g] It seems unlikely that Dewey would have cared much if Burlington, Vermont, had suffered this fate, or that he would have found golf "a cheap ending to the story."

Whitehead, however, did not live solely in the past; nor was he uninterested in contemporary social problems. On the contrary, he had a very lively interest in such problems and wrote with power and insight on such subjects as education. Nevertheless, for Whitehead, philosophy was primarily a cognitive enterprise, and his primary interest was metaphysical. In a sense both he and Dewey wanted their theories to perform a social function. They wanted to make human life richer and more significant by helping us understand our experience. But whereas Dewey thought of this task primarily in terms of solving a variety of fairly immediate, concrete problems, Whitehead thought of it in terms of a long-range and systematic interpretation of the whole range of experience. Because he was a systematizer, his point of view was less "modern" than Dewey's; on the other hand, he belongs to the great tradition that has always regarded the role of philosophy as more a matter of understanding the world than of changing it.

If Dewey represented the empirical spirit of the modern mind, modified, as has been seen, by his sense of humankind's functional and active relation to the data of experience, Whitehead can be fairly said to have represented the rationalist tradition. But his relation to this tradition must be stated with care. To begin with, like every other philosopher of the last century, he took process very seriously. This serves to distinguish him from the rationalists of the Enlightenment, but not from Hegel. The chief differences between Whitehead and Hegel are, first, that Whitehead was not a constructivist but conceived philosophy in the realistic spirit that animated Moore, Russell, and the other philosophers who were attempting to break out of the Kantian paradigm and reaffirm objectivity; second, that he drew his conceptual scheme from the physical sciences instead of from "pure" logic; and third, that there is no Whiteheadian "dialectic." In addition, Whitehead was quite clear that his conceptual scheme was not the final answer,

---

[19] Alfred North Whitehead (1861–1947) was born in England and educated at Trinity College, Cambridge. After teaching mathematics there for some years, he moved to London, where he continued teaching and writing on scientific subjects. In 1924, at an age when most people would be thinking of retiring, he became a professor at Harvard and subsequently published most of his work on purely philosophical subjects.

whereas Hegel sometimes slipped into thinking of his in this way. Whitehead's thought about his own thinking was open-ended like Dewey's rather than dogmatic, as the traditional rationalism tended to be.

The Function of Philosophy

Philosophy, Whitehead held, is simply the search for the pattern in the universe. In one sense people always have the pattern in their grasp; in another sense it forever eludes them. Philosophy works with feeble instruments, but it perfects these instruments as it goes. It is an "attempt to express the infinity of the universe in terms of the limitations of language."[h] It is the enemy of half-truths, dogmatic generalizations, watertight compartmentalizations, and doctrinaire solutions. It knows that "all general truths condition each other; and the limits of their application cannot be adequately defined apart from their correlation by yet wider generalities."[i] To perform this never-ending work of criticism and revision, to move forward to ever less inadequate formulations of the underlying pattern, is the task of philosophy.

> Philosophy is an attitude of mind towards doctrines ignorantly entertained. By the phrase "ignorantly entertained" I mean that the full meaning of the doctrine in respect to the infinitude of circumstances to which it is relevant, is not understood. . . .
>
> The use of philosophy is to maintain an active novelty of fundamental ideas illuminating the social system. It reverses the slow descent of accepted thought towards the inactive commonplace. If you like to phrase it so, philosophy is mystical. For mysticism is direct insight into depths as yet unspoken. But the purpose of philosophy is to rationalize mysticism: not by explaining it away, but by the introduction of novel verbal characterizations, rationally coördinated.
>
> Philosophy is akin to poetry, and both of them seek to express that ultimate good sense which we term civilization. In each case there is reference to form beyond the direct meanings of words. Poetry allies itself to metre, philosophy to mathematic pattern.[j]

It will be seen how close Whitehead's view of language is to Eliot's. He would have agreed with Eliot that language is "a raid on the inarticulate," which inevitably deteriorates into a "general mess of imprecision of feeling."[20] Thus, though Whitehead shared Russell's realism, he was almost diametrically opposed to Russell's view of philosophy. It is not the business of philosophy, as Russell held, to ascertain, by means of an analysis of the logic of language, the simple facts into

[20] See p. 7.

which the world divides.[21] Rather, it is the business of philosophy, and of the sciences and the arts—indeed, as we shall see, it is the whole business of life—to render some welter of feeling articulate. But as often as some welter of feeling is articulated, it collapses into the "inarticulate commonplace," and the process must begin anew. Hence, because he saw philosophy as "akin to poetry" and to mysticism, rather than to logic, Whitehead could afford to be speculative, as Russell could not.

FAITH IN A PATTERN

Whitehead was convinced that, though we can never formulate it completely or finally, there *is* a pattern—that is the realistic strain in his thought. On the one hand, "the ultimate natures of things lie together in a harmony which excludes mere arbitrariness."[k] On the other hand, since "we are finite beings," the *complete* grasp of this pattern "in its totality is denied us."[l] It follows that belief in an order of nature, belief that "at the basis of things we shall not find mere arbitrary mystery," is, in the final analysis, an "act of faith." But Whitehead's faith was not remotely like Kierkegaard's leap of faith. Whitehead's was a faith in the continuity of things—a faith that the patterns already discovered are the basis for patterns yet to be found. Kierkegaard's faith involved a quantum jump, a complete break with the evidence. Whitehead's was a faith in an objective truth, in a cosmological principle. Kierkegaard's faith claimed only subjective truth; although for Kierkegaard it "made all the difference," the difference it made was entirely in his own life. Finally, and most important, Whitehead's was a faith that the human mind and the universe are interfused in harmony; Kierkegaard's faith presupposed that an abyss separates them.

Guided by his faith in the ultimate rationality of the universe, Whitehead held that philosophy is "to seek the forms in the facts"[m] and to display these forms in their systematic interconnections. Since Whitehead believed that the pattern thus revealed has affinities with the pattern found in mathematics, it is important to understand what he conceived the nature of mathematics to be. The following passage should be contrasted with Dewey's account of mathematics, which has already been examined.[22]

> The science of Pure Mathematics, in its modern developments, may claim to be the most original creation of the human spirit. . . . [Its] originality consists in the fact that in mathematical science connections between things are exhibited which, apart from the agency of human reason, are extremely unobvious. . . .
>
> The point of mathematics is that in it we have always got rid of the particular instance, and even of any particular sorts of entities. . . . All

---

[21] See pp. 172–73.
[22] See pp. 49–50.

you assert is, that reason insists on the admission that, if any entities whatever have any relations which satisfy such-and-such purely abstract conditions, then they must have other relations which satisfy other purely abstract conditions.

In the pure mathematics of geometrical relationships, we say that, if *any* group [of] entities enjoy *any* relationships among its members satisfying *this* set of abstract geometrical conditions, then such-and-such additional abstract conditions must also hold for such relationships. But when we come to physical space, we say that some definitely observed group of physical entities enjoys some definitely observed relationships among its members which do satisfy this above-mentioned set of abstract geometrical conditions. We thence conclude that the additional relationships which we concluded to hold in *any* such case, must therefore hold in *this particular* case. . . .

Pure mathematics . . . is a resolute attempt to go the whole way in the direction of complete analysis, so as to separate the elements of mere matter of fact from the purely abstract conditions which they exemplify. . . .

The exercise of logical reason is always concerned with these absolutely general conditions. In its broadest sense, the discovery of mathematics is the discovery that the totality of these general abstract conditions, which are concurrently applicable to the relationships among the entities of any one concrete occasion, are themselves inter-connected in the manner of a pattern with a key to it. . . .

The key to the patterns means this fact:—that from a select set of those general conditions, exemplified in any one and the same occasion, a pattern involving an infinite variety of other such conditions, also exemplified in the same occasion, can be developed by the pure exercise of abstract logic. Any such select set is called the set of postulates, or premises, from which the reasoning proceeds. . . .

The complete pattern of general conditions, thus exemplified, is determined by any one of many select sets of these conditions. These key sets are sets of equivalent postulates. This reasonable harmony of being, which is required for the unity of a complex occasion, together with the completeness of the realisation (in that occasion) of all that is involved in its logical harmony, is the primary article of metaphysical doctrine. It means that for things to be together involves that they are reasonably together. This means that thought can penetrate into every occasion of fact, so that by comprehending its key conditions, the whole complex of its pattern of conditions lies open before it. It comes to this:—provided we know something which is perfectly general about the elements in any occasion, we can then know an indefinite number of other equally general concepts which must also be exemplified in that same occasion.[n]

It is clear from this passage that Whitehead belonged to the Platonic tradition. He would not have denied, of course, that mathematics can have a purely calculative role of the kind that nominalists assign to it; he would have agreed that from this point of view it is "a way of avoiding reasoning." But it is, he believed, *also* an insight into real connections. Whitehead held, as Descartes did, that it is necessary to distinguish between (1) the movement of thought or inference in our own minds, (2) the eternal objects thought about, whose real connections are revealed when we think truly, and (3) the possible exemplification of these connections in the physical world. One of the tasks of the "philosophy of organism" (as Whitehead called his view) is to put these three factors back into organic unity instead of leaving them separate as Descartes had been obliged to do. But the point to understand here is simply that in Whitehead's view mathematical reasoning is more than a mere computation of the agreements and disagreements of names; it traverses an objectively real pattern. This pattern is something we *find* (we "seek the forms in the facts"), not a subjective order that we impose on experience.

But what is the source of the concepts that constitute this pattern, or categorial scheme—that is, what are those highest and pervasive concepts that apply to all experience whatever and thus "never fail of exemplification"? It was once thought that such highest forms had a "peculiar certainty and initial clarity," that they could therefore easily be recognized as self-evident axioms, and that, once they had been ascertained, the task of philosophy was "to erect upon those premises a deductive system of thought." Unfortunately, according to Whitehead, there are no intrinsically clear and certain starting points. Theorems derived in one system can become postulates in another, and "the verification of a rationalistic scheme is to be sought in its general success," that is, in the way in which a deductive structure is developed. Until such a structure emerges, "every premise . . . is under suspicion."°

INCLUSIVENESS: THE CRITERION

Since there are no self-evident axioms, it is necessary (Whitehead held) to make a start with the concepts that seem to form a satisfactory pattern for some less inclusive region of experience (such as physics). The next step is to try to show that this set of concepts is also adequate for the interpretation of other regions of experience. Eventually the concepts may prove to be the categorial scheme that is being sought. All claimants to categorial status must be challenged to show their relevance to *all* the facts.

> Speculative Philosophy is the endeavour to frame a coherent, logical, necessary system of general ideas in terms of which every element of our experience can be interpreted. By this notion of "interpretation" I mean that everything of which we are conscious, as enjoyed, perceived, willed, or thought, shall have the character of a particular instance of the general scheme. . . .

"Coherence," as here employed, means that the fundamental ideas, in terms of which the scheme is developed, presuppose each other so that in isolation they are meaningless. . . .

The term "logical" has its ordinary meaning, including "logical" consistency, or lack of contradiction. . . . It will be observed that logical notions must themselves find their places in the scheme of philosophic notions.

It will also be noticed that this ideal of speculative philosophy has its rational side and its empirical side. The rational side is expressed by the terms "coherent" and "logical." The empirical side is expressed by the terms "applicable" and "adequate."ᵖ

THE ROLE OF IMAGINATION

But though the verification of a proposed categorial scheme is straightforwardly empirical, the initial formulation of the scheme is not. It is more like poetic insight than like generalization from the enumeration of instances. This is the case because of the very great generality of the concepts contained in a categorial scheme. Normally, science and common sense alike proceed by the method of difference: the range of a generalization is specified by noting the cases for which it does not hold. But metaphysical principles, precisely because they are categorial, hold universally.

We habitually observe by the method of difference. Sometimes we see an elephant, and sometimes we do not. The result is that an elephant, when present, is noticed. . . .

The metaphysical first principles can never fail of exemplification. We can never catch the actual world taking a holiday from their sway. Thus, for the discovery of metaphysics, the method of pinning down thought to the strict systematization of detailed discrimination, already effected by antecedent observation, breaks down. This collapse of the method of rigid empiricism is not confined to metaphysics. It occurs whenever we seek the larger generalities. In natural science this rigid method is the Baconian method of induction, a method which, if consistently pursued, would have left science where it found it. What Bacon omitted was the play of a free imagination, controlled by the requirements of coherence and logic. The true method of discovery is like the flight of an aeroplane. It starts from the ground of particular observation; it makes a flight in the thin air of imaginative generalization; and it again lands for renewed observation rendered acute by rational interpretation. The reason for the success of this method of imaginative rationalization is that, when the method of difference fails, factors which are constantly present may yet be observed under the influence of imaginative thought. Such thought supplies the differences which the direct observation lacks. It can even play with inconsistency; and can thus throw light on the consistent, and persistent, elements in experience by comparison with what in imagination is inconsistent with them. . . . The success of the imaginative experiment is always to be tested by the applicability of its results beyond the restricted locus from which it originated. . . . The partially successful philosophic generalization will, if derived from physics, find applications in fields of experience beyond physics. It will enlighten observation in those remote fields, so that general principles can be discerned as in process of illustration, which in the absence of the imaginative generalization are obscured by their persistent exemplification. . . .

There may be rival schemes, inconsistent among themselves; each with its own merits and its own failures. It will then be the purpose of research to conciliate the differences. Metaphysical categories are not dogmatic statements of the obvious; they are tentative formulations of the ultimate generalities.

If we consider any scheme of philosophic categories as one complex assertion, and apply to it the logician's alternative, true or false, the answer must be that the scheme is false. . . .

The scheme is true with unformulated qualifications, exceptions, limitations, and new interpretations in terms of more general notions. . . . [It] is a matrix from which true propositions applicable to particular circumstances can be derived. We can at present only trust our trained instincts as to the discrimination of the circumstances in respect to which the scheme is valid. . . .

Rationalism is an adventure in the clarification of thought, progressive and never final. But it is an adventure in which even partial success has importance.[q]

This notion of imaginative rationalization, with the related ideas of adventure, poetic vision, and instinct, is one of the major clues to understanding Whitehead's conception of philosophy and his constant emphasis on growth and openness.

THE UTILITY OF METAPHYSICS

The chief criticisms of such an attempt at speculative philosophy, Whitehead believed, will be (1) that it is impossible and (2) that even if it is possible it is useless. It is a sign of the marked empiricism and pragmatism of one aspect of contemporary culture that Whitehead felt he had to defend himself on the second, as well as on the first, of these scores. As regards the claim that speculative philosophy is impossible, Whitehead believed that "all constructive thought is dominated by some such scheme, unacknowledged but no less influential in guiding the imagination." Thus philosophy has an important role to perform in making "such schemes explicit and thereby capable of criticism and improvement."[r]

Obviously, this is also a reply to the charge that speculative philosophy is useless. If it is true that constructive thought is always guided by some underlying metaphysical scheme, any improvement of the scheme by means of philosophical criticism should result in an improved empirical understanding of the world about us.

> The main objection . . . is that we ought to describe detailed matter of fact, and elicit the laws with a generality strictly limited to the systematization of these described details. General interpretation, it is held, has no bearing upon this procedure; and thus any system of general interpretation, be it true or false, remains intrinsically barren. Unfortunately for this objection, there are no brute, self-contained matters of fact, capable of being understood apart from interpretation as an element in a system. Whenever we attempt to express the matter of immediate experience, we find that its understanding leads us beyond itself, to its contemporaries, to its past, to its future, and to the universals in terms of which its definiteness is exhibited. . . . When thought comes upon the scene, it finds the interpretations as matters of practice. Philosophy does not initiate interpretations. Its search for a rationalistic scheme is the search for more adequate criticism, and for more adequate justification, of the interpretations which we perforce employ. . . .
>
> The useful function of philosophy is to promote the most general systematization of civilized thought. There is a constant reaction between specialism and common sense. It is the part of the special sciences to modify common sense. Philosophy is the welding of imagination and common sense into a restraint upon specialists, and also into an enlargement of their imaginations.[5]

Criticism of the Dominant Philosophical Scheme

According to Whitehead, then, all thought has as its underlying presupposition some categorial scheme. These categorial schemes are often largely unconscious and chaotic; yet each one shapes the actual concepts, hypotheses, and theories by means of which the scientists—as well as the ordinary people—of any age seek to understand themselves and the world they live in.

Stated in this general way, Whitehead's assertion is clearly an echo of Hegel's contention that what we experience is in part a product of the mind's activity, and that the mind's role in this production has a history. But in one respect Whitehead was perhaps closer to Nietzsche than to any of the other nineteenth-century philosophers who held this kind of view. He agreed with Nietzsche that the categorial scheme underlying modern thought was the product in large measure of seventeenth-century physics; he agreed, too, that although this scheme had worked reasonably well for a long time in the field of physics, its application to other fields—psychology, ethics, and theory of knowledge, for instance—was never even remotely adequate. Further, Whitehead pointed out that relativity theory and quantum physics (which Nietzsche, of course, had not known) demonstrated that the dominant categorial scheme was no longer adequate even in its own sphere.

But although Nietzsche and Whitehead agreed that the dominant categorial scheme had collapsed, Nietzsche was content merely to suggest a new one in a cursory and sketchy fashion. Whitehead, for his part, regarded this collapse as an occasion for the exercise of those constructive functions that he assigned to speculative philosophy. These radically different attitudes toward the role of speculative philosophy reflect, once again, two persistently different personality types that have appeared again and again in Western culture. Nietzsche was too deeply concerned with his existential problem—with the need to affirm life despite its horrors—to be seriously interested in cosmology. Moreover, he believed that all categorial schemes—including, of course, any that he himself might put forward—were mechanisms designed to protect philosophers from insecurity, and he held that it was more noble and "masterly" to face insecurity boldly than to invent a categorial defense against it. In contrast, Whitehead's faith in a pattern led him to believe that categorial schemes are not merely products of insecurity; they are also expressions of the human passion to understand. In his view, since the schemes can come to correspond more and more adequately to the "facts" of the cosmological pattern, this passion is reasonable; it is capable of progressive, though never complete, satisfaction. But not only did Whitehead believe that the application of intelligence can result in improved categorial schemes; he also had surplus energy to expend on that improvement because he was not deeply immersed in an existential problem of his own.

Whitehead's philosophy of organism thus falls into two parts. First, he undertook to demonstrate the incompetence of the existing categorial scheme. Second, he sought to develop a new scheme that would avoid the difficulties of the existing one.

THE NOTION OF SIMPLE LOCATION

Whitehead believed that the root idea, and the source of much of the trouble, in the dominant categorial scheme was the notion of "simple location."

> One . . . assumption [underlying] the whole philosophy of nature during the modern period . . . is embodied in the conception which is supposed to express the most concrete aspect of nature. The Ionian philosophers asked, What is nature made of? The answer is couched in terms of stuff, or matter, or material—the particular name chosen is indifferent—which has the property of simple location in space and time, or, if you adopt the more modern ideas, in space-time. What I mean

by matter, or material, is anything which has this property of *simple location.* . . .

The characteristic common both to space and time is that material can be said to be *here* in space and *here* in time, or *here* in space-time, in a perfectly definite sense which does not require for its explanation any reference to other regions of space-time. Curiously enough this character of simple location holds whether we look on a region of space-time as determined absolutely or relatively. . . .

This fact that the material is indifferent to the division of time leads to the conclusion that the lapse of time is an accident, rather than of the essence, of the material. The material is fully itself in any sub-period however short. . . .

The answer, therefore, which the seventeenth century gave to the ancient question of the Ionian thinkers, "What is the world made of?" was that the world is a succession of instantaneous configurations of matter—or of material, if you wish to include stuff more subtle than ordinary matter, the ether for example.

We cannot wonder that science rested content with this assumption as to the fundamental elements of nature. . . . This is the famous mechanistic theory of nature, which has reigned supreme ever since the seventeenth century. It is the orthodox creed of physical science. Furthermore, the creed justified itself by the pragmatic test. It worked. . . . But the difficulties of this theory of materialistic mechanism very soon became apparent. The history of thought in the eighteenth and nineteenth centuries is governed by the fact that the world had got hold of a general idea which it could neither live with nor live without.[t]

THE PROBLEM OF INDUCTION

In Whitehead's view, the first thing wrong with the dominant scheme is that developments in physics in the twentieth century (such as discoveries about the properties of electrons) made interpretation in terms of simple location hopelessly complex and even contradictory. People used to think that it would someday be possible to give a mechanical explanation of all natural phenomena—this was the "ideal" of science. But "what is the sense of talking about a mechanical explanation when you do not know what you mean by mechanics?"[u]

But apart from such difficulties posed by twentieth-century discoveries, the dominant scheme is ill equipped even for dealing with the kind of world it supposes itself to be facing. "It is obvious," for instance, "that the concept of simple location is going to make great difficulties for induction." For the assumption that there is no inherent connection between heres and theres or between nows and thens means that inference from what happened at one instantaneous configuration of matter to what may happen at another is quite impossible.

The governing principle underlying [the orthodox] scheme is that extension, namely extension in time or extension in space, expresses disconnection. This principle issues in the assumptions that causal action between entities separated in time or in space is impossible and that extension in space and unity of being are inconsistent. . . . This governing principle has to be limited in respect to extension in time. The same material exists at different times. This concession introduces the many perplexities centering round the notion of change. . . .

The ultimate fact embracing all nature is (in this traditional point of view) a distribution of material throughout all space at a durationless instant of time, and another such ultimate fact will be another distribution of the same material throughout the same space at another durationless instant of time. The difficulties of this extreme statement are evident and were pointed out even in classical times when the concept first took shape. . . .

We must therefore in the ultimate fact, beyond which science ceases to analyse, include the notion of a state of change. But a state of change at a durationless instant is a very difficult conception. It is impossible to define velocity without some reference to the past and the future. Thus change is essentially the importation of the past and of the future into the immediate fact embodied in the durationless present instant.

This conclusion is destructive of the fundamental assumption that the ultimate facts for science are to be found at durationless instants of time. . . .

In biology the concept of an organism cannot be expressed in terms of a material distribution at an instant. The essence of an organism is that it is one thing which functions and is spread through space. Now functioning takes time. Thus a biological organism is a unity with the spatio-temporal extension which is of the essence of its being. This biological conception is obviously incompatible with the traditional ideas. This argument does not in any way depend on the assumption that biological phenomena belong to a different category to other physical phenomena. The essential point of the criticism on traditional concepts which has occupied us so far is that the concept of unities, functioning and with spatio-temporal extensions, cannot be extruded from physical concepts.[v]

Of course, as Whitehead pointed out, such "theoretical difficulties . . . have never worried practical scientists."[w] Scientists are content to operate pragmatically; they do not worry that their tacit assumption of arbitrariness and disconnectedness undermines the rationale of their procedure. For they have quietly gone on *believing* in the rationality of the universe even while *saying* that it is irrational. "It does not matter what men say in words, so long as their activities are controlled by settled instincts. . . . Since the time of Hume, the fashionable scientific philosophy has been such as to deny the rationality of science. . . . But scientific faith has risen to the occasion, and has tacitly removed the philosophic mountain."[x]

Nevertheless, however pragmatically minded practicing scientists may be, no one can enjoy operating from contradictory premises. If it is the notion of simple location that is responsible for "this strange contradiction in scientific thought," the sensible procedure is to abandon the concept in question.

THE "BIFURCATION OF NATURE"

Another difficulty with the concept of simple location is connected with the theory of perception. The minds that observe nature are supposed to be different sorts of things from the nature they observe. This notion of "bifurcation of nature," which is another by-product of the assumption of simple location, is hopelessly contradictory. According to this view, the ordinary objects of sense perception (for example, the castle seen at a distance, the planet in the sky) are unreal. They are actually only material particles that cause changes in the observer via his or her sense organs and cortex. But

> the difficulty to be faced is just this. We may not lightly abandon the castle [and] the planet, . . . and hope to retain the eye, its retina, and the brain. Such a philosophy is too simple-minded—or at least might be thought so, except for its wide diffusion.
>
> Suppose we make a clean sweep. Science then becomes a formula for calculating mental "phenomena" or "impressions." But where is science? In books? But the castle and the planet took their libraries with them.
>
> No, science is in the minds of men. But men sleep and forget, and at their best in any one moment of insight entertain but scanty thoughts. Science therefore is nothing but a confident expectation that relevant thoughts will occasionally occur. . . . Yet this won't do; for this succession is only known by recollection, and recollection is subject to the same criticism as that applied . . . to the castle [and] the planet. . . . In their departure "you" also have accompanied them; and I am left solitary in the character of a void of experience without significance.[y]

CONFLICTS WITH ESTHETIC AND MORAL VIEWS OF THE WORLD

Even apart from such epistemological puzzles, the dominant view of the world is "quite unbelievable." According to Whitehead, ordinary, everyday experience—including even the ordinary, everyday experience of those physicists and philosophers who affirm the "truth" of the dominant categorial scheme—is not experience of temporally and spatially discrete entities that are wholly without sensuous differentiations. Everyone's experience includes continuity, endurance, value, and sensuous detail. But according to the dominant scheme, nature is "a dull affair, soundless, scentless, colourless; merely the hurrying of material endlessly, meaninglessly." From this point of view it is we, not the rose, who should get the credit for its scent; we, not the nightingale, the credit for its song. "The poets are entirely mistaken. They should address their lyrics to themselves, and should turn them into odes of self-congratulation on the excellency of the human mind."[z]

But Whitehead held the poets to be right in refusing to believe this scientific dogma about the unreality of secondary qualities. Moreover, by insisting on the endurance and interpenetration of things, poets "bear witness that nature cannot be divorced from its aesthetic values; and that these values arise from the cumulation, in some sense, of the brooding presence of the whole on to its various parts."[a]

In addition to conflicting with the esthetic view, the old scientific scheme is incompatible with the moral and religious view of the world. The problem of free will is an example. According to the scientific scheme,

> each molecule blindly runs. The human body is a collection of molecules. Therefore, the human body blindly runs. . . .
>
> There are then two possible theories as to the mind. You can either deny that it can supply for itself any experiences other than those provided for it by the body, or you can admit them.
>
> If you refuse to admit the additional experiences, then all individual moral responsibility is swept away. If you do admit them, then a human being may be responsible for the state of his mind though he has no responsibility for the actions of his body. . . .
>
> The question as to the metaphysical status of molecules does not come in. The statement that they are mere formulae has no bearing on the argument. For presumably the formulae mean something. If they mean nothing, the whole mechanical doctrine is likewise without meaning, and the question drops. But if the formulae mean anything, the argument applies to exactly what they do mean. The traditional way of evading the difficulty—other than the simple way of ignoring it—is to have recourse to some form of what is now termed "vitalism." This doctrine is really a compromise. It allows a free run to mechanism throughout the whole of inanimate nature, and holds that the mechanism is partially mitigated within living bodies. I feel that this theory is an unsatisfactory compromise. The gap between living and dead matter is too vague and problematical to bear the weight of such an arbitrary assumption, which involves an essential dualism somewhere.[b]

Whitehead's position can be summarized by saying that the metaphysical scheme based on simple location, which modern science inherited from the seventeenth century and which it is still trying to apply, is far too narrow to serve as a satisfactory categorial scheme; it is even too narrow for science itself. What is required is "an alternative cosmological doctrine, which shall be wide enough to include what is fundamental both for science and for its critics."[c] Such a scheme will first replace the concept of simple location by concepts more adequate to the new developments in physics and then try to show that these new concepts are also more adequate for interpreting esthetic, moral, and religious experience.

Whitehead's New Categorial Scheme

The new categorial scheme that Whitehead constructed is not only the center of his own philosophy; it also represents the last of the great efforts of speculative philosophy. Unfortunately, it is as difficult and obscure as anything in modern philosophy.[23] The concepts that form the core of Whitehead's view are those of event (or occasion), prehension, eternal object, and organism.

EVENTS

According to Whitehead, the notion of a thing as existing at a particular here and enduring through a succession of instantaneous nows must be replaced by the concept of event. Here again the pervasive influence of the idea of process can be seen. Like Dewey, Whitehead held that the concept of event involves the notions of beginning, ongoing, and consummation. But the measure of Whitehead's greater metaphysical interest is the more thorough analysis to which he subjected these ideas.

A Whiteheadian event is "the ultimate unit of natural occurrence." The simplest example is any act of perception. I say that from the top of this hill I see a castle across the valley, or that I see a planet in the sky. Thinking in terms of the old scheme of simple location, I regard myself as wholly "here" and the castle and the planet as wholly "there," with all the ensuing difficulties that have been pointed out. But let me abandon the notion of simple location. Then the things "grasped into a realized unity" here and now are not the castle and the planet simply in themselves; they are the castle and the planet from the point in space and time of my here and now. And there are innumerable other points from which other aspects of castle and planet are grasped and with which they are united in similar ways. What, indeed, are *the* castle and *the* planet except the endless variety of standpoints (including, if they were conscious, their "own" standpoints) from which, and into which, they are perceived? And what is this "here and now" from which I am perceiving? The phrase used above was that "from the top of this hill"

---

[23] Whitehead's most systematic treatment of his proposed scheme is contained in *Process and Reality,* in which the "category of the ultimate" ("creativity," "many," "one"), eight "categories of existence," twenty-seven "categories of explanation," and nine "categoreal obligations" are defined and elaborated. For the most part, however, the present account will follow the somewhat simpler, but sufficiently abstruse, version given in *Science and the Modern World.*

I saw the castle. But hill is "too wide for our peculiar *locus standi.*" What I am conscious of is merely the relation of my "bodily events to the simultaneous events throughout the rest of the universe."[d] Hence an event is the interpenetrating of all the infinitely various aspects of the universe at some particular standpoint.

PREHENSIONS

Applied to events at the level of human perceivings, Whitehead's conception is most interesting and ingenious, but difficulties arise as soon as we try to pass from the level of human perception (which leaves us in "idealism") to the "realism" Whitehead wanted to maintain. According to him, these graspings into unity are not merely ways by which the human mind synthesizes its materials; they are objective occurrences going on all over the universe at all sorts of levels below the level of conscious comprehension. Thus, while I am perceiving the castle and the planet, they are prehending (feeling) me. But that does not mean a radical difference between their mode of experiencing me and my mode of experiencing them, for there is much about them that I am merely feeling rather than perceiving, and feeling at much the same level that they are feeling me.

Most unifyings, that is, are simply felt; they take place without consciousness of the fact of unification. This is why Whitehead talked about "prehendings" instead of "perceivings." He intended, on analogy with "apprehension," that the term "prehension" suggest the unifying function of perception and consciousness, but without definitely implying the perception and consciousness. In this way, he believed he had obtained a concept that would serve equally well for interpreting such diverse phenomena as an electron and my view of the castle. "Prehension" and "event" are categorial concepts precisely because (Whitehead believed) they hold good for—that is, are exemplified in—the whole of nature.

Unfortunately, one cannot escape the feeling that categorial interpretation is secured by a verbal trick. Is the electron a prehension into unity in the sense in which my view of the castle is? If so, how do we know that it is? The terminological relationship between "prehension" and "apprehension" suggests somewhat facilely an objective relationship about whose existence not everyone will be persuaded. But is it in fact possible to have any clear idea at all, verbal relationship apart, of a prehension that is not an *ap*prehension? Thus the *effect* of categoriality is achieved, but the cost is ambiguity.

Applications of the Categorial Scheme

So much for two of the main elements in the scheme itself. The next step is to see how they are applied. This examination should make the concept more intelligible and perhaps clear up some of the ambiguity. To begin with, how does the concept of event fit in with developments in quantum physics?

One of the most hopeful lines of explanation [in quantum physics] is to assume that an electron does not continuously traverse its path in space. The alternative notion as to its mode of existence is that it appears at a series of discrete positions in space which it occupies for successive durations of time. It is as though an automobile, moving at the average rate of thirty miles an hour along a road, did not traverse the road continuously; but appeared successively at the successive milestones, remaining for two minutes at each milestone. . . .

But now a problem is handed over to the philosophers. This discontinuous existence in space, thus assigned to electrons, is very unlike the continuous existence of material entities which we habitually assume as obvious. The electron seems to be borrowing the character which some people have assigned to the Mahatmas of Tibet. . . .

There is difficulty in explaining the paradox, if we consent to apply to the apparently steady undifferentiated endurance of matter the same principles as those now accepted for sound and light. A steadily sounding note is explained as the outcome of vibrations in the air: a steady colour is explained as the outcome of vibrations in ether. If we explain the steady endurance of matter on the same principle, we shall conceive each primordial element as a vibratory ebb and flow of an underlying energy, or activity. . . . Accordingly there will be a definite period associated with each element; and within that period the stream-system will sway from one stationary maximum to another stationary maximum. . . . This system, forming the primordial element, is nothing at any instant. It requires its whole period in which to manifest itself. . . .

Accordingly, in asking where the primordial element is, we must settle on its average position at the centre of each period. If we divide time into smaller elements, the vibratory system as one electronic entity has no existence. The path in space of such a vibratory entity— where the entity is *constituted by* the vibrations—must be represented by a series of detached positions in space, analogously to the automobile which is found at successive milestones and at nowhere between. . . .

[This] hypothesis of essentially vibratory existence is the most hopeful way of explaining the paradox of the discontinuous orbit.

In the second place, a new problem is now placed before philosophers and physicists, if we entertain the hypothesis that the ultimate elements of matter are in their essence vibratory. By this I mean that apart from being a periodic system, such an element would have no existence. With this hypothesis we have to ask, what are the ingredients which form the vibratory organism. We have already got rid of the matter with its appearance of undifferentiated endurance. . . . The field is now open for the introduction of some new doctrine of organism which may take the place of the materialism with which, since the seventeenth century, science has saddled philosophy.[e]

What is here called an organism is simply an event—that is, a coming into being of a prehensive unity, whose present includes its past and looks ahead into its future. The organism's life has a structure, or pattern, that arises from the particular way it prehends into unity all the manifold aspects of nature that it includes. Its endurance through time is simply the successive prehension of past patterns along with present aspects.

> For example, a molecule is a pattern exhibited in an event of one minute, and of any second of that minute. It is obvious that such an enduring pattern may be of more, or of less, importance. It may express some slight fact connecting the underlying activities thus individualised; or it may express some very close connection. . . . [In the latter case] there is then an enduring object with a certain unity for itself and for the rest of nature. Let us use the term physical endurance to express endurance of this type. Then physical endurance is the process of continuously inheriting a certain identity of character transmitted throughout a historical route of events. This character belongs to the whole route, and to every event of the route. This is the exact property of material. If it has existed for ten minutes, it has existed during every minute of the ten minutes, and during every second of every minute. Only if you take *material* to be fundamental, this property of endurance is an arbitrary fact at the base of the order of nature; but if you take *organism* to be fundamental, this property is the result of evolution. . . .
>
> Endurance is the repetition of the pattern in successive events. Thus endurance requires a succession of durations, each exhibiting the pattern.[f]

In contrast to the very simple, material points that the old scheme took as its ultimate reals, events are thus very complex affairs. What physics studies is only a part of the total complex. Of the manifold aspects of nature prehended into an event, physics is concerned only with "their effects on patterns and on locomotion [insofar as they] are expressible in spatio-temporal terms. . . . An electron for us is merely the pattern of its aspects in its environment, so far as those aspects are relevant to the electromagnetic field." In other words, Whitehead replaced the old notion that "happenings of nature are to be explained in terms of the locomotion of material" with the notion of two radically different kinds of locomotion—the "vibratory locomotion of a given pattern as a whole" and the "vibratory change of pattern."[g]

Thus physics is simply an abstraction from the full nature of an organism, that is, from all the other aspects that are relevant in other ways to other fields. Hence there is no fundamental difference between, for instance, physics and biology. "Science is taking on a new aspect which is neither purely physical, nor purely biological. It is becoming the study of organisms. Biology is the study of the larger organisms; whereas physics is the study of the smaller organisms."[h] Nor is there any difference, ultimately, between the relatively simple organisms studied in physics and biology and those much larger and richer organisms called human beings. Beginning with the simplest event, or prehension into unity, we can advance into more and more complex organic structures, as a given structure at one level is prehended into a higher structure at another level.

In this way, eventually, the level of ordinary everyday experience is reached, from which (as has just been seen) physics is an abstraction. One of the troubles with the dominant metaphysical scheme was precisely its failure to see that it was dealing with an abstraction. Since, according to that scheme, the abstract, simply located material particles were "real," it was necessary to relegate the concrete, sensuous world to "appearance." Whitehead called this the Fallacy of Misplaced Concreteness, the mistake of treating an abstraction as if it were a concrete fact. One of the advantages claimed by Whitehead for his philosophy of organism was that it enables us to escape this particular fallacy. Once philosophers understand that they are dealing with prehendings into unity, they will no longer feel that scientific objects and everyday objects are in competition as rival claimants to an exclusive reality. On the contrary, they will see that a so-called scientific object— electron, molecule, and so on—is simply a selection from the full diversity of aspects that are being prehended into unity here and now. Hence the poetic-esthetic view of the world, as well as the everyday view, is rehabilitated. Indeed, Whitehead believed that what the poets express in their imaginative language is precisely that interpenetration of aspects and prehension into unity that he himself was describing in abstract and philosophical prose.

Whitehead's Account of Value

One of the most fundamental aspects of everyday, as well as of poetic and religious, experience is the experience of value. Whitehead believed that one main advantage of his philosophy of organism was its ability to make a place for value in a world of fact. In order to deal with this question it is necessary to describe an aspect of prehension into unity that has so far been omitted from the discussion. What is it that is prehended? Up to now the answer has been simply "aspects of nature." It is time to examine this matter more precisely. Some organisms obviously prehend other organisms, but what about those simpler organisms that are the prehensions prehended by more-complex organisms? Eventually, we have to face the question, "Of what are the simplest events the prehension?" Whitehead's answer was "eternal objects"—but what is an eternal object?

ETERNAL OBJECTS

An eternal object is "any entity whose conceptual recognition does not involve a necessary reference to any definite actual entities of the temporal world."[1] Some entities—a fire engine, for example—are obviously cognized in spatiotemporal relations to other events: the garage in which it is housed, those who operate it, the citizens who pay for it, and so forth. The color "fire engine red" has a different status. It "ingresses" into many particular, actual occasions, including the fire engine. But its nature is what it is, indifferent to any of the occasions into which it ingresses. As has been seen, events change and endure; eternal objects are the eternal elements that become the ingredients of various transitory events.

> Enduring things are thus the outcome of a temporal process; whereas eternal things are the elements required for the very being of the process. . . .
>
> Every scheme for the analysis of nature has to face these two facts, *change* and *endurance*. There is yet a third fact to be placed by it, *eternality,* I will call it. The mountain endures. But when after ages it has been worn away, it has gone. If a replica arises, it is yet a new mountain. A colour is eternal. It haunts time like a spirit. It comes and it goes. But where it comes, it is the same colour. It neither survives nor does it live. It appears when it is wanted. The mountain has to time and space a different relation from that which colour has. . . .
>
> In any occasion of cognition, that which is known is an actual occasion of experience, as diversified by reference to a realm of entities which transcend that immediate occasion in that they have analogous or different connections with other occasions of experience. For example a definite shade of red may, in the immediate occasion, be implicated with the shape of sphericity in some definite way. But that shade of red, and that spherical shape, exhibit themselves as transcending that occasion, in that either of them has other relationships to other occasions. Also, apart from the actual occurrence of the same things in other occasions, every actual occasion is set within a realm of alternative interconnected entities. This realm is disclosed by all the untrue propositions which can be predicated significantly of that occasion. . . . It is the foundation of the metaphysical position which I am maintaining that the understanding of actuality requires a reference to ideality. The two realms are intrinsically inherent in the total metaphysical situation. The truth that some proposition respecting an actual occasion is untrue may express the vital truth as to the aesthetic achievement. . . . An event is decisive in proportion to the importance (for it) of its untrue propositions: their relevance to the event cannot be dissociated from what the event is in itself by way of achievement. These transcendent entities . . . are thus, in their nature, . . . comprehensible without reference to some one particular occasion of experience. . . . But to transcend an actual occasion does not mean being disconnected from it. On the contrary, I hold that each eternal object has its own proper connection with each such occasion.[j]

POSSIBILITY, LIMITATION, AND VALUE

The realm of eternal objects is the realm of possibility; the realm of events is the realm of actuality. Since there are always possibilities not realized in the complex of interlocking events, a principle of selection is necessary. Prehending unities, that is, are not merely passive contemplators of "aspects of nature"; they are at the same time includings and excludings of eternal objects. Every realized, actual occasion is a limitation. This is the basis for Whitehead's conception of value.

> The element of value, of being valuable, of having value, of being an end in itself, of being something which is for its own sake, must not be omitted in any account of an event as the most concrete actual something. "Value" is the word I use for the intrinsic reality of an event. . . . But there is no such thing as mere value. Value is the outcome of limitation. The definite finite entity is the selected mode which is the shaping of attainment; apart from such shaping into individual matter of fact there is no attainment. The mere fusion of all that there is would be the nonentity of indefiniteness. . . . That which endures is limited, obstructive, intolerant, infecting its environment with its own aspects. But it is not self-sufficient. The aspects of all things enter into its very nature. It is only itself as drawing together into its own limitation the larger whole in which it finds itself. Conversely it is only itself by lending its aspects to this same environment in which it finds itself. The problem of evolution is the development of enduring harmonies of enduring shapes of value, which merge into higher attainments of things beyond themselves. Aesthetic attainment is interwoven in the texture of realisation. The endurance of an entity represents the attainment of a limited aesthetic success, though if we look beyond it to its external effects, it may represent an aesthetic failure.[k]

An organism, then, is a "unit of emergent value, a real fusion of the characters of eternal objects, emerging for its own sake." This, once again, is easier to understand if we think of it at the human level (for example, the esthetic process going on in the mind of the artist—what emerges is a work of art, a "fusion" of selected eternal objects) than if we try to think of it as a universal ontological principle. But the latter is the way we must think of it if we want to follow Whitehead. Thus an electron is just as much a unit of emergent value (and for the same reason) as is Michelangelo's "David" or Socrates' decision to sit in prison instead of fleeing to Megara.

GOD: THE ULTIMATE PRINCIPLE OF CHOICE

The realm of possibility, of eternal objects, is not a hodgepodge of diverse entities. The eternal objects are arranged in orders and hierarchies. If some are selected, others must be excluded—as a child soon enough finds out when first confronted with the hard fact of alternatives. And ultimately, of course, these are not merely matters of private choice. There is a metaphysical principle at work, and this is God.

> We require God as the Principle of Concretion. This position can be substantiated only by the discussion of the general implication of the course of actual occasions—that is to say, of the process of realisation.
>
> We conceive actuality as in essential relation to an unfathomable possibility. Eternal objects inform actual occasions with hierarchic patterns, included and excluded in every variety of discrimination. Another view of the same truth is that every actual occasion is a limitation imposed on possibility, and that by virtue of this limitation the particular value of that shaped togetherness of things emerges. . . .
>
> Consider an occasion α:—we have to enumerate how other actual occasions are in α, in the sense that their relationships with α are constitutive of the essence of α. What α is in itself, is that it is a unit of realised experience; accordingly we ask how other occasions are in the experience which is α. . . .
>
> There is also in α . . . the "abrupt" realisation of finite eternal objects. . . . This abrupt synthesis of eternal objects in each occasion . . . is how the actual includes what (in one sense) is not-being as a positive factor in its own achievement. It is the source of error, of truth, of art, of ethics, and of religion. By it, fact is confronted with alternatives. . . .
>
> Restriction is the price of value. There cannot be value without antecedent standards of value, to discriminate the acceptance or rejection of what is before the envisaging mode of activity. Thus there is an antecedent limitation among values, introducing contraries, grades, and oppositions. . . .
>
> [Eventually there must be] a ground for limitation . . . for which no reason can be given: for all reason flows from it. God is the ultimate limitation, and His existence is the ultimate irrationality. For no reason can be given for just that limitation which it stands in His nature to impose. God is not concrete, but He is the ground for concrete actuality. No reason can be given for the nature of God, because that nature is the ground of rationality. . . .
>
> We have come to the limit of rationality. . . . What further can be known about God must be sought in the region of particular experiences, and therefore rests on an empirical basis. In respect to the interpretation of these experiences, mankind have differed profoundly. He has been named respectively, Jehovah, Allah, Brahma, Father in Heaven, Order of Heaven, First Cause, Supreme Being, Chance. Each name corresponds to a system of thought derived from the experiences of those who have used it.[1]

COMMENT ON WHITEHEAD'S ACCOUNT OF VALUE

It will be noted that Whitehead's theory of value depends on the doctrine of eternal objects, and it should be clear that eternal objects are nothing but Platonic forms. But if this is true, why not call them "universals" and be done with it? Whitehead answered, "I prefer to use the term 'eternal objects,' in order to disengage myself from presuppositions which cling to the former term [universals] owing to its prolonged philosophical history."[m] It is certainly easy to sympathize with a philosopher's desire to escape the difficulties clustering around the problems of universals. But can one "disengage" merely by using a different term? It is difficult to see how Whitehead's "prehensions" and "events" resolve the old difficulties about participation, or indeed why Whitehead's theory of knowledge requires eternal objects at all. Though it is impossible to go into this matter here, it should be noted that any difficulties with Whitehead's eternal objects will "infect" his account of value.

Even apart from this consideration, his theory of value is in trouble. For one thing, it is not clear whether value is a structure or a feeling, that is, whether value resides in the limitation—the structure achieved—or in the idea that in this structure the aim of some feeling happens to be realized. In the latter case, that is, if a structure is valuable insofar as it facilitates the achievement of some feeling's aim, Whitehead's values are indistinguishable from Dewey's enjoyings; and it is not at all evident that Whitehead would have found congenial the relativistic and empirical naturalism that Dewey openly espoused.[24] On the other hand, if feelings are valuable only insofar as they are realized in certain structures, objectivity is attained. But what does it mean to say that such-and-such a structure is valuable in itself, apart from any interest or need that is thereby satisfied? It would seem that if ontological significance is attributed to values by defining them in terms of structure, they lose just those characteristics that, in most people's view, make them valuable. Whitehead's predominant metaphysical interest naturally inclined him to put the emphasis on structure rather than on feeling:

> All value is the gift of finitude which is the necessary condition for activity. Also activity means the origination of patterns of assemblage. . . .
> Thus the infusion of pattern into natural occurrences, and the stability of such patterns, and the modification of such patterns, is the necessary condition for the realization of the Good.[n]

And again:

> Value is in its nature timeless and immortal. Its essence is not rooted in any passing circumstance. The immediacy of some mortal circumstance is only valuable because it shares in the immortality of some value.[o]

[24] See pp. 57–64.

Of course, no sooner had Whitehead erected this dualism of a "world of value" and a "world of fact" than he tried to break it down. Either "considered by itself is an abstraction"; they "require each other, and together constitute the concrete universe. . . . The value inherent in the Universe has an essential independence of any moment of time; and yet it loses its meaning apart from its necessary reference to the World of passing fact. Value refers to Fact, and Fact refers to Value."

Religion

Obviously Whitehead was confronted with Plato's old problem—the question of the relation between the forms and the particulars that supposedly "participate" in them. Reformulation of this puzzle in terms of the ingression of eternal objects into events hardly clears the matter up. Nevertheless, let us assume for the sake of argument that God somehow performs the metaphysical role that Whitehead assigned to him as the principle of concretion—that he effects the transition between the eternal and the actual. Then the metaphysical scheme satisfies the demands of logic, but does it satisfy the requirements of feeling? Is the principle of concretion "available for religious purposes"? This depends in part on what one means by religion. According to Whitehead,

> religion is the vision of something which stands beyond, behind, and within, the passing flux of immediate things; something which is real, and yet waiting to be realised; something which is a remote possibility, and yet the greatest of present facts; something that gives meaning to all that passes, and yet eludes apprehension; something whose possession is the final good, and yet is beyond all reach; something which is the ultimate ideal, and the hopeless quest. . . .
>
> The fact of the religious vision, and its history of persistent expansion, is our one ground for optimism. Apart from it, human life is a flash of occasional enjoyments lighting up a mass of pain and misery, a bagatelle of transient experience.p

Eloquent as this passage is, it misses both the personality and the providence, as well as the theological precision, that some people require in religion. On the whole, it would seem that Whitehead was correct in remarking that "it may be doubted whether any properly general metaphysics can ever, without the illicit introduction of other considerations, get much further than Aristotle," who certainly did not get "very far towards the production of a God available for religious purposes."q Although Whitehead put forward a more available God in *Process and Reality,* it was one that seems to have been reached by "the illicit introduction of other considerations." But Whitehead was not the first philosopher to find it difficult to reconcile religious demands with the requirements of philosophical consistency.[25]

Perhaps enough has been said to suggest that there are difficulties with White-head's categorial scheme. But Whitehead would not have expected it to be otherwise. The whole point of his position was that philosophical thinking, like all other thinking, is open-ended. "A clash of doctrines is not a disaster—it is an opportunity. . . . The clash is a sign that there are wider truths and finer perspectives within which a reconciliation . . . will be found."[r] Although Whitehead would not, therefore, have regarded deficiency as per se an objection to his view, he surely hoped that his categorial scheme would be more "coherent" than it seems to be. His emphasis was always (and rightly) on inclusiveness. Yet inclusiveness is just where the scheme is weakest: he wanted his concept of God to be available for religious purposes as well as necessary for metaphysical purposes; he wanted his concept of event to be relevant to everyday experience as well as to quantum physics; and so on. That these concepts are not so inclusive as Whitehead believed them to be was hidden from him by the ambiguity of such terms as "prehension," which allowed him to think that he had hit on a generic relationship that transcended "apprehension" while including it.

But such criticisms as these are in some respects beside the point. Philosophers who admire Whitehead and who are impressed by the boldness of his categorial scheme will rightly regard his majestic vision of a single explanatory system for the universe as being of central importance; criticism of this or that detail will seem to them trivial. On the other hand, philosophers who are indifferent or hostile to metaphysics will say that it is a waste of time to attack specific points in Whitehead's categorial scheme; the whole enterprise, they will hold, is mistaken from start to finish.

Here again, clearly, we have reached a fundamental parting of the ways in philosophy. An antimetaphysical spirit is probably dominant in contemporary philosophy, at least in the United States and Great Britain. The remark just made, and so often repeated in this *History*, that we have now reached a "parting of the ways," surely reflects this spirit: if there are fundamental partings of the ways, the pursuit of an all-inclusive, systematic metaphysical scheme is certainly illusory. But *are* there fundamental partings of the ways in philosophy? Though this seems to be a straightforward empirical question, it involves deep metaphysical issues. Thus, as Dewey discovered, even the most determined of antimetaphysicians is likely to find himself or herself doing metaphysics in the course of demonstrating that it is not "do-able." For this reason, although metaphysics has been "killed off" many times in the history of Western thought, it has always revived. Metaphysicians need not be distressed by these swings. Indeed if, like Whitehead, they take process seriously, they will expect them and seek to explain them by means of a meta-metaphysical scheme.

[25] See Vol. IV, pp. 62 and 93–95.

CHAPTER 3

Moore and the Revival of Realism

The Analytic Tradition

Analytic philosophy was a central movement in the English-speaking world (and beyond) throughout the twentieth century. It is, however, an odd sort of movement, since many of the characteristic features of analytic philosophy as practiced in the first half of the century were explicitly attacked and rejected by philosophers engaged in analytic philosophy in the second half of the century. Because a fundamental shift has taken place in the analytic movement, it is obviously misleading to speak about analytic philosophy in a general and unqualified manner. We shall therefore distinguish, in an admittedly rough-and-ready way, two phases in the development of analytic philosophy: the early or classic analytic philosophy of the first half of the century, and the late or new analytic philosophy of the second. This chapter and the four that follow are concerned with classic analytic philosophy; Chapters 11 through 13 consider the new form of analytic philosophy that arose in opposition to classic analytic philosophy.

Classic analytic philosophy is committed to a set of more or less implicit assumptions about the nature of the world and about the nature of philosophical inquiry, assumptions that can be traced far back into the past—to Hume, beyond Hume to Locke, and beyond Locke to Hobbes. One of the main features of twentieth-century philosophy has been the reemergence, or revival, of this tradition after a period of quiescence during most of the nineteenth century. We shall first examine the theories of a number of philosophers who, while differing in many respects, may all be said, without stretching the definition, to belong to the analytic tradition.[1]

A chief characteristic of the analytic tradition is its commitment to atomicity, that is, to the belief that the universe consists of a very large number of independent, encapsulated entities. Analytic philosophers have conceived of these entities in various ways—as material particles, as sense data, as impressions, as "facts." But common to all philosophers of this tradition is the conviction that the ultimate entities of which the universe is composed are only externally related—that they are, in Hume's language, "loose and separate."

From this basic assumption follows the importance of analysis for these philosophers: the primary task of philosophy, they held, is the analysis of complex entities into the simple entities of which they are composed. Because the simple entities *are* simple they are directly understandable whenever they are encountered. A complex entity is explained only when its analysis into simples has been correctly carried out. They thus completely reversed the direction of explanation as it was understood by contextual philosophers such as Bradley, Dewey, and Heidegger.[2] For such philosophers a simple is unintelligible; it becomes intelligible only when it is seen in the larger context in which it operates. The direction of explanation is from simple to complex, from the small entity to the larger entity that includes it. For the analytic philosophers, in contrast, the direction of explanation is from the large to the small.

Philosophers of the analytic tradition thus put a very high valuation on "clarity," the pursuit of which has been, as we have seen, one of the main preoccupations of twentieth-century thought. It seemed to philosophers of the analytic

---

[1] We use the term "tradition" instead of "school" because it suggests a looser relationship. No two philosophers discussed in these five chapters are representative of the analytic tradition in exactly the same way. Rather, they only shared a family resemblance (see p. 401), and the resemblance became more attenuated as time passed. From this point of view, as from so many others, *Philosophical Investigations* was a turning point. Post-Wittgensteinian analysis has been very different from pre-Wittgensteinian analysis, but these later developments do not come within the purview of this volume.
[2] See pp. 54–57 and 325–31.

persuasion, as to poets like Wallace Stevens,[3] that most of our experience is anything but clear; on the contrary, most of our experience is an encounter with large, vaguely bounded, and complex conglomerates. Further, our experience of these conglomerates is notoriously affected by our beliefs about them and our attitudes toward them: this is why no two observers are likely to agree about the foreign policy of Russia or even about the character of a mutual acquaintance. Clarity is achieved, in the first place, when such a conglomerate is analyzed into the set of unambiguous simples of which it is composed, each one of which (to expropriate a phrase of Bishop Butler's, which he used in a different connection) "is what it is, and not another thing." And in the second place, clarity is achieved when the mind is brought directly into the presence of each of these simples—that is, when its experience is a direct confrontation, unmediated and uncontaminated by our hopes or our fears. These two requirements for clarity are closely connected: it is possible to have a direct, unmediated experience of the simples on which analysis terminates precisely because, since they are simples, there is nothing about them to arouse our hopes or fears. We are able to contemplate them in their essential nature for what they are in themselves, without reacting to them and so confusing them with our feelings about them.

The analytic philosophers' pursuit of clarity led them to a great concern about language, a concern that, as we have seen, is another characteristic preoccupation of the twentieth century.[4] In the view of the analytic philosophers most of our language is seriously inadequate. This follows from everyday language suggesting that the universe consists of untidy conglomerates such as dogs and cats and apples and oranges, instead of such neat, encapsulated, atomistic entities as sweetness, redness, and sphericity. Accordingly, these philosophers were convinced that before philosophical inquiry can begin, everyday language must be refined and purified. For want of this preliminary work, they believed, many philosophers have ended in blind alleys and confusion; but if this work is carefully performed, most philosophical questions can be rather easily answered. This attitude was expressed by Thomas Hobbes:

> Seeing that truth consists in the right ordering of names in our affirmations, a man that seeks precise truth had need to remember what every name he uses stands for and to place it accordingly, or else he will find himself entangled in words as a bird in lime twigs, the more he struggles the more belimed. . . . By this it appears how necessary it is for any man that aspires to true knowledge to examine the definitions of former authors, and either to correct them where they are negligently set down or to make them himself. For the errors of definitions multiply themselves according as the reckoning proceeds, and lead men into absurdities.[a]

[3] See p. 6.
[4] See pp. 6–8.

And by John Locke:

> It is ambition enough to be employed as an under-labourer in clear-
> ing the ground a little, and removing some of the rubbish that lies in the
> way to knowledge. . . . Vague and insignificant forms of speech, and
> abuse of language, have . . . long passed for mysteries of science; and
> hard or misapplied words, with little or no meaning, have [been] mis-
> taken for deep learning. . . . They are but the covers of ignorance, [and]
> hindrance of true knowledge.[b]

And by Bishop Berkeley:

> We need only to draw the curtain of words, to behold the fairest tree
> of knowledge, whose fruit is excellent, and within the reach of our
> hand.[c]

It is this interest in language, this conviction that philosophical problems are
best approached by a tough-minded, critical examination of linguistic usage, that
chiefly distinguishes analytic philosophers from other post-Kantians. Once Kant
had drawn the distinction between phenomena and noumena, the basic choice for
philosophers was either to reaffirm that some sort of knowledge of noumena is
possible or to confine their attention to phenomena.[5] Most nineteenth-century
philosophers unhesitatingly rejected the former alternative: unknowable things-
in-themselves seemed to them to be useless and redundant.

But a major division soon developed among the philosophers who rejected
Kant's noumena and concentrated on his phenomena: some concerned themselves primarily with the observable phenomena and the various spatiotemporal
relations in which they stood; and some focused on the part of Kant's doctrine that
held phenomena and their spatiotemporal relations to be the products, at least in
part, of the synthesizing activities of mind. The latter school, among them the
Hegelians, Marxists, and Nietzscheans, were naturally led in the direction of social psychology, anthropology, and cultural history. From the point of view of the
analytic philosophers this whole development was a disaster. In the first place, the
inquiries generated in this way were not philosophy at all—that is, of course, not
as the analytic philosophers conceived philosophy. In the second place, the metaphysical and epistemological assumptions underlying these inquiries seemed to
the analytic philosophers to be self-stultifying, since they ended in skepticism and
relativism. The analytic philosophers therefore put themselves squarely in the
other post-Kantian camp: the one that concentrated on the phenomena themselves, just as we experience them. Indeed, for the analytic philosophers, since
noumena are meaningless nonsense, it is a mistake to talk about phenomena at all,
for this term inevitably suggests something less than wholly real. Once noumena
are eliminated from the inventory of realities, what Kant called phenomena are

[5] See Vol. IV, p. 101.

not appearances of something more basic but the only reals that there are. Further, by an easy move, the analytic philosophers identified these reals with the unambiguous simples that are the termini of the process of analysis. Now the central problem of philosophy is the problem of finding a language that is itself simple enough and clear enough to reflect the simplicity and clarity of those unambiguous simples in which reality, on this view, consists.

Just at this point, by a happy coincidence, new developments occurred in logic that provided the analytic philosophers with a more powerful instrument of linguistic analysis and thus gave early-twentieth-century versions of analytic philosophy their characteristic form. As long as logic had been dominated by the Aristotelian conviction that all propositions are reducible to the subject-predicate form, it was easy to assume that words are the names of objects and that they mean the objects that they name. This assumption about naming (evident in the passage quoted above from Hobbes) and the assumption about atomicity reinforce each other. Since words are clearly atomistic units, it seemed evident that corresponding to the words there must be self-enclosed, encapsulated entities named by them. These assumptions occasioned a number of paradoxes that preoccupied analytic philosophers at the beginning of this century, and the emergence of relational logic seemed to them to make the resolution of these paradoxes possible.[6] But this new start was made within the framework of the analytical-linguistic tradition; that is, it was taken for granted that complexes could be, and should be, analyzed into simples and that the proper method of attack was to uncover the "true meaning" of the language that we ordinarily use loosely and ambiguously. The chief innovation of the new, twentieth-century version of the tradition was that the new, relational logic was to be the instrument of analysis.

In what other ways is the analytic tradition to be characterized? The analytic philosophers doubtless had existential problems, as all individuals presumably do. But like Dewey, Whitehead, and Bergson, and unlike Kierkegaard and Nietzsche, they kept these problems under reasonably adequate control and out of their philosophical writings. For them philosophy was primarily a cognitive enterprise, not, as with James, a therapeutic one.

Again, although they were interested in science, differences in temperament also marked the analytic philosophers from other thinkers who were sympathetic to the scientific viewpoint. For example, even though Whitehead started as a physicist and joined with Russell in pioneering important studies of logic, he and Russell subsequently moved in very different directions. Whitehead used the concepts of physics as a "categoreal scheme" for a new metaphysics of the traditional type; Russell employed the concepts of logic as the basis for clearing up puzzles about "meaning" occasioned by people's slipshod use of language.

In addition, philosophers of the analytic tradition were almost untouched by the idea of process; certainly they were not in the least moved by the vision of development and the emergence of new forms of life that we found in the writings of Hegel and Karl Marx and that we find again in Bergson and Whitehead. One

[6] See pp. 174–87.

reason for this is undoubtedly the analytic commitment to atomicity: the ultimate simples by definition do not undergo internal change; they are whatever they are. Therefore, though they endure through time, they do not, in the strict sense of the word, have a history. New forms of life occur, but their "emergence" is merely the arrangement of the changeless simples in different combinations.

Further, the philosophers of the analytic tradition have generally not been deeply interested in social reform. There are exceptions, of course—for instance, Russell.[7] But Russell the reformer and Russell the philosopher were much more sharply distinguished (and not merely so far as writing goes) than were, say, Dewey the reformer and Dewey the philosopher. Dewey was essentially a social philosopher—his "reconstruction of philosophy" was part and parcel of his whole program of social reform; Russell was a philosopher who happened also to be a passionate critic of the economic and social status quo and a courageous political activist. But the reforming zeal of most analytic philosophers has been largely focused on philosophy itself—not in the interest of improving our "traffic with nature" but simply in the interest of obtaining "clarity."

Finally, whereas the idealists and constructivists undermined the concept of truth—each, of course, in a different way—and replaced it with the concept of interpretation, the philosophers of the analytic tradition wholly rejected this procedure as "psychologizing." They wanted, not to abandon the notion of truth, but to refine it. In doing so they certainly exposed many old "truths"; their assault on traditional metaphysics was every bit as radical as was that of the pragmatists. But the spirit of their attack was quite different from that of the pragmatists because, like the traditional pre-Kantian metaphysicians, they were realists. They took it for granted that there is an objective world that is independent of us but nonetheless accessible to us. The task of philosophy, they held, is to replace false or mistaken assertions about the nature of reality by true ones, attained by means of rigorous analysis. Here again the ideal of clarity is central. According to the analytic tradition, things are what they are; we have only to get clear in our minds about their nature.

Moore and Analysis

Philosophers agree that Moore[8] was one of the leaders in the revival of the analytic tradition in our time. Indeed, though Moore himself protested that he never

---

[7] See pp. 210–13.

[8] G. E. Moore (1873–1958) was born and brought up in a suburb of London. He was educated at Dulwich College, a private school near his home, and at Cambridge, where he studied classics and philosophy and where he first met Russell, who was two years his senior. Moore spent almost the whole of his long life at Cambridge, first as a research Fellow at Trinity, then as a lecturer, and finally as a professor. After his retirement in 1939 he visited the United States several times and taught at a number of institutions in this country. His influence on Anglo-American philosophy was great.

maintained that "analysis is the only proper business of philosophy,"[d] most of the philosophers influenced by his writings have been more impressed by his method than by the positive conclusions he reached by means of that method. We shall therefore begin our discussion of Moore with an account of his method. It is somewhat ironic, in view of Moore's insistence on clarity, that it is by no means clear exactly what "analysis" meant to Moore. Even Moore himself on occasion professed not to understand what his method was. "I used to hear them speak of 'The Method' sometimes, and understood that it was regarded as mine, but I never did know what it was."[e]

The "them" referred to in this rather giveaway remark included John Maynard Keynes,[9] and Keynes has left us a vivid description of the method of analysis as Moore practiced it in 1903, when he was a young Fellow of Trinity and Keynes was a precocious undergraduate.

> How did we know what states of mind were good? This was a matter of direct inspection, of direct unanalysable intuition about which it was useless and impossible to argue. In that case who was right when there was a difference of opinion? There were two possible explanations. It might be that the two parties were not really talking about the same thing, that they were not bringing their intuitions to bear on precisely the same object. . . . Or it might be that some people had an acuter sense of judgment, just as some people can judge a vintage port and others cannot. . . .
>
> We regarded [such questions] as entirely rational and scientific in character. Like any other branch of science, it was nothing more than the application of logic and rational analysis to the material presented as sense-data. Our apprehension of good was exactly the same as our apprehension of green, and we purported to handle it with the same logical and analytical technique which was appropriate to the latter. . . .
>
> It was all under the influence of Moore's method, according to which you could hope to make essentially vague notions clear by using precise language about them and asking exact questions. It was a method of discovery by the instrument of impeccable grammar and an unambiguous dictionary. "What *exactly* do you mean?" was the phrase most frequently on our lips. If it appeared under cross-examination that you did not mean *exactly* anything, you lay under a strong suspicion of meaning nothing whatever.[f]

Though Keynes, naturally, was not concerned with philosophical fine points, the main features of analysis, as Moore practiced it, are quite evident in his account. Analysis is a form of division, in which something complex is taken to

[9] J. M. Keynes (1883–1946) was born in Cambridge and educated there. His economic theories, and especially his *General Theory of Employment, Interest, and Money* (1936), have had great influence in Western Europe and the United States.

pieces in order to ascertain how its constituent parts have been put together. As a result of this taking to pieces, we are in a position to inspect the constituent parts in a way that was impossible as long as they were assembled in the compound from which analysis started. The whole method is in fact dominated by two metaphors—first, the metaphor of disassembling some complex physical object, such as a watch or a diesel engine; second, the metaphor of visual perception. As a result of analysis the object whose nature we want to understand is before the mind in the way in which a physical object is before our eyes, and the process of analysis is talked about as if it were analogous to bringing that object into sharper focus, getting closer to it, getting it into a good light, getting it separated from the background, and so on.

With this general description of analysis in mind, it will be useful to watch the method in action, as Moore tackles the question of the relation between being and existence—a question that has always baffled philosophers, but that Moore held to be a puzzle only because in the past philosophers had failed to do the essential preliminary work of "analysis and distinction." [10]

BEING

> The first and most fundamental property which I wish to call attention to . . . is just this one which *does* belong to *what* we believe in, whenever our belief is true, and which does *not* belong to *what* we believe in, whenever our belief is false. I propose to confine the name *being* to this property; and I think you can all see what the property in question is. If, for instance, you are believing now that I, while I look at this paper, am directly perceiving a whitish patch of colour, and, if your belief is true then there *is* such a thing as *my being now directly perceiving* a whitish patch of colour. And I think you can all understand in what sense there is such a thing. . . . This property, then, which does so plainly belong to this event (or whatever you like to call it) is the one I am going to call "being." [g]

EXISTENCE

Next, as regards existence: How is the property that is denoted by the verb "is" related to the property denoted by the noun "being"?

> As regards this question, I used to hold very strongly, what many other people are also inclined to hold, that the words "being" and "existence" do stand for two entirely different properties; and that though everything which exists must also "be," yet many things which "are"

[10] See p. 99.

nevertheless do emphatically *not* exist. . . . But nevertheless, I am inclined to think that I was wrong, and that there is no such distinction between "being" and "existence" as I thought there was. There is, of course, a distinction of usage, but I am inclined to think that this distinction is only of the same kind as that holding between "being" and "being a fact."[11] That is to say, when we say of a thing that it exists, we don't, I think, mean to attribute to it any property different from that of "being"; all that we mean to say of it is simply that it *is* or is a constituent of the Universe. . . . In merely saying that there is a class of things, to which we tend to confine the word "existence," we are, of course, saying that these things have some common property, which is *not* shared by other constituents of the Universe. . . . The important thing is to recognise as clearly as possible *that* there is such a property, and *what* it is. . . .

And I think the best way of doing this is to point out what are the classes of things in the Universe, of which we *cannot* quite naturally say that they "exist." And so far as I can see we can divide these into two classes. The first is simply the class of things which I have just called "facts." It is in the highest degree unnatural to say of these that they exist. No one, for instance, would think of saying that the fact that lions exist, *itself* exists; or that the fact that $2 + 2 = 4$ exists. We do, therefore, I think, certainly tend to apply the word "existence" *only* to constituents of the Universe, *other* than facts.

But there is, it seems to me, also another class of things, which really are constituents of the Universe, in the case of which it is also unnatural, though not, perhaps, quite so unnatural, to say that they "exist." The class of things I mean is the class of things which Locke and Berkeley and Hume called "general ideas" or "abstract ideas," and which have been often called by that name by other English philosophers. This is, I think, their most familiar name.[h]

THE PRESUPPOSITIONS OF ANALYSIS

Analysis, then, is the process of isolating for inspection—holding up before our eyes, as it were—one or another of the various entities that, collectively, make up the universe. That division of complex entities into simple ones and inspection of these simple items are the two essential steps in the method follows from Moore's assumption that the universe consists of a vast number of absolutely simple items and that analysis, if carried far enough, always terminates on one of these items. For any such simple item, precisely because it is simple, is absolutely unambiguous and so requires only inspection to be fully grasped and understood.

---

[11] [In another discussion Moore had argued that the difference in usage between "being" and "being a fact" expresses "not a difference of *predicate*, but a difference in the character of the *subjects* to which it is applied"—AUTHORS.]

It follows again that philosophical difficulties and disagreements

> are mainly due to a very simple cause: namely to the attempt to answer questions, without first discovering precisely *what* question it is which you desire to answer. I do not know how far this source of error would be done away, if philosophers would *try* to discover what question they were asking, before they set about to answer it; for the work of analysis and distinction is often very difficult: we may often fail to make the necessary discovery, even though we make a definite attempt to do so. But I am inclined to think that in many cases a resolute attempt would be sufficient to ensure success; so that, if only this attempt were made, many of the most glaring difficulties and disagreements in philosophy would disappear. At all events, philosophers seem, in general, not to make the attempt; and, whether in consequence of this omission or not, they are constantly endeavouring to prove that "Yes" or "No" will answer questions, to which *neither* answer is correct, owing to the fact that what they have before their minds is not one question, but several, to some of which the true answer is "No," to others "Yes."[i]

It is not the world or the sciences that suggest philosophical problems to us—at least not to minds like Moore's[j]—but only the writings of those philosophers who ignore analysis and who demand of the universe more "symmetry and system" than it possesses. And this demand is in the highest degree unreasonable: "To search for 'unity' and 'system,' at the expense of truth, is not, I take it, the proper business of philosophy, however universally it may have been the practice of philosophers."[k]

But what seemed so unreasonable to Moore was eminently reasonable to philosophers who, like Bradley,[12] start from the assumption that reality is a complex unity, not a collection of simples. Whereas for Moore, and for the analytic tradition generally, analysis gets us back to those real simples, for Bradley and philosophers of his school, analysis only fragments a real unity: they share Wordsworth's belief that we murder to dissect. For Moore, to understand any item is to inspect that item in splendid isolation from every other item; for Bradley, to be forced to contemplate such an isolated item is to *mis*understand it: every "bare conjunction" is a standing contradiction.[13]

A PUZZLE ABOUT CLARITY

Here, then, we have reached another major parting of the ways in philosophy. But even from within the general framework of the analytic tradition there are some serious questions about analysis as Moore practiced it. In the first place, it does not follow, just because we feel clear about something, that the thing we feel

[12] See Vol. IV, Ch. 9.
[13] See Vol. IV, p. 343.

clear about is clear. Moore wanted to hold, in opposition to extreme constructivists such as Nietzsche, that clarity is a property of things, not a reflection of our
attitudes toward them. But even granting Moore's basic assumption (which the
constructivists would of course have rejected) that there are entities so simple that
when we inspect them they are perfectly clear, it is still possible on any particular
occasion that the clarity we experience is subjective, not objective. Moore himself, in a passage already quoted,[14] admitted to having once believed himself to be
clear about something (that there is a difference between the property denoted
by "being" and the property denoted by "exist") about which he subsequently
came to hold that he had been mistaken. And we shall encounter other instances
of such confusions. Accordingly, no matter how sure we may feel that an analysis
has yielded clarity, we may be mistaken.

A PUZZLE ABOUT PROPOSITIONS AND THEIR VERBAL EXPRESSION

In the second place, what exactly (to borrow one of Moore's favorite adverbs)
is being analyzed when an analysis is taking place? Sometimes Moore wrote as if
what is being analyzed is the "meaning" of such a word as "is" or "exists"; sometimes, as if what is being analyzed is the "property denoted" by the word; sometimes, indeed, as if what is being analyzed is the verbal expression.[15] These shifts
gave rise to a request from friendly critics that Moore clarify the relations among
meanings, properties, and verbal expressions, that is, that he undertake an analysis of what analysis is.[l] When he did so, he concluded that, though he had sometimes written in ways that could give rise to a false impression, he never intended
to make analyses of verbal expressions.

> There is, of course, a sense in which verbal expressions can be
> "analysed." . . . Consider the verbal expression "x is a small y." I should
> say that you could quite properly be said to be analysing this expression
> if you said of it: "It contains the letter 'x', the word 'is', the word 'a',
> the word 'small', and the letter 'y'; and it begins with 'x', 'is' comes next in
> it, then 'a', then 'small', and then 'y'." It seems to me that nothing but
> making some such statement as this could properly be called "giving an
> analysis of a verbal expression."[m]

We may agree, first, that if this is what analyzing a verbal expression amounts
to, Moore certainly never analyzed verbal expressions, and, second, that it would
be a very trivial thing to do. But, as we shall see, there is a different way in which
one might go about analyzing a verbal expression: one might undertake to show,
not the constituent physical parts of the expression, but the various contexts in
which the expression occurs and the way in which these contexts affect the use of
the expression.

[14]See pp. 97–98.
[15]See p. 105.

As regards "meaning," Moore concluded that it is too subjective a term and for it he therefore substituted the term "proposition," defined as the thing that is apprehended when someone says to us (or we read) a sentence that we understand.[16,n]

Accordingly, if Moore's analysis of analysis is correct, whenever an analysis is undertaken it is a proposition that is being analyzed.[17] But what is the relation between the proposition that is being analyzed and the verbal expression that we necessarily use to express it? Moore assumed that the verbal expression of a proposition denotes the proposition it expresses. Thus, on his view, language is anything but "a raid on the inarticulate."[18] Rather, it is just a label that we attach to the proposition in order to identify it for people with whom we want to communicate. Some interesting consequences follow, among them that we can have independent knowledge of a proposition before finding the right label for it. Indeed, it would seem that we *must* have such prior independent knowledge of the proposition; otherwise how do we know which label is the right one?

> Just as we apprehend propositions in exactly the same sense . . . whether we hear spoken sentences which express them, or *see* these sentences written or printed, so also, obviously, we very often apprehend propositions in exactly the same sense, when we *neither* hear nor see any words which express them. . . . No doubt when we do thus apprehend propositions, without either hearing or seeing any words which express them, we often have before our minds the *images* of words, which would express them. But it is, I think, obviously possible that we should apprehend propositions, in exactly the same sense, without even having before our minds *any images* of words which would express them. We may thus apprehend a proposition, which we desire to express, before we are able to think of any sentence which would express it. We apprehend the proposition, and desire to express it, but none of the words we can think of will express exactly *the* proposition we are apprehending and desiring to convey.[o]

---

[16]This is all straightforward enough, but unfortunately Moore also used the term "proposition" in a different way. Since he held in *that* sense there simply are no propositions, readers are likely to become confused unless they keep these two senses of "proposition" distinct.

[17]What Moore actually says, in "A Reply to My Critics," in *The Philosophy of G. E. Moore*, edited by P. A. Schilpp (Tudor, New York, 1952), p. 661, is that what is being analyzed is always either "an idea or concept or proposition," but since, according to him, ideas and concepts are no more "mental facts" than are propositions, this does not affect the general thesis. They are indeed constituents of propositions and therefore as independent of minds as are propositions. Thus we could undertake an analysis of the concept expressed by "brother," and we could also undertake an analysis of the proposition expressed by "Sons of brothers are first cousins," in which the concept expressed by "brother" is a constituent.

[18]See p. 7.

Again, it follows that a given verbal expression may be the label for two or more quite different propositions—for instance, "That is a red" may express a proposition about somebody's political affiliation and also a proposition about the locus of some color in the spectrum. This is obviously a source of possible confusion, which analysis is intended to clear up. From the detachability of verbal expressions it also follows that a number of quite different verbal expressions can be equally correct labels for the same proposition. The most obvious instances of this are verbal expressions in different languages. Thus "Red is a color" and "Rot ist eine Farbe" are labels for exactly the same proposition. Finally, we can know that two verbal expressions express the same proposition (for example, we can know that "Rot" means what is meant by "red") without knowing what color is named by both of these terms. To put this differently, we can employ correct usage without knowing how to analyze the proposition expressed in this usage. For instance, I can know that Tom, Dick, and Harry are brothers, and I can use the term "brother" correctly with reference to them (I can say, correctly, "Tom is a brother of Dick's") without in the least knowing that the concept "being a brother" is identical with the concept "being a male sibling," which is the correct analysis of "brother."p All these assumptions about the relation between verbal expression and proposition appear in the following passage.

> The preceding discussion concerned the meaning of certain words. I said I proposed to raise the question: What is the meaning of the words "real," "exists," "is," "is a fact," "is true"? But I think this was perhaps an unfortunate way of describing the question which I really wished to discuss. Obviously there can be no need for me to explain to you the meaning of the word "real," in the sense in which it might be necessary for me to explain its meaning if I were trying to teach English to some foreigner who did not know a word of the language. . . .
>
> Just as, if I were trying to tell you some facts about the anatomical structure of horses, I should suppose that the word "horse" had already called up to your mind the object I was talking about, and just as, unless it had, you would not understand a word that I was saying; so I am now supposing that the word "real" has already called up to your mind the *object* or *objects* I wish to talk about—namely the property or properties which you wish to assert that a thing possesses when you say that it *is real*—and unless the word has called up before your mind this property or properties, everything that I say will be quite unintelligible. The fact is then, that I am solely concerned with the object or property or idea, which is what is called up to your mind by the word "real," if you understand the English language: it is solely some questions about this object or property or notion or idea that I wish to investigate. . . . What is this notion or property, which we *mean* by the word real? But you see, the question, in this sense, is an *entirely* different question from that which would be expressed in the same words if a Polynesian,

who knew no English, asked: "What is the meaning of the word 'real'?"
So far as I can see, the Polynesian's question would be simply equivalent to saying: Please, call up before my mind the notion which Englishmen express by the word "real." So soon as you had done this, you would
have completely answered his question. Whereas this is by no means all
that I want to do when I ask: What is the meaning of the word "real"?
What I want to do is to raise certain questions about the nature of this
notion, which is called up by the word "real," not merely to call it up. . . .

So far as we assert: the notion or notions in question *are* conveyed
by the word "real," we are asserting something which presupposes a
knowledge of English. But I want to insist that as regards part, and the
most important part, of its meaning, my question is a question which
can be raised *without* a knowledge of English. All that it requires is that
we should have before our minds the notion or notions which are in fact
expressed to Englishmen by the word "real": it does not require that we
should *know* the fact that these notions are expressed to Englishmen by
the word "real." A person may quite well investigate the differences between a horse and a donkey, without knowing at all that these objects
are called "horse" and "donkey" in English. And similarly a person who
had never heard the word "real" might have before his mind the rough
notion or notions, which are conveyed by this word to us, and might ask:
Is it the same notion I have before my mind now, as I had just now, or
is it a different one? . . . If you ask yourself: Is the notion conveyed to
my mind by the word "real" in *that* sentence, the same as that conveyed
to it by the word "real" in *this* sentence? it is not always easy to be sure
whether it is the same or not. . . . A philosopher may say: When I use
the word "real," this is what I mean by it; and yet he may be wrong:
what he says he means by it may not, in fact, be what he does mean by
it. It may be the case that the thought which is before his mind, when
he uses the word "real," and which he expresses by it, is in fact different from that which is conveyed by the words of his definition, only that
he has made the mistake of thinking they are the same. . . . And just as
a philosopher may think that the thought which he is expressing by two
different words, or by the same word on two different occasions, is the
same, when in fact it is different; so conversely he may think that there
is a difference between what he is expressing by a word on one occasion and what he expresses by the same or a different word on another,
when in fact there is *no* difference—when the two thoughts, which he
thinks are different, are, in fact, the same. . . . This would be an instance
of making a distinction without a difference—of making a merely verbal distinction, an offence of which some philosophers have often
accused others and probably sometimes with justice, though I think
philosophers are certainly more often guilty of the opposite offence—
that of supposing that there is no difference, where there is one.q

An analogy may be helpful. Let us therefore return to the three brothers, Tom, Dick, and Harry. Because they are brothers they resemble one another, and Tom and Dick, who are twins, resemble each other more closely than either resembles Harry. It is possible that acquaintances who do not know them well (or even friends who look at them hastily or in a poor light) may mistake one for another. To mistake them is to misname them. An acquaintance may for instance call Dick "Tom" and Tom "Dick." Or again he may encounter Dick on two separate occasions and call him (correctly) "Dick" on the first and (incorrectly) "Tom" on the second: he may mistakenly believe he has encountered two brothers when he has in fact encountered only one. Conversely, he may encounter Dick on one occasion and Tom on another, and call them both "Dick": he may believe himself to have talked with one brother when he has in fact talked with two. Finally, corresponding to the English names of the brothers there are French, German, and Italian names, and a man might know that "Heinrich" is German for "Harry," and so know that the brother who is called "Harry" in English would be called "Heinrich" in German, without having the least idea which of the three brothers is Harry/Heinrich.

Moore's account of language as denotative is plausible as long as we are thinking about people and their names. Each of the brothers is obviously himself and not another one of the brothers; their names are detachable labels that they could change. And obviously we could know a lot about Tom, Dick, and Harry (how tall they are, how much they weigh, whether they are good at sports, how much their salaries are) without knowing that they are called "Tom," "Dick," and "Harry." The same is true for horses and donkeys. There are obviously horse-things— things that we can see, smell, and touch quite independently of knowing that these horse-things are called "horses." And if there are horse-things in Polynesia, then we can point to those horse-things and ask what they are called in Polynesian. We shall then know the label in Polynesian for the things that we label in English by the word "horse."

The question is, how far can this account of language be generalized? Granted that in some situations language functions denotatively, does language always function in this way? For instance, is there a Polynesian equivalent—as Moore assumed there must be—for "real"? And how would we go about finding out? Or to take an easier case, suppose a man says to us, "Numbers are real," and we wonder what he means. It would seem that the only way we can find out what he means by "real" in this sentence is by taking note of the contexts in which he says this sentence, that is, by studying his usage. Moore has maintained that to ascertain meaning is to ascertain the proposition that is expressed by a sentence. If, however, usage determines meaning, there is no need to postulate the existence of propositions. It would seem that propositions are redundant; they are not needed to give an account of meaning.[19]

---

[19] It was Wittgenstein who first posed the kinds of question raised in this paragraph. See pp. 396–401.

Now, if propositions are redundant, what happens to analysis as Moore practiced it? Evidently, if there are no propositions Moore cannot have been doing what he thought he was doing, that is, dividing a complex proposition into its constituent parts. It would seem that Moore's analysis turns out to be an examination of the ways in which certain English terms are actually used and a recommendation to confine our own usage to one of these ways rather than to any other. For instance, on this analysis of Moore's analysis, he was not displaying, as he believed himself to be doing, the property denoted by "is" and the property denoted by "exists" and showing us that they are exactly the same property. Instead, he was urging us to agree to use "is" and "exists" interchangeably.

But if this is what Moore was doing, why did he not see it himself? The answer appears to be as follows. If the objects we think about exist independently of our thoughts about them, it is plausible to regard thought (and perception) as contemplation, not activity, and language then functions merely ex post facto to label objects already fully apprehended. But, as we have seen, Moore's temperament was fundamentally realistic. As Keynes perceptively wrote, "Moore had a nightmare once in which he could not distinguish propositions from tables. But even when he was awake, he could not distinguish love and beauty and truth from the furniture. They took on the same definition of outline, the same stable, solid, objective qualities and common-sense reality."[r] For Moore, that is to say, "Our apprehension of good [is] exactly the same as our apprehension of green."[s] Thus Moore's view that language is denotative, on which his analysis of analysis depends, rests in turn on his realism. It is time, then, to examine his argument for realism and against idealism.

Realism

THE REFUTATION OF IDEALISM

In our discussion of the Kantian paradigm[20] we said that the attempt to break out of it took three main forms—one a revival of realism, another based on a revolution in logic, and a third based on phenomenological observation and bracketing. Moore played no substantial part in the second of these movements, but his article "The Refutation of Idealism," published in 1903, was one of the earliest, and also one of the most influential, contributions to the revival of realism.

> If I can refute a single proposition which is a necessary and essential step in all Idealistic arguments, then, no matter how good the rest of these arguments may be, I shall have proved that Idealists have *no reason whatever* for their conclusion. . . .

[20] See pp. 8–14.

[There is] a matter upon which not Idealists only, but all philosophers and psychologists also, have been in error, and from their erroneous view of which they have inferred (validly or invalidly) their most striking and interesting conclusions. . . . It will indeed follow that all the most striking results of philosophy—Sensationalism, Agnosticism and Idealism alike—have, for all that has hitherto been urged in their favour, no more foundation than the supposition that a chimera lives in the moon. It will follow that, unless new reasons never urged hitherto can be found, all the most important philosophic doctrines have as little claim to assent as the most superstitious beliefs of the lowest savages.[t]

The step in the idealist argument that Moore selected for attack is the claim that to be is to be experienced, or, in Berkeley's formulation, *esse est percipi,* and since from Berkeley[21] to Bradley[22] this had been an essential part of the idealist case, it was shrewd of Moore to focus on it.

That wherever you can truly predicate *esse* you can truly predicate *percipi,* in some sense or other, is, I take it, a necessary step in all arguments, properly to be called Idealistic, and, what is more, in all arguments hitherto offered for the Idealistic conclusion. If *esse* is *percipi,* this is at once equivalent to saying that whatever is, is experienced; and this, again, is equivalent, in a sense, to saying that whatever is, is something mental. But this is not the sense in which the Idealist *conclusion* must maintain that Reality is *mental.* The Idealist *conclusion* is that *esse* is *percipere;* and hence whether *esse* be *percipi* or not, a further and different discussion is needed to show whether or not it is also *percipere.* . . .

But now: Is *esse percipi?* There are three very ambiguous terms in this proposition, and I must begin by distinguishing the different things that may be meant by some of them.

And first with regard to *percipi.* This term need not trouble us long at present. It was, perhaps, originally used to mean "sensation" only; but . . . the distinction between sensation and thought need not detain us here. For, in whatever respects they differ, they have at least this in common, that they are both forms of consciousness or, to use a term that seems to be more in fashion just now, they are both ways of experiencing. Accordingly, whatever *esse* is *percipi* may mean, it does *at least* assert that whatever is, is *experienced.* . . . I shall undertake to show that what makes a thing real cannot possibly be its presence as an inseparable aspect of a sentient experience.[u]

---

[21] See Vol. III, p. 287.
[22] See Vol. IV, pp. 357–58.

So much for *percipi*. Next Moore considered the ambiguity of "is."

> What can be meant by saying that Esse *is* percipi? There are just
> three meanings, one or other of which such a statement *must* have, if it
> is to be true; and of these there is only one which it can have, if it is to
> be important. (1) The statement may be meant to assert that the word
> "esse" is used to signify nothing either more or less than the word "per-
> cipi": . . . that what is meant by *esse* is absolutely identical with what is
> meant by *percipi*. I think I need not prove that the principle *esse* is *per-
> cipi* is *not* thus intended merely to define a word. . . . But if it does *not*
> mean this, only two alternatives remain. The second is (2) that what is
> meant by *esse*, though not absolutely identical with what is meant by
> *percipi*, yet *includes* the latter as a *part* of its meaning. If this were the
> meaning of "esse is percipi," then to say that a thing was real would not
> be the same thing as to say that it was experienced. . . . From the fact
> that a thing was real we should be able to infer, by the law of contra-
> diction, that it was experienced; since the latter would be *part* of what
> is meant by the former. But, on the other hand, from the fact a thing
> was experienced we should *not* be able to infer that it was real.[v]

That is to say, although from xy we can infer y, from y we cannot infer x. But
the idealist of course does not want to infer y from xy, that is, infer *percipi* from
esse and *percipi* together—that would be the most trivial conclusion. He wants to
infer *percipi* from *esse* alone, that is, y from x. "This is (3) the third possible meaning of the assertion *esse* is *percipi*: and [it is] the only important one. *Esse* is *percipi* asserts that wherever you have an x you also have *percipi*, that whatever has
the property x also has the property that it is experienced."[w]

Moore has now formulated the doctrine that he believed idealists wanted to
maintain—that "whatever is experienced, is *necessarily so*"—and that they formulated, in a very muddled way, by saying that "the object of experience is
inconceivable apart from the subject." And this assertion, so far from being obviously true as the idealists suppose, is actually self-contradictory.

How can the idealists have made such a colossal mistake? The reason is that
they have never looked at experience carefully enough to see that subject and object are two completely distinct things.

> I am suggesting that the Idealist maintains that object and subject are
> necessarily connected, mainly because he fails to see that they are *dis-
> tinct*, that they are *two*, at all. When he thinks of "yellow" and when he
> thinks of the "sensation of yellow," he fails to see that there is anything
> whatever in the latter which is not in the former. This being so, to deny
> that yellow can *ever be apart* from the sensation of yellow is merely to
> deny that yellow can ever be other than it is; since yellow and the sen-
> sation of yellow are absolutely identical. To assert that yellow is neces-
> sarily an object of experience is to assert that yellow is necessarily

yellow—a purely identical proposition, and therefore proved by the law of contradiction alone. Of course, the proposition also implies that experience is, after all, something distinct from yellow—else there would be no reason for insisting that yellow is a sensation: and that the argument thus both affirms and denies that yellow and sensation of yellow are distinct, is what sufficiently refutes it.[x]

In a word, *esse* and *percipi* are actually just as different from each other as are green and sweet, and there is therefore no more reason "to believe that what *is* is *also* experienced than to believe that whatever is green is also sweet."[y]

But now what is that property, missed altogether by the idealist, that, being actually present in the sensation of yellow and absent in yellow, makes subject and object into two quite distinct things? The answer is, consciousness.

> We all know that the sensation of blue differs from that of green. But it is plain that if both are *sensations* they also have some point in common. What is it that they have in common? And how is this common element related to the points in which they differ?
>
> I will call the common element "consciousness" without yet attempting to say what the thing I so call *is*. We have then in every sensation two distinct terms, (1) "consciousness," in respect of which all sensations are alike; and (2) something else, in respect of which one sensation differs from another. It will be convenient if I may be allowed to call this second term the "object" of a sensation: this also without yet attempting to say what I mean by the word. . . .
>
> Accordingly to identify either "blue" or any other of what I have called "*objects*" of sensation, with the corresponding sensation is in every case, a self-contradictory error. It is to identify a part either with the whole of which it is a part or else with the other part of the same whole. If we are told that the assertion "Blue exists" is *meaningless* unless we mean by it that "The sensation of blue exists," we are told what is certainly false and self-contradictory. . . . We can and must conceive that blue might exist and yet the sensation of blue not exist. For my own part I not only conceive this, but conceive it to be true.[z]

This, then, is Moore's refutation of idealism: idealism is refuted by showing that one of the principal links in the proof is self-contradictory, and the self-contradictoriness of this link is shown, in its turn, by pointing out the two distinct things—(1) consciousness and (2) the object of consciousness—which the idealist has confusedly identified. We have quoted Moore's case against idealism in detail not only because it is historically important but also, and especially, because it is an excellent example of analysis as Moore practiced it. The critical move in the whole argument is the uncovering for inspection of an entity (consciousness) that Moore held to be clearly visible as soon as we look in the right place but that eludes those who do not take care to analyze the complex entity "experience" into its constituent parts. The idealists' mistake is thus, in Moore's view, a classical instance of one of the most common of philosophical mistakes, identifying two things that are superficially similar but really very different.[23] It corresponds, that is, to the mistake made by the man who, failing to see that he has encountered twins, calls both of them "Dick."[24]

A PUZZLE ABOUT CONSCIOUSNESS

But *is* consciousness as clear and unambiguous an item in experience as Moore claimed it to be? James, who was certainly an acute observer, was unable to find any such element when *he* introspected, and he concluded that people who think that they are conscious of consciousness are mistaken. What they are really aware of, he thought, is their breathing.[25] Thus, though James was as hostile to idealism as was Moore, he would have said that it was Moore, not the idealists, who were mistaken about the makeup of experience; there was, as it were, only one man, whom Moore called by two different names because he erroneously believed that this man had a brother.

Moore himself allowed that

> the element which I have called "consciousness" . . . is extremely difficult to fix. . . . It seems, if I may use a metaphor, to be transparent— we look through it and see nothing but the blue. . . . The moment we try to fix our attention upon consciousness and to see *what,* distinctly, it is, it seems to vanish: it seems as if we had before us a mere emptiness. When we try to introspect the sensation of blue, all we can see is the blue: the other element is as if it were diaphanous. Yet it *can* be distinguished if we look attentively enough, and if we know that there is something to look for.[a]

The operative phrase here is "if we know that there is something to look for." Certainly, if we *know* that there is something to look for, we are much more likely to find it than if we do not know. On the other hand, however, if we very much want to find something, we may persuade ourselves we have found it when in fact it is not there to be found. This is one reason that the experience of clarity is not infallible evidence that what we feel clear about is in fact the case. Moore of course had a very strong motive for wanting to find consciousness: it enabled him both to refute idealism and also, as we shall shortly see, to prove realism.

[23] See p. 104.
[24] See p. 104.
[25] See Vol. IV, p. 306.

THE EVIDENCE OF BRENTANO[26]

It would be unfair, however, to suggest that Moore had nothing to go on but his own introspection. On the contrary, the psychological studies of Franz Brentano, in contrast to those of James, lent support to the thesis that something real and important is named by the term "consciousness." Indeed, Brentano's studies suggested that James had failed to find consciousness because he had been looking for the wrong sort of thing, a thesis that resonated, of course, with Moore's belief that philosophers go wrong because they fail to isolate those simple items that are there to be inspected. What, then, is consciousness, according to Brentano? Not an idea, not a representation, not a state, but a direction. Consciousness is intentional in nature and simply "points toward an object." Since James was looking for a psychic state it is no wonder he could not find consciousness. Had he looked for a direction, instead of a psychic state, he would have found it.

Brentano's account of consciousness—and it must be emphasized that this was a psychological description, not a piece of philosophical theorizing—seemed to hold out a way of reviving realism without slipping back into the paradox of Cartesianism. The problem for Cartesianism had always been to explain how, if we are directly conscious only of our own mental states, we can ever know that these states represent an objective world. But if Brentano was correct, to be conscious of something (say, my desk) is not to contemplate a private inner representation of the desk; it is simply for me to be directed toward the desk, to "intend" the desk.

More important in the present connection is that Brentano's account of consciousness as intentional suggested a way of avoiding the subjectivism in which the whole post-Kantian philosophy had become enmeshed. It now seemed possible to agree with Kant that human experience is limited to things-for-consciousness while denying to consciousness any role in constructing these things. If Brentano was correct, consciousness does not *do* anything; it merely discloses, or displays, things to us.

Although, as we shall see when we begin to trace the development of phenomenology,[27] Moore's was not the only possible conclusion to be derived from Brentano's account of consciousness, what Moore saw in it was a way of eliminating any kind of intermediary between our minds and their objects. What we are aware of when we are conscious of something is what Wallace Stevens also sought[28]—the very thing itself, unmediated and uncontaminated by any sort of

---

[26] Franz Brentano (1838–1917) was a Catholic priest for nearly ten years but resigned his priesthood because he refused to accept some of the fundamental dogmas of the Church. He taught at Würzburg and at Vienna, but his independence of mind cost him both posts, and he spent the last twenty years of his life in Italy and Switzerland. His lectures on "descriptive psychology" were given at Vienna in 1888–89.

[27] See pp. 272–76.

[28] See pp. 6–7.

mental activity whatsoever. Anybody, Moore thought, who attends carefully to very simple experiences—such as the experience first of a green sense datum and then of a blue one—will see that this is the case, and what is true of very simple experience is equally true of complex perceptions and cognitions, though in such cases careless observers may be misled.

THE PROOF OF REALISM

So far Moore has merely insisted that the sensation of blue and the sensation of green have something in common, which he called "consciousness," and something in respect to which they differ, which he called "object,"[29] but of which he has not yet given an account. This was enough to refute idealism but not to establish realism.

> The point I had established so far was that in every sensation or idea we must distinguish two elements, (1) the "object," or that in which one differs from another; and (2) "consciousness," or that which all have in common—that which makes them sensations or mental facts. . . .
>
> The analysis hitherto accepted of the relation of what I have called "object" to "consciousness" in any sensation or idea . . . is . . . that what I call the object is merely the "content" of a sensation or idea. It is held that in each case we can distinguish two elements and two only, (1) the fact that there is feeling or experience, and (2) *what* is felt or experienced; the sensation or idea, it is said, forms a whole, in which we must distinguish two "inseparable aspects," "content" and "existence." I shall try to show that this analysis is false. . . .
>
> We have it, then, as a universally received opinion that blue is related to the sensation or idea of blue, as its *content,* and that this view, if it is to be true, must mean that blue is part of *what* is said to exist when we say that the sensation exists. To say that the sensation exists is to say both that blue exists and that "consciousness," whether we call it the substance of which blue is *the* content or call it another part of the content, exists too. Any sensation or idea is a *"thing,"* and what I have called its object is the quality of this thing. Such a "thing" is what we think of when we think of a *mental image.* . . .
>
> What I wish to point out is that we have no reason for supposing that there are such things as mental images at all—for supposing that blue *is* part of the content of the sensation of blue. . . .
>
> The true analysis of a sensation or idea is as follows. The element that is common to them all, and which I have called "consciousness," really *is* consciousness. A sensation is, in reality, a case of "knowing" or "being aware of" or "experiencing" something. When we know that the

[29] See p. 108.

sensation of blue exists, the fact we know is that there exists an awareness of blue. And this awareness is not merely, as we have hitherto seen it must be, itself something distinct and unique, utterly different from blue: it also has a perfectly distinct and unique relation to blue, a relation which is *not* that of thing or substance to content, nor of one part of content to another part of content. This relation is just that which we mean in every case by "knowing." To have in your mind "knowledge" of blue, is *not* to have in your mind a "thing" or "image" of which blue is the content. To be aware of the sensation of blue is *not* to be aware of a mental image—of a "thing," of which "blue" and some other element are constituent parts in the same sense in which blue and glass are constituents of a blue bead. It is to be aware of an awareness of blue; awareness being used, in both cases, in exactly the same sense. This element, we have seen, is certainly neglected by the "content" theory: that theory entirely fails to express the fact that there is, in the sensation of blue, this unique relation between blue and the other constituent. . . .

It being the case, then, that the sensation of blue includes in its analysis, beside blue, *both* a unique element "awareness" *and* a unique relation of this element to blue, . . . [it follows] that what is called the *content* of a sensation is in very truth what I originally called it—the sensation's *object*.

But, if all this be true, what follows? . . .

What my analysis of sensation has been designed to show is, that whenever I have a mere sensation or idea, the fact is that I am then aware of something which is equally and in the same sense *not* an inseparable aspect of my experience. The awareness which I have maintained to be included in sensation is the very same unique fact which constitutes every kind of knowledge: "blue" is as much an object, and as little a mere content, of my experience, when I experience it, as the most exalted and independent real thing of which I am ever aware. There is, therefore, no question of how we are to "get outside the circle of our own ideas and sensations." Merely to have a sensation is already to *be* outside that circle. It is to know something which is as truly and really *not* a part of *my* experience, as anything which I can ever know.[b]

This, then, is Moore's proof of realism. On the one hand, consciousness is real and not a case of mistaken identity, as James had held; on the other hand, it is not an organizing activity, as the idealists had held. It is just the nature of consciousness to be *of,* so that we mean exactly what we say when we say that we are "conscious of" blue: when we are conscious of blue, it is blue we are conscious *of*—blue itself, and not another thing.

Further, what is true about blue is, of course, equally true of all other things—they are all equally independent of us and our thoughts about them. The universe contains in fact an immense variety of different kinds of entities. For instance: My mind, any particular thought, a perception of mine, the quality which distinguishes an act of volition from a mere act of perception, the Battle of Waterloo, the process of baking, the year 1908, the moon, the number 2, the distance between London and Paris, the relation of similarity—all of these are contents of the Universe, all of them are contained in it.[c]

These items divide into two main classes—items that are "mental" (or "psychical") and items that are not. Some of the items that are not mental are physical objects; some are not. But all of these items—including such mental items as my thoughts and sensations—have the characteristic of being, in their nature, independent of minds. My awareness of blue, for instance (just as much as the moon or the number 2), is just what it is, a fact uncontaminated and untouched by my awareness that I am aware of blue. What is more, the objective and public world which is thus revealed to view is just the world that common sense believes in. Finally, that all this is true Moore held to be completely obvious to anyone who takes the trouble to look carefully at his or her experience.

It would be difficult to exaggerate the effect of this analysis on those who had been disturbed by the subjectivism of idealism. Russell's response was typical:

> G. E. Moore . . . took the lead in rebellion, and I followed, with a sense of emancipation. Bradley had argued that everything common sense believes in is mere appearance; we reverted to the opposite extreme, and thought that *everything* is real that common sense, uninfluenced by philosophy or theology, supposes real. With a sense of escaping from prison, we allowed ourselves to think that grass is green, that the sun and stars would exist if no one was aware of them [and that] mathematics would be *quite* true, and not merely a stage in dialectic.[d]

THE STATUS OF SENSE DATA

It was not long, however, before Moore—and Russell too—began to see grave difficulties in the new view. As long as we concentrate on sense data, realism is persuasive, for it seems plausible to say that when I am sensing a blue sense datum, it is the blue sense datum itself, directly and in its entirety as it were, that I am aware of. But it is only under rather unusual circumstances that I actually ever experience a blue sense datum; what I usually experience are blue things—blue beads, blue flowers, blue ribbons, and the like. I do not experience any such object all at once, and it may even be doubted whether I experience any of it *directly*.

When, for instance, I see a dime and a quarter lying on the ground in front of me, I am not directly aware of the whole of either coin—I do not see the other side of either, still less the inside of either. Further, if the coins are a little way off I am directly aware of two elliptical sense data (though the coins themselves are round), and, if the dime happens to be nearer than the quarter, the sense datum associated with the dime may be larger than the sense datum associated with the quarter. But how are these sense data related to the coins? What, exactly, does "associated" mean?

One way of dealing with this problem is to define a physical object (for instance, a coin) as the whole set of sense data that all possible observers would experience under all possible conditions of observation. Then the elliptical sense datum would be related to the coin by the well-known relation of class membership. This, as we shall see, is the type of solution for which Russell opted, but since Moore's main aim was to "vindicate" common sense, and since he believed that common sense holds material objects to be more than mere collections of sense data, he could not take this way out.

> It is obvious that, on this view, though we shall still be allowed to say that the coins *existed* before I saw them, are *circular,* etc., all these expressions, if they are to be true, will have to be understood in a Pickwickian sense. When I know that the coins existed before I saw them, what I know will not be that anything whatever existed at that time, in the sense in which those elliptical patches of colour exist now. *All* that I know will be simply that, since the elliptical patches exist now, it is true, that, *if* certain unrealised conditions had been realised, I should have had certain sensations that I have not had; or, *if* certain conditions, which may or may not be realised in the future, were to be so, I *should* have certain experiences. . . . In other words, to say of a *physical object* that it *existed* at a given time will always consist merely in saying of some sensible, *not* that *it* existed at the time in question, but something quite different and immensely complicated. . . .
>
> The fact that these assertions that the coins exist, are round, etc., will, on this view, only be true in this outrageously Pickwickian sense, seems to me to constitute the great objection to it. But it seems to me to be an objection only, so far as I can see, because I have a "strong propensity to believe" that, when I know that the coins existed before I saw them, *what* I know is that something existed at that time, in the very same sense in which those elliptical patches now exist. And, of course, this belief *may* be a mere prejudice. It *may* be that when I believe that I *now* have, in my body, blood and nerves and brain, *what* I believe is only true if it does *not* assert, in the proper sense of the word "existence," the *present* existence of anything whatever, other than sensibles which I directly apprehend, but only makes assertions as to the kind of experiences a doctor *would* have, if he dissected me. But I cannot feel at all sure that my belief . . . is a mere prejudice.[e]

What, then, is the alternative for a realist? In the end Moore inclined to a position "roughly identical with Locke's view," that at least some of the sense data "resemble" the physical objects that are their "source." But, as Moore recognized, this seems indistinguishable from just that representative theory of perception that Moore's own original formulations were designed to avoid: "How can I ever come to know that these sensibles have a 'source' at all? And how do I know that these 'sources' are circular?"[f] Moore confessed that he did not know how to answer these questions. Of course, if, along with our experience of the sensibles, we had an "immediate awareness" that the sources of these sensibles exist and that they are circular, the problem would be solved. But do we have such an immediate awareness? Analysis, Moore had to admit, did not disclose any such immediate awareness to inspection. But of course the fact that analysis has not yet disclosed something does not prove that a more careful analysis would not lay it bare. Thus, the most Moore felt he could claim was that there is no *conclusive* evidence against the Lockean view.

It has to be allowed that this is a somewhat inconclusive conclusion, but it is not the only problem about sense data that realism had to face: When a color-blind man looks at a traffic signal, where are the gray sense data that he sees? If they are objective, as Moore's theory must hold them to be, they must be somewhere in physical space. Are they in the same region of space as the red and green sense data that the person with normal vision sees? How can this be? And what about the silvery circular sense datum that we see when we look at the moon? Where is it? Out there, where the moon itself is—250,000 miles away?

Still another set of problems emerged in connection with developments of modern physics. For physics the coin was neither the solid material object that common sense believes it to be nor yet the collection of sense data that, as we have just seen, one philosophical theory held it to be. On the contrary, for physics, it seemed, the coin was mostly empty space, occupied here and there by electrical charges. Thus arose what Sir Arthur Eddington called "the two-tables problem": What is the relation between the table of physics and the table of common sense? If the former is real, must not the latter be an illusion? Since these are all questions to which Russell addressed himself, we may postpone further consideration of them until Chapter 5.

THE FALSE, THE IMAGINARY, AND THE CONTRADICTORY

As we have just seen, perceptual illusions, foreshortenings, hallucinations, and the like create problems for any view, like Moore's, that holds us to be aware of something real, objective, and independent of ourselves, since there is a puzzle about where these illusory or mistaken sensory experiences are located. There is an analogous puzzle about imaginary, self-contradictory, and nonexistent objects. What am I thinking about when I think about such objects? On Brentano's account of consciousness as consciousness-*of,* it seems to follow there must be something that is the object of consciousness whenever we are conscious, even when we are conscious of (thinking about) centaurs, chimeras, round squares, and the present king of France.

Given Moore's strong tendency to hypostatize everything from green to good, he naturally sympathized with this point of view.[30] As he wrote in a passage already quoted,[31] he initially drew a sharp distinction between "being" and "existence," and his first account of the nature of truth conformed. Every assertion, he argued, refers to a proposition, and all propositions without exception, both true propositions and false ones, have the "ultimate and unanalysable property of 'being.'" True propositions, however, have in addition a second equally ultimate and unanalyzable property, which, he said, may be called "truth." Thus the propositions referred to in assertions about fictitious or contradictory objects have but one property ("being"), whereas the propositions referred to in factual assertions have two properties ("being" and "truth").

By 1910 Moore had decided that this theory was mistaken, though he still held that it is "a very simple and a very natural one; and I must confess I can't find any conclusive arguments against it."[g] The main objection is that propositions turn out to be redundant. Suppose that Moore were now hearing the noise of a brass band. It would follow that there is in the universe the fact that Moore is hearing the noise of a brass band. But now suppose that Moore (or somebody else) were to assert, "Moore is now hearing the noise of a brass band." On the theory we are considering, a proposition would be referred to in this assertion, the proposition, namely, that Moore is now hearing the noise of a brass band. Thus, on this theory, there are in the universe two "different facts having the same name—the proposition, on the one hand, and the fact on the other."[h] Therefore it seemed reasonable to Moore to drop propositions from the inventory of items in the universe. There are no more any true propositions than there are any false propositions. "There simply are no such things as propositions."[32] Moore's objection to the theory gives us an interesting insight into his underlying assumptions about the nature of the world, assumptions that are reflected in his conception of analysis. He was not at all disturbed by the notion of "ultimate and unanalysable properties"—a notion that many philosophers would regard as prima facie suspect. What disturbed *him* was the thought of "two different facts that have the same name."

But now, if there are not propositions, then "belief does *not* consist, as the former theory held, in a relation between the believer, on the one hand, and another thing which may be called the proposition believed."[i] In what, then, does belief consist? And, more especially, what is it that makes some beliefs true if it is not having for their objects propositions possessing the unanalyzable property "truth"?

---

[30] See p. 105.

[31] See p. 97.

[32] In the discussion being summarized here Moore is using the term "proposition" in a different sense from that in which he maintained that the object of analysis is a proposition. See pp. 101–02.

Let me try to state the matter quite precisely, and to explain what I think is quite certain about truth. . . . To say that a belief is true is to say that the *fact to which it refers is* or has being; while to say that a belief is false is to say that the fact to which it refers is not—that there is no such fact. Or, to put it another way, we might say: Every belief has the property of *referring to* some particular fact, every different belief to a different fact; and *the* property which a belief has, when it is true—*the* property which we name when we call it true, is the property which can be expressed by saying that *the* fact to which it refers *is*. . . . Obviously this expression "referring to" stands for some relation which each true belief has to one fact and to one only; and which each false belief has to no fact at all; and the difficulty [is] to define this relation. Well, I admit I can't define it, in the sense of analysing it completely. . . . But obviously from the fact that we can't analyse it, it doesn't follow that we may not know perfectly well *what* the relation is; we may be perfectly well *acquainted* with it; it may be perfectly familiar to us; and we may know both that there is such a relation, and that this relation is essential to the definition of truth. And what I want to point out is that we do in this sense *know* this relation; that we are perfectly familiar with it; and that we can, therefore, perfectly well understand this definition of *truth*, though we may not be able to analyse it down to its simplest terms.[j]

So much for truth. But what about falsity? It may seem quite plausible to say that a true belief refers to "a fact that is or has being." But if *every* belief refers, to what does a false belief refer, since Moore has now abandoned the propositions to which, on the old view, a false belief refers? It certainly seems odd to say, as Moore does, that a false belief refers to a fact that is not, and it is typical of Moore's intellectual honesty that he pointed out this difficulty as clearly and incisively as the most severe critic of realism could possibly have done.

If you consider what happens when a man entertains a false belief, it . . . seems . . . as if the thing he was believing, the *object* of his belief, were just *the* fact which certainly is *not*—which certainly is not, because his belief is false. This, of course, creates a difficulty, because if the object certainly is *not*—if there *is* no such thing, it is impossible for him or for anything else to have any kind of relation to it. In order that a relation may hold between two things, both the two things must certainly be; and how then is it possible for any one to believe in a thing which simply has no being? This is the difficulty, . . . and I confess I do not see any clear solution. . . .

What I think is quite certain is that when we have before us a *sentence*—a form of words—which *seems* to express a relation between two objects, we must not always assume that the names, which seem to be names of objects between which a relation holds, are always really names of any object at all. . . .

For instance, one of my friends might be believing of me now, *that I am not in London.* This is a belief which certainly might quite easily be now occurring. And yet there certainly is no such thing as my *not* being now in London. I *am* in London; and that settles the matter. . . . We must, therefore, I think, admit that we can, in a sense, think of things which absolutely have no being. We must *talk* as if we did. And when we so talk and *say* that we do, we certainly do mean *something* which is a fact, by so talking. When, for instance, my friend believes that I am *not* in London, whereas in fact I am, he *is* believing that I am not in London: there is no doubt of that. That is to say this whole expression "he believes that I am not in London" does express, or is the name for, a fact. But the solution of the difficulty seems to me to be this, namely that this whole expression does *not* merely express, as it seems to, a relation between my friend on the one hand and a fact of which the name is "that I am not in London" on the other. It does *seem* to do this; and that is where the difficulty comes in. It does seem as if the words "that I am not in London" *must* be a name for something to which my friend is related, something which certainly *has being.* But we must admit, I think, that these words may not really be a name for anything at all. Taken by themselves they are not a name for anything at all, although the whole expression "he believes that I am not in London" is a name for something. This fact that single words and phrases which we use will constantly seem to be names for something, when in fact they are not names for anything at all, is what seems to me to create the whole difficulty. Owing to it, we must, in talking of this subject, constantly seem to be contradicting ourselves. And I don't think it is possible wholly to avoid this appearance of contradiction. . . . I think it is quite plain that wherever we entertain a false belief—whenever we make a mistake—there really is, in a sense, no such thing as *what* we believe in; and though such language does *seem* to contradict itself, I don't think we can express the facts at all except by the use of language which does seem to contradict itself; and if you understand what the language means, the apparent contradiction doesn't matter.[k]

The notion that a whole expression (for example, "that there is no such thing as a chimera") can be the name of something, while a part of that same expression (that is, "chimera") is not the name of anything, is far from clear and requires further analysis, which, as Moore readily acknowledged, he did not "pretend to be able" to provide. Again, Moore's idea that, "if we know what we mean, the apparent contradiction doesn't matter" is troubling. It might be questioned whether we really do know what we mean until we manage to remove the contradiction and so show that it is only "apparent." And we cannot do that, surely, until we find language that does not contradict itself, as this language does. These are problems that have preoccupied many philosophers, among them, notably, Russell. And since Russell carried the analysis further than Moore, we may once again postpone further discussion.

Ethics

In 1903, the year in which "The Refutation of Idealism" appeared, Moore also published *Principia Ethica,* another landmark in the development of twentieth-century philosophy. But in ethics as in epistemology, what has had a lasting influence is less his answers to ethical questions than the acuity with which he exposed confusions in the answers that philosophers—including Moore himself—have given to ethical questions. Indeed, *Principia Ethica* begins from the thesis we have already encountered, that "everybody" really knows the answers to the important questions in ethics and that they have become confused only because philosophers have failed to formulate the questions carefully.[33] What, then, are those central questions of moral ethics, which philosophers have so badly muddled?

> I have tried in this book to distinguish clearly two kinds of question, which moral philosophers have always professed to answer, but which, as I have tried to shew, they have almost always confused both with one another and with other questions. These two questions may be expressed, the first in the form: What kind of things ought to exist for their own sakes? the second in the form: What kind of actions ought we to perform? I have tried to shew exactly what it is that we ask about a thing, when we ask whether it ought to exist for its own sake, is good in itself or has intrinsic value; and exactly what it is that we ask about an action, when we ask whether we ought to do it, whether it is a right action or a duty.[1]

WHAT IS RIGHT?

Let us take up these two central questions of moral philosophy in turn, and let us begin with the second. What it is right to do in any particular set of circumstances (alternatively, what we ought to do, or again, what it is our duty to do) is the act that will produce more good (or less evil) than any other act open to us in those circumstances. Though this may sound straightforward, it requires a good deal of analysis, as a result of which some seemingly paradoxical conclusions emerge, among them the conclusion that we can never *know* what we ought to do.

[33] See p. 99.

To begin with, to be able to ascertain what our duty is, we need to know not only what is good but also what effects, both long-range and short-range, our actions will have.

> Whenever we judge that a thing is "good as a means," we are making a judgment with regard to its causal relations: we judge *both* that it will have a particular kind of effect, *and* that that effect will be good in itself. But to find causal judgments that are universally true is notoriously a matter of extreme difficulty. . . . We cannot even discover hypothetical laws of the form "Exactly this action will always, under these conditions, produce exactly that effect." But for a correct ethical judgment with regard to the effects of certain actions we require more than this in two respects. (1) We require to know that a given action will produce a certain effect, *under whatever circumstances it occurs.* But this is certainly impossible. It is certain that in different circumstances the same action may produce effects which are utterly different in all respects upon which the value of the effects depends. . . . With regard then to ethical judgments which assert that a certain kind of action is good as a means to a certain kind of effect, none will be *universally* true; and many, though *generally* true at one period, will be generally false at others. But (2) we require to know not only that *one* good effect will be produced, but that, among all subsequent events affected by the action in question, the balance of good will be greater than if any other possible action had been performed. In other words, to judge that an action is generally a means to good is to judge not only that it generally does *some* good, but that it generally does the greatest good of which the circumstances admit.[m]

It follows that the so-called moral laws that Kant characterized as categorical imperatives are at best only rules of thumb, and that "duty," which he exalted as "sublime," is only equivalent to "useful." This is easily shown. Since our duty

> can only be defined as that action which will cause more good to exist in the Universe than any possible alternative, [it follows that] when Ethics presumes to assert that certain ways of acting are "duties" it presumes to assert that to act in those ways will always produce the greatest possible sum of good. If we are told that to "do no murder" is a duty, we are told that the action, whatever it may be, which is called murder, will under no circumstances cause so much good to exist in the Universe as its avoidance.
>
> But, if this be recognised, several most important consequences follow, with regard to the relation of Ethics to conduct.
>
> (1) It is plain that no moral law is self-evident, as has commonly been held by the Intuitional school of moralists. . . .

(2) In order to shew that any action is a duty, it is necessary to know both what are the other conditions, which will, conjointly with it, determine its effects; to know exactly what will be the effects of these conditions; and to know all the events which will be in any way affected by our action throughout an infinite future. We must have all this causal knowledge, and further we must know accurately the degree of value both of the action itself and of all these effects; and must be able to determine how, in conjunction with the other things in the Universe, they will affect its value as an organic whole. And not only this: we must also possess all this knowledge with regard to the effects of every possible alternative; and must then be able to see by comparison that the total value due to the existence of the action in question will be greater than that which would be produced by any of these alternatives. But it is obvious that our causal knowledge alone is far too incomplete for us ever to assure ourselves of this result. Accordingly it follows that we never have any reason to suppose that an action is our duty: we can never be sure that any action will produce the greatest value possible.[n]

But though "no sufficient reason has ever yet been found for considering one action more right or more wrong than another," we can nevertheless find "actions which are *generally* better as means than any probable alternative," and this gives us the practical guidance we need.[o] The actions that are generally better are for the most part just those actions that are "most universally enforced by legal sanctions, such as respect of property." It is possible, regarding such actions, to show that "a *general observance* of them *would* be good as a means,"[p] and from this it follows that we should never violate these rules—whether from altruistic motives or because we choose to make an exception of ourselves.

Two possible difficulties with this conclusion may be pointed out. First, it is far from obvious that a violation of some "legally sanctioned rules" can *never* be productive of more good than conformity to those rules. It is surely arguable, for instance, that if the attempt to assassinate Hitler in the summer of 1944 had succeeded, a great deal of evil that befell many Europeans during the next year would never have occurred and that the net result of the assassination would therefore have been a decided gain. Second, it is not obviously wrong, as Moore supposed, to make an exception of oneself. Moore had originally believed that it is self-contradictory to hold both (1) that one ought to do act A, that maximizes one's own good and (2) that A lessens the total amount of good in the universe. But in the end Moore concluded that it is merely odd to hold these views; no contradiction is involved.

WHAT IS GOOD?

On Moore's view, "right" is a subordinate notion, in the sense that in order to ascertain what we ought to do we need information not only about what empirical effects our acts are likely to have but also about what is good. Let us turn therefore to the question "What is good?" Moore begins by pointing out that, as it stands, this question is ambiguous. "What is good?" may mean (1) "What particular things are good?" (2) "What sorts of things are good?" or (3) "What does the word 'good' mean?"—that is, how is the word "good" to be defined? To the first question there are literally "many millions of answers," and it is not the business of "scientific Ethics" to try to supply them. The second question, in contrast, is within the domain of ethics, and in the final chapter of *Principia Ethica* Moore listed some of the chief sorts of good thing. But it is the third question that is absolutely basic to moral philosophy. Unfortunately, "How is 'good' to be defined?" is itself ambiguous and in its turn requires analysis.

> A definition does indeed often mean the expressing of one word's meaning in other words. But this is not the sort of definition I am asking for. Such a definition can never be of ultimate importance in any study except lexicography. If I wanted that kind of definition I should have to consider in the first place how people generally used the word "good"; but my business is not with its proper usage, as established by custom. . . . My business is solely with that object or idea, which I hold, rightly or wrongly, that the word is generally used to stand for. What I want to discover is the nature of that object or idea. . . .
>
> But, if we understand the question in this sense, my answer to it may seem a very disappointing one. If I am asked "What is good?" my answer is that good is good, and that is the end of the matter. Or if I am asked "How is good to be defined?" my answer is that it cannot be defined, and that is all I have to say about it. . . .
>
> When we say, as Webster says, "The definition of horse is 'A hoofed quadruped of the genus Equus,'" we may, in fact, mean three different things. (1) We may mean merely: "When I say 'horse,' you are to understand that I am talking about a hoofed quadruped of the genus Equus." This might be called the arbitrary verbal definition: and I do not mean that good is indefinable in that sense. (2) We may mean, as Webster ought to mean: "When most English people say 'horse,' they mean a hoofed quadruped of the genus Equus." This may be called the verbal definition proper, and I do not say that good is indefinable in this sense either; for it is certainly possible to discover how people use a word: otherwise, we could never have known that "good" may be translated by "gut" in German and by "bon" in French. But (3) we may, when we define horse, mean something much more important. We may mean that a certain object, which we all of us know, is composed in a certain manner: that it has four legs, a head, a heart, a liver, etc., etc., all of them arranged in definite relations to one another. It is in this sense that I deny good to be definable. I say that it is not composed of any parts, which we can substitute for it in our minds when we are

thinking of it, . . . and that is what I mean, when I say that good is indefinable.⁹

GOOD IS A SIMPLE PROPERTY

Good, then, is a simple property that belongs to, or is attached to, many millions of things in the universe. The word "good" is, Moore thought, parallel to the word "yellow." "Yellow" is an adjective, the name of a simple (and thus indefinable) quality that innumerable objects—buttercups, primroses, crocuses, for instance—possess. If someone does not understand what property is named by the adjective "yellow," we can point to an object having this property and say, "That is yellow." It is unfortunately true that if that person is blind, there is no possibility of his or her understanding what "yellow" means. But if the person has normal vision and looks in the right direction when we say "That is yellow," he or she will understand the meaning of "yellow." We must only take care to "isolate" the instance of yellow to which we point; for example, we must see to it that when we say "That is yellow," the person looks at a primrose, not at the violet that is growing beside it.

All of this holds equally of "good." It too is an adjective; it too names a simple (and thus indefinable) quality that cannot be defined but that can be pointed to. If someone professes not to know what "good" means, we can call his or her attention to something that has the property of being good, such as some pleasurable experience or some beautiful object. That person will then apprehend the simple, self-identical property good that inheres in pleasurable experiences and in beautiful objects in exactly the way that yellow inheres in primroses and crocuses, but not in violets or camellias. The only difference between "good" and "yellow" is that "yellow" is the name of a natural property and "good" of a nonnatural property.

Moore regarded all this as self-evident—that is, evident as soon as we attend closely to good things and isolate the property in virtue of which they are, in fact, good. Beyond this direct appeal to intuition, Moore offers no argument for the simplicity (hence, indefinability) of the property of being good.

MOORE'S ANTINATURALISM

Moore not only held that good is a simple property; more famously, he held that it is a *nonnatural* property. What, exactly, did Moore have in mind when he spoke of a nonnatural property? A nonnatural property is clearly a property that is not natural, but that hardly helps until we are told what this contrast amounts to. Moore had no difficulty in presenting what he took to be clear examples of both natural properties and nonnatural properties. Being yellow and being pleasurable are, for Moore, examples of natural properties. Being good and being beautiful are, for him, examples of nonnatural properties. When, however, he tried to go beyond presenting examples to offer an analysis of the difference between natural and nonnatural properties, he was never able to come up with anything that satisfied him.

At first Moore held that it is one that is not "the subject-matter of the natural sciences [or] psychology." Thus yellow is a natural, not a nonnatural, property because it is a matter for investigation in physics and in physiological psychology. But this will hardly do, for the yellow that we experience (the felt, or sensed, yellow) can no more be investigated than can the good that we experience. The circumstance under which we experience yellow (for instance, what happens in the nervous system and in the cortex) can certainly be studied, but this holds for good as much as for yellow. Hence good and yellow seem to be on the same footing; if the latter is a natural property, so is the former.[r]

Next, Moore suggested that natural properties are those that can "exist in time by themselves" and nonnatural properties are those that cannot so exist. But on further consideration he concluded that the distinction, as he tried to draw it, was "utterly silly and preposterous."[s] Finally, after attempting to distinguish natural properties as "intrinsic" and nonnatural properties are not intrinsic, he decided that the difference may be that natural properties "describe, at least to some extent," and that nonnatural properties "do not describe at all."[t] But this far from satisfied him, for he allowed that this account is "vague and not clear," and that "to make it clear it would be necessary to specify the sense of 'describe' in question; and I am no more able to do this now than I was then."

Ultimately, Moore left the contrast between natural and nonnatural properties at an intuitive level.

Even if Moore was not able to produce an analysis of natural and nonnatural properties that satisfied him, he was, he thought, able to provide a number of considerations that would show, for example, that the hedonist's identification of goodness with pleasure cannot be correct. More generally, he thought that he could show that any theory that identified goodness with some natural property must be mistaken. We will let his attack on hedonism serve as a model for his general attack on all the theories that he deemed naturalistic.

It is important to be clear about the target of Moore's attack. It is *analytic* hedonism—that is, the view that the words "good" and "pleasant" simply mean the same thing. Because it is a thesis about the meaning of ethical terms, it is sometimes called a *metaethical* theory. Analytic hedonism stands in contrast with what might be called *normative* hedonism—the view that pleasure, and pleasure alone, is intrinsically good. Whereas analytic hedonism is a metaethical thesis concerning the meaning of words, normative hedonism is a substantive thesis concerning what things are good. Moore, in fact, rejected both analytic hedonism and normative hedonism. He rejected normative hedonism because he thought that other things besides pleasure were good—knowledge, for example. But Moore is best remembered for his attacks on analytic hedonism, and, by extension, on analytic naturalism in general.

Moore employed two arguments in his attempt to refute analytic hedonism. The first involves the so-called *naturalistic fallacy;* the second has come to be known as the *open-question argument*—although Moore himself never used this label. As we shall see, it is the open-question argument, and not the naturalistic fallacy, that carries the main burden of Moore's attempted refutation of naturalism.

Moore is famous for having formulated the naturalistic fallacy, but if we examine the text closely, it is not immediately clear what he had in mind when he said that a theory committed this fallacy. Sometimes when Moore spoke of the naturalistic fallacy, he seemed to have in mind the error (assuming it is one) of identifying goodness with some natural property. This is sometimes more loosely described as the fallacy (again assuming it is one) of *reducing* values to facts. This is the common way of understanding what Moore meant by the naturalistic fallacy. There are, however, passages that suggest a different interpretation: the naturalistic fallacy is a tempting form of invalid reasoning (hence, literally a fallacy) that has misled philosophers to define good in terms of some natural property, for example, pleasure.

In order to sort all this out, it will be helpful to examine exactly how the naturalistic fallacy first appears in the text. Just before introducing the naturalistic fallacy, Moore draws a distinction between two sorts of definitions:

> But I am afraid I have still not removed the chief difficulty which may prevent acceptance of the proposition that good is indefinable. I do not mean to say that *the* good, that which is good, is thus indefinable; if I did think so, I should not be writing on Ethics, for my main object is to help towards discovering that definition. It is just because I think there will be less risk of error in our search for a definition of "the good," that I am now insisting that *good* is indefinable. I must try to explain the difference between these two. I suppose it may be granted that "good" is an adjective. Well "the good," "that which is good," must therefore be the substantive to which the adjective "good" will apply: it must be the whole of that to which the adjective will apply, and the adjective must *always* truly apply to it. But if it is that to which the adjective will apply, it must be something different from that adjective itself; and the whole of that something different, whatever it is, will be our definition of *the* good. Now it may be that this something will have other adjectives, beside "good," that will apply to it. It may be full of pleasure, for example; it may be intelligent: and if these two adjectives are really part of its definition, then it will certainly be true, that pleasure and intelligence are good. And many people appear to think that, if we say "Pleasure and intelligence are good," or if we say "Only pleasure and intelligence are good," we are defining "good." Well, I cannot deny that propositions of this nature may sometimes be called definitions; I do not know well enough how the word is generally used to decide upon this point. I only wish it to be understood that that is not what I mean when I say there is no possible definition of good, and that I shall not mean this if I use the word again. I do most fully believe that

some true proposition of the form "Intelligence is good and intelligence alone is good" can be found; if none could be found, our definition of *the* good would be impossible. As it is, I believe *the* good to be definable; and yet I still say that good itself is indefinable.[u]

The difference between defining good and defining *the* good seems to come to this: A definition of good would have this form:

(1) The property of being good is a whole made up of parts A, B, C, etc.

whereas a definition of *the* good would have quite a different form:

(2) Something is good if and only if it has features A, B, C, etc.

Moore holds that the simplicity of good precludes definitions of the first kind, though he thinks, indeed hopes, that definitions of the second kind are possible.

It is important to see that this discussion of simplicity, and hence indefinability, has absolutely no bearing on the question whether goodness is a natural or a nonnatural property. For all that has been said so far, goodness may be a simple (hence, indefinable) natural property, for it is clear from the examples he uses that Moore thinks that such simple natural properties do exist. What is needed, then, is an argument with the consequence that good cannot be a natural property of any kind, including a *simple* natural property. Moore makes the transition from indefinability to antinaturalism following a curious route:

Consider yellow, for example. We may try to define it, by describing its physical equivalent; we may state what kind of light-vibrations must stimulate the normal eye, in order that we may perceive it. But a moment's reflection is sufficient to shew that those light-vibrations are not themselves what we mean by yellow. *They* are not what we perceive. Indeed we should never have been able to discover their existence, unless we had first been struck by the patent difference of quality between the different colours. The most we can be entitled to say of those vibrations is that they are what corresponds in space to the yellow which we actually perceive.

Yet a mistake of this simple kind has commonly been made about "good." It may be true that all things which are good are *also* something else, just as it is true that all things which are yellow produce a certain kind of vibration in the light. And it is a fact, that Ethics aims at discovering what are those other properties belonging to all things which are good. But far too many philosophers have thought that when they named those other properties they were actually defining good; that these properties, in fact, were simply not "other," but absolutely and entirely the same with goodness. This view I propose to call the "naturalistic fallacy" and of it I shall now endeavour to dispose.[v]

Here the naturalistic fallacy is clearly identified as a faulty inference from the claim that certain properties belong to all things that are good to the conclusion that these properties are identical with the property of being good. Or to use Moore's somewhat strange terminology, it involves a faulty inference from a definition of *the* good (or that which is good) to a definition of goodness itself. Read this way, as a particular kind of faulty inference, it does not matter whether goodness is a nonnatural property or not—for the fallacy will be the same in either case. Moore sees this, and makes the point explicitly.

> When I say "I am pleased," I do *not* mean that "I" am the same thing as "having pleasure." And similarly no difficulty need be found in my saying that "pleasure is good" and yet not meaning that "pleasure" is the same thing as "good," that pleasure *means* good, and that good *means* pleasure. If I were to imagine that when I said "I am pleased," I meant that I was exactly the same thing as "pleased," I should not indeed call that a naturalistic fallacy, although it would be the same fallacy as I have called naturalistic with reference to Ethics.[w]

Or again:

> As for the reasons why good is not to be considered a natural object, they may be reserved for discussion in another place. . . . Even if [good] were a natural object, that would not alter the nature of the fallacy nor diminish its importance one whit. All that I have said about it would remain quite equally true: only the name which I have called it would not be so appropriate as I think it is.[x]

If we have correctly identified the naturalistic fallacy as a particular kind of faulty inference—one that is called the naturalistic fallacy when it is committed by a naturalist doing ethics—then it follows that it *cannot* be used to show that naturalism is false. The point is quite simple: an argument can be fallacious but still have a true conclusion. (If this were not the case, it would be possible to refute a claim simply by presenting a fallacious argument in its behalf.) Pointing out a fallacy blocks a route to a conclusion; it does not show that this conclusion is false. Moore is completely clear about this, for notice that the last passage cited begins with the remark that "the reasons why good is not to be considered a natural object . . . may be reserved for discussion in another place." Even with both the discussion of the indefinability of good and the presentation of the naturalistic fallacy behind us, naturalism in ethics, as Moore plainly sees, remains to be refuted.

Moore does, however, present another argument against analytic naturalism that, if correct, would refute analytic naturalism. It has come to be known as the *open-question argument.* It exerted a profound influence on twentieth-century reflection on the meaning of evaluative terms. An analytic naturalist holds that the term "good" is synonymous with some purely naturalistic or descriptive term—

for example, "pleasurable." Against any such claim, Moore responds in the following way:

> It is very natural to make the mistake of supposing that what is universally true is of such a nature that its negation would be self-contradictory: the importance which has been assigned to analytic propositions in the history of philosophy shews how easy such a mistake is. And thus it is very easy to conclude that what seems to be a universal ethical principle is in fact an identical proposition; that, if, for example, whatever is called "good" seems to be pleasant, the proposition "Pleasure is the good" does not assert a connection between two different notions, but involves only one, that of pleasure, which is easily recognised as a distinct entity. But whoever will attentively consider with himself what is actually before his mind when he asks the question "Is pleasure (or whatever it may be) after all good?" can easily satisfy himself that he is not merely wondering whether pleasure is pleasant. And if he will try this experiment with each suggested definition in succession, he may become expert enough to recognise that in every case he has before his mind a unique object, with regard to the connection of which with any other object, a distinct question may be asked.[y]

The argument here is remarkably simple. An analytic naturalist holds that the term "good" is synonymous with some purely naturalistic or descriptive term, for example, "pleasurable." If this theory is right, however, then the following sentence,

> (1) That which is pleasurable is good.

would be analytic—an empty redundancy—and say nothing more than the following sentences:

> (2) That which is pleasurable is pleasurable.
> (3) That which is good is good.

Yet, according to Moore, it is simply obvious that the first sentence is not analytic (or an empty redundancy) in the way in which the last two sentences are. From this it follows that analytic hedonism is false. More generally, whatever descriptive property we assign to a thing, it remains an *open question*—that is, a question we can *significantly ask*—whether that thing is good or not.

The open-question argument is one main support of Moore's case against naturalism. His commitment to a denotationalist account of meaning is another. Combined with his distinction between natural and nonnatural properties, we get an argument that, if sound, provides a decisive refutation of analytic naturalism in ethics:

> In saying that something is good, we are ascribing a property to it.
> That property is either a natural or a nonnatural property.
> That property cannot be a natural property.

Therefore:

> In saying that something is good, we are ascribing a nonnatural property to it.

At the time Moore wrote *Principia Ethica*—and for some time after—the first premise of this argument was accepted as a matter of course. The second premise is a truth of logic. The open-question argument seems to establish the truth of the third premise. Accepting these three premises makes Moore's conclusion that goodness is a nonnatural property completely unavoidable.

None of this, however, settles the matter in Moore's favor; instead, it leaves us with a series of choices. We can accept the premises and find ourselves committed to Moore's doctrine of nonnatural properties. Alternatively, we can reject the conclusion and then seek good reasons for rejecting at least one of the premises that leads to it. This provides a set of choices of its own. A staunch naturalist could reject the third premise, claiming not to be convinced by the open-question argument. More strongly, the naturalist could argue that the only thing that he or she finds in good things in virtue of which they are good is that they are pleasant (or desired or whatever); and the naturalist finds nothing corresponding to Moore's strange notion of a nonnatural property. It is also possible to reject the second premise on the grounds that the distinction between natural and nonnatural properties has never been drawn in a satisfactory way. Perhaps the most radical move is to reject the first premise by maintaining that evaluative terms do not refer to properties of *any* kind, either natural or nonnatural. This is the view of the *emotivists* (and, more generally, of the *noncognitivists*) in ethics. We will return to this story when we examine emotivism in Chapter 7.

Moore's Philosophy of Common Sense

From what we have seen so far, it would seem peculiar to associate Moore's philosophy with common sense. His complex reflections on perception and existence—not to mention his commitment to nonnatural properties—seem wholly remote from the beliefs of daily life. Yet, from early in his career, Moore showed a deep respect for commonsense beliefs and, corresponding to this, a deep suspicion of philosophical theories that ran counter to them. Here, for instance, is Moore's reply to the phenomenalists' argument that material objects are nothing but "bundles" of perception.

> You have all probably often travelled in a railway-train. And you would agree that a railway-train is one specimen of the sort of things which we call material objects. And you would agree that, when you travel in a railway-train, you may, if you happen to think of it, believe in the existence of the train you are travelling in. . . .

But now, what does [phenomenalism] say? It says that . . . the existence of the train simply consists in the existence of the sense-data
which you and the other people travelling in it are at the moment directly apprehending; in this together with the fact that, *if,* in succession
to those, you were to directly apprehend certain others, you would, or
would probably, directly apprehend still others. But to suppose that
your carriage, while you sit in it, really is running on wheels, or that it
really is coupled to other carriages in the train or to the engine—this,
it says, is a complete mistake. . . . All that you really believe in, and certainly all that you can possibly know, is not that there are any wheels existing at the moment, but merely that you *would,* in the future, if you
were first to apprehend certain other sense-data, also directly apprehend those sense-data which we call the visible appearances of wheels,
or those which you would feel, if you did that which we call touching
them. . . .

But now, I ask, is this, in fact, what you believe, when you believe you
are travelling in a train? Do you not, in fact, believe that there really are
wheels on which your carriage is running at the moment? . . . [Phe-
nomenalism] does, I think, plainly give an utterly false account of what
we do believe in ordinary life. . . . So long as it is merely presented in
vague phrases such as: All that we know of material objects is the orderly succession of our own sensations, it does, in fact, sound very plausible. But, so soon as you realise what it means in particular instances
like that of the train—how it means that you cannot possibly know that
your carriage is, even probably, running on wheels, or coupled to other
carriages—it seems to me to lose all its plausibility.[z]

This, then, is Moore's first, and chief, argument against philosophical theories
that run counter to common sense. It consists simply in showing the enormous
number of beliefs that must be false if these theories are true. Moore called this
"translating into the concrete."

Of course, Time, with a big T, seems to be a highly abstract kind of
entity, and to define *exactly* what can be meant by saying of an entity of
that sort that it is unreal does seem to offer difficulties. But if you try
to translate the proposition into the concrete, and to ask what it *implies,*
there is, I think, very little doubt as to the sort of thing it implies. . . . If
Time is unreal, then plainly nothing ever happens before or after anything else; nothing is ever simultaneous with anything else; it is never
true that anything is past; never true that anything will happen in the
future; never true that anything is happening now; and so on.[a]

Of course, pointing out that a philosophical position has consequences that
seem odd or paradoxical from a commonsense standpoint is not likely to lead a
philosopher who holds such a position to give it up. On the contrary, it is often

just these odd and paradoxical features that make a philosophical position seem exciting or give it an appearance of depth. If a philosopher succeeds, for example, in proving that time is unreal or proving that we can have no knowledge of the external world, then we seem to accept these results no matter how odd or paradoxical they may seem. Against this, Moore made a move that became a central part of his philosophical position for the remainder of his career.

A second strategy notes that philosophers maintaining these paradoxical theses usually contradict themselves. Idealists, for instance, are capable of writing, "I shall next proceed to demonstrate the unreality of time," thus affirming temporal succession even as they deny it. A third line of argument points out that these theses are all *conclusions*—the conclusions of long, complicated, and often obscure chains of reasoning, no link in which is remotely so persuasive as the beliefs that it is proposed to replace.

WHAT IS COMMON SENSE?

What, for Moore, is common sense, and why does he give it priority in deciding philosophical issues? Moore's most sustained attempt to answer these questions occurs in his essay "A Defence of Common Sense." After some preliminary remarks, Moore produces a rather long list of what he calls "truisms," every one of which he claims to know and know with certainty. He refers to this list as (1).

> (1) I begin, then, with my list of truisms, every one of which (in my own opinion) I *know*, with certainty, to be true. The propositions to be included in this list are the following:
>
> There exists at present a living human body, which is *my* body. This body was born at a certain time in the past, and has existed continuously ever since, though not without undergoing changes; it was, for instance, much smaller when it was born, and for some time afterwards, than it is now. Ever since it was born, it has been either in contact with or not far from the surface of the earth; and, at every moment since it was born, there have also existed many other things, having shape and size in three dimensions (in the same familiar sense in which it has), from which it has been *at various distances* (in the familiar sense in which it is now at a distance both from that mantelpiece and from that bookcase, and at a greater distance from the bookcase than it is from the mantelpiece); also there have (very often, at all events) existed some other things of this kind with which it was *in contact* (in the familiar sense in which it is now in contact with the pen I am holding in my right hand and with some of the clothes I am wearing). Among the things which have, in this sense, formed part of its environment (i.e. have been either in contact with it, or at *some* distance from it, however *great*) there have, at every moment since its birth, been large numbers of other living human bodies, each of which has, like it, (*a*) at some time been born, (*b*) continued to exist from some time after birth, (*c*) been,

at every moment of its life after birth, either in contact with or not far from the surface of the earth; and many of these bodies have already died and ceased to exist. But the earth had existed also for many years before my body was born; and for many of these years, also, large numbers of human bodies had, at every moment, been alive upon it; and many of these bodies had died and ceased to exist before it was born. Finally (to come to a different class of propositions), I am a human being, and I have, at different times since my body was born, had many different experiences, of each of many different kinds: e.g. I have often perceived both my own body and other things which formed part of its environment, including other human bodies; I have not only perceived things of this kind, but have also observed facts about them, such as, for instance, the fact which I am now observing, that that mantelpiece is at present nearer to my body than that bookcase; I have been aware of other facts, which I was not at the time observing, such as, for instance, the fact, of which I am now aware, that my body existed yesterday and was then also for some time nearer to that mantelpiece than to that bookcase; I have had expectations with regard to the future, and many beliefs of other kinds, both true and false; I have thought of imaginary things and persons and incidents, in the reality of which I did not believe; I have had dreams; and I have had feelings of many different kinds. And, just as my body has been the body of a human being, namely myself, who has, during his lifetime, had many experiences of each of these (and other) different kinds; so, in the case of very many of the other human bodies which have lived upon the earth, each has been the body of a different human being, who has, during the lifetime of that body, had many different experiences of each of these (and other) different kinds.[b]

Having completed this list of beliefs, which all, in one way or another, are keyed on Moore himself, he adds a further truism concerning *other* people that he also claims to know and know with certainty, namely, that many other people, though not all, know of themselves just the sorts of things that Moore knows about himself. He calls this further truism (2). In his words:

What (2) asserts is only (what seems an obvious enough truism) that each of *us* . . . has frequently *known,* with regard to *him*self or *his* body . . . everything which, in writing down my list of propositions in (1), I was claiming to know about *my*self or *my* body.[c]

Before we examine the way in which Moore attempts to use his list of truisms for philosophical purposes, we can first note some features they all share. First, unlike truths of logic or mathematical truths, not one of these truisms is *necessarily* true. Though Moore did live for many years near or close to the surface of the earth, it is not necessarily true that he did so. We can at least conceive of a world where Moore had quite extraordinary powers of flight. For that matter, we can also conceive of a world where Moore never existed at all. Moore's truisms are, one and all, contingencies. Second, none of these seems self-evident in the sense that it can be seen to be true simply by reflecting on the content of the proposition itself. Third, none of these truisms has the form of a weak, highly protected proposition. One way to approach certainty is to restrict oneself to highly guarded propositions such as: "It seems to me now that I am aware of something that may be red." In contrast, Moore's truisms are robust, unqualified claims about the world he inhabits. Fourth, these truisms do not involve specialized knowledge; they are all items of *commonplace* knowledge. Moore, for example, would probably claim to know with certainty that there are more than seven planets, but this is not the sort of thing that Moore puts on his list. The items on Moore's list are all things that any mentally competent adult will know. They are *common* features of the world, and are things, according to (2), that we know in common with others.

Of course, many philosophers might agree that at a practical, day-to-day level we can be said to know all these things to be true, but they might still insist that, *strictly speaking,* none of these so-called truisms is *wholly* true. This is the position of the British Idealists, who held that truth can be assigned only to the total (or absolute) system of beliefs. Individual beliefs, for them, could, at most, only be *partially* true. Moore will have none of this. "I am maintaining," he tells us, "that all the propositions in (1), and also many propositions corresponding to each of these, are *wholly* true."[d] Moore also rejects a subtle variation on this doctrine of partial truth, which he describes as follows:

> Some philosophers seem to have thought it legitimate to use such expressions as, e.g. "The earth has existed for many years past," as if they expressed something which they really believed, when in fact they believe that every proposition, which such an expression would *ordinarily* be understood to express, is, at least partially, false; and all they really believe is that there is some *other* set of propositions, related in a certain way to those which such expressions do actually express, which, unlike these, really are true.[e]

Over against this, Moore tells us:

> I wish . . . to make it quite plain that I was not using the expressions I used in (1) in any such subtle sense. I meant by each of them precisely what every reader, in reading them, will have understood me to mean.[f]

Moore's thesis, then, is that the items in (1), understood in the ordinary or popular manner, are wholly true.

Moore realizes that his appeal to the ordinary or popular meaning of the items in (1) can itself be a target of criticism. Many philosophers have held that ordinary language, because of its inherent vagueness and ambiguity, often does not convey exact meanings. To this, Moore responds in the following way:

In what I have just said, I have assumed that there is some meaning which is *the* ordinary or popular meaning of such expressions as "The earth has existed for many years past." And this, I am afraid, is an assumption which some philosophers are capable of disputing. They seem to think that the question "Do you believe that the earth has existed for many years past?" is not a plain question, such as should be met either by a plain "Yes" or "No," or by a plain "I can't make up my mind," but is the sort of question which can be properly met by: "It all depends on what you mean by 'the earth' and 'exists' and 'years': if you mean so and so, and so and so, and so and so, then I do; but if you mean so and so, and so and so, and so and so, or so and so, and so and so, and so and so, or so and so, and so and so, and so and so, then I don't, or at least I think it is extremely doubtful." It seems to me that such a view is as profoundly mistaken as any view can be. Such an expression as "The earth has existed for many years past" is the very type of an unambiguous expression, the meaning of which we all understand. Anyone who takes a contrary view must, I suppose, be confusing the question whether we understand its meaning (which we all certainly do) with the entirely different question whether we *know what it means,* in the sense that we are able to *give a correct analysis* of its meaning. The question what is the correct analysis of *the* proposition meant *on any occasion* (for, of course, as I insisted in defining [2], a different proposition is meant at every different time at which the expression is used) by "The earth has existed for many years past" is, it seems to me, a profoundly difficult question, and one to which, as I shall presently urge, no one knows the answer. But to hold that we do not know what, in certain respects, is the analysis of what we understand by such an expression, is an entirely different thing from holding that we do not understand the expression.[g]

This is an important passage—one that deserves very close reading. Moore begins by rejecting the idea that whether a statement is true or not simply depends on how one *chooses to interpret* the meaning of the words it contains. On this view, if words are interpreted one way, a statement might be true; interpreted another way, perhaps, false. On this view, no statement will be determinately true or false. It is probably because of this relativistic consequence that he tells us that this view "is as profoundly mistaken as any view can be." For Moore, meanings are not something we decide on arbitrarily; they are things we learn when acquiring a language.

Having insisted on the nonarbitrariness of meaning, the passage then takes a remarkable turn. If we do, in fact, understand the meaning of the items in (1), should we not be able to say what those meanings are? Moore's answer is no. For him, it is possible to understand what a proposition means without being able to state what its meaning is—without, that is, being able to offer an adequate analysis of the proposition. More strongly, Moore says that the question of the correct analysis of a proposition such as "The earth has existed for many years past" is not only profoundly difficult but one to which "no one knows the answer."

This doctrine that we can understand the meaning of a proposition without being able to offer an analysis of it certainly casts the project of analytic philosophy in a peculiar light. It seemed that analytic philosophy would be of service just because it would clarify the meanings of the propositions that we employ and, in doing so, contribute to the solution of philosophical problems. This, as we shall see in the next chapter, was Russell's attitude. For him, most of the propositions formulated in everyday language are inherently inexact. It is the task of analytic philosophy, he thought, to clarify them and, when necessary, replace them with something better. Moore, in contrast, holds that the sentence "The earth has existed for many years past" is *the very type of an unambiguous expression, the meaning of which we all understand.* Furthermore, we can understand it without being able to analyze it; indeed, we can understand it even if we are convinced that no adequate analysis exists or is ever likely to exist. Here Moore notes that his position is the reverse of that held by many other philosophers.

> I am not at all sceptical as to the *truth* of such propositions as "The earth has existed for many years past". . . . i.e. propositions which assert the existence of material things: on the contrary, I hold that we all know, with certainty, many such propositions to be true. But I am very sceptical as to what . . . the correct *analysis* of such propositions is. And this is a matter as to which I think I differ from many philosophers. Many seem to hold that there is no doubt at all as to [the] *analysis* . . . of the proposition "Material things have existed,". . . [whereas] I hold that the analysis of the proposition in question is extremely doubtful; and some of them . . . while holding that there is no doubt as to [the] *analysis,* seem to have doubted whether any such propositions are *true.* I, on the other hand, while holding that there is no doubt whatever that many such propositions are wholly true, hold also that no philosopher . . . has succeeded in suggesting an analysis of them . . . which comes anywhere near to being certainly true.[h]

Moore, then, does not employ the methods of analysis in the process of establishing the truth of the items that he lists in (1). For him, our ability to understand these propositions and know them to be true is wholly independent of our ability to provide them with a proper analysis. This may seem an odd position for someone who is generally considered a founder of twentieth-century analytic philosophy.

Moore's position is peculiar in another way. When people claim to know certain things, we often ask them *how* they know, and if they cannot provide a reasonable answer to this question, we are often inclined to say that they do not know what they claim to know. Moore seems unconcerned with challenges of this kind.

He, in fact, acknowledges that, with respect to some of the propositions on his list, he is not able to explain how he is able to know them to be true.

> It is, indeed, obvious that, in the case of most of them, I do not know them *directly:* that is to say, I only know them because, in the past, I have known to be true *other* propositions which were evidence for them. If, for instance, I do know that the earth had existed for many years before I was born, I certainly only know this because I have known other things in the past which were evidence for it. And I certainly do not know exactly what the evidence was. Yet all this seems to me to be no good reason for doubting that I do know it. We are all, I think, in this strange position that we do *know* many things, with regard to which we *know* further that we must have had evidence for them, and yet we do not know *how* we know them, i.e. we do not know what the evidence was.[i]

In this passage Moore freely acknowledges that he cannot explain how he knows that the earth had existed for many years before his birth. But instead of taking this as grounds for saying that he does not know it, he takes his knowing it as grounds for saying that one can know something without knowing how one knows it.

With this battery of truisms in place, Moore has little difficulty in dismissing philosophical views opposed to his own. For Moore, anyone who adopts the truisms he has presented thereby adopts what he calls the Common Sense view of the world. "I am," Moore tells us, "one of those philosophers who have held that the 'Common Sense view of the world' is, in certain fundamental features, *wholly* true."[j] Furthermore, by the truism he labeled (2), Moore attributes this Common Sense view of the world to a great many other people as well—presumably to all competent adult human beings. In doing this, however, Moore seems to ignore the plain fact that many reputable philosophers (whose mental competence is not at issue) have explicitly rejected various aspects of the Common Sense view of the world. Moore claims, however, that those philosophers who reject aspects of the Common Sense view of the world also accept them:

> According to me, *all* philosophers, without exception, have agreed with me in [accepting the Common Sense view of the world]: and that the real difference [between me and some other philosophers] is only a difference between those philosophers, who have *also held* views inconsistent with these features in "the Common Sense view of the world," and those who have not.[k]

This is an ingenious maneuver, for it has the immediate result that any philosopher who holds beliefs incompatible with Moore's commonsense beliefs must thereby hold views incompatible with some of his or her own beliefs. Moore shows great ingenuity in ringing changes on this basic pattern of criticism.

For many, it is hard to read Moore's defense of common sense without the sense that none of his arguments is really persuasive. They seem somehow question-begging, but it is hard to make such a charge stick. Perhaps we can understand the source of this dissatisfaction by noting that at the heart of Moore's position we find a *refusal* to do things that philosophers have commonly thought essential to philosophy itself. In freeing himself from the necessity of giving an *analysis* of the propositions he claims to know, and, further, in freeing himself from the necessity of providing *reasons* for the things he claims to know, Moore has significantly lightened his philosophical burden. Indeed, it comes very close to a refusal to accept a philosophical burden at all. Looked at this way, Moore has not begged any philosophical questions; he has simply rejected the claim that he is under any obligation to answer them.

Moore's Influence

Moore is generally regarded as one of the most influential philosophers in the first half of this century. How can this be if his conclusions were so often, as we have had to point out, inconclusive? The answer is that what philosophers noted was not so much that his conclusions were inconclusive but that he *knew* that they were and freely admitted it. What impressed philosophers was his intellectual honesty, his integrity, and his persistence.

They were also impressed by his concentration on method. Method always becomes important at the end of a period in which the results have been less than what was expected, as at the end of the Middle Ages, when it became clear that scholasticism had failed. Similarly, the nineteenth century had been a period of great hopes unfulfilled—a period of vast philosophical syntheses that, because they were constructed too rapidly and without sufficient preparation, collapsed of their own weight even before they had been completed. Philosophers were therefore ready for thinkers like Moore who maintained that we should not move too fast, that we should divide large, messy problems into smaller, more precise ones, and that we should not try to make an advance until we are sure of the basis from which it is to be launched. They were impressed by the way Moore sought to narrow down issues by specifying all alternatives and then eliminating them in turn. They saw that Moore was a master of the closely reasoned argument, and they took him for a model.

But philosophers were by no means impressed only by Moore's methodology. He was, as we have already seen, one of the leaders in the attempt to revive realism, but even philosophers who had no interest in realism were struck by the prominence of sense data in his theory and by his attention to common sense. Though Moore was interested in sense data chiefly because, as he thought, they lead us to physical objects, he did hold that the existence of objectively real and independent sense data is particularly easy to verify.[34] It was natural, then, that philosophers who were aware of the difficulty of getting from sense data to physical objects, who were in pursuit of absolutely certain knowledge, and who did not share Moore's confidence in common sense would fasten onto what Moore had to say about sense data as the starting point for a view that turned out to be radically different from his. This development led, through Russell, to Logical Positivism. On the other hand, those who were less insistent on certainty (or even doubtful about the possibility of achieving it), but who were impressed by what Moore said about common sense, moved in a different direction. When they, in harmony with the general shift of the culture toward an interest in language, began to translate substantive philosophical questions into linguistic questions, Moore's common-sense philosophy was then developed into a philosophy of ordinary language. Since Logical Positivism and ordinary-language philosophy were important influences on Anglo-American philosophy in the second half of the twentieth century, it is fair to call Moore one of the fathers of twentieth-century philosophy. It is true that Moore repudiated both of these developments, but has it not often been the fate of fathers to disown, and to be disowned by, their children?

[34] See pp. 113–15.

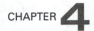

Frege and the Revolution in Logic

The revival of realism, whose beginnings we have just studied in the philosophy of G. E. Moore, was the first of three main routes out of the Kantian paradigm.[1] The second route was opened up by a revolution in logic that occurred at about the same time. The details of this revolution are part of the development of logic and as such lie outside the purview of this history. Here we have to examine only the impact of this revolution on those central metaphysical and epistemological problems that have been our theme from the beginning.

[1] See p. 14.

Aristotelian Logic and Its Critics

For two thousand years after Aristotle first put together his views on logic in the *Analytics* and other works, it was felt that he had said virtually everything that needed saying about this discipline. Early in the nineteenth century, it is true, there had been a revolt against Aristotle, and, as a result of the influence of Hegel, a "new" logic had emerged, which was dialectical and dynamic and regarded contradiction as merely a stage in thought that could be transcended and harmonized in a higher synthesis.[2] But the revolt that we have now to consider was far more radical and attacked both the Aristotelian and the Hegelian logics, the former on the ground that it was too narrow, the latter on the ground that it was not logic at all but psychology. Let us examine these criticisms in turn, starting with a brief account of the features of Aristotelian logic against which the revolution was directed.

Aristotle was chiefly interested in the ways in which different types of judgment can be combined so as to yield valid conclusions. For this purpose he classified judgments in various ways: they are either affirmative (All men are mortal) or negative (No men are mortal); either universal (All men are mortal), particular (Some men are mortal), or individual (Socrates is mortal). He assumed that all judgments without exception are predicative. That is, he assumed that when we judge we are always either (1) attributing a predicate (some property or quality) to a subject or (2) denying that the subject has this predicate. Thus "Socrates is mortal" and "Socrates is not a Spartan" are, for Aristotle, typical, or representative, judgments. And judgments that do not at first sight seem to have a subject-predicate form (Whales suckle their young; The cow jumped over the moon) can easily be rephrased to bring out the idea that in them we are nonetheless predicating a quality or property of a subject (Whales are young-suckling creatures; The cow is a jumping-over-the-moon animal).

Further, Aristotle thought that the standard unit of reasoning (to which he gave the name "syllogism") consists in three judgments: two premises and a conclusion. So the question is, which combinations of premises, affirmative and negative, universal, particular, and individual, yield valid conclusions, and which yield invalid ones? Consider, for instance, the following arguments:

> (1)   All men are mortal
>   All Greeks are men
>   —————————————————
>   All Greeks are mortal

> (2)   All men are mortal
>   All Greeks are Europeans
>   —————————————————
>   All Greeks are mortal

[2] See Vol. IV, pp. 124–34.

(3)   No mortals are angels
         All men are mortal
         _____
         No men are angels

(4)   No men are angels
         No centaurs are men
         _____
         No centaurs are angels

Which of these syllogisms are valid? Which are invalid, and why? Aristotle was not concerned with the particular conclusions of particular arguments, but with those arrangements of subjects and predicates in the premises—which he called "figures"—that yield valid conclusions. For instance, in the two premises there must be a "middle" term, and the position of this middle is one feature of an argument that determines whether the conclusion is valid. In the first syllogism the middle is "men," and in all syllogisms of this figure—where the premises are two universal affirmative judgments—the middle must be the subject of the first premise and the predicate of the second premise. Thus (1) is valid and (2) is invalid—actually, in (2) there is no middle at all. Or consider a different figure, as in (3), where one of the premises is a universal negative and the other is a universal affirmative judgment. Here again there must be a middle, and the middle must again appear as the subject of the first premise and the predicate of the second. Since "mortal" occupies these positions in (3), this is a valid syllogism. In contrast, (4) is invalid because no conclusion may be drawn from two negative premises.[3]

Logicians after Aristotle's day refined his account, but no one—not even the Hegelian logicians—questioned Aristotle's fundamental thesis that all judgments are predicative in form. As long as mathematics and logic were viewed as completely different disciplines there was no reason to challenge this assumption, and since logic was held to be the science of the laws of thought, while mathematics was the science of number and quality, it seemed evident that they were indeed wholly autonomous sciences.

The first step in what proved to be the merging of mathematics and logic was taken quite unintentionally. Mathematicians had long been dissatisfied with the postulate of parallels, which seemed to them less certain than the Euclidean axioms—which is why they called it a "postulate" rather than an "axiom." They sought to prove the postulate by means of a standard strategy of proof: one assumes that the proposition one wants to prove is false and then shows that on the assumption of its falsity a contradiction emerges. But to everybody's surprise, when this *reductio* strategy was applied to the postulate of parallels, no contradiction was generated. Instead, what was generated, as geometers gradually came to see, was an internally consistent set of theorems different from the Euclidean theorems—a non-Euclidean geometry, in fact. And from each different set of

[3] For a more detailed account of Aristotle's logic, see Vol. I, pp. 244–54.

axioms a different geometry could be generated. From this it followed that geometry is not, as had always been supposed, the science of space—at least not if space is conceived in the Newtonian fashion as an independently existing three-dimensional box in which events occur. But if geometry is not the science of space, what is it? It began to look surprisingly like logic, but the logic it looked like was not the old syllogistic, predicative logic of Aristotle.

While geometry was thus being shaken to its foundations, conceptions of arithmetic were undergoing an equally radical transformation, though as a result of a very different line of investigation, whose aim was to "formalize" arithmetic. It is unnecessary for us to go into these developments in detail,[4] but the result was to demonstrate that the line between logic and mathematics is essentially arbitrary. However—and this is the relevant point—the logic to which arithmetic was being reduced, like that which geometry was beginning to resemble, was very far from the traditional Aristotelian logic. Indeed, as soon as mathematicians began to think seriously about logic, the limitations of Aristotle's account of reasoning became evident.

When we assert, for instance, that Plato is taller than Socrates, we have certainly said something about Plato, and we can, in fact, express this in the traditional Aristotelian way by saying that Plato has the specific *property* of being taller than Socrates. If we call this property of being taller than Socrates H, then the assertion that Plato is taller than Socrates can be expressed in the simple subject-predicate statement:

> Plato is H.

Similarly, the assertion that Aristotle is taller than Plato can be put into subject-predicate form by symbolizing the property of being taller than Plato by G:

> Aristotle is G.

In a certain sense, there is nothing wrong with these symbolizations. Being taller than Socrates may have been a property that Plato possessed and being taller than Plato may have been a property that Aristotle possessed, and if we want to assign symbols to these properties, nothing stops us from doing so. The difficulty with this way of symbolizing these assertions is not that it is illegitimate but that it fails to bring out important logical relationships between them. To see this, we need only compare the following clearly valid argument (1) with its translation into a subject-predicate form (2):

(1) Aristotle is taller than Plato.   (2) Aristotle is G.
    Plato is taller than Socrates.   Plato is H.

Therefore: Therefore:

    Aristotle is taller than Socrates   Aristotle is H.

[4] However, see p. 146 ff.

The argument on the right does not give us a clue why the argument on the left is valid. The situation is altered in a fundamental way if we introduce *relational* terms. The statement "x R y" says that x stands in the relation R to y. For example, we can take "x T y" as a way of saying that x is taller than y. Using this notation, we now get a new symbolization for the above argument:

Aristotle is taller than Plato.	Aristotle T Plato.
Plato is taller than Socrates.	Plato T Socrates.
Therefore:	Therefore:
Aristotle is taller than Socrates.	Aristotle T Socrates.

In this case, the symbolization on the right does bring out the logical structure in virtue of which the argument on the left is valid. We see that the validity of this argument depends on the logical properties of the relational term "taller than."

If the validity of some arguments depends on relational rather than predicative structures, it follows that some reasoning is not syllogistic, for a syllogism presupposes, as we have seen, that the two premises consist of subjects, predicates, and middles arranged in certain regular patterns. The argument we have just considered does not have this form. Nor do these two arguments: (1) If New York is east of Chicago, and Chicago is east of Los Angeles, then New York is east of Los Angeles. (2) If Aristotle was before Hegel, and Hegel was before Russell, then Aristotle was before Russell. What we are dealing with in all of these arguments are relations characterized by transitivity, and the conclusion follows in each argument because the relation asserted between the terms is transitive. Let us use the symbol ">" to refer to any transitive relation; we can now write "If x > y, and y > z, then x > z," and this will represent the logical form of a class of arguments that is not reducible to a syllogistic figure.

So far as such considerations as these dethroned syllogism, they constituted a formidable attack on Aristotelian logic. But in one important respect they were a reaffirmation of Aristotle, as against Hegel and his followers. Aristotle, like these late-nineteenth-century logicians, and unlike the Hegelians, had concentrated on logical form. What had interested him was precisely what interested them—the *formal* properties of arguments in virtue of which they are valid and therefore fit guides for reasoning. The application of mathematical models to logic enabled logicians to bring out the formal properties of arguments much more powerfully than Aristotle had been able to do, but the mathematical logicians were at one with him in holding that the business of logic is not to tell us how people actually happen to think but to tell us how we must think if we are to think correctly. Logic, that is, is a normative, not a descriptive, science. Alternatively, logic is not to be confused with psychology. It does not describe how people actually happen to think but provides instead the criteria for distinguishing between correct and incorrect thinking.

This brings us to the attack on post-Hegelian, idealist logic. In the first place, Hegel was by no means so revolutionary as he thought he was. As Russell remarked, "There is some sense in which the traditional logic, with all its faults, is uncritically and unconsciously assumed throughout his reasoning." That is, like Aristotle, Hegel assumed "the universality of the subject-predicate form."ᵃ But, in the second place, the Hegelians fell into a mistake from which Aristotle himself was exempt. Hegelian logic did not merely give a deficient account of logical form; it virtually ignored logical form. That it should do so was of course almost inevitable, for if mind constructs its world, as the idealists held, then the focus of attention is on the mind's constructive activity, and logic becomes simply a description of this activity. We have seen this tendency in Bradley, despite his efforts to resist it;[5] in Dewey it became open and explicit.[6] For Dewey, indeed, thought is simply the process of problem solving, and there are as many different techniques of problem solving as there are types of problems to be solved. It is the business of logic, he held, to describe these techniques, not to evaluate them, for they are to be evaluated not on the basis of abstract logical form but simply on the basis of whether or not the outcomes are successful. Which techniques solve the problems to which they have been applied, and which do not? This indeed was the whole thrust of Dewey's "instrumentalism." From the viewpoint of the mathematical logicians this idealist logic was not merely mistaken in the way Aristotelian logic was mistaken. It was wrongheaded, and what is more, wrongheaded in a deep and fundamental way.

Thus, the motive of the logicians was very similar to the motive that animated those philosophers who were reviving realism: opposition to contructivism. Like the realists, the mathematical logicians believed that for knowledge to be possible there must be an objective universe, independent of us and of our constructions. But though the revolution in logic was inspired by the same pursuit of objectivity, the mathematical logicians provided philosophers influenced by the revolution in logic with a new route out of the Kantian paradigm. Moore's refutation of idealism consisted in an attack on idealist epistemology, specifically in an analysis of experience that purported to show that mind *does* nothing; it merely contemplates an object held before it in consciousness. Moore simply offered a new answer to the old epistemological question, "How do we know?"—the question with which philosophy, since the time of Descartes, had been obsessed.

In contrast, the new attack on idealism bypassed epistemology altogether and thus broke new ground. The philosophers influenced by the mathematical logicians fully shared the realists' thesis—Wallace Steven's thesis[7]—that when we *know* something it is the very thing itself that is present in the mind, not some idea or mental representation of it. So, in effect, they said, since it is the very thing itself that is present in our minds when we know, let us undertake an analysis of the language in which our knowledge claims are expressed—the language, that is, of assertion. If by means of such an analysis we can ascertain the logical form of

[5] See Vol. IV, p. 340.
[6] See p. 53.
[7] See pp. 6–7.

true assertions, we shall *eo ipso* be acquiring information about the logical structure of the universe. For it is the structure of the universe that is revealed in these assertions as the "meaning" expressed in them.

These philosophers pointed out that what metaphysicians have believed about logical form has always determined their view of the universe. The only differences between themselves and earlier metaphysicians, they held, were, first, that they were aware of the relationship between logical form and metaphysical theory whereas earlier metaphysicians had been unaware of it, and second, that they had an instrument, which earlier philosophers had lacked, for analyzing logical form correctly and hence for ascertaining the true nature of the universe.

Let us spell this out in a bit more detail: as we have seen, all philosophers up to the "revolution" had assumed that all judgments are predicative—that they predicate properties of subjects. Since we can, at least on occasion and in principle, make true judgments about the world, it follows that the world about which we judge truly must consist of substances that own properties. The only question is how many such substances there are—many or one? If many, then each substance is an isolated individual, for the only relationship that this logic recognizes is the relationship of predication. If one, then this one substance is an all-encompassing subject of which the seemingly separate things are really only predicates. Thus, as long as the subject-predicate logic was unquestioned there were but two options: Leibniz's monads or Spinoza's god, though the philosophers in question had no idea that their logic was thus limiting their options.[8]

The revolution in logic, then, proposed to free philosophy from these limitations by exploding the myth that all judgments are predicative in form. Of course, when these philosophers talked about an analysis of the logic of assertions, they were not thinking of studying the ordinary language in which people actually make assertions, for this language is often muddled and incoherent, and it is always multifunctional. Their approach was normative, not descriptive. Their aim was to uncover the form that language must have if it is to be capable of conveying truths about the world. Hence what we learn about the universe through this analysis is its general nature, not its specific features.

Naturally not all of these long-range implications of the revolution in logic were seen at the outset, but the initial moves were nevertheless made very early—and also very clearly—by Frege.[9] Frege was first and foremost a mathematician and mathematical logician, but his work in these highly specialized fields had important applications to questions of general philosophical interest—applications on which this account will concentrate.

---

[8] See Vol. III, pp. 224–29 and 196–202.
[9] Gottlob Frege (1848–1925) taught mathematics at the University of Jena from 1879 until his retirement in 1918. His two chief works were *The Foundations of Arithmetic* (1884) and *The Basic Laws of Arithmetic* (Vol. I, 1893; Vol. II, 1903). He received almost no recognition during his lifetime, and it was chiefly owing to Russell's efforts that his work became known.

Frege on the Nature of Number

Although Frege's views about the nature of language and the nature of meaning are of central importance for us, we shall begin where Frege began, with a study of the nature of number. Frege's reason for starting here was his desire to establish arithmetic on a secure basis.

> The charm of work on arithmetic and analysis is, it seems to me, easily accounted for. We might say, indeed, almost in the well-known words: the reason's proper study is itself. In arithmetic we are not concerned with objects through the medium of the senses, but with objects given directly to our reason and, as its nearest kin, utterly transparent to it.[b]

Like Plato, that is, Frege held that the objects of mathematical thought are nonsensible entities that are completely independent of our thoughts about them: "The mathematician cannot create things at will, any more than the geographer can; he too can only discover what is there and give it a name."[c] In other words, from the outset Frege adopted an anticonstructivist stance. His stance is equally in the spirit of what we have called the analytic tradition, as the following passage shows.

> When we ask someone what the number one is, or what the symbol 1 means, we get as a rule the answer "Why, a thing." And if we go on to point out that the proposition
>
> "the number one is a thing"
>
> is not a definition, because . . . it only assigns the number one to the class of things, without stating which thing it is, then we shall very likely be invited to select something for ourselves—anything we please—to call one. Yet if everyone had the right to understand by this name whatever he pleased, then the same proposition about one would mean different things for different people—such propositions would have no common content. . . .
>
> Is it not a scandal that our science should be so unclear about the first and foremost among its objects, and one which is apparently so simple? . . . If a concept fundamental to a mighty science gives rise to difficulties, then it is surely an imperative task to investigate it more closely until those difficulties are overcome; especially as we shall hardly succeed in finally clearing up negative numbers, or fractional or complex numbers, so long as our insight into the foundation of the whole structure of arithmetic is still defective. . . .
>
> In order, then, to dispel this illusion that the positive whole numbers really present no difficulties at all, . . . I have adopted the plan of

criticizing some of the views put forward by mathematicians and philosophers on the questions involved. . . . My object in this is to awaken a desire for a stricter enquiry. At the same time this preliminary examination of the views others have put forward should clear the ground for my own account, by convincing my readers in advance that these other paths do not lead to the goal, and that my opinion is not just one among many all equally tenable; and in this way I hope to settle the question finally, at least in essentials.

. I realize that, as a result, I have been led to pursue arguments more philosophical than many mathematicians may approve; but any thorough investigation of the concept of number is bound always to turn out rather philosophical. It is a task which is common to mathematics and philosophy.[d]

It is easy to see why Frege would appeal so strongly to philosophers in the analytic tradition. There is the same demand for clarity, the same emphasis on rigor, the same insistence on clearing the ground and on securing an absolutely firm base before seeking to make any advance, however small. Moreover, there is the same assumption of objectivity. Indeed, Frege's whole criticism of then current views of the nature of number turned on their failure to satisfy the Platonic requirements of objectivity and certainty. He ruled out formalist theories on the ground that they failed to meet the first requirement; empirical theories, on the ground that they failed to meet the second; psychologizing theories, on the ground that they met neither. Let us first examine Frege's criticism of psychologizing.

CRITICISM OF PSYCHOLOGIZING THEORIES

The predominance in philosophy of psychological methods of argument . . . [has] penetrated even into the field of logic. With this tendency mathematics is completely out of sympathy. . . . When . . . our ideas of numbers [are called] motor phenomena and [are made] dependent on muscular sensations, no mathematician can recognize his numbers in such stuff. . . . No, sensations are absolutely no concern of arithmetic. No more are mental pictures, formed from the amalgamated traces of earlier sense-impressions. All these phases of consciousness are characteristically fluctuating and indefinite, in strong contrast to the definiteness and fixity of the concepts and objects of mathematics. It may, of course, serve some purpose to investigate the ideas and changes of ideas which occur during the course of mathematical thinking; but psychology should not imagine that it can contribute anything whatever to the foundation of arithmetic. . . . Never let us take a description of the origin of an idea for a definition, or an account of the mental and physical conditions on which we become conscious of a proposition for a proof of it. A proposition may be thought, and again it may be true; let us never confuse these two things. We must remind ourselves, it seems, that a proposition no more ceases to be true when I cease to think of it than the sun ceases to exist when I shut my eyes. Otherwise, in proving Pythagoras' theorem we should be reduced to allowing for the phosphorous content of the human brain; and astronomers would hesitate to draw any conclusions about the distant past, for fear of being charged with anachronism—with reckoning twice two as four regardless of the fact that our idea of number is a product of evolution and has a history behind it. . . . The historical approach, with its aim of detecting how things begin and of arriving from these origins at a knowledge of their nature, is certainly perfectly legitimate; but it has also its limitations. If everything were in continual flux, and nothing maintained itself fixed for all time, there would no longer be any possibility of getting to know anything about the world and everything would be plunged in confusion.[e]

Thus psychologizing theories totally misunderstand the nature of mathematics—as Frege understood the nature of mathematics. At best, such theories merely tell us why, in terms of personal biography or the circumstances of the culture, a particular mathematician (say, Pythagoras) undertook to prove a particular theorem at a particular time. Mathematics is concerned with whether the proof of the theorem is valid. "A proposition may be thought, and again it may be true; let us never confuse these two things." There could hardly be a more succinct statement of the difference between a psychological or sociological inquiry into the causes of beliefs and a logical inquiry into the validity of inference.

CRITICISM OF FORMALIST THEORIES

Formalism escapes psychologizing only at the cost of trivializing mathematics. Parrots learn to articulate words, but they do not think, for they do not realize that the noises they articulate are *signs.* Nor are we thinking, unless the words we utter and the marks we make on paper are signs. Accordingly, mathematics cannot be, as the formalists hold, merely the manipulation of marks in accordance with certain arbitrarily chosen rules. In that case mathematics would not involve thought. Mathematical thinking is *thinking* only because the marks the mathematician manipulates are signs of real entities and because his or her manipulation of these marks reflects the real nature of these real entities.

It is possible, of course, to operate with figures mechanically, just as it is possible to speak like a parrot: but that hardly deserves the name of thought. It only becomes possible at all after the mathematical notation has, as a result of genuine thought, been so developed that it does the thinking for us, so to speak.[f]

CRITICISM OF EMPIRICAL THEORIES

The empiricists for their part avoid the mistake of the formalists—they recognize that mathematics is not merely the manipulation of marks on paper. But though they understand that mathematics is about real entities of which these marks are the signs, unfortunately they suppose these real entities to be sensible properties of sensible things. Their view may seem faintly plausible if we confine ourselves to the positive integers; then someone with no real feeling for mathematics might conclude that, just as "red" is the name of a property of some sensible things and "blue" is the name of another, so "two" is the name of a property of some agglomerations and "three" is the name of a property of other agglomerations. But their view is wholly implausible as an account of the irrationals. Those who think that three is a property of aggregates having three parts may be challenged to present us with instances of aggregates having $\sqrt{-1}$ parts. However, in fact, this "gingerbread and pebble arithmetic," as Frege contemptuously described it, is inadequate even for the positive integers, in part because the number of an agglomeration depends on how we choose to think about it. What, for instance, is the number of that agglomeration known as Homer's *Iliad*? It is one poem, twenty-four books, a very large number of verses, and a still larger number of words.

> Mill is, of course, quite right that two apples are physically different from three apples, and two horses from one horse; that they are a different visible and tangible phenomenon. But are we to infer from this that their twoness or threeness is something physical? *One* pair of boots may be the same visible and tangible phenomenon as *two* boots. Here we have a difference in number to which no physical difference corresponds; for *two* and *one pair* are by no means the same thing, as Mill seems oddly to believe.[g]

Underlying Frege's criticism of empiricism is a typically Platonic attitude: sensible objects are too transitory, too fluctuating, to have the permanence and objectivity required for those entities of which the marks the mathematician makes on paper are the signs. Those sensible things are but the shadows and reflections of these real objects, and to take the former for the latter is a most grievous error. In Mill's gingerbread and pebble arithmetic "we see everything as through a fog, blurred and undifferentiated. It is as though everyone who wished to know about America were to try to put himself back in the position of Columbus at the time when he caught the first dubious glimpse of his supposed India."[h]

NUMBERS ARE NONSENSIBLE OBJECTS

The chief reason for the persistence of these three mistaken theories, despite their obvious inadequacies, is simply that

> there is at present a very widespread tendency not to recognize as an object anything that cannot be perceived by means of the senses; this

leads here to numerals' being taken to be numbers, the proper objects of our discussion; and then, I admit, 7 and 2 + 5 would indeed be different. But such a conception is untenable, for we cannot speak of any arithmetical properties of numbers whatsoever without going back to what the signs stand for. For example, the property belonging to 1, of being the result of multiplying itself by itself, would be a mere myth; for no microscopical or chemical investigation, however far it was carried, could ever detect this property in the possession of the innocent character that we call a figure one. . . . The characters we call numerals have . . . physical and chemical properties depending on the writing material. One could imagine the introduction some day of quite new numerals, just as, e.g., the Arabic numerals superseded the Roman. Nobody is seriously going to suppose that in this way we should get quite new numbers, quite new arithmetical objects, with properties still to be investigated. Thus we must distinguish between numerals and what they stand for; and if so, we shall have to recognize that the expressions "2," "1 + 1," "3 − 1," "6 ÷ 3" stand for the same thing, for it is quite inconceivable where the difference between them could lie. . . . The different expressions correspond to different conceptions and aspects, but nevertheless always to the same thing.[i]

If people can only overcome their prejudice against nonsensible objects, they will see at once the "number is neither a collection of things nor a property of such, [nor] a subjective product of mental processes," but a nonsensible object. "A statement of number asserts something objective of a concept."[j]

As an example, consider $1000^{1000^{1000}}$. Is this

an empty symbol? Not at all. It has a perfectly definite sense, even although, psychologically speaking and having regard to the shortness of human life, it is impossible for us ever to become conscious of that many objects; in spite of that, $1000^{1000^{1000}}$ is still an object, whose properties we can come to know, even though it is not intuitable. To convince ourselves of this, we have only to show, introducing the symbol a^n for the nth power of a, that for positive integral a and n this expression always refers to one and only one positive whole number.[k]

For our purposes it is unnecessary to follow Frege's discussion of number any further,[10] except to emphasize once more the extent to which, in his view, the distinction between knowledge and belief on the one hand and the objectivity of number, on the other, are bound up together. Since it is possible to *prove*, for all values of a and n, that a^n is a positive whole number, we know—not merely believe—that $1000^{1000^{1000}}$ is an object, for we could not know this unless there is a real entity, independent of ourselves, of which $1000^{1000^{1000}}$ is the sign.

[10] See, however, pp. 176–77, note 7.

Ordinary Language and Formalized Language

To say that "$1000^{1000^{1000}}$" and "2" and "$\sqrt{-1}$" are signs of real, objective entities is to say that mathematics is a language, and this powerfully suggests that the superiority of mathematics as a way of knowing, which Frege so strongly felt, is reflected in the language that mathematics uses. Thus we find him drawing a distinction between ordinary language and the special, formalized language in which, as a result of logical analysis, the general principle of mathematics can be set out.

A distinction of *subject* and *predicate* finds *no place* in my way of representing a judgment. In order to justify this, let me observe that there are two ways in which the content of two judgments may differ: it may, or it may not, be the case that all inferences that can be drawn from the first judgment when combined with certain other ones can always also be drawn from the second when combined with the same other judgments. The two propositions "the Greeks defeated the Persians at Plataea" and "the Persians were defeated by the Greeks at Plataea" differ in the former way; even if a slight difference of sense is discernible, the agreement in sense is preponderant. Now I call the part of the content that is the same in both the *conceptual content. Only this* has significance for our symbolic language; we need therefore make no distinction between propositions that have the same conceptual content. . . . In [ordinary] language the place occupied by the subject in the word-order has the significance of a *specially important* place; it is where we put what we want the hearer to attend to specially. This may, e.g., have the purpose of indicating a relation between this judgment and others, and thus making it easier for the hearer to grasp the whole sequence of thought. All such aspects of language are merely results of the reciprocal action of speaker and hearer; e.g. the speaker takes account of what the hearer expects, and tries to set him upon the right track before actually uttering the judgment. In my formalized language there is nothing that corresponds; only that part of judgments which affects the *possible inferences* is taken into consideration. Whatever is needed for a valid inference is fully expressed; what is not needed is for the most part not indicated either; *no scope is left for conjecture.* In this I follow absolutely the example of the formalized language of mathematics; here too, subject and predicate can be distinguished only by doing violence to the thought. We may imagine a language in which the proposition "Archimedes perished at the capture of Syracuse" would be expressed in the following way: "The violent death of Archimedes at the capture of Syracuse is a fact." You may if you like distinguish subject and predicate even here; but the subject contains the whole content, and the only purpose of the predicate is to present this in the form of a judgment. *Such a language would have only a single predicate for all judgments, viz. "is a fact."* We see that there is no question here of subject and predicate in the ordinary sense.[1]

This passage is interesting for a number of reasons. In the first place, within the notion of "sense"—or, as we might say, "meaning"—Frege draws a distinction between what is "conceptual content" and what is not conceptual content. Though, as far as conceptual content goes, there is no difference between the active and passive voices of the verb, yet there *is* a difference. It reflects or expresses what the speaker regards as the important feature of the battle of Plataea. He will use the active voice if what impresses him is that the Greeks won the battle and the passive voice if what impresses him is that it was lost by the Persians. But this sort of difference is unimportant for Frege; he introduces it only in order to exclude it from further discussion. What interests him is what (in this early version of his theory) he calls conceptual content. This is defined as the part of the sense of a sentence on which valid inference depends, and in Frege's formalized language two sentences are to count as the same, however much they may differ in other respects, if all the inferences that can be drawn from one of the sentences can also be drawn from the other sentence. In the second place, the passage is worth noting because, though Frege recognized that ordinary language does much more than express valid inferences, in his formalized language, expression is confined to what is needed for inference.

Notice that Frege does not consider it a *defect* that assertions in ordinary language do more than express what he calls conceptual, or logical, content. In fact, he would certainly acknowledge it as one of the strengths of ordinary language that it contains devices that assist "reciprocal action of speaker and hearer." Frege considered aspects that are not part of a sentence's conceptual content so that he could set them aside as irrelevant to his *logical* concerns. All the same, he often showed considerable originality and sophistication in analyzing these nonconceptual aspects of sentences, and many of his ideas about them, which he sometimes seemed to produce just in passing, were incorporated into works by philosophers not committed to Frege's logical program—indeed, sometimes by those opposed to it.[11]

But even if ordinary language is, in its way, serviceable for ordinary activities, it does not, according to Frege, provide a symbolism adequate for logical purposes. Specifically, instead of making logical form clear, its grammar often hides it. In contrast, Frege's *Begriffsschrift*—literally, his concept writing—is a symbolism concerned *solely* with conceptual content and intended to present that content in a clear and rigorously defined format.

---

[11] Many of Frege's ideas about the nonconceptual aspects of sentences reappear, in various ways, in the works of the so-called ordinary-language philosophers—a group largely, although not completely, opposed to the use of the methods of formal logic in philosophy. See Chapter 12.

FUNCTIONS AND ARGUMENTS

Frege's discussion of the difference between a mathematical function and its argument will serve as an example of how it is possible to use the analysis of mathematical form as the basis for making a point about the logic of assertions generally. Frege began by pointing out that the distinction between a function and an argument is one about which mathematicians themselves are far from clear. Thus everybody agrees that the expression $2.x^3 + x$ (that is, two *times* x to the third power, plus x) is a function of x, and some mathematicians, arguing on analogy, would allow that $2.2^3 + 2$ is a function of 2. This, according to Frege, is a muddle that logical analysis can clear up and, in clearing it up, can lead us to a correct understanding of what a function is and how it differs from an argument. Consider, then, the expressions

$$2.1^3 + 1$$
$$2.2^3 + 2$$
$$2.4^3 + 4$$

These expressions stand for numbers, namely, 3, 18, and 132. If they were also functions, there would be no difference between numbers and functions, and "nothing new would have been gained for arithmetic" by speaking of functions. It follows, therefore, that there must be a difference between a function and a number. What is it?

> Admittedly, people who use the word "function" ordinarily have in mind expressions in which a number is just indicated indefinitely by the letter x, e.g.
>
> $$\text{``}2.x^3 + x\text{''};$$
>
> but that makes no difference; for this expression likewise just indicates a number indefinitely, and it makes no essential difference whether I write it down or just write down "x."
>
> All the same, it is precisely by the notation that uses "x" to indicate [a number] indefinitely that we are led to the right conception. People call x the argument, and recognize the same function again in
>
> $$\text{``}2.1^3 + 1,\text{''}$$
> $$\text{``}2.4^3 + 4,\text{''}$$
> $$\text{``}2.5^3 + 5,\text{''}$$
>
> only with different arguments, viz. 1, 4, and 5. From this we may discern that it is the common element of these expressions that contains the essential peculiarity of a function; i.e. what is present in
>
> $$\text{``}2.x^3 + x\text{''}$$

over and above the letter "x." We could write this somewhat as follows:

$$\text{``}2.(\quad)^3 + (\quad).\text{''}$$

I am concerned to show that the argument does not belong with the function, but goes together with the function to make up a complete whole; for the function by itself must be called incomplete, in need of supplementation, or "unsaturated." And in this respect functions differ fundamentally from numbers. . . .

The two parts into which the mathematical expression is thus split up, the sign of the argument and the expression of the function, are dissimilar; for the argument is a number, a whole complete in itself, as the function is not.[m]

Accordingly, if we continue to say, as we did at the start, that the expression "$2.x^3 + x$" is a function of x, it is essential to remember that "x must not be considered as belonging to the function; this letter only serves to indicate the kind of supplementation that is needed; it enables one to recognize the places where the sign for the argument must go in."[n]

In bringing out the difference between complete ("saturated") and incomplete ("unsaturated") expressions, Frege's point was not merely that these *expressions* are different but that these different expressions represent (are the signs of) fundamentally different sorts of entities. Thus the expressions "$2.1^3 + 1$" and "3," which look very dissimilar, are both signs of the same sort of entity, namely number, and indeed of the very same entity, 3, whereas the expressions "$2.1^3 + 1$" and "$2.(\quad) + (\quad)$," which look very similar, are signs of very different sorts of entity, the former being a sign of a number and the latter the sign of a function. The mistake committed by those who identify functions and numbers is thus first to confuse a sign with the thing that it signifies and then to conclude that when signs differ, different things are signified and that when signs are similar, similar things are signified. "It is as though one wanted to regard the sweet-smelling violet as differing from *Viola odorata* because the names sound different. Difference of sign cannot by itself be a sufficient ground for difference of the thing signified."[o]

TRUTH-VALUES

Frege next introduced the notion of truth-values. He began by defining "the value of a function for an argument" as "the result of completing the function with the argument. Thus, 3 is the value of the function $2.x^3 + x$ for the argument 1, since we have: $2.1^3 + 1 = 3$."[p] This leads to the question, "What are the values of a function—say, $x^2 = 1$—for different arguments?"

Now if we replace x successively by -1, 0, 1, and 2, we get:

$$(-1)^2 = 1,$$
$$0^2 = 1,$$
$$1^2 = 1,$$
$$2^2 = 1.$$

Of these equations the first and third are true, the others false, I now say: "the value of our function is a truth-value" and distinguish between the truth-values of what is true and what is false. I call the first, for short, the True; and the second, the False. Consequently, e.g., "$2^2 = 4$" stands for the True as, say, "2^2" stands for 4. And "$2^2 = 1$" stands for the False. Accordingly

$$\text{"}2^2 = 4\text{," "}2 > 1\text{," "}2^4 = 4^2\text{,"}$$

stand for the same thing, viz. the True, so that in

$$(2^2 = 4) = (2 > 1)$$

we have a correct equation.

The objection here suggests itself that "$2^2 = 4$" and "$2 > 1$" nevertheless make quite different assertions, express quite different thoughts; but likewise "$2^4 = 4^2$" and "$4.4 = 4^2$" express different thoughts; and yet we can replace "2^4" by "4.4," since both signs have the same reference. Consequently, "$2^4 = 4^2$" and "$4.4 = 4^2$" likewise have the same reference. We see from this that from identity of reference there does not follow identity of the thought [expressed]. If we say "the Evening Star is a planet with a shorter period of revolution than the Earth," the thought we express is other than in the sentence "the Morning Star is a planet with a shorter period of revolution than the Earth"; for somebody who does not know that the Morning Star is the Evening Star might regard one as true and the other as false. And yet both sentences must have the same reference; for it is just a matter of interchanging the words "Evening Star" and "Morning Star," which have the same reference, i.e. are proper names of the same heavenly body. We must distinguish between sense and reference. "2^4" and "4^2" certainly have the same reference, i.e. they are proper names of the same number; but they have not the same sense; consequently, "$2^4 = 4^2$" and "$4.4 = 4^2$" have the same reference, but not the same sense (which means, in this case: they do not contain the same thought). . . .

We saw that the value of our function $x^2 = 1$ is always one of the two truth-values. Now if for a definite argument, e.g. -1, the value of the function is the True, we can express this as follows: "the number -1 has the property that its square is 1"; or, more briefly, "-1 is a square root of 1"; or "-1 falls under the concept: square root of 1." If the value of the function $x^2 = 1$ for an argument, e.g. for 2, is False, we can express this as follows: "2 is not a square root of 1" or "2 does not fall under the concept: square root of 1." We thus see how closely that which is called a concept in logic is connected with what we call a function.q

CONCEPTS AND OBJECTS

Passing over, for the moment, the distinction just drawn between sense and reference, we can note the conclusion reached: a function is like a concept in that it has an empty place that must be filled to make it complete; an argument is like an object in that it "falls under" a concept and thereby makes it complete. We have reached the point where it is possible to extend the notions of function and argument to nonmathematical language.

We shall not stop at equations and inequalities. The linguistic form of equations is a statement. A statement contains (or at least purports to contain) a thought as its sense; and this thought is in general true or false; i.e. it has in general a truth-value, which must be regarded as the reference of the sentence, just as (say) the number 4 is the reference of the expression "2 + 2," or London of the expression "the capital of England."

Statements in general, just like equations or inequalities or expressions in Analysis, can be imagined to be split up into two parts; one complete in itself, and the other in need of supplementation, or "unsaturated." Thus, e.g., we split up the sentence

"Caesar conquered Gaul"

into "Caesar" and "conquered Gaul." The second part is "unsaturated"—it contains an empty place; only when this place is filled up with a proper name, or with an expression that replaces a proper name, does a complete sense appear. Here too I give the name "function" to what this "unsaturated" part stands for. In this case the argument is Caesar.

We see that here we have undertaken to extend [the application of the term] in the other direction, viz. as regards what can occur as an argument. Not merely numbers, but objects in general, are now admissible; and here persons must assuredly be counted as objects. The two truth-values have already been introduced as possible values of a function; we must go further and admit objects without restriction as values of functions. To get an example of this, let us start, e.g., with the expression

"the capital of the German Empire."

This obviously takes the place of a proper name, and stands for an object. If we now split it up into the parts

"the capital of" and "the German Empire"

. . . I call

"the capital of x"

the expression of a function. If we take the German Empire as the argument, we get Berlin as the value of the function.

When we have thus admitted objects without restriction as arguments and values of functions, the question arises what it is that we are here calling an object. I regard a regular definition as impossible, since we have here something too simple to admit of logical analysis. It is only possible to indicate what is meant. Here I can only say briefly: An object is anything that is not a function, so that an expression for it does not contain any empty place.

A statement contains no empty place, and therefore we must regard what it stands for as an object. But what a statement stands for is a truth-value. Thus the two truth-values are objects.[r]

In these paragraphs Frege was discussing, in his own terms, what in the history of philosophy is known as the problem of universals.[12] But notice how his linguistic approach differed from the usual epistemological approach, and how the problem is thereby transformed. From Frege's point of view there is no question about the "status" of universals or about their relation to particulars. Universals (or "concepts" in his terminology) are those entities of which unsaturated expressions are the signs. Thus, for Frege the much-debated question whether universals exist was easily answered. That there are, and must be, such entities follows directly from the idea that unsaturated expressions occur as components in significant assertions, sentences that are either true or false. These sentences would not be *significant* if the expressions that occur in them were not *signs,* that is, if these expressions did not refer to reals. What the metaphysical nature of these entities may be (which is the traditional puzzle) is simply bypassed.

The same is true for particulars. A particular (or "object") is an entity that saturates a concept by falling under it, that is, by serving as the argument that completes some function and gives it a truth-value. Since *anything* that completes a function is an object, the variety of objects is immense: men, cities, planets, points in space, proofs of theorems—all these and more are objects. Hence it is idle to inquire about the metaphysical status of particulars. But the existence of particulars is not problematic, as some philosophers have supposed. That there are particulars (objects) follows directly from the occurrence of proper names in significant assertions.

Sense and Reference

As we have seen, Frege introduced a distinction between sense and reference in his treatment of functions and concepts, but in that discussion he did not fully explain what he meant by it. In his effort to do so, Frege produced one of the undisputed classics of early analytic philosophy, an essay he published in 1892 with the

[12] For a discussion of the problem of universals in its historical context, see Vol. II, pp. 185–90. For contemporary critiques, see this volume, p. 49.

German title *Über Sinn und Bedeutung*. The title, in fact, produces a problem of translation that is not easily solved in a satisfactory way. Because the German words *Sinn* and *Bedeutung* both literally mean "meaning," we can wind up with the translation "On meaning and meaning," thus burying whatever distinction Frege was trying to draw. *Sinn* has been uniformly translated as "Sense." *Bedeutung* has been variously translated as "meaning," "reference," and, using a fancy Latin word, "nominatum." We have chosen to translate *Bedeutung* as "reference," for, even if it is not what the word literally means, it seems to bring out the contrast with "sense" that Frege had in mind.[13]

"On Sense and Reference" begins in the following way:

> EQUALITY[14] gives rise to challenging questions which are not alto-
> gether easy to answer. Is it a relation? A relation between objects, or be-
> tween names or signs of objects? In my *Begriffsschrift* I assumed the
> latter. The reasons which seem to favour this are the following: $a=a$
> and $a=b$ are obviously statements of differing cognitive value; $a=a$
> holds *a priori* and, according to Kant, is to be labelled analytic, while
> statements of the form $a=b$ often contain very valuable extensions of
> our knowledge and cannot always be established *a priori*. The discov-
> ery that the rising sun is not new every morning, but always the same,
> was one of the most fertile astronomical discoveries. Even to-day the
> identification of a small planet or a comet is not always a matter of
> course. Now if we were to regard equality as a relation between that
> which the names "a" and "b" designate, it would seem that $a=b$ could
> not differ from $a=a$ (i.e. provided $a=b$ is true). A relation would
> thereby be expressed of a thing to itself, and indeed one in which each
> thing stands to itself but to no other thing. What is intended to be said
> by $a=b$ seems to be that the signs or names "a" and "b" designate the
> same thing, so that those signs themselves would be under discussion;
> a relation between them would be asserted. But this relation would
> hold between the names or signs only in so far as they named or desig-
> nated something. It would be mediated by the connexion of each of the
> two signs with the same designated thing. But this is arbitrary. Nobody
> can be forbidden to use any arbitrarily producible event or object as a
> sign for something. In that case the sentence $a=b$ would no longer re-
> fer to the subject matter, but only to its mode of designation; we would
> express no proper knowledge by its means. But in many cases this is just
> what we want to do. If the sign "a" is distinguished from the sign "b"

---

[13] For this reason we have cited the first edition rather than the second edition of *Translations from the Philosophical Writings of Gottlob Frege*, edited by Peter Geach and Max
Black (Philosophical Library, New York, 1952). In the first edition, *Bedeutung* is translated as "reference"; in the second edition, it is translated as "meaning."

[14] I use this word in the sense of identity and understand "$a = b$" to have the sense of
"a is the same as b" or "a and b coincide."

only as object (here, by means of its shape), not as sign (i.e. not by the manner in which it designates something), the cognitive value of $a=a$ becomes essentially equal to that of $a=b$, provided $a=b$ is true. A difference can arise only if the difference between the signs corresponds to a difference in the mode of presentation of that which is designated. Let a, b, c be the lines connecting the vertices of a triangle with the midpoints of the opposite sides. The point of intersection of a and b is then the same as the point of intersection of b and c. So we have different designations for the same point, and these names ("point of intersection of a and b," "point of intersection of b and c") likewise indicate the mode of presentation; and hence the statement contains actual knowledge.

It is natural, now, to think of there being connected with a sign (name, combination of words, letter), besides that to which the sign refers, which may be called the reference of the sign, also what I should like to call the *sense* of the sign, wherein the mode of presentation is contained. In our example, accordingly, the reference of the expressions "the point of intersection of a and b" and "the point of intersection of b and c" would be the same, but not their senses. The reference of "evening star" would be the same as that of "morning star," but not the sense.[s]

The contrast between sense and reference is most easily shown by using a descriptive phrase such as "the tallest building in the world." The sense of this expression is what we might call its cognitive content or even it meaning. Sense is what a competent speaker of some language understands by a word or longer expression in that language. Notice that a competent speaker of English can understand the expression "the tallest building in the world" even if she does not know which building it is. That is, it is possible to know the *sense* of this expression without knowing its *reference*. Furthermore, the reference of this expression changes over time as progressively taller buildings are constructed.

The distinction between sense and reference seems unproblematic when applied to descriptive phrases such as "the tallest building in the world." One of Frege's innovations was to extend its use in ways that seem, at first glance, quite unnatural. He not only applied it to descriptive phrases of the kind just examined, but he also applied it to proper names. It does, in fact, seem odd to ask what a name *means*. For example, to the question "What do the words 'John F. Kennedy' mean?" the natural response is that they do not *mean* anything, they *name* someone, in particular, John F. Kennedy. In Fregean terminology, while proper names have a reference,[15] they seem not to have a sense. Yet Frege thought that proper names must have a sense as well as a reference, for it was the only way he could find to solve a problem he encountered concerning identity statements.

[15] Proper names of fictitious persons raise problems that we cannot discuss here.

The problem with identity statements, which is still with us today, is this: Suppose we identify the meaning of a proper name with the object it stands for—that is, with its reference. In that case, two proper names referring to the same thing would have the same meaning. For example, all the following names refer to the very same thing:

> The Morning Star
> The Evening Star
> Venus

Since all these names name the same thing, all the following identity statements are true:

> The Morning Star is Venus.
> The Evening Star is Venus.
> The Morning Star is the Evening Star.
> Venus is Venus.

The fourth item seems peculiarly uninformative, but—and here is Frege's problem—if the meaning of a proper name is simply its reference, then all of these sentences would mean the same thing, and thus be equally uninformative. This, however, seems plainly wrong, for the claim that the Morning Star and the Evening Star are the same thing seems altogether different from the claim that the Morning Star and the Morning Star are the same thing. This, then, is Frege's puzzle: how can an identity statement of the form "$a = b$," if true, be any more informative than the trivialities "$a = a$" and "$b = b$"?

One answer to this puzzle is to treat identity statements as statements *about* names. This is not wholly implausible and, as the passage just cited indicates, Frege was tempted by this way out of his problem. After all, an identity statement will be *true* just in case the names on each side of the identity sign refer to the same thing. This suggests an analysis of the following kind:

> "$a = b$" means "The names 'a' and 'b' refer to the same thing."

Although something might be said for an analysis developed along these lines, Frege rejects it, for, as it seems to him, it would make all identity statements rely on arbitrary linguistic conventions. To vary one of Frege's own examples, we can imagine an astronomer in the nineteenth century discovering a comet and naming it after herself: Comet Wilkinson. A hundred years later another astronomer discovers a comet and names it in his honor: Comet Nakamura. The question then arises whether the comets Wilkinson and Nakamura are the same comet. There is, in fact, a conventional element here: Wilkinson named the comet after herself; Nakamura named it after himself. But, as Frege saw, the question also involves an issue in astronomy. We want to know whether the comet that was named Wilkinson and the comet that was named Nakamura are, in fact, the very same comet.

This is not a question of linguistic convention. It was considerations of this kind that led Frege to abandon the sort of linguistic analysis sketched above, and put in its place the doctrine that a proper name has a sense as well as a reference.

What, then, does Frege mean by the sense of an expression? He describes a sense as a "mode of presentation of the thing designated," but does not fully explain what he means by this. He does, however, provide an elegant example of what he has in mind, referring to the following diagram:

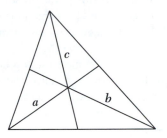

It is a theorem of geometry that, for a triangle constructed in this way, where each line bisects the opposing side of the triangle, the three lines must—as the diagram indicates—intersect at the same point. (The proof of this is not altogether trivial.) If we use Xxy as a way of representing the intersection of lines x and y, then the following identities hold:

$$Xab = Xbc$$
$$Xab = Xac$$
$$Xbc = Xac$$

Unlike $Xab = Xab$, these are all significant truths of geometry, because the intersecting point is presented to us in different ways on each side of the identity sign.

We can now examine the various ways in which a *name*, its *sense*, and its *reference* (if any) can be related to one another. In the simplest and standard case, a name has a sense that relates it to a single reference:

$$\text{Name} \longrightarrow \text{Sense} \longrightarrow \text{Reference}$$

For example, for the name "Moses," its sense is something like *the person who led the Jews out of Egypt, etc.;* its reference is the man Moses himself. We also have cases of the following kind:

$$\text{Name} \longrightarrow \text{Sense} \nrightarrow \text{No Reference}$$

This is an instance of reference failure. The name "Loch Ness Monster" may fit this pattern, for it has a sense, but, perhaps, the Loch Ness Monster does not exist. Frege saw that reference failures of this kind are not uncommon in ordinary language, but he thought they should be avoided in a proper logical notation.

The following pattern often arises in everyday language:

Name
→ Sense (1) ⟶ Reference (1) (If any)
→ Sense (2) ⟶ Reference (2) (If any)

This is a case of ambiguity. There are, for example, a great many different senses associated with the name "John Smith," and in virtue of these different senses, the name has different referents. "Prester John" presents an interesting example of a name with more than one sense and perhaps no reference at all. Various incompatible stories are told about this legendary medieval figure, but, still, he may never have existed.

Turning again to identity statements, such a statement will be true just in case the names on each side of the identity sign have the same reference. That is, "$a = b$" will be true just in case the following situation obtains:

"a"
"b"
Referent

This suggests—and we have seen that Frege was at first tempted by this idea—that identity statements simply say that two different names have the same reference. This, however, does not explain the difference between trivial and non-trivial identity statements. By introducing the distinction between sense and reference, Frege thought that he could show how the claim that a is identical with b can be significant in a way that the claim that a is identical with a is not:

"a" ⟶ Sense (a)
"b" ⟶ Sense (b)
Referent

This contrasts with the trivial claim that a is identical with a, which can be represented as follows:

"a"
"a" [16]
Sense (a) ⟶ Referent

This, then, is Frege's solution to the problem posed by significant identity claims: They are true just in case the terms flanking the identity sign have the same reference; they are significant just in case they have different senses.

---

[16] If "a" is, in fact, an ambiguous sign, namely a sign having two different senses, then an identity statement of the form "$a = a$" could be significant, but here we can ignore this possibility.

So far we have been told that the sense of a proper name is the mode of presentation of the thing designated, and we have been given some examples of what this means. Beyond this, Frege says little in the way of offering a positive account of what he means by a sense. He does, however, warn against a possible misunderstanding of his position. Although he acknowledges that different people may associate somewhat different senses with a proper name (the name "Aristotle," for example), he rejects the idea that senses are subjective. Frege is a Platonist with respect to senses. For him, senses are objective entities that exist independently of the mind that, on occasion, apprehends them. Senses, then, are not to be identified with the subjective *ideas* that occur in this or that mind on various occasions:

> The reference of a proper name is the object itself which we designate by its means; the idea, which we have in that case, is wholly subjective; in between lies the sense, which is indeed no longer subjective like the idea, but is yet not the object itself. The following analogy will perhaps clarify these relationships. Somebody observes the Moon through a telescope. I compare the Moon itself to the reference; it is the object of the observation, mediated by the real image projected by the object glass in the interior of the telescope, and by the retinal image of the observer. The former I compare to the sense, the latter is like the idea or experience. The optical image in the telescope is indeed one-sided and dependent upon the standpoint of observation; but it is still objective, inasmuch as it can be used by several observers. At any rate it could be arranged for several to use it simultaneously. But each one would have his own retinal image. On account of the diverse shapes of the observers' eyes, even a geometrical congruence could hardly be achieved, and an actual coincidence would be out of the question. This analogy might be developed still further, by assuming A's retinal image made visible to B; or A might also see his own retinal image in a mirror. In this way we might perhaps show how an idea can itself be taken as an object, but as such is not for the observer what it directly is for the person having the idea. But to pursue this would take us too far afield.[t]

Frege first applied his distinction between sense and reference to proper names in order to explain how identity statements could be cognitively significant. He then went on to apply this distinction to sentences as a whole with, as we shall see, some quite remarkable results. He identified the sense of a sentence with the *thought* it expressed. Like other senses, thoughts are objective and should not be confused with psychological states. Frege held that two people can quite literally entertain the same thought. There can also be thoughts that no one has ever entertained and that never will be entertained. That there is a zebra wearing pajamas standing on top of a bus in Times Square is almost certainly a thought that was never entertained before this paragraph was written. There must also be endlessly many such thoughts that will never be entertained by anyone, though of course it is not possible to produce an example of such a thought without thereby entertaining it.

If the thought is the sense of a sentence, we might ask whether a sentence has a reference as well, and, if so, what it is. On the face of it, it does not seem obvious that a sentence as a whole should refer to some particular object. Parts of sentences may refer to particular things, and in that sense we might say that sentences refer to particular things. Our question here, however, is whether sentences as a whole can have a reference distinct from the reference of the terms they contain, and it is far from obvious that they can. Frege, as we shall see, will argue that sentences as a whole can have referents, namely one of two abstract entities he calls the True and the False. Every true sentence names the True, and every false sentence names the False.

Before considering Frege's claim that sentences name the True and the False, we must first consider his reasons for saying that they are names at all. They certainly do not look like names. Names are the sort of thing people get when baptized, they are spelled using capital letters, and so on. Sentences are not like that. Part of the problem here is that Frege uses the notion of a name in a very wide sense to cover any expression intended to pick out a unique reference. Thus, for him, "the last man off the ship" counts as a name. We can remove some of the oddness from this discussion by introducing a less misleading label for expressions that function to pick out particular objects. We will call them *uniquely referring expressions* (UREs).[17] Proper names are UREs, but so too are descriptive phrases such as "the last man off the ship" and also demonstrative phrases such as "that man" or "this book."

Reformulated, our first question is this: Why does Frege hold that sentences as a whole are UREs? The argument here is rather complex, so we will take it slowly. As we have already seen, UREs with different senses can have the same reference. (That was the key element in Frege's treatment of significant identity statements.) For example, the following UREs have different senses but the same reference:

> "George Washington"
> "the first president of the United States"
> "the American commander at the Battle of Valley Forge"

We will call terms like this that have the same reference *coreferential* terms. Next, we can construct UREs that themselves contain UREs as parts. For example:

> "the spouse of George Washington"

The reference of this URE is Martha Washington. Thus, "the spouse of George Washington" and "Martha Washington" are coreferential terms.

---

[17] This terminology is derived from P. F. Strawson. His views on reference are examined in detail in Chapter 12.

With this background we can introduce one of Frege's fundamental principles (though not using his terminology):

> If a URE contains a URE as a part, then substituting a coreferential URE for the contained URE will not change the reference of the total URE.

A bit more simply:

> When coreferential terms are substituted one for another, the reference of the total expression remains unchanged.[18]

For example, "the spouse of George Washington" is a complex URE containing the URE "George Washington" as a part. This principle tells us that the reference of the larger URE will not change when a coreferential term is substituted for the contained URE. Our example bears this out:

> "the spouse of George Washington"
> "the spouse of the first president of the United States"
> "the spouse of the American commander at the Battle of Valley Forge"

Although the sense changes under substitution, the reference of these expressions remains the same, namely, Martha Washington.

We are now in a position to follow Frege's two-stage argument intended to show that the reference of an entire assertive sentence is a truth-value. The first stage of the argument is intended to show that such sentences do, indeed, have a reference:

> So far we have considered the sense and reference only of such expressions, words, or signs as we have called proper names. We now inquire concerning the sense and reference for an entire declarative sentence. Such a sentence contains a thought.[19] Is this thought, now, to be regarded as its sense or its reference? Let us assume for the time being that the sentence has reference. If we now replace one word of the sentence by another having the same reference, but a different sense, this can have no bearing upon the reference of the sentence. Yet we can see that in such a case the thought changes; since, e.g., the thought in the sentence "The morning star is a body illuminated by the Sun" differs from that in the sentence "The evening star is a body illuminated by the Sun." Anybody who did not know that the evening star is the

---

[18] In the second part of "On Sense and Reference," Frege examines and attempts to deal with a whole series of apparent counterexamples to this principle. His discussion shows a sophisticated understanding of the workings of ordinary language and has had an enormous influence on the work of later analytic philosophers. Unfortunately, these matters cannot be pursued here.

[19] By a thought I understand not the subjective performance of thinking but its objective content, which is capable of being the common property of several thinkers.

morning star might hold the one thought to be true, the other false. The thought, accordingly, cannot be the reference of the sentence, but must rather be considered as the sense. What is the position now with regard to the reference? Have we a right even to inquire about it? Is it possible that a sentence as a whole has only a sense, but not reference? At any rate, one might expect that such sentences occur, just as there are parts of sentences having sense but no reference. And sentences which contain proper names without reference will be of this kind. The sentence "Odysseus was set ashore at Ithaca while sound asleep" obviously has a sense. But since it is doubtful whether the name "Odysseus," occurring therein, has reference, it is also doubtful whether the whole sentence has one. Yet it is certain, nevertheless, that anyone who seriously took the sentence to be true or false would ascribe to the name "Odysseus" a reference, not merely a sense; for it is of the reference of the name that the predicate is affirmed or denied. Whoever does not admit the name has reference can neither apply nor withhold the predicate. But in that case it would be superfluous to advance to the reference of the name; one could be satisfied with the sense, if one wanted to go no further than the thought. If it were a question only of the sense of the sentence, the thought, it would be unnecessary to bother with the reference of a part of the sentence; only the sense, not the reference, of the part is relevant to the sense of the whole sentence. The thought remains the same whether "Odysseus" has reference or not. The fact that we concern ourselves at all about the reference of a part of the sentence indicates that we generally recognize and expect a reference for the sentence itself. The thought loses value for us as soon as we recognize that the reference of one of its parts is missing. We are therefore justified in not being satisfied with the sense of a sentence, and in inquiring also as to its reference.[u]

Having shown to his satisfaction that entire sentences must have a reference as well as a sense, Frege next argues that this reference can only be a truth-value:

But now why do we want every proper name to have not only a sense, but also a reference? Why is the thought not enough for us? Because, and to the extent that, we are concerned with its truth-value. This is not always the case. In hearing an epic poem, for instance, apart from the euphony of the language we are interested only in the sense of the sentences and the images and feelings thereby aroused. The question of truth would cause us to abandon aesthetic delight for an attitude of scientific investigation. Hence it is a matter of no concern to us whether the name "Odysseus," for instance, has reference, so long as we accept the poem as a work of art. It is the striving for truth that drives us always to advance from the sense to the reference.

> We have seen that the reference of a sentence may always be sought, whenever the reference of its components is involved; and that this is the case when and only when we are inquiring after the truth-value.
>
> We are therefore driven into accepting the *truth-value* of a sentence as constituting its reference. . . . If . . . the truth-value of a sentence is its meaning [reference], then on the one hand all true sentences have the same meaning [reference] and so, on the other hand, do all false sentences.[v]

Putting all these pieces together, we arrive at the following argument:

1. We are interested in the reference of a contained expression if and only if we are interested in the reference of the whole expression in which it occurs.
2. We are interested in the reference of a term within a sentence if and only if we are concerned with the truth-value of the sentence.
3. Whatever the reference of a sentence might be, it must remain unchanged under substitution of coreferential terms for the referential terms it contains.
4. Truth-values, and seemingly nothing else, possess this last feature.
5. "We are therefore driven into accepting the *truth-value* of a sentence as constituting what it means [what it refers to]."

This argument seems to give surprisingly strong support to a thesis that, on its face, seems quite implausible. Each of these premises is, however, open to criticism by those who are opposed to Platonism—or are at least opposed to Frege's rather exotic form of Platonism. Even so, Frege's discussion of sense and reference was a remarkable achievement. If nothing else, it set up a challenge that has dominated much of twentieth-century analytic philosophy: to accomplish what Frege accomplished without introducing a superabundance of exotic Platonic entities. That challenge has not proved easy to meet. In fact—more than a hundred years after Frege wrote "On Sense and Reference"—no philosopher has been able to meet this challenge in a way that has gained general acceptance.

Summary

Frege was one of the founders of philosophy of language, which has become a major preoccupation of philosophers in the twentieth century. Frege not only made important contributions to methods of linguistic analysis; more important—at least from our point of view—is the basic conception of the relation between language and the world that is implicit in his approach. Like the epistemological and metaphysical realists, Frege assumed that our minds are in contact with an objective world; like them he assumed this because he wanted to draw a firm distinction between knowledge and belief. But his approach differed from, say, Moore's in two respects. In the first place, he held that the logic of the signs in which we express our knowledge reflects the structure of the objects we know. That this should be the case follows from the realistic thesis that when we know, we are in direct contact with the object known. In the second place, where Moore began with our commonsense belief, Frege began with mathematics. He started from the Platonic assumption that in mathematics, if anywhere, we attain knowledge in contrast to mere belief. Hence, if we want to discover what characteristics the world must have for our thinking about it to be knowledge, not mere belief, we should examine the nature of our thinking in mathematics and generalize about all thought from this "best" type of thinking. But, once again, we think in signs, or at least we express our thoughts in signs. Hence, the logic of mathematical signs became the primary clue that led to what may be called a linguistic, as distinct from an epistemological, route out of the Kantian paradigm.

Russell

Russell and Moore

When philosophers mention Moore, they are likely to add "and Russell"; when they mention Russell,[1] they are likely to add "and Moore." The reasons for this strong association are obvious: Moore and Russell were almost exact contemporaries at Cambridge; they were friends; together they went through a period in which they "more or less" believed in Hegel and from which they emerged

---

[1] Bertrand A. W. Russell (1872–1970) was brought up in the home of his grandfather, who was a son of the duke of Bedford and who had been prime minister under Queen Victoria. Russell was educated at Trinity College, Cambridge, where he subsequently taught for some years. In 1931 he succeeded to the peerage, on the death of his elder brother, as third earl of Russell. In 1950 he was awarded the Nobel Prize for literature.

together, cured and, as it were, "whole." They not only agreed on rejecting ideal-ism, they also agreed on the reasons for doing so: first, because of its construc-tivism—because it holds that minds construct their experience rather than contemplate it; second, because of its monism—because, as Russell said, it makes the world into "a pot of treacle." Though Moore—at least according to Russell—was most concerned with the rejection of constructivism, "while I was most in-terested in the rejection of monism,"[a] they were both leaders in the revival of realism and the analytic tradition. That is, they both held that the universe is a col-lection of wholly independent, discrete entities and that "analysis" is the method by which we can come to know the nature of these atomic entities.

Despite all these similarities they differed so much temperamentally that they ended up in very different philosophical positions. Moore's objection to idealism was that it conflicts with our ordinary beliefs about the world.[2] This was Russell's objection too, but be put greater emphasis on idealism undermining the objectiv-ity of mathematics.

> Various things caused me to abandon both Kant and Hegel. . . . I thought that all that [Hegel] said about mathematics is muddle-headed nonsense. I came to disbelieve Bradley's arguments against relations, and to distrust the logical basis of monism. I disliked the subjectivity of the "Transcendental Aesthetic.". . . Moore took the lead in rebellion, and I followed, with a sense of emancipation. . . . With a sense of es-caping from prison, we allowed ourselves to think that grass is green, that the sun and stars would exist if no one was aware of them, and also that there is a pluralistic timeless world of Platonic ideas. . . . Mathe-matics could be *quite* true, and not merely a stage in dialectic.[b]

Thus the driving force behind Russell's interest in mathematics was his pur-suit of certainty, an interest as powerful as that which had animated Descartes. "I came to philosophy through mathematics or rather through the wish to find some reason to believe in the truth of mathematics."[c] And, looking back on his life in his old age, he described as "a great event" his discovery of geometry in 1883, when he was eleven:

> When I had got over my disappointment in finding that [Euclid] be-gan with axioms, which had to be accepted without proof, I found great delight in him. . . . This interest was complex: partly mere pleasure in discovering that I possessed a certain kind of skill, partly delight in the power of deductive reasoning, partly the restfulness of mathematical certainty; but more than any of these (while I was still a boy) the belief that nature operates according to mathematical laws, and that human actions . . . could be calculated if we had sufficient skill.[d]

[2] See pp. 129–37.

Russell's passion for certainty explains why he could never be satisfied, as Moore was, merely by justifying common sense against the arguments of the Hegelians. It explains, too, why, unlike Moore, he was a metaphysician. Russell adopted Moore's definition of the business of philosophy—"to give a general description of the whole universe," an inventory of the kinds of entities that make up the universe. But whereas Moore held that common sense provides the answers, Russell began with what the sciences tell us, and what they tell us, he thought, was problematic. Hence, though he certainly agreed with Moore that many so-called philosophical problems are generated by the mistakes and the carelessnesses of philosophers, he did not think that all are. On the contrary, there are real puzzles about what is real, which it is urgent to try to resolve. The "constant preoccupation" of his life, he said, had been "to discover how much we can be said to know and with what degree of certainty or doubtfulness."[e] "I wanted certainty in the kind of way in which people want religious faith."[f] And since Russell was never able to satisfy this deep metaphysical interest, since he was "unwillingly forced to the conclusion that most of what passes for knowledge is open to reasonable doubt,"[g] he experienced a kind of existential loneliness that was wholly foreign to the nature of one who, like Moore, was as persuaded of the existence of good as of green.[3]

Finally, Moore and Russell differed because Russell was an activist, as Moore was not.

> Ever since boyhood [I have had] two different objects which for a long time remained separate and have only in recent years united into a single whole. I wanted, on the one hand, to find out whether anything could be known; and, on the other hand, to do whatever might be possible toward creating a happier world.[h]

By the time he was fourteen he had abandoned in succession belief in free will, immortality, and God, and found himself "much happier" as a result. When he undertook to persuade people that they too would be happier if they abandoned these beliefs he naturally incurred the enmity of authorities.[4] During the First World War he was imprisoned for pacifism and for encouraging conscientious objectors. In 1940 he was forbidden to teach at City College in New York on the grounds that his views on morals and politics might corrupt innocent young minds. In the 1950s and 1960s, as he became increasingly concerned about the threat of thermonuclear war, he participated in various disarmament and passive disobedience demonstrations in England, for which at the age of ninety he was once again, but only briefly, imprisoned.

---

[3] See p. 105.

[4] In a 1959 BBC interview Russell said, "I had a letter from an Anglican bishop not long ago in which he said that *all* my opinions on *everything* were inspired by sexual lust, and that the opinions I expressed were among the causes of the Second World War."

Though Russell hated tradition and though his views on almost every subject were anathema to the social class into which he was born, in a curious way he remained loyal to his heritage. "My family during four centuries was important in the public life of England, and I was brought up to feel a responsibility which demanded that I express my opinions on political questions."[i] But Russell was too much attracted by the "lure of philosophy," too committed to the quest for certainty, too skeptical of its outcome, ever to become a politician in the traditional sense.

> When I come to what I myself can do or ought to do about the world situation, I find myself in two minds. A perpetual argument goes on within me between two different points of view which I will call that of the Devil's Advocate and that of the Earnest Publicist. . . . The voice of the Devil's Advocate is, at least in part, the voice of reason. "Can't you see," says this cynical character, "that what happens in the world does not depend upon you? Whether the populations of the world are to live or die rests with the decisions of Khrushchev, Mao Tse-tung and Mr. John Foster Dulles, not with ordinary mortals like ourselves. If they say 'die,' we shall die. If they say 'live,' we shall live. They do not read your books, and would think them very silly if they did. You forget that you are not living in 1688, when your family and a few others gave the king notice and hired another. It is only a failure to move with the times that makes you bother your head with public affairs." Perhaps the Devil's Advocate is right—but perhaps he is wrong. Perhaps dictators are not so all-powerful as they seem; perhaps public opinion can still sway them, at any rate in some degree; and perhaps books can help to create public opinion. And so I persist, regardless of his taunts. There are limits to his severities. "Well, at any rate," he says, "writing books is an innocent occupation and it keeps you out of mischief." And so I go on writing books, though whether any good will come of doing so, I do not know.[j]

Thus, irony and commitment, skepticism and a desire for certainty, scientific objectivity and deep passion were all intertwined in his nature. As we shall see, these complexities added their own shadings and tonality to his philosophical program and to its outcome.

Russell's Program

The project of making an inventory of the kinds of entities that collectively make up this world proved far more difficult than at the outset Russell thought it would be, and he changed his mind many times about what types of entity really belong in the inventory and what types, as a result of linguistic confusions, only seem to belong there and can therefore be eliminated from it. At the outset he thought the inventory consists in minds, material objects, universals, particulars, and the laws of logic. Subsequently, as we shall see, he dropped material objects from the inventory, and still later, minds. Particulars were replaced by qualities, and, as regards universals, he concluded that only one is indispensable, the universal called "similarity."

All these shifts and changes in position make it difficult to give an account of Russell's views in short compass. For the most part, therefore, we shall concentrate on a small number of persistent theses that together constitute the core of his program, rather than on the successive solutions that he from time to time put forward.

The first aspect of the program that Russell never abandoned was the distinction he and Moore had drawn between those entities about whose existence we are absolutely certain because we are directly aware of them and those entities of whose existence we are less certain because we are led to believe in their existence as a result of an inference. The former are "hard data"; the latter are "soft data." Though Russell changed his mind a number of times about what the things are of which we are directly aware, he never doubted that there is a distinction between knowledge by acquaintance and knowledge by description.

A second element in the core of Russell's program was pluralism, and a third was the importance of analysis. These, of course, are central features of the analytic way of thought.

> Although I have changed my opinion on various matters, . . . I still hold to the doctrine of external relations and to pluralism, which is bound up with it. I still hold that an isolated truth may be quite true. I still hold that analysis is not falsification. I still hold that any proposition other than a tautology, if it is true, is true in virtue of a relation to *fact*, and that facts in general are independent of experience. I see nothing impossible in a universe devoid of experience. . . . On all these matters my views have not changed since I abandoned the teachings of Kant and Hegel.[k]

Analysis was important to Russell because it enabled him to reduce the number of kinds of independent entities and so keep the inventory small. His drive for certainty and his demand for simplicity made him want to show that a large number of different kinds of inferred entities ("soft data") could all be accounted for in terms of a few kinds of hard data. In other words, Russell was a strong advocate of the maxim called Occam's razor: "Do not multiply entities beyond necessity."[5]

> When, however, after 1910, I had done all that I intended to do as regards pure mathematics, I began to think about the physical world and,

[5] See Vol. II, p. 322.

largely under Whitehead's influence, I was led to new applications of Occam's razor, to which I had become devoted by its usefulness in the philosophy of arithmetic. . . . As in all uses of Occam's razor, one was not obliged to deny the existence of the entities with which one dispensed, but one was enabled to abstain from ascertaining it. This had the advantage of diminishing the assumptions required for the interpretation of whatever branch of knowledge was in question.[1]

We may, then, call Occam's razor a fourth persistent element in Russell's program. A fifth was the conviction that ordinary language is so incoherent that it has badly misled philosophers: it disguises logical form. Here, of course, Russell differed from Moore, who held that most philosophical problems could be solved if only philosophers would return to ordinary language and to the ordinary beliefs expressed in that language. A sixth and final element in Russell's program—and another respect in which he differed from Moore—was his strategy of concentrating on logical form. A correct analysis, one that reveals logical form, will lead us directly to the solution of metaphysical problems and so bypass the great traditional question, "How do we know?" The contrast between Russell's logical orientation and Moore's epistemological orientation shows up very clearly in "My Present View of the World," written in 1959; but it had existed, really, from the start.

> I reverse the process which has been common in philosophy since Kant. It has been common among philosophers to begin with how we know and proceed afterwards to what we know. I think this a mistake, because . . . it tends to give to knowing a cosmic importance which it by no means deserves, and thus prepares the philosophical student for the belief that mind has some kind of supremacy over the non-mental universe, or even that the non-mental universe is nothing but a nightmare dreamt by mind in its unphilosophical moments. This point of view is completely remote from my imaginative picture of the cosmos. . . . There is no evidence of anything mental except in a tiny fragment of space-time, and the great processes of nebular and stellar evolution proceed according to laws in which mind plays no part.[m]

Though Russell and Moore agreed on the importance of analysis, their views of what analysis is differed considerably, inasmuch as Russell came to philosophical analysis from mathematical logic and Moore did not.

Logical Analysis

In a lecture called "Logic as the Essence of Philosophy," given in Boston in 1914, Russell laid it down categorically that "every philosophical problem, when it is subjected to the necessary analysis and purification, is found either to be not really philosophical at all, or else to be, in the sense in which [I am] using the word, logical." But, he immediately added, "as the word 'logic' is never used in the same sense by two different philosophers, some explanation of what I mean by the word is indispensable."[n]

> Logic, we may say, consists of two parts. The first part investigates what propositions are and what forms they may have; this part enumerates the different kinds of atomic propositions, of molecular propositions, of general propositions, and so on. The second part consists of certain supremely general propositions, which assert the truth of all propositions of certain forms. . . . The first part, which merely enumerates forms, is the more difficult, and philosophically the more important; and it is the recent progress in this first part, more than anything else, that has rendered a truly scientific discussion of many philosophical problems possible.[o]

The traditional Aristotelian logic, Russell concluded, "put thought in fetters, while the new logic gives it wings."[p] An example of the "fetters" that Russell had in mind is the old logic's assumption that all judgments are predicative in form. This, as we have seen, committed philosophers in advance to a substantive metaphysics and limited them to two options, monism or pluralism—either everything is an attribute of one substance or else there are many substances, each so independent of the others that interaction among them is impossible.[6] As for the way the new logic gives thought "wings," we shall give some examples of age-old philosophical problems that are solved by the new method of analysis.

THE THEORY OF TYPES

In our discussion of Frege we have already seen the interest of mathematicians in providing an anchor for mathematics in logic, instead of leaving it floating on a sea of vague and unanalyzed assumptions. Russell, who began life as a mathematician and who fully shared this Cartesian interest in certainty and clarity, was one of the first, and for some time one of the few, of Frege's contemporaries to recognize his genius and originality. The first step in giving mathematics a secure foundation was (to quote Russell's later description of the work of analysis) to show that "all traditional pure mathematics, including analytical geometry, may be regarded as consisting wholly of propositions about the natural numbers."[q] The second step was to show that "the entire theory of the natural numbers could be derived from three primitive ideas and five primitive propositions in addition to those of pure logic. These three ideas and five propositions thus became, as it

---

[6] See p. 145. Russell had discovered the way an assumption about logical form limits metaphysical options in the course of writing *A Critical Exposition of the Philosophy of Leibniz,* which was published in 1900.

were, hostages for the whole of traditional pure mathematics. If they could be defined and proved in terms of others, so could all pure mathematics." Here the operative words are "derived" and "defined." The next step was to show that the three primitive ideas (0, number, successor) are definable in terms of *class, belonging to a class,* and *similarity*—all of which are purely logical notions.[r] Here is Russell's definition of number.

> Many philosophers, when attempting to define number, are really setting to work to define plurality, which is quite a different thing. *Number* is what is characteristic of numbers, as *man* is what is characteristic of men. A plurality is not an instance of number, but of some particular number. A trio of men, for example, is an instance of the number 3, and the number 3 is an instance of number; but the trio is not an instance of number. . . .
>
> Number is a way of bringing together certain collections, namely, those that have a given number of terms. We can suppose all couples to be in one bundle, all trios in another, and so on. In this way we obtain various bundles of collections, each bundle consisting of all the collections that have a certain number of terms. Each bundle is a class whose members are collections, *i.e.* classes; thus each is a class of classes. . . .
>
> Two classes are said to be "similar" when there is a one-one relation which correlates the terms of the one class each with one term of the other class. . . .
>
> We may thus use the notion of "similarity" to decide when two collections are to belong to the same bundle. . . . We want to make one bundle containing the class that has no members: this will be for the number 0. Then we want a bundle of all the classes that have one member: this will be for the number 1, . . . and so on. Given any collection, we can define the bundle it is to belong to as being the class of all those collections that are "similar" to it. . . .
>
> We naturally think that the class of couples (for example) is something different from the number 2. But there is no doubt about the class of couples: it is indubitable and not difficult to define, whereas the number 2, in any other sense, is a metaphysical entity . . . which must always remain elusive. Accordingly we set up the following definition:—
>
> *The number of a class is the class of all those classes that are similar to it.* . . .
>
> At the expense of a little oddity, this definition secures definiteness and indubitableness; and it is not difficult to prove that numbers so defined have all the properties that we expect numbers to have.[7,s]

---

[7]This account may be compared with Frege's (see pp. 149–50). Where Russell made the notion of "similarity" fundamental, Frege introduced the notion of "capable of being recognized again." Number, he said, is "an object that can be recognized again, though not

Russell was soon to realize that the "oddity" was much more serious than he had supposed. To define number as the class of all classes is to say that number is a class. Some classes are members of themselves (for instance, the class of all classes, being a class, is a member of itself), and some are not members of themselves (for instance, the class of all men, not being a man, is not a member of itself). But what about the class, W, of all classes that are not member of themselves? Is W a member of itself? Unfortunately, however we answer, we contradict ourselves. Suppose we start by assuming that W is a member of itself. Then, being a member of itself, it cannot be a member of the class of classes that are not members of themselves. Therefore, contrary to assumption, W is not a member of itself. Very well, then, let us try the alternative—W is not a member of itself. But then, obviously, it is a member of the class of classes that are not members of themselves. Therefore, contrary to assumption, W is a member of itself. In a word, W is both a member of itself and not a member of itself, which is a contradiction.

Paradoxes of this kind have long been objects of curiosity and puzzlement. Consider the following assertion: "This sentence is false." Since every assertion is either true or false, this assertion is either true or false. Suppose it to be false. Then, since what it asserts is that it is false, it is false that it is false—that is, it is true. Now suppose that it is true. Then, since, once again, what it asserts is that it is false, it is true that it is false—that is, it is false. In both cases, we have contradicted ourselves. Or consider the claim made by Epimenides the Cretan that all Cretans are liars. Suppose Epimenides is not making merely the dispositional assertion that Cretans tend to lie, but the strong claim that no Cretan ever tells the truth. Then we have to ask whether Epimenides is telling the truth or lying. If he is telling the truth when he says that Cretans always lie, then it is not the case that Cretans always lie, for Epimenides is a Cretan and he is telling the truth now. He had falsified his own statement that Cretans always lie. On the other hand, if he is lying when he says that Cretans always lie, then Cretans are not always liars. Once again he has falsified his statement.

Solution of the paradox about the class of classes that are not members of themselves was urgent if Russell's attempt to provide a logical foundation for mathematics was not to collapse.[8] His solution was to introduce the notion of a hierarchy of types. There is, he said, a basic type of proposition that simply asserts

---

as a physical or even a merely spatial object, nor yet as one of which we can form a picture by means of our imagination. . . . The problem, therefore, was now this: to fix the sense of a numerical identity, that is, to express that sense without making use of number words," and so gave only a circular definition. This was accomplished by showing that "it is possible to correlate one to one the objects falling under a concept F with those falling under a concept G," and to define this possibility as numerical identity. Thus Russell and Frege made exactly parallel moves in defining number.

[8] The same was true for Frege, of course. Russell notified Frege of the paradox as soon as he discovered it, and Frege, who had just finished his *Basic Laws of Arithmetic,* could only remark, in an appendix, that nothing was more unfortunate for a writer "than to have one of the foundations of his edifice shaken after the work is finished."

something, for instance, "S." Then there is a second level that asserts something of S, for instance, "S is true." Then there is a third level that asserts "(S is true) is true," and a fourth level that asserts "([S is true] is true) is true," and so on. Paradoxes arise only when these levels are not distinguished, and they are resolved as soon as we see that a generalization (S is true) about an assertion (S) is not at the level of those assertions it is about but is always at a higher level. Hence the proposition that makes an assertion about a class of assertions is not included in that class of assertions. For instance, there is a class of assertions made by Cretans. Let us assume that these assertions are all at, say, level n, and let us suppose that all them are lies. Then there is an assertion made by Epimenides about this class of assertions to the effect that they are lies. That assertion is at level $n + 1$, and so is not one of the assertions that are being characterized by him as being lies. A contradiction seemed to arise only because this assertion was supposed to be at the same level as that of the assertions it was *about*.

The following theory of symbolic logic recommended itself to me in the first instance by its ability to solve certain contradictions. . . . But the theory in question seems not wholly dependent on this indirect recommendation; it has also, if I am not mistaken, a certain consonance with common sense which makes it inherently credible. This, however, is not a merit upon which much stress should be laid; for common sense is far more fallible than it likes to believe. I shall therefore begin by stating some of the contradictions to be solved, and shall then show how the theory of logical types effects their solution.

(1) The oldest contradiction of the kind in question is the *Epimenides*. Epimenides the Cretan said that all Cretans were liars, and all other statements made by Cretans were certainly lies. Was this a lie? The simplest form of this contradiction is afforded by the man who says "I am lying"; if he is lying, he is speaking the truth, and vice versa.

(2) Let w be the class of all those classes which are not members of themselves. Then, whatever class x may be, "x is a w" is equivalent to "x is not an x." Hence, giving to x the value w, "w is a w" is equivalent to "w is not a w.". . .

In the above contradictions (which are merely selections from an indefinite number) there is a common characteristic, which we may describe as self-reference or reflexiveness. The remark of Epimenides must include itself in its own scope. If *all* classes, provided they are not members of themselves, are members of w, this must also apply to w; and similarly for the analogous relational contradiction. . . . Let us go through the contradictions one by one and see how this occurs.

(1) When a man says "I am lying," we may interpret his statement as: "There is a proposition which I am affirming and which is false." All statements that "there is" so-and-so may be regarded as denying that the opposite is always true; thus "I am lying" becomes: "It is not true of

all propositions that either I am not affirming them or they are true"; in other words, "It is not true for all propositions p that if I affirm p, p is true." The paradox results from regarding this statement as affirming a proposition, which must therefore come within the scope of the statement. This, however, makes it evident that the notion of "all propositions" is illegitimate; for otherwise, there must be propositions (such as the above) which are about all propositions, and yet can not, without contradiction, be included among the propositions they are about. Whatever we suppose to be the totality of propositions, statements about this totality generate new propositions which, on pain of contradiction, must lie outside the totality. It is useless to enlarge the totality, for that equally enlarges the scope of statements about the totality. Hence there must be no totality of propositions, and "all propositions" must be a meaningless phrase. . . .

Thus all our contradictions have in common the assumption of a totality such that, if it were legitimate, it would at once be enlarged by new members defined in terms of itself.

This leads us to the rule: "Whatever involves *all* of a collection must not be one of the collection"; or, conversely: "If, provided a certain collection had a total, it would have members only definable in terms of that total, then the said collection has no total."[9]

We can now sum up our whole discussion. After stating some of the paradoxes of logic, we found that all of them arise from the fact that an expression referring to *all* of some collection may itself appear to denote one of the collection; as, for example, "all propositions are either true or false" appears to be itself a proposition. We decided that, where this appears to occur, we are dealing with a false totality, and that in fact nothing whatever can significantly be said about *all* of the supposed collection. In order to give effect to this decision, we explained a doctrine of *types* of variables, proceeding upon the principle that any expression which refers to *all* of some type must, if it denotes anything, denote something of a higher type than that to all of which it refers.[t]

Although, as Russell remarked, "this theory of types raises a number of difficult philosophical questions concerning its interpretation,"[u] we will not go into these complications. Instead, we will conclude this discussion—from which we have omitted all of the symbolic logic and much else besides—by noting two points that bear on Russell's general philosophical position. First, just as with Moore's quite different method of analysis, the results of Russellian analysis are supposed to be completely evident once they are pointed out to us. For instance, that a class composed of individuals belongs to a different logical type from a class

---

[9]When I say that a collection has no total, I mean that statements about *all* its members are nonsense.

composed of classes of individuals is "plain common sense, but unfortunately almost all philosophy consists in an attempt to forget it."ᵛ That the end results of logical analysis are evident follows, it should be noted, from the fundamental assumption of the analytic tradition that analysis terminates in simples.

Second, the paradoxes that have just been examined and solved are by no means the only philosophical puzzles caused by the incoherence of ordinary language. All such puzzles, which are wholly incapable of solution by traditional methods and have therefore plagued philosophy since the beginning, are to be resolved by means of mathematical logic. Thus the method used to generate the theory of types, and so resolve the paradox of Epimenides, became paradigmatic for Russell's whole program.

THE THEORY OF DESCRIPTIONS

Our second example of the way in which the new logic releases thought from the fetters in which the old logic had imprisoned it concerns a question that had perplexed Moore, namely, "What is the object of our thought when we are judging that chimeras do not exist, or that round squares do not exist, or, for that matter, that there is no present king of France?" On the realistic view that holds that the very thing itself is before our minds when we judge, nonexistent objects create a very difficult problem.[10]

Characteristically, Russell tackled this problem in its most general form. Since "the round square," "the golden mountain," and "the present king of France" are descriptions, instead of examining such phrases as these in isolation, he attacked the whole question of how descriptions, or as he called them, "denoting phrases," function.

> By a "denoting phrase" I mean a phrase such as any one of the following: a man, some man, any man, every man, all men, the present King of England, the present King of France, the centre of mass of the solar system at the first instant of the twentieth century, the revolution of the earth round the sun, the revolution of the sun round the earth. Thus a phrase is denoting solely in virtue of its *form*. We may distinguish three cases: (1) A phrase may be denoting, and yet not denote anything; e.g., "the present King of France." (2) A phrase may denote one definite object; e.g., "the present King of England" denotes a certain man. (3) A phrase may denote ambiguously; e.g., "a man" denotes not many men, but an ambiguous man. . . .
>
> The subject of denoting is of very great importance . . . in theory of knowledge. For example, we know that the centre of mass of the solar system at a definite instant is some definite point, and we can affirm a number of propositions about it; but we have no immediate

---

[10] For Moore's attempts to deal with this problem, see pp. 115–19.

acquaintance with this point, which is only known to us by description. The distinction between *acquaintance* and *knowledge about* is the distinction between the things we have presentations of, and the things we only reach by means of denoting phrases. It often happens that we know that a certain phrase denotes unambiguously, although we have no acquaintance with what it denotes; this occurs in the above case of the centre of mass. In perception we have acquaintance with the objects of perception, and in thought we have acquaintance with objects of a more abstract logical character; but we do not necessarily have acquaintance with the objects denoted by phrases composed of words with whose meanings we are acquainted. To take a very important instance: there seems no reason to believe that we are ever acquainted with other people's minds, seeing that these are not directly perceived; hence what we know about them is obtained through denoting. All thinking has to start from acquaintance; but it succeeds in thinking *about* many things with which we have no acquaintance.ʷ

It is commonly thought, and ordinary usage certainly suggests, that each denoting phrase denotes some object—for instance, that "my desk" denotes the desk that is mine and "the father of his country" denotes the man, whoever he may have been, who was the father of his country. That is, it is supposed that "denoting phrases [stand] for genuine constituents of the propositions in whose verbal expressions they occur."ˣ Russell undertook to show that this is a mistaken view, and that, on the contrary, "denoting phrases never have any meaning in themselves,"ʸ even though the propositions in which they occur do have meaning.

The strategy by means of which he undertook to prove this was, in essence, simple. It consisted in showing that, after a correct analysis, the denoting phrase disappears. Since the meaning of the proposition nevertheless remains intact, it follows that the denoting phrase, appearances to the contrary, does not denote. We shall have to examine this argument in detail, but before we do so, we should look at the "unavoidable difficulties" to which the alternative view—that denoting phrases have meaning—gives rise.

Russell criticized two versions of this alternative view. The simpler

is that of Meinong.[11] This theory regards any grammatically correct denoting phrase as standing for an *object.* Thus "the present King of France," "the round square," etc., are supposed to be genuine objects. It is admitted that such objects do not *subsist,* but nevertheless they are supposed to be objects. This is in itself a difficult view; but the chief

---

[11] [Alexis Meinong (1853–1921) was a student of Brentano's (see pp. 110–11). His "theory of objects"—an object being anything whatever intended by consciousness—influenced the development of phenomenology, which may be said to be an attempt to get at Meinong's objects and isolate them for inspection by a method called "bracketing" (see pp. 287–88)—AUTHORS.]

objection is that such objects, admittedly, are apt to infringe the law of contradiction. It is contended, for example, that the existent present King of France exists, and also does not exist; that the round square is round, and also not round, etc. But this is intolerable.[z]

That was one difficulty with Meinong's solution. Another was that, quite apart from the contradictions generated by certain descriptions, Meinong's account of descriptions offended against Occam's razor, since, according to this account, there must be an object (even if a nonexistent, nonsubsistent one) that is named by every description, however fantastic. As Russell wrote, "The desire to avoid Meinong's unduly populous realm of being led me to the theory of descriptions."[a]

The more complex version of this view that Russell criticized is that of Frege. Frege's solution avoids Meinong's "breach of the law of contradiction, but is involved in difficulties of its own."

> He distinguishes, in a denoting phrase, two elements, which we may call the *meaning* and the *denotation*.[12] Thus "the centre of mass of the solar system at the beginning of the twentieth century" is highly complex in *meaning*, but its *denotation* is a certain point, which is simple. The solar system, the twentieth century, etc., are constituents of the *meaning*; but the *denotation* has no constituents at all. . . .
>
> One of the first difficulties that confront us, when we adopt the view that denoting phrases *express* a meaning and *denote* a denotation, concerns the cases in which the denotation appears to be absent. If we say "the King of England is bald," that is, it would seem, not a statement about the complex *meaning* "the King of England," but about the actual man denoted by the meaning. But now consider "the King of France is bald." By parity of form, this also ought to be about the denotation of the phrase "the King of France." But this phrase, though it has a *meaning* provided "the King of England" has a meaning, has certainly no denotation, at least in any obvious sense. Hence one would suppose that "the King of France is bald" ought to be nonsense; but it is not nonsense, since it is plainly false.[b]

Here Russell seems to misunderstand Frege's position in a fundamental way. From what we saw in the previous chapter, Frege would simply say that the expressions "the king of France" and "the queen of England" are both meaningful, in that they both have senses. Furthermore, for Frege, an expression can have a sense without having a reference, so there is no need to introduce a strange (Meinongian) reference for the expression "the king of France." Russell would have done better by arguing that senses themselves are mysterious entities.

---

[12] [In the passages from Frege quoted on p. 157 ff, the German word *Sinn*, which Russell here translates as "meaning," is rendered as "sense," and the German word *Bedeutung*, which Russell translates as "denotation," is rendered as "reference"—AUTHORS.]

From Meinong's and Frege's difficulties Russell concluded that it is impossible to provide a denotation for phrases such as "the round square" and "the present king of France." But if they do not denote, then there is no reason to suppose that such descriptive phrases as "my desk" or "the father of his country" denote. The result is an immense reduction in the inventory of the universe, for we drop out of the universe at one stroke all the objects seemingly denoted by all those phrases—"the father of his country," "the owner of Mount Vernon," "the first president," "the chopper-down of cherry trees," "the man who never told a lie"— that denote George Washington. Thus an analysis of denoting phrases that eliminates the need to assign to them what Frege called their reference not only solves the puzzle about sentences such as "Round squares do not exist," it also satisfies the principle of Occam's razor and Russell's own desire to hold to a minimum the number of kinds of basic entities.

So much, then, for Russell's aim. His strategy, as we have said, was to show that denoting phrases can be eliminated from the sentences in which they occur without changing the meaning of those sentences. Russell deals first with "everything," "nothing," and "something," which he calls "the most primitive of denoting phrases"; then with indefinite descriptions, or denoting phrases such as "a man," and finally with definite descriptions such as "the man who. . . ."

> My theory, briefly, is as follows. I take the notion of the *variable* as fundamental; I use "$C(x)$" to mean a proposition in which x is a constituent, where x, the variable, is essentially and wholly undetermined. Then we can consider the two notions "$C(x)$ is always true" and "$C(x)$ is sometimes true." Then *everything* and *nothing* and *something* (which are the most primitive of denoting phrases) are to be interpreted as follows:
>
> C (everything) means "$C(x)$ is always true";
> C (nothing) means "'$C(x)$ is false' and is always true";
> C (something) means "It is false that '$C(x)$ is false' is always true."
>
> Here the notion "$C(x)$ is always true" is taken as ultimate and indefinable, and the others are defined by means of it. *Everything, nothing,* and *something* are not assumed to have any meaning in isolation, but a meaning is assigned to *every* proposition in which they occur. This is the principle of the theory of denoting I wish to advocate: that denoting phrases never have any meaning in themselves, but that every proposition in whose verbal expression they occur has a meaning. The difficulties concerning denoting are, I believe, all the result of a wrong analysis of propositions whose verbal expressions contain denoting phrases. The proper analysis, if I am not mistaken, may be further set forth as follows.
>
> Suppose now we wish to interpret the proposition, "I met a man." If this is true, I met some definite man; but that is not what I affirm. What I affirm is, according to the theory I advocate:

> "'I met x, and x is human' is not always false."
>
> Generally, defining the class of men as the class of objects having the predicate *human,* we say that: "C(a man)" means "'$C(x)$ and x is human' is not always false." This leaves "a man," by itself, wholly destitute of meaning, but gives a meaning to every proposition in whose verbal expression "a man" occurs.[c]

In other words, a correct analysis shows that indefinite descriptions can be eliminated without affecting in any way the meaning of the sentences in which they occur. It follows that the indefinite descriptions have no independent meaning. That is, if they are taken as distinct components in the sentences in which they occur, they are meaningless. They are "incomplete symbols." So much for indefinite descriptions. Now for definite descriptions, which, as Russell says, "are by far the most interesting and difficult of denoting phrases." Consider, as an example of a definite description, the phrase "the author of *Waverley.*"

> According to the view which I advocate, a denoting phrase is essentially *part* of a sentence, and does not, like most single words, have any significance on its own account. If I say "Scott was a man," that is a statement of the form "x was a man," and it has "Scott" for its subject. But if I say "the author of *Waverley* was a man," that is not a statement of the form "x was a man," and does not have "the author of *Waverley*" for its subject. . . . We may put, in place of "the author of *Waverley* was a man," the following: "One and only one entity wrote *Waverley,* and that one was a man.". . . And speaking generally, suppose we wish to say that the author of *Waverley* had the property Φ, what we wish to say is equivalent to "One and only one entity wrote *Waverley,* and that one had the property Φ."[d]

Once again, the denoting phrase has been eliminated without altering the meaning of the sentence. It follows that the denoting phrase, appearances to the contrary, does not denote.

This leaves, finally, phrases such as "the golden mountain" and "the present king of France"—that is, phrases that, according to the old theory, denote nonexistent objects—to be dealt with. They, too, do not denote. But the question is, how are they to be eliminated? Before we can answer this, we must distinguish between what Russell calls the primary and secondary occurrences of a denoting phrase.

> The difference of primary and secondary occurrences of denoting phrases is as follows:
>
> When we say: "George IV wished to know whether so-and-so," or when we say "So-and-so is surprising" or "So-and-so is true," etc., the "so-and-so" must be a proposition. Suppose now that "so-and-so" contains a denoting phrase. We may either eliminate this denoting

phrase from the subordinate proposition "so-and-so," or from the whole proposition in which "so-and-so" is a mere constituent. Different propositions result according to which we do. . . . When we say, "George IV wished to know whether Scott was the author of *Waverley*," we normally mean "George IV wished to know whether one and only one man wrote *Waverley* and Scott was that man"; but we *may* also mean: "One and only one man wrote *Waverley*, and George IV wished to know whether Scott was that man." In the latter, "the author of *Waverley*" has a *primary* occurrence; in the former, a *secondary*. The latter might be expressed by "George IV wished to know, concerning the man who in fact wrote *Waverley*, whether he was Scott." This would be true, for example, if George IV has seen Scott at a distance, and had asked, "Is that Scott?" A *secondary* occurrence of a denoting phrase may be defined as one in which the phrase occurs in a proposition *p* which is a mere constituent of the proposition we are considering, and the substitution for the denoting phrase is to be effected in *p*, not in the whole proposition concerned. . . .

The distinction of primary and secondary occurrences enables us to deal with . . . the logical status of denoting phrases that denote nothing. If "*C*" is a denoting phrase, say "the term having the property *F*," then "*C* has the property Φ" means "one and only one term has the property *F*, and that one has the property Φ." If now the property *F* belongs to no terms, or to several, it follows that "*C* has the property Φ" is false for *all* values of Φ. Thus "the present King of France is bald" is certainly false; and "the present King of France is not bald" is false if it means "There is an entity which is now King of France and is not bald," but is true if it means "It is false that there is an entity which is now King of France and is bald." That is, "the King of France is not bald" is false if the occurrence of "the King of France" is *primary*, and true if it is *secondary*. Thus all propositions in which "the King of France" has a primary occurrence are false; the denials of such propositions are true, but in them "the King of France" has a secondary occurrence.[e]

Though these paragraphs may seem a bit dense, Russell's point is readily grasped, for everyone distinguishes without difficulty between asking whether Scott was the author of *Waverley* and asking whether, if *Waverley* had one author,[13] his name was Scott. That is, everyone understands the difference between (1) a proposition in which what is predicated is a denoting phrase and (2) a proposition containing a subproposition in which the denoting phrase is predicated. In Russell's terminology, the denoting phrase has secondary occurrence in the latter

---

[13]We might be wondering whether *Waverley* was written by one man or by a committee, or whether it was composed by a man or by a group of monkeys hammering out letters at random on dozens of typewriters, or whether it was a real production or only a fictitious novel referred to in a novel that has a novelist for a hero.

case, since it is only a part, not the whole, of what is asserted or denied, whereas the denoting phrase has primary occurrence in the former case, since it is the whole of what is asserted or denied.

So much, in general, for the distinction Russell has drawn. Now for the problem of phrases that (according to the old theory) denote nonexistent objects. According to Russell, propositions in which such denoting phrases have primary occurrence are false; those in which they have secondary occurrence are true. Here again, common sense concurs. Suppose someone says to us, "The present king of France is not bald. True or false?" We should not try to reply until the assertion has been rephrased, for what exactly is being negated? There are two possibilities:

> (1) The present king of France is (not bald).
> (2) Not (the present king of France is bald).

Rephrased in this way, we have no problem, for evidently (1) is false and (2) is true. In (1) the denoting phrase ("the present king of France") has primary occurrence; in (2) it has secondary occurrence, since it is merely a part of the whole package being asserted. Thus, though common sense may not formulate the distinction between primary and secondary occurrence explicitly, common sense is not in the least muddled by it. Only old-fashioned logicians think that there must be a present king of France for us to be able to deny that the present king of France is bald.

In addition to clearing up the puzzle about phrases that seem to denote nonexistent objects, the theory of descriptions has other advantages, two of which may be mentioned. First, it explains "the usefulness of identity."

> The usefulness of *identity* is explained by the above theory. No one outside a logic-book ever wishes to say "*x* is *x*," and yet assertions of identity are often made in such forms as "Scott was the author of *Waverley*" or "thou art the man." The meaning of such propositions cannot be stated without the notion of identity, although they are not simply statements that Scott is identical with another term, the author of *Waverley*, or that thou art identical with another term, the man. The shortest statement of "Scott is the author of *Waverley*" seems to be "Scott wrote *Waverley*; and it is always true of *y* that if *y* wrote *Waverley*, *y* is identical with Scott." It is in this way that identity enters into "Scott is the author of *Waverley*"; and it is owing to such uses that identity is worth affirming.[14,f]

Second, it clears up puzzles about "existence" and "being" that have preoccupied metaphysicians since the days of Plato and Aristotle.[15] Consider the sentence

---

[14] Russell recognized that Frege's solution, which he criticized on other grounds, also had this advantage. See p. 157 ff.

[15] See pp. 97–98 for Moore's very different analysis.

"The author of *Waverley* exists." This analyzes into (1) "At least one person wrote *Waverley*," and (2) "At most one person wrote *Waverley*." In other words, by means of analysis we remove "exists" from the sentence, yet do not alter its meaning. Next, consider the sentence "Scott exists." Unless this is equivalent to "The author of *Waverley* exists," it is nonsense. Hence, once again, "exists" drops out; "exists" in the sentence "Scott exists" does not refer to a property of Scott, as "roar" in the sentence "Lions roar" refers to a property of lions. Though the two sentences look alike grammatically, the theory of descriptions shows that they are very different in logical form.

> An important consequence of the theory of descriptions is that it is meaningless to say "A exists" unless "A" is (or stands for) a phrase of the form "the so-and-so." If the so-and-so exists, and *x* is the so-and-so, to say "*x* exists" is nonsense. Existence, in the sense in which it is ascribed to single entities, is thus removed altogether from the list of fundamentals. The ontological argument and most of its refutations are found to depend upon bad grammar.[g]

Philosophy as Criticism

Since in Russell's view much of what has traditionally passed for profound philosophical speculation has resulted from logical confusions as elementary as this muddle over how "exists" functions in sentences, it is not surprising that Russell believed the primary business of modern philosophy to be criticism.

> The business of philosophy, as I conceive it, is essentially that of logical analysis, followed by logical synthesis. . . . Although . . . comprehensive construction is part of the business of philosophy, I do not believe it is the most important part. The most important part, to my mind, consists in criticizing and clarifying notions which are apt to be regarded as fundamental and accepted uncritically. As instances I might mention: mind, matter, consciousness, knowledge, experience, causality, will, time. I believe all these notions to be inexact and approximate, essentially infected with vagueness, incapable of forming part of any exact science.[h]

The last phrase is important. Science had the place in Russell's thought that common sense had in Moore's. But whereas Moore used analysis to restore our confidence in common sense, a confidence that has been shaken by philosophical confusion, Russell used analysis to purify science and purge it of the errors to which, as the heir of common sense, it was the unwitting victim.

> There are two different ways in which a philosophy may seek to base itself upon science. It may emphasize the most general *results* of

science, and seek to give even greater generality and unity to these results. Or it may study the *methods* of science, and seek to apply these
methods, with the necessary adaptations, to its own peculiar province.
Much philosophy inspired by science has gone astray through preoccupation with the *results* momentarily supposed to have been achieved. It
is not results, but *methods,* that can be transferred with profit from the
sphere of the special sciences to the sphere of philosophy. . . .

The special sciences have all grown up by the use of notions derived
from common sense, such as things and their qualities, space, time, and
causation. Science itself has shown that none of these common-sense
notions will quite serve for the explanation of the world; but it is hardly
the province of any special science to undertake the necessary reconstruction of fundamentals. This must be the business of philosophy. . . .
I believe that the philosophical errors in common-sense beliefs not only
produce confusion in science, but also do harm in ethics and politics, in
social institutions, and in the conduct of everyday life.[i]

This passage sounds very much like Dewey's attack on traditional philosophy,
but though Dewey and Russell both recommended that philosophy adopt the
methods of science, they perceived these methods quite differently. For Dewey
the important element in scientific method was its experimentalism and its tenta-
tiveness. He was not only content with provisional and probable conclusions; he
would have deeply distrusted conclusions of any other kind. Russell, in contrast,
believed that the sciences yield, or can yield, the truth about things. Hence his
criticisms of the traditional metaphysics consisted in arguing that its conclusions
about the world were *false*—not, as with Dewey, that they were neither true nor
false but merely fictions generated by the human quest for certainty.

CRITICISM OF TRADITIONAL METAPHYSICS

As has already been seen, in Russell's view the ascription of predicates to
subjects is but one of many logical relations. The old logic's restriction of "form"
to this relation is only one example of the pernicious influence of ordinary language on philosophy. It is "doubtful" whether the subject-predicate logic "would
have been invented by a people speaking a non-Aryan language," yet this subject-
predicate logic gave rise to a substance-attribute metaphysics that left philosophers no other option than that between Spinozistic monism and Leibnizian
pluralism.[16]

Further, the subject-predicate logic forced philosophers to deny the reality
of space and time; it therefore "rendered them incapable of giving any account
of the world of science and daily life." As we have seen, spatial relations (above,

[16] See p. 175.

below) and temporal relations (before, after) are transitive and cannot be reduced to subject-predicate relations.[17] Hence philosophers who cling to the old logic must deny spatial and temporal relations.

> Asymmetrical relations are involved in all series—in space and time, greater and less, whole and part, and many others of the most important characteristics of the actual world. All these aspects, therefore, the logic which reduces anything to subjects and predicates is compelled to condemn as error and mere appearance. To those whose logic is not malicious, such a wholesale condemnation appears impossible.[j]

Leibniz and Spinoza were among those whose metaphysics was "shattered" by the discoveries of mathematical logic, but in Russell's view Hegel was the worst offender. Consider the crucial concept of identity-in-difference:

> Hegel's argument . . . depends throughout upon confusing the "is" of predication, as in "Socrates is mortal," with the "is" of identity, as in "Socrates is the philosopher who drank the hemlock." Owing to this confusion, he thinks that "Socrates" and "mortal" must be identical. Seeing that they are different, he does not infer, as others would, that there is a mistake somewhere, but that they exhibit "identity in difference." Again, Socrates is particular, "mortal" is universal. Therefore, he says, since Socrates is mortal, it follows that the particular is the universal—taking the "is" to be throughout expressive of identity. But to say "the particular is the universal" is self-contradictory. Again Hegel does not suspect a mistake, but proceeds to synthesise particular and universal in the individual, or concrete universal. This is an example of how, for want of care at the start, vast and imposing systems of philosophy are built upon stupid and trivial confusions, which, but for the almost incredible fact that they are unintentional, one would be tempted to characterise as puns.[k]

Though Russell's main attack was directed against rationalistic metaphysics and its claim "that by mere thinking . . . the whole of reality could be established with a certainty which no contrary observations could shake,"[l] this was merely because he regarded it as his most formidable and most plausible antagonist. He had no more use for rationalism's rivals—pragmatism and Bergsonianism.

CRITICISM OF PRAGMATISM

> As applied to the general hypotheses of science and religion, there is a great deal to be said for [pragmatism]. Given a careful definition of

---

[17] See pp. 142–43.

what is meant by "working," and a proviso that the cases concerned are those where we do not really know the truth, there is no need to quarrel with the doctrine in this region. . . .

In practice, however, pragmatism has a more sinister side. The truth, it says, is what pays in the way of beliefs. Now a belief may be made to pay through the operation of the criminal law. In the seventeenth century, Catholicism paid in Catholic countries and Protestantism in Protestant countries. Energetic people can manufacture "truth" by getting hold of the Government and persecuting opinions other than their own.[m]

In short, Russell shared pragmatism's skepticism about whatever is not accessible to science, for example, rationalistic metaphysics and dogmatic theology. Like the pragmatists, he held that the "truth" of assertions in such fields is related to emotional and temperamental needs. But he was unwilling to accept the kind of account of "experience" Dewey gave,[18] for he wanted to draw a sharp distinction between beliefs and facts. Beliefs, he held, are "vague and complex"; facts are just precisely whatever they are. Beliefs do depend on "human occurrences"; they are relative to cultural conditions; and so on. But facts are "only within our control to a certain very limited extent, as regards some of the minor circumstances on or near the surface of a certain planet." The pragmatists went wrong first by confusing beliefs with facts[19] and then by concentrating their attention on events at or near the earth's surface. Such events are doubtless of great practical importance to men and women, but a sound theory of knowledge cannot be based on them alone. Since many facts have no relevance to us and our needs, a sound theory of knowledge must admit that truth resides in correspondence rather than in "workability"—in the correspondence of our beliefs to the facts of the case.

CRITICISM OF BERGSONIANISM

Despite its inadequacy as a theory of knowledge and its dangerous social implications, pragmatism "has certain important merits." But according to Russell there is nothing whatever to be said in favor of Bergsonianism:

> A great part of Bergson's philosophy is merely traditional mysticism expressed in slightly novel language. The doctrine of interpenetration, according to which different things are not really separate, but are merely so conceived by the analytic intellect, is to be found in every mystic, eastern or western, from Parmenides to [the Hegelians]. . . .
>
> In this part of his philosophy, apart from phraseology, Bergson has added nothing to Plotinus. The invention of the phraseology certainly

[18] See pp. 47 and 54–55.
[19] From Russell's point of view, this was another trouble with the Hegelians.

shows great ability, but it is that of the company-promoter rather than the philosopher. . . .

[But] if one might venture to apply to Bergson's philosophy so vulgar a thing as logic, certain difficulties would appear in this [adaptation]. If the new elements which are added in later states of the world are not external to the old elements, there is no genuine novelty, creative evolution has created nothing, and we are back in the system of Plotinus. Of course Bergson's answer to this dilemma is that what happens is "growth" [that is, "duration"], in which everything changes and yet remains the same. This conception, however, is a mystery, which the profane cannot hope to fathom.[n]

Philosophy as Synthesis

From criticism we turn to synthesis. As we have seen, Russell assigned synthesis a less important role than criticism. This assessment accorded with the temper of the times, which, in reaction to the system building of the nineteenth century, was ready to settle for positive results, however small and modest these might be. Russell certainly shared this temper. Thus, he roundly declared that the main business of philosophy "consists in criticizing and clarifying notions which are apt to be regarded as fundamental and accepted uncritically."[o] And when he was attacking the metaphysical syntheses of others he insisted that "the type of philosophy that I wish to advocate . . . represents . . . the substitution of piecemeal, detailed, and verifiable results for large untested generalities recommended only by a certain appeal to imagination."[p] But, despite these disclaimers, Russell was deeply interested in metaphysics. It was, as we have seen, the pursuit of certainty that had originally launched him into philosophical inquiry. Here, then, as so often, Russell's attitude was complex and ambivalent. There is in fact a tension running through all of his writings between criticism, at which he was a master, and synthesis, about which he was forever having to change his mind but which, nonetheless, he was unwilling to give up. We may suspect, therefore, that his assessment of the relative importance of criticism and synthesis is an expression of what he was gradually forced to conclude could be achieved rather than of what he had originally hoped might be accomplished.

LOGICAL CONSTRUCTION

For a philosopher in quest of certainty synthesis starts from indubitables; for a philosopher in the analytic tradition synthesis starts from simples; for a philosopher who draws a fundamental distinction between acquaintance and knowledge about, synthesis starts from entities with which we are directly acquainted.

Putting these together, we can say that for Russell synthesis started from simples with which we are directly acquainted and which, therefore, are indubitable. The aim of inquiry, then, is to ascertain which of our manifold beliefs about the world—both those of common sense and those of science—are true, and this amounts to ascertaining whether the objects of these beliefs can be analyzed into still simpler entities with which we are directly acquainted.

> When there is anything with which we do not have immediate acquaintance, but only definition by denoting phrases,, then the propositions in which this thing is introduced by means of a denoting phrase do not really contain this thing as a constituent, but contain instead the constituents expressed by the several words of the denoting phrase. Thus in every proposition that we can apprehend (i.e. not only in those whose truth or falsehood we can judge of, but in all that we can think about), all the constituents are really entities with which we have immediate acquaintance. Now such things as matter (in the sense in which matter occurs in physics) and the minds of other people are known to us only be denoting phrases, i.e. we are not *acquainted* with them, but we know them as what has such and such properties. Hence, although we can form propositional functions $C(x)$ which must hold of such and such a material particle, or of So-and-so's mind, yet we are not acquainted with the propositions which affirm these things that we know must be true, because we cannot apprehend the actual entities concerned. What we know is "So-and-so has a mind which has such and such properties" but we do not know "A has such and such properties," where A *is* the mind in question. In such a case, we know the properties of a thing without having acquaintance with the thing itself, and without, consequently, knowing any single proposition of which the thing itself is a constituent.[q]

It seemed obvious to Russell that we are not directly acquainted with electrons, protons, or other "scientific" objects, and that they are inferred entities. But no more are we—and here Russell differed from Moore—directly acquainted with the objects of commonsense experience. When a dog crosses my path and I notice it, I am not directly acquainted with the dog, but only with "a canoid patch of colour."[r] The expression "the dog" is a denoting phrase, and the dog is an inferred entity, just as the expressions "the electron" and "the proton" are denoting phrases, and the electrons and protons are inferred entities.

We may now rephrase the aim of inquiry. In accordance with the principle of Occam's razor, we want to reduce to a minimum the number of kinds of simple entities that have to be admitted into the inventory of the universe. We do this by showing that entities with which we may seem to be directly acquainted are in fact only inferred and so are reducible to more-ultimate entities: we do not, for instance, have to include dogs and cats in the inventory, but only canoid and feloid patches of color. On the other hand, we want to be able to show that the inferences involved in the "construction" of dogs and cats, electrons and protons, are justified. Otherwise we would have to conclude that our beliefs about all of these entities are unwarranted. This double enterprise is what Russell called logical construction.[20]

RUSSELL'S INITIAL VIEW

At the outset Russell held that what we are directly acquainted with are universals and particulars. And since nominalism denies the existence of universals, it was necessary for him not only to prove that there are universals but to show that we are directly acquainted with some universals. The nominalist case against universals is that universals are redundant. We do not need a universal yellow of which each particular yellow is an instance; we need only the set of particular colors that are similar to each other in a certain respect, namely their yellowness.

> In order to make the theory of Berkeley and Hume workable, [the nominalist] must assume an ultimate relation of colour-likeness, which holds between two patches which would commonly be said to have the same colour. Now, prima facie, this relation of colour-likeness will itself be a universal or an "abstract idea," and thus we shall still have failed to avoid universals. But we may apply the same analysis to colour-likeness. We may take a standard particular case of colour-likeness, and say that anything else is to be called a colour-likeness if it is exactly like our standard case. It is obvious, however, that such a process leads to an endless regress: we explain the likeness of two terms as consisting in the likeness which their likeness bears to the likeness of two other terms, and such a regress is plainly vicious. Likeness at least, therefore, must be admitted as a universal, and, having admitted one universal, we have no longer any reason to reject others. Thus the whole complicated theory, which had no motive except to avoid universals, falls to the ground. Whether or not there are particulars, there must be relations which are universals in the sense that (a) they are concepts, not percepts; (b) they do not exist in time; (c) they are verbs, not substantives.[s]

[20] It is important not to confuse construction in Russell's sense with the radically different constructivism of idealism, which was anathema to Russell. What Russell meant is better suggested by "reduction," "elimination," or "symbolic substitution." Whereas the idealists held that experience is a product of mental activity and is in that sense a construction, Russell held that nouns such as "dog" and "electron" are as much descriptions as "present king of France" and "author of *Waverley*"—they do not directly denote but can be analyzed into elements that do denote. Construction, in Russell's sense, is the process of carrying out this analysis.

In other words, the nominalists' own argument against such universals as yellow or blue presupposes the existence of at least one other universal, namely, similarity. As regards the question whether we are ever directly acquainted with universals, Russell held that we are certainly directly acquainted with such rational universals as "above," "larger than," and "earlier than." For instance, when we hear the bang of an explosion after we have seen the flash, we are directly acquainted with the universal "later than."

As regards particulars, at this time Russell held that we are acquainted with sense data, with the "I" who is aware of the sense data, and with the various mental states of this "I," its believings, hopings, doubtings, and the like. The ultimate constituents of the universe, then, are neither the physical objects (tables, chairs, sun, moon) of ordinary experience nor the "scientific" objects of physical theory (electrons, protons). They are

> a multitude of entities which . . . I shall call "particulars.". . . The particulars are to be conceived, not on the analogy of bricks in a building, but rather on the analogy of notes in a symphony. The ultimate constituents of a symphony (apart from relations) are the notes, each of which lasts only for a very short time. We may collect together all the notes played by one instrument: these may be regarded as the analogues of the successive particulars which common sense would regard as successive states of one "thing." But the "thing" ought to be regarded as no more "real" or "substantial" than, for example, the role of the trombone.[t]

Since each note, in this analogy, corresponds to a sense datum that some observer has directly experienced, a physical object, for instance, the moon, is not the single, persistent entity located some 250,000 miles away from us; the moon is a vast assemblage of sense data of many different shapes, sizes, and colors—the assemblage that all possible observers have experienced and will yet experience of the moon. Each observer's sense data fall into a pattern, or "perspective," like the pattern of notes that constitute the role of the trombone. My sense data of the moon are within my private three-dimensional spatial perspective, and every other observer's are within his or her private perspective, but all of these private spaces fit into the public space of the real world.

> What physics regards as the sun of eight minutes ago will be a whole assemblage of particulars, existing at different times, spreading out from a centre with the velocity of light, and containing among their number all those visual data which are seen by people who are now looking at the sun. Thus the sun of eight minutes ago is a class of particulars, and what I see when I now look at the sun in one member of this class. The various particulars constituting this class will be correlated with each other by a certain continuity and certain intrinsic laws of variation as we pass outwards from the centre. . . .

The *prima facie* difficulties in the way of this view are chiefly derived from an unduly conventional theory of space. It might seem at first sight as if we had packed the world much fuller than it could possibly hold. . . . Throughout the world, everywhere, there will be an enormous number of particulars co-existing in the same place. But these troubles result from contenting ourselves too readily with the merely three-dimensional space to which schoolmasters have accustomed us. The space of the real world is a space of six dimensions,[21] and as soon as we realize this we see that there is plenty of room for all the particulars for which we want to find positions. In order to realise this we have only to return for a moment from the polished space of physics to the rough and untidy space of our immediate sensible experience. The space of one man's sensible objects is a three-dimensional space. It does not appear probable that two men ever both perceive at the same time any one sensible object; when they are said to see the same thing or hear the same noise, there will always be some difference, however slight, between the actual shapes seen or the actual sounds heard. . . . There are therefore a multitude of three-dimensional spaces in the world: there are all those perceived by observers, and presumably also those which are not perceived, merely because no observer is suitably situated for perceiving them.

But although these spaces do not have to one another the same kind of spatial relations as obtain between the parts of one of them, it is nevertheless possible to arrange these spaces themselves in a three-dimensional order. . . .

There are two ways of classifying particulars: we may take together all those that belong to a given "perspective," or all those that are, as common sense would say, different "aspects" of the same "thing." For example, if I am (as is said) seeing the sun, what I see belongs to two assemblages: (1) the assemblage of all my present objects of sense, which is what I call a "perspective"; (2) the assemblage of all the different particulars which would be called aspects of the sun of eight minutes ago—this assemblage is what I define as *being* the sun of eight minutes ago. Thus "perspectives" and "things" are merely two different ways of classifying particulars.[u]

Similarly, for time, just as every physical object occupies, or lies along, a vast series of spatial perspectives, so every physical object endures through a vast

[21] [Russell is not adding two mysterious new dimensions to the four-dimensional space-time continuum. The six dimensions specified here are simply the minimum number of coordinates needed to order all of the particulars (each of which is itself ordered in its own three-dimensional array) in a single array. As Russell says, "Six coordinates will be required to assign its position in its own space and three more to assign the position of its space among the other spaces" (p. 134)—AUTHORS.]

series of "biographies." For instance, in each of these biographies the sense data that, collectively, are the moon occur at times that are earlier than, later than, or simultaneous with other sense data. But in different biographies the temporal order may be different. In my biography a particular sound may occur a moment earlier than the glimpse that I catch of the moon. In your biography the sound may occur a moment later than your glimpse of the moon. But these biographies, with their private temporal orders, can be correlated into a public time.

> The one all-embracing time, like the one all-embracing space, is a construction; there is no *direct* time-relation between particulars belonging to my perspective and particulars belonging to another man's. On the other hand, any two particulars of which I am aware are either simultaneous or successive, and their simultaneity or successiveness is sometimes itself a datum to me. We may therefore define the perspective to which a given particular belongs as "all particulars simultaneous with the given particular," where "simultaneous" is to be understood as a direct simple relation, not the derivative constructed relation of physics. . . .
> The sum-total of all the particulars that are (directly) either simultaneous with or before or after a given particular may be defined as the "biography" to which that particular belongs. It will be observed that, just as a perspective need not be actually perceived by any one, so a biography need not be actually lived by any one. Those biographies that are lived by no one are called "official."[v]

This witticism about official biographies—so characteristic of Russell—presupposes the realistic stance that Russell shared with Moore. That is, there are temporal and spatial perspectives in which no one happens to live, and in these perspectives there occur sense data that are real, even though no one happens to experience them. But whereas Moore held that physical objects (the moon, the dog that crosses my path) are independent existents as well as sense data, Russell held that physical objects are "logical constructions" (or "logical fictions"). They are not, however, mind-dependent in the way that idealism held them to be. For, though it is true that they are only "classes or series of particulars collected together on account of some property which makes it convenient to be able to speak of them as wholes," the particulars that are the members of the classes in question are not to be construed as in any sense "mental."[w]

> When I see a flash of lightning, my seeing of it is mental, but what I see, although it is not quite the same as what anybody else sees at the same moment, . . . is not mental. I maintain . . . that if my body could remain in exactly the same state in which it is, although my mind had ceased to exist, precisely that object which I now see when I see the flash would exist, although of course I should not see it, since my seeing is mental.[x]

This analysis enabled Russell to give an account of what, and where, hallucinations and illusions are. The dagger that Macbeth saw and could not touch was just as real, no more and no less, than the dagger that he wore at his side. It differed from that dagger only in that the sense data constituting it did not fit into any perspective; it was, therefore, objective, but "wild."[y] There is no a priori necessity that every sense datum fit into some perspective or other.

> I have talked so far about the unreality of the things we think real. I want to speak with equal emphasis about the reality of things we think unreal, such as phantoms and hallucinations. Phantoms and hallucinations, considered in themselves, are . . . on exactly the same level as ordinary sense-data. They differ from ordinary sense-data only in the fact that they do not have the usual correlations with other things. In themselves they have the same reality as ordinary sense-data. They have the most complete and absolute and perfect reality that anything can have. They are part of the ultimate constituents of the world, just as the fleeting sense-data are. Speaking of the fleeting sense-data, I think it is very important to remove out of one's instincts any disposition to believe that the real is the permanent. There has been a metaphysical prejudice always that if a thing is really real, it has to last either forever or for a fairly decent length of time. That is to my mind an entire mistake. The things that are really real last a very short time. Again I am not denying that there *may* be things that last forever, or for thousands of years; I only say that those are not within our experience, and that the real things that we know by experience last for a very short time, one tenth or half a second, or whatever it may be. Phantoms and hallucinations are among those, among the ultimate constituents of the world. The things that we call real, like tables and chairs, are systems, series of classes of particulars, and the particulars are the real things, the particulars being sense-data when they happen to be given to you.[z]

Moore's worry[22] about where the gray sense data of a color-blind man are located can be dealt with in the same way. These data lie in the private three-dimensional space of the color-blind man, which (along with the private three-dimensional spaces of individuals with normal vision) fits into the public six-dimensional space.

This, then, in brief is Russell's early metaphysics. He did not claim that it "is *certainly* true," but only that "it *may* be true. . . . I recommend it to attention as a hypothesis and a basis for further work."[a]

But is this hypothesis plausible enough to be adopted as a basis for further work? One's answer to this question probably depends in large part on one's attitude toward common sense. Certainly it is, as Moore would way, "Pickwickian."[23]

[22] See p. 115.
[23] See p. 114.

And beyond this it might also be thought that a theory that reduces physical objects to "constructions" is hardly consonant with that "robust sense of reality" that, according to Russell's own account, caused his revulsion from idealism. However this may be, the view that we have just described did not long survive Russell's own application of Occam's razor to the list of basic entities. He was, as we shall now see, to move further from the realistic thesis that he originally shared with Moore.

NEUTRAL MONISM

Realism is essentially dualistic: there are minds and there is an independent world of objects that minds contemplate. In the view we have just sketched, Russell has already dissolved the independent objects into "particulars," but an attenuated dualism persists: there are minds, on the one hand, and sense data, on the other. It is true that other people's minds are, like physical objects, inferred entities that we have knowledge about by means of descriptive phrases.[24] But the "I" that encounters the sense data and the mental states of this "I" are still held to be particulars and are included in the inventory of the universe.

These were the next to go, converted by means of logical analysis into inferred entities, thereby reducing the number of types of basic entity with which we are directly acquainted.

> Sensations are obviously the source of our knowledge of the world, including our own body. It might seem natural to regard a sensation as itself a cognition, and until lately I did so regard it. . . . This view, however, demands the admission of [a conscious] subject, or act [of awareness]. . . . If there is a subject, it can have a relation to the patch of colour, namely, the sort of relation which we might call awareness. In that case, the sensation, as a mental event, will consist of awareness of the colour, while the colour itself will remain wholly physical, and may be called the sense-datum, to distinguish it from the sensation. The subject, however, appears to be a logical fiction, like mathematical points and instants. It is introduced, not because observation reveals it, but because it is linguistically convenient and apparently demanded by grammar. Nominal entities of this sort may or may not exist, but there is no good ground for assuming that they do. The functions that they appear to perform can always be performed by classes or series or other logical constructions, consisting of less dubious entities. If we are to avoid a perfectly gratuitous assumption, we must dispense with the subject as one of the actual ingredients of the world.[b]

If we eliminate the subject, the whole dualistic distinction between the mental and the nonmental can be dispensed with. The ultimate constituent of the

24 See pp. 191–92.

universe is a "neutral stuff" out of which both minds and physical objects can be constructed. The neutral entities are like the names in a postal directory in which the same names occur in two listings, one alphabetical, one geographical. "We may compare the alphabetical order to the mental and the geographical order to the physical." Russell has now adopted James's "neutral monism,"[25] a view that, earlier on, he had severely criticized.

You all know the American theory of neutral monism, which derives really from William James and is also suggested in the work of Mach, but in a rather less developed form. The theory of neutral monism maintains that the distinction between the mental and the physical is entirely an affair of arrangement, that the actual material arranged is exactly the same in the case of the mental as it is in the case of the physical, but they differ merely in the fact that when you take a thing as belonging in the same context with certain other things, it will belong to psychology, while when you take it in a certain other context with other things, it will belong to physics, and the difference is as to what you consider to be its context. . . . It is just like rows or columns: in an arrangement of rows and columns, you can take an item as either a member of a certain row or a member of a certain column; the item is the same in the two cases, but its context is different.

[As an example, consider] . . . the appearances that a chair presents. If we take any one of these chairs, we can all look at it, and it presents a different appearance to each of us. Taken all together, taking all the different appearances that that chair is presenting to all of us at this moment, you get something that belongs to physics. So that, if one takes sense-data and arranges together all those sense-data that appear to different people at a given moment and are such as we should ordinarily say are appearances of the same physical object, then that class of sense-data will give you something that belongs to physics, namely, the chair at this moment. On the other hand, if instead of taking all the appearances that that chair presents to all of us at this moment, I take all the appearances that the different chairs in this room present to me at this moment, I get quite another group of particulars. All the different appearances that different chairs present to me now will give you something belonging to psychology, because that will give you my experiences at the present moment. Broadly speaking . . . that should be the definition of the difference between physics and psychology. . . .

There is no simple entity that you can point to and say: this entity is physical and not mental. According to William James and neutral monists that will not be the case with any simple entity that you may take. Any such entity will be a member of physical series and a member of mental series. . . .

[25] See Vol. IV, pp. 299–303.

I ought to proceed to tell you that I have discovered whether neutral monism is true or not, because otherwise you may not believe that logic is any use in the matter. But I do not profess to know whether it is true or not. I feel more and more inclined to think that it may be true.[c]

Next to go are particulars, which are replaced by qualities:

I propose to abolish what are usually called "particulars," and be content with certain words that would usually be regarded as universals, such as "red," "blue," "hard," "soft," and so on. . . .

I wish to suggest that . . . what would commonly be called a "thing" is nothing but a bundle of co-existing qualities such as redness, hardness, etc. . . .

Let us give the name "qualities" to specific shades of colour, specific degrees of hardness, sounds completely defined as to pitch and loudness and every other distinguishable characteristic, and so on. Although we cannot, in perception, distinguish exact from approximate similarity, whether in colour or in any other kind of quality, we can, by experience, be led to the conception of exact similarity, since it is transitive, whereas approximate similarity is not. . . .

Common sense regards a "thing" as having qualities, but not as defined by them; it is defined by spatio-temporal position. I wish to suggest that, wherever there is, for common sense, a "thing" having the quality C, we should say, instead, that C itself exists in that place, and that the "thing" is to be replaced by the collection of qualities existing in the place in question. Thus "C" becomes a name, not a predicate.

The main reason in favour of this view is that it gets rid of an unknowable. We experience qualities, but not the subject in which they are supposed to inhere. The introduction of an unknowable can generally, perhaps always, be avoided by suitable technical devices, and clearly it should be avoided whenever possible.[d]

RUSSELL'S "FINAL" VIEW

Reality has become thinner and more attenuated, under the applications of Occam's razor. But the process did not stop at this point. We conclude this brief account of the changes in Russell's view with some passages from "My Present View of the World." Though it was published in 1959, when he was eighty-seven, the title characteristically suggests that further changes were still possible. It is to be noted that Russell not unnaturally regarded all these changes as a consistent logical development, not as the series of twists and turns that critics perceive them to be.

The view to which I have been gradually led is one which has been almost universally misunderstood and which, for this reason, I will try to state as simply and clearly as I possibly can. . . . It is a view which results from a synthesis of four different sciences—namely, physics, physiology, psychology and mathematical logic. . . .

What sort of picture of the universe do these [sciences] invite us to construct? . . . For present purposes I shall content myself by treating as fundamental the notion of "event." I conceive each event as occupying a finite amount of space-time and as overlapping with innumerable other events which occupy partially, but not wholly, the same region of space-time. . . .

The world of which we have been speaking hitherto is entirely an inferred world. We do not perceive the sort of entities that physics talks of. . . .

But our world is not wholly a matter of inference. There are things that we know without asking the opinion of men of science. If you are too hot or too cold, you can be perfectly aware of this fact without asking the physicist what heat and cold consist of. . . .

We may give the name "data" to all the things of which we are aware without inference. They include all our observed sensations—visual, auditory, tactile, etc. Common sense sees reason to attribute many of our sensations to causes outside our own bodies. . . .

I maintain an opinion which all other philosophers find shocking: namely, that people's thoughts are in their heads. The light from a star travels over intervening space and causes a disturbance in the optic nerve ending in an occurrence in the brain. What I maintain is that the occurrence in the brain *is* a visual sensation. . . . If the location of events in physical space-time is to be effected, as I maintain, by causal relations, then your percept, which comes after events in the eye and optic nerve leading into the brain, must be located in your brain. . . .

We may define a "mind" as a collection of events connected with each other by memory-chains backwards and forwards. We know about one such collection of events—namely, that constituting ourself—more intimately and directly than we know about anything else in the world. In regard to what happens to ourself, we know not only abstract logical structure, but also qualities—by which I mean what characterizes sounds as opposed to colours, or red as opposed to green. This is the sort of thing that we cannot know where the physical world is concerned.

There are three key points in the above theory. The first is that the entities that occur in mathematical physics are not part of the stuff of the world, but are constructions composed of events and taken as units for the convenience of the mathematician. The second is that the whole of what we perceive without inference belongs to our private world. . . . The third point is that the causal lines which enable us to be aware of a diversity of objects, though there are some such lines everywhere, are apt to peter out like rivers in the sand. That is why we do not at all times perceive everything.

I do not pretend that the above theory can be proved. What I contend is that, like the theories of physics, it cannot be disproved, and gives an answer to many problems which older theorists have found puzzling. I do not think that any prudent person will claim more than this for any theory.[e]

After all the twists and turns of this long development, a number of themes persisted. First, there was the distinction between hard and soft data, between entities with which we are directly acquainted and inferred entities that we know only by description. Second, there was the attempt, for the sake of simplicity, to reduce the number of kinds of hard data to a minimum. Third, there was the attempt to show that our inferences from hard data to soft data—our inferences from entities with which we are directly acquainted to the inferred entities—are warranted. If inquiry starts from entities that we can surely know because we are directly acquainted with them, and if it proceeds by means of warranted inferences, though our quest for certainty may not be *fully* satisfied, it will be as nearly satisfied as is possible in this world.

But *are* the inferences on which Russell's whole synthesis depends warranted? Here we must distinguish between (1) particular inferences to particular conclusions, to which differing degrees of probability might be assigned depending on the evidence for each, and (2) the basic form of inference from hard to soft data. Obviously, it is the latter that is the fundamental question for Russell's whole program. As he himself put it, "The problem really is: Can the existence of anything other than our own hard data be inferred from the existence of those data?"[f]

NONDEMONSTRATIVE INFERENCE

Restated, the problem is that "if we know only what can be experienced and verified,"[g] most of what passes for knowledge, and what everybody confidently believes is knowledge, is not knowledge at all. If we know only what can be verified in experience, we know, for instance, only canoid color patches, not dogs. Even though we are perfectly confident that a dog, not merely a canoid color patch, is approaching us, we cannot be *certain* that this is so. Or, to take another example, "if at one moment, you see your cat on the hearth-rug and, at another you see it in a doorway," you are doubtless confident that it "has passed over intermediate positions although you did not see it doing it."[h] Nevertheless, you do not *know* that it did. Or again,

suppose you are walking out-of-doors on a sunny day; your shadow walks with you; if you wave your arms, your shadow waves it arms; if you jump, your shadow jumps; for such reasons you unhesitatingly call it *your* shadow and you have no doubt whatever that it has a causal connection with your body. But, although the inference is one which no sane man would question, it is not logically demonstrative. It is not logically impossible that there should be a dark patch going through movements not unlike the movements of your body, but having an independent existence of its own.[i]

It was considerations of this kind that led Russell to examine the problem of nondemonstrative, or nondeductive, inference. Clearly, deductive inference, to which he had earlier devoted so much attention, is of very limited scope, being confined to logic and pure mathematics, and "all the inferences used both in common sense and in science are of a very different sort."[j] But what are the principles underlying this latter sort of inference—such as the inference from a canoid color patch to a dog or from my body to my shadow? What must be the case about the world for nondeductive inferences of the kinds we constantly make to be warranted? And what grounds do we have for holding that what must (logically) be the case is indeed the case—that is, that nondeductive inference *is* warranted?

Russell's procedure was first to collect instances (such as those just given) "where we make inferences that we feel to be quite valid," and then to "discover by analysis what extra-logical principles must be true if we are not mistaken in such cases. The evidence in favor of the principles is derived from the instances and not vice versa."[k] For instance, if we are not mistaken in our inference about the cat's movement from hearth-rug to doorway, there must be (in some sense) enduring things, and the cat must be one of them. If we are not mistaken in our inference from our bodies to our shadows, there must be causal lines in nature, and so on. Can such admittedly vague notions as "thing" and "cause" be made more precise? Russell thought that they could be, and in an attempt to do so he formulated five principles, or postulates, that underlie nondemonstrative inference. "The purpose of my postulates is to substitute something more precise and more effective in the place of such vague principles" as "causality" and "the uniformity of nature."[l]

He called the first of his five postulates "the postulate of quasi-permanence":

> The chief use of this postulate is to replace the common-sense notion of "thing" and "person" in a manner not involving the concept of "substance." The postulate may be enunciated as follows:
> *Given any event A, it happens very frequently that, at any neighboring time, there is at some neighboring place an event very similar to A.*
> A "thing" is a series of such events. It is because such series of events are common that "thing" is a practically convenient concept.[m]

He called his second principle "the postulate of separable causal lines":

> This postulate has many uses, but perhaps the most important is in connection with perception—for example, in attributing the multiplicity of our visual sensations in looking at the night sky to a multitude of stars as their causes. The postulate may be enunciated as follows:

> *It is frequently possible to form a series of events such that from one or two members of the series something can be inferred as to all the other members.*
>
> The most obvious example is motion, particularly unimpeded motion such as that of a photon in interstellar space.[n]

The third postulate is that of "spatio-temporal continuity":

> This postulate is concerned to deny "action at a distance," and to assert that when there is a causal connection between two events that are not contiguous, there must be intermediate links in the causal chain such that each is contiguous to the next, or (alternatively) such that there is a process which is continuous in the mathematical sense. . . . This postulate presupposes causal lines, and is only applicable to them.[o]

Russell's fourth principle is called "the structural postulate":

> *When a number of structurally similar complex events are ranged about a center in regions not widely separated, it is usually the case that all belong to causal lines having their origin in an event of the same structure at the center. . . .*
>
> The phrase "grouped about a center" is intentionally vague, but in certain cases it is capable of a precise meaning. Suppose a given object to be simultaneously seen by a number of people and photographed by a number of cameras. The visual percepts and the photographs can be arranged by the laws of perspective, and by the same laws the position of the object seen and photographed can be determined.[p]

The last postulate—"the postulate of analogy"—is:

> Given two classes of events A and B, and given that, whenever both A and B can be observed, there is reason to believe that A causes B, then if, in a given case, A is observed, but there is no way of observing whether B occurs or not, it is probable that B occurs; and similarly if B is observed, but the presence or absence of A cannot be observed.[q]

Here, then, are the five postulates that, according to Russell, underlie non-demonstrative inference. Russell did not claim to have formulated them absolutely correctly; he merely claimed that postulates of this general sort are needed to justify such inference.

> I feel no great confidence in the precise postulates above enumerated, but I feel considerable confidence that something of the same sort is necessary if we are to justify the non-demonstrative inferences concerning which none of us, in fact, can feel any doubt.[r]

Granted that principles of this general sort are needed if nondemonstrative inference is warranted, the question is whether we have, or can ever have, evidence that the principles are true, and so that nondemonstrative inference is warranted. That is to say, it is one thing to show that such-and-such principles are needed *if* nondemonstrative inference is warranted; it is another thing to show that, *because* these principles are true, nondemonstrative inference is warranted. Though Russell had to allow that the principles "cannot be proved in any formal sense,"[s] he held that we may nonetheless be said to know them, rather than merely believe them or hope them to be true. How can this be?

> In what sense can we be said to "know" the above postulates, or whatever substitutes may hereafter be found preferable? . . . Knowledge of general connections between facts is more different than is usually supposed from knowledge of particular facts. Knowledge of connections between facts has its biological origin in animal expectations. An animal which experiences an A expects a B; when it evolves into a primitive man of science it sums up a number of particular expectations in the statement "A causes B." It is biologically advantageous to have such expectations as will usually be verified; it is therefore not surprising if the psychological laws governing expectations are, in the main, in conformity with the objective laws governing expected occurrences.
>
> We may state the matter as follows. The physical world has what may be called "habits," i.e., causal laws; the behavior of animals has habits, partly innate, partly acquired. The acquired habits are generated by what I call "animal inference," which occurs when there are the data for an induction, but not in all cases where there are such data. Owing to the world being such as it is, certain kinds of induction are justified and others are not. If our inductive propensities were perfectly adapted to our environment, we should only be prone to an induction if the case were of the sort which would make the induction legitimate. . . .
>
> I think, therefore, that we may be said to "know" what is necessary for scientific inference, given that it fulfills the following conditions: (1) it is true, (2) we believe it, (3) it leads to no conclusions which experience confutes, (4) it is logically necessary if any occurrence or set of occurrences is ever to afford evidence in favor of any other occurrence. I maintain that these conditions are satisfied.[t]

Doubtless, as Russell says here, the five postulates (or something like them) are "logically necessary if any occurrence or set of occurrences is ever to afford evidence in favor of any other occurrence." They are necessary, that is to say, if science is not "moonshine."[u] But it was Hume's thesis that, for all the evidence to the contrary, science may be moonshine. Hume did not believe that science is moonshine, but he saw no way of *proving* that it may not be. What Russell offers us as evidence that science is not moonshine is the fact that certain expectations (of animals and of scientists) have in the past turned out to be "biologically advantageous." It is easy to understand why animals and scientists with these expectations have survived and perpetuated their kind, and why those with different expectations (or with no expectations) have not survived. But certain expectations having had survival value in the past is not evidence that they will have survival value in the future, unless we assume the uniformity of nature, which is just the point at issue.

To sum up, nondemonstrative inference turns out to differ not qualitatively, but only in scope and stability, from animal inference, but animal inference is not inference in any strict sense. It is merely a matter of possessing advantageous habits, or expectations. However, to talk about our having knowledge, when knowledge is reduced to expectations, is a radical departure from what most scientists and philosophers have meant by knowledge, and it is as radical a departure from what Russell himself, in another mood, insisted that knowledge is. This is why, whenever he claimed that we have knowledge of the five postulates, he tended to put the word in quotation marks. Doing so was in effect an admission that he was using "knowledge" in a Pickwickian sense. Thus, for all that he gave a more rigorous analysis of the notion of the uniformity of nature and a more elaborate account of expectations than Hume and linked this up with Darwinian ideas to show why we have certain expectations and not others, Russell really did not get beyond Hume.

ASSESSMENT OF RUSSELL'S SYNTHESIS

Russell's synthesis involves, as we have seen, distinguishing between logic and pure mathematics, on the one hand, and science (and common sense), on the other. Logic and pure mathematics, being analytic and a priori, gave him no particular trouble, but science, being empirical, was quite another matter for a philosopher who took knowledge claims as seriously as Russell did. The problem was to show that inferences from supposedly hard data to admittedly soft data are warranted. Alternatively, it was to show that empiricism is compatible with claims to a knowledge of general truths about nature. This was the problem that Kant had sought to solve by means of his transcendental deduction of the categories; since Russell's aim was to break out of the Kantian paradigm, it was necessary for him to find another solution. At the end of the discussion of nondemonstrative inference that we have been following, Russell had to admit his failure:

> Although our postulates can . . . be fitted into a framework which has what may be called an empiricist "flavor," it remains undeniable that our knowledge of them, in so far as we do know them, cannot be based upon experience. . . . In this sense, it must be admitted, empiricism as a theory of knowledge has proved inadequate, though less so than any other previous theory of knowledge.[v]

There is thus a conflict at the heart of Russell's whole synthesis. On the one hand, the view that he put forward as a reasonable hypothesis "resulted," as he said, "from a synthesis of four sciences—physics, physiology, psychology and mathematical logic." On the other hand, analysis demonstrated that science is "at war with itself: when it most means to be objective, it finds itself plunged into subjectivity against its will. Naive realism leads to physics, and physics, if true, shows that naive realism is false. Therefore naive realism, if true, is false; therefore it is false."ᵂ

It seems to follow that Russell's account of the "business of philosophy" is mistaken. How can philosophy model itself on science if science is "at war with itself"? Although Russell frequently referred to Descartes and although he probably hoped to play the role in twentieth-century philosophy that Descartes had sought to play—and had failed to bring off—in seventeenth-century philosophy, his doubt was less like Descartes's than like Hume's. It was less a mere methodological tool than it was a settled conviction. Whereas Descartes believed he had established the existence of a real world, Hume knew that he had not. But Hume had been reasonably content with his "mitigated" skepticism. Since Russell, in contrast, hoped that his logical analysis would take him beyond Hume and validate inferences from sense data to the world of physics, Russell was a disappointed Descartes.

Again, though Russell constantly spoke a realistic, objectivist language, his whole position was infected by a subjectivism from which he extricated himself only by an appeal to irrational belief.

> In ontology, I start by accepting the truth of physics. . . . Philosophers may say: What justification have you for accepting the truth of physics? I reply: merely a common-sense basis. . . .
>
> I believe (though without good grounds) in the world of physics as well as in the world of psychology. . . .
>
> If we are to hold that we know anything of the external world, we must accept the canons of scientific knowledge. Whether . . . an individual decides to accept or reject these canons, is a purely personal affair, not susceptible to argument.ˣ

This amounts to making science as subjective as Russell held ethics to be.

Ethics

In Russell's view, there is nothing to be said about ethics as a philosophical theory—though as an activist, a reformer, and an ardent supporter of unpopular causes, he had a great deal to say about ethics as a practical matter and a way of life.

As far as theory goes, then, Russell was very cavalier. "Ethics is traditionally a department of philosophy, and that is my reason for discussing it. I hardly think myself that it ought to be included in the domain of philosophy."[y] The reasons for this attitude are obvious: All our knowledge is limited to science, and "science has nothing to say about values."[z]

> When we assert that this or that has "value," we are giving expression to our own emotions, not to a fact which would still be true if our personal feelings were different. To make this clear, we must try to analyse the conception of the Good. . . .
>
> When a man says "this is good in itself," he *seems* to be making a statement, just as much as if he said "this is square" or "this is sweet." I believe this to be a mistake. I think that what the man really means is: "I wish everybody to desire this," or rather "Would that everybody desired this." If what he says is interpreted as a statement, it is merely an affirmation of his own personal wish; if, on the other hand, it is interpreted in a general way, it states nothing, but merely desires something. The wish, as an occurrence, is personal, but what it desires is universal. It is, I think, this curious interlocking of the particular and the universal which has caused so much confusion in ethics. . . .
>
> The consequences of this doctrine are considerable. . . . Our values have been evolved along with the rest of our constitution, and nothing as to any original purpose can be inferred from the fact that they are what they are.[a]

If Russell's analysis of the nature of ethical statements is correct, he was obviously right in holding that ethics is not a "department" of philosophy. It belongs in the field of propaganda, or (to use a more pleasant word) "persuasion," and the importance of ethics arises because individuals' various desires conflict. Ethics is simply the art of inducing others to desire what we want them to desire.

Let us spell this out in a bit more detail.

> Man is a part of Nature, not something contrasted with Nature. His thoughts and his bodily movements follow the same laws that describe the motions of stars and atoms. The physical world is large compared with Man. . . .
>
> But . . . Nature is only a part of what we can imagine; everything, real or imagined, can be appraised by us, and there is no outside standard to show that our valuation is wrong. We are ourselves the ultimate and irrefutable arbiters of value, and in the world of value Nature is only a part. Thus in this world we are greater than Nature. In the world of values, Nature in itself is neutral, neither good nor bad, deserving of neither admiration nor censure. It is we who create value and our desires which confer value. In this realm we are kings, and we debase our king-

ship if we bow down to Nature. It is for us to determine the good life, not for Nature—not even for Nature personified as God.[b]

Values, then, are not a part of the inventory of the universe, in the way in which redness, blueness, and similarity are parts of that inventory. There are only individual desirings (appreciatings, enjoyings), and these differ markedly from culture to culture.

> When we study in the works of anthropologists the moral precepts which men have considered binding in different times and places we find the most bewildering variety. . . . The Aztecs held that it was a duty to sacrifice and eat enemies captured in war, since otherwise the light of the sun would go out. The Book of Leviticus enjoins that when a married man dies without children his brother shall marry the widow, and the first son born shall count as the dead man's son. The Romans, the Chinese, and many other nations secured a similar result by adoption. This custom originated in ancestor-worship; it was thought that the ghost would make himself a nuisance unless he had descendants (real or putative) to worship him. In India the remarriage of widows is traditionally considered something too horrible to contemplate. Many primitive races feel horror at the thought of marrying anyone belonging to one's own totem, though there may be only the most distant blood-relationship. After studying these various customs it begins at last to occur to the reader that possibly the customs of his own age and nation are not eternal, divine ordinances, but are susceptible of change, and even, in some respects, of improvement. . . .
>
> It is not the province of science to decide on the ends of life. Science can show that an ethic is unscientific, in the sense that it does not minister to any desired end. Science also can show how to bring the interest of the individual into harmony with that of society. We make laws against theft, in order that theft may become contrary to self-interest. We might, on the same ground, make laws to diminish the number of imbecile children born into the world. There is no evidence that existing marriage laws, particularly where they are very strict, serve any social purpose; in this sense we may say that they are unscientific. But to proclaim the ends of life, and make men conscious of their value, is not the business of science; it is the business of the mystic, the artist and the poet.[c]

In other words, when people happen to agree on ends and differ only on means their disagreements are amenable to being reconciled by scientific procedures, that is, by an appeal to empirical evidence. But when they differ regarding ends, no argument, but only persuasion, is possible.

There are two chief ways of winning people over to desiring what we want them to desire: the "way of the legislator" and the "way of the preacher." The legislator persuades people to follow his way of thinking by promulgating a code of laws and punishments and, generally, by instituting "a system of moral instruction." Insofar as he "makes men feel wicked if they pursue other purposes than his" he is successful. The preacher desires to produce the same result (to persuade others to desire what he desires), but since he "does not control the machinery of the State," he must use different means. His appeal is to the emotions (often disguised as an appeal to "evidence"); he knows how, by means of the "moving effect of rhythmical prose," to rouse feelings similar to his own in other minds.[d]

THE GOOD LIFE

It is evident that since Russell was not a legislator he was a preacher. What, then, were the ethical beliefs Russell desired us to accept? His own view was that "the good life is one inspired by love and guided by knowledge." Naturally, he could not prove that his view of the good life was right; he could only state it "and hope that as many as possible will agree."

> Knowledge and love are both indefinitely extensible; therefore, however good a life may be, a better life can be imagined. Neither love without knowledge, nor knowledge without love can produce a good life. In the Middle Ages, when pestilence appeared in a country, holy men advised the population to assemble in churches and pray for deliverance; the result was that the infection spread with extraordinary rapidity among the crowded masses of supplicants. This was an example of love without knowledge. The late war [the First World War] afforded an example of knowledge without love. In each case, the result was death on a large scale.
>
> Although both love and knowledge are necessary, love is in a sense more fundamental. . . .
>
> Love at its fullest is an indissoluble combination of the two elements, delight and well-wishing.[e]

REFORM: SEX, EDUCATION, PROPERTY

It should be obvious now why Russell was a passionate reformer, and his case against contemporary society can be stated succinctly. It was that our social institutions and the lives we live under them are neither animated by love nor guided by knowledge. A few paragraphs from Russell's writings on sex, education, and property will give the flavor of his views on a range of issues. If some of these criticisms and recommendations today seem commonplace, this merely shows how far we have moved from the decades before the Second World War, in which

Russell was writing. It is not unfair to attribute some of the credit for this shift in public opinion to Russell's effectiveness as a "preacher."

First, then, a passage concerning sex from *Marriage and Morals:*

> If sex is not to be an obsession, it should be regarded by the moralists as food has come to be regarded. . . . Sex is a natural human need like food and drink. It is true that men can survive without it, whereas they cannot survive without food and drink, but from a psychological standpoint the desire for sex is precisely analogous to the desire for food and drink. . . . Healthy, outward-looking men and women are not to be produced by the thwarting of natural impulse, but by the equal and balanced development of all the impulses essential to a happy life.
>
> I am not suggesting that there should be no morality and no self-restraint in regard to sex, any more than in regard to food. In regard to food we have restraints of three kinds, those of law, those of manners, and those of health. We regard it as wrong to steal food, to take more than our share at a common meal, and to eat in ways that are likely to make us ill. Restraints of a similar kind are essential where sex is concerned, but in this case they are much more complex and involve much more self-control. Moreover, since one human being ought not to have property in another, the analogue of stealing is not adultery, but rape, which obviously must be forbidden by law. The questions that arise in regard to health are concerned almost entirely with venereal disease.[f]

As for education, since "authority is to some extent unavoidable in dealing with children," it should be balanced by reverence.

> A man who is to educate really well, and is to make the young grow and develop into their full stature, must be filled through and through with the spirit of reverence. It is reverence towards others that is lacking in those who advocate machine-made cast-iron systems: militarism, capitalism, Fabian scientific organization and all the other prisons into which reformers and reactionaries try to force the human spirit. In education, with its codes of rules emanating from a Government office, its large classes and fixed curriculum and overworked teachers, its determination to produce a dead level of glib mediocrity, the lack of reverence for the child is all but universal. Reverence requires imagination and vital warmth; it requires most imagination in respect of those who have least actual achievement or power. . . .
>
> Passive acceptance of the teacher's wisdom is easy to most boys and girls. It involves no effort of independent thought, and seems rational because the teacher knows more than his pupils; it is moreover they way to win the favour of the teacher unless he is a very exceptional man. Yet the habit of passive acceptance is a disastrous one in later life. It

causes men to seek a leader, and to accept as a leader whoever is established in that position. . . .

Above all, there [should] be an endeavour to rouse and stimulate the love of mental adventure. The world in which we live is various and astonishing: some of the things that seem plainest grow more and more difficult the more they are considered; other things, which might have been thought quite impossible to discover, have nevertheless been laid bare by genius and industry. The powers of thought, the vast regions which it can master, the much more vast regions which it can only dimly suggest to imagination, give to those whose minds have travelled beyond the daily round an amazing richness of material, an escape from the triviality and wearisomeness of familiar routine, by which the whole of life is filled with interest, and the prison walls of the commonplace are broken down. . . .

It will be said that the joy of mental adventure must be rare, that there are few who can appreciate it, and that ordinary education can take no account of so aristocratic a good. I do not believe this. The joy of mental adventure is far commoner in the young than in grown men and women. Among children it is very common, and grows naturally out of the period of make-believe and fancy. It is rare in later life because everything is done to kill it during education. . . .

The wish to preserve the past rather than the hope of creating the future dominates the minds of those who control the teaching of the young. Education should not aim at a passive awareness of dead facts, but at an activity directed towards the world that our efforts are to create.[g]

Finally, as regards property and industrial society:

In judging of an industrial system, whether the one under which we live or one proposed by reformers, there are four main tests which may be applied. We may consider whether the system secures (1) the maximum of production, or (2) justice in distribution, or (3) a tolerable existence for producers, or (4) the greatest possible freedom and stimulus to vitality and progress. We may say, broadly, that the present system aims only at the first of these objects, while Socialism aims at the second and third. . . . I believe that the fourth is much the most important of the objects to be aimed at, that the present system is fatal to it, and that orthodox Socialism might well prove equally fatal.

One of the least-questioned assumptions of the capitalist system is, that production ought to be increased in amount by every possible means. . . . The belief in the importance of production has a fanatical irrationality and ruthlessness. So long as something is produced, what it is that is produced seems to be thought a matter of no account. . . .

The time which is now spent in producing luxuries could be spent partly in enjoyment and country holidays, partly in better education, partly in work that is not manual or subserving manual work. We could, if we wished, have far more science and art, more diffused knowledge and mental cultivation, more leisure for wage-earners, and more capacity for intelligent pleasures. . . .

The most important purpose that political institutions can achieve is to keep alive in individuals creativeness, vigour, vitality, and the joy of life. These things existed, for example, in Elizabethan England in a way in which they do not exist now. They stimulated adventure, poetry, music, fine architecture and set going the whole movement out of which England's greatness has sprung in every direction in which England has been great. These things co-existed with injustice, but outweighed it, and made a national life more admirable than any that is likely to exist under Socialism.[h]

Although there may be differences of opinion about the quality of life in Elizabethan England, most people will surely agree with Russell that diffusing knowledge and encouraging creativity are good things and that war and poverty are bad things. Further, it may be allowed in a general way that we have the knowledge necessary to bring the good things about and to eliminate the bad things. Why, then, are we so far from achieving what we all want? Russell's answer is that we do not desire these good things strongly enough. What "keeps evil in being" is the fact that "we have less desire for the welfare of our friends than for the punishment of our enemies." But though the passion of hate is very strong, it is capable of being changed.[26] This brings us back to love, the second component in the good life. What is needed to dissipate hatred and "generate" goodness is a "very simple and old-fashioned thing. . . . It is love, Christian love, or compassion. If you feel this, you have a motive for existence, a guide in action, a reason for courage, an imperative necessity for intellectual honesty. If you feel this, you have all that anybody should need in the way of religion."[i]

Religion

It is necessary, Russell held, to distinguish between "personal religion as a way of feeling" and the formal, historical religions. Each of the formal religions "has three aspects: (1) a church, (2) a creed, and (3) a code of personal morals"; and each has "three central doctrines—God, immortality, and freedom." The

---

[26] Of course, the essay in which all of this was described was itself an effort to change passion—to cause the reader to desire what Russell desired.

doctrines of formal religion can be neither proved nor, in the strict sense, disproved. On the whole, formal religion has had a pernicious influence, insofar as it has persistently tried to limit the freedom of inquiry that is the essence of science. Writing in 1935, Russell seemed to believe that science had for some years been almost continuously victorious in its warfare with formal religion, "but the rise of new religions in Russia and Germany, equipped with new means of missionary activity provided by science, has again put the issue in doubt."[j]

In contrast to formal religion, personal religion is valuable;[27] far from being in conflict with science, it is inspired by science. The essence of personal religion is not merely compassion; it is also humility. By revealing the "vastness of the universe," science inspires us with "a new form of humility to replace that which atheism has rendered obsolete." This feeling of what can fairly be described as sublimity was always very strong in Russell. It accounts for the attraction Hegelianism had for him as a young man; in Hegel's conception of the absolute as "one single harmonious system . . . there is undeniably something sublime, something to which we could wish to yield assent." As an expression of his own, "feeling about the universe and about human passions," Russell quoted Leopardi's poem *The Infinite:*

> And then I call to mind eternity,
> And the ages that are dead, and this that now
> Is living, and the noise of it. And so
> In this immensity my thought sinks drowned:
> And sweet it seems to shipwreck in this sea.[k]

Yet Russell would not, or could not, assent; evidence was lacking. "When the arguments . . . are carefully examined," they are all seen to involve "confusion and many unwarrantable assumptions." The result of his insisting on "indubitableness" was therefore a romantic, almost melodramatic, conception of our relation to the cosmos.

> Brief and powerless is Man's life; on him and all his race the slow, sure doom falls pitiless and dark. Blind to good and evil, reckless of destruction, omnipotent matter rolls on its relentless way; for Man, condemned to-day to lose his dearest, to-morrow himself to pass through the gate of darkness, it remains only to cherish, ere yet the blow falls, the lofty thoughts that ennoble his little day; disdaining the coward terrors of the slave of Fate, to worship at the shrine that his own hands have built; undismayed by the empire of chance, to preserve a mind free from the wanton tyranny that rules his outward life; proudly defiant of the irresistible forces that tolerate, for a moment, his knowledge and his condemnation, to sustain alone, a weary but unyielding Atlas,

---

[27] Russell often wrote as if it were valuable in some other sense than merely as something desired by him and by other people.

the world that his own ideals have fashioned despite the trampling march of unconscious power.[1]

It is not clear why it is appropriate for us to react in this way to "the world which Science presents for our belief," or on what grounds, if anyone were to react differently, it would be possible for Russell to "convict him of intellectual error." Indeed, it would seem, on Russell's own premises, that *all* reactions of whatever kind must be as "devoid of meaning" as the universe itself it supposed to be. Human reactions are included in the universe. Like it, therefore, they are merely phases of "Nature's secular hurryings through the abysses of space."

To understand the curious ambivalence in Russell's position—an ambivalence that is shared by many people today—it is necessary to see that, like Kierkegaard and Nietzsche, Russell experienced existential anguish, but that unlike them he was also a rationalist, a logician, and a social critic and reformer. To bring out still another aspect of Russell's complex personality, he was in many respects a Humean. But Hume would never have written about "a free man's worship." He had no sense of the sublime and the transcendent that Russell felt so strongly but to which he was unwilling to commit himself fully. Hume was content in his skepticism; Russell was unhappy in his. Whether this made Russell a better philosopher than he would otherwise have been is perhaps an open question, but there is no doubt that it made him an antimetaphysician in spite of himself.

The Russell who was admired by his contemporaries and who so greatly influenced the younger philosophers growing up around him was the Humean Russell who conceived philosophy as criticism. But there was also, as we have just seen, a Kierkegaardian Russell, and we must not forget the Cartesian Russell, who hoped to vindicate the claims of physics, and who in the end had to confess that he believed in the world of physics "without good grounds."

Toward the end of Russell's life, these three Russells wrote:

> My intellectual journeys have been, in some respects, disappointing. When I was young I hoped to find religious satisfaction in philosophy; even after I had abandoned Hegel the eternal Platonic world gave me something non-human to admire. I thought of mathematics with reverence, and suffered when Wittgenstein led me to regard it as nothing but tautologies. I have always ardently desired to find some justification for the emotions inspired by certain things that seemed to stand outside human life and to deserve feelings of awe. . . . Those who attempt to make a religion of humanism, which recognizes nothing greater than man, do not satisfy my emotions. And yet I am unable to believe that, in the world as known, there is anything that I can value outside human beings, and, to a much lesser extent animals. . . . And so my intellect goes with the humanists, though my emotions violently rebel. In this respect, the "consolations of philosophy" are not for me.[m]

The *Tractatus*

Wittgenstein's [1] *Tractatus*—the *Tractatus Logico-Philosophicus,* to refer to it for once by its full name—was in many respects the culmination of the logical route, as distinct from the realist and the phenomenological routes, out of the Kantian paradigm—the route that Frege had first developed and that Russell had carried forward. The *Tractatus* is a work of great difficulty, over which controversy still rages; almost the only points on which commentators agree are that it is subtle

---

[1] Ludwig Wittgenstein (1889–1951) was born in Vienna into a wealthy and cultivated family. After studying engineering in Austria, he went in 1911 to Manchester to continue his studies and to do research in the design of airplane propellers and engines. Soon his interests shifted to mathematics and logic, and he moved to Cambridge, where he was a pupil of Russell's. While serving in the Austrian army during the First World War, he finished his *Tractatus Logico-Philosophicus.* Though at the time he thought

and complex and of great importance. Here we can set out only a few of the major themes, omitting complicating details. Even regarding the points that we present here there have been, and will probably continue to be, major disagreements.

The Basic Orientation

In the Preface, Wittgenstein stated the purpose of his work in the following way:

> The book deals with the problems of philosophy, and shows, I believe, that the reason why these problems are posed is that the logic of our language is misunderstood. The whole sense of the book might be summed up in the following words: what can be said at all can be said clearly, and what we cannot talk about we must pass over in silence.
>
> Thus the aim of the book is to set a limit to thought, or rather—not to thought, but to the expression of thoughts: for in order to be able to set a limit to thought, we should have to find both sides of the limit thinkable (i.e., we should have to be able to think what cannot be thought).
>
> It will therefore only be in language that the limit can be set, and what lies on the other side of the limit will simply be nonsense.[a]

Thus, in 1918, the year in which the Preface was written, Wittgenstein already had adopted an explicitly linguistic approach. The *Tractatus* is thus one of the earliest evidences of that profound shift in viewpoint that we have characterized as a major feature of twentieth-century culture.[2]

Wittgenstein distinguished, then, between what can be said and what cannot be said. This reminds us of Kant, who made a similar, and equally fundamental, distinction between what can be known and what is unknowable. Granted that Wittgenstein poses the distinction in linguistic terms, the basic orientation is much the same: a distinction is drawn between what is accessible to us and what must remain forever inaccessible. Again, Wittgenstein's approach to what can be said is similar to Kant's approach to what can be known; both ask what we can

---

he had solved all philosophical problems, he gradually came to question many of the doctrines of the *Tractatus*. Accordingly, he returned to Cambridge in 1929 and resumed the study and teaching of philosophy. He had given away the fortune he had inherited from his father and lived in great simplicity. Except for a single article Wittgenstein later repudiated, the *Tractatus* was the only philosophical work he published during his lifetime. However, his posthumous works run to many volumes. This material is derived from three sources: notes taken by students attending his lectures, notes he dictated to selected students, and a large body of manuscripts later edited and published by his literary executors.

[2] See p. 6.

infer about the nature of what is accessible from the sheer fact that it is accessible. But Kant posed this question in terms of physics—assuming that in physics we have an a priori knowledge of nature, he asked in effect what must be the case about our minds and their relation to the world to make this knowledge possible. Wittgenstein for his part started from logic, not from physics. He asked what follows about the world from the idea that *something* can be said about it—not what follows if this or that particular assertion is made about it, for nothing follows about the world from *that,* but what follows about the world from the idea that it is possible for us to frame assertions about it that are either true or false. Wittgenstein was very close to Frege in that he assumed that, since we can make assertions about the world, an examination of the logic of assertions will disclose the general features that the world must have for any assertion about it to be true.

Two more similarities between Wittgenstein and Kant may be mentioned. Both were concerned with the boundary between what can be said (known) and what cannot be said (known). This was not a central issue for Kant; it appears in his writings chiefly in connection with the regulative use of reason. But for Wittgenstein it is fundamental. How do we talk about what is unsayable?—for it seems that we must in some sense talk about it, if only to say that it is unsayable.

Finally, Wittgenstein and Kant were both convinced that the domain of the inaccessible is of great importance; it is, for instance, the domain of ethics and religion. Kant believed that the transcendental deduction not only validates physics but also makes a secure place for ethics and religion; he had, he believed, limited knowledge to make a place for faith. No such line of reasoning was available to Wittgenstein. Because he was interested in the inaccessible and because it was nonetheless necessary, as he thought, to pass it over in silence, he seems to have experienced deep disquietudes—disquietudes that he must have hoped the arguments of the *Tractatus*[3] would allay. This feature of his personality, along with the fact, as we believe, that the disquietudes were never successfully allayed, adds a dimension to his thought—a depth and a pathos—that we do not find in Frege or the positivists. Wittgenstein, for all the clarity, precision, and toughness of his mind, was also, in James's terminology, tender-minded.[4]

What Can Be Said about the World

1[5]	The world is all that is the case.
1.1	The world is the totality of facts, not of things.
1.11	The world is determined by the facts, and by their being *all* the facts.

[3] See pp. 236–37 and pp. 425–27.
[4] See Vol. IV, p. 297.
[5] [There are seven main propositions in the *Tractatus*, which are numbered from 1 to 7. Everything else is either a comment on one of these seven propositions (in which case it

1.12	For the totality of facts determines what is the case, and also whatever is not the case.
1.13	The facts in logical space are the world.
1.2	The world divides into facts.
1.21	Each item can be the case or not the case while everything else remains the same.
2	What is the case—a fact—is the existence of states of affairs.
2.01	A state of affairs (a state of things) is a combination of objects (things).
2.011	It is essential to things that they should be possible constituents of states of affairs. . . .
2.0141	The possibility of its occurring in states of affairs is the form of an object.
2.02	Objects are simple. . . .
2.022	It is obvious that an imagined world, however different it may be from the real one, must have *something*—a form—in common with it.
2.023	Objects are just what constitute this unalterable form. . . .
2.0271	Objects are what is unalterable and subsistent; their configuration is what is changing and unstable.
2.0272	The configuration of objects produces states of affairs.
2.03	In a state of affairs objects fit into one another like the links of a chain. . . .
2.061	States of affairs are independent of one another.
2.062	From the existence or non-existence of one state of affairs it is impossible to infer the existence or non-existence of another.[b]

These opening propositions about the world probably sound obscure; they also sound dogmatic. But Wittgenstein held them to be conclusions following from the theory of meaning that he had adopted. He was indeed arguing from what he took to be the conditions that must obtain if any proposition is meaningful. A complex proposition—and all of the propositions that occur in ordinary language, even the simplest, are complex from Wittgenstein's point of view—is meaningful only if it is analyzable into simpler propositions and eventually into elementary propositions that consist only in names. These names are not analyzable; they are the termini of analysis, and analysis must have termini. It must, that is, end somewhere, and it cannot end if there remains something that *might* be

---

is given a number with one decimal place—for example, 1.1, 2.1), or it is a comment on one of these comments (in which case it is given a number with two decimal places—for instance, 1.11, 2.11), or it is a comment on one of the comments on a comment (in which case it is given a number with three decimal places), and so on. Thus, 2.0121 is a comment on 2.012, which is a comment on 2.01, which is a comment on 2. This elaborate architectonic is largely a façade; the comments are too short and epigrammatic for there to be any neat relation of logical subordination—AUTHORS.]

analyzed, that is theoretically analyzable. Hence analysis ends in simples. What each name refers to must itself be simple. The simple names, that is to say, must be the signs of simple objects.

> 3.25 A proposition has one and only one complete analysis.
>
> 3.251 What a proposition expresses it expresses in a determinate manner, which can be set out clearly: a proposition is articulated.
>
> 3.26 A name cannot be dissected any further by means of a definition: it is a primitive sign. . . .
>
> 4.21 The simplest kind of proposition, an elementary proposition, asserts the existence of a state of affairs.
>
> 4.22 An elementary proposition consists of names. It is a nexus, a concatenation, of names.
>
> 4.221 It is obvious that the analysis of propositions must bring us to elementary propositions which consist of names in immediate combination.[c]

There has been much debate about exactly what sort of an entity a Wittgensteinian object is, and about the relation of objects to the facts, things, and states of affairs that are also mentioned in the passages quoted. But about one characteristic of objects there can be no doubt: they are simple, and being simple, they cannot be defined or talked about. That there are simples can only be shown. Thus, unless a sentence can be analyzed into a series of simple symbols ("primitive names"), each of which refers to a simple object that can be "elucidated" by primitive propositions, the sentence is meaningless. But at least some sentences are meaningful. It follows, therefore, that there must be simple objects.

> 4.2211 Even if the world is infinitely complex, so that every fact consists of infinitely many states of affairs and every state of affairs is composed of infinitely many objects, there would still have to be objects and states of affairs.[d]

We seen, then, that the *Tractatus* is set firmly in the analytic tradition, and this is one of the reasons why it appealed so greatly to the positivists and why it also found favor with Russell.

Logical and Pictorial Form

That there must be simple objects is not the only, nor the most important, consequence of Wittgenstein's theory of meaning, and we shall have to examine some of the other consequences later. But since so much depends on this view of meaning, we should first ask ourselves why it seemed so plausible, so overwhelmingly obvious, to Wittgenstein—at least when he wrote the *Tractatus*.

Wittgenstein, it appears, had been impressed by an account of a trial arising out of an automobile accident, in which the lawyers used dolls and miniature cars to represent the real people and real automobiles involved in the accident.[e] It seemed to him that propositions must represent the world in the same way. "We picture facts to ourselves," he wrote, and the picture "must have something in common with what it depicts."[f] What it has in common is its "pictorial form."[g] If the doll used in the trial occupies the same place in the miniature car that the real driver occupied in the real car, it represents the accident truly; otherwise not. "A picture agrees with reality or fails to agree; it is correct or incorrect, true or false."[h]

Thus it is in virtue of its pictorial form that a picture represents correctly or incorrectly, as the case may be. If it lacked pictorial form, it would not represent at all, neither correctly nor incorrectly; it would not be a picture. So, in an exactly analogous way, it is by virtue of its logical form that a proposition is either true or false. If it lacks logical form it would be neither true nor false; it would not be a proposition but some other sort of utterance. It might look, grammatically, like a proposition, but it would not be one because, lacking logical form, it would assert nothing about the world.

2.1	We picture facts to ourselves.
2.12	A picture is a model of reality.
2.13	In a picture objects have the elements of the picture corresponding to them. . . .
2.14	What constitutes a picture is that its elements are related to one another in a determinate way. . . .
2.15	The fact that the elements of a picture are related to one another in a determinate way represents that things are related to one another in the same way.
	Let us call this connexion of its elements the structure of the picture, and let us call the possibility of this structure the pictorial form of the picture.
2.151	Pictorial form is the possibility that things are related to one another in the same way as the elements of the picture.
2.161	There must be something identical in a picture and what it depicts, to enable the one to be a picture of the other at all.
2.17	What a picture must have in common with reality, in order to be able to depict it—correctly or incorrectly—in the way it does, is its pictorial form. . . .
2.22	What a picture represents it represents independently of its truth or falsity, by means of its pictorial form.[i]

In a word, a proposition is, quite literally, a picture.

2.18   What any picture, of whatever form, must have in common with reality, in order to be able to depict it—correctly or incorrectly—in any way at all, is logical form, i.e. the form of reality.

2.181   A picture whose pictorial form is logical form is called a logical picture.

2.182   Every picture is *at the same time* a logical one. (On the other hand, not every picture is, for example, a spatial one.)ʲ

That pictures (and models, diagrams, architects' blueprints, maps) look like the things they represent, everyone will agree, but to claim, as Wittgenstein did, that propositions also represent their objects sounds odd, even mistaken. Perhaps it will help if we say that, generally, A represents B (A, in some sense, looks like B) when there is a rule by which we can get, systematically, from A to B and back again. "Form" provides us with, or is, the rule, and in the case of propositions, as much as in the case of pictures, blueprints, and models, a rule exists. In the case of paintings the rule may be the "laws" of perspective; without an understanding of these laws we would never get from the blobs of pigment on the canvas to the landscape represented—without them the landscape would not be represented in the painting at all. In the case of propositions, the rule is the syntax of the language in which the propositions occur. Without these semantic "laws" the propositions would not represent—would not be propositions; with them they do represent, just as much as the paintings represent.

4.011   At first sight a proposition—one set out on the printed page, for example—does not seem to be a picture of the reality with which it is concerned. But no more does musical notation at first sight seem to be a picture of music. . . .

4.014   A gramophone record, the musical idea, the written notes, and the sound-waves, all stand to one another in the same internal relation of depicting that holds between language and the world.

They are all constructed according to a common logical pattern. . . .

4.0141 There is a general rule by means of which the musician can obtain the symphony from the score, and which makes it possible to derive the symphony from the groove on the gramophone record, and, using the first rule, to derive the score again. That is what constitutes the inner similarity between these things which seem to be constructed in such entirely different ways. And that rule is the law of projection which projects the symphony into the language of musical notation. It is the rule for translating this language into the language of gramophone records. . . .

4.016   In order to understand the essential nature of a proposition, we should consider hieroglyphic script, which depicts the facts that it describes.

And alphabetic script developed out of it without losing what was essential to depiction.[k]

The General Form of a Proposition

Wittgenstein recognized, of course, that our everyday sentences do not reveal *how* they picture the world. He held that language gets hooked up to the world by way of the picturing relationship that holds between elementary propositions and states of affairs. This, however, raises a further question. Plainly, our everyday sentences are not themselves elementary propositions. They do not consist wholly of names; the names they contain do not name simples; and so on. What, then, is the relationship between elementary propositions and the sentences that we actually employ? We have already been told (at 4.221) that "it is obvious that the analysis of propositions must bring us to elementary propositions." We now want to know exactly what form this analysis takes. Wittgenstein's answer to this question introduces perhaps the most innovative idea in the *Tractatus:*

5.   A proposition is a truth-function of elementary propositions.[l]

Avoiding technical details as much as possible, we can next examine what Wittgenstein meant by a *truth-function.*

Suppose we are given three elementary propositions, each composed of only two names: "AB," "CD," and "EF." Suppose further that the first two elementary propositions are true and the third is false. Starting with these elementary propositions, we can use the conjunction "and" to construct other propositions that are complex rather than elementary:

"AB and CD"
"AB and EF"
"CD and EF"
"CD and EF and AB"
"CD and CD and AB"
And so on indefinitely.

These are not elementary propositions because they contain the expression "and," which, according to Wittgenstein, is not the name of any object. For Wittgenstein there is no entity that the word "and" stands for. More generally, no logical terms (or, as he calls them, logical constants) refer to, or represent, objects:

4.0312   My fundamental idea is that the "Local constants" [e.g., "and," "or," "not," etc.] are not representatives.[m]

But if the word "and" does not stand for anything, how can it be meaningful? To understand Wittgenstein's answer to this question, we can note that the complex propositions in the above list share the following feature: because we have been given the truth-values of the elementary propositions they contain, we are in a position to determine the truth-value of each complex proposition. More technically, the truth-value of each complex proposition is a *function of the truth-values of the elementary propositions it contains.* In particular, a conjunction is true just in case its conjuncts are both true; it is false otherwise. We can capture this idea by employing a format—invented by Wittgenstein—that has come to be known as a truth table.

AB	CD	AB and CD
T	T	T
T	F	F
F	T	F
F	F	F

Here the two columns on the left specify all the possible ways that truth-values can be assigned to the two elementary propositions "AB" and "CD"; the column on the right gives the truth-value of the conjunction "AB and CD" for each assignment. We can now answer the question that first concerned us: If the word "and" does not stand for anything or refer to anything, how can it be meaningful? The answer is this: The word "and" allows us to construct a complex proposition out of two other propositions where this complex proposition is counted as true just in case the original propositions are both true, but counted as false otherwise. A conjunction of elementary propositions provides our first example of a proposition that is a truth-function of elementary propositions.

We can use a similar truth-table technique for defining the negation of a proposition. The negation of a proposition is true just in case the proposition negated is false; it is true otherwise. Using the elementary proposition "AB" as an example, the following truth table illustrates how negation functions:

AB	Not-AB
T	F
F	T

In short, negating a proposition produces another proposition that has the reverse truth-value of the proposition negated.

Although this is not precisely the way Wittgenstein made the point, we are now in a position to make sense of the fundamental thesis stated in proposition 5, namely, that every "proposition is a truth-function of elementary propositions." For Wittgenstein, the only thing that a proposition can indicate is that certain simple objects either are or are not combined in certain ways. If that is correct, then every proposition, in principle at least, can be represented using nothing more than elementary propositions and the truth-functional notions of conjunction and negation. In particular, every proposition, in principle, can be analyzed into a conjunction consisting only of elementary propositions or the denials of elementary propositions. Thus the analysis of a nonelementary proposition might look something like this:

AB and BC and Not-DE . . .

Furthermore, in principle, we could get a complete description of the world by constructing a very large (perhaps infinitely large) conjunction containing every elementary proposition or its denial, depending on which is true. Such a superconjunction would consider every possible combination of basic objects and tell us which ones hold and which ones do not. This superconjunction would contain all the news about the universe—or at least all the news expressible in language.

It is important to note that the phrase "in principle" occurs repeatedly in the above paragraph. Wittgenstein, in fact, nowhere suggests that such a reduction of everyday propositions to truth-functions of elementary propositions could actually be carried out. The thesis that every proposition is a truth-function of elementary propositions is not the result of an empirical investigation of language. It is, instead, the result of thinking through what language *must* be like in order for us to be able to picture the world at all—either truly or falsely. The argument here is an a priori transcendental argument.

Logical Propositions

Broadly speaking, Wittgenstein's notion of an elementary proposition provides the foundation for his picture theory of meaning, for, strictly speaking, only elementary propositions enter into the picturing relationship with the world in a direct way. We can also say that Wittgenstein uses the notion of an elementary proposition to explain how propositions can have a significant content. Although his notion of truth-functions plays an important role in explaining the possibility of complex pictures of the world, its main attraction for Wittgenstein is that it gives an account of the status of *logical* propositions.

Again, our discussion will be simpler than Wittgenstein's, but it will give at least a general idea of the way he dealt with the propositions of logic. We can begin by again considering the elementary proposition "AB." It will be true just in case the objects named by "A" and "B" are appropriately combined. To use a somewhat technical term, the truth or falsity of "AB" is *contingent* on the combination or noncombination of these objects. Furthermore, according to Wittgenstein, there is no way of knowing a priori whether these objects are or are not combined in this way. Even if true, "AB" could not be known a priori to be true.

For Wittgenstein, it is a feature of *all* elementary propositions that, even if true, they are only contingently true and cannot be known a priori to be true.

Many truth-functional complexes of elementary propositions have these same features of being contingent and not capable of being known a priori. For example, a conjunction of two elementary propositions is, if true, only contingently true and its truth cannot be known a priori. This, however, is not true of all truth-functions of elementary propositions, as the following truth table shows. Starting with the single elementary "AB," we can construct truth-functions from it in the following way:

(1)	(2)	(3)	(4)
AB	Not-AB	AB and Not-AB	Not-(AB and Not-AB)
T	F	F	T
F	T	F	T

Here proposition 1 is a contingent proposition. It will be true just in case the objects the names refer to are combined in the world. Whether this is so or not can not be known a priori. Proposition 2 is also a contingent proposition, but its truth-conditions are just the reverse of proposition 1's: it will be true just in case the objects the names refer to are not combined in the world. Again, this is not something that can be known a priori. Given the definitions of conjunction and negation, we can see that proposition 3 will be false no matter how the objects in the world are connected or disconnected. That this is so is something that *can* be known a priori. Propositions of this kind are called *contradictions*. Proposition 4 is the negation of proposition 3 and has the reverse property: it will be true no matter how objects in the world are connected or disconnected. This can also be known a priori. Propositions of this kind are called *tautologies*.

We can next notice that propositions 3 and 4 have the following important feature: since their truth-value does not depend on the arrangement of objects in the world, they cannot be *pictures* of reality. Wittgenstein says this explicitly:

> 4.46   Among the possible groups of truth-conditions there are two extreme cases.
>
> In one of these cases the proposition is true for all the truth-possibilities of the elementary propositions. We say that the truth-conditions are *tautological*.
>
> In the second case the proposition is false for all the truth-possibilities: the truth-conditions are *contradictory*.
>
> In the first case we call the proposition a tautology; in the second, a contradiction.
>
> 4.461 Propositions show what they say: tautologies and contradictions show that they say nothing.
>
> A tautology has no truth-conditions, since it is unconditionally true: and a contradiction is true on no condition.
>
> Tautologies and contradictions lack sense. . . .

(For example, I know nothing about the weather when I know that it is either raining or not raining.)

4.4611   Tautologies and contradictions are not, however, nonsensical. They are part of the symbolism, just as "0" is part of the symbolism of arithmetic.

4.462   Tautologies and contradictions are not pictures of reality. They do not represent any possible situations. For the former admit *all* possible situations, and the latter *none*.[n]

How exactly does this discussion bear upon the status of laws of logic? To answer this we can look again at proposition 4:

Not-(AB and Not-AB)

This proposition is an instance of a fundamental law of logic, namely the law of noncontradiction. In its general form, this law states that, for any proposition p, whether it is elementary or complex,

Not-(p and Not-p)

Thus it turns out that the law of noncontradiction, often thought to be *the* fundamental law of logic, is a mere tautology. The law of excluded middle has also been taken to be a fundamental law of logic. In its general form it states that for any proposition p, whether it is elementary or complex,

p or Not-p

Using further developments of Wittgenstein's truth-table techniques, this can be shown to be tautological as well. These results led Wittgenstein to his ultimate solution concerning the status of propositions of logic:

6.1   The propositions of logic are tautologies.

6.11   Therefore the propositions of logic say nothing. (They are the analytic propositions.) . . .

6.113   It is the peculiar mark of logical propositions that one can recognize that they are true from the symbol alone, and this fact contains in itself the whole philosophy of logic. And so too it is a very important fact that the truth or falsity of non-logical propositions *cannot* be recognized from the proposition alone.

6.12   The fact that the propositions of logic are tautologies *shows* the formal—logical—properties of language and the world. . . .

6.124   The propositions of logic describe the scaffolding of the world, or rather they represent it. They have no "subject-matter." They presuppose that names have meaning and elementary propositions sense; and that is their connexion with the world. It is clear that something about the world must be indicated by the fact that certain combinations of symbols—whose essence involves the possession of a determinate character—are tautologies. This contains the decisive point. We have said that some things are arbitrary in the symbols that we use and that some things are not. In logic it is only the latter that express: but that means that logic is not a field in which *we* express what we wish with the help of signs, but rather one in which the nature of the natural and inevitable signs speaks for itself. If we know the logical syntax of any sign-language, then we have already been given all the propositions of logic.°

A number of important facts follow from this account of logic: first, that there are no logical primitives—we can start anywhere; second, that the notion of self-evidence can be eliminated; and third, that proof in logic is purely mechanical—we merely substitute equalities for each other according to some rule.

6.127   All the propositions of logic are of equal status: it is not the case that some of them are essentially primitive propositions and others essentially derived propositions. . . .

6.1271   It is clear that the number of the "primitive propositions of logic" is arbitrary, since one could derive logic from a single primitive proposition, e.g. by simply constructing the logical product of Frege's primitive propositions. (Frege would perhaps say that we should then no longer have an immediately self-evident primitive proposition. But it is remarkable that a thinker so rigorous as Frege appealed to the degree of self-evidence as the criterion of a logical proposition.)

6.126   One can calculate whether a proposition belongs to logic, by calculating the logical properties of the *symbol.*

     And this is what we do when we "prove" a logical proposition. For, without bothering about sense or meaning, we construct the logical proposition out of others using only *rules that deal with signs.* . . .

6.1261   In logic process and result are equivalent. (Hence the absence of surprise.)

6.1262   Proof in logic is merely a mechanical expedient to facilitate the recognition of tautologies in complicated cases.ᵖ

Since "mathematics is a logical method,"�q what has been said about logic applies also to mathematics.

6.22   The logic of the world, which is shown in tautologies by the propositions of logic, is shown in equations by mathematics. . . .

6.2321   And the possibility of proving the propositions of mathe-
           matics means simply that their correctness can be perceived
           without its being necessary that what they express should it-
           self be compared with the facts in order to determine its
           correctness. . . .

6.234   Mathematics is a method of logic.

6.2341   It is the essential characteristic of mathematical method that
           it employs equations. For it is because of this method that
           every proposition of mathematics must go without saying.

6.24   The method by which mathematics arrives at its equations
           is the method of substitution.

           For equations express the substitutability of two expres-
           sions and, starting from a number of equations, we advance
           to new equations by substituting different expressions in ac-
           cordance with the equations.[r]

This account of mathematics greatly pleased the positivists. If mathematics is
thought to fall within the domain of significant propositions, one has either to
claim that mathematical propositions are mere empirical generalizations (which
did not seem plausible) or else admit that there is a class of propositions—and an
important class, too—to which the verifiability principle does not apply. But if,
as Wittgenstein purported to show, mathematics is tautological, the question
whether it is an embarrassing exception to the positivists' claim for the verifiability principle simply does not arise.

Natural Science

This brings us to natural science, and to the third class of expression that Wittgenstein allowed: propositions with sense, that is, expressions that are pictures and
are true or false depending on whether they represent correctly or incorrectly. In
the first place, "outside logic everything is accidental."[s] That this is the case follows directly from the idea that, as we have already seen, everything—every object, every state of affairs—is independent of every other: "From the existence or
non-existence of one state of affairs it is impossible to infer the existence or nonexistence of another."[t] And this in turn follows from the basic assumption of the
whole analytic tradition that the world consists in a collection of wholly independent, wholly encapsulated simples. In separating the a priori from the empirical
and in ruling out the possibility of an a priori knowledge of nature, Wittgenstein
was drawing explicitly a conclusion that was implicit in the analytic tradition from
the start.

2.225   There are no pictures that are true *a priori*. . . .

5.134   One elementary proposition cannot be deduced from an-
           other.

5.135   There is no possible way of making an inference from the existence of one situation to the existence of another, entirely different situation.

5.136   There is no causal nexus to justify such an inference.

5.1361   We *cannot* infer the events of the future from those of the present.

        Belief in the causal nexus is *superstition.* . . .

6.37   There is no compulsion making one thing happen because another has happened. The only necessity that exists is *logical* necessity.ᵘ

As regards the "laws of nature," Wittgenstein did not hold that they are not *laws,* but that they do not hold of nature. Or, more exactly, he held that we have, and can have, no *evidence* that they hold of nature. We are justified in using them when and to the extent that they "work"—that is, we are justified in using them when they enable us to make predictions from what has happened to what will happen; to this extent Wittgenstein was a pragmatist. But that they are useful now is not evidence that they will be useful in the future; nor is the idea that they may turn out to be useful in the future evidence that there is any necessity, or "compulsion," in things that makes them happen as they do happen.

6.363   The procedure of induction consists in accepting as true the *simplest* law that can be reconciled with our experiences.

6.3631   This procedure, however, has no logical justification but only a psychological one.

        It is clear that there are no grounds for believing that the simplest eventually will in fact be realized.

6.36311   It is an hypothesis that the sun will rise tomorrow: and this means that we do not *know* whether it will rise.ᵛ

All of this, evidently, is merely the spelling out in detail of the consequences of the chasm between the logical and the empirical. On one side of the chasm are the various conceptual schemata (for example, the laws of mechanics) that scientists from time to time work out; on the other side are the loose and separate (to use Hume's phrase) facts. The schemata are like grids that we draw on a surface, systems of coordinates by means of which we locate features of the surface and describe their relations to each other. Given a knowledge of the principles (the "laws") by which a grid system has been designed, we can deduce from certain known characteristics of a grid what other characteristics of this grid are. But since the surface on which the grid has been imposed is wholly independent of any and all grids that we inscribe on it, we cannot deduce what any features of the surface are.

6.341   Newtonian mechanics, for example, imposes a unified form on the description of the world. Let us imagine a white surface with irregular black spots on it. We then say that whatever kind of picture these make, I can always approximate as closely as I wish to the description of it by covering the surface with a sufficiently fine square mesh, and then saying of every square whether it is black or white. In this way I shall have imposed a unified form on the description of the surface. The form is optional, since I could have achieved the same result by using a net with a triangular or hexagonal mesh. Possibly the use of a triangular mesh would have made the description simpler: that is to say, it might be that we could describe the surface more accurately with a coarse triangular mesh than with a fine square mesh (or conversely), and so on. The different nets correspond to different systems for describing the world. Mechanics determines one form of description of the world by saying that all propositions used in the description of the world must be obtained in a given way from a given set of propositions—the axioms of mechanics. It thus supplies the bricks for building the edifice of science, and it says, "Any building that you want to erect, whatever it may be, must somehow be constructed with these bricks, and with these alone."

(Just as with the number-system we must be able to write down any number we wish, so with the system of mechanics we must be able to write down any proposition of physics that we wish.) . . .

6.343   Mechanics is an attempt to construct according to a single plan all the *true* propositions that we need for the description of the world. . . .

6.35   Although the spots in our picture are geometrical figures, nevertheless geometry can obviously say nothing at all about their actual form and position. The network, however, is *purely* geometrical; all its properties can be given *a priori*.

Laws like the principle of sufficient reason, etc. are about the net and not about what the net describes.ʷ

In a word, principles like the law of least action, which classical physics and the philosophy based on it had supposed to be a priori true of nature, are only a priori true of the grids we construct. They are, as it were, a part of the set of necessary conditions that must obtain if a grid is to be a grid of the kind that, so far at least, has characterized fruitful scientific theories.

Thus the whole post-Cartesian conception of nature was profoundly mistaken—profoundly mistaken, that is, if the theory of logic and the theory of meaning put forward in the *Tractatus* are correct. It was once held that the laws of nature formulate the way nature necessarily behaves and hence that reference to these laws provides an ultimate and complete explanation of why things happen as they do. But if the *Tractatus* is correct, the laws of nature explain nothing. To appeal to them is like appealing to God or to Fate, but worse, since the ancients who appealed to God or to Fate at least recognized that they were appealing to the inscrutable and the unintelligible, whereas those who talk about the laws of nature suppose themselves to be offering intelligible explanations.

> 6.371   The whole modern conception of the world is founded on the illusion that the so-called laws of nature are the explanations of natural phenomena.
>
> 6.372   Thus people today stop at the laws of nature, treating them as something inviolable, just as God and Fate were treated in past ages.
>
> And in fact both are right and both wrong: though the view of the ancients is clearer in so far as they have a clear and acknowledged terminus, while the modern system tries to make it look as if *everything* were explained.[x]

Although, as we have suggested,[6] there is striking similarity between the basic orientations of Kant and Wittgenstein, inasmuch as they both adopted a "critical" approach to the problem of defining the limit between what is knowable (sayable) and what is unknowable (unsayable), nothing could be more different than the conclusions they reached. Kant, for his part, had set out to meet Humean skepticism regarding the possibility of a rational knowledge of nature, and he saw that to do so it was necessary to establish some sort of bridge over the chasm that Hume had exposed between logic and experience. This bridge, according to Kant, was the activity of a logical and rational mind constructing a logical and rational world. The "Transcendental Aesthetic" and the "Transcendental Logic,"[7] which were the marshaling in detail of the evidence that there is such a bridge, seemed to Kant to prove that synthetic a priori judgments are possible both in mathematics and in physics. In *Tractarian* terminology Kant's position was that both mathematics and physics give us a priori pictures of the world. Wittgenstein's position, as we have just seen, is that "there are no pictures that are true *a priori.*"[y] Physics pictures the world but is not a priori; mathematics is a priori but does not picture anything.

Philosophy

And now what of philosophy? What sort of discourse is philosophical discourse? To begin with:

[6] See p. 217.
[7] See Vol. IV, pp. 27–61.

4.111   Philosophy is not one of the natural sciences. . . .

4.112   Philosophy aims at the logical clarification of thoughts. . . .

4.002   Language disguises thought. So much so, that from the outward form of the clothing it is impossible to infer the form of the thought beneath it, because the outward form of the clothing is not designed to reveal the form of the body, but for entirely different purposes.

　　　　　The tacit conventions on which the understanding of everyday language depends are enormously complicated.

4.003   Most of the propositions and questions to be found in philosophical works are not false but nonsensical. Consequently we cannot give any answer to questions of this kind, but can only establish that they are nonsensical. Most of the propositions and questions of philosophers arise from our failure to understand the logic of our language.

　　　　　(They belong to the same class as the question whether the good is more or less identical than the beautiful.)

　　　　　And it is not surprising that the deepest problems are in fact *not* problems at all.[z]

So far, Wittgenstein is a Russellian, and the positivists of course welcomed him as an ally in their battle against metaphysics. But the last two paragraphs in 4.003 sound a different note and suggest a different view, both of philosophy and of the world, and one that was not at all Russellian or positivistic.

This arises because Wittgenstein was concerned, as Russell and the positivists were not, with the unsayable, with what lies on the other side of the boundary between the knowable and the unknowable. The general thesis, to which Wittgenstein returns again and again, is that there is a profound dichotomy between what can be said and what can only be shown. On the one hand, "What *can* be shown, *cannot* be said."[a] On the other hand, what cannot be said, about which we must perforce be silent, may yet be shown. We have already seen that objects, being wholly simple entities, cannot be defined. "Objects can only be *named.* Signs are their representatives. I can only speak *about* them: I cannot *put them into words.* Propositions only say *how* things are, not *what* they are."[b] And again, "A proposition *shows* its sense. [It] shows how things stand *if* it is true. And it *says that* they do so stand."[c]

It is impossible, that is to say, to frame a proposition about the relation between a proposition and what that proposition means: pictorial and logical form can only be shown. Suppose someone paints a picture of a landscape. One can look at the picture and look at the landscape and *see* that the picture represents it. But can one represent the way the picture represents the landscape? No, one cannot. One could photograph the painting and the landscape and compare them. But that would be comparing two representations. The photograph would not represent the relation of representation that holds between the painting represented in the photograph and the landscape. *That* relation—the relation of representation—can be displayed (pointed to), but it cannot be represented, for, being a relation between a representation and what is represented, it falls outside all representation.

> 4.12   Propositions can represent the whole of reality, but they cannot represent what they must have in common with reality in order to be able to represent it—logical form.
>
>   In order to be able to represent logical form, we should have to be able to station ourselves with propositions somewhere outside logic, that is to say outside the world.
>
> 4.121   Propositions cannot represent logical form: it is mirrored in them.
>
>   What finds its reflection in language, language cannot represent.
>
>   What expresses *itself* in language, *we* cannot express by means of language.
>
>   Propositions *show* the logical form of reality. They display it. . . .
>
> 2.172   A picture cannot, however, depict its pictorial form: it displays it.[d]

In other words, if Kant's attempt to construct a bridge between logic and experience was defeated by showing that there is no synthetic a priori, every other proposal to construct a bridge is foreclosed by the distinction between saying and showing. *That* language has a relation to the world can be shown; *what* the relation is cannot be said. This is a very radical conclusion indeed, and one that Russell naturally resisted. Though metaphysical truth eluded him, he was loath to accept a position that excluded even its possibility.[8] His countersuggestion was that, though Wittgenstein might be correct in holding that the relation between any given language and the world cannot be said in that language, it is sayable in a metalanguage "dealing with the structure of the first language and having a new structure." . . . "To this hierarchy of languages," he added, "there may be no limit."[e]

This solution did not satisfy Wittgenstein. Russell was in effect telling him that there is no limit to the number of specific things we can say about (that is, *within*) the world; Wittgenstein was concerned that we can say nothing about the world *as a whole*. Russell was interested in solving a logical problem not unlike the problem solved by the theory of types, and his proposed solution was analogous. Wittgenstein was certainly concerned with the logical problem to which Russell was addressing himself, but he was also concerned with a human problem. We may call it a problem of human finitude. One feature of this finitude is our imprisonment in language. Our world, the world of each of us, is bounded by our language. *"The limits of my language* mean the limits of my world."[f]

[8] See pp. 191, 205–06, and 215.

We are now in a position to return to the question, "What sort of discourse is philosophy?" We have already said that one of its functions is to expose the mistakes of earlier philosophers, but we can now see that their mistakes were not due merely to a confusion between grammatical and logical structure. More profoundly, the mistakes of earlier philosophers arose because they were trying to say the unsayable. Accordingly, the correct account of philosophy is to say that it is not *discourse* at all; it is an activity, the activity of displaying the limits of what can be said.

> 4.112   Philosophy is not a body of doctrine but an activity.
>
>   A philosophical work consists essentially of elucidations.
>
>   Philosophy does not result in "philosophical propositions," but rather in the clarification of propositions.
>
>   Without philosophy thoughts are, as it were, cloudy and indistinct: its task is to make them clear and to give them sharp boundaries. . . .
>
> 4.113   Philosophy sets limits to the much disputed sphere of natural science.
>
> 4.114   It must set limits to what can be thought; and, in doing so, to what cannot be thought.
>
>   It must set limits to what cannot be thought by working outwards through what can be thought.
>
> 4.115   It will signify what cannot be said, by presenting clearly what can be said.g

But does this not involve Wittgenstein in a contradiction? Is he not trying to say the unsayable when he *says* that it is unsayable? If philosophy is not discourse but an activity, what of the *Tractatus*? It is not an activity, but a piece of discourse. Wittgenstein's answer is that the discourse in the *Tractatus* is designed to show his readers that he cannot discourse to them about, but only show them, the boundary between the sayable and the unsayable. When Wittgenstein—or any other philosopher—has discoursed enough to make this clear, he can stop discoursing, and his readers, once they have seen what he is pointing out to them, can stop reading. They and he can discard his discourse; it no longer has a place in his or their scheme of things.

> 6.53   The correct method in philosophy would really be the following: to say nothing except what can be said, i.e. propositions of natural science—i.e. something that has nothing to do with philosophy—and then, whenever someone else wanted to say something metaphysical, to demonstrate to him that he had failed to give a meaning to certain signs in his propositions. Although it would not be satisfying to the other person—he would not have the feeling that we were teaching him philosophy—*this* method would be the only strictly correct one.

6.54 My propositions serve as elucidations in the following way: anyone who understands me eventually recognizes them as nonsensical, when he has used them—as steps—to climb up beyond them. (He must, so to speak, throw away the ladder after he has climbed up it.)

He must transcend these propositions, and then he will see the world aright.

7 What we cannot speak about we must pass over in silence.[h]

The Mystical

Wittgenstein's term for "things that cannot be put into words" but that "make themselves manifest" is "the mystical."[i] Among these things are the values that people try—and of course fail—to express in ethical and religious discourse.

6.41 The sense of the world must lie outside the world. In the world everything is as it is, and everything happens as it does happen: *in* it no value exists—and if it did exist, it would have no value.

If there is any value that does have value, it must lie outside the whole sphere of what happens and is the case. For all that happens and is the case is accidental. . . .

6.421 It is clear that ethics cannot be put into words. Ethics is transcendental.

(Ethics and aesthetics are one and the same.) . . .

6.423 It is impossible to speak about the will in so far as it is the subject of ethical attributes. . . .

6.43 If the good or bad exercise of the will does alter the world, it can alter only the limits of the world, not the facts—not what can be expressed by means of language.

In short the effect must be that it becomes an altogether different world. It must, so to speak, wax and wane as a whole.

The world of the happy man is a different one from that of the unhappy man.

6.431 So too at death the world does not alter, but comes to an end. . . .

6.432 *How* things are in the world is a matter of complete indifference for what is higher. God does not reveal himself *in* the world. . . .

6.44 It is not *how* things are in the world that is mystical, but *that* it exists.[j]

This notion of the mystical left Russell, no one will be surprised to learn, "with a certain sense of intellectual discomfort." It is unlikely that Wittgenstein himself found it satisfying, though it is probable that the discomfort he felt was moral or human, rather than merely intellectual. Indeed, we may believe that the source of one of the deepest of Wittgenstein's "deep disquietudes" was precisely his conviction that meaning is limited to propositions with sense (that is, to expressions that picture the world), and accordingly that we can say nothing whatever about those matters that mean (in another sense of "mean") most to us. Wittgenstein's temperament was very different from Hume's; he could never have been content with the latter's "mitigated scepticism."[9]

Accordingly, Wittgenstein attempted to allay his distress by assuring himself that Humean skepticism is nonsensical: we can be skeptical only about the possibility of answering some questions, but no question can be framed regarding those matters—such as the existence of God—about which Hume believed himself to be skeptical.

> 6.51 Scepticism is *not* irrefutable, but obviously nonsensical, when it tries to raise doubts where no questions can be asked.
>
> For doubt can exist only where a question exists, a question only where an answer exists, and an answer only where something *can be said*.
>
> 6.52 We feel that even when *all possible* scientific questions have been answered, the problems of life remain completely untouched. Of course there are then no questions left, and this itself is the answer.
>
> 6.521 The solution of the problem of life is seen in the vanishing of the problem.
>
> (Is not this the reason why those who have found after a long period of doubt that the sense of life became clear to them have then been unable to say what constituted that sense?)[k]

As we read these paragraphs and listen to how what is said is said, we may doubt whether Wittgenstein was successful in exorcising his demons; doubts persisted even though Wittgenstein told them they were really not questions. Wittgenstein, we may feel, was not one of those lucky ones who emerged from "a long period of doubt" to find that his "sense of life" had become "clear." If this is the case, it may explain in part why in *Philosophical Investigations* he was led to make a new start.[10]

---

[9] See Vol. III, pp. 349–51.
[10] See Ch. 11.

Logical Positivism

The Vienna Circle

In the early 1920s a group of Viennese intellectuals, including at the outset mathematicians, physicists, sociologists, and economists but no professional philosophers, began meeting weekly under the leadership of Moritz Schlick,[1] the newly appointed professor of the philosophy of the inductive sciences at the University of Vienna. The group, which had a strong sense of identity and mission, called

---

[1] Moritz Schlick (1892–1936) was born in Berlin and studied physics under Max Planck. He went to Vienna as a professor in 1922 and was killed fourteen years later by a student who had earlier made an unsuccessful attempt on Schlick's life and who was under psychiatric observation at the time.

itself the Vienna Circle. Later on, after it acquired adherents elsewhere in Europe and the United States, the geographically limited name was no longer felt to be appropriate, and the members of the Circle began to call their movement variously "Logical Empiricism," "Scientific Empiricism," and "Logical Positivism." Although the last is the name that stuck, the alternatives also tell us something about the Circle's view of what was important and characteristic about it: "empiricism" because the movement insisted that our knowledge of synthetic propositions can be gained only through experience; "positivism" because the members recognized the influence of Mach, Pearson, and other late-nineteenth-century positivists,[2] "logical" because the members of the Circle took seriously, and built on, the logical revolution described in the previous three chapters.

Although the positivists were thus empirical in outlook, they were anything but skeptics, relativists, or subjectivists, as many empiricists tended to be. They were contemptuous of attempts to justify the sciences on pragmatic or instrumentalist grounds. They wanted to show that the cognitive claims of the sciences are fully warranted, and they believed they had found a way of doing this.

This way of putting the sciences on an absolutely secure footing had the added advantage, from the positivists' view, of eliminating everything transcendental, everything otherworldly, everything supernatural. Positivism was, in fact, determinedly—one could fairly say, passionately—antimetaphysical. The positivists' attitude toward metaphysics was similar to that of the Marxists toward Christianity—and for much the same reason. If the Marxists held that religion is the opiate of the masses, the positivists held that metaphysics—and especially the idealist metaphysics that still dominated German universities—is, in effect, a tool of social and political conservatives. From the positivists' point of view metaphysicians were not merely mistaken; they were the instruments of reaction. Hence the positivists did not share Russell's hopes for a philosophical synthesis; they wanted to use philosophy to destroy all of philosophy except the part that can be called the logic of the sciences.

Finally, and in terms of James's classification of temperaments,[3] the positivists were tough-minded, rather than tender-minded. They were also cocky, self-assured, and optimistic. At the start, everything seemed simple and straightforward, and it was only gradually that they discovered they had imprudently set out to sea in an unfinished and leaking ship. Most of their energy was consumed in emergency repairs, and then repairs to the emergency repairs. In the process they fell into sharp disagreements, and by the mid-1930s positivism as a united front had begun to disintegrate.

For these reasons, in this chapter we shall adopt a different approach from the one we have usually followed. Instead of taking a single positivist for detailed study, as we took Moore to represent the realists, we shall draw on the writings of a number of positivists, with the aim, first, of bringing into focus the beliefs and

[2] See Vol. IV, pp. 202–05.
[3] See Vol. IV, p. 297.

attitudes that they all shared and, second, of examining the small set of closely related problems to which most of the positivists devoted most of their attention.

The Verifiability Principle

All the positivists agreed that, except in mathematics and logic, it is only in the sciences—and especially in physics—that we have anything that can properly be called *knowledge*. If we want to increase the amount of reliable information available to us, we should therefore extend the use of the scientific method in all domains. Why is it that science yields reliable information? It is because all assertions made in the sciences are warranted by experiment and controlled observation. Consider, for instance, the question, which was once much debated, whether the ether exists. For the positivists—if not for Michelson and Morley themselves—the Michelson-Morley experiment settled the issue.[4] In the test case no observable data (such as discernible differences in time) were found to which the term "ether" could be assigned. It should therefore be eliminated from the vocabulary of science as a meaningless word.

Generalizing from what they thus took to be the essential feature of scientific method, the positivists formulated a criterion of meaning that came to be called the "Verifiability Principle." This asserted that the meaning of a proposition is its mode of verification. Since it follows that propositions for which no means of verification exist are literally meaningless, the positivists saw that they had in their hands an instrument that would totally destroy metaphysics.

Schlick's essay "Positivism and Realism" is an early version of the Verifiability Principle and an application of it to a typical metaphysical problem: the dispute about the reality and/or ideality of the world. Positivism, he said, neither asserts the existence of an external world as the realists do nor denies it as the idealists do, for positivism holds that the question "Is there an external world?" is meaningless and so cannot be answered. "The whole business is much ado about nothing, for the 'problem of the reality of the external world' is a meaningless pseudo-problem."[a] That this is the case can "be made evident" by giving an account of the meaning of propositions.

> It is the peculiar business of philosophy to ascertain and make clear the *meaning* of statements and questions. The chaotic state in which

[4]In 1887 Albert Michelson and Edward Morley conducted an experiment designed to ascertain the speed of light relative to the ether. They reasoned that if a beam of light were transmitted first across and then along the direction of the flow of ether, there would be a difference in the times of transmission. Since no difference was observed, they concluded that their experiment had failed. It was not until later that Einstein interpreted the experiment as supporting the thesis of relativity theory that light has a uniform velocity.

philosophy has found itself during the greater part of its history is due to the unfortunate fact that, in the *first* place, it took certain formulations to be real questions before carefully ascertaining whether they really made any sense, and, in the *second* place, it believed that the answers to the questions could be found by the aid of special philosophical methods, different from those of the special sciences. But we cannot by philosophical analysis decide whether anything is real, but only what it *means* to say that it is real; and whether this is then the case or not can be decided only by the usual methods of daily life and of science, that is, through *experience*. . . .

When, in general, are we sure that the meaning of a question is clear to us? Evidently when and only when we are able to state exactly the conditions under which it is to be answered in the affirmative, or, as the case may be, the conditions under which it is to be answered in the negative. By stating these conditions, and by this alone, is the meaning of a question defined.

It is the first step of any philosophizing, and the foundation of all reflection, to see that it is simply impossible to give the meaning of any statement except by describing the fact which must exist if the statement is to be true. If it does not exist then the statement is false. The meaning of a proposition consists, obviously, in this alone, that it expresses a definite state of affairs. And this state of affairs must be pointed out in order to give the meaning of the proposition. One can, of course, say that the proposition itself already gives this state of affairs. This is true, but the proposition indicates the state of affairs only to the person who understands it. But when do I understand a proposition? When I understand the meanings of the words which occur in it? These can be explained by definitions. But in the definitions new words appear whose meanings cannot again be described in propositions, they must be indicated directly: the meaning of a word must in the end be *shown,* it must be *given.* This is done by an act of indication, of pointing; and what is pointed at must be given, otherwise I cannot be referred to it.

Accordingly, in order to find the meaning of a proposition, we must transform it by successive definitions until finally only such words occur in it as can no longer be defined, but whose meanings can only be directly pointed out. The criterion of the truth or falsity of the proposition then lies in the fact that under definite conditions (given in the definition) certain data are present, or not present. If this is determined then everything asserted by the proposition is determined, and I know its meaning. . . .

The content of our insight is indeed quite simple (and this is the reason why it is so sensible). It says: a proposition has a statable meaning only if it makes a verifiable difference whether it is true or false. A proposition which is such that the world remains the same whether it be true or false simply says nothing about the world; it is empty and communicates nothing; I can give it no meaning. . . .

The results of our discussion may be summarized as follows. . . . The justified unassailable nucleus of the "positivistic" tendency seems to me to be the principle that the meaning of every proposition is completely contained within its verification in the given. . . .

The chief opposition to our view derives from the fact that the distinction between the falsity and the meaninglessness of a proposition is not observed. The proposition "Discourse concerning a metaphysical external world is meaningless" does *not* say: "There is no external world," but something altogether different. The empiricist does not say to the metaphysician "what you say is false," but "what you say asserts nothing at all!" He does not contradict him, but says "I don't understand you."[b]

That the Verifiability Principle was the "nucleus" of positivism everyone agreed; unfortunately, it proved to be anything but "unassailable." Indeed, as we shall see,[5] much of the history of positivism was a series of attempts to defend the principle against attack.

Logical Construction

The second point on which the positivists agreed was the importance of "modern" logic and the analysis that it made possible. Here, of course, they learned much from Russell. The aim of logical analysis, according to the positivists, is to clarify the statements that are made in the sciences, in order to reveal their true cognitive content. We have seen that, though "The author of *Waverley* is Scott" is true, unwary readers—even the literary historian who makes the assertion—may attribute a false cognitive content to it until its precise cognitive content has been exposed by analysis.[6] The positivists recognized that scientists could go astray in a similar way. Without a logical analysis there was a danger that physicists themselves—let alone philosophers and laypersons—might misread such true statements as "Electrons exist" or "The ether does not exist" and attribute a metaphysical content to them.

Taken together, the Verifiability Principle and the conception of logical construction defined the nature of the program the positivists hoped to carry out. This was to start from elements so simple that our experience of them is incorrigible and to construct the propositions that form the content of the several

[5] See pp. 267–70.
[6] See p. 184.

sciences. Or, to put matters the other way around, it was to start from the propositions of the sciences and by means of analysis show that these are all reducible to observation statements about directly experienced simples.

The outline of this program is contained implicitly in the passage from Schlick that we have already quoted. For if the Verifiability Principle asserts, as Schlick held, that "the meaning of a word must in the end be *shown*, it must be *given*," then it becomes necessary to "transform" every sentence that does not directly refer to the given into a sentence that does directly refer to the given. As Schlick wrote, "In order to find the meaning of a proposition, we must transform it by successive definitions until finally only such words occur in it as can no longer be defined, but whose meanings can only be directly pointed out."

The Unity of Science

Theoretically, the dual objective of eliminating nonsense and of securing sense would be satisfied if the various sentences tested by the Verifiability Principle were traced back, each to its own area of the given. Being incorrigible, each such experience would secure the sentence being analyzed. Every science would then have its own foundation. But it was much more economical—and also more elegant—to "reduce" the several sciences to one science, and the only plausible candidate for this role was physics. The attempt to reduce the languages of the various subsciences—from chemistry and biology to psychology and sociology—to that of physics was called the "unity of science" movement, and the thesis underlying this movement was "physicalism."

> The thesis of *physicalism* maintains that the physical language is a universal language of science—that is to say, that every language of any sub-domain of science can be equipollently translated into the physical language. From this it follows that science is a unitary system within which there are no fundamentally diverse object-domains, and consequently no gulf, for example, between natural and psychological sciences. This is the thesis of the *unity of science.*[c]

The goal of the unity-of-science movement was to be achieved by first ascertaining what the "basic objects" are that together form the "basis of the system" and by then constructing objects of successively higher levels from these objects "by a step-by-step procedure." We can say at once that though they devoted much energy and ingenuity to designing "reduction procedures" and "ascension forms," the positivists were never able to carry out this ambitious project. And in any case they soon became increasingly involved in coping with fundamental questions that placed the whole undertaking in jeopardy. Nevertheless, the spirit of the movement and its early assurance are well conveyed in the following passage:

The new type of philosophy has arisen in close contact with the work of the special sciences, especially mathematics and physics. . . . The individual no longer undertakes to erect in one bold stroke an entire system of philosophy. Rather, each works at his special place within the one unified science. For the physicist and the historian this orientation is commonplace, but in philosophy we witness the spectacle (which must be depressing to a person of scientific orientation) that one after another and side by side a multiplicity of incompatible philosophical systems is erected. If we allot to the individual in philosophical work as in the special sciences only a partial task, then we can look with more confidence into the future: in slow careful construction insight after insight will be won. Each collaborator contributes only what he can endorse and justify before the whole body of his co-workers. Thus stone will be carefully added to stone and a safe building will be erected at which each following generation can continue to work.[d]

Although this passage shows how much the positivists' program was dominated by a quest for certainty, their talk about the "reduction" of complex statements to observation statements, or about the "construction" of higher-level objects out of basic objects, was not intended to be a claim that basic objects are more real than, or in any sense ontologically superior to, higher-level objects. From the positivists' point of view, of course, questions about the reality or ontological status of any object are ruled out as meaningless—for instance, Moore's worry about the relation between sense data and physical objects was misplaced.[7] Properly understood, it is not a philosophical question at all, but merely a question as to whether a translation is possible from the sense-data language to the physical-object language. Nevertheless, if the unity-of-science movement was not an old-fashioned ontological inquiry into what the ultimate elements in the universe are, neither was it intended to be merely an exercise in the construction of a unifying language. The unity-of-science movement started from an analysis of the logical structure of scientific propositions, and it started there because it made the fundamental assumption that an isomorphism exists between the structure of "the" language and the structure of the world described in the language. That there is a language that is *the* language they did not question, being persuaded by Fregean considerations—above all, by Frege's contention that all assertions have a necessary structure that analysis can expose to view.

These assumptions were to prove much more slippery than the positivists initially believed, and there was always a danger, even while explicitly denying ontological intentions, of slipping unconsciously into ontological commitments. It is difficult, for instance, to resist the conclusion that Schlick, at least some of the time, regarded his ineffable "given" as not merely epistemologically more certain, but somehow ontologically superior.

[7] See pp. 113–15.

How the Positivists Read the Tractatus

In their attempt both to define and to carry out their program, the positivists were greatly influenced by Wittgenstein's *Tractatus*. Soon after its publication in 1921 the Vienna Circle was reading it aloud and analyzing it sentence by sentence. By this time Wittgenstein had returned to Austria, and he and members of the Circle met from time to time for discussions. His style and outlook were so different from that of most of the members of the Circle that these meetings were unsuccessful. To Wittgenstein it probably seemed that they oversimplified his position; to them he seemed oracular, his attitudes toward people and problems being "much more similar to those of a creative artist than to that of a scientist, one might almost say, similar to those of a religious prophet or seer."[e] And, personalities aside, there were certainly features of the *Tractatus* with which they disagreed. They were utterly uninterested in the idea of showing the unsayable. As regards the unsayable, the positivists thought it quite sufficient to demonstrate that metaphysics is unsayable. There is nothing to be shown. The mystical, in a word, seemed to them disreputable—something to be ignored, not passed over in silence.

But what Wittgenstein said about the sayable was quite another matter. The positivists' program rested, first, on the basic assumption of the whole analytic tradition that analysis terminates in simples and, second, on the special assumption generated by the logical investigations of Frege and Russell, that when language has been correctly analyzed it will be isomorphic with the world; the structures of the sentences in which we make assertions about the world must exactly mirror the structures that characterize the world about which these assertions are made. These were just the two theses held by the positivists that the argument of the *Tractatus* put beyond question. As Russell wrote in his introduction, "In order that a certain sentence should assert a certain fact there must, however the language may be constructed, be something in common between the structure of the sentence and the structure of the fact." That, Russell said, is "perhaps the most fundamental thesis of Mr. Wittgenstein's theory."[f]

Putting the picturing thesis and the atomistic thesis together, we get the thesis that since logical analysis terminates in simple names, the world consists of a set of atomic facts that these names designate. The names, being simple, cannot be defined; hence they must be "explained by means of elucidations." "Elucidations are propositions that contain the primitive signs." The names that occur in elucidations "are like points," and the propositions in which the names occur "are like arrows."[8,g] In short, the function of elucidations is to draw our attention to those simple, atomic facts of which the world consists and out of which the complex things of ordinary experience are constructed, just as the names themselves are the simple elements into which the complex propositions of ordinary and of scientific discourse can be analyzed.

---

[8] See pp. 219–20 for the context of these sentences.

This is the way the positivists read the *Tractatus,* and no wonder they were impressed. It provided the philosophical rationale for their program, the basis from which it could be securely launched.

What Do the Elucidations Elucidate?

The positivists, then, believed that they could in effect begin where the *Tractatus* left off. Since the *Tractatus* was a work on logic, not on the foundations of the sciences, the positivists recognized that it was enough for Wittgenstein to show that there must be atomic facts. The positivists, however, were interested in logic chiefly as a preliminary for, and a clarification of, the sciences, and it was necessary for them to go beyond the *Tractatus* and ascertain the nature of the atomic facts. But the positivists had quite specific notions about what the clarification of the sciences consists in. In accordance with the requirements of the Verifiability Principle, to clarify the sciences—to put them on a secure basis—is to show that all scientific propositions, however complex, are reducible to empirically verifiable assertions. Accordingly, if Wittgenstein's atomic facts were to be of any use to the positivists, they must be empirically observable occurrences. And again, if the sciences are to be put on a secure basis, the elucidations by means of which we become acquainted with the atomic facts must be incorrigible. These two requirements greatly restricted the positivists' freedom to work within the logical framework of the *Tractatus,* and the questions "What is the nature of what is elucidated?" and "What sorts of propositions are the elucidations themselves?" proved much more difficult to answer than the positivists initially supposed.

The essay by Schlick from which we have already quoted was an early answer to both questions, and the extent to which he had been influenced by Wittgenstein is evident. Schlick held his "given" to be the terminus of the definition process; being given, it cannot itself be defined but only shown—but, being given, it does not need to be defined, since the showing of it is enough. In a word, his given is evidently the object named by one of Wittgenstein's primitive signs, which must be explained by elucidations, since analysis or definition of an object is impossible.

But can the given be elucidated in a way that provides a secure basis for the sciences? Since, according to Schlick, the given is "what is most simple and no longer questionable,"[h] it follows that electrons and other "scientific" objects are not given, nor are ordinary objects that we encounter in everyday life. Thus, in terms of Russell's distinction between dogs and canoid color patches,[9] it is the latter, not the former, that are given. But since, in opposition to Russell (and to Moore), Schlick held that sense data are not public but private and incommunicable, a

[9] See p. 192.

difficulty arises. There is, Schlick thought, a radical difference—"a difference in principle," he said—between (1) my observing two pieces of paper and noting that they are both green, and (2) my showing "one of these two pieces of paper to a second observer and ask[ing] the question: does he see the green as I do?" My observation that the two pieces are both green is infallible; so, too, presumably is his. But I can never know whether he is having the same experience—experiencing the same quality—that I am experiencing. He *says* "green" when I say "green," but "I cannot infer from this that he experiences this same quality. It could be the case that on looking at the green paper he would have a color experience which I would call 'red,'" and that "when I see red he would see green, calling it 'red' of course, and so on."[i]

But if this is the case, the Verifiability Principle's appeal to experience amounts to no more than this: I verify the complex assertions of the sciences in *my* experience and you verify them in *yours*. But since your experiences and mine are incomparable, the attempt to found the sciences on the given may seem to have collapsed.

Not so, according to Schlick. Though the sense data themselves are incomparable, the relational structures into which these sense data fit are comparable. Though I can never know whether what you call green is what I call green, I can observe that what you call green is related to what you call yellow and what you call blue in the same way that what I call green is related to what I call yellow and what I call blue. Thus, even though the quality of my experience may differ so much from the quality of another man's that

> my color experiences correspond to his tone experiences, . . . nevertheless . . . we should always understand one another perfectly . . . if the inner *order* of his experience agreed with that of mine. There is no question here of their "quality," all that is required is that they can be arranged into systems in the same manner. . . . A statement concerning the similarity of the experiences of two persons has no other *communicable* meaning than a certain agreement of their reactions.[j]

And since reactions are, of course, observable facts, intersubjective verifiability has been restored.

This solution did not satisfy the Circle. The sciences, they agreed, are concerned with order—however, not with order in the abstract but with the ordering of real, concrete things. To exclude quality would be to suspend science in an ideal domain; it is and ought to be about the actual. On the other hand, to allow quality was to bring in, on Schlick's own account, the incommunicable and the unverifiable, in fact, the metaphysical. It seemed to follow that Schlick's distinction between order and quality was a blind alley, and if this was the outcome of an appeal to the given, Schlick's approach must be abandoned and a wholly new start made.

PROTOCOL SENTENCES

To get around the hazards of defining verification in terms of the given, Neurath[10] introduced the concept of protocol sentences. All sentences, he said, fall into one of two classes, tautologies or factual sentences, and the latter are further subdivided into protocol sentences and nonprotocol sentences. Of course, the vast majority of factual sentences are nonprotocol sentences; indeed, protocol sentences are the invention of Neurath to escape Schlick's dilemma. But the point is that such sentences *can* be constructed, that they are factual sentences, and that all other factual sentences can be reduced to them and so verified by means of them. That, at least, was Neurath's claim.

The distinguishing feature of protocol sentences is that

> in them, a personal noun always occurs several times in a specific association with other terms. A complete protocol sentence might, for instance, read: "Otto's protocol at 3:17 o'clock: [At 3:16 o'clock Otto said to himself: (at 3:15 o'clock there was a table in the room perceived by Otto)]." This factual sentence is so constructed that, within each set of brackets, further factual sentences may be found, *viz.*: "At 3:16 o'clock Otto said to himself: (At 3:15 o'clock there was a table in the room perceived by Otto)" and "At 3:15 o'clock there was a table in the room perceived by Otto."[k]

We can see what Neurath wanted to do: to construct sentences that report very precisely the occurrence of minimal (that is, atomistic) events. For this purpose the bracketed phrases serve well, but (as Neurath himself says) "'Otto' itself is in many ways a vague term."[l] Very well, then, it is possible to devise more-precise locutions. For instance,

> one may introduce a system of physicalistic designations in place of "Otto," and this system of designations may, in turn, further be defined by referring to the "position" of the name "Otto" in a group of signs composed of the names "Karl," "Heinrich," etc.[m]

And this process can be continued until we reach any level of precision in phraseology we desire.

> The phrase "Otto is observing" could be replaced by the phrase "The man, whose carefully taken photograph is listed no. 16 in the file, is observing": but the term "photograph listed no. 16 in the file" still has to be replaced by a system of mathematical formulae, which is

[10]Otto Neurath (1882–1945) was a sociologist and economist. During the First World War he was a civil servant in Bavaria; he was imprisoned when the communist regime that had been set up after the German defeat was overthrown. He moved to Vienna in 1920 after his release. In the mid-1930s he emigrated to the United States.

unambiguously correlated with another system of mathematical formulae, the terms of which take the place of "Otto," "angry Otto," "friendly Otto," etc.[n]

But reduction of ambiguity is one thing; incorrigibility is another. And it was incorrigibility that was needed if the sciences were to be assured the foundation for which the positivists were looking. But *are* protocol sentences incorrigible? Neurath thought not and was prepared to accept the consequences.

> *There is no way of taking conclusively established pure protocol sentences as the starting point of the sciences.* No *tabula rasa* exists. We are like sailors who must rebuild their ship on the open sea, never able to dismantle it in dry-dock and to reconstruct it there out of the best materials. . . . Vague linguistic conglomerations always remain in one way or another as components of the ship. If vagueness is diminished at one point, it may well be increased at another.[o]

It follows that a complex proposition is not verified by reducing it to elementary propositions and then showing that they state atomistic facts, but by ascertaining whether any proposed new sentence agrees with, or conflicts with, the whole system of sentences that form the body of the science at this time. And here we always have an option. If the new sentence conflicts with the system, we can, and often do, abandon the sentence as "false." But if we prefer, we hold that the sentence is "true" and alter the system enough to make the sentence consistent with it.

> The transformation of the sciences is effected by the discarding of sentences utilized in a previous historical period, and, frequently, their replacement by others. Sometimes the same form of words is retained, but their definitions are changed. *Every law and every physicalistic sentence of unified-science or of one of its sub-sciences is subject to such change. And the same holds for protocol sentences.*
>
> In unified-science we try to construct a non-contradictory system of protocol sentences and non-protocol sentences (including laws). When a new sentence is presented to us we compare it with the system at our disposal, and determine whether or not it conflicts with that system. If the sentence does conflict with the system, we may discard it as useless (or false), as, for instance, would be done with "In Africa lions sing only in major scales." One may, on the other hand, *accept* the sentence and so change the system that it remains consistent even after the adjunction of the new sentence. The sentence would then be called "true."[p]

Readers of this passage were astonished to find a positivist reverting to a theory of truth associated with the much-scorned objective idealism,[11] and Schlick, for his part, was horrified:

---

[11] See Vol. IV, Ch. 9.

What was originally meant by "protocol statements," as the name indicates, are those statements which express the *facts* with absolute simplicity, without any moulding, alteration or addition, in whose elaboration every science consists, and which precede all knowing, every judgment regarding the world. It makes no sense to speak of uncertain facts. . . . If we succeed therefore in expressing the raw facts in "protocol statements," without any contamination, these appear to be the absolutely indubitable starting points of all knowledge. . . .

Surely the reason for bringing in the term "protocol statement" in the first place was that it should serve to mark out certain statements by the truth of which the truth of all other statements comes to be measured, as by a measuring rod. But according to [Neurath's] viewpoint . . . all statements shall accord with one another, with the result that every single one is considered as, in principle, corrigible, [and] truth can consist only in a *mutual agreement of statements.* . . .

The only way to avoid this absurdity is not to allow any statements whatsoever to be abandoned or altered, but rather to specify those that are to be maintained, to which the remainder have to be accommodated.q

"CONFIRMATION" STATEMENTS

Schlick therefore introduced another distinction, this time between protocol sentences and what he called "confirmation" sentences. The latter, not the former, are those incorrigible propositions that form the bedrock on which the sciences rest and to which all other propositions have to be accommodated. Let "M. S. perceived blue on the nth of April 1934 at such and such a time and such and such a place" be a protocol sentence. Then "Here now blue" (uttered at some particular time) is the corresponding confirmation statement. The protocol "is equivalent to 'M. S. made . . . (here time and place are to be given) the confirmation "here now blue."'"r

Protocol sentences, then, are in effect hypotheses; they therefore cannot serve as "the ultimate basis of all knowledge." But confirmation sentences have the advantage of being absolutely certain.

While in the case of all other synthetic statements determining the meaning is separate from, distinguishable from, determining the truth, in the case of [confirmations] they coincide, just as in the case of analytic statements. However different therefore "confirmations" are from analytic statements, they have in common that the occasion of understanding them is at the same time that of verifying them: I grasp their meaning at the same time as I grasp their truth. In the case of a confirmation it makes as little sense to ask whether I might be deceived regarding its truth as in the case of a tautology. Both are absolutely valid. However, while the analytic, tautological statement is empty of content, the observation statement supplies us with the satisfaction of genuine knowledge of reality.[s]

Thus it might seem that confirmation sentences provide the secure basis for which we have been looking. Unfortunately,

> a genuine confirmation cannot be written down, for as soon as I inscribe the demonstratives "here," "now," they lose their meaning. Neither can they be replaced by an indication of time and place, for as soon as one attempts to do this, the result . . . is that one unavoidably substitutes for the observation statement a protocol statement which as such has a wholly different nature.[t]

It looks, then, as if we face a dilemma. Confirmation sentences are incorrigible, but wholly unverifiable; they are personal, momentary, and private. Protocol sentences are verifiable, but never completely so; they remain hypotheses "characterized by uncertainty." But this uncertainty is irrelevant to the practicing scientist, according to Schlick. What is all-important to him is the "moment of fulfillment and combustion" that is conveyed in a confirmation statement.

This may be a correct account of the psychological motivation of many scientists. What matters to them may well be the joy of discovery, the thrill of having some guess, some intellectual gamble, pay off. But the Circle was not interested in the personal psychology of scientists; it was interested in the foundations of science—a quite different matter. If the aim of *science*, as distinct from the aim of individual scientists, is to reach a secure knowledge of the world, Schlick's confirmation sentences were unsatisfactory.

PHYSICALISM

Neurath's protocol sentences always included an observer, and even though he introduced ways of specifying the observer unambiguously and so securing an intersubjective consensus about who the observer is, there remained the problem of reference by this observer to the observer's experience. Carnap[12] thought the way out of this difficulty was to recast protocol sentences so that they report not an observer's experiences but observable physical changes. For instance, instead of writing "Otto sees yellow bordering on blue here and now," we could instruct Otto (in ordinary language) to press a lever or a button whenever (in the ordinary way of speaking) he sees yellow bordering blue. Our protocol sentence could then report the occurrence of such and such specific bodily movements at

---

[12] Rudolf Carnap (1891–1970) was educated at Freiburg and Jena, where he studied mathematics, physics, and philosophy. Frege was one of his teachers. He went to Vienna in 1926 at Schlick's invitation and came to the United States nine years later, where he taught at the University of Chicago and at UCLA.

such and such times, thereby eliminating "Otto," "sees," "yellow," and "blue," and giving us a completely verifiable, because completely objective, proposition. Similarly, instead of writing "Otto feels pain here and now" we could report such and such changes in blood pressure, respiration rate, and so on.

But are sentences about experiences fully translatable into sentences about physical changes? Many people would hold, at least initially, that they are not. It seems obvious, they would say, that seeing yellow bordering blue is not the same as pressing a button or pulling a lever and that what is meant by "pain" is quite different from what is meant by "increase in blood pressure." But if psychological propositions are not equivalent to physiological or physical propositions, then, whatever may be true of physiology and physics, psychology has certainly not been provided with a secure basis in the form of incorrigible protocol sentences.

Accordingly, it was essential for Carnap to be able to show that the psychological language (the language in which we talk, for instance, about pain) is reducible to a behavioristic language (in which we talk about observations of changes in blood pressure). For this purpose Carnap needed a general definition of reducibility and rules for carrying out a reduction.

> We know the meaning (designatum) of a term if we know under what conditions we are permitted to apply it in a concrete case and under what conditions not. . . . If now a certain term x is such that the conditions for its application (as used in the language of science) can be formulated with the help of the terms y, z, etc., we call such a formulation a *reduction statement* for x in terms of y, z etc., and we call x *reducible* to y, z, etc. There may be several sets of conditions for the application of x; hence x may be reducible to y, z, etc., and also to u, v, etc., and perhaps to other sets. There may even be cases of mutual reducibility, e.g., each term of the set x_1x_2, etc., is reducible to y_1y_2, etc.; and, on the other hand, each term of the set y_1y_2, etc., is reducible to x_1x_2, etc.
>
> A *definition* is the simplest form of a reduction statement. For the formulation of examples, let us use "$\equiv$" (called the symbol of equivalence) as abbreviation for "if and only if." Example of a definition for "ox": "x is an ox $\equiv x$ is a quadruped and horned and cloven-footed and ruminant, etc." This is also a reduction statement because it states the conditions for the application of the term "ox," saying that this term can be applied to a thing if and only if that thing is a quadruped and horned, etc. By that definition the term "ox" is shown to be reducible to— moreover definable by—the set of terms "quadruped," "horned," etc. . . .
>
> A general way of procedure which enables us to find out whether or not a certain term can be applied in concrete cases may be called a *method of determination* for the term in question. The method of determination for a quantitative term (e.g., "temperature") is the method of measurement for that term. Whenever we know an experimental method of determination for a term, we are in a position to formulate a reduction statement for it. . . .

Sometimes we know several methods of determination for a certain term. For example, we can determine the presence of an electric current by observing either the heat produced in the conductor, or the deviation of a magnetic needle, or the quantity of a substance separated from an electrolyte, etc. Thus the term "electric current" is reducible to each of many sets of other terms. Since not only can an electric current be measured by measuring a temperature but also, conversely, a temperature can be measured by measuring the electric current produced by a thermo-electric element, there is mutual reducibility between the terms of the theory of electricity, on the one hand, and those of the theory of heat, on the other. The same holds for the terms of the theory of electricity and those of the theory of magnetism. . . .

If a certain language (e.g., a sublanguage of the language of science, covering a certain branch of science) is such that every term of it is reducible to a certain set of terms, then this language can be constructed on the basis of that set by introducing one new term after the other by reduction statements. In this case we call the basic set of terms a *sufficient reduction basis* for that language.[11]

So much for reduction statements in general. Carnap proceeded to tackle psychological terms. His first move was to distinguish between being able to carry out a reduction in detail and knowing in principle how to go about it.

Let us take as an example the term "angry." If for anger we knew a sufficient and necessary criterion to be found by a physiological analysis of the nervous system or other organs, then we could define "angry" in terms of the biological language. The same holds if we knew such a criterion to be determined by the observation of the overt, external behavior. But a physiological criterion is not yet known. And the peripheral symptoms known are presumably not necessary criteria because it might be that a person of strong self-control is able to suppress these symptoms. If this is the case, the term "angry" is, at least at the present time, not definable in terms of the biological language. But, nevertheless, it is reducible to such terms. It is sufficient for the formulation of a reduction sentence to know a behavioristic procedure which enables us—if not always, at least under suitable circumstances—to determine whether the organism in question is angry or not. And we know indeed such procedures; otherwise we should never be able to apply the term "angry" to another person on the basis of our observations of his behavior, as we constantly do in everyday life and in scientific investigation. A reduction of the term "angry" or similar terms by the formulation of such procedures is indeed less useful than a definition would be, because a definition supplies a complete (i.e., unconditional) criterion for the term in question, while a reduction statement of the conditional form gives only an incomplete one. But a criterion, conditional or not, is all we need for ascertaining reducibility. Thus the result is the following: If for any psychological term we know either a physiological or a behavioristic method of determination, then that term is reducible.[v]

But what about our introspective knowledge of psychological states? When I am angry, surely I know that I am angry, and I know this "without applying any of those procedures which another person would have to apply," that is, without having to look in the mirror in order to see the way my face grimaces. Does this not invalidate the claims for reducibility? No, not at all. For reducibility to obtain, it is not necessary to exclude introspection: "It will suffice to show that in every case, no matter whether the introspective method is applicable or not, the behavioristic method can [also] be applied." There may indeed just possibly be some processes that have no behavioral symptoms at all and that therefore are accessible only by means of introspection. However, what is at issue here are not processes but the *terms* that designate processes, and the thesis of physicalism is simply that "there cannot be a term in the psychological language, taken as an intersubjective language for mutual communication, which designates a kind of state or event without any behavioristic symptom."[w]

But "symptom" evades the issue. Few people would deny the claim that psychological processes have observable, behavioristic symptoms. The Freudians, for instance, would allow—indeed, insist on—symptoms. The real question is whether the psychological process is *reducible* to the symptom: whether, for instance, the male patient's Oedipus complex is the same thing as his violent physical attack on his father. Not everyone would agree that it is, and some psychologists and philosophers of science would go so far as to say, not only that the process and the symptom are not identical, but that it is impossible even to talk about the symptom (as a physical event) without presupposing the process (as a psychological event). Radical behaviorism of the Carnapian variety, they would say, puts the cart before the horse.[13]

Thus one more attempt to define elucidations in a way that puts the sciences on a secure basis has broken down, or at least remains inconclusive. Meanwhile, Carnap's own position began to shift so much that the whole question of the nature both of elucidations and of what they elucidate was transformed.

The Shift toward Linguistic Analysis

The *Logical Syntax of Language* shows the results of this change in viewpoint. In it Carnap maintained that the intra-Circle disagreements, which he had earlier regarded as substantive issues, were only disputes over the choice of language.

---

[13] See pp. 306–07.

On the view here expounded the domain of the scientific sentences is not so restricted as on the one formerly held by the Vienna Circle. It was originally maintained that every sentence, in order to be significant, must be *completely verifiable;* . . . every sentence therefore must be a molecular sentence formed of concrete sentences. . . . On this view there was no place for the *laws of nature* amongst the sentences of the language. Either these laws had to be deprived of their unrestricted universality and be interpreted merely as report-sentences, or they were left their unrestricted universality, and regarded not as proper sentences of the object-language, but merely as directions for the construction of sentences. . . . In accordance with the principle of tolerance, we will not say that a construction of the physical language corresponding to this earlier view is inadmissible; it is equally possible, however, to construct the language in such a way that the unrestrictedly universal laws are admitted as proper sentences. The important difference between laws and concrete sentences is not obliterated in this second form of language, but remains in force. It is taken into account in the fact that definitions are framed for both kinds of sentences, and their various syntactical properties are investigated. The choice between the two forms of language is to be made on the grounds of expedience.[x]

THE PRINCIPLE OF TOLERANCE

It will be seen that Carnap called the insight that animated this shift the "Principle of Tolerance."

> We have discussed several examples of negative requirements . . . by which certain common forms of language—methods of expression and of inference—would be excluded. Our attitude to requirements of this kind is given a general formulation in the *Principle of Tolerance: It is not our business to set up prohibitions, but to arrive at conventions.*
>
> Some of the prohibitions which have hitherto been suggested have been historically useful in that they have served to emphasize important differences and bring them to general notice. But such prohibitions can be replaced by a definitional differentiation. In many cases, this is brought about by the simultaneous investigation (analogous to that of Euclidean and non-Euclidean geometries) of language-forms of different kinds—for instance, a definite and an indefinite language, or a language admitting and one not admitting the Law of Excluded Middle. . . . Thus, for example, . . . we shall differentiate between limitedly universal sentences, analytic unlimitedly universal sentences, and synthetic unlimitedly universal sentences, whereas Wittgenstein . . . and Schlick all exclude sentences of the third kind (laws of nature) from language altogether, as not being amenable to complete verification.

> *In logic, there are no morals.* Everyone is at liberty to build up his own
> logic, i.e. his own form of language, as he wishes. All that is required of
> him is that, if he wishes to discuss it, he must state his methods clearly,
> and give syntactical rules instead of philosophical arguments.[y]

Both the Circle and the *Tractatus* had uncritically assumed that it was "a question of '*the* language' in an absolute sense; it was thought possible to reject both
concepts and sentences if they did not fit into *the* language."[z] It is rather a question, Carnap now saw, of choosing from among a variety of languages, in each of
which, if they are properly constructed, everything that can be said can be said.
Hence we choose from among them not on truth-grounds but on grounds of
"expedience." In order to bring out forcefully a thesis that seems particularly important to some individual writer, it may be desirable to express oneself in a particular way—for instance, it may be desirable to construct a language in which the
possibility of syntactical a priori sentences is excluded. But it is quite possible to
construct a second language, with different syntactical rules, in which syntactical
a priori sentences are permitted. The only requirement is that the syntactical
rules permitting or excluding this class of sentences be clearly stated so that we
can see both what is going on in the language and why it is going on.

Carnap was still a long way from the later Wittgenstein and his language
games,[14] for he was not thinking of ordinary language and the manifold uses to
which it is constantly being put, but of "constructed" languages. It is characteristic that the example of linguistic diversity he cites is the Euclidean and non-
Euclidean geometries, which, starting from different axioms and definitions,
permit or exclude different sentences. Thus Euclidean geometry permits sentences about parallels that non-Euclidean geometries exclude. If the definitions
were not explicitly stated, we might suppose that the geometries contradict each
other, and we would then face the problem of deciding which was "true" and
which "false." As it is, since the definitions are explicit, we see that it is not at all
a question of truth or falsity, but of whether or not the different sentences about
parallels are developed consistently in accordance with the different syntactical
rules of the different geometries.

Nevertheless, when all this is said, there has still been a drastic change in viewpoint. For instance, the question whether protocol sentences are incorrigible has
been dissolved. For the assertion that protocol sentences are incorrigible is now
not a substantive claim whose truth or falsity has, if possible, to be ascertained but
only a linguistic recommendation that is to be accepted or rejected on grounds of
expedience.

THE MATERIAL AND FORMAL MODES OF SPEECH

Clearly, Carnap was moving away from a strictly positivistic, and toward a
more linguistic, approach to the problems of philosophy. In this respect he was

[14]See pp. 400–04.

reflecting, and also doubtless contributing to, a general shift in the orientation of the whole culture. Another sign of this shift in Carnap's point of view is the distinction he drew between the material and the formal modes of speech and the consequences that followed from it.

As a start we may say that sentences are in the material mode when they are about the world—for instance, "London is the capital of Britain"—and that sentences are in the formal mode when they are about words, sentences, or other linguistic features—for instance, "'London' is the correct spelling in English of the capital of Britain." The point of insisting on the distinction is this: some sentences that seem to be in the material mode are really in the formal mode. These sentences, which Carnap calls pseudo-object sentences, are the source of much grief to philosophers.

> To this intermediate field we will assign the sentences which are formulated as though they refer (either partially or exclusively) to objects, while in reality they refer to syntactical forms, and, specifically, to the forms of the designations of those objects with which they appear to deal. Thus these sentences are syntactical sentences in virtue of their content, though they are disguised as object-sentences. We will call them *pseudo-object-sentences.* If we attempt to represent in a formal way the distinction which is here informally and inexactly indicated, we shall see that these pseudo-object-sentences are simply *quasi-syntactical sentences of the material mode of speech.* . . .
>
> To this middle territory belong many of the questions and sentences relating to the investigation of what are called philosophical foundations. We will take a simple example. Let us suppose that in a philosophical discussion about the concept of number we want to point out that there is an essential difference between numbers and (physical) things, and thereby to give a warning against pseudo-questions concerning the place, weight, and so on of numbers. Such a warning will probably be formulated as a sentence of, say, the following kind: "Five is not a thing but a number" ($\mathfrak{S}_1$). Apparently this sentence expresses a property of the number five, like the sentence "Five is not an even but an odd number" ($\mathfrak{S}_2$). In reality, however, $\mathfrak{S}_1$ is not concerned with the number five, but with the word "five"; this is shown by the formulation $\mathfrak{S}_3$ which is equipollent to $\mathfrak{S}_1$: "'Five' is not a thing-word but a number-word." While $\mathfrak{S}_2$ is a proper object-sentence, $\mathfrak{S}_1$ is a pseudo-object-sentence; $\mathfrak{S}_1$ is a quasi-syntactical sentence (material mode of speech), and $\mathfrak{S}_3$ is the correlated syntactical sentence (formal mode of speech).
>
> We have here left out of account those logical sentences which assert something about the *meaning, content,* or *sense* of sentences or linguistic expressions of any domain. These also are pseudo-object-sentences. Let us consider as an example the following sentence, $\mathfrak{S}_1$: "Yesterday's

lecture was about Babylon." $\mathfrak{S}_1$ appears to assert something about Babylon, since the name "Babylon" occurs in it. In reality, however, $\mathfrak{S}_1$ says nothing about the town Babylon, but merely something about yesterday's lecture and the word "Babylon." This is easily shown by the following non-formal consideration: for our knowledge of the properties of the town Babylon it does not matter whether $\mathfrak{S}_1$ is true or false. Further, that $\mathfrak{S}_1$ is only a pseudo-object-sentence is clear from the circumstance that $\mathfrak{S}_1$ can be translated into the following sentence of (descriptive) syntax: "In yesterday's lecture either the word 'Babylon' or an expression synonymous with the word 'Babylon' occurred" ($\mathfrak{S}_2$).

Accordingly, we distinguish *three kinds of sentences:*

1. *Object-sentences*	2. *Pseudo-object-sentences* = quasi-syntactical sentences	3. *Syntactical sentences*
	Material mode of speech	*Formal mode of speech*
Examples: "5 is a prime number"; "Babylon was a big town"; "lions are mammals."	Examples: "Five is not a thing, but a number"; "Babylon was treated of in yesterday's lecture."	Examples: "'Five' is not a thing-word, but a number-word"; "the word 'Babylon' occurred in yesterday's lecture."[a]

Armed with these distinctions Carnap proceeded to attack a whole series of traditional philosophical problems—about meaning, about universals, about the status of sense data and physical objects, for instance. In each case he argued, first, that the problem arises only because philosophers cast their talk about the topic in the material mode of speech and, second, that it disappears when this talk is translated into the formal mode of speech.

We shall give a few examples, from a list many pages long, of Carnap's method of translating from the material mode into the formal mode. The first examples are concerned with meaning. Sentences containing such expressions as "means," "signifies," "names," "is a name for," and "designates" all suggest that meaning is a special sort of extralinguistic entity whose nature we, as philosophers, ought to investigate. Translation into the formal mode exposes this as an illusion. The great philosophical problem of the meaning of meaning simply evaporates.

Material mode of speech (quasi-syntactical sentences)	Formal mode of speech (the correlated syntactical sentences)
2a. The word "daystar" *designates* (or: *means;* or: *is a name for*) the sun.	2b. The word "daystar" is synonymous with "sun."
3a. The sentence $\mathfrak{S}_1$ *means* (or: *asserts;* or: has the *content;* or; has the *meaning*) that the moon is spherical.	3b. $\mathfrak{S}_1$ is equipollent to the sentence "The moon is spherical."
4a. The word "luna" in the Latin language *designates* the moon.	4b. There is an equipollent expressional translation of the Latin into the English language in which the word "moon" is the correlate of the word "luna."

The following examples, 6 and 7, show how the difference between the *meaning of an expression* and the *object designated by the expression* can be formally represented. . . .[15]

6a. The expressions "merle" and "blackbird" have the same *meaning* (or: *mean* the same; or: have the same *intensional object*).	6b. "Merle" and "blackbird" are L-synonymous.
7a. "Evening star" and "morning star" have a different meaning, but they *designate* the same object.	7b. "Evening star" and "morning star" are not L-synonymous, but P-synonymous.[16,b]

The next examples concern universal words. When philosophers talk in the material mode of speech, these words almost inevitably suggest to some of them that there must be abstract objects to name by these words; these philosophers therefore become metaphysical realists. Philosophers who are skeptical of the existence of such abstract objects become metaphysical nominalists; they maintain that universal words are the names of classes of particulars, instead of denying, as they should, that universal words are names. In this way the great philosophical problem of the "status" of universals was generated. Translation into the formal mode of speech dissolves it at once.

[15] [This shows Carnap's way of dealing with Frege's distinction between "sense" and "reference" (see p. 157). For his reference to the phenomenologists and their very different treatment of the same distinction, see p. 296—AUTHORS.]

[16] ["L-rules" is Carnap's shorthand for referring to the logicomathematical transformation rules of a language; "P-rules" refers to all the other syntactical rules of the language—AUTHORS.]

Sentences with universal words	Syntactical sentences
(Material mode of speech)	(Formal mode of speech)
17a. The moon is a *thing;* five is not a thing but a *number.*	17b. "Moon" is a thing-word (thing-name); "five" is not a thing-word, but a number-word.

In 17a, as contrasted with sentences like "the thing moon, . . ." "the number five, . . ." the universal words "thing" and "number" are independent.

18a. A property is not a *thing.*	18b. An adjective (property-word) is not a thing-word.

· ·

19a. Friendship is a *relation.*	19b. "Friendship" is a relation-word.
20a. Friendship is not a *property.*	20b. "Friendship" is not a property-word.[c]

INTERNAL AND EXTERNAL QUESTIONS CONCERNING LANGUAGE

As a final example of Carnap's shift toward a linguistic point of view, we may mention still another distinction that he came to draw, this time between internal and external questions about language. Once again, according to Carnap, failure to observe this distinction has led to endless, and quite unnecessary, controversy.

> Are there properties, classes, numbers, propositions? In order to understand more clearly the nature of these and related problems, it is above all necessary to recognize a fundamental distinction between two kinds of questions concerning the existence or reality of entities. If someone wishes to speak in his language about a new kind of entities, he has to introduce a system of new ways of speaking, subject to new rules; we shall call this procedure the construction of a linguistic *framework* for the new entities in question. And now we must distinguish two kinds of questions of existence: first, questions of the existence of certain entities of the new kind *within the framework;* we call them *internal questions;* and second, questions concerning the existence or reality *of the system of entities as a whole,* called *external questions.* Internal questions and possible answers to them are formulated with the help of the new forms of expressions. The answers may be found either by purely logical methods or by empirical methods, depending upon whether the framework is a logical or a factual one. An external question is of a problematic character which is in need of close examination.[d]

Leaving aside logical languages, such as mathematics, let us consider a factual language, and the simplest example is the ordinary language in which we talk about everyday things. Once we have accepted this language with its framework of things, we can answer internal questions, such as whether King Arthur ever existed, whether unicorns and centaurs are real, and whether there is a piece of white paper on the floor in the dark corner. That is, the "thing language" provides us with rules for deciding whether such and such a thing is real or imaginary or a hallucination. These rules include looking things up in an encyclopedia or other reference book, turning on the light, looking more closely, and so on.

> To recognize something as a real thing or event means to succeed in incorporating it into the system of things at a particular space-time position so that it fits together with the other things recognized as real, according to the rules of the framework.
>
> From these questions we must distinguish the external question of the reality of the thing world itself. In contrast to the former questions, this question is raised neither by the man in the street nor by scientists, but only by philosophers. Realists give an affirmative answer, subjective idealists a negative one, and the controversy goes on for centuries without ever being solved. And it cannot be solved because it is framed in a wrong way. . . . Those who raise the question of the reality of the thing world itself have perhaps in mind not a theoretical question as their formulation seems to suggest, but rather a practical question, a matter of a practical decision concerning the structure of our language. We have to make the choice whether or not to accept and use the forms of expression in the framework in question. . . .
>
> We are free to choose to continue using the thing language or not; in the latter case we could restrict ourselves to a language of sense-data and other "phenomenal" entities, or construct an alternative to the customary thing language with another structure, or, finally, we could refrain from speaking. If someone decides to accept the thing language, there is no objection against saying that he has accepted the world of things. But this must not be interpreted as if it meant his acceptance of a *belief* in the reality of the thing world; there is no such belief or assertion or assumption, because it is not a theoretical question. To accept the thing world means nothing more than to accept a certain form of language, in other words, to accept rules for forming statements and for testing, accepting, or rejecting them.[e]

Exactly similar considerations apply to abstract entities. Just as the question "Do things exist?" is meaningless and must be replaced by the question "Will you accept our recommendation to employ a language in which the term 'thing' occurs, together with rules for its use?" so it is meaningless to ask whether abstract entities exist. It is simply a question of whether it is worth our while to introduce the term "abstract entity" into our language, with appropriate rules for its use.

For those who want to develop or use semantical methods, the decisive question is not the alleged ontological question of the existence of abstract entities but rather the question whether the use of abstract linguistic forms . . . is expedient and fruitful for the purposes for which semantical analyses are made. . . .

The acceptance or rejection of abstract linguistic forms, just as the acceptance or rejection of any other linguistic forms in any branch of science, will finally be decided by their efficiency as instruments, the ratio of the results achieved to the amount and complexity of the efforts required. To decree dogmatic prohibitions of certain linguistic forms instead of testing them by their success or failure in practical use, is worse than futile; it is positively harmful because it may obstruct scientific progress. The history of science shows examples of such prohibitions based on prejudices deriving from religious, mythological, metaphysical, or other irrational sources, which slowed up the developments for shorter or longer periods of time. Let us learn from the lessons of history. Let us grant to those who work in any special field of investigation the freedom to use any form of expression which seems useful to them; the work in the field will sooner or later lead to the elimination of those forms which have no useful function. *Let us be cautious in making assertions and critical in examining them, but tolerant in permitting linguistic forms.*[f]

All this follows from the Principle of Tolerance. Carnap was well aware of its importance. As early as 1934, he wrote:

The first attempts[17] to cast the ship of logic off from the *terra firma* of the classical forms were certainly bold ones, considered from the historical point of view. But they were hampered by the striving after "correctness." Now, however, that impediment has been overcome, and before us lies the boundless ocean of unlimited possibilities.[g]

The consequences of the Principle of Tolerance were indeed radical. The program that the Vienna Circle had laid down in the twenties, and which Carnap[18] and others had sought to carry out, had presupposed that there is an ideal language whose structure is revealed by logical analysis and that exactly mirrors the world. It now appears that there is a variety of languages, none of which is isomorphic with the world, and all of which can be recommended—but on different grounds.

[17][For instance, those of Frege, Russell, and the *Tractatus*—AUTHORS.]
[18]In *The Logical Structure of the World,* published in 1928.

Noncognitivism in Ethics and Religion

While the attempt to justify their program and render it coherent was thus leading some positivists to transform it, others continued to preach the orthodox doctrine of the Circle against traditional views about the nature of ethics, theology, and metaphysics. The basic strategy adopted was simple: it was to draw a sharp distinction between cognitive and noncognitive expressions. The former, being factual, are either true or false; they set out to give us information about the world, and if they are true they actually do so. The latter, being nonfactual, are neither true nor false. Since the two types of expression look alike it has been easy for philosophers to suppose that expressions containing ethical, theological, and metaphysical terms are cognitive. It can be shown, however, that all such expressions are nonfactual; if they have any function at all in the human economy it is certainly not to give us information about the world. Representative of this side of positivism was A. J. Ayer's [19] *Language, Truth, and Logic* (1936), in which the self-confidence and cockiness of the early years of positivism were still much in evidence.

THE EMOTIVE THEORY OF ETHICS

Since according to the Verifiability Principle all meaningful assertions must be capable of verification by empirical observation, it seemed to Ayer to follow that ethical assertions (for example, assertions of the form "X is right"; "Y is wrong") are either (1) empirically verifiable or (2) nonsense. It is true that expressions of this form are sometimes used empirically, both by ethical philosophers and by ordinary people. When, for instance, someone says, "Looking after one's old parents is right, but murder is wrong," he may intend to convey to us merely that most people approve of the one kind of action and disapprove of the other. If *that* is what he intends to say his assertion is indeed empirical, but it is not ethical. He is making an ordinary sociological observation that is verifiable in the usual way. But if we ask whether this is what he means and intends to convey to us, he perhaps replies indignantly, "No, no! I'm saying that murder is really wrong, and what people think about it is beside the point. Even if everyone approved of it, it would still be wrong." In this case, he is making a specifically ethical claim. The question is, what, if anything, can he mean?

Ayer's account of expressions of the form "X is right" and "Y is wrong" is an early version of the noncognitivist, or emotivist, theory of ethics. "Noncognitivist" because it maintains that ethical expressions assert nothing, "emotivist" because it maintains that what these expressions actually do is give vent to feelings.

---

[19] Alfred Jules Ayer was born in 1910 and was educated at Eton and Oxford. In 1933 he was in Vienna studying with the Circle. He taught at Oxford until the outbreak of the war and subsequently in London. He was knighted in 1970.

We begin by admitting that the fundamental ethical concepts are unanalysable, inasmuch as there is no criterion by which one can test the validity of the judgments in which they occur. So far we are in agreement with the absolutists. But, unlike the absolutists, we are able to give an explanation of this fact about ethical concepts. We say that the reason why they are unanalysable is that they are mere pseudo-concepts. The presence of an ethical symbol in a proposition adds nothing to its factual content. Thus if I say to someone, "You acted wrongly in stealing that money," I am not stating anything more than if I had simply said, "You stole that money." In adding that this action is wrong I am not making any further statement about it. I am simply evincing my moral disapproval of it. It is as if I had said, "You stole that money," in a peculiar tone of horror, or written it with the addition of some special exclamation marks. The tone, or the exclamation marks, adds nothing to the literal meaning of the sentence. It merely serves to show that the expression of it is attended by certain feelings in the speaker.

If now I generalise my previous statement and say, "Stealing money is wrong," I produce a sentence which has no factual meaning—that is, expresses no proposition which can be either true or false. It is as if I had written "Stealing money!!"—where the shape and thickness of the exclamation marks show, by a suitable convention, that a special sort of moral disapproval is the feeling which is being expressed. . . .

It is worth mentioning that ethical terms do not serve only to express feeling. They are calculated also to arouse feeling, and so to stimulate action. Indeed some of them are used in such a way as to give the sentences in which they occur the effect of commands. Thus the sentence "It is your duty to tell the truth" may be regarded both as the expression of a certain sort of ethical feeling about truthfulness and as the expression of the command "Tell the truth." The sentence "You ought to tell the truth" also involves the command "Tell the truth," but here the tone of the command is less emphatic. In the sentence "It is good to tell the truth" the command has become little more than a suggestion. And thus the "meaning" of the word "good," in its ethical usage, is differentiated from that of the word "duty" or the word "ought." In fact we may define the meaning of the various ethical words in terms both of the different feelings they are ordinarily taken to express, and also the different responses which they are calculated to provoke.[h]

What about the claim, made by Moore and many other philosophers, that, since we argue about values, there must be something objective for us to argue about? The answer is that we never do argue about values.

When someone disagrees with us about the moral value of a certain action or type of action, we do admittedly resort to argument in order to win him over to our way of thinking. But we do not attempt to show by our arguments that he has the "wrong" ethical feeling towards a situation whose nature he has correctly apprehended. What we attempt to show is that he is mistaken about the facts of the case. . . . We do this in the hope that we have only to get our opponent to agree with us about the nature of the empirical facts for him to adopt the same moral attitude towards them as we do. And as the people with whom we argue have generally received the same moral education as ourselves, and live in the same social order, our expectation is usually justified. But if our opponent happens to have undergone a different process of moral "conditioning" from ourselves, so that, even when he acknowledges all the facts, he still disagrees with us about the moral value of the actions under discussion, then we abandon the attempt to convince him by argument. We say that it is impossible to argue with him because he has a distorted or undeveloped moral sense; which signifies merely that he employs a different set of values from our own. We feel that our own system of values is superior, and therefore speak in such derogatory terms of his. But we cannot bring forward any arguments to show that our system is superior.[i]

RELIGION

So much, then, for expressions containing ethical terms. Expressions containing religious terms obviously can be analyzed in the same way. Religion is as much a noncognitive, emotive enterprise as is ethics. This position must not be confused with either atheism or agnosticism.

For it is characteristic of an agnostic to hold that the existence of a god is a possibility in which there is no good reason either to believe or disbelieve; and it is characteristic of an atheist to hold that it is at least probable that no god exists. And our view that all utterances about the nature of God are nonsensical, so far from being identical with, or even lending any support to, either of these familiar contentions, is actually incompatible with them. For if the assertion that there is a god is nonsensical, then the atheist's assertion that there is no god is equally nonsensical, since it is only a significant proposition that can be significantly contradicted. As for the agnostic, although he refrains from saying either that there is or that there is not a god, he does not deny that the question whether a transcendent god exists is a genuine question. He does not deny that the two sentences "There is a transcendent god" and "There is no transcendent god" express propositions one of which is actually true and the other false. All he says is that we have no means of telling which of them is true, and therefore ought not to commit ourselves to either. But we have seen that the sentences in question do not express propositions at all. And this means that agnosticism also is ruled out.

Thus we offer the theist the same comfort as we gave to the moralist. His assertions cannot possibly be valid, but they cannot be invalid either. As he says nothing at all about the world, he cannot justly be accused of saying anything false, or anything for which he has insufficient grounds.[j]

That, as far as Ayer was concerned, is the end of it. Carnap, however, thought there was a good deal more to say. In the first place, though metaphysical expressions (among which religious expressions are included) are without theoretical content, he allowed that they are not sheerly nonsensical; they are in fact a kind of poetry. In the second place, he gave an explanation to metaphysicians of why they have mistakenly supposed themselves to be doing a superior sort of science, instead of recognizing that they are composing an inferior sort of verse.

How could it be explained that so many men in all ages and nations, among them eminent minds, spent so much energy, nay veritable fervor, on metaphysics if the latter consisted of nothing but mere words, nonsensically juxtaposed? And how could one account for the fact that metaphysical books have exerted such a strong influence on readers up to the present day, if they contained not even errors, but nothing at all? These doubts are justified since metaphysics does indeed have a content; only it is not theoretical content. The (pseudo) statements of metaphysics do not serve for the *description of states of affairs*, neither existing ones (in that case they would be true statements) nor nonexisting ones (in that case they would be at least false statements). They serve for the *expression of the general attitude of a person towards life*. . . .

Metaphysics . . . arises from the need to give expression to a man's attitude in life, his emotional and volitional reaction to the environment, to society, to the tasks to which he devotes himself, to the misfortunes that befall him. This attitude manifests itself, unconsciously as a rule, in everything a man does or says. It also impresses itself on his facial features, perhaps even on the character of his gait. Many people, now, feel a desire to create over and above these manifestations a special expression of their attitude, through which it might become visible in a more succinct and penetrating way. If they have artistic talent they are able to engross themselves by producing a work of art. . . . What is here essential for our considerations is only the fact that art is an adequate, metaphysics an inadequate means for the expression of the basic attitude. Of course, there need be no intrinsic objection to one's using any means of expression one likes. But in the case of metaphysics we find this situation: through the form of its works it pretends to be something that it is not. . . . The metaphysician believes that he travels in territory in which truth and falsehood are at stake. . . . He polemicizes against metaphysicians of divergent persuasion by attempting to refute their assertions in his treatise. Lyrical poets, on the other hand, do not try to refute in their poem the statements in a poem by some other lyrical poet; for they know they are in the domain of art and not in the domain of theory.[k]

Though Carnap's analysis is more subtle than Ayer's, they are in basic agreement. And how different their positions are from Wittgenstein's in the *Tractatus*! Formally, all three make the same disclaimer—religion and metaphysics lie in the domain of the unsayable. But what a difference between, for this reason, characterizing them as nonsense or bad poetry and characterizing them as mystical!

Verifiability Again

Early in this chapter we said that everyone would agree with Schlick that the Verifiability Principle was the nucleus of positivism, that this nucleus proved anything but unassailable, and that the history of the movement was a series of attempts to get the principle right. It may seem that we have failed to record this history, but though we have not talked about the principle directly, it was at the center of the whole struggle over elucidations. For that was an attempt to save the principle from the threat of a vicious regress. The principle asserts that the meaning of a proposition is its method of verification. Very well, then, let us start with any proposition we like. We verify it by reference to other propositions. But these propositions now require verification, and this is accomplished by reference to other propositions, and these in their turn to still others, and so on without end, unless there are ultimate verifiers on which the process of verification can terminate. Hence the importance of incorrigible protocol sentences. As we have seen, this difficulty about the Verifiability Principle was never resolved.

TESTABILITY AND MEANING

Other difficulties with the initial formulation of the principle soon turned up. In its original version the principle asserted that the meaning of a proposition is its method of verification. But since normally we think of meaning as what requires verification, meaning and method of verification cannot be identical. What, then, is the relation between them? Again, though the principle talks about verifying a proposition, it is sentences that have meaning, and, at least in the technical vocabulary of Moore and Russell,[20] "proposition" is the term that designates this meaning. Once again, there seems to be a difference between verification and meaning.

[20] See pp. 100–01.

Further, and passing over this problem, does the meaning of a proposition (or sentence) consist in actually verifying it or merely in there being the possibility of verifying it? And is it in a complete verification or only in a partial verification? As regards the first question, it seems clear that many propositions that have never been tested, and even seem incapable of being tested, are nonetheless meaningful. For instance, propositions about the far side of the moon (such as "There are craters on the far side of the moon similar to those on the visible side") are certainly meaningful, although in the 1930s, when this matter was being hotly debated, it seemed likely that there would never be any way of testing them. Hence it was necessary to introduce the qualification that propositions are meaningful if they are in principle verifiable. But "in principle" left plenty of room for argument and was a disappointing complication of a claim whose chief attraction lay in its seeming simplicity.

As regards the second question, generalizations in the sciences are never completely verifiable, since some subsequent event may possibly disprove them; they are, and remain, hypotheses. Hence, if complete verification is insisted on, we have reached the surprising conclusion that generalizations in the sciences (including the so-called laws of physics) are one and all meaningless. The way out of this paradox was to introduce the notion of confirmability, alongside the notion of verification, and to insist only on the former, not the latter. But confirmation is not the clear-cut, all-or-none matter that verification suggested and that the positivists preferred. Confirmation is always only a matter of degree, and about differences of degree there can be disagreements. Once again, the simplicity of the principle has been compromised.

In the following passage from one of Carnap's papers (published in 1936) we see the Verifiability Principle in transition.

> If by verification is meant a definitive and final establishment of truth, then no (synthetic) sentence is ever verifiable, as we shall see. We can only confirm a sentence more and more. Therefore we shall speak of the problem of *confirmation* rather than of the problem of verification. We distinguish the *testing* of a sentence from its confirmation, thereby understanding a procedure—e.g. the carrying out of certain experiments—which leads to a confirmation in some degree either of the sentence itself or of its negation. We shall call a sentence *testable* if we know such a method of testing for it; and we call it *confirmable* if we know under what conditions the sentence would be confirmed. . . .
>
> The connection between meaning and confirmation has sometimes been formulated by the thesis that a sentence is meaningful if and only if it is verifiable, and that its meaning is the method of its verification. The historical merit of this thesis was that it called attention to the close connection between the meaning of a sentence and the way it is confirmed. This formulation thereby helped, on the one hand, to analyze the factual content of scientific sentences, and, on the other hand,

to show that the sentences of trans-empirical metaphysics have no cognitive meaning. But from our present point of view, this formulation, although acceptable as a first approximation, is not quite correct. By its oversimplification, it led to a too narrow restriction of scientific language, excluding not only metaphysical sentences but also certain scientific sentences having factual meaning. Our present task could therefore be formulated as that of a modification of the requirement of verifiability. . . .

If verification is understood as a complete and definitive establishment of truth then a universal sentence, e.g. a so-called law of physics or biology, can never be verified, a fact which has often been remarked. Even if each single instance of the law were supposed to be verifiable, the number of instances to which the law refers—e.g. the space-time-points—is infinite and therefore can never be exhausted by our observations which are always finite in number. We cannot verify the law, but we can test it by testing its single instances, i.e. the particular sentences which we derive from the law and from other sentences established previously. If in the continued series of such testing experiments no negative instance is found but the number of positive instances increases then our confidence in the law will grow step by step. Thus, instead of verification, we may speak here of gradually increasing *confirmation* of the law.[1]

WHAT IS THE STATUS OF THE VERIFIABILITY PRINCIPLE?

According to the principle itself, all meaningful assertions are either tautologies or empirical hypotheses. Which is the principle itself, a tautology or an empirical hypothesis? The positivists did not like either alternative. If the principle were a tautology it would tell us nothing about the world and so would be irrelevant as a test of meaning. If it were an empirical hypothesis, it would require verification, and it is not easy to attempt to verify how the principle itself could escape circularity.

The way out of this dilemma was suggested by the Principle of Tolerance. Carnap had pointed out that if sentences in the formal mode of speech are not specifications holding for some existing language or languages, they are recommendations regarding some proposed language. If the Verifiability Principle were in the formal mode of speech, it would function not to make "assertions" about the world but only to make "suggestions" about how to use the terms "meaningful" and "meaningless." Thus we slip through the horns of the dilemma, but at heavy cost. We can no longer say that those who reject the Verifiability Principle are in error; we have to recognize that they have simply rejected our recommendation and chosen to use the terms "meaningful" and "meaningless" in a different way. The result of this linguistic shift is another, and radical, retreat from positivist principles. Indeed, Schlick's nucleus has disintegrated.

Bearing in mind Ayer's own early and wholehearted advocacy of positivism, we may say that he really wrote its epitaph in 1959, and it is to be noted that in doing so he carefully dissociated himself from the deceased. "The Vienna Circle," he observed, "tended to ignore" the whole question of the status of the Verifiability Principle. But

> it seems to me fairly clear that what they were in fact doing was to adopt the verification principle as a convention. . . .
>
> But why should this [convention] be accepted? The most that has been proved is that metaphysical statements do not fall into the same category as the laws of logic, or as scientific hypotheses, or as historical narratives, or judgments of perception, or any other common sense descriptions of the "natural" world. Surely it does not follow that they are neither true nor false, still less that they are nonsensical.
>
> No, it does not follow. Or rather, it does not follow unless one makes it follow. The question is whether one thinks the difference between metaphysical and common sense or scientific statements to be sufficiently sharp for it to be useful to underline it in this way. The defect of this procedure is that it tends to make one blind to the interest that metaphysical questions can have.[m]

The Ayer of 1959 had certainly traveled a long way from the Ayer of 1936, who thought that metaphysics was obviously sheer nonsense.

The End of Positivism

Ayer is not the only positivist who made this journey. Indeed, by the mid-1930s, as a result of the linguistic shift and of internal pressures, it had been transformed beyond recognition. But if positivism was only an *entre deux guerres* phenomenon, it nevertheless has an important place in Western history. Positivism was one of the last survivors of eighteenth- and nineteenth-century culture. Like the men and women of those times, the positivists lived in an aboveground, sunlit world; as far as they were concerned, Dostoevsky's *Notes from Underground* might never have been written. Though they differed from Dewey in many ways, especially in their rejection of his emphasis on results rather than on truth, they shared his conviction that all our problems can be solved by the application of a rational intelligence, armed with a scientific methodology. For them as for him, all problems are technological, not intrinsically human. It was in this respect that they differed most markedly from Wittgenstein, who resonated as much with the tone of the new culture as they did with the old.

And, though positivism as the particular doctrine associated with the Vienna Circle will probably not be revived, whenever and wherever the analytic tradition survives there will be sympathy with the positivistic temper—with its hard-nosed, empirical, debunking, no-nonsense point of view. Given all the superstitions in which people still persist, all the myths to which they still fall victim, all the spells and incantations to which they still commit themselves, it will surely always be useful to have some people around who rather nastily demand, "What exactly do you mean by that?"

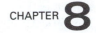

Husserl and the Phenomenological Tradition

The Phenomenological Tradition

In the previous five chapters we have been examining views that, however they may differ in important respects, share a number of basic assumptions—those we described as constituting the analytic tradition. In this and the next two chapters we will examine three views that, once again, differ greatly among themselves but share another set of basic assumptions—those we will call the "phenomenological tradition."

To move from a study of philosophers of the analytic tradition to those of the phenomenological tradition is to enter a wholly different world—a world of pure intuitions, apodeictic certainties, and transcendental egos. But though the world of phenomenology looks very different—indeed, *is* very different—from the sparsely populated world of the analytic tradition, with its hard data and its "neutral stuff," some future historian, looking at these two movements from the perspective of several centuries, may well discern more similarities than differences. Just as the disputes between the Stoics and the Epicureans appear to us, from the distance of two thousand years, to have been conducted within the basic framework of post-Aristotelianism and to reflect the profound cultural changes that were occurring in the late-classical world, so we may hazard the prediction that the historian of the future will view the analytic tradition and the phenomenological tradition as merely two variants of the same basically anti-Kantian stance.

The phenomenologists, just as much as the analytic philosophers, rejected the constructivism that, as they saw it, had "infected" nineteenth-century culture: it failed to distinguish between belief and knowledge. But though they held it responsible for this mistake, the phenomenologists—again like the analytic philosophers—saw that the Copernican revolution had been an attempt to avoid the paradoxes of Cartesian dualism. They did not want to enter that blind alley. Hence, in rejecting the Kantian paradigm, they took care not to become entangled once again in representative theories of perception. This they sought to do by arguing that the things themselves appear in (or to) consciousness. This position was quite different from the pre-Kantian view, for it required that consciousness be taken account of. Thus, despite major differences in *how* the two traditions dealt with consciousness, they were basically similar in that both accepted a "things-for-consciousness" orientation. Hence the fundamental question for both schools was: "How can things be *for* consciousness and yet not in any sense constructed by consciousness?"

Finally, both schools found the clue to the answer to this question in Brentano's approach to psychology.[1] As we have seen, instead of describing consciousness as consisting in "ideas" or "representations," he described it as intentional in nature, a direction, not a state. If it is only a direction, then it does not construct its object; it merely discloses, or displays, it. Hence it seemed possible to agree with Kant that human experience is limited to phenomena (that is, to things-for-consciousness) while denying that the objects thus experienced are constructs. This was a starting point for the phenomenologists as well as the analytic philosophers. But if the analysts and the phenomenologists thus not only had similar anticonstructivist motives but also shared a starting point, how did they come to diverge so radically?

First of all, the whole orientation of the traditions differed. The analysts found British empiricism, especially that of Hume, congenial. When they asked what the objects of consciousness are, they naturally thought of Hume's impressions, though of course, thanks to Brentano's insight, these impressions were no longer regarded as mental states; they were held to be "neutral stuff." That part of Brentano's view that appealed to the analysts was the notion that consciousness is transparent; indeed, to them it was so transparent that they in effect passed

[1] See pp. 110–11.

through it and fixed their attention exclusively on its objects. This point of view—
that consciousness can safely be ignored—was reinforced later on by a behaviorism that, starting from James, sanctioned by Russell, and supported by the
positivists' Verifiability Principle, maintained that sentences about inner states
can be eliminated without loss of meaning and replaced by sentences about bodily states.[2]

For the phenomenologists this was not only an appalling mistake, it was a de-
liberate blindness. They held that if one learns to attend carefully—if one culti-
vates a special attitude, which they called "reduction"[3]—one discovers that one is
directly aware of an immense variety of entities and acts. The analytic philosophers—precisely because of their analytic presupposition that the world consists
in a number of encapsulated simple items—wholly overlooked this vast realm.

When the analytic philosophers thought of Hume, the phenomenologists
thought of Hegel. But they believed that Hegel had not realized that consciousness is intentional. Since it seemed to them that he had missed its essential
nature, they proposed (and this, of course, was why they called themselves "phenomenologists") to make an improved study of consciousness—to do better than
Hegel what Hegel had sought to do. For this reason alone it is obvious that the
paths taken by the analytic tradition and by the phenomenological tradition had
to diverge: the former regarded the intentionality of consciousness as a reason for
ignoring consciousness; the latter regarded this intentionality as a justification for
concentrating on consciousness.

Second, the analytic philosophers believed (as has been seen) that each of the
real entities of which the universe is composed is itself and not another thing.
Since in their opinion explanation consists in the analysis of complexes into their
parts, there must be—if completely satisfactory explanations are to be possible—
encapsulated entities that are absolutely simple. (Here again Hume's "loose and
separate" impressions were their model.) In contrast, the phenomenological philosophers were impressed by the interconnectedness of things—for them experience was a river, not a collection of "loose and separate" sense data.

Third, the analytic philosophers and the phenomenologists differed about
the status of the world of everyday experience. The analytic philosophers recognized that there is a puzzle about the relation between the world that physics
discloses and the world of ordinary perception—the world of shoes, ships, and
cabbages that even physicists encounter in their daily round. But they thought this
puzzle could be disposed of by a properly rigorous logical analysis of language.
For the most part they were either epistemologists or logicians, and they were
not much interested (apparently) in humanity's existential, or moral, relation to
the aseptic world disclosed by physics. Thus Russell held that "when we assert
that this or that has 'value,' we are giving expression to our own emotions."[4] The

[2] See pp. 252–53.
[3] This is quite different, of course, from the positivists' "reduction," which was a program,
  not an attitude. See pp. 287–88.
[4] See p. 207.

phenomenologists were unwilling to write off as "subjective" the experiential world of lovely, hateful, enduring, and transitory things; hence, they took their stand on this experiential world—our "life-world," as they called it. In this respect they were very close to Whitehead. Like him they rejected that bifurcation of nature to which, it seemed, physics had committed modern culture.[5] They shared with Whitehead the sense, so vividly expressed by the Romantic poets, that all things are "interfused" together. Had the phenomenologists read Wordsworth, they would have noted with approval his

> . . . observation of affinities
> In objects where no brotherhood exists
> To passive minds.[a]

For, like him, they

> . . . felt the sentiment of Being spread
> O'er all that moves and all that seemeth still;
> O'er all that, lost beyond the reach of thought
> And human knowledge, to the human eye
> Invisible, yet liveth to the heart;
> O'er all that leaps and runs, and shouts and sings,
> Or beats the gladsome air; o'er all that glides
> Beneath the wave, yea, in the wave itself,
> And mighty depth of waters.[b]

The phenomenologists, that is, shared Wordsworth's sense of the presence in everything of everything else, his feeling that into every here and now are synthesized not only past experiences but anticipated future ones. The phenomenologists believed philosophy should, and could, take account of all this ambience—not merely reduce it to the association of disconnected simples.

A difference in attitude toward language is another reason why the two movements developed in opposite directions from a similar starting point. Both movements believed there is a barrier between our minds and things and that it is the business of philosophy to overcome this barrier. For the analytic philosophers the barrier was sloppy language; hence they focused their attention on clarifying linguistic muddles and confusions. At least initially—this is true of Frege, Russell, and the early positivists—they held that all or most philosophical problems simply disappear when ordinary language is replaced by an ideal language that reflects the logic of assertions. Because they sought in their own writings to approximate as closely as possible this ideal language, their terminology became sparse, and precise. For the phenomenologists the barrier consisted less in language than in preconceptions—such as the atomistic preconception that

[5] See p. 77.

dominated much of the thinking of the earlier analytic philosophers. Thus clarity was their aim too, but it was to be achieved by looking at things directly, instead of indirectly through a pair of philosophical spectacles. They felt no particular need to prune language; indeed, their method actually encouraged it to flourish. Their effort to describe the unusual and surprising things they encountered when they *did* succeed in looking at things directly, led them to employ a terminology so complex, elaborate, and esoteric that it repulsed philosophers of the analytic persuasion.

Husserl and the Quest for Certainty

The animating force in Husserl's[6] life and thought was a deep need for certainty. In 1906 he wrote in his diary, "I have been through enough torments from lack of clarity and from doubt that wavers back and forth. . . . Only one need absorbs me: I must win clarity, else I cannot live; I cannot bear life unless I can believe that I shall achieve it."[c] Clarity, Husserl thought, guarantees certainty because when something becomes completely clear to us it stands before us in a way that it is impossible for us to doubt: it is "self-given" in its completeness and simplicity.

> If we see an object standing out in complete clearness, if . . . we have carried out processes of discrimination and conceptual comprehension, . . . the statement faithfully expressing this has then its justification. If we ask why the statement is justified, and ascribe no value to the reply "I see that it is so," we fall into absurdity.[d]

It was this passion for clarity and certainty that led Husserl from mathematics to logic, from logic to philosophy, and from philosophy in general to phenomenology as a special kind of seeing that, he believed, could be cultivated by training and practice.

Attitudes toward the quest for certainty vary; indeed, they constitute a major parting of the ways in contemporary culture. Kierkegaard, for instance, fully

[6] Edmund Husserl (1859–1938) was born in Czechoslovakian Moravia, at that time a part of the Austrian empire. He studied mathematics, physics, and astronomy at the Universities of Leipzig, Berlin, and Vienna and wrote his dissertation on the calculus of variations. From early on, however, he was interested in philosophy, and abandoning his plans to be a teacher of science, he returned to Vienna in 1884 to attend Brentano's lectures (see p. 110, note 26) and to finish his education in philosophy. Subsequently, Husserl taught at Halle, Göttingen, and Freiburg. His production was immense, especially after his retirement in 1928. Though much of his work has been published, even more remains in manuscript—as much as 45,000 pages in the shorthand that Husserl used. All this material is preserved in the Husserl Archives in Louvain and is carefully supervised by faithful disciples.

shared Husserl's passion for certainty, but unlike Husserl he was convinced that individuals cannot attain certainty by their own efforts. The best that they are capable of, according to Kierkegaard, is an approximation process, and the end result of such a process is as far from certainty as is total ignorance. Hence his leap of faith. Another possible attitude is Dewey's. He was quite satisfied with approximation processes, since he believed they yield all that one can reasonably ask for—continually improved conditions of life. He held that the quest for certainty is a symptom of a mild neurosis. And there is Nietzsche, who did not believe even in the possibility of approximation processes. He regarded the belief that the truth can be gradually approximated as itself a symptom of neurosis, and he held that the capacity to *enjoy* uncertainty (as distinct from merely accepting it, as with Dewey) is a sign of strength, an expression of our will to power.

It is interesting in this connection to contrast Husserl's and Nietzsche's use of the same metaphor. In his *Cartesian Meditations* Husserl likened his position to that of Descartes, pointing out that both he and Descartes not only sought certainty but also found it in the transcendental ego. Unfortunately, however, Descartes went wrong by misinterpreting the transcendental ego.[7] Correct interpretation of the transcendental ego is, then, the critical stage in the quest for certainty:

> When making certain of the transcendental ego, we are standing at an altogether dangerous point. . . . It is as though we were on the brink of a precipice, where advancing calmly and surely is a matter of philosophical life and death. . . . [Descartes stood] on the threshold of the greatest of all discoveries . . . yet . . . he [did] not pass through the gateway that leads into genuine transcendental philosophy.[e]

Nietzsche too once represented himself as standing at a gateway.[8] But the name of Nietzsche's gateway was "Moment"; and far from passing through to rest on the other side in indubitable certainty, he passed through only to continue forever on the path he had already been traveling. Nietzsche had abandoned the notion of "advance," as well as the notion of "end," as an illusion. Both he and Husserl were aware of precipices, but whereas Nietzsche rejoiced in them, Husserl hoped to get beyond the danger point as quickly as possible—as if, from Nietzsche's point of view, there were a "beyond the danger point."

Every reader's own attitude toward certainty will probably determine his or her overall assessment of Husserl's version of phenomenology. Those who agree with Dewey and Nietzsche that the quest for certainty is illusory will perceive Husserl's elaborate investigations as a complicated exercise in self-deception.

---

[7] For a discussion of the transcendental ego and Descartes's mistake, see pp. 293–94. Here the point is simply to see the difference between Husserl's attitude and Nietzsche's, and for this an understanding of the details of Husserl's doctrine is not necessary.

[8] See Vol. IV, pp. 254–55.

Those who hold, with Kierkegaard, that it is essential to confess that humans are "always in the wrong" will view these same investigations as one more demonstration of the utter failure of "objectivity" and of the "speculative point of view." Such people might indeed allow that Husserl's phenomenological method could make useful contributions to psychology and to the social sciences, but only those who share his need for certainty and who also regard this quest as rational will sympathize with what Husserl himself took to be his main contribution to culture.

Criticism of Relativism

Before examining Husserl's account of his method, we should take a look at the case he made for the possibility of "universally valid truth." In an essay published in 1911 Husserl attacked both "the flood of positivism and pragmatism, which latter exceeds the former in its relativism," and historicism, that "romantic philosophy" that rejects "any belief whatever in an absolute philosophy" and offers instead "the relative justification of every philosophy in its own time."[f] The pragmatist argues that what is true is what works; but since what works at one time and in one context may not work at another time and in another context, the pragmatist's argument involves the admission that truth is relative. The historicist also holds that truth is relative—not to what works, but to social or cultural context. What does the historicist's argument amount to?

> He will point to changes in scientific views—how what is today accepted as a proved theory is recognized tomorrow as worthless, how some call certain things laws that others call mere hypotheses, and still others vague guesses, etc. [But] does that mean that in view of this constant change in scientific views we would actually have no right to speak of sciences as objectively valid unities instead of merely as cultural formations? [No; for] it is easy to see that historicism, if consistently carried through, carries over into extreme sceptical subjectivism. The ideas of truth, theory, and science would then, like all ideas, lose their absolute validity. . . . There would be no unqualified validity, or validity-in-itself, which is what it is even if no one has achieved it and though no historical humanity will ever achieve it. . . . It is not necessary to go further. . . . We shall certainly have said enough to obtain recognition that no matter what great difficulties the relation between a sort of fluid worth and objective validity, between science as a cultural phenomenon and science as a valid systematic theory, may offer an understanding concerned with clarifying them, the distinction and opposition must be recognized. . . . .The mathematician will not turn to historical science to be taught about the truth of mathematical theories. It will not occur to him to relate the historical development of mathematical

representations with the question of truth. How, then, is it to be the historian's task to decide as to the truth of given philosophical systems and, above all, as to the very possibility of a philosophical science that is valid in itself? . . .

The unconditional affirmation that any scientific philosophy is a chimaera, based on the argument that the alleged efforts of millennia make probable the intrinsic impossibility of [any absolutely valid scientific] philosophy, is erroneous not merely because to draw a conclusion regarding an unlimited future from a few millennia of higher culture would not be a good induction, but erroneous as an absolute absurdity, like $2 \times 2 = 5$. And this for the indicated reason: if there is something there whose objective validity philosophical criticism can refute, then there is also an area within which something can be found as objectively valid. If problems have demonstrably been posed "awry," then it must be possible to rectify this and pose straight problems. If criticism proves that philosophy in its historical growth has operated with confused concepts, has been guilty of mixed concepts and specious conclusions, then if one does not wish to fall into nonsense, that very fact makes it undeniable that, ideally speaking, the concepts are capable of being pointed, clarified, distinguished, that in the given area correct conclusions can be drawn. Any correct, profoundly penetrating criticism itself provides means for advancing and ideally points to correct goals, thereby indicating an objectively valid science.g

The arguments presented in this passage are of very different worth. As regards the contention that historical evidence cannot establish that any particular theory T is false, this seems correct. Historical evidence can establish, for instance, that during some particular period of time P_1 people disbelieved T, that during a subsequent period P_2 they believed T, and that during another period P_3 they again disbelieved T. But since no one—not even that "flood of positivists and pragmatists"—equates "T is false" simply with "People disbelieved T at P_1," historical evidence does not show that theories are false. This distinction clearly is important, for people often become muddled about what the "historical argument" shows.

Husserl was also correct in pointing out that an inductive argument that runs from past failures to prospective future failures does not yield the absolutely certain conclusion that there is no absolutely certain truth—for *no* inductive argument yields more than probability. But past failures (coupled with historical evidence about the special psychological and sociological factors that make T persuasive at P_2) can make this conclusion probable—which is all that most positivists and pragmatists would want to maintain.

But what about the argument that anyone who denies the possibility of absolute truth is involved in contradiction? Is it the case that anyone who criticizes a claim must logically allow the existence of "an objectively valid science"? It is not difficult to reconstruct how Dewey or Nietzsche would have dealt with this contention. They would have looked for the need being expressed in Husserl's rather emotional affirmation of absolute validity. Approaching the matter from a psychological, or even psychoanalytic, point of view, they would have maintained that, appearances to the contrary, Husserl's talk about an "absolutely objective science" was not actually talk about an absolutely objective science, in the way that talk about Bucephalus is presumably talk about Bucephalus. On the contrary, it was expressive or revelatory of Husserl's state of mind (in this case, his fear of uncertainty), in the same way that talk to the effect that "So-and-so is a dirty Red" is not a comment on So-and-so's political opinions but a reflection of the speaker's dislike or fear of So-and-so.

As for Wittgenstein, he would have characterized Husserl's whole discussion as nothing but another example of the "subliming" of logic.[9] He would have pointed out that criticism of an argument no more depends on there being an objectively valid science than criticism of a game of chess depends on there being an objectively valid set of rules for chess playing—or than criticism of an ambiguous signpost depends on there being an absolutely unambiguous set of directions.

The Crisis of European Man

In addition to arguing that relativism is self-contradictory, Husserl maintained that it has deleterious social consequences. Writing in 1935, when the Nazis had been in power for two years, Husserl saw that Europe was in crisis, and he thought that the gradual decay of belief in rational certainty was responsible for that crisis. The revival of this belief therefore seemed to him essential.

Husserl's exposition of the belief in rational certainty led him back to the Greeks. The ideal of rational certainty was their discovery, and Europe's inheritance of it had unified Western culture for centuries. According to Husserl, what the Greeks had actually done was to anticipate the basic insight of phenomenology. The rehabilitation of the ideal of rational certainty could therefore be accomplished by returning to the phenomenological method, which the Greeks had only dimly understood, and perfecting it. For when phenomenology was perfected it would demonstrate that the quest for certainty was not in vain; it would do this by actually establishing a secure foundation for the sciences. Husserl's account of the Greek discovery may not be historically accurate, but it does at least throw light on his view of the nature of phenomenology and shows the context of values and goals in which he developed his method.

What was it, then, that distinguished the Greeks' "overall orientation" toward the world from that of other peoples, not only primitive races but also "the wise

---

[9] The later Wittgenstein, that is; not the Wittgenstein of the *Tractatus*. See p. 412.

Egyptians, Babylonians," and so on? Whereas the attitude of other groups was either practical or "mythico-religious," the Greek attitude was "theoretical"—the Greeks were curious about the world; they wanted to understand it.

> There is a sharp cleavage, then, between the universal but mythico-practical attitude and the "theoretical," which by every previous standard is unpractical, the attitude of *thaumazein* [Greek: to wonder], to which the great men of Greek philosophy's first culminating period, Plato and Aristotle, trace the origin of philosophy. Men are gripped by a passion for observing and knowing the world, a passion that turns from all practical interests and in the closed circle of its own knowing activities, in the time devoted to this sort of investigation, accomplishes and wants to accomplish only pure *theoria*. In other words, man becomes the disinterested spectator, overseer of the world, he becomes a philosopher. More than that, from this point forward his life gains a sensitivity for motives which are possible only to this attitude, for novel goals and methods of thought. . . .
>
> With an attitude such as this . . . there arises the distinction between the represented and the real world, and a new question is raised concerning the truth—not everyday truth bound as it is to tradition but a truth that . . . is identical and universally valid, a truth in itself.[h]

This description of the Greek attitude coincides completely with Dewey's.[10] But whereas Husserl praised the disinterested attitude and the spectator point of view, Dewey condemned them. Both philosophers agreed that the spread of this attitude, with the accompanying belief in a "universally valid truth," led in the course of time to "a transformation of human existence and of man's entire cultural life."[i] But whereas Dewey regarded this transformation as an unmitigated misfortune and wanted philosophy to adopt the methods of natural science and to turn to practical problems connected with our traffic with nature, Husserl held that it is the methods of natural science that are responsible for the "crisis of European man," and that the only hope for Europe was a revival of the disinterested attitude and a return to rationality "in that noble and genuine sense, the original Greek sense."[j]

THE RISE OF "NATURALISM"

The root of the crisis, Husserl thought, lay in the ideal of rationality, the ideal of disinterested theory, having gradually become identified with a set of assumptions that Husserl called "naturalism." Naturalism is the belief that "the extraordinary successes of natural knowledge are now to be extended to knowledge of the spirit."[k] This belief is understandable, for the natural sciences have had

---

[10] See pp. 44–45.

enormous success in their own field. Nevertheless, such an extension is an "aberration," because the least amount of attention given to psychic processes as they actually occur in experience (instances of willing, thinking, imagining, and the like) shows them to be utterly different in nature from the material objects studied in physics. To extend the methods of natural science to the psychic life is to "objectivize" that life; it is to treat psychic processes as if they were material objects existing in the same public space and time as the bodies with which these processes are associated. Because rationality has quite mistakenly come to be associated with this extension and because (as Husserl pointed out) the consequences of the extension are grave, it is not surprising that rationality too has been attacked.

> With this [extension of the methods of the natural sciences to psychic processes] the interpretation of the world immediately takes on a predominantly dualistic, i.e., psychophysical form. The same causality—only split in two—embraces the one world; the sense of rational explanation is everywhere the same but in such a way that all explanation of spirit,[11] in the only way in which it can be universal, involves the physical. There can be no pure, self-contained search for an explanation of the spiritual, no purely inner-oriented psychology or theory of spirit beginning with the ego in psychical self-experience and extending to the other psyche. The way that must be traveled is the external one, the path of physics and chemistry. . . . This objectivism or this psychophysical interpretation of the world, despite its seeming self-evidence, is a naive one-sidedness. . . . To speak of the spirit as [an] annex to bodies and having its supposedly spatiotemporal being within nature is an absurdity. . . . .
>
> There are all sorts of problems that stem from naiveté, according to which objectivistic science holds what it calls the objective world to be the totality of what is, without paying any attention to the fact that no objective science can do justice to the subjectivity that achieves science. One who has been trained in the natural sciences finds it self-evident that whatever is merely subjective must be eliminated and that the method of natural science, formulated according to a subjective mode of representation, is objectively determined. By the same token, it is taken for granted that the subjective, eliminated by the physical scientist, is, precisely as psychic, to be investigated in psychophysical psychology. The investigator of nature, however, does not make it clear to himself that the constant foundation of his admittedly subjective thinking activity is the environing world of life. The latter is constantly

---

[11] [If "spirit" has any supernatural or religious connotations for the reader, it is a bad translation of *Geist*, the rather vague term that Husserl used; "psychic" would be better—AUTHORS.]

presupposed as the basic working area, in which alone his questions and his methodology make sense. Where, at the present time, is that powerful bit of method that leads from the intuitive environing world to the idealizing of mathematics and its interpretation as objective being, subjected to criticism and clarification? Einstein's revolutionary changes concern the formulas wherein idealized and naively objectivized nature (*physis*) is treated. But regarding the question of how formulas or mathematical objectification in general are given a sense based on life and the intuitive environing world, of this we hear nothing. Thus Einstein does nothing to reformulate the space and time in which our actual life takes place.

Mathematical science of nature is a technical marvel for the purpose of accomplishing inductions whose fruitfulness, probability, exactitude, and calculability could previously not even be suspected. As an accomplishment it is a triumph of the human spirit. With regard to the rationality of its methods and theories, however, it is a thoroughly relative science. It presupposes as data principles that are themselves roughly lacking in actual rationality. Insofar as the intuitive environing world, purely subjective as it is, is forgotten in the scientific thematic, the working subject is also forgotten, and the scientist is not studied.[1]

In the paragraphs just quoted, as well as in those that follow, a number of theses can be distinguished. First, there is the contention that the natural sciences are uncritical. For instance, scientists have never so much as asked what sort of entity a spatiotemporal object is; they have simply plunged ahead into investigating the interrelations, causal and otherwise, among such objects. Further, the natural sciences all assume a very naïve form of dualism, according to which the physical world that they study is mind-independent. Second, there is the contention that psychology in particular has been misguided. Having made the mistake of distinguishing sharply between minds and bodies, psychologists have then proceeded to compound this mistake by treating minds as if they were like bodies. Third, a program is sketched for a radically different method that would avoid all these errors. Fourth, it is proposed that the findings of this new method should become the foundation stones for a reconstruction of all the sciences, including physics. It may be said at once that there will be more agreement among philosophers about the two critical theses than about the two proposals for reform and reconstruction.

It is true that . . . there is psychology, which . . . claims . . . to be the universal fundamental science of the spirit. Still, our hope for real rationality, i.e., for real insight, is disappointed here as elsewhere. The psychologists simply fail to see that they too study neither themselves nor the scientists who are doing the investigating nor their own vital environing world. They do not see that from the very beginning they necessarily presuppose themselves as a group of men belonging to their own environing world and historical period. By the same token they do not see that in pursuing their aims they are seeking a truth in itself universally valid for everyone. By its objectivism psychology simply cannot make a study of the soul in its properly essential sense, which is to say, the ego that acts and is acted upon. Though by determining the bodily function involved in an experience of evaluating or willing, it may objectify the experience and handle it inductively, can it do the same for purposes, values, norms? . . . Completely ignored is the fact that objectivism, as the genuine work of the investigator intent upon finding true norms, presupposes just such norms. . . . More and more perceptible becomes the overall need for a reform of modern psychology in its entirety. As yet, however, it is not understood that psychology through its objectivism . . . simply fails to get at the proper essence of spirit; that in isolating the soul and making it an object of thought . . . it is being absurd. . . .

In our time we everywhere meet the burning need for an understanding of spirit, while the unclarity of the methodological and factual connection between the natural sciences and the sciences of the spirit has become almost unbearable.[m]

CRITICISM OF NATURAL SCIENCE

As regards Husserl's first contention, little need be said. Writers as diverse in other respects as Whitehead and Nietzsche agreed that nineteenth- and early-twentieth-century physics assumed a whole mass of highly questionable concepts—from the notion of simple location to that of causality.[12] But the main thrust of Husserl's attack on natural science differed in an important way from that of most other critics. Whitehead, for instance, argued that because the basic concepts of physics had become inadequate, an improved set of concepts was necessary. Whitehead derived such a set from quantum physics, and he hoped it would prove to be "categorial," that is, applicable also to biology and the social sciences. From Husserl's point of view this proposed reform remained completely "naturalistic" and "objectivistic," for Whitehead never questioned the essential rightness of the experimental method used in biology and psychology as well as in physics. Further, Whitehead did not think of his categorial scheme as complete and absolutely valid. The complete pattern, he believed, always eludes us; philosophy must remain open-ended. Therefore, from Husserl's point of view, to the other deficiencies of the philosophy of organism must be added "relativism." Husserl was not looking for a revised conceptual scheme that would enable scientists to achieve more-reliable, but still always tentative, interpretations of the evidence supplied by the experimental method; he was looking for apodeictically

[12] See pp. 73–79 and Vol. IV, pp. 242–43.

certain evidence, and he saw that to find such evidence he needed a method radically different from that of the natural sciences. The experimental method might indeed have a suitable place in scientific research, but only after a secure foundation had been laid by the new phenomenological method. Thus Husserl's critique of the natural sciences was far more drastic than Whitehead's and called for very different measures of reform.

CRITICISM OF PSYCHOLOGY

This brings us to Husserl's criticism of psychology, a science that had gone wrong, he held, because it aped the methods of the natural sciences. As a laboratory science committed to experimentation, it generally focused its attention on measuring bodily changes held to be related in some way to mental states. Pavlov's experiments on the conditioned reflex are a classic example of the kind of psychology Husserl condemned. In such experiments changes in the rate of a dog's salivation are correlated with the change from visual and olfactory stimuli (food actually present) to an auditory stimulus (the ringing of a bell, which has previously become "associated" with the presence of food).

The trouble with experimental psychology, from Husserl's point of view, is that it apes the natural sciences. In attempting to be "objective" like physics, it ignores that it is dealing with a living subject who is not simply reacting automatically to external stimuli but responding to its own perception of what these stimuli mean. In Husserl's view, it is bad enough that physics ignores that its mathematical method is itself the product of the human spirit—bad enough that Einstein revolutionized the concept of objective space and time but said nothing whatever about lived-through space and lived-through time. But it is deplorable that psychology, which is supposed to be the science of the human spirit, makes the same mistake. Husserl considered it ironic that the psychologists who devise and conduct all these experiments forget that they "are a group of men belonging to their own environing world and historical period."

Husserl's manner of criticism may suggest that his approach was what is now called the sociology of knowledge. However, Husserl would have held that the sociology of knowledge possessed the same fatal defect as historicism—that is, relativism. But the sociology of knowledge studies the norms of scientists, and Husserl wanted psychology to study, among other psychic activities, the scientists' setting of norms for themselves. What, then, is the difference? Why would he have criticized the sociology of knowledge? The sociology of knowledge studies scientific norms from the *outside;* it asks, for instance, how these norms are related to the social class from which scientists are drawn. It is possible to think of an experiment designed to ascertain whether scientific norms change as individuals from lower social strata infiltrate the scientific establishment. Husserl would have held this point of view to be as naturalistic as physiological psychology. In contrast, he wanted psychology to observe norm setting from the *inside,* as one of the ways in which the ego acts. As a universal human phenomenon, norm setting has, he thought, an essential nature that can be grasped if, and only if, we attend to it in the right way—that is, if we use the phenomenological method for studying specifically psychic phenomena. The essence of norm setting is an absolute that characterizes every actual instance of norm setting, regardless (for instance) of the social class of the scientists who happen to be setting the norms by which laboratory experiments are devised and conducted. And this essence, when it is uncovered by observation, is precisely one of those fundamental facts on which the sciences should be built. Of course, norm setting is only one of the activities of the ego; it is simply an example of the investigations that psychology should undertake. The starting point for all investigations must be this special method of phenomenological observation that Husserl had discovered.

The Phenomenological Method

CONTRAST WITH THE NATURAL STANDPOINT

Essential to Husserl's method was what may be called the phenomenological stance. In order to describe it, Husserl contrasted it with what he called "the natural standpoint," that is, the stance toward the world that most people adopt all the time and that all people, even phenomenologists, adopt most of the time.

> Our first outlook upon life is that of natural human beings, imagining, judging, feeling, willing, *"from the natural standpoint."* Let us make clear to ourselves what this means in the form of simple meditations which we can best carry on in the first person.
>
> I am aware of a world, spread out in space endlessly, and in time becoming and become, without end. I am aware of it, that means, first of all, I discover it immediately, intuitively, I experience it. Through sight, touch, hearing, etc., in the different ways of sensory perception, corporeal things somehow spatially distributed are *for me simply there*, in verbal or figurative sense "present," whether or not I pay them special attention by busying myself with them, considering, thinking, feeling, willing. . . .
>
> [Further,] what is actually perceived, and what is more or less clearly co-present and determinate (to some extent at least), is partly pervaded, partly girt about with a *dimly apprehended depth or fringe of indeterminate reality*. I can pierce it with rays from the illuminating focus of attention with varying success. . . .
>
> As it is with the world in its ordered being as a spatial present—the aspect I have so far been considering—so likewise is it with the world in respect to its *ordered being in the succession of time*. This world now present to me, and in every waking "now" obviously so, has its temporal horizon, infinite in both directions. . . .

[Moreover,] this world is not there for me as a mere *world of facts and affairs*, but, with the same immediacy, as a *world of values*, a *world of goods*, a *practical world.* . . . I find the things before me furnished not only with the qualities that befit their positive nature, but with value-characters such as beautiful or ugly, agreeable or disagreeable, pleasant or unpleasant, and so forth. . . .

We emphasize a most important point once again in the sentences that follow: I find continually present and standing over against me the one spatio-temporal fact-world to which I myself belong, as do all other men found in it. . . . This "fact-world," as the word already tells us, I find to *be out there,* and also *take it just as it gives itself to me as something that exists out there.* All doubting and rejecting of the data of the nat- ural world leaves standing the *general thesis of the natural standpoint.* "The" world is as fact-world always there; at the most it is at odd points "other" than I supposed, this or that under such names as "illusion," "hallucination," and the like, must be struck *out of it,* so to speak; but the "it" remains ever . . . a world that has its being out there. To know it more comprehensively, more trustworthily, more perfectly than the naive lore of experience is able to do . . . is the goal of the *sciences of the natural standpoint.*[n]

Husserl's point in the last paragraph is that, although we often come to suspect (and eventually to reject) this or that particular segment of experience, we simply and unquestioningly accept the world as a whole. This is surely correct, and com- monly we do not even come to suspect a particular segment of experience unless and until it conflicts with some other segment (for example, our visual perception of an oar in water as bent conflicts with our tactile perception of the oar as straight). Indeed, most people would probably say that there is something a bit neurotic about doubting any experience until we have reason to do so—that is, until it conflicts with some other experience.

Those who find this position reasonable will experience great difficulty in making the move (which Husserl recommends) from the natural standpoint to the phenomenological stance. For it would seem to follow from what has just been said, both about the way doubt arises and about our ways of dealing with it, that unless we accept the world as a whole we cannot in any meaningful way doubt a part of it. Yet to doubt the world as a whole is precisely what Husserl asks us to do.

BRACKETING

Instead now of remaining at this [that is, the natural] *standpoint, we propose to alter it radically.* Our aim must be to convince ourselves of the possibility of this alteration on grounds of principle.

The General Thesis according to which the real world about me is at all times known . . . as a fact-world *that has its being out there,* does *not* consist of course in *an act proper,* in an articulated judgment *about* existence. . . .

[Nevertheless] we can treat the potential and unexpressed thesis exactly as we do the thesis of the explicit judgment. A procedure of this sort, *possible at any time,* is, for instance, *the attempt to doubt everything.* . . .

Rather is [such doubt] *something quite unique. We do not abandon the thesis we have adopted, we make no change in our conviction.* . . . And yet the thesis undergoes a modification—whilst remaining in itself what it is, *we set it as it were "out of action," we "disconnect it," "bracket it."* It still remains there like the bracketed in the bracket, like the disconnected outside the connexional system. We can also say: The thesis is experience as lived (*Erlebnis*), *but we make "no use of it,"* and by that, of course, we do not indicate privation (as when we say of the ignorant that he makes no use of a certain thesis); in this case, rather, as with all parallel expressions, we are dealing with indicators that point to a definite but *unique form of consciousness,* which clamps on to the original simple thesis . . . and transvalues it in a quite peculiar way. *This transvaluing is a concern of our full freedom.* . . .

In relation to *every* thesis and wholly uncoerced we can use this *peculiar ἐποχή,*[13] *a certain refraining from judgment which is compatible with the unshaken and unshakable because self-evidencing conviction of Truth.* . . .

We put out of action the general thesis which belongs to the essence of the natural standpoint, we place in brackets whatever it includes respecting the nature of Being: *This entire natural world therefore,* which is continually "there for us," "present to our hand," and will ever remain there, is a "fact-world" of which we continue to be conscious, even though it pleases us to put it in brackets.

If I do this, as I am fully free to do, I do *not* then *deny* this "world," as though I were a sophist. *I do not doubt that it is there* as though I were a sceptic; but I use the "phenomenological" *ἐποχή* which *completely bars me from using any judgment that concerns spatio-temporal existence (Dasein).*°

It is important to understand both what Husserl meant by "doubt" and also how radical was the doubt that he wished us to learn to cultivate. To begin with, at least as far as this passage goes, doubt does not mean disbelieving something but rather suspending judgment about it. It is obviously possible to bracket *particular* beliefs within the natural standpoint, and we often do so if we cannot get a clear view of some object. If, for instance, I am at the theater, I may wonder

---

[13][*Epoche* was the term used by the Greek skeptics to designate the attitude that they recommended one adopt in the face of a world of doubt and uncertainty, an attitude of noncommitment and suspension of judgment—AUTHORS.]

whether the books in a bookcase on the set are real or painted, and not being able to get on the stage I may simply suspend judgment, neither believing nor disbelieving that they are painted. Or if I am walking down a London street on a foggy day I may wonder whether the object approaching is a bus or a truck; not being able to get a clear view, I suspend judgment. But Husserl wants me to suspend judgment not only in cases where I cannot get a clear and unimpeded view of something, but even in cases where, for instance, I am standing beside the bus and about to board it, and where the book is not on the stage but in my hand. Of course, I am not to suspend the *experience* of standing beside the bus or of holding the book in my hand. But I *am* to suspend judgment about whether I am actually standing beside the bus and about whether I actually have the book in my hand. To put this in Husserl's technical language, I am not to doubt the being of the book; I am to doubt that the book has being in the mode of existence, for it may have being in the mode of a dream.

To suspend belief in such cases as these, where the experience is clear and not in the least ambiguous, seems difficult enough. However, phenomenological doubt requires much more of us—it is not merely suspension of belief with respect to this or that experience within the natural standpoint; it is suspension of belief in the natural standpoint itself. But is it really possible—let alone desirable—to bracket the whole natural world?

Husserl would not have denied that such an attitude is unusual; indeed, he would have insisted on its rarity—and also on its difficulty. Otherwise phenomenology would not have had to wait so long for its discoverer. But though universal doubt is unusual, it was essential to his whole position that it be psychologically possible. This is presumably an empirical question, but it is not exactly an easy one to settle. And some people will be tempted to reply that, even if it is psychologically possible to doubt everything, to do so would be to fall into a serious psychosis. These people may therefore question whether Husserl himself ever actually carried out his program of bracketing. They will suspect that it was never more than an elaborate bit of playacting (by which Husserl himself was taken in).

Perhaps it will be possible to make the notion of bracketing more intelligible by emphasizing the aspect of detachment. As soon as we do so we understand why Husserl regarded the ideal of rationality as the Greeks' greatest legacy to Europe. Both Plato and Aristotle had distinguished between the pure theoretical reason that contemplates the world and the practical reason that seeks to change it. Though Plato's and Aristotle's notion of disinterested contemplation was a long way from Husserl's *epoche,* it at least involved a detachment from involvement in the world.

Even more interesting is the parallel that can be drawn with Schopenhauer and Bergson, philosophers whose views were otherwise very different from Husserl's. Schopenhauer's description of the "pure knowing subject" who has freed himself from the influence of his will was not unlike Husserl's description of the detachment involved in bracketing. Similarly, for Bergson intuition was a pure and detached state. What was common to all three of these thinkers was their distrust of epistemological theories based on the model of physics. Like Husserl, Schopenhauer and Bergson were reacting against the tendency in nineteenth-century culture to equate all knowledge with the kind of knowledge that is possible in the natural sciences. All three found what they believed to be a superior kind of knowledge in a type of direct and immediate experience, in contrast to the discursive, conceptual form of experience. But, whereas Bergson and Schopenhauer (and Plato and Aristotle as well) believed that what is encountered in this deeper form of cognition is a separate realm of metaphysically real existents, Husserl denied this, for he accepted the Kantian prohibition against the possibility of knowledge of things-in-themselves. Nevertheless, all three thinkers shared the conviction that when we suspend the truth-claims of our everyday cognitive processes, far from being (as might be supposed) in a state of not knowing anything, we find ourselves in the presence of truths of great importance that would otherwise wholly escape our attention.

This is perhaps what Husserl meant, in the passage just quoted, when he linked bracketing with "our full freedom." Similarly, he maintained elsewhere that much more is involved in bracketing than mere suspension of belief; what is needed is a "personal transformation" so complete that it is comparable "to a religious conversion." But this, to nonphenomenologists, makes bracketing even more suspect, and certainly more difficult to cultivate.

However this may be, it is evident why, in Husserl's view, the phenomenological stance is so important. As we learn to carry through bracketing more and more skillfully, we finally succeed in suspending belief in everything that can possibly be doubted. What in the end survives bracketing is thus literally indubitable and therefore absolutely certain. Thus absolute subjectivity, defined as the condition furthest removed from the natural standpoint, is the basis for absolute objectivity, the basis, that is, for that apodeictic science that neither Russell nor Whitehead—still less Dewey or the positivists—could offer us. The phenomenological stance is all-important, then, precisely because in it we encounter those apodeictic truths that European thought has been seeking. Phenomenology is thus the "rigorous science" that is needed to resolve the crisis of our culture.

But what, according to Husserl, does survive the "attempt to doubt everything"? The general answer is that what survives is consciousness.

> We have learnt to understand the meaning of the phenomenological ἐποχή, but we are still quite in the dark as to its serviceability. . . . For *what can remain over when the whole world is bracketed, including ourselves and all our thinking (cogitare)?* . . .
>
> *Consciousness in itself has a being of its own which in its absolute uniqueness of nature remains unaffected by the phenomenologic disconnexion.* It therefore remains as a *"phenomenological residuum,"* as a region of Being which is in principle unique, and can become in fact the field of a new science—the science of Phenomenology.P

"Residuum" is an unfortunate term; it is not Husserl's view that a part of the content of experience is lost in the course of bracketing and that a part remains. No content is lost; everything remains. Yet as a result of bracketing everything is different.

> Let us suppose that we are looking with pleasure in a garden at a blossoming apple-tree, at the fresh young green of the lawn, and so forth. . . . From the natural standpoint the apple-tree is something that exists in the transcendent reality of space, and the perception as well as the pleasure [is] a psychical state which we enjoy as real human beings. Between . . . the real man on the one hand and the real apple-tree on the other, there subsist real relations. . . . Let us now pass over to the phenomenological standpoint. The transcendent world enters its "bracket"; in respect of its real being we use the disconnecting *epoché*. . . . Together with the whole physical and psychical world the real subsistence of the objective relation between perception and perceived is suspended; and yet a relation between perception and perceived (as likewise between the pleasure and that which pleases) is obviously left over, a relation which in its essential nature comes before us in "pure immanence."q

Because my attitude has become wholly disinterested as a result of bracketing, I observe that which I never before observed, the essential nature of "pure" consciousness. In this transcendentally reduced observation I encounter a multitude of mental acts—perceivings, thinkings, imaginings, dreamings, and the like—and a multitude of different objects intended by these diverse acts. Consciousness, that is, involves both an act of intending and the intended object of this act. Here is an example: What you now see is a page of white paper with the words "What you now see . . ." printed on it. When we are in the natural standpoint it never occurs to us to doubt such a fact—after all, we see it. But we *can* doubt it—at least Husserl said we can. Perhaps what you are now seeing are not the printed words "What you now see . . ." but black dots floating before your eyes. However, it is not possible to doubt the experience of having seen printed words on the page. *That* this experience occurred is indubitable. Further, within this experience of printed words on a page it is possible to distinguish the intentional objects (the printed words) from the act of intending them. *What* I experience, when I bracket, is both my experiencing (that is, intending) printed words on a page and also the printed words as experienced (that is, as intended) by me.

It is important that both poles of consciousness-of can be bracketed, for each becomes a special domain for phenomenological investigation. Thus when we are in the natural standpoint we can certainly reflect on our experience. It is possible, while in the natural standpoint, not only to experience the printed words on the page but also to experience yourself experiencing them—to say, or think to yourself, "I am now reading the words 'What you now see. . . .'" But just as bracketing is needed to bring out the true character of the objects we intend, so bracketing is needed to bring out the true nature of these acts of reflection. In short, "from the natural standpoint nothing can be seen except the natural world." So entrenched are the habits of this standpoint that

> we take all these data of psychological reflexion as real world-events, as the experiences (*Erlebnisse*) of animal beings. . . . We fail to notice that it is from out of these centres of experience (*Erlebnisse*) themselves that through the adoption of the new standpoint the new domain emerges. Connected with this is the fact that instead of keeping our eyes turned toward these centres of experience, we turned them away and sought the new objects in the ontological realms of arithmetic, geometry, and the like, whereby indeed nothing truly new was to be won.[14]
>
> [Thus] the "phenomenological" ἐποχή [is] the necessary operation which *renders "pure" consciousness accessible to us, and subsequently the whole phenomenological region.* . . . So long as the possibility of the phenomenological standpoint was not grasped, and the method of relating the objectivities which emerge therewith to a primordial form of apprehension has not been devised, the phenomenological world must needs have remained unknown, and indeed barely divined at all.[r]

To repeat, there are two correlated domains of investigation—the acts of the ego as it thinks, wills, doubts, fears, believes, hopes, and loves (acts that are revealed in reflection and then held in suspension by bracketing) and the objects of these acts of thinking, willing, doubting, fearing, believing, hoping, and loving (objects that in turn are held in suspension by bracketing). At the outset of his phenomenological investigation, Husserl focused his attention chiefly on the intended entities. When some of these are held for inspection by bracketing, they prove to be "essences." For instance, if you bracket your experience on the page of printed matter, you encounter the essence "page" and also the essences "white," "black," and "rectangular."[15]

What is an essence? Is it that about an object which makes it this sort of object rather than another sort of object—that about a page which makes it a page and not an apple tree, that about an apple tree which makes it an apple tree and not a page. Since essences also have the property of being completely present on each occasion that they are present at all, it was highly fortunate for Husserl that he was able to discover essences in transcendentally reduced experience. It was this discovery of essences that enabled him to claim that we are directly aware of objects, not merely of their appearances.

[14] [Here Husserl was presumably thinking of Plato, who, instead of directing his disinterested, contemplative gaze toward consciousness, turned it toward mathematics and thus derived his abstract, otherworldly forms—AUTHORS.]

[15] Husserl held that essences are disclosed in a special form of bracketing that he called "eidetic reduction."

Consider once again this page of printed matter at which you are now looking. If all that you were experiencing were simply this particular page (an individual object) you would certainly not be seeing the whole object (you are not, for instance, seeing both sides at once, nor the inside as well as the surface), and, according to some philosophers, you would not be experiencing *any* part of the object (you are not even experiencing its surface; you are experiencing only the appearance of its surface under such and such conditions of illumination). Thus, to have had to allow that we experience only particulars, and not essences, would have involved Husserl in all the puzzles that had plagued Moore—for instance, what is the relation between the elliptical appearance of a coin and the circular coin that is presumably its cause?[16] One of the great virtues of phenomenology, in Husserl's view, is that transcendentally reduced experience "consists in the self-appearance, the self-exhibiting, the self-giving" of objects themselves. That is, in transcendentally reduced experience we do not have to infer the existence of a coin (or an apple tree, or a page) that is not directly present from data that are directly present; we directly intuit the essence of the coin (as it appears). Transcendentally reduced experience brings us back from sense data to the thing itself—not to Kant's unknown and unknowable thing-in-itself, but to Stevens's "very thing itself and nothing else."

Reflection on the way in which objects are present to consciousness led Husserl to devote more attention to the opposite pole of consciousness-of, that is, acts of intending. Bracketing disclosed to him various activities of the ego (such as, in the example given above, synthesis of successive partial presentations of the page); and beneath such relatively accessible activities he found still other, deeper levels of ego activity, all supposedly revealed by rigorous bracketing. We need not follow Husserl into these ramifications and refinements; indeed, he insisted that it was impossible to follow him without extensive practice and training in phenomenological reduction. It will be enough for our purposes to understand the phenomenological method in a general way and to consider its implications for philosophy.

For these purposes let us consider Husserl's account of how his method differs from that of Descartes. That there are parallels is obvious, for Descartes too sought certainty and found it in the absolute indubitability of the *cogito*, the "I think." By focusing on the points at which Husserl parted company from Descartes we can begin to understand Husserl's conception of phenomenology.

DESCARTES'S DISCOVERY AND HIS MISTAKES

France's greatest thinker, René Descartes, gave transcendental phenomenology new impulses through his *Meditations*. . . . One might almost call transcendental phenomenology a neo-Cartesianism, even

<hr>

[16] See pp. 113–15.

though it is obliged—and precisely by its radical development of Cartesian motifs—to reject nearly all the well-known doctrinal content of the Cartesian philosophy. . . .

Every beginner in philosophy knows the remarkable train of thoughts contained in the *Meditations*. Let us recall its guiding idea. The aim of the *Meditations* is a complete reforming of philosophy into a science grounded on an absolute foundation. That implies for Descartes a corresponding reformation of all the sciences, because . . . only within the systematic unity of philosophy can they develop into genuine sciences. As they have developed historically, on the other hand, they lack that scientific genuineness which would consist in their complete and ultimate grounding on the basis of absolute insights, insights behind which one cannot go back any further. Hence the need for a radical rebuilding. . . . With Descartes this demand gives rise to a philosophy turned toward the subject himself. . . .

The *Meditations* were epoch-making in a quite unique sense, and precisely because of their going back to the pure *ego cogito*. Descartes, in fact, inaugurates an entirely new kind of philosophy. Changing its total style, philosophy takes a radical turn: from naive objectivism to transcendental subjectivism. . . . And so we make a new beginning, each for himself and in himself, with the decision of philosophers who begin radically: that at first we shall put out of action all convictions we have been accepting up to now, including all our sciences. . . .

Logic must be included among the sciences overthrown in overthrowing all science. Descartes himself presupposed an ideal of science, the ideal approximated by geometry and mathematical natural science. As a fateful prejudice this ideal determines philosophies for centuries and hiddenly determines the *Meditations* themselves. . . . For him a role similar to that of geometrical axioms in geometry is played in the all-embracing science by the axiom of the ego's absolute certainty of himself. . . .

None of that shall determine our thinking. As beginning philosophers we do not as yet accept any normative ideal of science; and only so far as we produce one newly for ourselves can we ever have such an ideal.

But this does not imply that we renounce the general aim of grounding science absolutely. The aim shall indeed continually motivate the course of our meditations, as it motivated the course of the Cartesian meditations; and gradually, in our meditations, it shall become determined concretely. . . .

At this point, following Descartes, we make the great reversal that, if made in the right manner, leads to transcendental subjectivity: the turn to the *ego cogito* as the ultimate and apodictically certain basis for judgments, the basis on which any radical philosophy must be grounded.[s]

Though the method of doubt thus brought Descartes to the very threshold of phenomenology,[17] Husserl claimed that from that point on he went badly wrong. First, he interpreted the "I think" substantively; second, he interpreted the objects of the "I think's" thoughts realistically, that is, as things-in-themselves. Since he did not have the advantage of Brentano's insight that consciousness is always consciousness-of, he failed to see both that the self is not a thing but a flow of intentional acts and also that things exist only in and for such acts, as objects intended by them.[18]

To put this differently, for Descartes the absolutely certain starting point on which the whole reconstruction of science had to depend was the single item, the self conceived of as a unitary substance. For Husserl, the absolutely certain starting point was a vast realm of intentions and intentional objects—the innumerable consciousnesses-of that come into view as a result of bracketing. Or, to put this in the Cartesian language that Husserl liked, for Descartes the starting point was simply the unitary *cogito* itself; for Husserl it was *ego cogito cogitatum,* an ego and its intended objects. This starting point gave Husserl a much broader base on which to construct his new sciences—a base that included all the manifold believings, rememberings, imaginings, and enjoyings encountered in bracketing and all the manifold objects (people, houses, trees, pages of printed matter, and so on) that can be remembered, thought about, imagined, and enjoyed.

> If we follow this methodological principle [of bracketing] in the case of the dual topic, *cogito-cogitatum* (*qua cogitatum*), there become opened to us, first of all, the general descriptions to be made, always on the basis of particular *cogitationes*, with regard to each of the two correlative sides. Accordingly, on the one hand, descriptions of the intentional object as such, with regard to the determinations attributed to it in the modes of consciousness concerned, attributed furthermore with corresponding modalities, which stand out when attention is directed to them. (For example: the "modalities of being," like certain being, possibly or presumably being, etc.; or the "subjective"—temporal modes, being present, past, or future.) This line of description is called *noematic.* Its counterpart is *noetic* description, which concerns the modes of the *cogito* itself, the modes of consciousness (for example: perception, recollection, retention), with the modal differences inherent in them (for example: differences in clarity and distinctness).[t]

Consider, for instance, the object we call a house—a particular house, like the house I live in now. This house can be intended in innumerable different acts: I

---

[17] See p. 277.

[18] Since this was a discovery Husserl himself did not make until he came to write the *Cartesian Meditations,* he was perhaps too critical of Descartes.

can look at it now, I can shut my eyes and imagine it, I can remember it, and so on. Corresponding to each of these modes of intending my house there is a uniquely determined essence, or meaning.

> Each *cogito,* each conscious process, we may also say, *"means" some-thing or other,* and bears in itself, in this manner peculiar to the *meant,* its particular *cogitatum.* Each does this, moreover, in its own fashion. The house-perception means a house—more precisely, as this indi-vidual house—and means it in the fashion peculiar to perception; a house-memory means a house in the fashion peculiar to memory; a house-phantasy, in the fashion peculiar to phantasy. A predicative judg-ing about a house, which perhaps is "there" perceptually, means it in just the fashion peculiar to judging; a valuing that supervenes means it in yet another fashion; and so forth.[u]

By collating all the ways in which the house means (the various meanings of the house) I can grasp what it is to be this house and, generally, what it is to be an object in the spatiotemporal world. I can, for instance, come to see that

> the object is, so to speak, a *pole of identity,* always meant expectantly as having a sense yet to be actualized; in every moment of consciousness it is an index, pointing to a noetic intentionality that pertains to it ac-cording to its sense, an intentionality that can be asked for and expli-cated. All this is concretely accessible to investigation.[v]

This is Husserl's way of dealing with the Fregean distinction between mean-ing and reference.[19] Frege's meaning has been replaced by a noema; his reference (which is a relation between a term and what the term designates) by a relation between a noema and its "pole of identity." Frege was concerned, characteristi-cally, with the relation between names and their references; Husserl, just as char-acteristically, with a relation that exists for consciousness, between an intentional act and its noema. A noema is anything but a name; it is the object of an inten-tional act, and each such act has its own noema. When I think about my house, this act has a thinking-about-the-house noema; when I value my house, this act has a valuing-the-house noema; when I remember my house, this act has a remembering-the-house noema, and so on. My house it the pole of identity for all these noemata, not in the sense that it is the independent object to which they re-fer (it is not a thing-in-itself that transcends all acts of intention), but only in the sense that it is not exhausted by any particular set of noemata, however large that set is. This is the case because, no matter how many times I may already have thought about, valued, and remembered my house, obviously I can think about it, value it, and remember it again. And each of these new acts of intentionality

---

[19] See pp. 157–67. For Carnap's version, see pp. 258–59.

would have its own noema, for which the house would also be the pole of identity. Nor do I *infer* the house for the noema. Rather, as we have seen,[20] I intuit the house itself as it appears in the noema. Thus to say that the house is not exhausted in any act of intentionality is quite compatible with saying that it is *for* consciousness. One must decide for oneself whether one prefers Frege's or Husserl's account of what Frege called meaning and reference.

So much for the noematic side of intentionality. As for the noetic side, by concentrating on it I can bracket various instances of, say, remembering—remembering the house, remembering the book I read yesterday, remembering the painting I saw two years ago in Paris, and so on. By collating these instances of remembering I can grasp the essential structure of the psychic process of remembering. Natural science studies material objects without knowing what a material object is; psychology studies psychic processes without having the least idea what a psychic process really is. No wonder these sciences lacked rigor! Husserl believed that phenomenology would provide them with the secure basis that they desperately needed. Descriptions from the side of the *cogitata* (noema) reveal the structures of the various kinds of states of affairs intended by the ego and hence provide an absolutely secure foundation for the natural sciences; descriptions from the side of the *ego cogito* (noesis) reveal the structure of the ego's intentional acts and hence provide corresponding foundations for empirical psychology.

EVIDENCE

In addition to mistakenly interpreting the "I think" as a unitary substance and the objects of the "I think's" thoughts as things-in-themselves, Descartes made a third mistake, according to Husserl. This was to adopt a geometric model for the rigorous new science that he was seeking. He regarded the *cogito* as an axiom and tried to deduce theorems from it. As Husserl pointed out in a passage quoted earlier, a thinker who aims at apodeictic certainty cannot afford to proceed in this careless way, but must subject the "normative ideal" of logic itself to criticism, not merely take it for granted. The Cartesian proofs of God and of the external world are suspect as long as the rules of evidence that guided these proofs have not themselves been exposed to universal doubt. Obviously, philosophy cannot simply take over the rules of evidence used in logic and in geometry; one of the tasks of philosophy as a rigorous science is to examine those rules of evidence in order to find for them too a secure foundation.

Husserl therefore proposed to be more careful than Descartes. According to his plan, phenomenology's ideal of evidence would not be assumed at the outset; on the contrary, it would "be determined concretely in the course of the investigations." Given Husserl's motivation, which he shared with Descartes, it is easy to sympathize with his desire to provide an assumption-free account of the nature of evidence. But is not this enterprise inevitably involved in circularity? Our

[20] See p. 293.

conclusion that certain evidence is adequate and that certain other evidence is not is the result of a reasoning process. But in order to know that this reasoning process is correct, must we not have been guided by some notion of what constitutes adequate evidence, a notion that was prior to our conclusion regarding what particular evidence is adequate? Husserl thought he could escape the danger of such a regress. The evidence that is disclosed by bracketing and that serves as the foundation of the reformed sciences is not the end result of any process of reasoning or inferring. It is simply present.

> Evidence is, in an *extremely broad sense,* an *"experiencing"* of something that is, and is thus; it is precisely a mental seeing of something itself. . . .
>
> In the broadest sense, evidence denotes a universal primal phenomenon of intentional life, namely . . . the quite pre-eminent mode of consciousness that consists in the *self-appearance,* the *self-exhibiting,* the *self-giving,* of an affair, an affair-complex (or state of affairs), a universality, a value, or other objectivity, in the final mode: "itself there," "immediately intuited," "given originaliter.". . . In the case of most objects, to be sure, evidence is only an occasional occurrence in conscious life; yet it is a possibility—and more particularly, one that can be the aim of a striving and actualizing intention—in the case of anything meant already or meanable. Thus it points to an essential *fundamental trait of all intentional life.* Any consciousness, without exception, either is itself already characterized as evidence (that is, as giving its object originaliter) or else has an essential tendency toward conversion into givings of its object originaliter.[w]

The term "collating," used above to describe the process by which we come to grasp the nature of such psychic processes as remembering and such states of affairs as spatiotemporal objects, will be misleading if it suggests that Husserl believed that what occurs is some sort of inferential process. Rather, when we put several instances of remembering side by side we simply intuit the essential nature of the psychic process of remembering, just as when we put several instances of whiteness together we intuit the essence of whiteness. It is simply true, he maintained, that in phenomenological observation we come to see clearly and unambiguously the true nature of different modes of being—the mode of being of a spatiotemporal object, the mode of being of a necessary object, the mode of being of a possible object, the mode of being of an ego, and so on. We do not have to deduce these; we do not have to infer them. We simply see them—when we have learned how to bracket our experience properly.

Phenomenology: The Science of Being

Phenomenology is thus the science of being; for this reason it serves as the foundation for all the special sciences. But phenomenology is the science of being in a radically different sense from that in which, for centuries, metaphysics had been regarded as the science of being. Beginning with Aristotle, philosophers had held that metaphysics is concerned with an ultimate reality that exists in and for itself. Kant had finally demolished the claims of this traditional metaphysics by showing that things-in-themselves (being-in-itself) are forever inaccessible to human minds. Accordingly, many philosophers concluded that the possibility of any science of being was thereby excluded. Knowledge, they thought, was limited to mind-dependent objects; thus they launched philosophy on the fatal path of relativism.

For Husserl, the beauty of the phenomenological method was that it made possible a new science of being.[21] It disclosed a realm of being that was ultimate, not in the sense that it existed beyond experience, but in the sense that it presented itself with absolute certainty within experience. To study being is not to turn to another reality (things-in-themselves, Platonic forms, élan vital); it is to penetrate deeper and deeper into the same—the one and only—reality (things-for-consciousness). Hence, Husserl liked to think of phenomenology as archaeology. The ruling idea in this metaphor was the notion of getting back to what is genuine, simple, and uncontaminated by later excrescences. In this respect Husserl's view was diametrically opposed to Nietzsche's; whereas Nietzsche held that there is no original text but only a series of interpretations, Husserl believed that, in the phenomenological method, he had found a way of reaching the original text, that is, the true meaning.

HOW THE PHENOMENOLOGICAL METHOD WORKS: AN EXAMPLE OF BRACKETING

So far, the account of Husserl's method has been set forth perforce in general terms. It may be useful to give an example of bracketing and of the results it is supposed to achieve. Consider the relatively simple object of a die that I hold in my hand. In the natural standpoint, I look at it. It is a cube; it has a certain color; it is of a certain size; on one surface there is a dot; on another surface there are two dots; and so on. There is nothing very interesting about it; perhaps I wonder where its mate is or toss it idly in my hand.

Now suppose I bracket this experience. At once everything is immensely more complex. Instead of the unitary, enduring, and unchanging die, there is a rapid and continuous flow of slightly changing colors as I move my hand toward the light; changing sizes as I move it toward my face; changing shapes as I rotate the die; and so on. Further, these appearances are not discrete units; each merges into the others. For instance, as I rotate the die through 180° the look of the die from one angle includes an anticipation, as it were, of the look of the die from succeeding angles of vision. Each look of the die implicitly contains other looks; the

---

[21] Given that the term "metaphysics" was closely associated with an alleged being beyond experience, the new phenomenological science of being could better have been called "ontology."

same is true for colors and shapes. This characteristic of experience (which is supposedly revealed only in the *epoche*) Husserl called "shadowing forth."

Further, my experience of the die is not just a matter of my experience at any particular time (say, the two or three seconds during which the die is lying in the palm of my hand). Memories of the die flow into present experiences, and future possible experiences are adumbrated in it. These aspects of intentionality (again revealed only in the *epoche*) Husserl called "horizons." Every individual object has infinitely open horizons; consequently no object can ever be experienced completely—though it can nonetheless be experienced "adequately."

Finally, all these experiences—past, present, and future—are being continuously "synthesized" so as to form, on the noematic side, the die that I have in my hand and, on the noetic side, the acts that constitute the self that perceives the die. Thus "synthesis," "horizons," and "shadowing forth" are features of the constitutional structure of intentionality. They and other features supposedly revealed in the *epoche* are described in the following passage. It should be noted that the descriptions move back and forth from the noetic to the noematic poles.

> Inquiry into consciousness concerns *two sides* . . . ; they can be characterized descriptively as *belonging together inseparably.* The sort of combination uniting consciousness with consciousness can be characterized as *synthesis,* a mode of combination exclusively peculiar to consciousness. For example, if I take the perceiving of this die as the theme for my description, I see in pure reflection that "this" die is given continuously as an objective unity in a multiform and changeable multiplicity of manners of appearing, which belong determinately to it. These, in their temporal flow, are not an incoherent sequence of subjective processes. Rather they flow away in the unity of a synthesis, such that in them "one and the same" is intended as appearing. The one identical die appears, now in "near appearances," now in "far appearances": in the changing modes of Here and There, over against an always co-intended, though perhaps unheeded, absolute Here (in my co-appearing organism). Furthermore, each continued manner of appearance in such a mode (for example: "the die here, in the near sphere") shows itself to be, in turn, the synthetic unity pertaining to a multiplicity of manners of appearance belonging to that mode. Thus the near-thing, as "the same," appears now from this "side," now from that; and the "visual perspectives" change—also, however, the other manners of appearance (tactual, acoustic, and so forth), as we can observe by turning our attention in the right direction. . . . Always we find the feature in question as a unity belonging to a passing "flow of multiplicities": Looking straightforwardly, we have perhaps the one unchanging shape or color; in the reflective attitude, we have its manners of appearance (orientational, perspectival, and so forth), following one another in continuous sequence. Furthermore, each of these manners of appearance (for example: the shadowing forth [*Abschattung*] of the

shape or color) is itself an *exhibition of* [*Darstellung von*] the shape, the color, or whatever the feature is that appears in it. Thus each passing cogito intends its cogitatum, not with an undifferentiated blankness, but as a cogito with a describable *structure of multiplicities,* a structure having a *quite definite* noetic-noematic composition, which, by virtue of its essential nature, pertains to just *this* identical cogitatum. . . .

Once we have laid hold of the phenomenological task of describing consciousness concretely, veritable infinities of facts—never explored prior to phenomenology—become disclosed. . . .

If we consider the *fundamental form of synthesis,* namely *identification,* we encounter it first of all as an all-ruling, *passively* flowing synthesis, in the form of the *continuous consciousness of internal time.* Every subjective process has its internal temporality. If it is a conscious process in which (as in the perception of the die) a worldly Object appears as cogitatum, then we have to distinguish the *Objective temporality that appears* (for example: the temporality of this die) from the "*internal*" *temporality of the appearing* (for example: that of the die-perceiving). This appearing "flows away" with its temporal extents and phases, which, for their part, are continually changing appearances *of* the one identical die. Their unity is a unity of synthesis: not merely a continuous connectedness of cogitationes (as it were, a being stuck to one another externally), but *a connectedness that makes the unity of one consciousness.* . . .

Now the same die (the same for consciousness) can be intended in highly diverse modes of consciousness—simultaneously, or else successively in *separated* modes of consciousness—for example: in separate perceptions, recollections, expectations, valuations, and so forth. Again it is a synthesis that, as a unitary consciousness *embracing* these separated processes, gives rise to the consciousness of identity and thereby makes any knowing of identity possible. . . .

Synthesis, however, does not occur just in every particular conscious process, nor does it connect one particular conscious process with another only occasionally. On the contrary, . . . the *whole of conscious life is unified synthetically.* Conscious life is therefore an all-embracing cogito. . . . The *fundamental form* of this universal synthesis, the form that makes all other syntheses of consciousness possible, is the all-embracing *consciousness of internal time.* . . .

The multiplicity of the intentionality belonging to any cogito . . . is a theme not exhausted with the consideration of cogitationes as *actual* subjective processes. On the contrary, *every actuality involves its potentialities,* which are not empty possibilities, but rather possibilities intentionally predelineated in respect of content. . . .

With that, *another fundamental trait of intentionality* is indicated. Every subjective process as a process "horizon," which changes with the alteration of the nexus of consciousness to which the process belongs and with the alteration of the process itself from phase to phase of its flow—an intentional *horizon of reference* to potentialities of consciousness that belong to the process itself. For example, there belongs to every external perception its reference from the "genuinely perceived" sides of the object of perception to the sides "also meant"—not yet perceived but only anticipated. . . . Furthermore, the perception has horizons made up of other possibilities of perception, as perceptions that we *could* have, if we *actively directed* the course of perception otherwise: if, for example, we turned our eyes that way instead of this. . . .

The horizons are "predelineated" potentialities. We say also: We can *ask any horizon what "lies in it,"* we can *explicate* or unfold it, and *"uncover"* the potentialities of conscious life at a particular time. . . . The predelineation itself, to be sure, is at all times imperfect; yet, with its *indeterminateness,* it has a *determinate structure.* For example: the die leaves open a great variety of things pertaining to the unseen faces; yet it is already "construed" in advance as a die, in particular as colored, rough, and the like, though each of these determinations always leaves further particulars open. This leaving open, prior to further determinings (which perhaps never take place), is a moment included in the given consciousness itself; it is precisely what makes up the "horizon.". . .

Thus, as consciousness of something, every consciousness has the essential property, not just of being somehow *able to change into continually new modes of consciousness of the same object* . . . , but of being able to do so according to—indeed, *only according to those horizon intentionalities.* The object is, so to speak, *a pole of identity,* always meant expectantly as having a sense yet to be actualized.[x]

COMMENT ON THIS PASSAGE

Perhaps enough has been quoted to indicate how Husserl practiced his phenomenological method. What are we to make of it? Does the method really uncover apodeictically certain truths about the nature of being?

To begin with, in some cases it is possible, even for those not adept at bracketing, to identify what Husserl is describing in this passage. But, one is tempted to ask, why use the language Husserl chose? As an example, consider Husserl's account of what he called "predelineated possibilities." What does this amount to? Apparently something like this: What I mean by "die" is, among numerous other things, that if I am looking at the one-dot surface, I will see the six-dot surface if I rotate the die through 180°. If on rotating it I were not to see the six-dot surface, I would say "Something has gone wrong," or "That's a dishonest die," or possibly "Why, that's not a die at all." In a word, to talk about "possibilities" in this case is to point out that, on the basis of prior experience, I believe that the die has another side; this being the case, I often anticipate seeing the other side while I am still looking at this one. To talk about "predelineation" is simply to point out that while I am looking at the one-dot side I anticipate seeing a configuration of six dots, and not, for example, the king of spades or General de Gaulle.

Husserl's description in terms of predelineated possibilities sounds much more impressive than this one, but is it *better*? Is it, for that matter, better than the one Husserl himself gave from the natural standpoint, in terms of a "fringe of indeterminate reality"?[22] Is it better than Whitehead's description in terms of prehendings into unity?[23] Both philosophers seem to be saying that if we attend to the die as we actually experience it we find that it is not *here* all at once; nor is it *now* all at once. Again, is Husserl's description of this experience of the interconnectedness of things better than the Romantic poet's description in terms of "affinities" that "passive minds" overlook?[24] Finally, is this description of what we experience when we look at a die better than Moore's account of what we see when we look at two coins?[25]

Husserl would claim that none of these descriptions is reliable; all are distorted by implicit, not fully articulated presuppositions. Doubtless he would be correct. Moore's, for instance, is certainly colored by the assumption, which he shared with other philosophers of the analytic tradition, that the universe consists in an immense number of atomistic, encapsulated items. But was Husserl's account not also, and equally, influenced by *his* implicit assumptions—for instance, his assumption that there must be essences, which more or less parallels Moore's assumption that there must be sense data? Philosophers who are unable to discover essences for *their* consciousness may be inclined to suspect that Husserl found them not because they were there waiting to be found but because they solved so conveniently an otherwise intractable philosophical problem. People who have no such philosophical axe to grind might prefer Dewey's or James's or Whitehead's descriptions of experience (though they too had philosophical axes to grind), as being less artificial than either Moore's or Husserl's.

PHENOMENOLOGY AS DESCRIPTION
AND PHENOMENOLOGY AS A QUEST FOR CERTAINTY

But we must remember that Husserl's interest was not merely to describe; he wanted also to satisfy the quest for certainty. And this is why directly present, and hence self-evident, intentional acts and intentional objects figure so prominently in his description of experience. They were to be the bases for that "objectively valid science" that was Husserl's goal. But unfortunately this science remained as programmatic as the very different program of the positivists. Instead, Husserl's

---

[22] See p. d286.
[23] The essences that Husserl believed come into view as a result of eidetic reduction (for instance, the red color of the die) are descriptions of the same aspects of experience that are called, in Whitehead's terminology, "eternal objects."
[24] See p. 275.
[25] See pp. 113–15.

energy was more and more distracted into the Pandora's box of metaphysical and epistemological puzzles that he thought his phenomenological method had forever eliminated.

In this connection it is interesting to contrast Dewey and Husserl. In one important respect they agreed: both maintained that minds and objects occur within experience, thus eliminating at one stroke the old mind-body dualism, which had posed for philosophers the hard choice between opting for mind (and saying with the idealists that all is mental) or for body (and saying with the materialists that all is physical). But for Dewey mind and body are "emergents"; for Husserl they are revealed once and for all in their essential purity. Dewey could accept that mind and body are emergents, that they have a natural history, because he was not looking for an apodeictically certain science; Husserl had to insist on essential purity, because he was looking for such a science.

One consequence of this emphasis on an apodeictic science was that, even within the phenomenological movement of which he was the founder, Husserl's position was unstable. There was, indeed, a deep and unresolved conflict at the heart of his thought between phenomenology as a method of describing experience more accurately and phenomenology as a quest for certainty.

Phenomenology as description has had a salutary effect on the social sciences.[26] But description, however accurate, can never establish the certainty of what is described. Though it can turn up *experiences* of certainty, whose structure can be explored, it never makes it certain that these experiences of certainty are certainly what they claim to be. This might not disturb psychologists or sociologists, especially those with instrumentalist leanings, but it was a fatal limitation for a philosopher in search of an absolutely valid science. Hence, as it seemed to many philosophers, Husserl increasingly inclined toward a Kantian type of solution to the problem of a priori knowledge; the findings of phenomenological description had to be guaranteed by the activities of a transcendental ego.

HUSSERL'S LAPSE INTO IDEALISM

Husserl would have objected strongly to a description of his later view as "inclining" toward a Kantian position. He continued to maintain—naturally—that he was neither an idealist nor a realist, he was a phenomenologist. In one place, it is true, he described phenomenology as *"eo ipso 'transcendental idealism,'"* but he added that it is idealism "in a fundamentally and essentially new sense."[y] He might just as well have described phenomenology as "realism in a fundamentally and essentially new sense"—better still, he might have pointed out that, whereas both idealism and realism attempt to stake out metaphysical claims on domains beyond experience, phenomenology is a doctrine of, and limited to, experience.

Thus Husserl's position was—at least in intent—radically different from Kant's, even though some of the elements disclosed by bracketing ("synthesis," for

[26]See p. 306.

example) sound remarkably Kantian and even though Husserl used a good deal of Kant's terminology. But for Kant "transcendental" meant "underlying" experience; for Husserl it meant "disclosed in experience by phenomenological analysis."[27] Kant called his investigations "transcendental logic," for he was setting out the logical conditions that make experience of the self and the world possible. Husserl, in contrast, held that his logical investigations were empirical and descriptive. What they disclosed was as much a part of the experiential world as are the tables and chairs that are disclosed from the natural standpoint. Thus whereas Kant had *deduced* this ego and its categorical syntheses (they were behind experience, but did not appear in it), Husserl's phenomenological method, which of course he never thought of abandoning, required him to find the synthesis operations of the transcendental ego in experience. Since they did not appear in transcendentally reduced observation as he had previously practiced it, more and more rigorous reductions became necessary to uncover more and more activities of the ego at supposedly deeper and deeper levels.[28]

From Husserl's own point of view these activities were all within experience, waiting to be disclosed; but they were so deeply hidden that they became accessible only through the most severe bracketing. But what about readers less adept than Husserl in the art of bracketing who were unable to uncover these deeper activities? If they did not want to cast doubt on the whole method, they had no recourse but to think of these activities as lying outside the phenomenal field altogether, that is, as "transcendent" in the Kantian sense. Hence, though Husserl himself thought he was bringing to light the "hidden achievements" of the ego, few of even the most devout phenomenologists were prepared to follow him. To them, this whole line of reasoning seemed a surrender to idealism. Husserl, they felt, had abandoned the quest for objectivity. Whereas, from Husserl's point of view, the transcendental ego's activities having been supposedly revealed in experience saved him from idealism, from the point of view of his phenomenologist critics, the transcendental ego ruined everything. Husserl wrote about its activities as "constituting" the experiential world; they saw little difference between constituting and constructing. Far from Wallace Stevens's pine being the very tree itself, it proved to have been constructed by Stevens's poetic imagination and, behind that, by anonymous and hidden activities.

Husserl's phenomenological method had appealed to those who, though they rejected the analytic philosophers' atomistic assumptions, shared these philosophers' dislike of constructivism, their desire to see things clearly and unambiguously, and hence their disposition to treat consciousness as transparent.[29] Husserl's method of bracketing had appealed precisely because it claimed to present "objects originaliter." To these phenomenologists it seemed that the attribution of

---

[27] According to Husserl, not only the intentional objects but also the underlying intentional acts are disclosed in experience.
[28] See p. 301.
[29] See pp. 91–92.

activities to the ego reintroduced ambiguity into the epistemological situation, which had seemed so simple and straightforward; it was a return to the slippery Hegelian slope. Thus phenomenology, like its archrival positivism—both of which had been launched as efforts to break out of the Kantian paradigm—threatened to collapse back into it.

Husserl's Influence

To allow these last comments to stand alone would be to create too negative an impression of Husserl's philosophy. Certainly, if his philosophy is judged by its own grandiose aims, its accomplishments are meager. But his influence on contemporary philosophy and on the social sciences has been great. Although he did not lay the foundation for a new ontology, he did found a school of psychology that, following his method more or less closely, has made detailed and often illuminating investigations of such phenomena as bad faith, anxiety, and time sense. And quite apart from the work of what may be called "armchair" psychology, phenomenology has had a salutary influence on experiential psychology in calling attention to the importance of "experiential variables," which tend to be overlooked by psychologists with a strongly behavioristic orientation. For instance, it has been pointed out that

> if we are to understand the world of color, we must first look carefully at the colors themselves, not just at their qualities, but at all the ways in which they appear. They usually appear as surfaces . . . ; but they may also have a filmy quality devoid of surface characteristics, or they may be seen as tridimensional or as lustrous or glowing. These are all different modes of appearance of the same color. . . . The same stimulus applied in different contexts may produce radically different perceptions of color. . . . The surface appearance is not a simple function of the wave length or intensity of incoming light; it is a complex function of many variables which contribute to the structuring of the visual world.[z]

Husserl saw that psychologists who attended only to external, physical "stimuli" that could be isolated and then correlated with other similarly isolated "responses" not only missed important variables altogether; in their desire to correlate variables, they did not see that they were ignoring context (even "physical" context) and thus creating a highly artificial situation. Because they had uncritically taken over the methods of physics they blandly regarded the limitations of these methods not as limitations but as the essence of science. Husserl helped free psychology from the dogma that all sciences should model themselves on physics; he taught psychologists to begin with the experiential field itself rather than with stimuli or hypothetical elements of sensation. In this sense he was far more empirical than many psychologists who prided themselves on their "empiricism."

Similarly, Husserl's influence has caused sociologists to attend to social experience as well as social structure—to the inner *Erlebnis,* the inner flow of our experience as we live and act in groups of various kinds, to our beliefs and value systems, and to our different ways of perceiving social realities, in addition to attending to our overt, "observable" interactions. Here too the result has been to start with problems and to devise means of dealing with them, instead of starting with a method that "predelineates" results in advance.

These achievements, which are of great importance, all flow from Husserl's empirical orientation and his repeated injunction to "return to the things themselves."[30] He was sufficiently freed from metaphysical dualism and from the "scientism" that infected the thinking of many of his contemporaries to take note of many ranges of facts that they ignored. But somehow this empirical approach became entangled in his urgent personal need for absolutes, with the unfortunate result that his experientialism was converted into ontology and the data of observation were dressed up as "objects originaliter." This, not the move from realism to idealism, is the most serious shift in Husserl's philosophy. It shows us once again the extent to which the quest for certainty has been a major factor in twentieth-century culture.

But Husserl's emphasis was on cognitive certainty. He thought of humans chiefly as observers, spectators, of reality, and this bias naturally colored his account of the subjective pole of pure consciousness. For many phenomenologists Husserl's version of phenomenology was therefore too intellectualistic. Whereas he concentrated on the possibility of knowledge, they despaired of knowledge and concentrated on how to act in an absurd world—especially in a world in which people know that they are going to die. Hence, though these phenomenologists shared Dewey's emphasis on a human being as a doer, not merely as a knower, they lacked Dewey's optimism and practicality. They perceived humans as aliens, cast into an indifferent universe where they are forced, willy-nilly, to act and to choose.

Thus the phenomenological movement underwent a dual development—first, in an attempt to found an ontology on the basis of phenomenological description; second, in the direction of an existential interpretation of consciousness. Since most phenomenologists shared these interests, the two developments were closely related. In this connection we will examine the theories of Heidegger in the next chapter, and, in Chapter 10, those of Sartre.

---

[30]*Not* to things-in-themselves.

Heidegger

Heidegger and the Phenomenological Tradition

Heidegger's[1] first introduction to philosophy was Thomism, in connection with his preparation for a theological career. But, as he says, "I [soon] gave up my

[1] Martin Heidegger was born in 1889 and grew up in Baden in southwest Germany. He was educated at the University of Freiburg and taught there and at the University of Marburg, where he knew Jaspers, Max Scheler, and Tillich. He was recalled to Freiburg in 1928 on Husserl's retirement, and in the spring of 1933, just after the Nazis came into power in Germany, he became rector of the university. At this time he was an ardent supporter of the Nazis, but his enthusiasm for the regime declined, and in 1935 he resigned as rector. Despite his earlier Nazi connections he did not lose his professorship at the end of the war; he continued to lecture until the normal time for retirement, but withdrew more and more into a secluded life on a mountaintop in the Black Forest. He died in 1976.

theological studies and dedicated myself entirely to philosophy."[a] The philosophy to which he initially dedicated himself was phenomenology in the Husserlian manner. Though he was never a pupil of Husserl's in the formal sense, when he was a young teacher at Freiburg he worked with Husserl, "primarily in his workshop," and was led by him through "a step-by-step training in phenomenological 'seeing.'"[b] Heidegger became so proficient in phenomenological seeing that Husserl thought he had found the heir he had been seeking, and he secured for Heidegger the succession to his professorship.

Alas for Husserl! Once established in Husserl's chair, Heidegger dissociated himself both from the phenomenological movement and from Husserl personally.[2] Husserl had failed to recognize that Heidegger's outlook was fundamentally different from his own. Heidegger's interests were from the start metaphysical. He had been concerned even at the time he was still a theology student with the question, "If being is predicated on manifold meanings, then what is its leading fundamental meaning? What does Being mean?"[c] That is pretty much the question Aristotle had first formulated and the question that preoccupied the medieval Scholastics. The novelty of Heidegger's approach was his proposal to apply the method of phenomenology to it.

This was a natural move for him to make. After all, Husserl's main thesis had been that transcendentally reduced experience "consists in the self-appearance, the self-exhibiting, the self-giving" of objects themselves. It is true that Husserl had focused the phenomenological method on the essences of such entities as dice and apple trees and that what interested Heidegger the metaphysician was Being as such. It was his conviction that Being, too, as well as "mere beings," exhibits itself, "gives" itself, to us in the phenomenological "seeing" that Husserl had taught. Husserl claimed that such experience is "pure" because it is wholly free from presuppositions; what we experience in it is the very thing itself. Heidegger accepted this claim but applied it to the reform of metaphysics rather than to the establishment of "rigorous science." In transcendentally reduced experience we free ourselves not only from the false preconceptions of empirical scientists but also from those of earlier metaphysicians. Therefore, in transcendentally reduced experience we encounter Being itself—not merely Being as it appeared to those metaphysicians, but the very Being they had been seeking but which, because of their erroneous preconceptions, they had failed to find.

Thus one important difference between Husserl's and Heidegger's versions of phenomenology lies in the object that is to be studied in this science: for Husserl it was (in Heidegger's terminology) beings; for Heidegger himself it was Being. This is why in the following passage Heidegger emphasizes that "phenomenology" is the name of a method, not of a subject matter.

[2] Despite Husserl's eminence and age, he, like other Jews, was subject to the anti-Semitic measures taken by the Nazis to purge the University of Freiburg. Granted that it would probably have taken courage to intervene on Husserl's behalf, still it is a fact that Heidegger did not do so, despite his leading position at the university.

"Phenomenology" neither designates the object of its researches, nor characterizes the subject-matter thus comprised. The word merely informs us of the *"how"* with which *what* is to be treated in this science gets exhibited and handled. To have a science "of" phenomena means to grasp its objects *in such a way* that everything about them which is up for discussion must be treated by exhibiting it directly and demonstrating it directly. The expression "descriptive phenomenology," which is at bottom tautological, has the same meaning. . . . That which remains *hidden* in an egregious sense, or which shows itself only *"in disguise,"* is not just this entity or that, but rather the *Being* of entities. . . . This Being can be covered up so extensively that it becomes forgotten and no question arises about it or about its meaning. . . .

Phenomenology is our way of access to what is to be the theme of ontology,[3] and it is our way of giving it demonstrative precision. *Only as phenomenology, is ontology possible.* In the phenomenological conception of "phenomenon" what one has in mind as that which shows itself is the Being of entities, its meaning, its modifications and derivatives. And this showing-itself is not just any showing-itself, nor is it some such thing as appearing. Least of all can the Being of entities ever be anything such that "behind it" stands something else "which does not appear."

"Behind" the phenomena of phenomenology there is essentially nothing else; on the other hand, what is to become a phenomenon can be hidden. And just because the phenomena are proximally and for the most part *not* given, there is need for phenomenology. Covered-up-ness is the counter-concept to "phenomenon."

There are various ways in which phenomena can be covered up. In the first place, a phenomenon can be covered up in the sense that it is still quite *undiscovered.* It is neither known nor unknown. Moreover, a phenomenon can be *buried over.* This means that it has at some time been discovered but has deteriorated to the point of getting covered up again. This covering-up can be complete; or rather—and as a rule—what has been discovered earlier may still be visible, though only as a semblance. Yet so much semblance, so much "Being." This covering-up as a "disguising" is both the most frequent and the most dangerous, for here the possibilities of deceiving and misleading are especially stubborn. . . .

Because phenomena, as understood phenomenologically, are never anything but what goes to make up Being, while Being is in every case the Being of some entity, we must first bring forward the entities

---

[3][Because of his differences from the classical metaphysicians, Heidegger preferred to use the term "ontology" to describe the type of inquiry he undertook—AUTHORS.]

themselves if it is our aim that Being should be laid bare; and we must do this in the right way. . . .

Ontology and phenomenology are not two distinct philosophical disciplines among others. These terms characterize philosophy itself with regard to its object and its way of treating that object. Philosophy is universal phenomenological ontology, and takes its departure from the hermeneutic of Dasein, which, as an analytic of *existence,* has made fast the guiding-line for all philosophical inquiry at the point where it *arises* and to which it *returns.*[d]

The term "Dasein"[4] in the last sentence points to another major difference between Heidegger and Husserl. Although Husserl too concentrated on human nature, he focused on what he called the noetic pole—on acts of attending, perceiving, recalling, and thinking about the world. For him the human being is chiefly a knower. For Heidegger, in contrast, the human being is not so much a knower as a concerned creature—concerned above all for its fate in an alien world. The human being, or Dasein, that Heidegger's phenomenological analysis discloses is thus very different from the human being that Husserl's phenomenological analysis discloses.

Further, since the being making the analysis is in its very nature a concerned being, its inquiry about its own nature and about the nature of Being generally is a concerned inquiry. Hence, though Heidegger often talks, as we have just been talking, about phenomenological "analysis," the term is misleading. Better perhaps are words such as "insight" and "sympathy"; better still, since these terms have psychological connotations, is an expression such as "empathetic understanding" if this suggests a kind of cognition in which the being who understands is not a mere knower but stands in a concerned relation to the object of its knowledge. A term that Heidegger himself sometimes used is "attunement," which shows how far he had moved from Husserl's notion of consciousness and mere directionality.

In view of these differences from Husserl, was Heidegger a phenomenologist? Although it is easy to see why he claimed that he was not, it is Heidegger the phenomenologist, not Heidegger the metaphysician and ontologist, who will probably have the greater impact on twentieth-century philosophy.[5] Though the discussion of Dasein in *Being and Time* (1927) was intended to be only preliminary, and thus subordinate, to ontology, this description of what it is to be human is more acute, more sensitive, altogether "deeper" than Husserl's. And what is more, it resonates in a powerful and evocative way with the mood of our times. Accordingly, in the

---

[4]"Dasein," which the translators like to retain because it had special connotations for Heidegger, means roughly "human being" or "the mode of being human."

[5]Since, as we have just seen, Heidegger identified ontology with phenomenology, he would not allow us this distinction. We can rephrase our comment in his terminology by saying that it is the ontical-existentiell level of this inquiry, not the ontological-existential, that will survive. See pp. 342–45.

following account of Heidegger's view we shall devote most of our attention to his phenomenology of human existence. But we shall begin with the question with which Heidegger himself began: "What is the meaning of Being?"

The Question of Being

Heidegger's chief work, *Being and Time*, opens with a quotation from Plato. "For manifestly you have long been aware of what you mean when you use the expression 'being.' We, however, who used to think we understood it, have now become perplexed."[e]

Heidegger then asks,

> Do we in our time have an answer to the question of what we really mean by the word "being"? Not at all. So it is fitting that we should raise anew *the question of the meaning of Being*. But are we nowadays even perplexed at our inability to understand the expression "Being"? Not at all. So first of all we must reawaken an understanding for the meaning of this question. Our aim in the following treatise is to work out the question of the meaning of *Being* and to do so concretely.[f]

The quotation from Plato sounds one of the leitmotifs of the whole work: reminding. To quote the passage is to remind us of Plato and his dialogues, which we may have forgotten. But what is said at just this point in this dialogue is itself an instance of reminding: the speaker is reminding his interlocutor of a still-earlier occasion on which something that had been forgotten has been recalled. And of what are we being reminded on this occasion by reference to those earlier remindings? It is our amazement—our wonder—about Being. The history of humankind, Heidegger is saying (or rather, not *saying*, but suggesting—and so, in a sense, reminding us), is the history of being amazed by Being, of forgetting and then recalling our wonder. In a sense, our amazement—our wonder—is always with us; we have only to look in order to rediscover it. But sometimes we become so involved in the affairs of the world that we are not only not amazed by Being, we do not even wonder at our lack of wonder.

But what *is* the question of Being? What is it about Being that would constantly amaze us, if only we were to direct our attention to it? It is just that there is anything at all, that anything at all *is*: "Why is there any Being at all—why not far rather Nothing?"[g] Put thus starkly, we may wonder what the pother is all about. What may amaze us is that Heidegger expects us to wonder about Being. But that is just the point, Heidegger would reply. It only proves what he had been contending, that twentieth-century humans did not understand the question of Being.

Let us begin by pointing out what the question of Being does not mean. It does not mean "Why should this or that particular thing be?" If, for instance, someone asks "Why are there earthquakes?" we turn to seismologists for an answer and are satisfied if they can give us an account in terms of differential movements of the earth's crust. We understand the occurrence of an earthquake in San Francisco in 1906 in terms of antecedent movements of the San Andreas Fault, and we understand these movements in terms of certain earlier events, and so on. But none of this has anything at all to do with Heidegger's question. Granting that this thing is because that thing is, he wants to know why anything at all is.

It is precisely because this kind of question cannot be dealt with by the sciences that the positivists ruled it out as meaningless. But if we think back over the history of culture, we see that positivists, and skeptics generally, have been greatly outnumbered by those who have been concerned by, haunted by, the question of Being, and who have sought, each in his or her own way, to answer it. Long ago the question was answered by myths—most peoples have had a creation myth of some sort, in which we can see reflected their amazement at Being. In Christianity the question was answered by reference to the goodness of God. When religious belief declined, metaphysics took over, and from Aristotle to Hegel metaphysicians sought to explain why something rather than nothing should exist.

Consequently, we can understand Heidegger's question in one sense—in the sense that it is a part of the history of culture. But to grasp the question of Being, it is not enough to understand it in this objective, neutral way. Consider the difference between a question about earthquakes and a question about love. If John, who does not love Mary, asks, "Why should I love Mary?" we cannot tell him. Suppose we point out that she is beautiful. He will reply, "Yes, I suppose she is, but why all the pother about beauty?" And so for anything else about Mary that we might mention in an attempt to persuade him that Mary is lovable. But if he falls in love with Mary, the situation is wholly different. Then the answer to the question "Why should I love Mary?" is transparently clear: Mary's lovability shines before him. So with the question of Being. It is not a question that we first understand and then later seek to answer. We cannot even begin to understand this question without already being able to answer it. That is, we cannot understand why we should wonder at Being without already wondering at it. And when we *do* wonder at Being, the question does not arise; the wonderability of Being shines before us.

For Heidegger, to be human is simply to be open to the presence of Being, and the mark of one's openness to Being is one's amazement. It seemed to him urgent to help us make ourselves into human beings by opening us to Being. No one will understand Heidegger—understand, that is, in the sense of entering into the meaning and grasping it—unless he or she feels the missionary zeal that suffuses all his writings. His aim was not merely to call attention to Being—that would be useless—but to evoke in us the amazement that he felt in the presence of Being. He wanted, as he said, to "stir us by the question of Being."[h] Thus the last word in the passage quoted above is the operative word: "concretely." It was the phenomenological method, Heidegger thought, that gave him the opportunity to "work out the question of the meaning of being concretely."

Philosophers of the Aristotelian-Scholastic tradition, in which he himself had been introduced to philosophy, had *talked* a lot about Being, but they had regarded it only as the highest genus, the most universal (and therefore the most empty) of concepts; they had no sense of the living presence of Beings in beings. In contrast to this abstract approach, the concrete approach recognizes that Being is not an entity at all; it is rather the light that illumines beings. Just as light is there, waiting to be looked at, instead of being merely looked with, so Being is always present to us, waiting for us to feel its presence in our lives. Or, to use another metaphor, Being is the soil that nourishes the tree of knowledge. If we look only at what is obvious we may think only of the branches, roots, and leaves, forgetting that it is the soil hidden away beneath the surface that nevertheless gives them strength. Given this view of the relation between Being and beings, it is easy to see why Heidegger believed that metaphysics must be "overcome" and replaced by a wholly different kind of thinking.

> Because metaphysics inquires about beings as beings, it remains concerned with beings and does not devote itself to Being as Being. . . .
>
> Insofar as a thinker sets out to experience the ground of metaphysics, insofar as he attempts to recall the truth of Being itself instead of merely representing beings as beings, his thinking has in a sense left metaphysics. From the point of view of metaphysics, such thinking goes back into the ground of metaphysics. . . . If our thinking should succeed in its efforts to go back into the ground of metaphysics, it might well help to bring about a change in human nature, accompanied by a transformation of metaphysics.
>
> If, as we unfold the question concerning the truth of Being, we speak of overcoming metaphysics, this means: recalling Being itself. . . .
>
> Why, however, should such an overcoming of metaphysics be necessary? . . . Are we trying to go back into the ground of metaphysics in order to uncover a hitherto overlooked presupposition of philosophy, and thereby to show that philosophy does not yet stand on an unshakable foundation and therefore cannot yet be the absolute science? No.
>
> It is something else that is at stake with the arrival of the truth of Being or its failure to arrive. . . . What is to be decided is nothing less than this: can Being itself, out of its own unique truth, bring about its involvement in human nature? . . .
>
> Due to the manner in which it thinks of beings, metaphysics almost seems to be, without knowing it, the barrier which keeps man from the original involvement of Being in human nature.
>
> What if the absence of this involvement and the oblivion of this absence determined the entire modern age? What if the absence of Being abandoned man more and more exclusively to beings, leaving him forsaken and far from any involvement of Being in his nature, while this

forsakenness itself remained veiled? What if this were the case—and had been the case for a long time now? What if there were signs that this oblivion will become still more decisive in the future? . . .

Thus everything depends on this: . . . The thinking which is posited by beings as such, and therefore representational and illuminating in that way, must be supplanted by a different kind of thinking which is brought to pass by Being itself and, therefore, responsive to Being. . . .

The question is: Why is there any being at all and not rather Nothing? Suppose that we do not remain within metaphysics to ask metaphysically in the customary manner; suppose we recall the truth of Being out of the nature and the truth of metaphysics; then this might be asked as well: How did it come about that beings take precedence everywhere and lay claim to every "is" while that which is not a being is understood as Nothing, though it is Being itself, and remains forgotten? How did it come about that with Being it really is nothing and that the Nothing really is not? Is it perhaps from this that the as yet unshaken presumption has entered into all metaphysics that "Being" may simply be taken for granted and that Nothing is therefore made more easily than beings? That is indeed the situation regarding Being and Nothing.[i]

The last paragraph is pure Heideggerese, and some readers may feel that, far from evoking Being, it evokes nothing—not Nothing, just nothing at all. In fairness to Heidegger, however, we must remember that we have not yet approached Being via his chosen route, the route of Dasein. We must now embark on this route ourselves, but before we do so we will call attention to a similarity between Heidegger and the Romantic poets that may throw a little light on the path ahead.

A POET MANQUÉ

In connection with our account of the underlying outlook of the phenomenological tradition, as contrasted with that of the analytic tradition, we have already quoted Wordsworth on the "sentiment of being" that he found "spread o'er all that moves and all that seemeth still."[6] When he was walking in the Wye Valley near Tintern, and on many other occasions as well, Wordsworth experienced

> A presence that disturbs me with the joy
> Of elevated thoughts; a sense sublime
> Of something far more deeply interfused,
> Whose dwelling is the light of setting suns,
> And the round ocean and the living air,
> And the blue sky, and in the mind of man.[j]

[6]See p. 275.

It seems likely that Heidegger had experiences of this kind, experiences that were of immense significance to him and that made him discontented with the Scholasticism in which he had been brought up and made him, too, when he came to do philosophy on his own, reject both the intellectualism of Husserl's phenomenology and the "abstract" approach of the traditional metaphysics. Though we know remarkably little about Heidegger's early life, we are told[k] that his father was the sexton of the Catholic church in a village in Baden and that Heidegger entered a Jesuit seminary with the intention of joining the order and becoming a priest. May we not conjecture that this abandonment of this career was connected with his sense of presence?

There have certainly been mystics and "romantics" in the Church, but they have always had a hard time staying there. From the point of view of the Church, with its commitment to a transcendent God, mysticism is tainted with pantheism;[7] from the point of view of the mystics, the official doctrine of God as *ens realissimum et perfectissimum* removes God's haunting presence from the setting sun, the living air, and the blue sky.

But if Heidegger shared this sentiment of being experienced by the mystics and the Romantic poets, he was not a mystic like St. John of the Cross or Meister Eckhart, and though on occasion he wrote verse, he was hardly a great poet. He was by inclination and by training a metaphysician, and however much he might repudiate the traditional philosophy, he was interested in questions that were of no concern whatever to mysticism and poets. He had, in fact, two aims that we may think proved to be incompatible. On the one hand, he wanted to evoke in others the sentiment of Being that he himself had felt; on the other hand, he wanted to found a new science of ontology. Therefore, whenever what Heidegger the ontologist says about Being seems impenetrable, the puzzled reader may find it helpful to try translating it into the language of religious mysticism. To do so may prove "illuminating," in much the same way that Heidegger himself held that Being illuminates beings.

Human Being in a Human "World"

Human beings have usually supposed that there is something that distinguishes them from other creatures. The only trouble is that they have never been able to agree on what this something is. Some say that what is unique about humans is that they were made in the image of God; others, that they have immortal souls; still others, that they are the only rational animals. They have variously characterized their species as *sapiens, habilis, faber, symbolicus.* Heidegger's writings

[7] See Vol. II, pp. 182–84 and 188.

constitute a major contribution to this long list of descriptions of what it is to be human. To be human is to have a world.

Heidegger's notion of world was derived from Husserl's "environing life world."[8] Naturally, in view of his differences from Husserl, his human world turns out to be by no means identical with Husserl's life world, but there are two respects in which they agreed. First, they were both convinced that the world that most scientists and many laypersons take to be the world is simply one environing life world among many, the one that is based on the presuppositions of Cartesian dualism. Second, they agreed it is actually a dehumanizing world. Both Heidegger and Husserl therefore asked us in effect to remove the Cartesian spectacles we have worn for so long and look at our world and ourselves afresh. Such looking would be the presuppositionless "seeing" that is the heart of the phenomenological method.

DASEIN AS THE CLUE TO BEING

If Heidegger's description of the nature of human beings may be called, broadly speaking, phenomenological anthropology, then it is important to see that Heidegger did not do anthropology for its own sake. Description of human nature was to lead to an understanding of human being, and an understanding of human being was to lead to an understanding of Being. In a word, phenomenological anthropology was merely a preliminary for fundamental ontology.

> The analytic of Dasein . . . is to prepare the way for the problematic of fundamental ontology—*the question of the meaning of Being in general.* . . .
> Dasein is an entity which does not just occur among other entities. Rather it is ontically distinguished by the fact that, in its very Being, that Being is an *issue* for it. But in that case, this is a constitutive state of Dasein's Being, and this implies that Dasein, in its Being, has a relationship towards that Being—a relationship which itself is one of Being. And this means further that there is some way in which Dasein understands itself in its Being, and that to some degree it does so explicitly. It is peculiar to this entity that with and through its Being, this Being is disclosed to it. *Understanding of Being is itself a definite characteristic of Dasein's Being.* Dasein is ontically distinctive in that it *is* ontological. . . .
> That kind of Being towards which Dasein can comport itself in one way or another, and always does comport itself somehow, we call "*existence.*" And because we cannot define Dasein's essence by citing a "what" of the kind that pertains to a subject-matter, and because its

---

[8] See pp. 282–83.

essence lies rather in the fact that in each case it has its Being to be, and has it as its own, we have chosen to designate this entity as "Dasein," a term which is purely an expression of its Being.

Dasein always understands itself in terms of its existence—in terms of a possibility of itself: to be itself or not itself. Dasein has either chosen these possibilities itself, or got itself into them, or grown up in them already. Only the particular Dasein decides its existence, whether it does so by taking hold or by neglecting. The question of existence never gets straightened out except through existing itself. . . .

Dasein takes priority over all other entities in several ways. The first priority is an *ontical* one: Dasein is an entity whose Being has the determinate character of existence. The second priority is an *ontological* one: Dasein is in itself "ontological," because existence is thus determinative for it. But with equal primordiality Dasein also possesses—as constitutive for its understanding of existence—an understanding of the Being of all entities of a character other than its own. Dasein has therefore a third priority as providing the ontico-ontological condition for the possibility of any ontologies. Thus Dasein has turned out to be, more than any other entity, the one which must first be interrogated ontologically.[1]

Though a great deal of the terminology is probably opaque, at least at this stage, and though some of the distinctions drawn—for instance, the fundamental distinction between ontological and ontical—will have to be postponed,[9] the main thrust of the passage is relatively clear. Heidegger is listing these features of Dasein's mode of being that distinguish it from the mode of being of any other entity and so make Dasein a clue to the meaning of Being.

First and foremost, then, it is a feature of Dasein's being that, unlike other kinds of being—say, plants or animals or the solar system—it "comports" itself toward the things in its world. Other beings react toward the stimuli they receive, and react automatically according to their nature and the nature of the stimuli. Dasein does not react, but *responds* in accordance with its perception of itself and of the stimuli. Dasein has attitudes toward its world, and these attitudes affect its response. That Dasein comports itself not only to beings but to Being—that it, and it alone, responds to Being—is of course one of the chief reasons why Dasein is a clue to the meaning of Being.

But is not Dasein, too, reacting according to its nature? Is it not simply the case that human beings react in a more flexible, less rigid way than other entities? No, it is not that Dasein has a nature that happens to be more complicated than that of other entities; that would imply only a difference in degree between Dasein and other entities. To be in the mode of Dasein is precisely not to *have* a nature that endures through time, but to be, at any particular time, the possibility of

[9] See pp. 342–45.

choosing to be something different at some future time. This is the second feature of Dasein that is a clue to an understanding of Being: Dasein is in the mode of choosing, of facing possibilities, and it cannot escape having its being in this mode of being. To neglect to choose, to refuse to choose, to fear to choose, are all ways of choosing.

Third, one of the ways in which Dasein comports itself toward its world is to "do" science—that is, to try to understand its world. And of course it is not merely the entities that are in its world alongside it that Dasein seeks to understand; it also seeks to understand Being. We cannot "interrogate" a plant about its attitude toward the soil in which it grows; it merely reacts to the soil in accordance with its nature and the soil's nature. But we can interrogate Dasein about Being. Because Dasein is interrogating itself about Being, Being will have something to say to us; it will respond to our interrogation, not merely react to it. It will enter into "dialogue" with us.

From this summary sketch, let us now turn to a more detailed examination of Dasein, bearing in mind always that in Heidegger's view this study of the mode of being that is characteristically human has been undertaken, not for its own sake, but to remind us of Being.

EXISTENCE

Though for the purposes of analysis it is necessary to take up the characteristics of Dasein separately, they are features, or aspects, of a single unitary mode of being, and the correct way, according to Heidegger, to characterize this mode of being is to say that Dasein, and only Dasein, exists. Other beings "are," but do not exist.

> Dasein exists. Furthermore, Dasein is an entity which in each case I myself am. Mineness belongs to any existent Dasein, and belongs to it as the condition which makes authenticity and inauthenticity possible. . . .
>
> But these are both ways in which Dasein's Being takes on a definite character, and they must be seen and understood *a priori* as grounded upon that state of Being which we have called "*Being-in-the-world*.". . .
>
> The compound expression "Being-in-the-world" indicates in the very way we have coined it, that it stands for a *unitary* phenomenon. This primary datum must be seen as a whole. But while Being-in-the-world cannot be broken up into contents which may be pieced together, this does not prevent it from having several constitutive items in its structure.ᵐ

BEING-IN

> What is meant by "*Being in*"? Our proximal reaction is to round out this expression to "Being-in 'in the world,'" and we are inclined to

understand this Being-in as "Being in something." This latter term des-ignates the kind of Being which an entity has when it is "in" another one, as the water is "in" the glass, or the garment is "in" the cupboard. By this "in" we mean the relationship of Being which two entities ex-tended "in" space have to each other with regard to their location in that space. Both water and glass, garment and cupboard, are "in" space and "at" a location, and both in the same way. . . .

All entities whose Being "in" one another can thus be described have the same kind of Being—that of Being-present-at-hand—as Things occurring "within" the world. Being-present-at-hand "in" something which is likewise present-at-hand, and Being-present-at-hand-along-with in the sense of a definite location-relationship with something else which has the same kind of Being, are ontological characteristics which we call *"categorial"*: they are of such a sort as to belong to entities whose kind of Being is not of the character of Dasein.

Being-in, on the other hand, is a state of Dasein's Being; it is an *exis-tentiale.* So one cannot think of it as the Being-present-at-hand of some corporeal Thing (such as a human body) "in" an entity which is present-at-hand. . . .

"Being alongside" the world in the sense of being absorbed in the world (a sense which calls for still closer interpretation) is an *exis-tentiale* founded upon Being-in. . . . This "Being-alongside" must be examined still more closely. We shall again choose the method of con-trasting it with a relationship of Being which is essentially different ontologically—*viz.* categorial—but which we express by the same lin-guistic means. . . .

As an *existentiale,* "Being alongside" the world never means anything like the Being-present-at-hand-together of Things that occur. There is no such thing as the "side-by-sideness" of an entity called "Dasein" with another entity called "world." Of course when two things are present-at-hand together alongside one another, we are accustomed to express this occasionally by something like "The table stands 'by' the door" or "The chair 'touches' the wall." Taken strictly, "touching" is never what we are talking about in such cases. . . . If the chair could touch the wall, this would presuppose that the wall is the sort of thing "for" which a chair would be *encounterable.* An entity present-at-hand within the world can be touched by another entity only if by its very nature the lat-ter entity has Being-in as its own kind of Being—only if, with its Being-there, something like the world is already revealed to it, so that from out of that world another entity can manifest itself in touching, and thus become accessible to its Being-present-at-hand.[n]

Heidegger's point is that people are usually too preoccupied with other mat-ters to look at their experience carefully, but when they do look they can see that there is a radical difference between the way human beings are in our world and the way in which water is in a glass or a shoe is in a shoe box. A man is alongside his desk in a different way from the way in which the desk is alongside him; one touches a sore tooth, or a lover's hand, in ways that, though they certainly differ among themselves, have something in common that distinguishes them from the way in which a shoe touches the box in which it lies or the desk touches the floor.

Surely we can agree that there is a difference, but what exactly is it? Heidegger proceeded to spell it out by introducing the concepts of readiness-to-hand, concern, living-ahead, and understanding. Human beings are in the world in the mode of finding the things in it ready-to-hand, in being concerned about them and for them, in facing a future that consists of alternatives and possibilities, and in seeking to understand the world in which they find themselves. We will deal in turn with these characteristics of existence.

READINESS-TO-HAND

"Readiness-to-hand" is the mode of being that objects have within a human world, and it is to be contrasted with "present-at-hand," which is the mode of being that Cartesian dualism and its various modern descendants attribute to the objects of our experience. On the latter view, the physical world consists in a vast number of "things." My body, to which my mind is somehow mysteriously attached, and your body, to which your mind is similarly attached, are items in this universe of things. These things all interact with each other and our bodies in complex ways which it is the business of science to study, by means of dissection, spectrometry, Skinner boxes, and the like.

This is what the theory tells us the things we encounter in our world are, and the theory is so powerful, so pervasive, and so seductive that we usually fail to recognize that what we really experience are not things that are present-at-hand but things that are ready-to-hand—things that are, as it were, for us or against us— things of which we do, or might, make some use. When we look at a hammer we see a possible driver-of-nails, or a possible hitter-on-the-head of some enemy or rival. When we look at a chair, we see something that is "inviting" (that opens its arms to us, cosily and protectingly) or something that repulses us by its hardness, rigidity, and stiffness. That things are experienced in this way as ready-to-hand, not as present-to-hand, is, then, a prime feature of existence, that is, of Dasein's human mode of being.

> The Being of those entities which we encounter as closest to us can be exhibited phenomenologically if we take as our clue our everyday Being-in-the-world, which we also call our *"dealings"* in the world and *with* entities within-the-world. Such dealings have already dispersed themselves into manifold ways of concern. The kind of dealing which is closest to us is as we have shown, not a bare perceptual cognition, but rather that kind of concern which manipulates things and puts them to use; and this has its own kind of "knowledge.". . .

We shall call those entities which we encounter in concern *"equipment."* In our dealings we come across equipment for writing, sewing, working, transportation, measurement. The kind of Being which equipment possesses must be exhibited. The clue for doing this lies in our first defining what makes an item of equipment—namely, its equipmentality. . . .

Equipment is essentially "something in-order-to.". . . A totality of equipment is constituted by various ways of the "in-order-to," such as serviceability, conduciveness, usability, manipulability.

In the "in-order-to" as a structure there lies an *assignment* or *reference* of something to something. . . . Equipment—in accordance with its equipmentality—always is *in terms of* its belonging to other equipment: ink-stand, pen, ink, paper, blotting pad, table, lamp, furniture, windows, doors, room. These "Things" never show themselves proximally as they are for themselves, so as to add up to a sum of *realia* and fill up a room. What we encounter as closest to us (though not as something taken as a theme) is the room; and we encounter it not as something "between four walls" in a geometrical spatial sense, but as equipment for residing. Out of this the "arrangement" emerges, and it is in this that any "individual" item of equipment shows itself. *Before* it does so, a totality of equipment has already been discovered. . . .

The peculiarity of what is proximally ready-to-hand is that, in its readiness-to-hand, it must, as it were, withdraw in order to be ready-to-hand quite authentically. That with which our everyday dealings proximally dwell is not the tools themselves. On the contrary, that with which we concern ourselves primarily is the work—that which is to be produced at the time; and this is accordingly ready-to-hand too. The work bears with it that referential totality within which the equipment is encountered.

The work to be produced, as the *"towards-which"* of such things as the hammer, the plane, and the needle, likewise has the kind of Being that belongs to equipment. The shoe which is to be produced is for wearing (footgear); the clock is manufactured for telling the time. . . .

But the work to be produced is not merely usable for something. The production itself is a using *of* something for something. In the work there is also a reference or assignment to "materials": the work is dependent on leather, thread, needles, and the like. Leather, moreover, is produced from hides. These are taken from animals, which someone else has raised. . . . Hammer, tongs, and needle, refer in themselves to steel, iron, metal, mineral, wood, in that they consist of these. In equipment that is used, "Nature" is discovered along with it by that use—the "Nature" we find in natural products.

Here, however, "Nature" is not to be understood as that which is just present-at-hand, nor as the *power of Nature*. The wood is a forest of timber, the mountain a quarry of rock; the river is water-power, the wind is wind "in the sails." As the "environment" is discovered, the "Nature" thus discovered is encountered too. If its kind of Being as ready-to-hand is disregarded, this "Nature" itself can be discovered and defined simply in its pure presence-at-hand. But when this happens, the Nature which "stirs and strives," which assails us and enthralls us as landscape, remains hidden. The botanist's plants are not the flowers of the hedgerow; the "source" which the geographer establishes for a river is not the "springhead in the dale."°

Thus it is not merely tools and other fabricated things that we experience in the mode of readiness-to-hand; we also experience so-called "inanimate" nature in the same way. We perceive deserts as sandy wastes that can be made to bloom, mountains as challenges, rivers as fordable, and so on. One of the characteristic aspects of the human mode of being, then, is to be within a world of things to which we respond because we perceive them as ready-to-hand, that is, as potentialities for us in various ways.

CONCERN

One fundamental feature, or aspect, of existence, then, is to experience things as ready-to-hand, instead of merely present-at-hand. The reason that this is a fundamental characteristic of existence is that Dasein does not passively react to its world but *does* something to, with, or about that world. The multiplicity of Dasein's ways of doing—which amount to a multiplicity of ways of Being-in—are all characterized by concern: they are modes, or ways, of being concerned. But what is concern?

> This term has been chosen not because Dasein happens to be proximally and to a large extent "practical" and economic, but because the Being of Dasein itself is to be made visible as *care*. This expression . . . has nothing to do with "tribulation," "melancholy," or the "cares of life," though ontically one can come across these in every Dasein. These— like their opposites, "gaiety" and "freedom from care"—are ontically possible only because Dasein, when understood *ontologically,* is care. Because Being-in-the-world belongs essentially to Dasein, its Being towards the world is essentially concern.
>
> From what we have been saying, it follows that Being-in is not a "property" which Dasein sometimes has and sometimes does not have, and *without* which it could *be* just as well as it could with it. It is not the case that man "is" and then has, by way of an extra, a relationship-of-Being towards the "world"—a world with which he provides himself occasionally. Dasein is never "proximally" an entity which is, so to speak, free from Being-in, but which sometimes has the inclination to take up a "relationship" towards the world. Taking up relationships towards the world is possible only *because* Dasein, as Being-in-the-world, is as it is.P

There are two points here that must be distinguished. Dasein's mode of being in the world is to be toward the world; that is, Dasein has an underlying attitude toward the world and this attitude issues in various doings. Second, this underlying attitude is one of concern. Many philosophers who would agree about the first point would reject the second. Some—Dewey, for instance—would say that "taking an interest in" or "being interested" is a more accurate way of describing the attitude that Heidegger calls being in the mode of being-toward. This is more than a mere semantic difference. "Being interested" puts the emphasis on intelligence, on the problem-solving capacity. "Concern" focuses on attitude, not on aptitude. To make use of a traditional distinction, what makes a human being human, in Heidegger's view, is not intelligence but will.

LIVING-AHEAD

Those who define being human in terms of taking an interest and those who define it in terms of caring at least agree on one point—that human beings are forward-looking, future-looking creatures. This is because taking account of possibilities, of alternatives, of what is not yet but may be, is an essential aspect both of taking an interest and of caring. Heidegger calls this feature of existence "living-ahead."

> Dasein is always "beyond itself," not as a way of behaving towards other entities which it is *not,* but as Being towards the potentiality-for-Being which it is itself. This structure of Being, which belongs to the essential "is an issue," we shall denote as Dasein's *"Being-ahead-of-itself."*. . .
>
> "Being-ahead-of-itself" means, if we grasp it more fully, *"ahead-of-itself-in-already-being-in-a-world."* As soon as this essentially unitary structure is seen as a phenomenon, what we have set forth earlier in our analysis of worldhood also becomes plain. The upshot of that analysis was that the referential totality of significance (which as such is constitutive for worldhood) has been "tied up" with a "for-the-sake-of-which." The fact that this referential totality of the manifold relations of the "in-order-to" has been bound up with that which is an issue for Dasein, does not signify that a "world" of Objects which is present-at-hand has been welded together with a subject. It is rather the phenomenal expression of the fact that the constitution of Dasein, whose totality is now brought out explicitly as ahead-of-itself-in-Being-already-in . . . is primordially a whole. . . .
>
> The formally existential totality of Dasein's ontological structural whole must therefore be grasped in the following structure: the Being of Dasein means ahead-of-itself-Being-already-in-(the-world) as Being-alongside (entities encountered within-the-world). This Being fills in the signification of the term *"care."*[q]

It is because Dasein's mode of being consists in living-ahead that Dasein does not have a nature. Unlike other entities that simply are whatever they happen to be throughout the whole time span in which they "are" at all, what Dasein "is" at any particular time is the possibility of being (of choosing to be) something at some future time. Dasein's now-being is indeterminate because it consists in living-ahead to further possibilities.

Heidegger is certainly not the only philosopher to emphasize living-ahead as a fundamental characteristic of being human. William James, for instance, was much struck by the indeterminacy of being human. But for him living into the future, the idea that we are forever confronting what he called "live options,"[10] made life an exciting adventure. In contrast, Heidegger wrote of "the burdensome character" of being human.[r] But Heidegger would not have regarded this as merely a difference in temperament, as James would have. James, Heidegger would have said, was mistaken. Care, not adventure, is "ontologically 'earlier'"[11] than other attitudes.

UNDERSTANDING

Our discussion of living-ahead, or living into the future, has put us in a position to give an account of understanding, the last feature of Dasein with which we have to deal. Of the many modes of Being-in, understanding is but one. It has no superior status. Unfortunately, the intellectualistic bias of philosophers has led them virtually to equate thinking with being human. So far, Heidegger might be Dewey.[12]

> The phenomenon of Being-in has for the most part been represented exclusively by a single exemplar—knowing the world. . . . Because knowing has been given this priority, our understanding of its own-most kind of Being gets led astray, and accordingly Being-in-the-world must be exhibited even more precisely with regard to knowing the world, and must itself be made visible as an existential "modality" of Being-in.[s]

That is the first mistake that philosophers have made—they have falsified the human situation by giving thinking a special promise. The second mistake is that they have identified thinking with abstract cognition (with "theoretical" understanding). But dealing with the world and having an attitude toward it are also ways of understanding it.

> If we look at Things just "theoretically," we can get along without understanding readiness-to-hand. But when we deal with them by using

[10] See Vol. IV, pp. 309–15.
[11] Once again we will postpone the ontological question and continue with phenomenological description. See pp. 342–45.
[12] See pp. 39–40 and 44–46.

them and manipulating them, this activity is not a blind one; it has its own kind of sight, by which our manipulation is guided and from which it acquires its specific Thingly character. Dealings with equipment subordinate themselves to the manifold assignments of the "in-order-to." And the sight with which they thus accommodate themselves is *circumspection.*

"Practical" behaviour is not "atheoretical" in the sense of "sightlessness." The way it differs from theoretical behaviour does not lie simply in the fact that in theoretical behaviour one observes, while in practical behaviour one *acts,* and that action must employ theoretical cognition if it is not to remain blind; for the fact that observation is a kind of concern is just as primordial as the fact that action has *its own* kind of sight.[t]

It will be seen that Heidegger totally rejected all theories of what Dewey called the "spectator" type, that is, all theories that assume knowledge is a matter of "beholding" from outside, whether this beholding be intellectual ("the kind of knowledge we get in mathematics and physics")[u] or perceptual in character. These theories, by placing the knower outside the object he or she knows, make it incomprehensible how we ever come to know anything at all.

If knowing "is" at all, it belongs solely to those entities which know. . . . Now, inasmuch as knowing belongs to these entities and is not some external characteristic, it must be "inside." Now . . . the problem[s] arise of how this knowing subject comes out of its inner "sphere" into one which is "other and external," of how knowing can have any object at all, and of how one must think of the object itself so that eventually the subject knows it without needing to venture a leap into another sphere. But in any of the numerous varieties which this approach may take, the question of the kind of Being which belongs to this knowing subject is left entirely unasked. . . . And no matter how this inner sphere may get interpreted, if one does no more than ask how knowing makes its way "out of" it and achieves "transcendence," it becomes evident that the knowing which presents such enigmas will remain problematical unless one has previously clarified how it is and what it is. . . .

If we now ask what shows itself in the phenomenal findings about knowing, we must keep in mind that knowing is grounded beforehand in a Being-already-alongside-the-world, which is essentially constitutive for Dasein's Being. Proximally, this Being-already-alongside is not just a fixed staring at something that is purely present-at-hand. Being-in-the-world, as concern, is *fascinated by* the world with which it is concerned. If knowing is to be possible as a way of determining the nature of the present-at-hand by observing it, then there must be a *deficiency* in our having-to-do with the world concernfully. When concern holds back from any kind of producing, manipulating, and the like, it puts itself into what is now the sole remaining mode of Being-in, the mode of just tarrying alongside. . . . Looking *at* something, [however, is usually] a definite way of taking up a direction towards something—of setting our sights towards what is present-at-hand. It takes over a "view-point" in advance from the entity which it encounters. . . . Perception is consummated when one *addresses* oneself to something as something and *discusses* it as such. This amounts to *interpretation* in the broadest sense; and on the basis of such interpretation, perception becomes an act of *making determinate.* What is thus perceived and made determinate can be expressed in propositions, and can be retained and preserved as what has been asserted. This perceptive retention of an assertion about something is itself a way of Being-in-the-world. . . .

When Dasein directs itself towards something and grasps it, it does not somehow first get out of an inner sphere in which it has been proximally encapsulated, but its primary kind of Being is such that it is always "outside" alongside entities which it encounters and which belong to a world already discovered. Nor is any inner sphere abandoned when Dasein dwells alongside the entity to be known, and determines its character; but even in this "Being-outside" alongside the object, Dasein is still "inside," if we understand this in the correct sense; that is to say, it is itself "inside" as a Being-in-the-world which knows. And furthermore, the perceiving of what is known is not a process of returning with one's booty to the "cabinet" of consciousness after one has gone out and grasped it; even in perceiving, retaining, and preserving, the Dasein which knows *remains outside,* and it does so *as Dasein.*[v]

Perhaps it will be helpful to translate out of Heideggerese into ordinary English, or at least into the kind of language in which most philosophers discuss epistemological problems. The first paragraph criticizes the view of knowledge as derived from Cartesian dualism. Dualism, according to Heidegger, leads to insuperable difficulties. Because it fails to distinguish the various modes of being-in that phenomenological analysis discloses, it supposes that a human being either is in the world or else is not in the world, in the way in which a penny either is in a piggy bank or else is not in that piggy bank. Once this false disjunction is set up, it becomes impossible to give an adequate account of knowledge. If we say that humans are in the world, we are committed to a constructivist theory of knowledge, with its relativistic consequences. On the other hand, if we say that they are not in the world, but metaphysically distinct from it, we are committed to the beholder, or spectator, theory of knowledge. Since the knowing subject is now wholly outside the object it seeks to know, it has access to the object only by looking at it.

The second and third paragraphs call for abandoning this muddled way of thinking about "in." Phenomenological analysis discloses the true nature of understanding by illuminating the way in which we are in the world when we come to understand something. We do indeed sometimes look at things in an *un*engaged, *dis*interested way (we sometimes "tarry alongside" an object), but such looking, such perceiving, is unusual, and it is also incomplete. Perception is "consummated" when, and only when, we make the object "determinate," and this can only occur when we become engaged with it, when we "address" ourselves to it. Being uninterested—tarrying alongside—is in fact a special mode, the limiting case, of being engaged. This is quite different from the way in which two entities that are only present-at-hand to each other are related—they cannot be uninterested in each other because they have never been interested in each other.

So far, then, we can conclude that we never understand anything unless we are dealing with it or have dealt with it; and if we are dealing with it, we always, at least to some extent, understand it. But what, then, are those specific features of any and all of our dealings with objects that result in our coming to understand those objects? Heidegger's answer is in terms of the closely related actions of projection, articulation, possibility, and significance.

> As a disclosure, understanding always pertains to the whole basic state of Being-in-the-world. As a potentiality-for-Being, any Being-in is a potentiality-for-Being-in-the-world. Not only is the world, *qua* world, disclosed as possible significance, but when that which is within-the-world is itself freed, this entity is freed for *its own* possibilities. That which is ready-to-hand is discovered as such in its servic*eability,* its us*ability,* and its detrimen*tality.* The totality of involvements is revealed as the categorial whole of a *possible* interconnection of the ready-to-hand. . . .
>
> Why does the understanding—whatever may be the essential dimensions of that which can be disclosed in it—always press forward into possibilities? It is because the understanding has in itself the existential structure which we call *"projection."* With equal primordiality the understanding projects Dasein's Being both upon its "for-the-sake-of-which" and upon significance, as the worldhood of its current world. . . . Projecting has nothing to do with comporting oneself towards a plan that has been thought out, and in accordance with which Dasein arranges its Being. On the contrary, any Dasein has, as Dasein, already projected itself; and as long as it is, it is projecting. As long as it is, Dasein always has understood itself and always will understand itself in terms of possibilities. . . .
>
> The ready-to-hand comes *explicitly* into the sight which understands. All preparing, putting to rights, repairing, improving, rounding-out, are accomplished in the following way: we take apart in its "in-order-to" that which is circumspectively ready-to-hand, and we concern ourselves with it in accordance with what becomes visible through this process. That which has been circumspectively taken apart with regard to its "in-order-to," and taken apart as such—that which is *explicitly*

understood—has the structure of *something as something*. The circumspective question as to what this particular thing that is ready-to-hand may be, receives the circumspectively interpretive answer that it is for such and such a purpose. . . . In dealing with what is environmentally ready-to-hand by interpreting it circumspectively, we "see" it *as* a table, a door, a carriage, or a bridge; but what we have thus interpreted need not necessarily be also taken apart by making an assertion which definitely characterizes it. Any mere pre-predicative seeing of the ready-to-hand is, in itself, something which already understands and interprets. But does not the absence of such an "as" make up the mereness of any pure perception of something? Whenever we see with this kind of sight, we already do so understandingly and interpretatively. In the mere encountering of something, it is understood in terms of a totality of involvements; and such seeing hides in itself the explicitness of the assignment-relations (of the "in-order-to") which belong to that totality. That which is understood gets Articulated when the entity to be understood is brought close interpretatively by taking as our clue the "something as something"; and this Articulation lies *before* our making any thematic assertion about it. In such an assertion the "as" does not turn up for the first time; it just gets expressed for the first time, and this is possible only in that it lies before us as something expressible. The fact that when we look at something, the explicitness of assertion can be absent, does not justify our denying that there is any Articulative interpretation in such mere seeing, and hence that there is any as-structure in it. . . . If the "as" is ontically unexpressed, this must not seduce us into overlooking it as a constitutive state for understanding, existential and *a priori*.[w]

The key word here is "as." We understand something x, when and to the extent that we see it "as" y, that is, *as* being useful, serviceable, or otherwise ready-to-hand. Here I stand, looking at a mountain across the valley from me. I may, in a fit of abstraction or of daydreaming, simply "tarry alongside it"; in those circumstances I do not understand it. I begin to understand it when I perceive it *as* a challenge to climb, *as* a possible source of precious minerals which I might mine, *as* a home of wild animals that I might hunt, *as* a barrier that I might fortify against an enemy on the opposite side.

That is to say, we understand things in virtue of the fact that we experience them as ready-to-hand. Understanding them is merely making explicit ("articulating") the various possibilities—the manifold for-the-sake-of-whiches—that we are implicitly aware of when we experience them as ready-to-hand, and things are "significant" if and to the extent that their possibilities have been articulated. Again, to say that understanding is "projection" is simply to bring out another facet of this complex phenomenon. To understand is to press forward actively into possibilities, not merely considering them abstractly as logically possible alternatives but viewing them with concern as alternatives that will matter one way or another in our lives. Ultimately, then, all meaning is meaning *for us*—not for you or me personally, but for Dasein, for human beings. To put this differently again, all meaning is circumspective.

In two important respects Heidegger's view is similar to Bradley's. For both, coming to understand is not a matter of moving from ignorance to knowledge; it is a matter of moving from one degree of knowledge, or familiarity, to another. It is a matter of moving around (as it were) in a region that, even at the outset, is not unfamiliar and that becomes more familiar as a result of making articulate the involvements we already have with that region. Understanding is a matter of becoming better acquainted with something we "fore-have," that is, with something we in a sense already possess, in advance of and prior to having come to understand it.

As Heidegger puts it, in language that is certainly different from Bradley's:

> The ready-to-hand is always understood in terms of a totality of involvements. This totality need not be grasped explicitly by a thematic interpretation. Even if it has undergone such an interpretation, it recedes into an understanding which does not stand out from the background. And this is the very mode in which it is the essential foundation for everyday circumspective interpretation. In every case this interpretation is grounded in *something we have in advance*—in a *fore-having*. . . . When something is understood but is still veiled, it becomes unveiled by an act of appropriation, and this is always done under the guidance of a point of view, which fixes that with regard to which what is understood is to be interpreted. In every case interpretation is grounded in *something we see in advance*—in a *foresight*. . . . In such an interpretation, the way in which the entity we are interpreting is to be conceived can be drawn from the entity itself, or the interpretation can force the entity into concepts to which it is opposed in its manner of Being. In either case, the interpretation has already decided for a definite way of conceiving it, either with finality or with reservation; it is grounded in *something we grasp in* advance—in a *fore-conception*.[x]

In the second place, Heidegger's notion of articulation is remarkably like Bradley's notion of judgment. Both start from a felt whole whose internal structure becomes progressively more and more explicit, and for both understanding is simply this process of making the structure of the whole articulate. Bradley and Heidegger are thus at the opposite pole, as we might expect, from the analytic philosophers. For the latter, we achieve understanding only when we have analyzed some whole into its simple constituents; it is the simples that are understandable, precisely because they are simple and so grasped in their entirety. For the former, a simple in itself is unintelligible: we can only "tarry alongside" it. We only begin to understand it when we see it *as* something else, that is, when we put it into some sort of context, however meager. Where the analytic philosophers put their emphasis on the articulated (that is, analyzed) parts, Bradley and Heidegger put their emphasis on the articulated (structured) whole. Where the former hold that our understanding of the analyzed parts renders the whole, conceived as an aggregate of the parts, understandable, the latter hold that our understanding of the articulated whole makes the parts understandable.[13]

This discussion of understanding completes our account of the structure of that aspect, or feature, of Dasein that Heidegger calls "existence." To exist (and it will be recalled that, for Heidegger, only human beings exist) is precisely to have one's being "in" a world of possibilities—of alternatives—among which one must choose, to experience the things in that world as ready-to-hand, to have manifold dealings with them, to feel concern, solicitude, and care for them, and to find them "significant." But existence is only one aspect of Dasein's mode of being. Dasein has two other "fundamental ontological characteristics"; facticity and Being-fallen.[y] Examination of these, to which we now turn, will bring into the foreground what we may call the human predicament—the burden of being human.

The Human Predicament

"Facticity" and "thrownness" are closely related terms. Both are designed to call our attention to a feature of human experience that Heidegger thinks we might otherwise overlook—indeed, to a feature of our experience that he thinks we deliberately avoid looking at. Insistence on the "facticity" of Dasein's existence is intended to bring out its sheer incomprehensibility; Dasein's existence is just a brute fact that is incapable of any logical, rational, scientific, or teleological explanation. Because we lack any such explanation, we feel ourselves simply to have been thrown into the world, ignorant of whence we have come or whither we will go. Given our mode of entry into it and our mode of exit from it—given our feeling that we are simply "there" in the world—the world is not the sort of place in which we can feel at home. We are, as it were, orphans and "homeless."

It is true, of course, that we are at home with many individual things in the world—that we are at home with them is part of what is meant by saying that we experience them as ready-to-hand, as serviceable. But the world as a whole is not ready-to-hand in this way; taken in its totality it is present-at-hand, a brute fact

---

[13] Though Heidegger shared Bradley's emphasis on context and his notion of understanding as being a matter of degree, he would have condemned Bradley's theory of knowledge as belonging to the "beholder" type. Whereas Bradley was content to talk about "judgment"—an intellectual act—Heidegger preferred to talk about concern and circumspection, as being truer to our phenomenological experience of coming to understand something. See Vol. IV, Ch. 9.

that we do not and cannot understand. Why it should be at all, rather than nothing, is, as we have seen, the great question. And, more particularly, we do not understand why *we* should be at all, or what our relation to the world is.

> Dasein understands its ownmost Being in the sense of a certain "factual Being-present-at-hand." And yet the "factuality" of the fact of one's own Dasein is at bottom quite different ontologically from the factual occurrence of some kind of mineral, for example. Whenever Dasein is, it is a Fact; and the factuality of such a Fact is what we shall call Dasein's *"facticity."* This is a definite way of Being, and it has a complicated structure which cannot even be grasped *as a problem* until Dasein's basic existential states have been worked out. . . . The pure "that it is" shows itself, but the "whence" and the "whither" remain in darkness. . . .
>
> This characteristic of Dasein's Being—this "that it is"—is veiled in its "whence" and "whither," yet disclosed in itself all the more unveiledly; we call it the "thrownness" of this entity into its "there"; indeed, it is thrown in such a way that, as Being-in-the-world, it is the "there." The expression "thrownness" is meant to suggest the *facticity of its being delivered over.* The "that it is and has to be" which is disclosed in Dasein's state-of-mind is not the same "that-it-is" which expresses ontologico-categorially the factuality belonging to presence-at-hand. This factuality becomes accessible only if we ascertain it by looking at it. The "that-it-is" which is disclosed in Dasein's state-of-mind must rather be conceived as an existential attribute of the entity which has Being-in-the-world as its way of Being. . . . The "that-it-is" of facticity never becomes something that we can come across by beholding it. . . .
>
> Dasein itself, as in each case my Dasein and this Dasein, *must* be; and in the same way the truth, as Dasein's disclosedness, *must be.* This belongs to Dasein's essential thrownness into the world. *Has Dasein as itself ever decided freely whether it wants to come into "Dasein" or not, and will it ever be able to make such a decision?* "In itself" it is quite incomprehensible why entities are to be *uncovered,* why *truth* and *Dasein* must be. . . .
>
> As something thrown, Dasein has been thrown *into existence.* It exists as an entity which has to be as it is and as it can be.[z]

ANXIETY

How do we come to recognize—to uncover—the facticity and thrownness of Dasein? The answer is that we come to understand our predicament in the mood that Heidegger calls "anxiety." That moods in general are cognitive follows from Heidegger's account of understanding. Understanding, we have already seen, is not a matter of beholding but of being involved. Understanding is, as it were, moody. To be in some particular mood is to be in attunement with some phase or aspect of the world. Because, and only because, we are in attunement with it, we understand it. So much in general as regards moods. Now as regards the mood Heidegger calls anxiety: when we experience anxiety we are in attunement with, and so understand, our human facticity and thrownness.

> How far is anxiety a state of mind which is distinctive? . . . *That in the face of which one has anxiety is Being-in-the-world as such.* What is the difference phenomenally between that in the face of which anxiety is anxious and that in the face of which fear is afraid? That in the face of which one has anxiety is not an entity within-the-world. Thus it is essentially incapable of having an involvement. This threatening does not have the character of a definite detrimentality which reaches what is threatened, and which reaches it with definite regard to a special factical potentiality-for-Being. That in the face of which one is anxious is completely indefinite. Not only does this indefiniteness leave factically undecided which entity within-the-world is threatening us, but it also tells us that entities within-the-world are not "relevant" at all. Nothing which is ready-to-hand or present-at-hand within the world functions as that in the face of which anxiety is anxious. . . .
>
> That in the face of which one has anxiety is characterized by the fact that what threatens is *nowhere.* Anxiety "does not know" what that in the face of which it is anxious is. "Nowhere," however, does not signify nothing. . . . That which threatens cannot bring itself close from a definite direction within what is close by; it is already "there," and yet nowhere; it is so close that it is oppressive and stifles one's breath, and yet it is nowhere. . . .
>
> Being-anxious discloses, primordially and directly, the world as world. It is not the case, say, that the world first gets thought of by deliberating about it, just by itself, without regard for the entities within-the-world, and that, in the face of this world, anxiety then arises; what is rather the case is that the *world as world* is disclosed first and foremost by anxiety, as a mode of state-of-mind. This does not signify, however, that in anxiety the worldhood of the world gets conceptualized.[a]

Anxiety, then, is a "distinctive" state of mind, or mood. It differs radically from fear, with which it has often been confused, in that fear is directed toward particular things that threaten us, whereas anxiety is directed toward nothing in particular. Some people might be inclined to say that, whereas and to the extent that fear alerts us to dangers, it has survival value and is therefore "rational," but that anxiety about nothing in particular is irrational and neurotic. Not at all, according to Heidegger. He is quite prepared to allow that "'real' anxiety is rare," and even that it is "often conditioned by 'physiological' factors." As for rarity, that is explained by our attempt to escape from it by masking it as something else: "Fear is anxiety, fallen into the 'world,' inauthentic, and, as such, hidden from itself." As for a physiological explanation, this puts the cart before the horse: "Only because Dasein is anxious in the very depths of its Being, does it become possible for anxiety to be elicited physiologically."[b]

For Heidegger, any merely "scientific" approach to the phenomenon of anxiety (whether it be physiological, psychoanalytic, or sociological) is inevitably superficial. Because all such approaches take moods to be the merely subjective "effects" of certain physiological, psychological, or sociological variables, they fail to grasp that moods are clues to our mode of being in the world. Those who "study" anxiety—that is, who observe it and describe it from outside—naturally conclude that it is a neurotic fear of nothing-in-particular and thus discount it as "neurotic." Only those who experience anxiety from inside, and who grasp that anxiety (along with other moods, of course) is cognitive, realize that anxiety is a disclosure of the true precariousness of our mode of being, a disclosure from which we usually attempt to flee.

INAUTHENTICITY: FALLENNESS AND THE "THEY"

In anxiety, then, we come to recognize the precariousness of our human mode of existence. We attempt to alleviate the burden of this knowledge in many ways, among them escape into the "they" self. The they self, essentially, is simply our social self, the self that, far from being pure potentiality, has a neat and tidy "nature"—the nature decreed for it by others, the anonymous "they." To understand the they and the they self that we acquire from the they, it is necessary to return to the distinction already noted between being alongside and being with: we are in the world with other people in a different way from the way in which we are in the world with entities merely ready-to-hand. For instance,

> along with the equipment to be found when one is at work, those Others for whom the "work" is destined are "encountered too.". . . When material is put to use, we encounter its producer or "supplier" as one who "serves" well or badly. When, for example, we walk along the edge of a field but "outside it," the field shows itself as belonging to such-and-such a person, and decently kept up by him; the book we have used was bought at So-and-so's shop and given by such-and-such a person, and so forth. The boat anchored at the shore is assigned in its Being-in-itself to an acquaintance who undertakes voyages with it; but even if it is a "boat which is strange to us," it still is indicative of Others. . . . Such "Things" are encountered from out of the world in which they are ready-to-hand for Others—a world which is always mine too in advance. . . .
>
> The kind of Being which belongs to the Dasein of Others, as we encounter it within-the-world, differs from readiness-to-hand and presence-at-hand. Thus Dasein's world frees entities which not only are quite distinct from equipment and Things, but which also—in

accordance with their kind of Being *as Dasein* themselves—are "in" the world in which they are at the same time encountered within-the-world, and are "in" it by way of Being-in-the-world. These entities are neither present-at-hand nor ready-to-hand; on the contrary, they are *like* the very Dasein which frees them, in that *they are there too, and there with it.* . . . .

Not only is Being towards Others an autonomous, irreducible relationship of Being: this relationship, as Being-with, is one which, with Dasein's Being, already is. Of course it is indisputable that a lively mutual acquaintanceship on the basis of Being-with, often depends upon how far one's own Dasein has understood itself at the time; but this means that it depends only upon how far one's essential Being with Others has made itself transparent and has not disguised itself. And that is possible only if Dasein, as Being-in-the-world, already is with Others.[c]

Thus, it is possible to live authentically, genuinely, in the mode of being-with-others. To live in this mode is to perceive men and women as others, that is, to perceive them as having their being, as we have ours, in the mode of Dasein. Unfortunately, our experience of others tends all too easily to collapse into experience of an anonymous they. We no longer perceive other people as Dasein, but as different from us, as apart from us, almost as merely present-at-hand. Our empathetic relation with others is replaced by a competitive relation with the they.

In one's concern with what one has taken hold of, whether with, for, or against, the Others, there is constant care as to the way one differs from them, whether that difference is merely one that is to be evened out, whether one's own Dasein has lagged behind the Others and wants to catch up in relationship to them, or whether one's Dasein already has some priority over them and sets out to keep them suppressed. The care about this distance between them is disturbing to Being-with-one-another, though this disturbance is one that is hidden from it. If we may express this existentially, such Being-with-one-another has the character of *distantiality.* . . .

But this distantiality which belongs to Being-with, is such that Dasein, as everyday Being-with-one-another, stands in *subjection* to Others. It itself *is* not; its Being has been taken away by the Others. Dasein's everyday possibilities of Being are for the Others to dispose of as they please. These Others, moreover, are not *definite* Others. On the contrary, any Other can represent them. . . . The "who" is not this one, not that one, not oneself, not some people, and not the sum of them all. The "who" is the neuter, *the "they."* . . .

The "they" has its own ways in which to be. That tendency of Being-with which we have called "distantiality" is grounded in the fact that Being-with-one-another concerns itself as such with *averageness,* which is an existential characteristic of the "they." The "they," in its Being, essentially makes an issue of this. Thus the "they" maintains itself factically in the averageness of that which belongs to it, of that which it regards as valid and that which it does not, and of that to which it grants success and that to which it denies it. In this averageness with which it prescribes what can and may be ventured, it keeps watch over everything exceptional that thrusts itself to the fore. Every kind of priority gets noiselessly suppressed. Overnight, everything that is primordial gets glossed over as something that has long been well known. Everything gained by a struggle becomes just something to be manipulated. Every secret loses its force. This care of averageness reveals in turn an essential tendency of Dasein which we call the "levelling down" of all possibilities of Being. . . .

   Thus the particular Dasein in its everydayness is *disburdened* by the "they." Not only that; by thus disburdening it of its Being, the "they" accommodates Dasein if Dasein has any tendency to take things easily and make them easy. And because the "they" constantly accommodates the particular Dasein by disburdening it of its Being, the "they" retains and enhances its stubborn dominion.[d]

The influence of the they on Dasein is as subtle as it is deleterious. Whether we feel superior to the they (experience ourselves as having "some priority" over the they) or inferior (experience ourselves as "lagging behind" and as wanting to "catch up"), it is the they, not we ourselves, who set the standards by which we estimate our progress or lack of it. The subversive influence of the they on Dasein is well brought out in the contrast between dialogue and idle talk. Dialogue, as we shall see, is the paradigmatic example of coming to understand, and it is possible only when we perceive those with whom we are communicating as others. When others become the they, dialogue collapses into "idle talk." The reason is that true discourse, or dialogue, is always concerned; each participant's concern is to help bring himself or herself and the other participants to a concerned understanding of that which is being talked about. Idle talk, in contrast, is a kind of speaking in which neither of the participants is concerned. Doubtless they "understand" each other, but only in a superficial sense, because they are exchanging verbal counters that are in common currency and because they never ask themselves what, if anything, these tokens really mean. In idle talk

what is said-in-the-talk gets understood; but what the talk is about is understood only approximately and superficially. We have *the same thing* in view, because it is *the same* averageness that we have a common understanding of what is said. . . . And because this discoursing has lost its primary relationship-of-Being towards the entity talked about, or else has never achieved such a relationship, it does not communicate in such a way as to let this entity be appropriated in a primordial manner, but communicates rather by following the route of *gossiping* and *passing the word along*. What is said-in-the-talk as such, spreads in wider circles and takes on an authoritative character. Things are so because one says so. Idle talk is constituted by just such gossiping and passing the word along—a process by which its initial lack of grounds to stand on becomes aggravated to complete groundlessness. . . .

The groundlessness of idle talk is no obstacle to its becoming public; instead it encourages this. Idle talk is the possibility of understanding everything without previously making the thing one's own. . . . Idle talk . . . releases one from the task of genuinely understanding.[e]

What is true of idle talk is equally true of every aspect of life at the level of the they self. Life at this level is a dimming down, a thinning down, an averaging down of experience to the expectations of the they—in effect, to the expectations of public opinion. We no longer feel sufficiently involved in our world to experience it as it is, in all its mystery, diversity, beauty, and terror; instead we experience only what the they decrees we ought to experience it to be.

How is it that the they exerts such a powerful influence on Dasein? The answer is not that Dasein simply allows the they to dominate it; rather it actively seeks the they as a way of escape from the mystery, diversity, beauty, and terror of Dasein's world as Dasein comes to understand that world in the mood called "anxiety."

Retreat into the they self absolves us from being free. The profound problem of what to be is put aside, replaced by a series of trivial questions about what to do. These questions are easily answered; we have merely to consult the they. What we have to do is decided by the norms provided for us by the social class into which we have been born, the ethnic group to which we belong, the profession we have adopted, the economic standing we have acquired.

"Fallenness" is the term Heidegger coined to characterize this mode of being.

> Idle talk, curiosity and ambiguity characterize the way in which, in an everyday manner, Dasein is its "there"—the disclosedness of Being-in-the-world. As definite existential characteristics, these are not present-at-hand in Dasein, but help to make up its Being. In these, and in the way they are interconnected in their Being, there is revealed a basic kind of Being which belongs to everydayness; we call this the *"falling"* of Dasein. . . .
>
> Dasein has, in the first instance, fallen away from itself as an authentic potentiality for Being its Self, and has fallen into the "world." "Fallenness" into the "world" means an absorption in Being-with-one-another, in so far as the latter is guided by idle talk, curiosity, and ambiguity. Through the Interpretation of falling, what we have called the "inauthenticity" of Dasein may now be defined more precisely. . . . "Inauthenticity" does not mean anything like Being-no-longer-in-the-

world, but amounts rather to a quite distinctive kind of Being-in-the-world—the kind which is completely fascinated by the "world" and by the Dasein-with of Others in the "they.". . .

Through the self-certainty and decidedness of the "they," it gets spread abroad increasingly that there is no need of authentic understanding or the state-of-mind that goes with it. The supposition of the "they" that one is leading and sustaining a full and genuine "life," brings Dasein a *tranquility,* for which everything is "in the best of order" and all doors are open. Falling Being-in-the-world, which tempts itself, is at the same time *tranquillizing.*

However, this tranquility in inauthentic Being does not seduce one into stagnation and inactivity, but drives one into uninhibited "hustle." Being-fallen into the "world" does not now somehow come to rest. . . . Versatile curiosity and restlessly "knowing it all" masquerade as a universal understanding of Dasein. But at bottom it remains indefinite *what* is really to be understood, and the question has not even been asked. Nor has it been understood that understanding itself is a potentiality-for-Being which must be made free in one's *ownmost* Dasein alone. When Dasein, tranquillized, and "understanding" everything, thus compares itself with everything, it drifts along towards an alienation in which its ownmost potentiality-for-Being is hidden from it. Falling Being-in-the-world is not only tempting and tranquillizing; it is at the same time *alienating.*[f]

Fallenness, then, is inauthenticity. It is that mode of being in which we are lost in, dominated by, the world. It is the condition in which we believe we understand everything but in which, because we have adopted a very superficial and external view of understanding, we really understand nothing. Least of all, when we have "fallen" into the world, do we understand our own Dasein, for we have turned away from it and toward the world and the they. Fallenness is in fact just that state of mind that has been admired and praised for the past four centuries as the "scientific" attitude—the attitude that Dewey urged us to adopt in our traffic with nature and with one another. The connotations of "traffic"—being busy, preoccupied, and manipulative—are precisely what, in Heidegger's eyes, make this attitude inauthentic and fallen.

AUTHENTICITY

If fallenness is inauthenticity, what is authenticity? It is living in and with anxiety; it is living in the full, moody understanding of our indeterminacy, our freedom. It is accepting, not trying to escape from, Dasein's mode of being. And what retrieves us from fallenness? What recalls us from inauthenticity to authenticity? It is the knowledge (the moody understanding) that we are going to die. For it is this knowledge, and this knowledge alone, that enables us to understand our Being fully, to grasp it as a whole and as a totality.

That is Heidegger's thesis. The reasoning seems to be as follows. Dasein alone of all entities knows that its Being will come to an end. Thus only Dasein has the possibility of understanding itself as a whole, of grasping its Being as a totality. This follows from what has already been said about the nature of understanding, articulation, and forehaving. To come to understand something explicitly is to articulate a whole that, in some sense, we already understand (are familiar with) implicitly. Dasein knows, even if only implicitly, that it is not the sort of being that endlessly is, but the sort of being that has an end. That is, Dasein knows, if only implicitly, that it is a whole, a totality. The only question is whether Dasein can articulate this implicit understanding of itself as a totality. This depends on whether or not Dasein can retrieve itself from fallenness, for in its fallen state it suppresses the knowledge that it is going to die and so does not even implicitly grasp itself as a totality.

> One thing has become unmistakable: *our existential analysis of Dasein up till now cannot lay claim to primordiality.* Its fore-having never included more than the *inauthentic* Being of Dasein, and of Dasein as *less* than a *whole.* If the Interpretation of Dasein's Being is to become primordial, as a foundation for working out the basic question of ontology, then it must first have brought to light existentially the Being of Dasein in its possibilities of *authenticity* and *totality.*
>
> Thus arises the task of putting Dasein as a whole into our fore-having. This signifies, however, that we must first of all raise the question of this entity's potentiality-for-Being-a-whole. As long as Dasein is, there is in every case something still outstanding, which Dasein can be and will be. But to that which is thus outstanding, the "end" itself belongs. The "end" of Being-in-the-world is death. This end, which belongs to the potentiality-for-Being—that is to say, to existence—limits and determines in every case whatever totality is possible for Dasein. If, however, Dasein's Being-at-an-end in death, and therewith its Being-a-whole, are to be included in the discussion of its possibly *Being-a-whole,* and if this is to be done in a way which is appropriate to the phenomenon, then we must have obtained an ontologically adequate conception of death—that is to say an *existential* conception of it. But as something of the character of Dasein, death *is* only in an existentiell *Being towards death.*[g]

The clue to understanding this passage is the notion of Being-toward-an-end. One lives authentically when, and only when, one lives in anticipation of death. This emphatically does not mean "preparing" for death—for instance, making one's will, designing one's tombstone, disposing of one's property, trying to arrange matters so that, even after death, one can manipulate one's successors. Rather it means doing, during all the days of one's life, whatever it is one is doing in the moody understanding that one is going to die, and this in its turn means, in Heidegger's language, living in "one's ownmost potentiality of being"—that is, living a life that is independent of the restrictions and limitations that the they constantly seeks to impose on one's freedom. Only when one is free from the they's domination—and one is free from the they's domination only when one lives in anticipation of death—can one realize one's ownmost potentiality of Being.

> The uttermost "not-yet" has the character of something *towards which* Dasein *comports itself.* The end is impending for Dasein. Dasein is not something not yet present-at-hand, nor is it that which is ultimately still outstanding but which has been reduced to a minimum. *Death is something that stands before us—something impending.* . . .
>
> Death is a possibility-of-Being which Dasein itself has to take over in every case. With death, Dasein stands before itself in its ownmost potentiality-for-Being. . . . As potentiality-for-Being, Dasein cannot outstrip the possibility of death. Death is the possibility of the absolute impossibility of Dasein. Thus death reveals itself as that *possibility which is one's ownmost, which is non-relational, and which is not to be outstripped.* . . .
>
> This ownmost possibility, however, non-relational and not to be outstripped, is not one which Dasein procures for itself subsequently and occasionally in the course of its Being. On the contrary, if Dasein exists, it has already been *thrown* into this possibility. Dasein does not, proximally and for the most part, have any explicit or even any theoretical knowledge of the fact that it has been delivered over to its death, and that death thus belongs to Being-in-the-world. Thrownness into death reveals itself to Dasein in a more primordial and impressive manner in that state-of-mind which we have called "anxiety." Anxiety in the face of death is anxiety "in the face of" that potentiality-for-Being which is one's ownmost, non-relational, and not to be outstripped. That in the face of which one has anxiety is Being-in-the-world itself. That about which one has this anxiety is simply Dasein's potentiality-for-Being. Anxiety in the face of death must not be confused with fear in the face of one's demise. This anxiety is not an accidental or random mood of "weakness" in some individual; but, as a basic state-of-mind of Dasein, it amounts to the disclosedness of the fact that Dasein exists as thrown Being *towards* its end.[h]

An existential knowledge of death, then, is that moody understanding that Heidegger characterized as anxiety—the mood that evokes and is evoked by our experience of being toward our end, together with the resultant experience of being perfectly free to be our ownmost potentiality of being. Death is a threat since it abolishes our Being, and this threat is constant, though the time of its coming is indefinite. To live authentically we must keep this constant indefinite threat before us. We must be constantly vigilant against the tendency to slip back into the safety and security—and the inauthenticity—of the they self and its dimmed-down, thinned-down mode of experience. To live authentically we must, as it were, live at the pitch, as a finely tuned instrument.

Doubtless we must. But how, as a practical matter, can fallen Dasein ever be recalled from its fallen state? The answer is that even in the depths of fallenness the voice of conscience attests to the possibility of an authentic life. This reference to conscience will have a rather old-fashioned sound to those brought up with sociological, psychological, or psychoanalytic explanations of conscience. But, of course, for Heidegger conscience is a primordial ontological structure.

> Because Dasein is *lost* in the "they," it must first *find* itself. In order to find *itself* at all, it must be "shown" to itself in its possible authenticity. In terms of its *possibility*, Dasein *is* already a potentiality-for-Being-its-Self, but it needs to have this potentiality attested.
>
> In the following Interpretation we shall claim that this potentiality is attested by that which, in Dasein's everyday interpretation of itself, is familiar to us as the *"voice of conscience."* That the very "fact" of conscience has been disputed, that its function as a higher court for Dasein's existence has been variously assessed, and that "what conscience says" has been interpreted in manifold ways—all this might only mislead us into dismissing this phenomenon if the very "doubtfulness" of this Fact—or of the way in which it has been interpreted—did not *prove* that here a *primordial* phenomenon of Dasein lies before us. In the following analysis conscience will be taken as something which we have in advance theoretically, and it will be investigated in a purely existential manner, with fundamental ontology as our aim. . . .
>
> The ontological analysis of conscience on which we are thus embarking is prior to any description and classification of Experiences of conscience, and likewise lies outside of any biological "explanation" of this phenomenon (which would mean its dissolution). But it is no less distant from a theological exegesis of conscience or any employment of this phenomenon for proofs of God or for establishing an "immediate" consciousness of God. . . .
>
> Conscience gives us "something" to understand; it *discloses*. . . . It is revealed as a *call*. Calling is a mode of *discourse*. The call of conscience has the character of an *appeal* to Dasein by calling it to its ownmost potentiality-for-Being-its-Self. . . .
>
> The call dispenses with any kind of utterance. It does not put itself into words at all; yet it remains nothing less than obscure and indefinite. *Conscience discourses solely and constantly in the mode of keeping silent.* . . . The fact that what is called in the call has not been formulated in words, does not give this phenomenon the indefiniteness of a mysterious voice, but merely indicates that our understanding of what is "called" is not to be tied up with an expectation of anything like a communication.

Yet what the call discloses is unequivocal. . . . One must keep in mind that when we designate the conscience as a "call," this call is an appeal to the they-self in its Self; as such an appeal, it summons the Self to its potentiality-for-Being-its-Self, and thus calls Dasein forth to its possibilities.[i]

Thus conscience is not evidence of some transcendental realm of being, whether this be the Christian heaven or a Platonic realm of forms. Still less is it evidence of some societal or psychological malfunctioning, such as an excessively strong superego. Conscience is not "evidence" at all; it is disclosure—the disclosure to Dasein of its fallenness, of its thrownness, and of its responsibility to itself to live resolutely in the face of that anxiety which its thrownness generates.

From the Ontical to the Ontological

We have now sketched some—by no means all—of the main features of Dasein, a unitary mode of being in which, nonetheless, three aspects can be distinguished: existence, thrownness, and fallenness. As we have seen, Heidegger did not undertake this long discussion of Dasein for its own sake, but because he held that Dasein's mode of being—its involvement with the world, its escape into everydayness, its recall to anxiety—was a clue that would lead him to Being as such. We shall have to ask whether this expectation was fulfilled, but before we do so we must pause briefly to assess what has been accomplished in this still preliminary stage of the whole investigation. This requires us to examine a distinction that has been referred to repeatedly in passages we have already quoted, the distinction between the ontical (alternatively, the "existentiell") and the ontological (alternatively, the "existential").

Heidegger claimed that at the ontical-existentiell level we obtain only a very superficial view of the varied and manifold entities—"houses, trees, people, mountains, stars"—that are the objects investigated in such sciences as botany, psychology, geology, and astronomy. In these and the other "positive" sciences we can and do

depict the way such entities "look," and we can give an account of occurrences in them and with them. This, however, is obviously a pre-phenomenological "business" which cannot be at all relevant phenomenologically. Such a description is always confined to entities. It is ontical. But what we are seeking is Being.[j]

As an example of inquiry at the ontical level Heidegger discusses the science of ethnology.

> Heretofore our information about primitives has been provided by
> ethnology. . . . Here too we are confronted with the same state of affairs
> as in the other [positive sciences]. Ethnology itself already presupposes
> as its clue an inadequate analytic of Dasein. But since the positive sci-
> ences neither "can" nor should wait for the ontological labours of phi-
> losophy to be done, the further course of research will not take the
> form of an "advance" but will be accomplished by *recapitulating* and by
> purifying it in a way which is ontologically more transparent.[k]

Ethnology, that is to say, claims to supply us with information about primitive
people, and so it does. But what it gives us is only information about how primitive people behave, information of the kind that an outsider can acquire by observation. It yields no insight at all regarding the Being of humans (Dasein). Still
less does it yield insight into the nature of Being as such. Nor is it just a matter of
waiting until ethnology makes an "advance." As in all the positive sciences the
methods of investigation used in ethnology will doubtless improve in the course
of time, but only in the sense of providing us with more, and more-refined, information about primitive peoples, not in the sense of ever yielding an understanding of Dasein. For that—for a grasp of the *meaning* of Dasein—a wholly different
method is needed, the method that, earlier in this account of Heidegger's position, we called moody understanding. Learning to look at human beings, whether
primitive or contemporary, with a moody understanding is what it takes to bring
us from the merely ontical level to the ontological level.

Consider, for instance, the contrast between an ontical and an ontological approach to the phenomenon of care. We know the way in which care is, or might
be, studied in the positive sciences: it is possible to give a neurophysiological account of the variables that are associated with the experience of care, or a sociological account of the same phenomenon, in which it is correlated with other
variables, or a psychoanalytic account, and so on. Heidegger's account of the ontical approach (as he calls it) is comprehensible enough, but only because we have
all had some experience of this kind of approach. Our problem is to understand
what is involved in passing to the ontological level. Heidegger has this to say about
the difference between an ontical and an ontological approach to care:

> As compared with [an] ontical interpretation, the existential-
> ontological Interpretation is not, let us say, merely an ontical general-
> ization which is theoretical in character. That would just mean that
> ontically all man's ways of behaving are "full of care" and are guided by
> his "devotedness" to something. The "generalization" is rather one that
> is *ontological and a priori*. What it has in view is not a set of ontical
> properties which constantly keep emerging, but a state of Being which
> is already underlying in every case, and which first makes it ontologi-
> cally possible for this entity to be addressed ontically as *"cura."* The
> existential conditions for the possibility of "the cares of life" and

"devotedness," must be conceived as care, in a sense which is primordial—that is ontological.

The transcendental "generality" of the phenomenon of care and of all fundamental *existentialia* is, on the other hand, broad enough to present a basis on which *every* interpretation of Dasein which is ontical and belongs to a world-view must move, whether Dasein is understood as affliction and the "cares of life" or in an opposite direction.[1]

In other words, descriptions of ontological structure differ from the generalizations of the positive sciences in at least two ways. First, though generalizations at the ontical level (for example, those of Freudian psychologists about the Oedipus complex; those of Marxist sociologists about the class struggle) are sometimes very broad and sweeping, they never claim absolute universality. Either they apply only to certain regions, as it were, of human nature—to certain institutions in certain cultures, in certain historical periods—or they are not limited specifically to human beings: for instance, something like the Oedipus complex and something like a class struggle seem to characterize the behavior of the higher animals. In contrast, Heidegger claims that his "fundamental existentialia" (for instance, care, thrownness, anxiety) are absolutely universal: no human being lacks them; nothing that is not a human being has them. In short, ontological structure is "*a priori* and primordial," whereas generalization at the ontical level is empirical and derived. Second, ontological structure is no mere generalization that we frame about phenomena; it is a real structure that is in, that appears in, all the diverse ontical phenomena. Of course, from Heidegger's point of view, to say that this structure "appears in" the phenomena is not to say that it somehow lies behind them; rather it is to say that they usually "cover" it and "disguise" it so that we may fail to recognize it.[14] Phenomenological seeing—moody understanding—is simply the method of uncovering and bringing into plain view what was there all the time, and this method, clearly, is radically different from generalizing from our observation of certain surface similarities that various phenomena happen to "have in common."

This, then, is how the ontological level, or approach, is supposed to differ from the ontical. We have to ask what sort of evidence Heidegger might adduce to support his claim that there is indeed a special ontological approach. That the so-called ontical interpretations are partial and limited, that each rests on a particular set of assumptions, on a particular "worldview," many people will allow. But these people will be disposed to say that Heidegger's ontological approach is just another interpretation at the ontical level, indeed, one that is more partial and limited—more "slanted"—than most. What justifies Heidegger's claim that his account is at an altogether different level—deep where those others are shallow, a priori where they are relative to a worldview?

---

[14] Compare p. 312.

We do not get an answer to this question from Heidegger. But in fairness it is necessary to add that in the nature of the case (his position being what it is) he cannot be expected to answer it. From his point of view we are either adept at moody understanding or we are not. If we are, no elucidation of the difference between the ontical and the ontological is necessary. Our moody understanding of, say, care itself elucidates the difference between levels. In moody understanding we *see* the ontological structure of care and see that it "recapitulates" and "purifies" the various ontical accounts of care. Unfortunately, if we are not adept at moody understanding, this difference eludes us. We are outside, and being outside, we may suspect that what purports to be revealed as the ontological structure of Dasein is really no more than a projection of Heidegger's biases, including an almost pathological anxiety.

In a word, these outsiders would say that Heidegger's account of the ontological structure of Dasein as revealed in the fundamental existentialia is simply a vivid account of how the world looks to Heidegger, an alienated and anxious man. And they might add, since as a matter of fact many men and women in our time do experience alienation and anxiety, the description is far from being merely idiosyncratic. But, they would conclude, here again Heidegger has only described one kind of experience—not *the* world, but simply the world of the anxious.

To such skeptics Heidegger's reply is at once simple and, in a sense, complete. It is that they have "not looked long enough."[m] Nor have they looked correctly; they have not used the method of phenomenological seeing. I *have* looked, he would say, and I have seen; if you have not looked and not seen, that is simply evidence of some deficiency in you, not in me. From Heidegger's point of view (which, from his point of view, was not a point of view) this reply is unassailable. From outside his point of view it is no reply at all: we have reached another parting of the ways.

The Call of Being

Heidegger's move from what he held to be a superficial ontical study of human beings to a deep ontological insight into Dasein's real structure was, as we have said, but the first step on a path that he believed would lead him from the human mode of being to Being as such. Whatever we think about the success of this first step on the path, even Heidegger had to admit in the end that the path itself proved to be a dead end. The second part of *Being and Time* (four out of the six "divisions" that he had optimistically projected at the start of the journey) was again and again postponed and, eventually, quietly abandoned. In its place there are only a number of essays, mostly published lectures, on a variety of topics. In these, the language has become, if possible, even more opaque. There is much more of what a hostile critic would call punning and what Heidegger himself regarded as etymology, that is, the uncovering of the true meaning that has been lost.[15] And the elaborate technical vocabulary has been replaced by a highly anthropomorphic one in which we are told that Being "calls" to us, that it on occasion "conceals" itself from us, and again "reveals" itself to us.

In these circumstances it is not surprising that Heideggerians disagree as to whether, and if so to what extent, the master's views changed after the publication of *Being and Time* in 1927. Rather than plunge into these heated debates we will concentrate on trying to make sense of a number of hints thrown out in these later writings. These are the relation between time and Being, the nature of poetry, and the limitations of language.

TIME AND BEING

We are repeatedly told in *Being and Time* that time is the "horizon" of Being. This apparently means that Being is to be understood in terms of time; it is as if a Keynesian were to write that fiscal policy is the horizon of inflation. That is to say, Being's being is not ahistorical, as the Christian God is thought to be, but historical, as Hegel's spirit would be if the dialectical process did not come to rest in a timeless and changeless Absolute.

Dasein's being is temporal through and through. To be Dasein, as we have seen, is not to have a nature that is (exists) throughout some period of time, but to live ahead, to live toward an end. We can see, then, why Heidegger could believe that Dasein's historicity would be a clue to the historicity of Being, for Being as such is no more indifferent to time than is Dasein. But this clue was never worked out in *Being and Time.* The book ends not with an answer but with three questions: "How is this mode of the temporalizing of temporality to be interpreted? Is there a way which leads from primordial *time* to the meaning of Being? Does *time* itself manifest itself as the horizon of Being?"[n]

In a lecture given in 1962 called "Time and Being," Heidegger took up the question of their relation again.

> What prompts us to name time and Being together? From the dawn of Western-European thinking until today, Being means the same as presencing. Presencing, presence speaks of the present. According to current representations, the present, together with past and future, forms the character of time. Being is determined as presence by time. That this is so could in itself be sufficient to introduce a relentless disquiet into thinking. This disquiet increases as soon as we set out to think through in what respect there is such a determination of Being by time.
>
> In what respect? Why, in what manner and from what source does something like time have a voice in Being? Every attempt to think adequately the relation of Being and time with the help of the current and imprecise representations of time and Being immediately be-

---

[15] See p. 347.

comes ensnared in a hopeless tangle of relations that have hardly been thought out.°

We already know what, according to Heidegger, are the "current and imprecise representations" of Being: they are the notion of Being as the highest genus (and therefore, the emptiest of concepts) or as that which lies beyond and behind the appearances. But what is the current and imprecise notion of time? It is the notion of clock time, of time as an even flow in which the present comes to us out of the future and flows away from us into the past. So viewed, Being and time seem utterly different. But grasped in their inner being, Being and time come together in the notion of presence.

> Being is not a thing, thus nothing temporal, and yet it is determined by time as presence.
>
> Time is not a thing, thus nothing which is, and yet it remains constant in its passing away without being something temporal like the beings in time. . . .
>
> We say of beings: they are. With regard to the matter "Being" and with regard to the matter "time," we remain cautious. We do not say: Being is, time is, but rather: there is Being and there is time. For the moment we have only changed the idiom with this expression. Instead of saying "it is," we say "there is," "it gives."
>
> In order to get beyond the idiom and back to the matter, we must show how this "there is" can be experienced and seen.ᴾ

Some people might think that there is nothing to get back to beyond the idiom; it just happens to be the case that in German one says "es gibt" (literally, "it gives"), whereas in English one says "there is." We can infer nothing about the nature of Being from this usage. Not so, according to Heidegger. German is far superior to English in depth and in insight into fundamental ontology. It is no accident that in German one says "es gibt"; Germans realize (even if only dimly) that it is not merely the case that something is there (hence they do not say "there is"), but that something is presenting itself, or offering itself, to us. The idiom conceals a profound insight into Being, and in uncovering the meaning of the idiom, we recover this lost insight.

> Being, by which all beings as such are marked, Being means presencing. Thought with regard to what presences, presencing shows itself as letting-presence. But now we must try to think this letting-presence explicitly insofar as presencing is admitted. Letting shows its character in bringing into unconcealment. To let presence means: to unconceal, to bring to openness. In unconcealing prevails a giving, the giving that gives presencing, that is, Being, in letting-presence.
>
> (To think the matter "Being" explicitly requires our reflection to follow the direction which shows itself in letting-presence. But from unconcealing speaks a giving, an It gives.) . . .

To think Being explicitly requires us to relinquish Being as the ground of beings in favor of the giving which prevails concealed in unconcealment, that is, in favor of the It gives. As the gift of this It gives, Being belongs to giving. As a gift, Being is not expelled from giving. Being, presencing is transmuted. As allowing-to-presence, it belongs to unconcealing; as a gift of unconcealing it is retained in the giving. Being *is* not. There is, It gives Being as the unconcealing; as the gift of unconcealing it is retained in the giving. Being *is* not. There is, It gives Being as the unconcealing of presencing.

This "It gives, there is Being" might emerge somewhat more clearly once we think out more decisively the giving we have in mind here. We can succeed by paying heed to the wealth of the transformation of what, indeterminately enough, is called Being, and at the same time is misunderstood in its core as long as it is taken for the emptiest of all empty concepts.q

The notion that an object is present to us when we perceive it is familiar to us from epistemological realism. In order to bring out his contention that the object is independent of our perception of it, an epistemological realist—Moore, for instance—might say that an object of perception is present to us. But he would not say, if he was Moore, that the object presents itself to us. This, however, is just what Heidegger did say: his position thus went far beyond epistemological realism. To perceive something—say, a coin—is to let that thing

take up a position opposite to us, as an object. The thing so opposed must, such being its position, come across the open towards us and at the same time stand fast in itself as the thing and manifest itself as a constant. This manifestation of the thing in making a move towards us is accomplished in the open, within the realm of the Overt. . . .

All behaviour is "overt" to what-is, and all "overt" relationship is behaviour. Man's "overtness" varies with the nature of what-is and the mode of behaviour. All working and carrying out of tasks, all transaction and calculation, sustains itself in the open, an overt region within which what-is can expressly take up its stand *as* and *how* it is *what* it is, and thus become capable of expression.r

But Being as presencing involves even more than an object's merely presenting itself to us, making a move toward us, and taking a stand. It involves the object giving and withdrawing itself, revealing and concealing itself. To those who might object that they never experience anything remotely like this when they look at objects, and that it sounds like the sheerest anthropomorphism, Heidegger would reply that if one does not experience Being as a revealing and concealing, a giving and withdrawing, that is because one is not open to the object.[16]

---

[16]To be "open" (the language of these later essays) seems about equivalent to the mode of authenticity described in *Being and Time.*

There is nothing difficult or esoteric about an encounter with Being. If we but open ourselves to any object whatever, any natural object or any artifact, we encounter Being. "We perceive presencing in every simple, sufficiently unprejudiced reflection on things of nature and artifacts. Things of nature and artifacts are both modes of presencing."[s] However, to encounter Being in any object, we must harken to its call, and in this dark age in which we live, few people actually listen to Being's call.

So much, for the moment, regarding Being as presencing. Let us turn to time. Time, it turns out, is also presencing. Of course, to the extent that we identify time with clock time, present, past, and future are distinct from each other—past is past, not present; future is future, not present. Understood in this way, the present (the now) is utterly different from the presencing of Being. This clock-time view of time is, however, very superficial. Rightly understood, any present (any now) includes both past and future.

> How are we to determine this giving of presencing that prevails in the present, in the past, in the future? Does this giving lie in this, that it reaches us, or does it reach us because it is in itself a reaching? The latter. Approaching, being not yet present, at the same time gives and brings about what is no longer present, the past, and conversely what has been offers future to itself. The reciprocal relation of both at the same time gives and brings about the present. . . .
>
> It is thus inadmissible to say that future, past and present are before us "at the same time." Yet they belong together in the way they offer themselves to one another. Their unifying unity can be determined only by what is their own; that they offer themselves to one another. But what do they offer to one another?
>
> Nothing other than themselves—which means: the presencing that is given in them. With this presencing, there opens up what we call time-space. But with the word "time" we no longer mean the succession of a sequence of nows. Accordingly, time-space no longer means merely the distance between two now-points of calculated time, such as we have in mind when we note, for instance, this or that occurred within a time-span of fifty years. Time-space now is the name for the openness which opens up in the mutual self-extending of futural approach, past and present. . . .
>
> Prior to all calculation of time and independent of such calculation, what is germane to the time-space of true time consists in the mutual reaching out and opening up of future, past and present.[t]

This is certainly difficult. But Heidegger seems to be talking, in typical Heideggerese, about a well-known psychological fact—that time is not experienced as a series of discrete, encapsulated nows that move along from future into past, like a string of freight cars past a station, but as a continuous flow in which any segment that we may select as now seems to contain future as well as present. For instance, if I repeat the line, "Of man's first disobedience and the fruit of that forbidden tree," when I get to the "dis" of "disobedience" I have finished saying "first." Yet the sound and the sense of "first" linger on, echoing in the "dis" that I am just now saying. And "obedience," which is yet to come, already colors "dis," rendering it different from what it would be if it were, say, the "dis" of "dismal."

This phenomenon is characterized as the "specious present."[17] Though this experiential specious present is actually very short, we can extend it metaphorically, and talk, for instance, about the distant past (say, a childhood Oedipal fixation) persisting into the present and of a remote future (say, graduating from college and going to work) affecting the present. We do not mean that the future event (going to work) is present, but only that a present thought of it affects what we do now. When we speak in this way, we might say we are talking in a deliberately metaphorical way.

That is what *we* might say. According to Heidegger, these descriptions are not metaphors; on the contrary, they uncover and lay bare the ontological structure of "true" time. A present that includes a not-yet and an over-and-done, far from being merely "specious," is real. What makes time time is just what makes the not-yet and the over-and-done present in the present, as a kind of revealing and concealing, a kind of giving and withdrawing. Because the future is not-yet and because the past is over-and-done, they are concealed from us, withheld from us, here and now in the present. Yet they are also here-and-now in the present; they are present in the present in the mode of being now the not-yet and now the over-and-done. Therefore, because they are present in the here-and-now, they are revealed, they are given to us.

Thus the structure of true time and the structure of Being are both a presencing that involves a revealing and a concealing, a giving and a withdrawing. Further, it is possible for us to grasp Being's being (if we may so speak) only because, and to the extent that, we are open to true time, that is, to a present that contains a future and a past. We grasp the being of Being in and through our grasp of the temporality of true (in distinction from clock) time. This is the sense in which one can say that time is the horizon of Being.

Heidegger does not deny that this account of the nature[18] of Being and time and of the relation between them is difficult. It is difficult, he says, because it is cast in the form of a lecture. "The form of a lecture remains an obstacle. . . . The lecture has been spoken merely in propositional statements." Hence if some critic

---

[17] James called it "specious" because he took the clock-time "now" as real, and because from this point of view what is past (for example, "first") and what is future (for example, "obedience") are not really present, but only seem to be present, along with "dis."

[18] Of course, it really does not do to talk, as we have, about Being's (or time's) "nature." This and similar terms are "preontological" survivals, and conceal more than they reveal. Being does not "have" a nature; Being *is* presencing. But even "is" is wrong; it, too, is a survival.

were to conclude that the lecture "says nothing at all," Heidegger would agree. "It does indeed say nothing so long as we hear a mere sentence in what was said, and expose that sentence to the cross-examination of logic. . . . The point is not to listen to a series of propositions but rather to follow the movement of showing."[u]

If "the form of a lecture is an obstacle," one may ask why Heidegger chose this form. If saying (that is, speaking propositions) is a wholly inadequate way of grasping Being, why not abandon the propositional path and seek some other path of Being? This is what, in effect, Heidegger increasingly did. He decided that poetry—and above all, the poetry of Hölderlin[19]—is a more promising path, for poetry does not say, it shows. Poets hear the call of Being and harken to it, whereas most people are deaf to it; poems have the power to make even the deaf hear. That, according to Heidegger, is what poetry does; that is the essence of poetry.

POETRY AS THE PATH TO BEING

In an essay called "Hölderlin and the Essence of Poetry" (1936) Heidegger commented on a number of "pointers," drawn from the writings of Hölderlin, all of which are concerned with—point to—the nature of language, and especially the language of poetry.

The five pointers, according to Heidegger, direct our attention to the idea that language has two very different functions, one obvious but superficial, the other much more important but much less obvious. The obvious function of language is to serve the purposes of communication; language makes social interaction possible by exchanging needed information. So far, language is a tool among other tools, a possession among other possessions. However, "this definition [of language] does not touch its essential essence, but merely indicates an effect of its essence. Language is not a mere tool, one of the many which man possesses; on the contrary, it is only language that affords the very possibility of standing in the openness of the existent."[v]

That is to say, it is language that makes possible Dasein's characteristic mode of being. It is language that makes it possible for us to ask "What is Being?"—not merely in the trivial sense that without language one could not verbalize this question, but in the deep sense that it is language that sets us enough apart from Being for us to be amazed by it. Other beings—"the rose, the swans, the stag in the forest"—are wholly immersed in Being, too immersed to be amazed by it. Language, by setting us apart, creates a human world, a world in which Being both gives and withholds itself. Since no other entity is worldly, since other entities merely "are," Being is not for them a "presence."

---

[19] Friedrich Hölderlin (1770–1843) was born in southwest Germany, the region of which Heidegger was a native. Hölderlin's poetic gifts were recognized early by Schiller and by Fichte, who encouraged him, but his career was plagued by ill health, disappointment in love, and recurring bouts of depression. In 1807 he became hopelessly insane.

The next pointer points to the contrast between what we have called "exchanging needed information" and what Heidegger calls a "conversation," or a dialogue. In a conversation, the participants share, participate in, a common subject and a common interest. To converse together, they must be attuned both to each other and to the subject of their conversation. As their conversation proceeds, this attunement is perfected by mutual tuning. That is to say, in the course of their conversation they reach an explicit understanding of what they have implicitly understood all along.[20]

So far, surely, everyone can agree; there are conversations like that—occasionally, we might want to add. But Heidegger goes much further. "We—mankind—are a conversation." There is, and has been, but one conversation, and the subject of this conversation is Being.

> The being of men is founded in language. But this only becomes actual in *conversation*. . . . But now what is meant by "a conversation"? Plainly, the act of speaking with others about something. Then speaking also brings about the process of coming together. But Hölderlin says: "Since we have been a conversation and have been able to hear from one another." Being able to hear is not a mere consequence of speaking with one another, on the contrary it is rather pre-supposed in the latter process. . . . We are a conversation—and that means: we can hear from one another. We are a conversation, that always means at the same time: we are a *single* conversation.[w]

Heidegger regarded his comments on Hölderlin's points as a conversation: the poet's share in this conversation was his verses; the philosopher's share was his exegesis of them. Both philosopher and poet were engaged in a joint undertaking, naming, or pointing at, that which is present to us, that which reveals itself to us and conceals itself from us. We already know that Heidegger's name for the subject, or topic, of this conversation was "Being." Hölderlin's name for it, according to Heidegger, was "the gods." Inasmuch as Hölderlin "tells us with the sure simplicity of the poet," are we to conclude that "gods" is a better name than "Being"? No, that would be an erroneous way of looking at the matter. It is not a question of which of several possible names of that which presences itself to us is the most accurate, as if it were a question of which of several possible labels correctly names the contents of a bottle or a box. That which the philosopher denominates "Being" and which the poet denominates "the gods," is, strictly speaking, unnameable—that is, in the sense that it can never be completely, perfectly, and exhaustively named. Yet that which eludes us in all names nevertheless also reveals itself in every name, providing that we "listen," that is, providing that we are participating in a conversation and not merely "exchanging needed information." Naming the unnameable is a matter of perfecting an attunement, of continuing a

[20] See pp. 330–31.

conversation, which we know can never be completed. But we also know that in this continuing conversation each namer is helped toward attunement with the unnameable by listening to the name that the other namer gives it, and by listening, too, to the unnameable that is seeking attunement with us while we seek attunement with it. The word by which each of us names it is our response both to the other namer's name for it and also to its own call. "The gods can acquire a name only by addressing and, as it were, claiming us. The word which names the gods is always a response to such a claim."[x] Thus, not only is there but a single conversation—a conversation that makes human beings human. It is also the case that Being participates in this conversation, and it is the participation of Being in it that makes us human.

The next pointer calls attention to the idea that poetic naming is not merely a matter of pointing to something already in existence; it is rather an "act of establishing."

> The poet names the gods and names all things in that which they are. This naming does not consist merely in something already known being supplied with a name; it is rather that when the poet speaks the essential word, the existent is by this naming nominated as what it is. So it becomes known *as* existent. Poetry is the establishing of being by means of the word.[y]

Naming, that is, is a creative act in which something is brought into existence. "When the gods are named originally and the essence of things receives a name, so that things for the first time shine out, human existence is brought into a firm relation and given a basis."[z] We expressed ourselves carelessly, therefore, when we wrote of the single conversation "having" a "subject." The conversation *makes* its subject as it develops. Dasein, that is to say, does not *have* a history, in the sense of enduring through time. Dasein *is* its history, and this history is not a straight-line linear affair; it is the alternating revealings and concealings of Being.

Finally, the last pointer points to the high role of the poet in the making of Dasein as history.

> Poetry is not merely an ornament accompanying existence. . . . Poetry is the foundation which supports history, and therefore it is not a mere appearance of culture, and absolutely not the mere "expression" of a "culture-soul."[a]

Poetry is the record of the poet's share in Dasein's conversation with Being; Dasein should, therefore, listen to poets at all times, but especially in this dark age, this age in which Being has withdrawn itself from Dasein.

> The time is needy and therefore its poet is extremely rich—so rich that he would often like to relax in thoughts of those that have been and in eager waiting for that which is coming and would like only to sleep

in this apparent emptiness. But he holds his ground in the Nothing of this night. Whilst the poet remains thus by himself in the supreme isolation of his mission, he fashions truth, vicariously and therefore truly, for his people.[b]

SILENCE

The discussion of poetry and its superiority to formal ontology rests on two assumptions: first, that, though language cannot name the unnameable with perfect completeness, it nonetheless can name it; second, that conversation is possible, that is, that the enterprise of naming the unnameable is a mutual undertaking in which the namers help each other to a closer attunement with what is being searched for. Underlying both of these assumptions is a more fundamental presupposition, namely, that there is one human world that all Dasein inhabits and in which the "articulation" that Heidegger calls understanding occurs. In a later essay, "A Dialogue on Language," it turns out that there is a radical problem of translation from one language to another, which renders conversation (at least as it was conceived in *Being and Time* and "The Essence of Poetry") impossible, and that the unnameable eludes all language, even the language of poetry. The solution is not saying, or even showing; it is silence.

We will consider these two points in turn. "A Dialogue on Language" purports to be a discussion between a Japanese student of Heidegger and an "Inquirer." We are told only that the "text originated in 1953/54, on the occasion of a visit by Professor Tezuka of the Imperial University, Tokyo."[c] The discussion begins, naturally enough, with the question whether, and to what extent, it is possible to translate a Japanese word such as *Iki* into a European language or a European word such as "aesthetics" into Japanese. Do not East Asians and Europeans live in fundamentally different "worlds"?

But the discussion of this translation problem soon uncovers a much deeper problem. Inquirer's earlier dialogues with Japanese visitors had revealed the difficulty of finding an adequate Japanese equivalent for certain European words and vice versa, but the correct dialogue with the new visitor now reveals that those earlier dialogues concealed a greater difficulty, a danger that was "all the more menacing just by being more inconspicuous."[d] What is this danger? It is difficult to say. But of course we—Inquirer and his current Japanese interlocutor—could not mention it to each other, if we had not, both of us, in some sense experienced it or at least "scented" it. As a start, we can say that the danger "was hidden in language itself, not in *what* we discussed, nor in the *way in which* we tried to do so."[e] Let us then—the current dialogue continues—try to uncover the danger that is concealed in this, and indeed in any, dialogue.

The danger concerns the way in which language is related to the subject of the dialogue, to what the participants are seeking to name in the language they are using, not the relation between one language and another. And the question is whether different languages are related to that subject in any common way. If not, translation is surely not merely difficult; it is impossible. And further, language is intrinsically inadequate to the task to which we have believed it is at least partially adequate—not this or that language, but language as such. The saying discussed in the dialogue, that "language is the house of Being,"[f] suggests that Being has several more or less interchangeable dwellings, each "a shelter erected earlier somewhere or other, in which Being, like a portable object, can be stored away."[g] That is a comforting idea, but a fundamentally false one.

Or to put the "danger" differently, Inquirer and his Japanese friend have been trying to formulate in language the relation between language and Being. That would seem to be impossible. They can, indeed, believe that in their different languages, and in all languages, "there sings something that wells up from a single source,"[h] but if so, they have to admit, this source remains concealed from the various "language worlds." They can indeed believe that the participants in a dialogue are, "without quite knowing it, obedient to what alone . . . allows a dialogue to succeed." They can believe this, but can they be sure? For instance, Inquirer and his Japanese interlocutor agree that they "have the Same in mind," that they are both "thinking . . . of the nature of language." But how, since they cannot define it, can they know that they are both thinking about the nature of language? They can only hope that "it is that undefined defining something [that] is defining our dialogue. But even so we must not touch it."[i] "The untouchable is veiled from us by the mystery of Saying."[j]

Or, to put the difficulty in a less picturesque way, it is impossible to formulate in language the relation between language and reality.[21] Yet that is just what we are trying to do in this dialogue when we talk together, as we have been doing, about the nature of language. Should we therefore cease? No, let us rather suggest hints to each other—though "even to talk of a hint is to venture too much." Nevertheless hints are suggestive, and so are gestures. "They are enigmatic. They beckon to us. They beckon *away*. They beckon us *toward* that from which they unexpectedly bear themselves toward us."[k] But chiefly this will be a dialogue, not of sayings, but of silences.

I: Speaking *about* language turns language almost inevitably into an object.

J: And then its reality vanishes.

I: We then have taken up a position above language, instead of hearing from it.

J: Then there would only be a speaking *from* language . . .

I: . . . in this manner, that it would be called *from out of* language's reality, and be led *to* its reality.

J: How can we do that?

[21] See pp. 232–36.

I: A speaking *from* language could only be a dialogue. . . .

J: But, patently, a dialogue altogether *sui generis.*

I: A dialogue that would remain originarily appropriated to Saying.

J: But then, not every talk between people could be called a dialogue any longer . . .

I: . . . if we from now on hear this word as though it named for us a focusing on the reality of language.

J: In this sense, then, even Plato's *Dialogues* would not be dialogues?

I: I would like to leave that question open, and only point out that the kind of dialogue is determined by *that which* speaks to those who seemingly are the only speakers—men.

J: Wherever the nature of language were to speak (say) to man as Saying, *it,* Saying, would bring about the real dialogue . . .

I: . . . which does not say "about" language but *of* language, as needfully used of its very nature.

J: And it would also remain of minor importance whether the dialogue is before us in writing, or whether it was spoken at some time and has now faded.

I: Certainly—because the one thing that matters is whether this dialogue, be it written or spoken or neither, remains constantly coming.

J: The course of such a dialogue would have to have a character all its own, with more silence than talk.

I: Above all, silence about silence . . .

J: Because to talk and write about silence is what produces the most obnoxious chatter . . .

I: Who could simply be silent of silence?

J: That would be authentic saying . . .

I: . . . and would remain the constant prologue to the authentic dialogue *of* language.[1]

Heidegger certainly moved a long way from Husserl. He had early become dissatisfied with Husserl's version of phenomenology because it yielded only "consciousness and its objectivity," not "the Being of beings in its unconcealedness and concealment."[m] But for a long time—for years after the publication of *Being and Time*—he still believed that his own form of phenomenology would result in a fundamental ontology. But the pursuit of Being in its purity and immediacy led away from ontology, past poetry, and finally to silence. And it is hard to see how the community of silence that is evoked in this dialogue as an opening toward Being differs in any way from mysticism. Unless one is content to achieve a mystical contact with reality, one must conclude that the phenomenological route out of the Kantian paradigm has reached a dead end in Heidegger. For all of his differences from the Logical Positivists, he concluded as they did—and just as regretfully as they did—that the ideal of a language isomorphic with reality is an illusion.

CHAPTER 10

Sartre

If Heidegger in a sense sat at Husserl's feet, Sartre[1] sat at Heidegger's; if Heidegger developed phenomenology in a direction that Husserl disowned, Sartre

[1] Jean-Paul Sartre was born in Paris in 1905. His father died when he was an infant and he was brought up in the home of his grandfather, who was a teacher of German. Sartre studied at the Ecole Normale Supérieure (1924–28) and at the Universities of Berlin and Freiburg (1933–35). After his graduate work, he taught at a number of French *lycées* until 1939 when he was called up for active duty at the outbreak of the war and sent to the Maginot Line. He was captured during the fall of France but was released the next year. He spent the rest of the war in Paris writing, teaching, and taking part in the Resistance. After the liberation he gave up teaching and devoted himself more and more to politics. In 1951 he helped found the *Rassemblement Démocratique Revolutionnaire,* a political movement aimed at regrouping the parties of the left, for which he incurred the enmity of the French Communist Party. He helped found, and edited, *Les Temps Modernes,* an influential journal of opinion with a strong leftist orientation. During the 1950s he opposed the French government's attempt to retain control of Algeria; during the 1960s he bitterly opposed United States intervention in Vietnam. He was a strong advocate of Castro's regime in Cuba and of the student uprising in Paris in May 1968. In 1964 he was awarded the Nobel Prize for Literature but refused to accept it. He died in 1980.

developed fundamental ontology in a fashion that Heidegger repudiated. Despite a common phenomenological orientation and a shared conviction that the human state is one of fallenness, Heidegger and Sartre were animated by profoundly different motives and influenced by very different experiences.

In the first place, Sartre seems to have been impervious to that romantic "sentiment of being" that so strongly affected Heidegger's thought. For Sartre, Being does not alternatively reveal itself to us and conceal itself from us; it is ontologically neutral, a Parmenidean "one." For Heidegger, the central—indeed, the only—moral issue is how we face the knowledge that we are going to die. For Sartre, the only issue is our human situation in a world without God. What is such a world? What is such a person? What, above all, is such a person to do in such a world? In this respect Sartre is far closer to Kierkegaard than to Heidegger. His outlook is intensely personal: What do I do? But his answers to these existential questions are very different from Kierkegaard's. For Sartre, as for Nietzsche, Kierkegaard's leap of faith was an act of cowardice and surrender. One does not *find* an integrating focus and a center for one's life; one must *make* a focus and a center. In Sartre's view it is impossible even to begin to do this until one has purged oneself of the illusions that cloud most people's vision of themselves and of their world. To know the world for what it is, is to experience despair. But this desperate knowledge is a necessary prelude to action. As Orestes says in Sartre's play *The Flies,* "Human life begins on the other side of despair."

In the second place, whereas for Heidegger the question is whether we succeed in living continuously in the mood he calls anxiety, for Sartre the question is what we do after we have experienced anxiety. Sartre, that is to say, is by nature and temperament an activist; Heidegger is a recluse.[2] After his love affair with the Nazis, Heidegger increasingly withdrew to his solitary mountaintop in the Black Forest; after the war, Sartre plunged ever more deeply into the politics of the French left. On the one hand, he felt a deep sympathy with Marxism as a philosophy and he shared many of the political aims of communism, especially its goal of overthrowing bourgeois capitalism. On the other hand, it was difficult to reconcile his emphasis on the individual with Marxism's emphasis on the group, his assertion of human freedom with Marxism's assertion of determinism, his conviction that our fundamental problems are existential and therefore irradicable (that is, they arise from our human nature) with Marxism's view that they are socioeconomic and therefore that if the modes of production and exchange are sufficiently altered a utopia on earth is possible. These issues, which became increasingly central for Sartre, hardly entered Heidegger's consciousness. For the latter this present age is a dark age because Being has withdrawn itself from us; we can only wait patiently until Being again reveals itself to us. Sartre certainly agrees that we live in a dark age; his concern is with how we can overthrow the political and economic regimes that created and perpetuate this darkness, and

---

[2] It is hard to think that Sartre would have walked by on the other side of the road, like the Pharisee, when the Nazis' anti-Semitic laws began to affect one of his former colleagues to whom he owed a debt of gratitude. See p. 308, note 1.

how we can join forces with other revolutionaries without losing our integrity as free individuals.

So far, it may seem that Sartre's orientation, with its focus on existential and political problems, is very different from that of the phenomenological tradition. But though Sartre is a moralist, he is also, like the phenomenologists, an epistemologist. He too holds that reality consists, not in Kantian things-in-themselves, but in phenomena, in consciousnesses-of. And he agrees with the standard phenomenological doctrine that consciousnesses-of involve not only intentions but also intentional objects. Hence he shares the view, widespread among phenomenologists, that Husserl fell from grace and slipped into idealism.[3] According to Sartre, the ego is an intentional object among other intentional objects. In Husserlian language, it is on the noematic rather than the noetic side. All that is left on the noetic side is a pure, impersonal spontaneity, a wind blowing toward objects. Thus for Sartre consciousness is as transparent as it was for Russell. But whereas for Russell the transparency of consciousness meant that consciousness could be ignored, for Sartre the "nothingness" of consciousness both creates our existential dilemma and provides such means as exist for resolving it.

This discovery about consciousness was the starting point for both Sartre the phenomenologist and Sartre the existentialist. For the one, the transparency of consciousness excluded all those "syntheses" that Husserl had emphasized and thus led to an ontology very different from that of Husserl. For the other, the nothingness of consciousness meant that we are not imprisoned in a ready-made self but are free to become the self of our choice. Whereas the phenomenological method had appealed to Husserl because it seemed to reveal those apodeictic evidences that satisfy our thirst for certainty, the method appealed to Sartre because it seemed to reveal those harsh existential truths that every individual must face and overcome to be an authentic individual, reconciled to living with uncertainty.

In addition to Sartre the phenomenologist, Sartre the politician, and Sartre the existentialist, there is Sartre the literary artist. Other philosophers, of course, have had high literary skills—Plato and Nietzsche, for instance. And other philosophers have carried on a literary career more or less concurrently with a philosophical career—Hume and Russell, for instance. But the literary and philosophical writings of most thinkers are quite independent of each other. Generally philosophers give us only the end products of their thinking; it is necessary to reconstruct from the finished philosophical treatise (insofar as this is possible) the vision of the world and of humankind that was the impetus, the starting point, for this treatise. In studying Sartre we have the advantage of literary works that are intensely personal documents revealing from inside his own experiences of the world and also philosophical treatises that are relatively neutral and objective accounts (from outside, as it were) of these experiences.

Although the literary works cannot justify the truth-claim that they make for his vision, they can persuade the reader by the vividness of their presentation, by

[3] See p. 306.

their concreteness, and by the overwhelming conviction of the author that he has *seen* the truth. The philosophical works, making the same truth-claim, attempt to substantiate it by incorporating it in an ontology that has been worked out systematically. For this reason—quite apart from one's evaluation of the truth-claim he has made—Sartre is a most instructive philosopher to read. We shall begin our examination of Sartre with the vision of the human condition as presented in his novels, for judging by the popularity of his writings, this vision is shared by many people today. We shall then proceed, by way of his writings on phenomenological psychology, to his ontological formulation of the vision.

The Human Condition

What is the human condition as it is revealed when phenomenological observation strips away the curtain of words, and with it all our presuppositions, theories, and hypotheses? In *Nausea* Sartre presents a dramatic account of one such revelatory encounter with reality, presumably very close to what Sartre himself had experienced.[4]

> Everywhere, now, there are objects like this glass of beer on the table there. . . . I have been *avoiding* looking at this glass of beer for half an hour. I look above, below, right and left; but I don't want to see *it*. And I know very well that all these bachelors [who are sitting at other tables in the restaurant] can be of no help. . . . They could come and tap me on the shoulder and say, "Well, what's the matter with that glass of beer?" It's just like all the others. It's bevelled on the edges, has a handle. . . . I know all that, but I know there is something else. Almost nothing. But I can't explain what I see. To anyone. There: I am quietly slipping into the water's depths, towards fear.[a]

It is evident that Roquetin is performing—quite unwittingly, of course—what Husserl called phenomenological reduction. But note that whereas Husserl held that it requires long and arduous preparation, Sartre believes that people may happen on it quite by accident, in the midst of other activities, and with literally shocking results to their sense of reality. Further, what Roquetin experiences is quite different from Husserl's apodeictically certain essences. Who is correct? One feels that whereas Husserl merely talked about bracketing and never really left the natural standpoint, Roquetin-Sartre must have actually had the experience of losing the whole world of stable, useful, familiar things, with their

---

[4]The novel, which is written in the form of a diary, takes place in Bouville, a thinly disguised Le Havre, where Sartre had taught. It is fair to say that Antoine Roquetin, the protagonist, is a thinly disguised Sartre.

complex relations among themselves ("causes" and "effects") and relations with us as instrumentalities of our purposes. To lose this stable, familiar world would surely be terrifying and nauseating—anything but reassuring, as Husserl supposed.

THINGS

What has happened, as Roquetin says, is that "things have become divorced from their names." What he used to see as he sat on a moving streetcar was (say) a house at the end of the street. Because he "knew" that it was a house, it only "seemed" to grow larger as the car advanced down the street. And because he knew that it was built of yellow bricks it only seemed in a particular light to be blue. But all this "knowing" depended on pinning down and fixing the fleeting consciousnesses-of by means of the name "house." Once they became divorced from the name everything changed: what before he had taken as real ("stationary yellow house") was suddenly revealed to be a fiction, a construction, a projection on the appearances that actually displayed themselves to him as the car moved down the street; what before he had believed to be "mere" appearances ("The house looks bluish in this light, but I know it is really yellow") are revealed to be, quite literally, all that there is—in other words, reality.

> Bluish objects pass the windows . . . blue this great yellow brick house advancing uncertainly, trembling, suddenly stopping and taking a nose dive. . . . [It] starts up again, it leaps against the windows. . . . It rises, crushing. . . . It slides along the car brushing past it. . . . Suddenly it is no longer there, it has stayed behind. . . .
>
> I lean my hand on the seat but pull it back hurriedly: it exists. This thing I'm sitting on, leaning my hand on, is called a seat. They make it purposely for people to sit on, they took leather, springs and cloth, they went to work with the idea of making a seat and when they finished, *that* was what they had made. . . . I murmur: "It's a seat," a little like an exorcism. But the word stays on my lips: it refuses to go and put itself on the thing. It stays what it is, with its red plush, thousands of little red paws in the air, all still, little dead paws. This enormous belly turned upward, bleeding, inflated . . . is not a seat. It could just as well be a dead donkey. . . . It seems ridiculous to call them seats or to say anything at all about them; I am in the midst of things, nameless things. Alone, without words, defenseless, they surround me, are beneath me, behind me, above me. They demand nothing, they don't impose themselves: they are there.[b]

In other words, that this plush red expanse is a streetcar seat is Roquetin's interpretation—an interpretation that imports an immense amount to the experience itself. It this sounds like Nietzsche, it is like Nietzsche, for Roquetin has made the same discovery that Nietzsche the classical philologist made—that there is no original text.

To illustrate this discovery, let us take another example connected with Roquetin. The Marquis of Rollebon, whose biography Roquetin is writing, is as inaccessible as any long-lost classical text, and what one thinks of as ascertaining the facts, as *re*constructing the life of this man, is sheerly constructing it. It is like writing a novel. After working for years on the life of the Marquis, Roquetin has accumulated an immense amount of material—letters, memoirs, secret reports, police reports. He knows more about Rollebon than he knows about any living person. But he comes to realize that he knows nothing at all about him. It is not just a question, he sees, of not being personally acquainted with Rollebon. All the testimony he possesses was written down by people who were personally acquainted with Rollebon. Had Roquetin himself known the Marquis, his knowledge of him would still have been from outside; it would have been only one more "report" to be added to the others.

> What is lacking in all this testimony is firmness and consistency. [The reports] do not contradict each other, neither do they agree with each other; they do not seem to be about the same person. . . .
>
> I am beginning to believe that nothing can ever be proved. These are honest hypotheses . . . but I sense so definitely that they come from me, and that they are simply a way of unifying my own knowledge. Not a glimmer comes from Rollebon's side. Slow, lazy, sulky, the facts adapt themselves to the rigour of the order I wish to give them; but it remains outside of them.[c]

THE SELF

The problem is not merely that the personality of others is inaccessible; the very notion of personality is just another product of words. Just as seathood was only an order, a pattern, that Roquetin imposed on his experience of red plushness in order to unify it, so the enduring personhood he has attributed to Rollebon is an order he imposed on those "sulky" reports. And, as Roquetin realizes, what applies to Rollebon applies equally to Roquetin himself; he too exists only in a momentary present. This is a truth that dawns on him when, after having interrupted his writing for a moment, he tries to resume.

> But as my eyes fell on the pad of white sheets, I was struck by its look and I stayed, pen raised, studying this dazzling paper: so hard and far seeing, so present. The letters I had just inscribed on it were not even dry yet and already they belonged to the past.
>
> "Care had been taken to spread the most sinister rumours. . . ." I had thought out this sentence, at first it had been a small part of myself. Now it was inscribed on the paper, it took sides against me. I didn't recognize it any more. I couldn't conceive it again. It was there, in front of me; in vain for me to trace some sign of its origin. Anyone could have written it. But *I* . . . *I* wasn't sure I wrote it. The letters glistened no

longer, they were dry. That had disappeared too; nothing was left but their ephemeral spark.[d]

Roquetin sees that the self he has attributed to himself—the self who is a historian, who has written other monographs, who has spent years on this biography of Rollebon—is a construction, like the construction that he calls "Rollebon." This self is something he has fashioned out of reports, other people's outside views of him, like his outside views of Rollebon. Stripping away all these interpretations, he is left only with fleeting, fugitive consciousnesses-of. In them he finds intentional objects in appalling abundance, including of course those intentional objects called memories. But he finds no enduring "I think," no transcendental ego, no synthesizing activities. Beyond the intentional objects there is only a thin transparency, a distance, a nothingness.

> Now when I say, "I," it seems hollow to me. I can't manage to feel myself very well. . . . And just what is Antoine Roquetin? An abstraction. A pale reflection of myself wavers in my consciousness. Antoine Roquetin . . . and suddenly the "I" pales, pales, and fades out.
>
> Lucid, static, forlorn, consciousness is walled-up; it perpetuates itself. Nobody lives there any more. A little while ago someone said "me," said *my* consciousness. Who? Outside there were streets, alive with known smells and colours. Now nothing is left but anonymous walls, anonymous consciousness. This is what there is: walls, and between the walls, a small transparency, alive and impersonal. . . . Consciousness . . . is conscious of being superfluous. It dilutes, scatters itself, tries to lose itself on the brown wall, along the lamp-post or down there in the evening mist. But it *never* forgets itself. That is its lot.[e]

The world as we have known it—a world of substantival Cartesian egos and subtantival Cartesian objects—has now disappeared. According to Sartre there is only the disgusting, overflowing abundance of existence, plus that transparent nothingness we call "consciousness" that separates us from this abundance. That is all. Words are simply devices by which we protect ourselves from seeing the world as it is; and though all words are therefore inadequate for describing it as it is, if we have to use any word at all, the best one is "absurd."

> Never until these last few days, had I understood the meaning of existence. . . . And then all of a sudden, there it was, clear as day: existence had suddenly unveiled itself. It had lost the harmless look of an abstract category: it was the very paste of things, this root [at the time Roquetin happened to be sitting in a public garden, looking at the roots of a tree] was kneaded into existence. Or rather the root, the park gates, the bench, the sparse grass, all that had vanished: the diversity of things, their individuality, were only an appearance, a veneer. This veneer had melted, leaving soft monstrous masses, all in disorder—naked, in a frightful, obscene nakedness. . . .

The word absurdity is coming to life under my pen; a little while ago, in the garden, I couldn't find it, but neither was I looking for it, I didn't need it: I thought without words, *on* things, *with* things. . . . Without formulating anything clearly, I understood that I had found the key to Existence, the key to my Nausea, to my own life. In fact, all that I could grasp beyond that returns to this fundamental absurdity. Absurdity: another word; I struggle against words; down there I touched the thing. But I wanted to fix the absolute character of this absurdity here. A movement, an event, in the tiny coloured world of men is only relatively absurd: by relation to the accompanying circumstances. A madman's ravings, for example, are absurd in relation to the situation in which he finds himself, but not in relation to his delirium. But a little while ago I made an experiment with the absolute or the absurd. This root—there was nothing in relation to which it was [not] absurd. Oh, how can I put it in words? Absurd: in relation to the stones, the tufts of yellow grass, the dry mud, the tree, the sky, the green benches. Absurd, irreducible; nothing—not even a profound, secret upheaval of nature—could explain it. . . . The world of explanations and reasons is not the world of existence. A circle is not absurd, it is clearly explained by the rotation of a straight segment around one of its extremities. But neither does a circle exist. This root, on the other hand, existed in such a way that I could not explain it. . . . This root, with its colour, shape, its congealed movement, was . . . below all explanation.[f]

This passage illustrates that the most unlikely people can be bedfellows: Roquetin-Sartre's world is very similar to Hume's. Everything is loose and separate from everything else. There is no reason why the world might be different in whole or in part from what it happens to be, for any reason to the contrary—for reasons belong to one realm and existence to another. The attempt made by philosophers such as Whitehead to answer Hume by showing that there is, after all, a rationale in things was wholly rejected by Sartre. He explicitly adopted Hume's radical distinction between "relations of ideas" and "matters of fact," a distinction from which all the Humean conclusions follow. The end of the passage just quoted repeats Hume's reasoning almost verbatim: we see why every point on the circumference of a circle is equidistant from its center, for this property follows logically from the definition of a circle. A circle therefore is not absurd, but a circle does not exist. On the other hand, relations between existing things—say, between being a root and being pink under a dark outer surface—are sheerly accidental. Since all relations among matters of fact ("existence") could be otherwise, existence is absurd.

Hume would have agreed. But far from finding this "obscene" (as Sartre did), he was completely composed.

Most fortunately it happens, that since reason is incapable of dispelling these clouds, nature herself suffices to that purpose, and cures

me of this philosophical melancholy and delirium. . . . I dine, I play a
game of backgammon, I converse, and am merry with my friends; and
when after three or four hours' amusement, I would return to these
speculations, they appear so cold, and strain'd, and ridiculous, that I
cannot find in my heart to enter them any further.

Here then I find myself absolutely and necessarily determin'd to live,
and talk, and act like other people in the common affairs of life.[g]

How are we to account for these astonishingly different responses to what both
Hume and Sartre agreed is the situation in which we find ourselves? This divergence is in part caused by their differing attitudes toward certainty. Sartre renounced it with regret; Hume renounced it willingly enough: "Experience is a
principle which instructs me in the several conjunctions of objects for the past."
In Hume's view, although experience may on occasion lead one astray in the future, it is nonetheless a sufficiently reliable guide. Their differing attitudes toward
what Husserl called the natural standpoint also contributed to the divergence of
their responses. For Hume "nature" and "natural" were still good words; he wrote
off deviant standpoints as "melancholy and delirium." He would have regarded
Roquetin as a psychotic personality desperately in need of clinical help, a man
whose vision of "obscene abundance" should not be taken seriously. In contrast,
the intervening century of constructivistic thinking led Sartre to conclude that the
natural standpoint is simply a reflection of bourgeois mentality, one of the many
devices that people use "to veil the enormous absurdity of their existence."[h] Accordingly, in his view Hume's decision to "act like other people in the common
affairs of life" was not prudence and good sense but an escape, an attempt to
avoid the painful knowledge of what the world really is. To Sartre this is how most
people have always dealt with their existential problems.

They have dragged out their life in stupor, and semisleep, they have
married hastily, out of impatience, they have made children at random.
They have met other men in cafés, at weddings and funerals. Sometimes, caught in the tide, they have struggled against it without understanding what was happening to them. . . . And then, around forty, they
christen their small obstinacies and a few proverbs with the name of experience;[5] they begin to simulate slot machines: put a coin in the left-
hand slot and you get tales wrapped in silver paper; put a coin in the
slot on the right and you get precious bits of advice that stick to your
teeth like caramels.[i]

At one point Roquetin visits the picture gallery where the portraits of local no-
tables are hung, the men who had "made Bouville the best equipped port in
France for unloading coal and wood." Here is a description of the portrait of Jean
Pacôme.

[5] [So much for experience as the "principle which instructs me"—AUTHORS.]

The slightest doubt had never crossed those magnificent grey eyes. Pacôme had never made a mistake. He had always done his duty, all his duty, his duty as son, husband, father, leader. He had never weakened in his demands for his due: as a child, the right to be well brought up, in a united family, the right to inherit a spotless name, a prosperous business; as a husband, the right to be cared for, surrounded with tender affection; as a father, the right to be venerated; as a leader, the right to be obeyed without a murmur. . . . He never told himself he was happy, and while he was enjoying himself he must have done so with moderation. . . . Thus pleasure itself, also becoming a right, lost its aggressive futility. On the left, a little above his bluish-grey hair, I noticed a shelf of books. The bindings were handsome; they were surely classics. Every evening before going to sleep, Pacôme undoubtedly read over a few pages of "his old Montaigne" or one of Horace's odes in the Latin text. Sometimes, too, he must have read a contemporary work to keep up to date.

He had never looked any further into himself; he was a leader.ʲ

Pacôme was a leader because he was perceived by other people as a leader; he had rights because other people accorded him rights. He never had to face any really moral decision; at every critical point he knew what to do, for this was decided for him in advance by society, which decreed what was expected of men of his class and position. He was in fact not a man but a social type. In contrast to people like Pacôme there are a few authentic individuals who have seen through the social self and who have surmounted the moral crisis that this revelation entails; they have experienced doubt and have suffered anguish in their attempt to discover who they are and what they ought to do.

The anguish is suffered because, when one has seen through the social self, one does not find, neatly tucked away beneath it and waiting to take over, an authentic self—one finds neither the Christian's immortal soul, nor Descartes's substantival *cogito,* nor Husserl's transcendental ego. One finds only the nothingness that is consciousness. This is the discovery of phenomenology as Sartre practiced it; this is the discovery that sets the existential problem as Sartre experienced it.

FREEDOM IN AN ABSURD WORLD

How is it possible under these circumstances to be an authentic self at all? How can nothingness be anything?

Sartre's answer is that the question is badly posed. Since the only self that one can be is the social self, one cannot *be* an authentic self at all. Authenticity is not a category of being; it is a category of acting, of becoming. A person is an authentic self in and through choices made on his or her own initiative, without adopting other people's standards or following their advice. By revealing that we do not "have" a nature and by releasing us from the straitjacket of the social self (and of course the metaphysical self), phenomenology frees us to become anything we choose. It is only nothingness that is free to be anything and everything.

But this perfect freedom is a heavy burden. To see through the social self is to become free to make an authentic self. Yet at the same time it is to lose the rationale for choosing among possible selves. In a world that is intrinsically absurd there is no *reason* for doing any one thing rather than another. Why not, then, do whatever enters one's head, providing only that it is sufficiently idiosyncratic not to be derived from one's social role? Why not indeed? As Roquetin sits in a restaurant eating dinner, he reflects on this idea.

> I feel as though I could do anything. For example, stab this cheese knife into [another diner's] eye. After that, all these people would trample me and kick my teeth out. But that isn't what stops me: a taste of blood in the mouth instead of this taste of cheese makes no difference to me.[k]

What stops Roquetin is the realization that he would only be playing another role—perhaps the role of the phenomenological observer or that of the despairing existentialist. Thus he would not achieve authenticity; or if he did momentarily achieve it he would promptly lose it. He still would be unable to accept himself.

Roquetin never finds a way of resolving this dilemma. At the end of the novel Sartre suggests, in a passage reminiscent of Nietzsche in his account of overman as a creative artist, that the solution may be "a book, a novel." But he puts this idea forward very tentatively; and if we are correct in identifying Sartre with Roquetin he *had* to be tentative, for *Nausea* was itself the novel that, in *Nausea,* is just about to be begun. Sartre could not know until the book was finished whether writing it would "save" Roquetin. As it turned out, it did not. Though Sartre continued to write novels and plays, he apparently came to feel that literary production was too detached a relation to the world. As involvement in the world—*engagement*—proved to be necessary in Sartre's own life, as he himself became more involved in politics, the characters in his later novels began to seek the solution for their existential problems in commitment rather than in "arid purity."

For instance, one of the chief characters of *The Reprieve,* Mathieu Delarue, is presented as a detached man of the Roquetin type who finds it impossible to commit himself to anything—to his mistress, to politics,[6] to the Second World War (or, alternatively, to protest against the war). Like Roquetin, Mathieu eventually comes to realize that he is completely free—free from obligations public and private, free from constraints of law or custom. And like Roquetin he experiences this freedom as anguish. What is he to do with his freedom? How can Mathieu become an authentic self now that he is freed from that social self in which he had

---

[6] Mathieu's friend Brunet constantly urges him to join the Communist Party, which Mathieu resists to his friend's disgust. But though Brunet is a "dedicated" Communist, he has by no means achieved existential commitment; he has simply accepted communism, much as Jean Pacôme had accepted the bourgeois culture in which he had been brought up.

been so long restrained? Late one night, after the outbreak of the war and several days after he should have reported for active duty, Mathieu almost reaches a decision that would indeed be definitive: to kill himself.

> Outside. Everything is outside. . . . Inside, nothing, not even a puff of smoke, there is no *inside,* there is nothing. Myself: nothing. I am free, he said to himself, and his mouth was dry.
>
> Halfway across the Pont-Neuf he stopped and began to laugh: liberty—I sought it far away; it was so near that I couldn't touch it, that I can't touch it; it is, in fact, myself. I am my own freedom. He had hoped that one day he would be filled with joy, transfixed by a lightning flash. But there was . . . only a sense of desolation, . . . an anguish. . . . Outside the world, outside the past, outside myself: freedom is exile, and I am condemned to be free.
>
> He walked on a few steps, stopped again, sat down on the parapet, and watched the water flowing past. What shall I do with all this freedom? What shall I do with myself? . . . Shall I take the train? What did it matter?—go or stay, or run away—acts of that kind would not call his freedom into play. And yet he must risk that freedom. He clutched the stone with both hands and leaned over the water. A plunge, and the water would engulf him, his freedom would be transmuted into water. Rest at last—and why not? This obscure suicide would *also* be an absolute, a law, a choice, and a morality. . . . Deep down within him he felt his heart throbbing wildly; one gesture, the mere unclasping of his hands and *I would have been* Mathieu. . . . Suddenly he *decided* not to do it. He decided: it shall merely be a trial. Then he was again upon his feet and walking on, gliding over the crest of a dead star. Next time, perhaps.[1]

The "next time" comes the following summer, 1940. The French army, Mathieu now included, is retreating in total confusion; Pétain is about to surrender unconditionally; the war is over. In these circumstances, Mathieu and several other soldiers suddenly decide to occupy the belfry of a village church and to attack a German column as it advances. On any utilitarian calculation the decision is obviously absurd; the men are "unbalanced." They will not only lose their own lives; they will cause great suffering for the villagers, who are their compatriots and to whom they are indebted for hospitality. Against these heavy costs they can chalk up only the killing (possibly) of a few Germans who have done them no personal harm. They will not alter the course of events in the slightest degree, or delay the German army.

Mathieu's "project" has become simply to hold out for fifteen minutes, but this is the first project to which he has ever been utterly committed.

> He made his way to the parapet and stood there firing. . . . Each one of his shots wiped out some ancient scruple. One for Lola, whom I

dared not rob, one for Marcelle, whom I ought to have ditched, one for Odette, whom I didn't want to screw. This for the books I never dared to write, this for the journeys I never made, this for everybody in general whom I wanted to hate and tried to understand. He fired, and the tables of the law crashed about him—Thou shalt love thy neighbor as thyself—bang! in that bastard's face—Thou shalt not kill—bang! at that scarecrow opposite. He was firing on his fellow men, on Virtue, on the whole world: Liberty is Terror. . . . He looked at his watch; fourteen minutes and thirty seconds. Nothing more to ask of fate now except one half-minute, just time enough to fire at that smart officer, at all the Beauty of the Earth, at the street, at the flowers, at the gardens, at everything he had loved. Beauty dived downwards obscenely, and Mathieu went on firing. He fired; he was cleansed, he was all-powerful, he was free.

Fifteen minutes.[m]

This, then, is Sartre's anguished discovery of our dreadful freedom in an absurd world. For a formal "account" of these matters, let us turn from the literary works to Sartre's psychological and philosophical writings, in which the nature of the self and the nature of its world are systematically worked out. We shall begin with his account of consciousness, the key concept both for his ontology and for his ethics.

Consciousness and Consciousness of Self

Sartre's method is empirical in the phenomenological sense. That is, he proposes to describe consciousness as it is, without allowing any metaphysical assumptions or Nietzschean interpretations to affect the description. This of course is exactly what Husserl had set out to do, but he went astray in supposing that some kind of synthesizing "I think" is necessary to make possible the multitude of consciousnesses-of. Without it, Husserl thought, there would be no unity by virtue of which all these consciousnesses-of are one's own. But according to Sartre every consciousness already contains self-consciousness. Hence Husserl's transcendental ego is unnecessary—it "has no *raison d'être.*"

But, in addition, this superfluous *I* would be a hindrance. If it existed it would tear consciousness from itself; it would divide consciousness; it would slide into every consciousness like an opaque blade. Indeed, the existence of consciousness is an absolute because consciousness is consciousness of itself. This is to say that the type of existence of consciousness is to be consciousness of itself. And consciousness is aware of itself *in so far as it is consciousness of a transcendent object.* All is

> therefore clear and lucid in consciousness: the object with its charac-
> teristic opacity is before consciousness, but consciousness is purely and
> simply consciousness of being consciousness of that object. This is the
> law of its existence.[n]

In other words, consciousness of self (self-consciousness) and consciousness
of objects are not different kinds of consciousness. Consciousness is a unique type
of existence: every consciousness of an object is *also* a consciousness of self. This
can be shown empirically by the following example. When I am intensely interested in what I am doing—say, in reading an exciting novel—I never think of myself as reading; I am fully occupied with the narrative. But if, after I have put the
book aside, someone asks me what I have been doing, I reply without hesitation,
"I was reading a book." Where does this knowledge come from? Careful introspection reveals that no "I" was actually present in my consciousness while I was
reading the book. Nevertheless I now know that at that time I was reading. Further, the "I" that is so seldom present is always available, on call. This too is shown
by introspection: I can at any time recall either *what* I experienced on a particular occasion in the past or the fact that it was *I* who experienced it.

> If, for example, I want to remember a certain landscape perceived
> yesterday from the train, it is possible for me to bring back the mem-
> ory of that landscape as such. But I can also recollect that *I* was seeing
> that landscape. . . . In other words, I can always perform any recollec-
> tion whatsoever in the personal mode, and at once the *I* appears.[o]

UNREFLECTED AND REFLECTIVE CONSCIOUSNESS

Here then is an apparent paradox—an "I" that is not present in consciousness
but that can nonetheless be brought into consciousness at will. How can the paradox be resolved? The solution is to distinguish between two *levels* of consciousness rather than to distinguish—as many philosophers in the past, even Husserl,
had done—between two *types* of consciousness. The two traditional types were,
of course, consciousness of objects and self-consciousness. Sartre's two levels are
"unreflected consciousness" and "reflective consciousness." At *both* levels consciousness is at once consciousness of objects and consciousness of self. This
distinction simply makes explicit Brentano's discovery of intentionality: every
consciousness involves both an intention and an intentional object. The difference
between the two levels is simply that at the unreflected level the self-conscious aspect of the consciousness is not "positional." That is, it is not an object in its own
field. At the reflective level, it is.

To repeat, all consciousness is consciousness of itself; that this is true follows
from the nature of consciousness's unique kind of existence. But under ordinary
circumstances, as when I am reading or looking out the train window, "this consciousness of consciousness is not *positional,* which is to say that consciousness
is not for itself its own object."[p] When, later on, I recall that it was I who was

reading or who saw that particular landscape, this consciousness of consciousness becomes positional in a second consciousness, just as the book or the landscape had been positional in the first consciousness. Meanwhile, of course, the second consciousness (the reflecting consciousness) contains its own nonpositional consciousness of consciousness.

> There is an indissoluble unity of the reflecting consciousness and the reflected consciousness (to the point that the reflecting consciousness could not exist without the reflected consciousness). But the fact remains that we are in the presence of a synthesis of two consciousnesses, one of which is conscious *of* the other. Thus the essential principle of phenomenology, "all consciousness is consciousness *of* something,"[7] is preserved. Now, my reflecting consciousness does not take itself for an object. . . . What it affirms concerns the reflected consciousness. Insofar as my reflecting consciousness is consciousness of itself, it is *nonpositional* consciousness. It becomes positional only by directing upon the reflected consciousness which itself was not a positional consciousness of itself before being reflected. Thus the consciousness which says *I Think* is precisely not the consciousness which thinks. Or rather it is not *its own* thought which it posits by this thetic act. . . . All reflecting consciousness is, indeed, in itself unreflected, and a new act of the third degree is necessary in order to posit it. [But] there is no infinite regress here, since a consciousness has no need at all of a reflecting consciousness in order to be conscious of itself. It simply does not posit itself as an object.[q]

THE TRANSCENDENT EGO

The upshot is that since there is no transcendental ego the only ego that exists is transcendent,[8] that is, an object that exists in the world and that is encountered there, along with other objects. Let us, then, consider the ego as it is revealed in phenomenological intuition along with such objects as tables, chairs, and trees. Of course, these objects are positional in unreflected consciousness. To describe the ego involves moving from this unreflected level, where consciousness is nonpositional, to the reflective level, where it becomes positional.

Consider, for instance, an unreflected consciousness of Peter being hated. I can turn my reflective consciousness on this hatred, in which case there is now a consciousness that it is I who hate Peter. But if I scrutinize the experiential field carefully, what is in my consciousness at this moment is my reflective awareness

---

[7][Sartre is quoting Husserl, of course—AUTHORS.]

[8]"Transcendental" is used by Sartre to designate what is outside consciousness; "transcendent" characterizes an object that is within consciousness but not wholly within it at any one time. Thus Sartre's criticism of Husserl can be rephrased by saying that Husserl mistakenly supposed the ego to be transcendental, whereas in fact it is transcendent.

that I am angry with Peter, or that I am disgusted with Peter. Unlike anger or disgust, hatred is a state that "implicates" the past and the future; if I refused to implicate the future I could not possibly hate Peter now. But I *do* experience hatred of Peter; therefore I do implicate the future. Hence consciousness is not a matter of instantaneous, encapsulated awarenesses. My hatred of Peter is

> given *in* and *by* each movement of disgust, of repugnance, and of anger, but at the same time it is *not* any of them. My hatred escapes from each of them by affirming permanence. . . . It overflows the instantaneousness of consciousness. . . . Hatred, then, is a transcendent object. Each *Erlebnis* reveals it as a whole, but at the same time the *Erlebnis* is a profile, a projection (an *Abschattung*). Hatred is credit for an infinity of angry or repulsed consciousness in the past and in the future. It is the transcendent unity of this infinity of consciousness. Thus, to say "I hate" or "I love" on the occasion of a particular consciousness of attraction or repugnance is to effect a veritable passage to infinity, rather analogous to that which we effect when we perceive *an* inkstand, or *the blue* of the blotter.[r]

In Sartre's view the ego (or more precisely, the *me*) stands in relation to a state like hatred in much the same way that the state of hatred stands to the instantaneous anger or disgust that I now feel. That is, the ego is a transcendent object that appears through the state of hatred but is not limited to that state, just as the state of hatred appears through the momentary repugnance but is not limited to that repugnance. This is why the ego is hard to find: usually we look for it *in* or *behind* the states, but in fact it is transcendent to them. For the most part we think of the ego as a kind of box (a Cartesian substance) that "contains" or "supports" psychic phenomena. But the ego

> is nothing outside of the concrete totality of states and actions it supports. Undoubtedly it is transcendent to all the states which it unifies, but not as an abstract X whose mission is only to unify: rather, it is the infinite totality of states and of actions which is never reducible to *an* action or to *a* state.[s]

NO PRIVILEGED ACCESS TO THE EGO

From this account of the ego some important conclusions follow. In the first place, no one has any special, or privileged, access to his or her own ego. Indeed,

> from this point of view my emotions and my states, my ego itself, cease to be my exclusive property. To be precise: up to now a radical distinction has been made between the objectivity of a spatio-temporal thing or of an external truth, and the subjectivity of psychical "states." It seemed as if the subject had a privileged status with respect to his own

states. When two men, according to this conception, talk about the same chair, they really are talking about the *same* thing. This chair which one takes hold of and lifts is *the same* as the chair which the other sees. There is not merely a correspondence of images; there is only one object. But it seemed that when Paul tried to understand a psychical state of Peter, he could not *reach* this state, the intuitive apprehension of which belonged only to Peter. . . . Psychological understanding occurred by analogy. Phenomenology has come to teach us that *states* are objects, that an emotion as such (a love or a hatred) is a transcendent object and cannot shrink into the interior unity of a "consciousness." Consequently, if Paul and Peter both speak of Peter's love, for example, it is no longer true that the one speaks blindly and by analogy of that which the other apprehends in full. They speak of the same thing. Doubtless they apprehend it by different procedures, but these procedures may be equally intuitional. And Peter's emotion is no more *certain* for Peter than for Paul. . . . There is no longer anything "impenetrable" about Peter; unless it is his very consciousness. But his consciousness is *radically* impenetrable. We mean that it is not only refractory to intuition, but to thought.[t]

That Peter's hatred (or love) is as accessible to Paul as it is to Peter himself follows directly from the nature of objects. Objects, whether egos or chairs, are present in intuition, but they are never wholly present in any one intuition or in any finite set of intuitions. If, for instance, Peter and Paul see a chair, it is indubitably the case that they have seen (had the experience of) a chair; but it is not indubitably the case that it was a chair that they saw, for the chair was not wholly present in this momentary experience. Only a "profile" was present, and what appeared in this profile may have been a hallucination, not a physical chair. Similarly, Peter and Paul may both experience Peter's anger. But this anger is a profile, and the psychic state that is appearing in it may not be hatred. Peter may be as mistaken as Paul about what psychic state is appearing in Peter's present anger.

The transcendent totality [that is, the ego] participates in the questionable character of all transcendence. This is to say that everything given to us by our intuitions of the ego is always given as capable of being contradicted by subsequent intuitions. For example, I can see clearly that I am ill-tempered, jealous, etc., and nevertheless I may be mistaken. In other words, I may deceive myself in thinking that I have *such a me*. . . . This questionable character of my ego—or even the intuitional error that I commit—does not signify that I have the *true me* which I am unaware of, but only that intended ego has in itself the character of dubitability (in certain cases, the character of falsehood).[u]

Thus Sartre's conclusion is that states of mind are no more and no less dubitable, and no more and no less accessible, than are any other objects. It is interesting to note that Wittgenstein reached this same conclusion, but by a very different route—by what was in effect an application of Carnap's Principle of Tolerance. For Wittgenstein (and for Carnap) it is not a question of what is really dubitable or how much is really accessible. It is simply a question of how we use the terms "dubitable" and "accessible"—and also, of course, the term "really." That is, it is a question not of ontology but of what language we choose to use and for what purpose.[9]

The second major conclusion that follows from Sartre's account of the ego as a transcendent object is that it is unknowable. This is because "the only method for knowing" any object (the chair, for instance) "is observation, approximation, anticipation, experience." But whereas these methods are adequate for knowing spatiotemporal objects such as chairs and planets, they are unsuitable for knowing the ego, which is an "intimate" object. The chair and the planet stay over there, far enough away for us to be able to get a good look at them. But the ego

is too much present for one to succeed in taking a truly external viewpoint on it. If we step back for vantage the *me* accompanies us in this withdrawal. It is infinitely near, and I cannot circle around it. Am I an idler or a hard worker? I shall doubtless come to a decision if I consult those who know me and get their opinion. Or again, I can collect facts concerning myself and try to interpret them *as objectively as if it were a question about someone else.* But it would be useless to address myself directly to the *me,* and to try to benefit from its intimacy in order to know it. For it is the *me,* on the contrary, which bars our way. Thus, "really to know oneself" is inevitably to take toward oneself the point of view of others, that is to say, a point of view which is necessarily false. And all those who have tried to know themselves will admit that this introspective attempt shows itself from the start as an effort to reconstitute from detached pieces, from isolated fragments, what is originally given *all at once,* at a stroke. Also, the intuition of the ego is a constantly gulling mirage, for it simultaneously yields everything and yields nothing. How could it be otherwise, moreover, since the ego is not the real totality of consciousness (such a totality would be a contradiction, like any infinite unity enacted), but the *ideal* unity of all the states and actions?[v]

Obviously Sartre is describing, in the neutral and objective language of phenomenological psychology, the truth that nauseated Roquetin when he actually encountered it. Having been brought up to believe in some sort of continuing self-identical ego that "inhabits" all of his consciousness, and by inhabiting them makes them his, Roquetin was inexpressibly shocked to discover that this inhabitant does not exist—to discover, first, that what exists (to put Roquetin's discovery in the language of phenomenological psychology) are only states and qualities (for example, the state of being an idler, the state of being a hater) and, second, that these states are not "inner" or directly accessible but only reconstituted by means of observation and inference.

SPONTANEITY

But what about the sense each of us has of generating our states and qualities? If, as it seems to me, I create my states spontaneously, my self is not merely social, not merely reconstituted by what I observe and by what people tell me about myself. Sartre would say in reply that it is necessary to distinguish between true spontaneity and pseudospontaneity.

> Everyone, by consulting the results of his intuition, can observe that the ego is given as producing its states. . . .
>
> We begin therefore with this undeniable fact: each new state is fastened directly (or indirectly, by the quality) to the ego, as to its origin. This mode of creation is indeed a creation *ex nihilo,* in the sense that the state is not given as having formerly been in the *me.* . . . The ego is the creator of its states and sustains its qualities in existence by a sort of preserving spontaneity. . . . It would be interesting to study the diverse types of progression from the ego to its states. Most of the time, the progression involved is magical. At other times it may be rational (in the case of reflective will, for example). But always there is a ground of unintelligibility. . . .
>
> But this spontaneity must not be confused with the spontaneity of consciousness. Indeed, the ego, being an object, is *passive.* It is a question, therefore, of a pseudo-spontaneity which is suitably symbolized by the spurting of a spring, a geyser, etc. This is to say that we are dealing here with a semblance only. Genuine spontaneity must be perfectly clear: it *is* what it produces and can be nothing else.[w]

Sartre's point here is that although I attribute spontaneity to myself (to the personal me), the only true spontaneity is absolutely impersonal. It cannot be attributed to anything; it simply occurs. Each consciousness is a totally new, totally fresh existence that simply emerges out of nothing; it has no real connection—causal, logical, or moral—with anything that has gone before or with anything that will come after. Each consciousness, then, is quite literally absurd. But how is it that this pure impersonal spontaneity comes to be experienced as personal?

As an example, consider some occasion of there being an experience of hatred of Peter. This hatred of Peter is a consciousness that emerges ex nihilo and at the unreflected level. Once it has emerged, however, it can be reflected on; and, if reflected on, I attribute it to my ego: it is I who hate Peter. This attribution is correct. The hatred of Peter belongs to my ego in the sense that, as has been seen, reflection reveals the self-consciousness that has been present all the time, but has not yet been posited, in this hatred of Peter. But though this hatred of Peter belongs to my ego, my ego has not *produced* it, in spite of appearances to the contrary. Indeed, far from producing this hatred, my ego (my social me) is itself being constituted in this and other acts of reflection. This production actually occurs in a direction contrary to that in which it seems to occur. In reality, consciousnesses are first; they emerge out of nothing with an impersonal spontaneity. Then in acts of reflection the ego is constituted. Finally, after the ego is constituted,

> consciousness projects its own spontaneity into the ego-object in order to confer on the ego the creative power which is absolutely necessary to it. But this spontaneity, *represented* and *hypostatized* in an object, becomes a degraded and bastard spontaneity, which magically preserves its creative power even while becoming passive. Whence the profound irrationality of the notion of an ego.[x]

But though the ego is irrational, it serves a very useful purpose; attribution of production to the ego protects us from realizing the true state of affairs. "Perhaps the essential role of the ego is to mask from consciousness its very spontaneity."[y]

Here again Sartre is describing in the language of phenomenological theory the dreadful, total freedom that Roquetin experienced when he inadvertently saw through the mask. It follows from this absolutely spontaneous and impersonal generation of consciousness that at any moment each of us could be totally different from what he or she is now. Thus it is no good to think complacently, as I read in the newspaper about some vicious crime. "*I* could never do that!" I *could,* and I might. The social self—that is, the only self that I "am"—is but a construction, a "reconstitution," from past accumulations of consciousness; every new consciousness is a totally new existence without connection with this past accumulation. There are, then, no bounds or limits—either psychological or ontological—to what I may become. As Sartre remarks (note the difference in tone from the cry of anguish in the novels),

> there is something distressing for each of us, to catch in the act this tireless creation of existence of which *we* are not the creators. At this level man has the impression of ceaselessly escaping from himself, of overflowing himself, of being surprised by riches which are always unexpected. . . . It seems to us that this monstrous spontaneity is at the origin of numerous psychasthenic ailments. Consciousness is frightened by its own spontaneity. . . . This is clearly seen in an example from Janet. A young bride was in terror, when her husband left her alone, of sitting at the window and summoning the passers-by like a prostitute. Nothing in her education, in her past, nor in her character could serve as an explanation of such a fear. . . . She found herself monstrously free, and this vertiginous freedom appeared to her *at the opportunity* for this action which she was afraid of doing. But this vertigo

is comprehensible only if consciousness suddenly appeared to itself as infinitely overflowing in its possibilities the *I* which ordinarily serves as its unity.[z]

We have now reached, by means of a psychological analysis, the question posed in the novels: "What shall I do?" That is, given my total freedom to become anything (as revealed through phenomenological analysis), what shall I become? Given the lack of psychological or ontological limits on what I *can* become, are there any moral limits on what I *may* become? Before examining this moral dilemma, it will be necessary to discuss briefly Sartre's ontology. What light does an examination of the nature of being throw on the human condition?

Sartre's Ontology

Ontology, as Sartre understands it, is the science of being. It is distinguished from metaphysics, which has traditionally been regarded as the science of being, first, in that it is purely descriptive, and second, in that it rejects things-in-themselves and takes its stand on phenomena. Thus Sartre's ontology eliminates the old dichotomy between appearance and reality. Since the phenomena are not the appearances of some "behind-the-scenes" reality, "the being of an existent is exactly what it appears." Nevertheless, Sartre's ontology introduces another dichotomy, for though the phenomena are not relative to a noumenal reality, they are relative to consciousness: "'To appear' supposes in essence somebody to whom to appear."[a]

There are, then, two sorts of being. To Sartre this seemed to follow from Brentano's and Husserl's central thesis that consciousness is consciousness-of. Thus the task of ontology, as the science of being, is to describe these two sorts of being—the being of consciousness and the being of that which appears to consciousness.

BEING-IN-ITSELF

Let us consider first the being of that which appears. What can be said about it beyond that it is that which appears? Sartre pointed out that what appears is never wholly or completely an object for any consciousness-of or any series of consciousnesses-of. That this is the case follows from what Sartre has already said about profiles.[10] This real existent—say, the chair over there at the other end of my room—is the intended object of an infinite number of rememberings, perceivings, imaginings, and other intentional acts. "Our theory of the phenomenon has replaced the *reality* of the thing by the *objectivity* of the phenomenon and . . .

[10] See p. 374.

has based this on an appeal to infinity."[b] Whereas the traditional versions of realism escaped subjectivity by alleging the chair to be an independently existing entity (a thing-in-itself), Sartre held it to be an intentional object with an infinity of profiles. It follows that being is "transphenomenal"; that is, "the being of that which *appears* does not exist *only* in so far as it appears. The transphenomenal being of what exists *for consciousness* is itself in itself (*lui-même en soi*)."[c]

Since being is transphenomenal it is possible to describe it as it is transphenomenally—as it is in itself, without consciousness. What, then, is being-in-itself? Sartre's answer sounds very much like an account of Parmenides' one. Being is "uncreated." It is not a cause, not even a cause of itself. It is neither passive nor active. It does not undergo change or transformation. One cannot say about the in-itself that it is not yet; and "when it gives way, one cannot even say that it no longer is." One can say only that "it was and at present other beings are."[d] Finally, the in-itself is contingent.

> Necessity concerns the connection between ideal propositions but not that of existents.[11] An existing phenomenon can never be derived from another existent qua existent. This is what we shall call the *contingency* of being-in-itself. But neither can being-in-itself be derived from a *possibility.* . . . Being-in-itself is never either possible or impossible. It *is*. This is what consciousness expresses in anthropomorphic terms by saying that being is superfluous (*de trop*)—that is, that consciousness absolutely cannot derive being from anything, either from another being, or from a possibility, or from a necessary law. Uncreated, without reason for being, without any connection with another being, being-in-itself is *de trop* for eternity.[e]

To sum up, the in-itself is undivided singleness—it is "massive," "solid," "glued to itself." This is why one can say nothing except that the in-itself is. For everything one says *about* it is true, not of the in-itself, but only of it as it is for consciousness.

BEING-FOR-ITSELF

This brings us to the for-itself, that is, conscious being. How is the mode of being of the for-itself to be characterized? Whereas the in-itself simply *is*, the for-itself "is what it is not and is not what it is." To understand this rather obscure saying it will be helpful to think of such typical human activities as imagining, asking questions, and telling lies. What is necessary for a person to be able to imagine a unicorn? It is necessary first to be able to make a realm of imaginary (in distinction from real) things and then to place the unicorn in that realm. But this realm of imagination is *not;* it is a realm of not-being. As for lying, to lie is to say

---

[11] [Compare what Roquetin said about the circle. See p. 365—AUTHORS.]

what is not the case; it is to appear to others what one is not. And to be capable of self-deception is to appear to oneself what one is not. Furthermore, to ask questions—to ask, for instance, "Is that a chair?"—is to raise the possibility of nonbeing. To be a human being is to be aware that *everything*, not merely the chair, might be otherwise than it appears to be; it is to be aware that everything might not-be. To be a human being in fact is to question what one encounters rather than merely to accept it at its face value.

Other human activities can be brought under this same rubric. Thus we are distinguished from, say, chairs not only by our capacity to imagine, to dissimulate, and to question but by our capacity for role-playing. A man may be, for instance, a waiter, a homosexual, a father. But no man's being is exhausted by his being a waiter or a homosexual or a father. The man who is a waiter is not a waiter in the same sense that a tree is a tree, for he is not only a waiter but a son. And since he is a son as well as a waiter, it is correct to say that he is not (merely) a waiter. Or consider the idea that a man lives into the future. He does not merely grow older as a chair does; he has a sense of the future as a not-yet-but-may-be. At any given point in his life he is not yet what he may become, and his thought about this not-yet (which, because it is a not-yet, is not) nonetheless affects what he now is and does.

Doubtless all these activities can be said to involve, in some sense or other, negation. But is this more than a series of plays on words? In Sartre's view, it is. According to him, he is calling attention to the fundamental characteristic of the mode of being of the for-itself. To be conscious is to be conscious *of* something; to be conscious of something is to be aware of that something as not oneself and of oneself as not that something. Thus the mode of being of the for-itself is not to be the objects it is conscious of, or as Sartre put it more succinctly but also more ambiguously, the mode of being of the for-itself is not-to-be.

This at least casts some light on the obscurity of Sartre's characterization of the for-itself as being that which "is what it is not and is not what it is." Do we, however, want to play this sort of language game—a game in which the for-itself "secretes" nothingness, "nihilates" the in-itself, and is "a hole of being at the heart of being"?[f] Whether we want to use this language probably turns on whether we think that ontology is a viable enterprise. But this is too large a question and involves too major a parting of the ways to be dealt with here.

It is possible, however, without raising this question and hence without leaving Sartre's frame of reference, to phrase his point in less picturesque language. It may be said that the mode of being of the for-itself differs from the mode of being of the in-itself precisely by the "*of*" in "consciousness-of." Consciousness does not make being; it makes meanings. When the for-itself "upsurges"[12] it makes a

---

[12] Ontology can give no account of why the for-itself upsurges. This would be the task of metaphysics. The most ontology can say is that "*everything takes place as if* the in-itself in a project to found itself gave itself the modification of the for-itself" (*Being and Nothingness*, p. 621). But to say "it is as if" is to say that it is a condition contrary to fact. In fact, the for-itself is as contingent as the in-itself; it simply upsurges, and on each occasion of its upsurge it makes a world.

world, a world of things that stand in complex spatiotemporal and causal relations to one another and in instrumental relations to the for-itself. Without the for-itself the in-itself does not "have" meanings or "stand in" relations; it simply *is.* Thus the for-itself lives in a world that it has created and for which, as the creator, it is responsible. Here again, stated this time in terms of ontology, is the source of Roquetin's anguish.

In Sartre's view his discovery that there are two modes of being—being-in-itself and being-for-itself—does away with the various dualisms that have plagued philosophy since its beginning: appearance and reality, attribute and essence, actuality and potentiality, idealism and realism. No one will deny that these issues have plagued philosophy; most philosophers who have aspired to philosophize in the grand manner have tackled them. In this sense Sartre is a philosopher in the Western tradition—in contrast, for instance, to Wittgenstein, who proposed not to solve these questions but to dissolve them by linguistic therapy.

It is impossible here to appraise Sartre's proposed solution, but we can at least consider the question of whether his "monism of the phenomenon" overcomes the new dualism that Sartre himself introduced. To many philosophers the in-itself and the for-itself are so different that placing them "under the same heading"g is merely a meaningless semantic gesture. However this may be, the discussion presented below will concentrate on those aspects of Sartre's ontology that help illuminate the nature of the human predicament. These are the nonexistence of God and the total freedom of the for-itself.

GOD DOES NOT EXIST

Whereas Hume modestly undertook to show only that the existence of God cannot be proved, and whereas Nietzsche simply announced God's death, Sartre set out to *prove* the nonexistence of God. One advantage of his ontology, from his point of view, is that it demonstrates that the idea of God is contradictory. God is defined by Sartre as being-in-itself-for-itself. This is merely a translation into Sartrean terms of the formulation of such Christian philosophers as St. Thomas. To define God as the Scholastics did—as his own essence, as a self-cause, or as perfect intelligence—is to say that he is being-in-itself-for-itself.

But as soon as God is defined in this way the contradiction is obvious. An in-itself that is for-itself is divided; this follows from the nature of the for-itself. If divided, it is not an in-itself; this follows from the nature of the in-itself. To be a cause, even a self-cause, is to be sufficiently divided for there to be a distinction between cause and effect. To know something, even only to know oneself, is to be sufficiently divided for there to be a distinction between subject and object. For instance,

> no consciousness, not even God's, can . . . apprehend the totality as
> such. For if God is consciousness, he is integrated in the totality. And if
> by his nature, he is a being *beyond consciousness* (that is, an in-itself
> which would be its own foundation) still the totality can appear to him

only as *object* (in that case he lacks the totality's internal disintegration as the subjective effort to reapprehend the self) or as subject (then since God *is not* this subject, he can only experience it without knowing it). Thus no point of view on the totality is conceivable.[h]

This gave Sartre still another way of characterizing the human predicament: we are not only the beings who ask questions, we are the beings who want answers. We do not want to be a chair or a tree—an in-itself that does not question.[13] Because we want answers, we must be questioners. And we want answers that are final and complete. That is, we are the beings who yearn passionately to be God. But since "the idea of God is contradictory," it follows that "man is a useless passion."[i]

Freedom and Action

According to Sartre, a human being has no substantival self. The only self that "is" is the reconstituted social self. Hence—and this follows from the mode of being of the for-itself—we *are* only insofar as we *act*. Action, of course, is not simply behaving or having things happen to one. A chair may fall or turn over; so may a person. But we do not act when we fall down, or when our leg jerks in response to a tap on the knee. Action—as a specifically human trait, like imagining, perceiving, lying, and role-playing—involves nihilation, nonbeing. When we imagine a unicorn we create an imaginary realm and place the unicorn in this realm. When we act (as distinct from simply reacting) we create a not-yet world and locate the act that we now do in this not-yet world (and hence nonworld) as a step toward the realization of it.

The world that we create when we act may be as small as this evening's dinner, or it may be as large as a flight to the moon. That is, our action may have only trivial or it may have momentous consequences. From the point of view of a Utilitarian such as Mill it is the consequences themselves that matter, not whether they have come about as a result of someone's action. From Sartre's point of view (and in this respect he is like Kant) consequences, whether momentous or trivial, are inconsequential. What matters is whether we have acted, for only in action—defined as the free adoption of a project—are we truly human beings. It is only when I *make* a world that I have being in the mode of the for-itself. Otherwise I have being in the mode of the in-itself, for then I am behaving in accordance with a *given* world instead of nihilating that given world in order to become a self.

> A first glance at human reality informs us that for it being is reduced to doing. . . . Thus we find no *given* in human reality in the sense that

13 But see pp. 389–90.

temperament, character, passions, principles of reason would be acquired or innate *data* existing in the manner of things. . . . Thus human reality does not exist first in order to act later; but for human reality, to be is to act, and to cease to act is to cease to be. . . .

Furthermore, . . . the act . . . must be defined by an *intention*. No matter how this intention is considered, it can be only a surpassing of the given toward a result to be obtained. This given . . . can not provide the reason for a phenomenon which derives all its meaning from a result to be attained; that is, from a non-existent. . . . Psychologists ought to have asked what could be the ontological structure of a phenomenon such that it makes known to itself what it is by means of something which does not yet exist. . . . [14]

Since the intention is a choice of the end and since the world reveals itself across our conduct, it is the intentional choice of the end which reveals the world, and the world is revealed as this or that (in this or that order) according to the end chosen. The end, illuminating the world, is a state *of* the world to be obtained and not yet existing. . . . Thus my *end* can be a good meal if I am hungry. . . . This meal which [is] beyond the dusty road on which I am traveling is projected as the *meaning* of this road. . . .

Thus the intention by a single unitary upsurge posits the end, chooses itself, and appreciates the given in terms of the end. Under these circumstances the given is appreciated in terms of something which does not yet exist; it is in the light of non-being that being-in-itself is illuminated. . . .

This characteristic of the for-itself implies that it is the being which finds *no help, no pillar of support* in what it *was*. But on the other hand, the for-itself is free and can cause there to be a world because the for-itself is *the being which has to be what it was in the light of what it will be*. Therefore the freedom of the for-itself appears as its *being*. . . . We shall never apprehend ourselves except as a choice in the making. But freedom is simply the fact that this choice is always unconditioned.

Such a choice made without base of support and dictating its own causes to itself . . . is absurd.[j]

Thus Sartre reverses the usual way of thinking about human behavior. Most people (not merely social scientists) assume that a man beats his wife and neglects his children because he is (say) a drunkard, and that he is a drunkard because (say) he grew up in a ghetto, without a "proper" upbringing. Thus most people believe that the state of the world (being a drunkard, having grown up in a ghetto)

---

[14] [Thus a phenomenon (for instance, a movement of my hand and arm through space) becomes the act it is (an offer to shake hands) by its projected end (getting someone to make up a quarrel). Given a different project, the *same* phenomenon might be, say, a threat—AUTHORS.]

determines what men do. Sartre holds, instead, that the project that we choose (the not-yet end) determines the actual world we live in. A man chooses to be a drunkard, and because he so chooses he lives in a drunkard's world, a world that includes wife beating and child neglect. He could choose to live in a different world—that is, he could drop this project and adopt a new one. And he *may* do so at any time; there is nothing in his past that makes this impossible or unlikely.

> The free project is fundamental, for it is my being. . . . [It] is a project concerning not my relations with this or that particular object in the world, but my total being-in-the-world. . . . However we need not understand by this that the fundamental project is coextensive with the entire "life" of the for-itself. Since freedom is a being-without-support and without-a-springboard, the project in order to be must be constantly renewed. I choose myself perpetually and can never be merely by virtue of having-been-chosen; otherwise I should fall into the pure and simple existence of the in-itself. . . . Since I am free, . . . I can always nihilate this first project and make it past. . . .
>
> No law of being can assign an a priori number to the different projects which I am.[k]

FUNDAMENTAL PROJECTS

Obviously, not every project is "fundamental"—the project of eating dinner at a certain restaurant this evening is not. But presumably there was a fundamental project, an "original upsurge," by which I chose the life (for example, that of a loafer and a carefree wanderer) that has brought me to this dusty road this afternoon. According to Sartre, a special method ("existential psychoanalysis") is necessary for uncovering a primary project of this kind. And in such a project we create a total world—the life of a drunkard, or a wanderer, or a homosexual, as the case may be. Since our choice of this fundamental project is absolutely spontaneous, we are wholly responsible for it. We cannot pass on the responsibility to others or excuse ourselves by blaming the time, the place, or the circumstances.

> Thus there are no *accidents* in a life; a community event which suddenly bursts forth and involves me in it does not come from the outside. If I am mobilized in a war, this war is *my* war; it is in my image and I deserve it. I deserve it first because I could always get out of it by suicide or by desertion. . . . For lack of getting out of it, I have *chosen* it. This can be due to inertia, to cowardice in the face of public opinion, or because I prefer certain other values to the value of the refusal to join in the war (the good opinion of my relatives, the honor of my family, etc.). Any way you look at it, it is a matter of a choice. This choice will be repeated later on again and again without a break until the end of the war.[l]

There is no way to escape from this freedom. I cannot evade responsibility by asking other people's advice about whether I should enlist or desert, for then I have chosen the people whose advice I solicit and I have chosen to follow their advice. If I kill myself in despair over the agonizing choice I face, I have chosen suicide.

Further, when I choose for myself, I also choose for all other people:

> If . . . existence precedes essence, and if we grant that we exist and fashion our image at one and the same time, the image is valid for everybody and for our whole age. Thus our responsibility is much greater than we might have supposed, because it involves all mankind. If I . . . choose to join a Christian trade-union rather than be a communist, and if by being a member I want to show that the best thing for man is resignation, . . . I am not only involving my own case—I want to be resigned for everyone. . . . If I want to marry, to have children, even if this marriage depends solely on my own circumstances or passion or wish, I am involving all humanity in monogamy and not merely myself. . . . I am creating a certain image of man of my own choosing. In choosing myself, I choose man.ᵐ

This sounds rather like Kant's categorical imperative, with its universalization principle.[15] But Kant of course held that the universalization principle shows that certain specific acts—truth telling and promise keeping, for instance—are always right and that others are always wrong. Sartre rejected this. In his view, each autonomous individual chooses and makes his or her own world—be it the world of the deserter or the world of the volunteer. What is universal for Sartre is only the respect that each free individual feels for the free choices of others. In the sense that one cannot say that it is universally wrong to desert and universally right to volunteer, Sartre is a subjectivist. But in one respect at least he is an objectivist. In his view, there is one kind of life that is categorically wrong—or at least "dishonest." This is the life that tries to escape responsibility by retreating into, or never emerging from, the social self. Sartre's argument is that to try to escape responsibility is to involve oneself in a logical contradiction—the contradiction of choosing not to choose.

It is true, Sartre says, that we cannot "pass judgment" either on the deserter who really chooses to desert or on the volunteer who really chooses to fight, for each of these men "sanely and sincerely involves himself and chooses his configuration." But we *can* pass judgment on the deserter who has merely followed the lead of his friends or on the volunteer who has unthinkingly accepted the claim his country makes on him.

> First, one can judge (and this is perhaps not a judgment of value, but a logical judgment) that certain choices are based on error and others

[15] See Vol. IV, pp. 72–78.

on truth. If we have defined man's situation as a free choice, with no excuses and no recourse, every man who takes refuge behind the excuse of his passions, every man who sets up a determinism, is a dishonest man.

The objection may be raised, "But why mayn't he choose himself dishonestly?" I reply that I am not obliged to pass moral judgment on him, but that I do define his dishonesty as an error. One can not help considering the truth of the matter. Dishonesty is obviously a falsehood because it belies the complete freedom of involvement. On the same grounds, I maintain that there is also dishonesty if I choose to state that certain values exist prior to me; it is self-contradictory for me to want them and at the same time state that they are imposed on me. Suppose someone says to me, "What if I want to be dishonest?" I'll answer, "There's no reason for you not to be, but I'm saying that that's what you are, and that the strictly coherent attitude is that of honesty."[n]

SOME DIFFICULTIES WITH THIS VIEW

That there is a logical contradiction may be true. But in an absurd world (it might be argued) it is not illogical to choose a logical contradiction. And absurdity apart, if one chooses a contradiction is one *morally* wrong—or is one merely muddleheaded? Perhaps the argument can be restated in a way that will bring out more clearly what seems to be Sartre's real position. Consider the Pacômes[16] of this world. Obviously Sartre detests them; obviously he wants to be able to justify this disgust, to hold that it is not merely prejudice. His argument is that a Pacôme-like existence is not really human. To be human is to make a world by adopting a project. Pacôme has not made a world; he has accepted the ready-made world of his social class—a given. He has not chosen capitalism; he *is* a capitalist. Thus the contradiction consists in Pacôme being a man who is not a man—a for-itself that does not have being in the mode of the for-itself but in the mode of the in-itself.

Sartre's position here is obviously close to Heidegger's.[17] Both would deny that they are making value judgments, still more that they are merely giving vent to a prejudice; both would claim to be asserting a fundamental fact about the ontological structure of human nature. But in Sartre's case, at least, the argument proves too much. Sartre holds that we yearn to be in the mode of the in-itself-for-itself, and that this is impossible. We may agree. Similarly, he holds that at least some individuals yearn, at least some of the time, to be in the mode of the in-itself. For instance, in *The Reprieve*, Mathieu's friend Daniel, a homosexual, wants to *be* a homosexual, that is, to "coincide" with himself. "Why can't I *be* what I am, *be* a pederast, villain, coward, a loathsome object that doesn't even manage to exist? . . . Just to be. In the dark, at random! To be homosexual just as the oak

[16] See pp. 366–67.
[17] See pp. 316–31.

is oak. To extinguish myself. Extinguish the inner eye."° Similarly, in *Nausea* Roquetin says, "I, too, wanted to *be*."ᴾ But to be in the mode of the in-itself, Sartre holds, is as impossible as to be in the mode of the in-itself-for-itself. Again we may agree. It is obvious that Pacôme is not a capitalist in the way in which a tree is a tree or an inkwell is an inkwell.

But what about the way in which a Communist is a Communist? Consider Brunet,[18] for instance. It is true that Brunet chose to be a Communist. He did not grow up as a Communist, nor did he drift into it, as we might suppose Pacôme slipped, without noticing, into being a capitalist. But the idea that Brunet chose makes no real difference, for once he became a Communist and accepted Party discipline he no longer made his world; communism became his "given." Nor does this problem exist only for Communists and for other people who accept an authoritarian code. A man who adopts desertion as his project is only too likely to slip from his freedom into playing the role of a deserter. Similarly, the man whose project is to become a soldier or the woman whose project is her own existential freedom is likely to slip from freedom. Doubtless some projects lend themselves more easily than others to slippage into bad faith. But no project, by its very nature as a project, is immune to such slippage.

It would seem, then, that it is no more possible (except in unusual circumstances and then only from moment to moment) to be in the mode of the for-itself, than to be in the mode of the in-itself or in the mode of the in-itself-for-itself. To live in the mode of the for-itself—to be in good faith, or to live authentically— may be an ethical ideal, but it seems that Sartre's ontology renders his ideal incapable of achievement.

The trouble is that Sartre's account of the for-itself commits him to holding that freedom is an all-or-none affair, whereas to many people it will seem a matter of degree. The same is true for humanity, and also for responsibility. Consider the question of responsibility. Most people hold that there are degrees of responsibility, corresponding roughly to the legal distinctions between first-degree murder, manslaughter, negligence, and innocence. Regarding the American atomic attack on Japan during the Second World War, they might say that President Truman and his advisers were "chiefly" responsible, that the scientists who designed the bomb and the aviators who flew the plane were "somewhat" responsible, and that the ordinary citizen, who did not even know that nuclear fission had been achieved, was "not at all" responsible. These are doubtless vague notions, but they represent an attitude toward morality that is profoundly different from Sartre's. In his view, since we are totally free we are wholly responsible; since every one of us could have made a world that excluded the atomic attack on Hiroshima, we are all equally responsible for that attack. To some this view will appear extreme.

Further, it could be argued plausibly that total freedom, far from entailing total responsibility, is actually incompatible with responsibility. It might be maintained that to be responsible for an act is to attribute this act to a self that, in some

---

[18] See p. 368, note 6.

sense or other, has endured from the past into the present that includes this act. An act that is simply the upsurge of a wholly impersonal spontaneity is not owned by anyone.

Sartre's reply would probably be, first, that phenomenological observation fails to disclose any such enduring self and, second, that it does disclose perfect freedom. Further, he would say that the critics' philosophical objections are only a subtle attempt to evade responsibility by closing their eyes to their own freedom.

Sartre and Marxism

But to what extent has Sartre, under the influence of Marxism, abandoned his existential commitment to human freedom? This is a hotly debated question, but, at least at first sight, it seems that in later writings such as the *Critique of Dialectical Reason,* he relaxed his earlier claim that human beings are totally free. Over the years he became more and more impressed by the problem of scarcity, not only by the growing scarcity of food as the population increases, but by all forms of scarcity. Scarcity, he concluded, leads us to regard others as mere objects whom we then "use" for our own ends, if we are able; hence scarcity leads inevitably to violence. Scarcity is, indeed, an aspect of what Sartre calls the "practico-inert," which is the tendency in human affairs for decisions made in the past to narrow down choices and opportunities in the present. The inevitable result of human practice is an inertia that limits human freedom. Current worries over the way the development of the internal combustion engine at the beginning of this century has resulted in air pollution on a large scale is a good example of the practico-inert. That development has limited our freedom to breathe good air, for instance, or to walk about the streets of a city in relative peace and quiet. Thus it is not only the present social order but the past that restricts our capacity to live in the mode of the for-itself.

This, according to Sartre, is the fault of capitalism; it keeps the vast majority of men and women in such a deprived condition economically and socially that they are unable to exercise their freedom. Marxism, by destroying the class structure, will make true freedom possible. This, then, was the source, or at least one of the chief sources, of the attraction for Sartre of Marxism. But is the freedom that capitalism denies and that communism opens up the existential freedom that Sartre had earlier described? Will the existential anguish experienced by Roquetin, Mathieu, and Sartre's other protagonists disappear in a classless society? Surely not. In the first place, the Sartrean human being is solitary. To commit oneself to a cause, however noble, one must join a group, one must combine with others—not only form a movement but institutionalize (and bureaucratize) it. This means surrendering one's freedom and hence becoming a thing. In the second place, anguish, at least as Sartre described it in his earlier works, has its source in human nature (the for-itself that yearns, impossibly, to be the in-itself-

for-itself), and not in socioeconomic conditions. But in the later works the difficulty of living in good faith turns out to be no longer an ontological problem but
only a function of scarcity.

Finally, there is the question whether Marxist determinism is compatible with
Sartrean spontaneity. In "Search for a Method," which is part of the *Critique of
Dialectical Reason,* Sartre adopts a Marxist interpretation of all philosophy, in-
cluding presumably his own existential phenomenology.

> You would never at the same time find more than *one* living philoso-
> phy. . . . Under certain well-defined circumstances *a* philosophy is de-
> veloped for the purpose of giving expression to the general movement
> of society. So long as a society is alive, it serves as a cultural milieu for
> its contemporaries. . . . A philosophy is first of all a particular way in
> which the "rising" class becomes conscious of itself. . . . Thus a philos-
> ophy remains efficacious so long as the *praxis* which has engendered it,
> which supports it, and which is clarified by it, is still alive.q

He then proceeds to argue that Marxism is *the* philosophy of our time. Since
the Renaissance there have been three philosophies that in turn have given expression to the general movement of society.

> Between the seventeenth century and the twentieth, I see three such
> periods, which I would designate by the names of the men who domi-
> nated them: there is the "moment" of Descartes and Locke, that of
> Kant and Hegel, finally that of Marx. These three philosophies become,
> each in its turn, the humus of every particular thought and the horizon
> of all culture; there is no going beyond them so long as man has not
> gone beyond the historical moment which they express. I have often re-
> marked on the fact that an "anti-Marxist" argument is only the appar-
> ent rejuvenation of a pre-Marxist idea. A so-called "going beyond"
> Marxism will be at worst only a return to pre-Marxism; at best, only the
> rediscovery of a thought already contained in the philosophy which one
> believes he had gone beyond.r

In short, all twentieth-century philosophers—Sartre and his blend of phenomenology and existentialism included—are inevitably Marxist, whether they
know it or not, whether they like it or not. But Marxism teaches us that the mode
of consciousness in a given period is only the reflection of the forms of production and exchange of the dominant class in that period. It seems to follow that the
notion of a pure spontaneity in which a new fundamental project upsurges is an
illusion—the illusion of a particular class in a particular period of time. Has Sartre
then abandoned his earlier position? No, apparently not. For Marx, at least according to Sartre, predicted an end to Marxism:

> As soon as there will exist *for everyone* a margin of *real* freedom
> beyond the production of life, Marxism will have lived out its span; a

philosophy of freedom will take its place. But we have no means, no intellectual instrument, no concrete experience which allows us to conceive of this freedom or of this philosophy.[s]

Thus spontaneity, not determinism, has the last word, as far as Sartre is concerned. Phenomenology, Marxism, and existentialism, from this point of view, are all unpredicted and unpredictable upsurgings ex nihilo, and a new upsurge may occur at any moment. In other words, we have to distinguish between existential phenomenology as a philosophical theory and the existential truth, as it were, of those original, spontaneous, wholly undetermined upsurges by which we make ourselves. Existential phenomenology as a philosophical theory is only the "rediscovery of a thought" already contained in the "moment" of Marxism. But Marxism itself is only a "moment" in the history of human freedom, the history, that is, of a human being as a sequence of these spontaneous "makings." At some point in this history, Marxism "will have lived out its span," and so, of course, will existential phenomenology. Both will be replaced by, or transcended in, a philosophy of freedom. But this "conclusion" is not the outcome of an analysis by Sartre the ontologist similar to those contained in *Being and Nothingness* and *The Transcendence of the Ego;* it is rather an existential commitment by Sartre the individual human being. Accordingly, to the question whether the existentialist view of the world or the Marxist view is correct, no objective definitive answer is possible. The "truth" of existential phenomenology is assured not by the weight of the evidence but by allegiance to the vision that had been so passionately affirmed and reaffirmed in the novels and the plays. Is this vision reliable? This is the sort of question that can be asked only from outside the vision, from outside one's commitment to it. From inside it is meaningless: "Suddenly, suddenly, the veil is torn away, I have understood, I have *seen.*"[t] From inside the commitment, learned discussions of whether Sartre has abandoned existentialism in favor of Marxism may be of some theoretical interest, but they are beside the point. Existentialism is true as a personal commitment even if it may be false as a theory.

CHAPTER 11

The Later Wittgenstein

When Wittgenstein finished the *Tractatus,* he believed he had demonstrated that philosophy was a matter of showing, not of saying. To gain insight into the nature of philosophy the reader will need the propositions of the *Tractatus,* but only as a ladder. He or she will "climb out" of philosophy by means of these propositions— "through them, on them, over them"; but when the reader has climbed out, he or she must "throw away the ladder." [a] True to this conception of the philosophical enterprise, Wittgenstein himself threw away the ladder, so to speak, when he finished the *Tractatus.* He abandoned philosophy, returned to Austria, and took up teaching school in a small village. Somewhere along the line, however, he began to have second thoughts—and, being Wittgenstein, third and fourth thoughts as well. But, though he had apparently concluded that one could after all "do" philosophy, his way of doing it was very different from that of most professors. Instead of giving formal lectures to large audiences of undergraduates, he conversed intensely with a few pupils in a highly Socratic manner.

This mode of teaching has survived in the conversational question-and-answer form of his *Philosophical Investigations,* which was not published until after his death. Whereas the argument of the *Tractatus* was marshalled into a tight hierarchical format, systematically divided and subdivided, the discussions of the *Investigations* proceed in a deliberately unsystematical way. Wittgenstein was at pains to point out the change. In the *Investigations* we

> travel over a wide field of thought criss-cross in every direction. The philosophical remarks in this book are, as it were, a number of sketches of landscapes which were made in the course of these long and involved journeyings.
>
> The same or almost the same points were always being approached afresh from different directions, and new sketches made. . . . Thus this book is really only an album.[b]

This striking stylistic difference is only a symptom of deeper differences, and although controversy rages over the extent to which *Philosophical Investigations* breaks with the doctrine of the *Tractatus,* about some points there can be no doubt. Though both books are concerned with the nature of language and with the nature of meaning, Wittgenstein's view of the relation between language and reality changed profoundly. This change corresponds, roughly, to the difference between Wallace Stevens's view and Eliot's. Like the Wallace Stevens of "Credences of Summer," the Wittgenstein of the *Tractatus* believed that it is possible to achieve an isomorphism between an ideal language and the very thing itself; like the Eliot of the *Quartets,* the Wittgenstein of the *Investigations* concluded that the notion of an ideal language is an illusion and the quest for isomorphism doomed to failure.[1]

This change in attitude toward language and the relation between language and the world was reflected in a changed conception of the nature of philosophy. In the *Tractatus,* insofar as philosophy had any positive role at all (insofar as it was not simply to disappear as the ladder was left behind), its role was to expose the grammatical confusions of earlier philosophers. That is, the *Tractatus* conceived of philosophy as linguistic analysis, in much the same way in which Russell and the positivists later conceived it. Now we can, without too much strain, call philosophy as analysis a form of therapy, in that it was intended to alleviate the worries of muddled thinkers. But this notion of philosophy as therapy was greatly deepened and extended in the *Investigations;* Wittgenstein moved toward Nietzsche and James and away from Russell and the positivists. He had never agreed with the latter that the worries of philosophers were merely silly, even while he agreed with them that these worries involved linguistic muddles. Rather, he held that the muddles are generated by "deep disquietudes," disquietudes that he certainly shared. Hence he did not think that the perplexities of philosophers would

[1] See p. 7.

easily disappear—and he did not find that his own disquietudes disappeared—when intellectual analysis pointed up the linguistic mistakes being made. This accounts for that last section of the *Tractatus* on the mystical. In it, Wittgenstein attempted to exorcise the disquietudes by arguing that questions can exist only when answers are possible and that answers are possible only when they can be framed clearly. The whole central doctrine of the *Tractatus*—the distinction between saying and showing—may be thought of as directed to this end: the cosmological, metaphysical, and religious questions over which philosophers torment themselves are not *questions* at all; but they are not nonsense either. They can be shown but not said.

We have suggested that this attempt to exorcise the disquietudes was unsuccessful. If this is so, it may explain why the method of therapy used in the *Tractatus* was abandoned and a new method introduced in the *Investigations*. However this may be, a new method was introduced, and this new method is connected with the changed view of language to which we have already referred. It is no longer claimed that philosophers must abjure saying and limit themselves to showing. On the contrary, the method of the *Investigations* is frankly linguistic. In this respect Wittgenstein was very close to Nietzsche. Like Nietzsche, Wittgenstein conducted his therapy by exposing the myths and fictions concealed within the standard philosophical vocabulary.[2] But Nietzsche's technique was almost amateurish as compared with the subtlety and finesse of Wittgenstein's. Nietzsche had anticipated Freud in suggesting that the language we use often expresses our unconscious needs; this was insightful, but speculative. Wittgenstein's approach, in contrast, was empirical. He saw that when language is performing its everyday practical functions, it is too busy to get into trouble. But sometimes, unfortunately, language "goes on holiday." Whenever it idles in this way, philosophical problems arise. The cure is to put language back into gear, as it were, by showing it at work in various concrete contexts relevant to the particular "holiday" that language happens to be taking. In collecting these contexts—in "assembling reminders" that were relevant to each of the classical philosophical problems—Wittgenstein showed the greatest skill.[c] By bringing together and comparing a large number of similar but slightly different cases, Wittgenstein displayed in a striking way the varied meanings that the same words have in different contexts and the many different uses to which they are put.

Thus, though his conception of philosophy as therapy was indeed very different from Russell's and from the usual analytic conception, his conviction that the proper method of philosophical inquiry is linguistic analysis revealed his relationship to this tradition and won a hearing for his views from tough-minded philosophers who would have considered listening to Nietzsche a waste of time. Even those who reject with disdain the notion that philosophy is a form of therapy, even those who have never experienced existential anxieties, agree that *Philosophical Investigations* is one of the most important works of our time.

[2] See Vol. IV, pp. 238–43.

The Nature of Language

Since the nature of language is the central theme both of the *Tractatus* and of the *Investigations,* we will begin with this topic, and we will start by examining the criticism in the latter work of the view taken for granted in the former.

THE PICTURE THEORY

Philosophical Investigations begins with a quotation from Augustine in which a view of language is stated that Wittgenstein proposed to criticize:

> When they (my elders) named some object, and accordingly moved towards something, I saw this and I grasped that the thing was called by the sound they uttered when they meant to point it out. Their intention was shewn by their bodily movements. . . . Thus, as I heard words repeatedly used in their proper places in various sentences, I gradually learnt to understand what objects they signified; and after I had trained my mouth to form these signs, I used them to express my own desires.[d]

To illustrate the view he was opposing, Wittgenstein might just as well have cited any one of a number of passages from the *Tractatus* or, for that matter, the passage from Hobbes that was quoted at the beginning of our discussion of the analytic tradition.[3] Although Augustine and Hobbes and the Wittgenstein of the *Tractatus* differed about almost everything else—from the nature of God to the nature of the earth—they had much the same view of language. This is a good example of the way in which certain very general assumptions about meaning may underlie theories of quite different types.

The particular assumptions common to Augustine, to Hobbes, and to the *Tractatus* (and of course to many other philosophers) are as follows. First, it is taken for granted that objects are perceived quite independently of language. Note that Augustine first saw the object and then "grasped that the thing was called by the sound." That is, he believed that before a child learns the word "chair," he or she sees a chair just as fully and completely as he or she sees the chair after learning its name. Language in no way affects what we experience; it affects only our ability to communicate to others what we have experienced. Second, it is assumed that individual words name objects. Every word thus has its own individual meaning that, once attached to it, stays with it. Not to use the word to name the object is to misuse the word; it is to equivocate, or simply to lie. Third, it is assumed that the object the word names is its meaning. (In some variations of this theory, a distinction is drawn between the object named by the word and the mental image of that object called up in the mind of the hearer; the meaning of the word is then identified with the image rather than with the object. But

---

[3] See p. 9.

even in this case meaning is regarded as determinate, specific, and fixed.) Fourth, it is held that sentences are combinations of such names and that the relations between the words in a sentence correspond to (that is, picture) the relations among the parts of the complex fact described in the sentence in question. And it is only because of this correspondence, or picturing, that sentences are meaningful and true.

If one thinks of such sentences as "The book is on the desk" or "Snoopy is lying on his doghouse," this theory has a certain plausibility; it is a theory of this general type that underlies the whole argument of the *Tractatus*. As we have seen, Wittgenstein had been influenced by a report he had read of a trial arising out of an automobile accident. In this trial dolls and miniature cars were used to represent the real people and automobiles involved in the accident, and it seemed to Wittgenstein at the time he wrote the *Tractatus* that sentences represent facts in much the same way as the arrangement of dolls and miniature cars represented facts—or in the way in which the spatial relations pictured in a portrait (for example, nose between eyes and mouth) correspond to the spatial relations among the features of the sitter's face. Thus he pictured language to himself as a kind of picture of reality.

He is said to have been jolted out of this picture theory of language by the challenge of a friend who made a familiar Neapolitan street gesture and asked, "What does *that* picture?" In any case, by the time he wrote *Philosophical Investigations* he had decided that this picture of language as a picture of reality was mistaken. The picture was inadequate not merely because it failed to correspond to reality (for if failure to conform to reality were the only problem, a more faithful picture could doubtless be designed that would correspond to the facts), but because the concept of language as being a picture of the facts was at best appropriate only for a very small part of the whole domain of language and meanings.

WITTGENSTEIN'S CRITICISM OF THE PICTURE THEORY

Wittgenstein did not deny that in some circumstances some words represent ("name," "signify") objects; nouns such as "chair," "table," and "bread" often do, as do proper names. Nor did Wittgenstein deny that we learn the meanings of some words in the way Augustine described, that is, by having other people point to the objects whose names they want us to learn. But Wittgenstein insisted that by no means all words function in this way; nor do we always learn the meanings of words by ostensive definition (by pointing). We learn them this way, for instance, when we are adding to our vocabulary in a language with which we are already familiar, but not (according to Wittgenstein) when we are learning a new language.

> Augustine, we might say, does describe a system of communication; only not everything that we call language is this system. And one has to say this in many cases where the question arises "Is this an appropriate

> description or not?" The answer is: "Yes, it is appropriate, but only for this narrowly circumscribed region, not for the whole of what you were claiming to describe."
>
> It is as if someone were to say: "A game consists in moving objects about on a surface according to certain rules . . . "—and we replied: You seem to be thinking of board games, but there are others. You can make your definition correct by expressly restricting it to those games.[e]

Wittgenstein observed that the tendency of people, including philosophers, to overgeneralize is unfortunately all too evident; Nietzsche had attributed this proclivity to our human sense of insecurity.[4] Whatever the psychological roots of the tendency, people are prone to conclude from a few cases that are striking in some way (or that are perhaps just the first cases they have encountered) that the properties characterizing these cases also characterize the whole class. Thus, according to Wittgenstein, the overgeneralization that Augustine (and Hobbes and many other philosophers) made about language and about meaning resulted from concentrating on nouns (which happen to be rather prominent in European languages). Because all words look more or less alike and because they sound more or less alike, Augustine (and Hobbes) assumed that all words mean in the same way that nouns mean. But if he had paid even the least attention to such words as "is," "not," "this," and "here"—let alone to the ways in which nouns themselves mean in many contexts—he would have come to realize the inadequacy of this theory of meaning.

Unfortunately, this overgeneralization "surrounds the working of language with a haze which makes clear vision impossible." How can this fog be dispersed? By considering a number of primitive languages—or, rather, a number of languages "in primitive kinds of application in which one can command a clear view of the aim and functioning of the words."[f]

Here is one such language:

> I send someone shopping. I give him a slip marked "five red apples." He takes the slip to the shopkeeper, who opens the drawer marked "apples"; then he looks up the word "red" in a table and finds a colour sample opposite it; then he says the series of cardinal numbers—I assume that he knows them by heart—up to the word "five" and for each number he takes an apple of the same colour as the sample out of the drawer.[g]

Here is another:

> Let us imagine a language which . . . is meant to serve for communication between a builder A and an assistant B. A is building with building stones: there are blocks, pillars, slabs, and beams. B has to pass the

---

[4] See Vol. IV, pp. 253–54.

stones, and that in the order in which A needs them. For this purpose they use a language consisting of the words "block," "pillar," "slab," "beam." A calls them out;—B brings the stone which he has learnt to bring at such-and-such a call.—Conceive this as a complete primitive language . . . the *whole* language of A and B; even the whole language of a tribe. The children are brought up to perform *these* actions, to use *these* words as they do so, and to react in *this* way to the words of others.

An important part of the training will consist in the teacher's pointing to the objects, directing the child's attention to them, and at the same time uttering a word; for instance, the word "slab" as he points to that shape. . . . This ostensive teaching of words can be said to establish an association between the word and the thing. But what does this mean? Well, it can mean various things; but one very likely thinks first of all that a picture of the object comes before the child's mind when it hears the word. But now, if this does happen—is it the purpose of the word?—Yes, it *can* be the purpose—I can imagine such a use of words (or series of sounds). (Uttering a word is like striking a note on the keyboard of the imagination.) But in the language [of the builder and the assistant] it is *not* the purpose of the words to evoke images. (It may, of course, be discovered that that helps to attain the actual purpose.)

But if the ostensive teaching has this effect, am I to say that it effects an understanding of the word? Don't you understand the call "Slab!" if you act upon it in such-and-such a way?—Doubtless the ostensive teaching helped to bring this about; but only together with a particular training. With different training the same ostensive teaching of these words would have effected a quite different understanding.

"I set the brake up by connecting up rod and lever."—Yes, given the whole rest of the mechanism. Only in conjunction with that is it a brake-lever, and separated from its support it is not even a lever; it may be anything, or nothing.[h]

Several important points are brought out in these examples. First, language arises in a particular social context—for instance, in an apple-buying context or in a building-construction context—and reflects that social context. Second, any system of signs is a language insofar as it facilitates the purpose implicit in the social context in which this system of signs is being used. Thus the color sample is as much a sign in the apple-buying language as the word "red" is in some other language. Furthermore, what looks like a word (for example, "Slab!"), and what might be only a word in some languages, is a sentence in the builder's language. Third, if the language (whatever it looks like and however odd it may seem when compared with standard written English as taught in schools) is effective in promoting the purpose for which the language has been introduced, then meaning is conveyed and understanding occurs. The critical point Wittgenstein is making here is that the test of meaningfulness is not whether a particular language conforms to some set of criteria that have been prescribed by logic[5] but, quite simply, whether it is successful in accomplishing whatever it set out to accomplish—buying five apples to bring home, getting the building materials to the building site in the right order, and so on.

Fourth, though the meaning of a word may occasionally be some image of the thing named by the word (one can think of social contexts in which the word "slab" is intended to call up in the mind of the hearer the mental image of a slab), this sort of meaning, far from being standard, is exceptional. In the social context of the builder and the assistant, the word "Slab!" spoken by the builder probably does not conjure up the mental image of a slab in the mind of the assistant; nor was it intended by the builder to do so. Are we to infer from the lack of an image being conjured up in the assistant's mind that "Slab!" has no meaning for him, that he does not understand what is said to him? To draw this conclusion is unduly and arbitrarily to restrict the meaning of "meaning." It is evident that he has understood, that the word is meaningful to him without an image having occurred, because he brings the item of building material that the builder wanted him to bring.

Finally, and most important, if we want to understand what understanding consists in, we must watch the way language functions in each particular circumstance in which it is actually used. We must look not to the meaning but to the use. In this aphorism Wittgenstein used "meaning" in the same sense as those philosophers who identify the meaning of a word either with the object named by the word or with the mental image of that object. It is in this limited sense of "meaning" that Wittgenstein says the meaning of a word must be ignored. However, Wittgenstein might just as well have expanded the meaning of "meaning" and said that there is no one standard meaning that is *the* meaning of a given word, but that each word or other sign has as many meanings as it has uses, and that these are countless.

> Think of the tools in a tool-box: there is a hammer, pliers, a saw, a screwdriver, a rule, a glue-pot, glue, nails and screws.—The functions of words are as diverse as the functions of these objects. (And in both cases there are similarities.)
>
> Of course, what confuses us is the uniform appearance of words when we hear them spoken or meet them in script and print. For their *application* is not presented to us so clearly. Especially not, when we are doing philosophy!
>
> It is like looking into the cabin of a locomotive. We see handles all looking more or less alike. (Naturally, since they are all supposed to be

---

[5] See pp. 412–15.

handled.) But one is the handle of a crank which can be moved continuously (it regulates the opening of a valve); another is the handle of a switch, which has only two effective positions, it is either off or on; a third is the handle of a brake-lever, the harder one pulls on it, the harder it brakes; a fourth, the handle of a pump: it has an effect only so long as it is moved to and fro.

When we say: "Every word in language signifies something" we have so far said *nothing whatever;* unless we have explained *exactly what* distinction we wish to make. . . .

Imagine someone's saying: "*All* tools serve to modify something. Thus the hammer modifies the position of the nail, the saw the shape of the board, and so on."—And what is modified by the rule, the gluepot, the nails?—"Our knowledge of a thing's length, the temperature of the glue, and the solidity of the box."—Would anything be gained by this assimilation of expressions?

The word "to signify" is perhaps used in the most straightforward way when the object signified is marked with the sign. Suppose that the tools A uses in building bear certain marks. When A shews his assistant such a mark, he brings the tool that has that mark on it.

It is in this and more or less similar ways that a name means and is given to a thing.—It will often prove useful in philosophy to say to ourselves: naming something is like attaching a label to a thing.

What about the colour samples that A shews to B: are they part of the *language?* Well, it is as you please. They do not belong among the words; yet when I say to someone: "Pronounce the word 'the,'" you will count the second "the" as part of the sentence. Yet it has a role just like that of a colour sample [in the apple-buying language]; that is, it is a sample of what the other is meant to say.

It is most natural, and causes least confusion, to reckon the samples among the instruments of the language. . . .

It will be possible to say: In [most languages] we have different *kinds of word.* . . . But how we group words into kinds will depend on the aim of the classification,—and on our own inclination.

Think of the different points of view from which one can classify tools or chess-men.

Do not be troubled by the fact that [some] languages . . . consist only of orders. If you want to say that this shews them to be incomplete, ask yourself whether our language is complete;—whether it was so before the symbolism of chemistry and the notation of the infinitesimal calculus were incorporated in it; for these are, so to speak, suburbs of our language. (And how many houses or streets does it take before a town begins to be a town?) Our language can be seen as an ancient city: a maze of little streets and squares, of old and new houses, and of houses with additions from various periods; and this surrounded by a multitude of new boroughs with straight regular streets and uniform houses.

It is easy to imagine a language consisting only of orders and reports in battle.—Or a language consisting only of questions and expressions for answering yes and no. And innumerable others.—And to imagine a language means to imagine a form of life. . . .

But how many kinds of sentence are there? Say assertion, question, and command?—There are *countless* kinds: countless different kinds of use of what we call "symbols," "words," "sentences." And this multiplicity is not something fixed, given once for all; but new types of language, new language-games, as we may say, come into existence, and others become obsolete and get forgotten. . . .

Here the term "language-*game*" is meant to bring into prominence the fact that the *speaking* of language is part of any activity, or of a form of life.

Review the multiplicity of language-games in the following examples, and in others:

Giving orders, and obeying them—
Describing the appearance of an object, or giving its measurements—
Constructing an object from a description (a drawing)—
Reporting an event—
Speculating about an event—
Forming and testing a hypothesis—
Presenting the results of an experiment in tables and diagrams—
Making up a story; and reading it—
Play-acting—
Singing catches—
Guessing riddles—
Making a joke; telling it—
Solving a problem in practical arithmetic—
Translating from one language into another—
Asking, thanking, cursing, greeting, praying—

It is interesting to compare the multiplicity of the tools in language and of the ways in which they are used, the multiplicity of kinds of word and sentence, with what logicians have said about the structure of language. (Including the author of the *Tractatus Logico-Philosophicus.*) . . .

One thinks that learning language consists in giving names to objects. Viz., to human beings, to shapes, to colours, to pains, to moods, to numbers, etc. To repeat,—naming is something like attaching a label to a thing. One can say that this is preparatory to the use of a word. But *what* is it a preparation *for*?

"We name things and then we can talk about them: can refer to them in talk."—As if what we did next were given with the mere act of naming. As if there were only one thing called "talking about a thing." Whereas in fact we do the most various things with our sentences. Think of exclamations alone, with their completely different functions.

Water!
Away!
Ow!
Help!
Fine!
No!

Are you inclined still to call these words "names of objects"? . . .
Naming is so far not a move in the language-game—any more than putting a piece in its place on the board is a move in chess. We may say: *nothing* has so far been done, when a thing has been named. It has not even *got* a name except in the *language-game.*[i]

Why do philosophers describe Wittgenstein's views as revolutionary? After all, what he says in this passage seems no more than commonplace. But that is precisely the point: to have introduced the commonplace into the esoteric domain of philosophy *was* revolutionary. It was the function of Wittgenstein's own version of philosophy to dissolve all those special, "philosophical" problems with which philosophy had traditionally been preoccupied and then, having dissolved them, to disappear. Let us then see how doing philosophy in Wittgenstein's way dissolves philosophical problems.

Universals and Family Resemblance

One question that philosophers have debated inconclusively since the time of Plato is the problem of universals. Plato's whole metaphysics, as well as his ethical and political philosophy, presupposed the existence of what he called forms. According to this view, in addition to such spatiotemporal entities as Dobbin, Bucephalus, Secretariat, and Swaps there is the form "horse." The form is the true reality; the individual flesh-and-blood horses encountered in this world gain what reality they possess by participating in the forms. Though few philosophers have accepted all the details of Plato's theory of forms, many, including Whitehead, have agreed that universals are real existents.

Wittgenstein's criticism of the picture theory of meaning both accounts for the persistence of this belief in real universals and suggests a possible alternative. According to the picture theory, every word names an individual object:

"Bucephalus" names the particular horse that was owned by Alexander the Great; "Swaps" the particular horse that is commemorated in bronze at Hollywood Park; and so on. But in addition to such words the English language contains the word "horse." What does "horse" name? To philosophers caught in the fly-bottle of the picture theory, the answer seemed obvious. Since every word names, unambiguously, a quite definite object, the word "horse" must name an entity of a very special kind, nonperceptible, nonspatial, and nontemporal. Whenever the word "horse" is used, this entity, the universal "horse," is always meant, just as whenever the word "Bucephalus" is mentioned, the physical object, Bucephalus, is always meant. The only difference is that whenever the word "Bucephalus" is mentioned the object always meant is a particular, whereas when the word "horse" is mentioned the object always meant is a universal.

This theory of universals can be plainly seen in the following argument by St. Anselm, in which he believed he had established the existence of a supremely good and powerful being, that is, God.

> Since there are goods so innumerable, whose great diversity we experience by the bodily sense, and discern by our mental faculties, must we not believe that there is some one thing, through which all goods whatever are good? . . . For, whatsoever things are said to be *just,* when compared one with another, whether equally, or more, or less, cannot be understood as just, except through the quality of *justness,* which is not one thing in one instance, and another in another. . . .
>
> But, since the reasoning which we have observed is in no wise refutable, necessarily, again, all things, whether useful or honorable, if they are truly good, are good through the same being through which all goods exist. . . . But who can doubt this very being, through which all goods exist, to be a great good? . . .
>
> It follows, therefore, that all other goods are good through another being than that which they themselves are, and this being alone is good through itself. Hence, this alone is supremely good, which is alone good through itself. But that which is supremely good, is also supremely great. There is, therefore, some one being which is supremely good, and supremely great, that is, the highest of all existing beings.j

This argument, which seemed to its author (and to many another philosopher) "irrefutable," depends for its plausibility on the picture theory of meaning.

The picture theory is not only responsible for a belief in universals (and the accompanying belief that God, as the most universal of universals, necessarily exists), it is also responsible for belief in the "subsistence" of such oddities as the present king of France, whose nonexistence happened to be affirmed.[6]

In the *Investigations* Wittgenstein, now released from the picture theory that had held him captive, was free to examine the ways in which people actually use

[6] See p. 186.

general terms in talking and writing, and to call attention to how varied these ways are. Words, he pointed out, are used in "countless" different ways, each of which constitutes a meaning of the word. No one meaning is intrinsically better, more meaningful, truer, or more really horselike than any other. These varied meanings need not have an identical entity (horseness) in common. Rather, Wittgenstein held, there are a number of similarities. None of the meanings is characterized by all these similarities, but every one of the meanings is characterized by some of them. It is as if they were all members of a human family, who are recognizable as members not because they all have an identical set of characteristics—red hair, Roman noses, and full lips being characteristic of this family—but because some members have Roman noses and full lips, others have full lips and red hair, and still others have red hair and Roman noses.

Wittgenstein's own example for his argument was what Plato would have called the form "game," what some epistemological realists call a universal, and what others would call the "essence" of games. Wittgenstein himself described it simply as the family resemblance among all the various uses (meanings) of the word "game."

> Someone might object against me: "You take the easy way out! You talk about all sorts of language-games, but have nowhere said what the essence of a language-game, and hence of language, is: what is common to all these activities, and what makes them into language or parts of language. . . . "
>
> And this is true.—Instead of producing something common to all that we call language, I am saying that these phenomena have no one thing in common which makes us use the same word for all,—but that they are *related* to one another in many different ways. And it is because of this relationship, or these relationships, that we call them all "language." I will try to explain this.
>
> Consider for example the proceedings that we call "games." I mean board-games, card-games, ball-games, Olympic games, and so on. What is common to them all?—Don't say: "There *must* be something common, or they would not be called 'games'"—but *look and see* whether there is anything common to all.—For if you look at them you will not see something that is common to *all*, but similarities, relationships, and a whole series of them at that. To repeat: don't think, but look!—Look for example at board-games, with their multifarious relationships. Now pass to card-games; here you find many correspondences with the first group, but many common features drop out, and others appear. When we pass next to ball-games, much that is common is retained, but much is lost.—Are they all "amusing"? Compare chess with noughts and crosses. Or is there always winning and losing, or competition between players? Think of patience. . . . Look at the parts played by skill and luck; and at the difference between skill in chess and skill in tennis. . . .

And we can go through the many, many other groups of games in the same way; can see how similarities crop up and disappear.

And the result of this examination is: we see a complicated network of similarities overlapping and criss-crossing: sometimes overall similarities, sometimes similarities of detail.

I can think of no better expression to characterize these similarities than "family resemblances"; for the various resemblances between members of a family: build, features, colour of eyes, gait, temperament, etc., etc., overlap and cross-cross in the same way.—And I shall say: "games" form a family. . . .

One might say that the concept "game" is a concept with blurred edges.—"But is a blurred concept a concept at all?"—Is an indistinct photograph a picture of a person at all? Is it even always an advantage to replace an indistinct picture by a sharp one? Isn't the indistinct one often exactly what we need? . . .

When philosophers use a word—"knowledge," "being," "object," "I," "proposition," "name"—and try to grasp the *essence* of the thing, one must always ask oneself: is the word ever actually used in this way in the language-game which is its original home?—

What *we* do is to bring words back from their metaphysical to their everyday use.[k]

Does this dissolve the problem of universals? No; at least not without a further step in the argument. For, though most concepts are clearly of the family-resemblance type, it is not obvious that all concepts, without exception, are of this type. And if some are not, then it could be the case that some concepts are such that in every case of our use of one of them we are referring to exactly the same set of properties. Suppose, for instance, that "square" is such a concept. "Square" would then differ from "game" in an important way, since in all circumstances "square" would have exactly the same meaning. But even granting this, it would not also follow, as epistemological realists have commonly supposed, that "square" is the name of some one thing that all squares have in common. As long as we distinguish between the definition of a term and what, if anything, that term names, we can allow that "square" applies to all and only to squares, without having to introduce a universal to account for this. One might indeed find *other* grounds for believing in universals, but, once the picture theory is abandoned, the chief consideration that makes them plausible disappears.[7]

[7] Philosophers of the nominalistic persuasion, who rightly found the notion of nontemporal, nonspatial, nonperceptible entities excessively odd, were also trapped in the fly-bottle of the picture theory. Though they rejected universals as the entities named by such words as "horse," most of them nevertheless took it for granted that "horse" must name a quite specific object and that this selfsame, identical entity is meant each time the word "horse" is used. Accordingly, they decided that "horse" names an image. This (they reasoned) must be an abstract image, since it can include only what is common to

The Question of Precision

In his discussion of family resemblance Wittgenstein pointed out that some concepts have blurred edges and that others have sharp edges. Philosophers have usually preferred those concepts with sharp edges. If we take seriously Nietzsche's and Dewey's psychological analyses, the explanation for this preference is obvious—it is connected with the philosophical quest for certainty. If a concept has vague, fuzzy boundaries a person cannot be certain whether the particular object he or she is considering belongs inside or outside the concept. If, for instance, the definition of "game" is open and indeterminate, it may be debatable whether a particular activity is a game. Whenever philosophers find themselves in such a situation, they tend to sharpen the edges of the concept, to define it in such a way that it becomes absolutely clear that the activity in question either is or is not a game. This move reduces philosophical anxiety, but only at the cost of creating an artificial situation.

This artificiality is just what the Romantic poets were objecting to when (as with Wordsworth) they condemned "that false secondary power by which we multiply distinctions." And it is what Schopenhauer criticized in his mosaic metaphor. A mosaicist puts together colored bits of stone (tesserae) to represent some object (say, a saint or an angel). No matter how small the tesserae the mosaicist uses, the surface of the mosaic consists of a number of wholly discrete objects. It therefore falsifies the object that it represents by introducing distinctions in kind (the abrupt jumps from one stone to another) where none exists, for the real object has a continuous surface.[8] It is instructive to compare Schopenhauer's approach with Wittgenstein's. Whereas his was metaphysical, Wittgenstein's was linguistic. Schopenhauer (and the Romantic poets) asked, "What is the real nature of things?" Their answer was, "Reality is continuous, and this is why clear-cut distinctions falsify." Wittgenstein, for his part, simply pointed out that in some language games sharp edges are appropriate and that in other games blurred edges are appropriate.

"BLURRED" VERSUS "SHARP" CONCEPTS

Since he happened to be arguing against the precisionists, Wittgenstein was chiefly concerned to show that we can get on very nicely with concepts whose

Bucephalus, Dobbin, Swaps, Secretariat, and all other particular horses. Hence the color of the image named by "horse" cannot be gray or black or roan, for these are the colors of particular horses. But what sort of color would a nonparticular, abstract color be? Clearly, these nominalists were involved in almost as many puzzles and paradoxes as were the realists.

[8] See Vol IV, pp. 146–47. According to von Wright, Wittgenstein said "he had read Schopenhauer's *Die Welt als Wille und Vorstellung* in his youth, and his first philosophy was a Schopenhauerian epistemological idealism"—in N. Malcolm, "Biographical Sketch," in *Ludwig Wittgenstein: A Memoir* (Oxford University Press, Oxford, 1966), p. 5.

edges are blurred—that is, we get along very nicely without knowing, or at least without being able to say, *exactly* what we mean. But this emphasis on the utility of blurred concepts was tactical; he did not mean that they are intrinsically better than sharply edged concepts, or that language games in which we cannot say what we know are somehow intrinsically better than those in which we can. As usual, he opposed the disposition to regard any one usage as "right," and he would have been as critical of the Romantics' disposition to say that reality *is* continuous as they were critical of their opponents' assumption that it consists in a number of discrete elements.

> I *can* give the concept "number" rigid limits, . . . but I can also use it so that the extension of concept is *not* closed by a frontier. And this is how we do use the word "game." For how is the concept of a game bounded? What still counts as a game and what no longer does? Can you give the boundary? No. You can *draw* one; for none has so far been drawn. (But that never troubled you before when you used the word "game.")
>
> "But then the use of the word is unregulated, the 'game' we play with it is unregulated."—It is not everywhere circumscribed by rules; but no more are there any rules for how high one throws the ball in tennis, or how hard; yet tennis is a game for all that and has rules too.
>
> How should we explain to someone what a game is? I imagine that we should describe *games* to him, and we might add: "This *and similar things* are called 'games.'" And do we know any more about it ourselves? Is it only other people whom we cannot tell exactly what a game is?—But this is not ignorance. We do not know the boundaries because none have been drawn. To repeat, we can draw a boundary—for a special purpose. Does it take that to make the concept usable? Not at all! (Except for that special purpose.) No more than it took the definition: 1 pace = 75 cm. to make the measure of length "one-pace" usable. And if you want to say "But still, before that it wasn't an exact measure," then I reply: very well, it was an inexact one.—Though you still owe me a definition of exactness. . . .
>
> What does it mean to know what a game is? What does it mean, to know it and not be able to say it? Is this knowledge somehow equivalent to an unformulated definition? So that if it were formulated I should be able to recognize it as the expression of my knowledge? Isn't my knowledge, my concept of a game, completely expressed in the explanations that I could give? That is, in my describing examples of various kinds of game; shewing how all sorts of other games can be constructed on the analogy of these; saying that I should scarcely include this or this among games; and so on.
>
> If someone were to draw a sharp boundary I could not acknowledge it as the one that I too always wanted to draw, or had drawn in my mind.

For I did not want to draw one at all. His concept can then be said to be not the same as mine, but akin to it. The kinship is that of two pictures, one of which consists of colour patches with vague contours, and the other of patches similarly shaped and distributed, but with clear contours. The kinship is just as undeniable as the difference. . . .

Compare *knowing* and *saying:*

how many feet high Mont Blanc is—
how the word "game" is used—
how a clarinet sounds.

If you are surprised that one can know something and not be able to say it, you are perhaps thinking of a case like the first. Certainly not of one like the third.

Consider this example. If one says "Moses did not exist," this may mean various things. It may mean: the Israelites did not have a *single* leader when they withdrew from Egypt————or: their leader was not called Moses————or: there cannot have been anyone who accomplished all that the Bible relates of Moses————or: etc., etc.—We may say, following Russell: the name "Moses" can be defined by means of various descriptions. . . .

But when I make a statement about Moses,—am I always ready to substitute some *one* of these descriptions for "Moses"? I shall perhaps say: By "Moses" I understand the man who did what the Bible relates of Moses, or at any rate a good deal of it. But how much? Have I decided how much must be proved false for me to give up my proposition as false? Has the name Moses got a fixed and unequivocal use for me in all possible cases?—Is it not the case that I have, so to speak, a whole series of props in readiness, and am ready to lean on one if another should be taken from under me and vice versa?

And this can be expressed like this: I use the name "N" without a *fixed* meaning. (But that detracts as little from its usefulness, as it detracts from that of a table that it stands on four legs instead of three and so sometimes wobbles.)

Should it be said that I am using a word whose meaning I don't know, and so am talking nonsense?—Say what you choose, so long as it does not prevent you from seeing the facts.[1]

DEFINITIONS AND RULES

A definition may be thought of as a rule, a rule for determining what circumstances are appropriate for the use of a word—for instance, for determining whether "horse" is the appropriate word to use when talking about that object over there in the field. Wittgenstein's point about definitions and concepts can therefore be restated in terms of rules. The rules of every game are subject to interpretation, and they change from time to time. Yet this does not make it impossible to play the game; we simply make up new rules as they are needed, to cover the doubtful cases, and proceed. Indeed, what sort of game would it be whose play was *absolutely* fixed by its rules?

> But what does a game look like that is everywhere bounded by rules? whose rules never let a doubt creep in, but stop up all the cracks where it might?—Can't we imagine a rule determining the application of a rule, and a doubt which it removes—and so on?
>
> But that is not to say that we are in doubt because it is possible for us to *imagine* a doubt. I can easily imagine someone always doubting before he opened his front door whether an abyss did not yawn behind it; and making sure about it before he went through the door (and he might on some occasion prove to be right)—but that does not make me doubt in the same case.ᵐ

To draw another analogy, definitions and rules are like signposts. Although a signpost gives a person direction, it can still leave that person in doubt. If it proves to be ambiguous, supplementary instructions can be added, but no matter how extensive these instructions are they cannot *guarantee* that no one ever loses the way. In any case, the pursuit of more and more precise signposts is not a philosophical matter but an empirical one.

This can be applied to such a problem as the meaning of "Moses." According to Wittgenstein, to seek an absolutely unambiguous meaning is a philosophical illness.

> Suppose I give this explanation: "I take 'Moses' to mean the man, if there was such a man, who led the Israelites out of Egypt, whatever he was called then and whatever he may or may not have done besides."— But similar doubts to those about "Moses" are possible about the words of this explanation (what are you calling "Egypt," whom the "Israelites" etc.?). Nor would these questions come to an end when we got down to words like "red," "dark," "sweet."—"But then how does an explanation help me to understand, if after all it is not the final one? In that case the explanation is never completed; so I still don't understand what he means, and never shall!"—As though an explanation as it were hung in the air unless supported by another one. Whereas an explanation may indeed rest on another one that has been given, but none stands in need of another—unless *we* require it to prevent a misunderstanding—one, that is, that would occur but for the explanation; not every one that I can imagine.
>
> It may easily look as if every doubt merely *revealed* an existing gap in the foundations; so that secure understanding is only possible if we first doubt everything that *can* be doubted, and then remove all these doubts.

The sign-post is in order—if, under normal circumstances, it fulfills its purpose.

If I tell someone "Stand roughly here"—may not this explanation work perfectly? And cannot every other one fail too?

But isn't it an inexact explanation?—Yes; why shouldn't we call it "inexact"? Only let us understand what "inexact" means. For it does not mean "unusable." . . .

We understand what it means to set a pocket watch to the exact time or to regulate it to be exact. But what if it were asked: is this exactness ideal exactness, or how nearly does it approach the ideal?—Of course, we can speak of measurements of time in which there is a different, and as we should say a greater, exactness than in the measurement of time by a pocket watch; in which the words "to set the clock to the exact time" have a different, though related meaning. . . . Now, if I tell someone: "You should come to dinner more punctually; you know it begins at one o'clock exactly"—is there really no question of *exactness* here? because it is possible to say: "Think of the determination of time in the laboratory or the observatory; *there* you see what 'exactness' means"?

"Inexact" is really a reproach, and "exact" is praise. And that is to say that what is inexact attains its goal less perfectly than what is more exact. Thus the point here is what we call "the goal." Am I inexact when I do not give our distance from the sun to the nearest foot, or tell a joiner the width of a table to the nearest thousandth of an inch?

No *single* ideal of exactness has been laid down; we do not know what we should be supposed to imagine under this head.[n]

Thus a definition—or a rule or a signpost—is "exact" if it is good enough for whatever purpose it has been introduced, and because purposes differ exactnesses too will differ. That is all there is to the question of precision. To ask for more is to become entangled in a whole nest of philosophical problems, all of which have their source in a quest for certainty. To realize this is to dissolve all these problems at one stroke.

Critique of Logical Atomism

At this point, Wittgenstein evidently had in mind the program that Russell had formulated and that the Logical Positivists were attempting to carry out—the project, that is, of analyzing all complex propositions into atomistic propositions about simple, elementary occurrences ("Blue here now," "Yellow here now," and the like), which could then be recombined according to the rules of a logically exact language.[9] In a word, the quest for certainty and precision had led these

[9] See pp. 246–54.

philosophers to logical atomism as a metaphysical doctrine and to analysis as a methodology.

In criticizing logical atomism Wittgenstein was of course attacking a contemporary version of the underlying theses of the analytic tradition—the assumptions (1) that the universe consists in a number of elementary, encapsulated entities, each itself and not another thing; (2) that everything that is not a simple is a composite composed of several such simples; and (3) that when we are confronted with a composite we can come to understand it by analyzing it into its constituent simples.[10] To these basic assumptions proponents of the picture theory added the doctrine that the simple elements can only be named (pointed to by ostensive definition); they cannot be described, for description involves analysis.

Let us first consider Wittgenstein's comments on analysis, bearing in mind that in the *Tractatus* he had himself put forward a view very similar to Russell's.

LIMITATIONS OF THE METHOD OF ANALYSIS

Characteristically, Wittgenstein pointed out that "analysis" has a variety of meanings, each appropriate in its own context, that is, in the language game in which it occurs. The logical atomists (Wittgenstein included, in his earlier work) had simply taken one of these meanings as *the* meaning of "analysis." The same was true for "composite" and the other terms in the lexicon of logical atomism. When this is understood, Wittgenstein held, it no longer seems plausible to characterize analysis as the ideal philosophical method.

> But what are the simple constituent parts of which reality is composed?—What are the simple constituent parts of a chair?—The bits of wood of which it is made? or the molecules, or the atoms?—"Simple" means: not composite. And here the point is: in what sense "composite"? It makes no sense at all to speak absolutely of the "simple parts of a chair."
>
> Again, Does my visual image of this tree, of this chair, consist of parts? And what are its simple constituent parts? Multi-colouredness is one kind of complexity; another is, for example, that of a broken outline composed of straight bits. And a curve can be said to be composed of an ascending and a descending segment.
>
> If I tell someone without any further explanation: "What I see before me now is composite," he will have the right to ask: "What do you mean by 'composite'? For there are all sorts of things that that can mean!"—The question "Is what you see composite?" makes good sense if it is already established what kind of complexity—that is, which particular use of the word—is in question. If it had been laid down that the visual image of a tree was to be called "composite" if one saw not just a single

[10] See pp. 90–92.

trunk but also branches, then the question "Is the visual image of this tree simple or composite?" and the question "What are its simple component parts?" would have a clear sense—a clear use. And of course the answer to the second question is not "The branches" (that would be an answer to the grammatical question: "What are here called 'simple component parts'?") but rather a description of the individual branches. . . .

We use the word "composite" (and therefore the word "simple") in an enormous number of different and differently related ways. (Is the colour of a square on a chessboard simple, or does it consist of pure white and pure yellow? And is white simple, or does it consist of the colours of the rainbow?—Is this length of 2 cm. simple, or does it consist of two parts, each 1 cm. long? But why not of one bit 3 cm. long, and one bit 1 cm. long measured in the opposite direction?)

To the *philosophical* question: "Is the visual image of this tree composite, and what are its component parts?" the correct answer is: "That depends on what you understand by 'composite.'" (And that is of course not an answer but a rejection of the question.)°

Diversity of meaning apart, analysis seems an ideal method only to those who have allowed a particular requirement to slip into their notion of what they are aiming at in the communications they make to other people. This, according to Wittgenstein, is the requirement of simplicity. But is simplicity always preferable? Suppose I ask someone to bring the broom from the kitchen. He must understand me, because he fetches the broom. Would I have made things clearer (to him? to myself?) if I had said "Bring me the broomstick and the brush that is fitted on it"? If I had said that would he not be likely to respond, "Do you want the broom? Why do you put it so oddly?" What would I have gained by the translation? The second sentence may be said to be a "further analysed form of the first one," in the sense that the requirement of greater simplicity has been met. But it achieves no more than the first sentence and it accomplishes its purpose only in a roundabout way; in this sense, the second sentence is not simpler but more complex.

So much for "simplicity." What of "further analysed form"? It is possible to think of two languages, in one of which, (a), the names of composites (such names as "broom") occur, and in the other of which, (b), only the names of simples (well, of such *relative* simples as "broomstick" and "brush") occur. What is meant by saying that (b) is an "analysed form" of (a)?

In what sense is an order in the second game an analysed form of an order in the first? Does the former lie concealed in the latter, and is it now brought out by analysis? . . .

To say . . . that a sentence in (b) is an "analysed" form of one in (a) readily seduces us into thinking that the former is the more fundamental form; that it alone shews what is meant by the other, and so on. For example, we think: If you have only the unanalysed form you miss the

> analysis; but if you know the analysed form that gives you everything.—
> But can I not say that an aspect of the matter is lost on you in the *lat-ter* case as well as the former?[p]

Possibly (b) is better for some purposes than (a), but is anyone going to argue that (b) is intrinsically superior to (a)? Everything depends on the context in which the language game is played, and in everyday contexts (such as asking someone to fetch a broom), (a) is preferable. It is much the same as in the case of the blurred and the sharply focused pictures. Something is gained when the picture is brought into focus, but something is lost.

IDEAL LANGUAGES

We come now to the question of ideal languages, or as Wittgenstein put it, the "subliming" of logic. It is often said that logic is a "normative science." It lays down the rules for correct—for valid—thinking. Once these rules are formulated it is possible to examine actual instances and accept or reject them, depending on how well they approximate the logical norms. Everything that Wittgenstein said about definitions and signposts, and about the "open" character of the rules by which games are played, naturally applies to logic and to the notion of an ideal language. Thus logic is indeed a normative science, in the sense that we can compare and criticize actual instances of thinking and everyday uses of language (just as, for that matter, we can compare and criticize actual instances of chess playing). But in Wittgenstein's view we do not need an absolutely definitive set of logical rules or an ideal language in order to make these comparisons (any more than we need an absolutely definitive set of rules about chess to criticize actual games of chess). Unfortunately, however, the phrase "normative sciences" suggests just such a set of rules.

> F. P. Ramsey once emphasized in conversation with me that logic was a "normative science." I do not know exactly what he had in mind, but it was doubtless closely related to what only dawned on me later: namely, that in philosophy we often *compare* the use of words with games and calculi which have fixed rules, but cannot say that someone who is using language *must* be playing such a game.—But if you say that our languages only *approximate* to such calculi you are standing on the very brink of a misunderstanding. For then it may look as if what we were talking about were an *ideal* language. . . . Here the word "ideal" is liable to mislead, for it sounds as if these languages were better, more perfect, than our everyday language; and as if it took the logician to shew people at last what a correct sentence looked like.[q]

In other words, the ideal of "exactness," which Wittgenstein had deflated insofar as it affected the notion of definition, has also infected our thinking about logic. That ideal has led to a conception of logic as "something sublime," as something having "peculiar depth" and "universal significance."[r] It has also led to a corresponding derogation of actual, everyday thought and language. As a result we tend to focus attention on what does not help us solve our philosophical problems and to neglect what can dissolve them.

Let us consider the way in which the ideal of exactness has led to the subliming of logic.

> Logic lay, it seemed, at the bottom of all the sciences.—For logical investigation explores the nature of all things. It seeks to see to the bottom of things and is not meant to concern itself whether what actually happens is this or that.—It takes its rise, not from an interest in the facts of nature, nor from a need to grasp causal connexions; but from an urge to understand the basis, or essence, of everything empirical. Not, however, as if to this end we had to hunt out new facts; it is, rather, of the essence of our investigation that we do not seek to learn anything *new* by it. We want to *understand* something that is already in plain view. For *this* is what we seem in some sense not to understand. . . .
>
> We feel as if we had to *penetrate* phenomena: our investigation, however, is directed not towards phenomena, but, as one might say, towards the *possibilities* of phenomena. . . .
>
> [Thus] it may come to look as if there were something like a final analysis of our forms of language, and so a *single* completely resolved form of every expression. That is, as if our usual forms of expression were, essentially, unanalysed; as if there were something hidden in them that had to be brought to light. When this is done the expression is completely clarified and our problem solved.
>
> It can also be put like this: we eliminate misunderstandings by making our expressions more exact; but now it may look as if we were moving toward a particular state, a state of complete exactness; and as if this were the real goal of our investigation. . . .
>
> Thought is surrounded by a halo.—Its essence, logic, presents an order, in fact the a priori order of the world: that is, the order of *possibilities*, which must be common to both world and thought. But this order, it seems, must be *utterly simple*. It is *prior* to all experience, must run through all experience; no empirical cloudiness or uncertainty can be allowed to affect it.—It must rather be of the purest crystal. . . .
>
> We are under the illusion that what is peculiar, profound, essential, in our investigation, resides in its trying to grasp the incomparable essence of language. That is, the order existing between the concepts of proposition, word, proof, truth, experience, and so on. This order is a *super*-order between—so to speak—*super*-concepts. Whereas, of course, if the words "language," "experience," "world," have a use, it must be as humble a one as that of the words "table," "lamp," "door."[s]

This placement of a halo around thought, this etherealization of logic into a superscience, results directly from the seemingly innocent assumption that "there can't be any vagueness in logic."ᵗ And where did we get this idea? Those crystal-clear rules of thought that logicians are forever polishing were not *discovered* by them as a result of any study of thought processes; they slipped unnoticed into the logicians' investigations at the outset as a requirement, a demand, that the logicians themselves imposed on their own investigations. Thus the assumption that there cannot be any vagueness in logic is but another reflection of the philosophical need for precision and exactness.

> The more narrowly we examine actual language, the sharper becomes the conflict between it and our requirement. (For crystalline purity of logic was, of course, not a *result of investigation:* it was a requirement.) The conflict becomes intolerable; the requirement is now in danger of becoming empty.—We have got on to slippery ice where there is no friction and so in a certain sense the conditions are ideal, but also, just because of that, we are unable to walk. We want to walk: so we need *friction.* Back to the rough ground!
>
> We see that what we call "sentence" and "language" have not the formal unity that I imagined, but are families of structures more or less related to one another.—But what becomes of logic now? Its rigour seems to be giving way here.—But in that case doesn't logic altogether disappear?—For how can it lose its rigour? Of course not by our bargaining any of its rigour out of it.—The *preconceived idea* of a crystalline purity can only be removed by turning our whole examination round. (One might say: the axis of reference of our examination must be rotated, but about the fixed point of our real need.)ᵘ

Thus Wittgenstein proposed a radical reform of logic: the purpose of logic was no longer to attempt to *correct* everyday language but to *understand* how everyday language functions. In a word, he proposed as the model for logic what he was doing in the *Investigations,* not the sort of analysis Russell had done, or that he himself had done in the *Tractatus.* This is what he meant by the rotation of the axis. Wittgenstein's contention was that everyday language is good enough for everyday purposes. Implicit in this position is a survival-of-the-fittest notion: everyday language would not have survived if it did not perform the functions for which it was introduced. In Wittgenstein's view we do not need a "sublimed" logic for everyday purposes. Nor do we need a sublimed logic to clear up the special philosophical problems that plague us. To dissolve *these* problems we need only to understand how everyday language actually functions, for it is our misunderstanding of how it functions that has created the problems.

> We must do away with all *explanation,* and description alone must take its place. And this description gets its light, that is to say its purpose—from the philosophical problems. These are, of course, not

empirical problems; they are solved, rather, by looking into the workings of our language, and that in such a way as to make us realize these workings: *in despite of* an urge to misunderstand them. The problems are solved, not by giving new information, but by arranging what we have always known. Philosophy is a battle against the bewitchment of our intelligence by means of language.[v]

Examples of How Philosophical Problems Are Dissolved

THE MIND-BODY PROBLEM

The mind-body problem is another typical philosophical puzzle that Wittgenstein undertook to dissolve. It is, in fact, a whole nest of puzzles. For instance, when I will to move my finger and it moves, how does my mind bring about this movement of my body on command? What sorts of processes, or mental states, are intending, hoping, expecting, imagining? What, in general, is the nature of thought, and how is thought related to the brain state that "causes" it or (possibly) that is "correlated" with it? Since my experiences (my psychic life) are private to me and inaccessible to others, how can anyone else ever know what I am experiencing—for instance, what my pain is like? And how can I know this about others?

Descartes's dual-substance theory, which dominated philosophy during most of the early modern period, made these questions wholly unanswerable. If there are two completely independent sorts of substance—mind and body—how can they interact? How can an entity that is nonmaterial (mind) cause changes in an entity that is material and that moves only on contact (body)? How can a change in body cause a change in mental state? That is, how does it happen that such a psychic event as seeing a red color-patch occurs as a result of some change in the physical condition of the cortex, a change itself caused by light waves impinging on the retina and thus setting up a movement along the optic nerve?

Hume reported that, even after careful introspection, he could observe no mental states. This was correct, but it did not occur to him that mental states are not the sort of thing that can be looked for. Had such a thought occurred to him, he might have been led to a new start. Instead, he argued that there are no mental states, which was merely a skeptical conclusion. Kant too attacked the Cartesian formula; he argued that we should think of mind and body as functions, not as independently existing substances. This was a more fruitful approach, but Kant and his successors still thought in terms of the Cartesian question "What sort of things, or processes, must mind and body *be*, for thoughts and acts of will to occur?" They simply gave a more sophisticated answer than did Descartes.

Wittgenstein regarded this whole approach as a blind alley. His own approach was, characteristically, linguistic. Instead of asking "What is thinking? What is willing?" he asked "How are words like 'thinking' and 'willing' actually used in everyday circumstances?" He held that because we have misunderstood the nature of language our thoughts about thinking are guided by misleading models. It is these models that have created the mind-body problem, and once we have managed to free ourselves from these models—by coming to understand the nature of language—the problem dissolves.

The root difficulty, according to Wittgenstein, is that we slip into supposing that thinking is some sort of special state (mental, psychic, or spiritual) that accompanies speech but is distinct from it and may occur independently (that is, in the absence of speech, when we think silently or "to ourselves"). The picture theory of meaning is responsible for our belief in mental states, as it is responsible for our belief in real universals, and for the same reason. Just as we suppose there is some specific entity named by "horse," which cannot be any of the particular horses named by "Bucephalus," "Dobbin," or "Swaps," so we suppose that there is some specific activity that always occurs whenever we correctly affirm that we are thinking.

> Because we cannot specify any *one* bodily action which we call pointing to the shape (as opposed, for example, to the colour), we say that a spiritual [mental, intellectual] activity corresponds to these words.
> Where our language suggests a body and there is none: there, we should like to say, is a *spirit*.[w]

Once the notion occurs to us that there is something (a spiritual activity) named by "thinking" (and of course other things named by "intending," "hoping," and "imagining"), we expect to be able to observe these processes. But realizing that they are very special and move very swiftly, we think we must catch them on the run, much as if we were astronomers who have to set up a telescope in order to see a meteor as it flashes past. To make these assumptions, Wittgenstein held, is to enter the path that leads to a Humean type of skepticism.

> Here it is easy to get into that dead-end in philosophy, where one believes that the difficulty of the task consists in this: our having to describe phenomena that are hard to get hold of, the present experience that slips quickly by, or something of the kind. Where we find ordinary language too crude, and it looks as if we were having to do not with the phenomena of every-day, but with ones that [as Augustine said] "easily elude us, and, in their coming to be and passing away, produce those others as an average effect."[x]

It might seem from such passages as these that Wittgenstein was a kind of cryptobehaviorist—that given the belief that "an 'inner process' stands in need of outward criteria,"[y] the next logical step would be to deny that an inner process, which cannot be observed, ever occurs. But behaviorism is a metaphysical position. The behaviorist starts from the basic Cartesian dichotomy between mind and body, and after eliminating mind, concludes that body alone is real. In contrast, Wittgenstein rejected the dichotomy and with it the metaphysical question of whether minds or bodies (or both) are real.

> "But you surely cannot deny that, for example, in remembering, an inner process takes place."—What gives the impression that we want to deny anything? . . .
>
> Why should I deny that there is a mental process? But "There has just taken place in me the mental process of remembering. . . . " means nothing more than: "I have just remembered. . . . " To deny the mental process would mean to deny the remembering; to deny that anyone ever remembers anything.
>
> "Are you not really a behaviorist in disguise? Aren't you at bottom really saying that everything except human behavior is a fiction?"—If I do speak of a fiction, then it is of a *grammatical* fiction.
>
> How does the philosophical problem about mental processes and states and about behaviorism arise?—The first step is the one that altogether escapes notice. We talk of processes and states and leave their nature undecided. Sometime perhaps we shall know more about them—we think. But that is just what commits us to a particular way of looking at the matter. For we have a definite concept of what it means to learn to know a process better. (The decisive movement in the conjuring trick has been made, and it was the very one that we thought quite innocent.) . . .
>
> Try not to think of understanding as a "mental process" at all—for *that* is the expression which confuses you. But ask yourself: in what sort of case, in what kind of circumstances, do we say, "Now I know how to go on."[z]

Instead of allowing himself to become involved in a sterile debate over whether minds and mental states are real, Wittgenstein examined the circumstances in which people have occasion to use words that may seem to designate mental states. He held that if we look closely at these occasions we find that the expressions used have perfectly straightforward, everyday meanings that do not involve any metaphysical issues at all. It is essential to remember that "we are not analysing a phenomenon (e.g., thought) but a concept (e.g., that of thinking), and therefore the use of a word."[a]

Under what circumstances would I say, for instance, that I was thinking about what time it was? Well, first, under what circumstances would I *not* say that I was thinking about what time it was? Suppose "I read this question in some narrative, or quote it as someone else's utterance." Or suppose I am "practicing the pronunciation of these words." In such circumstances I would not say that I was thinking about what time it was. On the other hand, I *would* say I was thinking of what time it was if "I was thinking about my breakfast and wondering whether it would be late today."[b]

The context in which I use the term "thinking" (and conversely, the context in which I do not use the term) reveals what I mean when I ascribe (or refuse to ascribe) thought to people. It turns out that we use the term in different circumstances and hence that thinking is a matter of family resemblance. This throws a new light on Wittgenstein's remark that inner processes need outward criteria. The point is that a mental state gets whatever specific character it has—as a thought or a feeling, a hope or a fear, an intention or an expectation—because of the context in which it occurs.

> Could someone have a feeling of ardent love or hope for the space of one second—*no matter what* preceded or followed this second?— What is happening now has significance—in these surroundings. The surroundings give it its importance. And the word "hope" refers to a phenomenon of human life. (A smiling mouth *smiles* only in a human face.)
>
> Now suppose I sit in my room and hope that N. N. will come and bring me some money, and suppose one minute of this state could be isolated, cut out of its context; would what happened in it then not be hope?—Think, for example, of the words which you perhaps utter in this space of time. They are no longer part of this language. And in different surroundings the institution of money doesn't exist either.
>
> A coronation is the picture of pomp and dignity. Cut one minute of this proceeding out of its surroundings: the crown is being placed on the head of the king in his coronation robes.—But in different surroundings gold is the cheapest of metals, its gleam is thought vulgar. There the fabric of the robe is cheap to produce. A crown is a parody of a respectable hat. And so on.[c]

Hence, when we hear an individual use such an expression as "I hope he'll come" or "I wonder what time it is," we have to look to the rest of that person's behavior: "The point is: what led up to these words?"[d] That is, we must look to the circumstances in which the words were used. Depending on the circumstances, we may ascribe thought to the individual (or hope, or expectation). Or we may conclude that he or she is not thinking but merely saying the words mechanically. To say that he or she is thinking is to say that a whole characteristic pattern of action is going forward—including, but not limited to, certain verbal expressions. That is why we do not ascribe thought to parrots or to phonographs (though they "talk"): their behavior lacks this characteristic pattern of action. And that pattern—not just an isolated psychic occurrence—is what we *mean* by "thought." Thus the metaphysical question (What is thought? What is mind?) is dissolved. We are left only with such straightforward empirical questions as "Was he thinking or was he just speaking mechanically?" Questions of this type, of course, are answered by reference to "what he tells us and the rest of his behavior."[e]

VOLUNTARY ACTS

Similar considerations apply to the age-old problems clustering around the nature of voluntary acts and around the supposed inaccessibility and privacy of pains and other sensations. As regards the former, Wittgenstein maintained that instead of looking for (and of course failing to find) a psychic cause of a peculiar kind, we should look at the way in which we ourselves and other people use the word "willing" in everyday speech. Under what circumstances does one say "I willed to raise my arm"? Under what circumstances does one say "My arm rose"? The differences in circumstances—inner and outer—are the meaning of "willing." One of these differences, and therefore one of the criteria of whether a voluntary act has occurred, is the absence of surprise.

> Examine the following description of a voluntary action: "I form the decision to pull the bell at 5 o'clock, and when it strikes 5, my arm makes this movement."—Is that the correct description, and not *this* one: " . . . and when it strikes 5, I raise my arm"? . . .
>
> So one might say: voluntary movement is marked by the absence of surprise. And now I do not mean you to ask "But *why* isn't one surprised here?"[f]

Thus the "philosophical" problem about the nature of an act of will is dissolved by taking note of the circumstances in which people use words such as "I decided" and the circumstances in which they do not use such words.

ARE SENSATIONS PRIVATE?

Philosophers have been puzzled for centuries about how we can know that other people feel pain and have other sensations. Their reasoning goes like this: Only I can know that I feel pain, for my pain is something that goes on inside me and is therefore inaccessible to anyone else. Other people's pain, if indeed they feel pain, is similarly private to them. I can therefore only surmise that they experience pain.

Wittgenstein used a number of strategies to dissolve this puzzlement. The first was simply to point out that if we use the word "know" in the everyday sense the situation is exactly reversed.

> If we are using the word "to know" as it is normally used (and how else are we to use it?), then other people very often know when I am in pain.—Yes, but all the same not with the certainty with which I know it myself!—It can't be said of me at all (except perhaps as a joke) that I *know* I am in pain. What is it supposed to mean—except perhaps that I *am* in pain?
>
> Other people cannot be said to learn of my sensations *only* from my behaviour,—for *I* cannot be said to learn of them. I *have* them.[g]

In a second argument Wittgenstein pointed out that if the situation were what philosophers say it is—if everyone knew only his or her own pain—it would be wholly irresponsible to infer anything at all about anyone else's experiences. It would be wildly speculative, for instance, for a physician to infer anything about a patient's condition from what the patient says about the pain he or she feels.

> Suppose everyone had a box with something in it: we call it a "beetle." No one can look into anyone else's box, and everyone says he knows what a beetle is only by looking at *his* beetle.—Here it would be quite possible for everyone to have something different in his box. One might even imagine such a thing constantly changing.—But suppose the word "beetle" had a use in these people's language?—If so it would not be used as the name of a thing. The thing in the box has no place in the language-game at all; not even as a *something:* for the box might even be empty.—No, one can "divide through" by the thing in the box; it cancels out, whatever it is.
>
> That is to say: if we construe the grammar of the expression of sensation on the model of "object and name" the object drops out of consideration as irrelevant.[h]

Wittgenstein's point is that if the philosophical doctrine of private sensations were right, the patient and the physician would be talking only about the word "pain"; they could not be discussing the patient's pain. Since everyone—not only the patient and the physician but even the philosophers themselves—believes the patient is discussing pain, not "pain," it follows that something is wrong with the doctrine in question.

Finally, Wittgenstein attacked the doctrine of privacy by arguing that the very notion of a private language in which a person talks about private sensations is meaningless. Although this criticism of private languages is involved and has occasioned much debate, the main line of the argument is fairly straightforward. According to Wittgenstein, since language is a social game it requires more than one player. The notion of a rule is fundamental to language, and a *private* rule is meaningless.

> Why can't my right hand give my left hand money?—My right hand can put it into my left hand. My right hand can write a deed of gift and my left hand a receipt.—But the further practical consequences would not be those of a gift. When the left hand has taken the money from the right, etc., we shall ask: "Well, and what of it?" And the same could be asked if a person had given himself a private definition of a word; I mean, if he has said the word to himself and at the same time has directed his attention to a sensation.[i]

Wittgenstein and Husserl

As another example of the Wittgensteinian method of dissolving philosophical problems, consider the dispute among phenomenologists over whether Husserl lapsed into idealism.[11] This dispute presupposes that realism and idealism are genuine philosophical alternatives. But practitioners of Wittgenstein's type of therapy would be disposed to reply in the following way: what is "hidden within" experience may, by a shift of metaphor, be thought of as "lurking behind" experience. With this shift the move is made from phenomenalism either to idealism or to realism, depending on the bias of the individual thinker. In either case it is a shift only from one picture frame to another. The question of whether Husserl was an idealist or a realist is thus not answered; it is dissolved.

Or again, consider the dispute between Husserl and his critics over transcendental reduction. Do the entities that phenomenologists find in reduced experience really exist or are they merely inventions of the phenomenologists? From the point of view of *Philosophical Investigations* this is not a substantive dispute, but a linguistic one. It is not, as the disputants themselves suppose, a question of whether the entities are in experience or not there; it is a question of what language is better for describing experience—Dewey's, for instance? or Whitehead's? or Moore's? or Husserl's?[12] And the answer to *this* question is another question: "Better for what?" Wittgenstein would have urged us, instead of disputing over which of these descriptions is correct, to examine the various language games in which the descriptions occur. Thus Whitehead's description is part of a language game designed to expound a new monistic metaphysics, and Husserl's is part of a language game designed to get rid of metaphysics and lay the foundations for his rigorous new science of human beings and nature. And so on.

Husserl of course would have none of this. His descriptions, he thought, were not merely better in the context of a particular language game; they were *true*. But whom are we to believe: Husserl or Wittgenstein? This turns on what we take to be the relation between philosophy and language—perhaps the major issue in twentieth-century philosophy. For Wittgenstein, all seeing is "languageified"; all seeing is relative to "frames"—to presuppositions, assumptions, and values that have become congealed in language. Hence philosophical inquiry is intrinsically linguistic in nature. In Husserl's view, there is a special kind of seeing, wholly free from language, that occurs when we bracket properly. First we see what is the case; then we look around for the right words to describe what we see. Doubtless it is not always easy to find the right words; indeed, Husserl's own difficulty in finding them is evident from the way in which his descriptions changed from book to book. But the problem of finding the right words is a subsidiary and completely separate task. In Husserl's view, philosophical inquiry itself is not in any sense linguistic.[13]

[11] See p. 306.
[12] See pp. 46–47, 79–80, 111–15, and 291–93.
[13] See p. 300. Husserl would, of course, have agreed with Wittgenstein that most philosophical theories—indeed, all philosophical theories before his own—present false and misleading pictures of reality. This is because he held none of them to be assumption-free. But it is one thing to agree that most pictures are false and another to say that the picture theory itself is a profound illusion.

If bracketing is, as Husserl claimed, a special kind of seeing that discloses objects *originaliter*, then Wittgenstein's view of the relation between philosophy and language is mistaken, and his whole program of therapy is undermined. Thus Husserl's phenomenology is, in effect and by anticipation, a direct answer to *Philosophical Investigations*. But now we have to ask whether Husserl's claims for bracketing are correct. This may seem like a straightforward (if admittedly difficult) empirical question. Are things "self-given" when we bracket or are they not? Suppose Wittgenstein had bracketed and reported that he did not find anything that was self-given. Husserl could have replied that this was merely evidence that Wittgenstein had failed to bracket successfully, for the procedure requires careful training. And Wittgenstein could have retorted that bracketing is only a particularly subtle sort of frame, that what seemed to be self-given and originaliter to Husserl looked that way only because Husserl identified so closely with his frame that he was wholly unconscious of it.

There is no way of adjudicating definitively between these interpretations. To hope to settle such an issue between Husserl and Wittgenstein by an appeal to the empirical evidence is naïve, for what is "empirical evidence" itself turns out to be at issue. What seems to one party apodeictically certain because it is "there" seems to the other party a projection of the quest for certainty. Here, then, we have reached another fundamental parting of the ways in philosophy. But to speak in this fashion is to side with Wittgenstein rather than with Husserl. For instance, the language just used about their difference being a matter of "interpretation" is language that is congenial to Wittgenstein, not to Husserl. Further, Wittgenstein could accept, and Husserl had to reject, the notion that what is "empirical evidence" remains an open issue; finally, Wittgenstein could agree, and Husserl could not, that there *are* partings of the ways.

Wittgenstein and Heidegger

It is difficult, at least on the surface, to think of two philosophers who have less in common than Wittgenstein and Heidegger. Consider, for instance, their views of time. There is no point at which their approaches intersect.[14] It is easy to find reasons for their differences. When Heidegger was preparing for the priesthood, Wittgenstein was studying engineering with a view to designing an airplane propeller. When Wittgenstein was reading Frege and Russell, Heidegger was reading Husserl. Where Wittgenstein started from a logistical frame of reference—the logic of assertions was to be analyzed to ascertain the basic structure of the world—Heidegger started from a phenomenological frame of reference—human experience was to be explored for the light it could cast on the nature of

[14] See pp. 346 and 418.

Being. But, under the pressure of those profound changes in the general culture that we described in Chapter 1,[15] both moved a long way from their starting points, and to a surprising degree their paths in the end converged.

Both experienced deep disquietudes, which, we may suspect, had similar roots; in both cases these disquietudes were generated at least in part by an uneasiness about the relation between language and reality. Both had started from the comfortable assumption that it is possible to find a language that will mirror the world. Though they certainly differed about what can be said and also about what saying it clearly consists in, both began by believing that what can be said can, with sufficient care and effort, be said clearly. But both came to the painful conclusion that what is most important in life cannot be said at all, and both concluded that among the most important things that cannot be said is the relation between language and reality. This conclusion obviously undermined the whole enterprise of philosophy as they had originally conceived it. Their reactions to this painful discovery differed: Wittgenstein wanted to cure us of our passion for saying the unsayable; Heidegger wanted to leave us exposed to this passion—that is, to leave us open to the "claim and call of Being." But the careers of both of these philosophers, it is clear, were deeply affected by the linguistic turn that Western culture took in this century.

Wittgenstein's Place in Twentieth-Century Philosophy

In many respects Wittgenstein—not only the Wittgenstein of the *Tractatus* but also the Wittgenstein of the *Investigations*—was a continuator of the analytic tradition. This can be seen, for instance, in his conviction that linguistic confusions are chiefly responsible for philosophical puzzles. But in other respects Wittgenstein revolutionized this tradition. At some important points Wittgenstein was much closer to Dewey than to any of the analytic philosophers—in his instrumentalism, in his emphasis on use, in his insistence that meaning is relative to social context. At other points Wittgenstein was close to Nietzsche. Like Nietzsche, he believed that philosophy is a form of therapy and that this therapy is successful when it brings us to the painful realization that what we have taken to be an account of the nature of the world is only and can be only an "interpretation."

Thus Wittgenstein did not say that the picture theory of meaning was *false*. He said that it was an interpretation that we have naïvely believed to be true: "A *picture* held us captive. And we could not get outside it, for it lay in our language and language seemed to repeat it to us inexorably."[j] Note that the illusion here lay not merely in supposing that a particular picture represents reality. The illusion was far deeper: it lay in supposing that *any* picture represents, or could represent,

---

[15] As it happens, they were born in the same year, 1889.

reality. What held us captive was the picture of a picture, the belief that language mirrors reality. Thus Wittgenstein quoted the doctrine of the *Tractatus*—"The general form of propositions is: This is how things are"—and commented, "That is the kind of proposition that one repeats to oneself countless times. One thinks that one is tracing the outline of the thing's nature over and over again, and one is merely tracing round the frame through which we look at it."[k]

There are many such "frames," each embedded in a particular language. The ideal of exactness is one. This is why it is so difficult to rid ourselves of the conviction that "there can't be any vagueness in logic." "The ideal, as we think of it, is unshakable. You can never get outside it; you must always turn back. There is no outside; outside you cannot breathe.—Where does this idea come from? Is it like a pair of glasses on our nose through which we see whatever we look at. It never occurs to us to take them off."[l]

Thus, like Nietzsche, Wittgenstein was far more radically antimetaphysical than were even such antimetaphysical philosophers as Bergson, Russell, and Dewey; the whole history of philosophy since Descartes can be viewed as a progressive erosion of the domain that philosophers have been willing to allot to metaphysics. Kant denied that we can know what ultimate reality is, but he took it for granted that we can at least know that "things-in-themselves" exist. Schopenhauer and Bergson, who maintained that ultimate reality is inaccessible to reason, thought that in intuition we know it to be will. Though Russell and the positivists curtailed the sphere of metaphysics still further, they held that by a rigorous logical analysis we can get back to "hard data." Even Dewey, despite his instrumentalism, worked out a doctrine of experience that he held to be a correct account of how things are. All these thinkers belonged to the major tradition in holding that philosophy is a cognitive enterprise—that its goal is to ascertain the truth about the universe, even though, in contrast to such earlier thinkers as Descartes and Aristotle, they believed there was little to be ascertained.

In conceiving of philosophy as a therapeutic rather than a cognitive enterprise, Nietzsche and Wittgenstein made a profound shift in orientation. For such thinkers, the existential problem comes to the fore: we must learn to live in a world in which God is dead; we must learn to get along without Truth, or rather, we must learn to live with the one truth that there is no Truth. This means that, for Wittgenstein as well as for Nietzsche, philosophy was an intensely serious matter; it was not something one "does," in the way in which one might "take up" painting or bird watching. Indeed, Wittgenstein was as passionately committed to philosophy as Kierkegaard was to God. In the *Investigations* he addressed his pupils as individuals. Though his rhetoric was certainly different from Kierkegaard's or Nietzsche's, he too aimed at edification. He wanted desperately to "cure" his pupils, to convert them, to save them from the "deep inquietudes"[m] from which they—and, it would seem, he too—suffered.

But Wittgenstein and Nietzsche differed in temperament. Nietzsche had certainly experienced "deep inquietudes," but he had seemingly overcome them; he had bitten the head of the snake that had bitten him. Wittgenstein, it would seem, did not accomplish this. Unlike Nietzsche, he could not wave away with a cavalier gesture the paradox of the truth that there is no Truth.[16] Yet neither could he make Kierkegaard's leap of faith. As a result, paradox haunts the pages of the *Investigations*. For instance, by making us aware of how language functions, therapy calls our attention to the glasses on our nose. Or, in terms of the picture metaphor, we suddenly see the "frame" and realize that we have been looking only at the picture, not at the landscape itself. But do we ever get an unimpeded view of the landscape? No, all views have frames around them; all views are through glasses. How, then, can we be sure that there is a landscape out there? Nietzsche avoided this difficulty by maintaining that we do not really *need* the notion of a landscape out there; he was quite willing to abandon the idea of an "inaccessible original" and got on satisfactorily with interpretations of interpretations. It is not clear, however, that Wittgenstein was willing to take this step.

FORMS OF LIFE

Consider, for instance, his remarkable—and remarkably Nietzschean—insight that "to imagine a language means to imagine a form of life."[n] Every language, that is, condenses and expresses some social group's characteristic way of doing things, of accomplishing its aims. From the group's language it is possible to "read back" to this mode of life, this way of organizing and carrying out the daily routine. In talking about forms of life Wittgenstein was doubtless thinking primarily about everyday practices such as buying apples, constructing buildings, and weighing cheese, rather than about worldviews and value systems. There is no reason, however, why his view of the relation between a language and a form of life cannot be extended (as Nietzsche extended the notion of interpretation) to differences between cultures—say, to the difference between the Hopi language and "standard, average European." But—this is the present point—cultural (or linguistic) relativism is implicit in the concept of forms of life, whether this be understood narrowly or broadly. The relativism only becomes more noticeable as forms of life diverge.

Agreements and disagreements that occur *within* a given form of life are not merely expressions of opinion; procedures for distinguishing the true from the false have been established in this form of life and are specified in its language. "'So you are saying that human agreement decides what is true and what is false?'—It is what human beings *say* that is true and false; and they agree in the *language* they use. That is not agreement in opinions but in form of life."[o] But what about disagreements *across* forms of life? Suppose that what is true in one form of life is false in another? What procedures exist to resolve such a conflict? "What has to be accepted, the given, is—so one could say—*forms of life*."[p] Is it possible to get beyond these given divergencies? This, of course, is where therapy

---

[16] See Vol. IV, pp. 247–48.

is supposed to come in. Therapy can show us that our conflict is not simply a disagreement about the facts; it is a disagreement about facts-through-frames. If I see a green color-patch where you see a red one, the situation looks hopeless until we suddenly realize that each of us is wearing glasses—your glasses have red lenses and mine have green.

The goal of Wittgensteinian therapy is to show us that we are trapped in language (a picture has held us captive) as a necessary preliminary to freeing us from that trap. His aim—as Wittgenstein expressed it in a striking phrase—was "to show the fly the way out of the fly-bottle"q—to *show* the way, not to say what the way is. But does Wittgenstein really succeed in showing us this? We may agree that therapy will show me that I am in my fly-bottle and that you are in yours, but will therapy get us out of our fly-bottles and into a common world? *Can* it get us into a common world, or does it only get us into still another fly-bottle? The *Investigations* leaves this question unanswered.

This difficulty can be put in another way in order to bring out the paradox more forcefully. Wittgenstein's whole method of dissolving philosophical problems consisted in referring back to everyday language. His procedure, he said, was "to bring words [for example, such words as 'thinking'] back from their metaphysical use to their everyday use."r To talk about everyday language in this way is to suggest that its use leads us into the common world outside all metaphysical fly-bottles. Now, people who use a language in common (whether everyday or not) will doubtless live in *a* common world—the world of their form of life. But it is not *the* common world; it is common only to the users of this language. Thus everyday language is just another "frame." And worse than that, everyday language is not *one* language; it is a whole family of languages—and of forms of life. Finally, is not Wittgenstein's own language a language, and hence still another "frame"?

Or consider Wittgenstein's view of philosophy as a ladder that we can eventually leave behind. It is easy to understand why he wanted to leave the ladder behind, for in that way one gets rid of the embarrassing frame. But leaving the ladder implies a "complete" cure, and the notion of a complete cure is another frame—very similar, indeed, to the frame of exactness that Wittgenstein himself had exposed. The goal of "complete clarity" (that is, of being freed from fly-bottles) is a survival in the *Investigations* of one of the analytic tradition's deepest convictions—the belief that the end result of linguistic analysis is Truth.

The vestiges of the view of the *Tractatus* survive at many points in the *Investigations,* as in this striking metaphor:

> Where does our investigation get its importance from, since it seems only to destroy everything interesting, that is, all that is great and important? (As it were all the buildings, leaving behind only bits of stone and rubble.) What we are destroying is nothing but houses of cards and we are clearing up the ground of language on which they stand.s

The suggestion here is that the inquiries undertaken in the *Investigations* were merely preparatory: Wittgenstein's intent was to demolish all the old buildings (false metaphysical theories) in order to provide a secure site for a new and permanent structure (the true theory). This is all very different from a ladder that disappears. Moreover, the procedure by which the old buildings are demolished actually reveals that *all* buildings, new as well as old, are houses made of cards; the bitter truth—carefully avoided in this passage—is that there exist only "bits of stone and rubble."

Thus there is an unresolved tension between the goal of therapy, as inherited from the *Tractatus* and its analytic forebears, and the new method of therapy, as worked out in the *Investigations*. Perhaps the deepest of Wittgenstein's disquietudes arose from this tension. If so, this is a disquietude that Western culture as a whole seems to share.

Finally, one more tension must be mentioned—one that not merely appears in Wittgenstein's writings but is reflected in the whole history of philosophy in the first half of the twentieth century. Philosophy in the twentieth century was a series of attempts to break out of the Kantian paradigm; realists such as Moore took one path, the logical analysts took a second, the phenomenologists took a third. None of these, it would seem from such perspective as we may have gained in the intervening period, was successful. It is not that philosophy slipped back into the Kantian form of constructivism; it is rather that the problem of the relation of mind to its objects has been replaced by the problem of the relation of language to the world. Despite all the efforts expended on escaping from the fly-bottle, we have so far only learned that the most dangerous, the most seductive, of all fly-bottles is the one labeled "I am not a fly-bottle."

CHAPTER 12

Ordinary-Language Philosophy

The Emergence of Ordinary-Language Philosophy

World War II preempted the activities of many of the philosophers examined in this volume. When the war ended, these figures returned to philosophy with the energy of those trying to make up for lost time.

One center of intense philosophical activity during these postwar years was Oxford University, where a style of doing philosophy emerged that came to be known as *ordinary-language philosophy,* or sometimes as *Oxford* ordinary-language philosophy in order to separate it from the style of philosophy practiced by Wittgenstein and his followers at Cambridge. It is not altogether easy to characterize what these Oxford philosophers were up to, since they often disagreed among themselves on important philosophical issues. They were at least united in the view that an examination of language is of fundamental importance to philosophy. Saying that, however, says little to distinguish them from other twentieth-century philosophers. It certainly does not separate the philosophical activities at Oxford from those under the influence of Wittgenstein at Cambridge. For that matter, it does not separate ordinary-language philosophy from what we might call classical analytic philosophy as practiced by the logical atomists[1] and the Logical Positivists,[2] since they were interested in the analysis of language as well. Perhaps we can get a sense of the intellectual "geography" of analytic philosophy by first contrasting ordinary-language philosophy (in both its Oxford and Cambridge forms) with pre–World War II classical analytic philosophy. That done, we can examine the differences between ordinary-language philosophy as practiced at Oxford (under the influence of Austin and others) and as practiced at Cambridge (under the dominating influence of Wittgenstein).

Though classical analytic philosophers were concerned with ordinary language, they were often highly critical of its lack of clarity and logical rigor. In the *Tractatus,* Wittgenstein complained about it in these words:

> Language disguises thought. So much so, that from the outward form of the clothing it is impossible to infer the form of the thought beneath it.[a]

Russell's writings contain numerous complaints about what he took to be the inadequacies of ordinary language; for example:

> The proposition "Socrates is a man" is no doubt *equivalent* to "Socrates is human," but it is not the same proposition. The *is* of "Socrates is human" expresses the relation of subject and predicate; the *is* of "Socrates is a man" expresses identity. It is a disgrace to the human race that it has chosen to employ the same word "is" for these two entirely different ideas—*a disgrace that symbolic logical language of course remedies.*[b]

For the classical analytic philosopher, our common language was, perhaps, adequate enough for the common affairs of life, but deeply lacking in the rigor and clarity needed for scientific and philosophical thought. It was the task of classical analytic philosophy to supply this clarity and rigor.

A distinctive feature of ordinary-language philosophy was a rejection of this indictment of our everyday language. Whatever their disagreements on particular subjects, they held that our common language provides us with a rich, subtle, and complex set of mechanisms almost always adequate to the tasks they are intended to perform. Austin puts it this way:

> Our common stock of words embodies all the distinctions men have found worth drawing, and the connexions they have found worth marking, in the lifetimes of many generations: these surely are likely to be

---

[1] See Chs. 5 and 6.
[2] See Ch. 7.

more numerous, more sound, since they have stood up to the long test of the survival of the fittest, and more subtle, at least in all ordinary and reasonably practical matters, than any that you or I are likely to think up in our arm-chairs of an afternoon—the most favored alternative method.[c]

For ordinary-language philosophers, our everyday, nontechnical language provides a source of philosophical insight. *It* is not the source of philosophical confusion; instead, the tendency of philosophers to *misuse* common language is what generates philosophical confusion.

If philosophical perplexities arise because philosophers misuse ordinary language, then it becomes important to understand how ordinary language actually works. Ordinary-language philosophers thought that this could only be accomplished by examining how words are actually used in their everyday circumstances. Thus, instead of asking such standard philosophical questions as "What is truth?" "What is knowledge?" or "What is reality?" these philosophers would ask questions of the following kind:

Under what circumstances do we use such words as "truth," "know," "real," and so forth? What tasks do these words perform? What rules govern their employment? And so forth.

We should proceed, as J. L. Austin put it, "by examining *what we should say when.* . . ."[d] Of course, the classic analytic philosophers also criticized their predecessors for misunderstanding the way our language really functions. This is a central claim in Russell's classic essay "On Denoting." Meinong, Russell argued, was led to introduce strange entities into his ontology because he misunderstood the underlying form of sentences containing definite descriptions. A common criticism among ordinary-language philosophers was that the classical analytic philosophers *themselves* often misunderstood the ways in which language functions, with the result that they generated philosophical confusions of their own.[3]

Ordinary-language philosophers not only rejected various doctrines of classical analytic philosophy, they also rejected the idea that symbolic logic provides the preferred method for understanding what a sentence means. With few exceptions, the *Oxford* ordinary-language philosophers were proudly ignorant of the methods of symbolic logic and, in any case, could not see its relevance to philosophy.[4] To understand what a sentence means, one need not translate it into a rigid, artificial notation—this, they thought, was more likely to confuse than to enlighten.

Ordinary-language philosophers had another objection to classical analytic philosophy: its tendency, most notably in the writings of Logical Positivists, to

---

[3] With Wittgenstein, this meant targeting his own *Tractatus* for such criticism.
[4] Paul Grice, as we shall see, was one of the exceptions.

dismiss large and seemingly important areas of language as *meaningless*.[5] Austin describes what he takes to be the strengths and the excesses of the verification movement in these words:

> First of all people began to say: "Well, if these things are true or false it ought to be possible to decide which they are, and if we can't decide which they are they aren't any good but are, in short, nonsense." And this new approach did a great deal of good; a great many things which probably are nonsense were found to be such. It is not the case, I think, that all kinds of nonsense have been adequately classified yet, and perhaps some things have been dismissed as nonsense which really are not; but still this movement, the verification movement, was, in its way, excellent.
>
> However, we then come to the second stage. After all, we set some limits to the amount of nonsense that we talk, or at least the amount of nonsense that we are prepared to admit we talk; and so people began to ask whether after all some of those things which, treated as statements, were in danger of being dismissed as nonsense did after all really set out to be statements at all.[e]

It is certainly correct that the classical analytic philosophers paid little attention to important uses of language that are not intended to assert anything either true or false. Beyond this, they often had a tendency to lump together all those uses of language that did not formulate verifiable assertions in a single category—the cognitively meaningless. That, according to the ordinary-language philosophers, was a mistake—a mistake that arose from paying insufficient attention to how our language actually functions.

Having given a broad sketch of the differences between ordinary-language philosophers and classical analytic philosophers, we can now turn to the second, more difficult, task of distinguishing the style of doing philosophy at Oxford by Austin and others from Wittgenstein's style of doing philosophy. It is important not to exaggerate these differences, as participants in the two camps tended to do. Here, similarities far outweigh differences. Even so, there are important differences in method and style between Wittgenstein's way of doing philosophy and that practiced, for example, by Austin. As we have seen, Wittgenstein was fond of broad proclamations about philosophy. For example:

> Philosophy is a battle against the bewitchment of our intelligence by means of language.[f]

Austin almost never makes statements at this level of generality. Speaking of his own procedures, Austin writes with more modesty. In the following passage he is speaking specifically about his treatment of the argument from illusion, but what

---

[5] See Ch. 5.

he says gives a good general characterization of his way of doing philosophy. Analyzing argument from illusion, he tells us,

> is a matter of unpicking, one by one, a mass of seductive (mainly verbal) fallacies, of exposing a wide variety of concealed motives—an operation which leaves us, in a sense, just where we began.

This, of course, still sounds much like Wittgenstein, but Austin then continues:

> In a sense—but actually we may hope to learn something positive in the way of a technique for dissolving philosophical worries (*some* kinds of philosophical worry, not the whole of philosophy); and also something about the meanings of some English words ("reality," "seems," "looks," &c.) which, besides being philosophically very slippery, are in their own right interesting.[g]

In this passage Austin makes it clear that he does not hold, as Wittgenstein sometimes seems to hold, that *all* philosophical problems are based on linguistic confusions and can be resolved by removing these confusions.

   This passage reveals another important difference between Austin's style of doing philosophy and that of Wittgenstein. Wittgenstein, for the most part, was interested in language only to the extent that it had a bearing on philosophical issues. Austin here indicates that the resolution of philosophical problems can reveal things about language that "are in their own right interesting." In fact, even though his examination of ordinary language was initially motivated by the desire to resolve or at least to clarify philosophical problems, the examination of ordinary language soon took on a life of its own. Austin was struck by the rich resources our language contains for dealing with the complications of our social lives. The richness—the diversity—of ordinary language is another idea found in Wittgenstein's writings. But Austin parted company with Wittgenstein in an important way. Wittgenstein, at least as many read him, rejected the idea that it was possible to produce a general theory of meaning. Though Wittgenstein identified the meaning of a word with its use in the language, he thought that the uses of language were too numerous and radically diverse to admit of theoretical understanding. In a famous passage, Wittgenstein writes:

> But how many kinds of sentence are there? Say assertion, question, and command?—There are *countless* kinds: countless different kinds of use of what we call "symbols," "words," "sentences."[h]

Austin disagreed. In the following passage Austin does not refer to Wittgenstein directly, but he obviously has him in mind.

> Certainly there are a great many uses of language. It's rather a pity that people are apt to invoke a new use of language whenever they feel so inclined, to help them out of this, that, or the other well-known philosophical tangle; we need more of a framework in which to discuss

these uses of language; and also I think we should not despair too easily and talk, as people are apt to do, about the *infinite* uses of language. Philosophers will do this when they have listed as many, let us say, as seventeen; but even if there were something like ten thousand uses of language, surely we could list them all in time. This, after all, is no larger than the number of species of beetle that entomologists have taken the pains to list.[i]

A third difference between Wittgenstein and Austin is temperamental—but not for that reason unimportant. Wittgenstein viewed philosophy as a disease—a deeply troubling malady that could only be cured by extreme mental exertion. There was no set procedure for doing this. The most that Wittgenstein thought he could do was leave records (or sketches) of his own attempts to reach philosophical emancipation. Ultimately, each person must shift for herself. Austin was plainly put off by this side of Wittgenstein's method and the influence it had on Wittgenstein's followers. Austin agreed that language is a complicated phenomenon—indeed, a *very* complicated phenomenon—but this in itself provides no reason for supposing that a great many people, working together diligently for a sustained period of time, could not make significant progress in developing a comprehensive theory of language.

Strawson v. Russell on Definite Descriptions

Returning to the differences between classical analytic philosophy and ordinary-language philosophy, there is, perhaps, no better example of an explicit break with the past than P. F. Strawson's essay "On Referring."[6] Its target was Russell's essay "On Denoting." Russell's essay is a model of an attempt to translate a class of sentences into a logically appropriate form and then draw strong philosophical conclusions based on this translation. Strawson rejected Russell's analysis. He was not, however, simply pointing to particular defects he found in it—defects that might be removed by a better logical analysis. He was attacking the underlying assumptions that produced Russell's problem in the first place—namely, how a referring expression can be meaningful when it lacks a referent. Strawson's essay "On Referring" did not fire the first salvo in the attack on traditional analytic philosophy.[7] It was, however, an early essay where lines are clearly drawn. For this reason, it provides a good entrée to the themes or motifs of ordinary-language philosophy.

[6] P. H. Strawson (1911–) was educated at Oxford University, where he remained as a member of the faculty, becoming the Waynflete Professor of Philosophy and Metaphysics.

[7] The credit for that goes to Wittgenstein, whose own reasons for rejecting the procedures of logical analysis were widely circulated in unpublished manuscripts. See Ch. 11.

As we saw in Chapter 5, Russell's "On Denoting" is not an altogether easy essay to understand. The writing is compressed, some of the technical language is daunting, and the analyses he offers are often more complex than they need be. Fortunately, it is possible to state the core idea of Russell's theory of definite descriptions in a relatively simple way. In effect, Russell held that sentences of the form "The king of France is wise" should be analyzed as saying:

(1)   There is a king of France.
(2)   There is not more than one king of France.
(3)   There is nothing that is king of France and is not wise.[8]

Russell, as noted in Chapter 5, saw a number of advantages in this method of analysis. First, the sentence "The king of France is wise" contains an apparently referring phrase, namely "the king of France," that refers to nothing at all, and for Russell it was problematic how such a phrase, in referring to nothing, could be meaningful. In contrast, in the analyzed form, no definite description occurs that lacks a reference—in fact, no definite description appears at all. In a sense, the definite description "the king of France" has *disappeared* under analysis, and is no longer around to cause trouble.[9] A second advantage of this analysis, as Russell saw it, is that it allows us to assign a definite truth-value to the sentence "The king of France is wise." Since there was no king of France when Russell considered this example, nothing satisfied the first clause in the analysis; the sentence "The king of France is wise" was then false. It is also false now, though it may have been true, say, during the reign of Louis XIV. Thus Russell's analysis seems to provide an elegant solution to two initially difficult problems: how to assign meaning to sentences containing apparent referring expressions with no reference, and how to assign truth-values to them.

Over against this, Strawson argues that Russell's analysis is wholly lacking in merit because the problems it addresses are themselves deeply confused. In particular, he thinks that the problems Russell attempts to solve are generated by Russell's failure to draw certain distinctions crucial for understanding how language functions. Strawson lays out his case against Russell in these words:

> As a step towards showing that Russell's solution of his problem is mistaken, and towards providing the correct solution, I want . . . to draw certain distinctions. . . . The distinctions are between:
>
> (A1)   a sentence
> (A2)   a use of a sentence
> (A3)   an utterance of a sentence

[8] Russell himself adopted this simpler way of presenting his position in his later writings. See, for example, his treatment of definite descriptions in his *Introduction to Mathematical Philosophy* (George Allen and Unwin, London, 1919), pp. 167–70.
[9] To see why the indefinite description "*a* king of France" causes no similar difficulties, again see the discussion in Ch. 5.

and, correspondingly, between:

(B1)   an expression
(B2)   a use of an expression
(B3)   an utterance of an expression

Consider . . . the sentence, "The king of France is wise." It is easy to imagine that this sentence was uttered at various times from, say, the beginning of the seventeenth century onwards, during the reigns of each successive French monarch; and easy to imagine that it was also uttered during the subsequent periods in which France was not a monarchy. Notice that it was natural to speak of "the sentence" or "this sentence" being uttered at various times during this period; or, in other words, that it would be natural and correct to speak of *one and the same* sentence being uttered on these various occasions. It is in the sense in which it would be correct to speak of one and the same sentence being uttered on all these various occasions that I want to use the expression (A1) "a sentence." There are, however, obvious differences between different *occasions of the use* of this sentence. For instance, if one man uttered it in the reign of Louis XIV and another man uttered it in the reign of Louis XV, it would be natural to say (to assume) that they were respectively talking about different people; and it might be held that the first man, in using the sentence, made a true assertion, while the second man, in using the same sentence, made a false assertion. If on the other hand two different men simultaneously uttered the sentence (e.g., if one wrote it and the other spoke it) during the reign of Louis XIV, it would be natural to say (assume) that they were both talking about the same person, and, in that case, in using the sentence, they *must* either both have made a true assertion or both have made a false assertion. And this illustrates what I mean by *a use* of a sentence. The two men who uttered the sentence, one in the reign of Louis XV and one in the reign of Louis XIV, each made a different use of the same sentence; whereas the two men who uttered the sentence simultaneously in the reign of Louis XIV, made the same use of the same sentence. Obviously in the case of this sentence, and equally obviously in the case of many others, we cannot talk of *the sentence* being true or false, but only of its being used to make a true or false assertion or (if this is preferred) to express a true or a false proposition. And equally obviously we cannot talk of *the sentence* being *about* a particular person, for the same sentence may be used at different times to talk about quite different particular persons, but only of *a use* of the sentence to talk about a particular person. Finally it will make sufficiently clear what I mean by an utterance of a sentence if I say that the two men who simultaneously uttered the sentence in the reign of Louis XIV made two different utterances of the same sentence, though they made the same *use* of the sentence.[j]

The key idea in this passage is that it is simply wrong to speak of a *sentence* being either true or false. It is the assertion made in using the sentence—not the sentence itself—that is either true or false. This is shown in that the very same sentence can be used to make different statements, where one can be true, the other false.

Turning now to referring expressions, Strawson notes that the very same referring expression can be used to refer to different things. Consider the following different utterances of the same sentence:

(1)   My mother is from Natchez. (Said by A)
(2)   My mother is from Natchez. (Said by B)

Suppose that A and B are unrelated. In that case, A and B are using the expression "my mother" to refer to two different women. All the same, although the expression "my mother" refers to different women when used by A and when used by B, the expression "my mother" has, Strawson would say, the same meaning in both cases. For both speakers, "mother" means "female parent." More interestingly, the word "my" indicates ownership by the person who employs the word. To use Strawson's own example, if you use the word "I" in a sentence and I use the word "I" in a sentence, we are referring to different people, but we each use the word in the same way—to refer to oneself. We might put the matter this way: expressions with the same meaning or the same function in the language can be used by different people to refer to different things. They can also be used by the same person to refer to different things on different occasions—for example, the expression "John's youngest child" changes reference, but not meaning, with each of his newborn children.

For Strawson, Russell's root mistake was to confuse the meaning of a referring expression with the reference it has when used.

> Generally, as against Russell, I shall say this. Meaning (in at least one important sense) is a function of the sentence or expression; mentioning and referring and truth or falsity are functions of the use of the sentence or expression. To give the meaning of an expression (in the sense in which I am using the word) is to give *general directions* for its use to refer to or mention particular objects or persons; to give the meaning of a sentence is to give *general directions* for its use in making true or false assertions. It is not to talk about any particular occasion of the use of the sentence or expression. The meaning of an expression cannot be identified with the object it is used, on a particular occasion, to refer to. The meaning of a sentence cannot be identified with the assertion it is used, on a particular occasion, to make. For to talk about the meaning of an expression or sentence is not to talk about its use on a particular occasion, but about the rules, habits, conventions governing its correct use, on all occasions, to refer or to assert. So the question of whether a sentence or expression *is significant or not* has nothing whatever to do

with the question of whether the sentence, *uttered on a particular occasion,* is, on that occasion, being used to make a true-or-false assertion or not, or of whether the expression is, on that occasion, being used to refer to, or mention, anything at all.

The source of Russell's mistake was that he thought that referring or mentioning, if it occurred at all, must be meaning.[k]

We can now return to the puzzle that generated Russell's analysis of definite descriptions. When employed in his time (the early twentieth century), France did not have a monarchy, so the sentence "The king of France is wise" contained an expression, "the king of France," that lacked reference. Russell reasoned that if this were a genuine referring expression, then, in lacking reference, it would be meaningless. But since the sentence is *not* meaningless, Russell concluded that, grammatical appearances to the contrary, it is not a genuine referring expression at all. Russell's theory of definite descriptions provided a way of restating the claim that the king of France is wise in a way that no referring expression lacking a reference occurs. Strawson's response is that Russell's project is fundamentally misconceived. The expression "the king of France" is a perfectly meaningful referring expression that in Russell's time (as now) simply lacks a reference. It cannot be used to speak about the king of France since there is no such king to speak about. Similarly, the sentence "The king of France is wise" is also meaningful even though right now it cannot be used to make an assertion that is either true or false. It cannot be used to say something either true or false, again, because there is no king of France to make this assertion about. Here is how Strawson puts this:

> Now suppose someone were in fact to say to you with a perfectly serious air: "The king of France is wise." Would you say, "That's untrue"? I think it is quite certain that you would not. But suppose he went on to *ask* you whether you thought that what he had just said was true, or was false; whether you agreed or disagreed with what he had just said. I think you would be inclined, with some hesitation, to say that you did not do either; that the question of whether his statement was true or false simply *did not arise,* because there was no such person as the king of France. You might, if he were obviously serious (had a dazed astray-in-the-centuries look), say something like: "I'm afraid you must be under a misapprehension. France is not a monarchy. There is no king of France."[1]

Notice that Strawson is not saying that sometimes the sentence "The king of France is wise" has been true (perhaps in the reign of Louis XIV) and sometimes false (perhaps in the reign of Louis XV). For Strawson sentences are *never* either true or false. It is not the sentence but the assertion made in using a sentence that is either true or false. For Strawson, sentences are bearers of meaning (but not truth-values), and assertions are bearers of truth-values (but not meaning). Once this distinction is clearly drawn, Russell, according to Strawson, will no longer have a problem to solve. If that is right, Russell's theory of definite descriptions was a wasted effort.

Before looking at Russell's reply to Strawson, we can note that Strawson does acknowledge that anyone who sincerely utters the sentence "The king of France is wise" does in *some* sense commit himself or herself to the existence of a king of France:

> To say "The king of France is wise" is, in some sense of "imply," to *imply* that there is a king of France. But this is a very special and odd sense of "imply." "Implies" in this sense is certainly not equivalent to "entails" (or "logically implies").[m]

Put somewhat differently, in asserting that the king of France is wise, we are supposing that a king of France exists, for if we did not suppose this, there would be no point in making this remark.

At a certain level, then, Russell and Strawson are in agreement. For both, if someone sincerely asserts that the king of France is wise, that person thereby *commits* himself or herself to the existence of a (unique) king of France. For Russell, this is part of what is *asserted* in claiming that the king of France is wise, and it therefore becomes part of his analysis of this sentence. For Strawson, this commitment is not part of what we actually assert and is therefore not part of the meaning of the sentence used in making the assertion. Russell, we might say, absorbs certain presuppositions of the use of a sentence into the meaning of the sentence itself. Strawson treats this as a fundamental mistake.

Suppose Strawson is right in his charges against Russell; how serious, from a philosophical point of view, would this be? That would depend on what Russell was trying to achieve by his theory of definite descriptions. If he was trying to give an accurate account of the meaning of such sentences as "The king of France is wise," then if Strawson is right (as he seems to be), Russell is wrong. In an effort to be more charitable toward Russell, we might say that his fundamental interests were not really linguistic at all, but, instead, ontological. His basic question was this: precisely what sorts of things do we commit ourselves to when we assert that the king of France is wise? Russell was able to answer that question in a way that both avoids the introduction of odd (Meinongian) entities[10] and preserves standard laws of logic. Viewed that way, Russell was not trying to analyze sentences of ordinary language; rather, he was attempting to transpose them into a notation that made transparent the commitments involved in their use. That this may have been Russell's way of viewing his analysis is suggested by the following remark in his response to Strawson:

> I . . . am persuaded that common speech is full of vagueness and inaccuracy, and that any attempt to be precise and accurate requires modification of common speech both as regards vocabulary and as regards syntax.[n]

---

[10] See pp. 181–82.

These reflections suggest that Russell and Strawson may only disagree because they are involved in fundamentally different lines of work. Strawson was primarily concerned with giving an accurate account of how certain sentences in our language actually function; Russell was not. Here, however, we are probably being too charitable to Russell. Recall that it was a central feature of Russell's analysis of definite descriptions to treat them as "incomplete symbols"—symbols that had no meaning on their own. To repeat a passage cited in Chapter 5:

> According to the view which I advocate, a denoting phrase is essentially *part* of a sentence, and does not, like most single words, have any significance on its own account. If I say "Scott was a man," that is a statement of the form "x was a man," and it has "Scott" for its subject. But if I say "the author of *Waverley* was a man," that is not a statement of the form "x was a man," and does not have "the author of *Waverley*" for its subject.[11]

Here Russell denies that "the author of *Waverley*" is the grammatical subject of "the author of *Waverley* was a man" because, in a parallel case, he could not see how "the king of France" could be the grammatical subject of "the king of France is wise." On this matter, Strawson holds that Russell is doubly wrong. "The author of *Waverley*" is, he maintains, the genuine subject of the first sentence, and "the king of France" is the genuine subject of the second sentence. If Strawson is correct in these claims, he has not simply found a difficulty with one aspect of Russell's theory of definite descriptions—he has refuted the very aspect of that theory that Russell stressed most when he first produced it.

Three Theories of Definite Descriptions

We have now examined in some detail three accounts of definite descriptions, given, respectively, by Frege,[12] Russell,[13] and Strawson. Here we can summarize how each would analyze the sentence "The present king of France is wise."

> Frege: The expression "the present king of France" is meaningful in virtue of having a sense associated with it; however, right now, it lacks a reference. For this reason, the entire sentence "The present king of France is wise" lacks a reference as well. But, since the reference of an assertive sentence, if any, is a truth-value, the sentence as a whole must lack a truth-value.

[11] See p. 184.
[12] See Ch. 4.
[13] See Ch. 5.

> Russell: In isolation, the expression "the present king of France" has no meaning. It is an incomplete symbol. Under analysis, however, the sentence "The present king of France is wise" is seen to contain no such incomplete symbol, and we evaluate this sentence as a whole as simply being false.

> Strawson: The expression "the present king of France" is meaningful in virtue of having certain conventions governing its use. Since there is no present king of France, the question whether he is wise or not simply does not arise.

Strawson's theory is obviously closer to Frege's than to Russell's. However, it differs from Frege's theory in two important respects. First, it does not treat the meaning of sense as an abstract object. Second, it does not say that sentences containing expressions that involve reference failure *lack* a truth-value since Strawson does not ascribe truth-values to sentences at all.

J. L. Austin

We have begun this examination of so-called ordinary-language philosophy with Strawson's attack on Russell's theory of definite descriptions because it exhibits in sharp relief the contrast between the older style of analytic philosophy that flourished in the first half of the twentieth century with the new style that came into prominence after World War II. Strawson was certainly an important early participant in this movement, but by general consensus J. L. Austin[14] was its central figure. He, more than anyone else, exemplified its central tendencies.

Austin published relatively little. His *Philosophical Papers* contains only seventeen articles—only seven published during his lifetime. His two brief books, *How to Do Things with Words* and *Sense and Sensibilia,* come to just over three hundred small-formatted pages. Much of Austin's influence was exerted in conversations and in the discussion groups that flourished in Oxford at the time. Inevitably, many of the details of these discussions have been lost.

The writings of Austin we shall examine fall into two broad categories: those whose emphasis is on understanding the way our ordinary language actually functions and those whose emphasis is on resolution or dissolution of standard philosophical problems. Here we must speak of two emphases, for some writings contain both. For example, *How to Do Things with Words* is predominantly a work of the first kind. It is an attempt to develop what later became known as a

---

[14]J. L. Austin (1911–1960) was educated at Oxford University, where he remained as a member of the faculty. At the time of his death, at age forty-nine, he held the Whites Chair of Moral Philosophy.

speech-act theory, yet this work is not without references to standard philosophical issues. *Sense and Sensibilia*[15] is primarily a destructive examination of the so-called problem of perception and the various answers that had been given to it, but, of necessity, this work also says important things about the actual use of perceptual terms that, according to Austin, philosophers have often misunderstood. At first, it was the destructive side of Austin's philosophy that attracted most attention—in part, because it seemed to liberate philosophy from the tedious gnawing-away at old issues or, in any event, to provide a fresh way of looking at them. From our present perspective, however, it is his constructive writing—chiefly his attempt to develop a theory of speech acts—that seems to have lasting importance. In what follows, we will look at both sides of his work, beginning with his essay "Other Minds," which contains both.

OTHER MINDS

The essay "Other Minds" was presented at a symposium on that topic at the Joint Session of the Mind Association and Aristotelian Society in 1946—the year after World War II ended. Like Russell's "On Denoting," which was a classic of traditional analytic philosophy, "Other Minds" is a classic of the philosophy of ordinary language. Also, like Russell's "On Denoting," it is a complicated essay pursuing a number of issues at once, with the result that it is not always clear what is going on, and sometimes clear that things have gone wrong.

The traditional problem of other minds arises when we ask, for example, how we can ever know that another person is angry since, as it is often put, we have no access to another person's mind and the feelings that occur in it. Austin's strategy in dealing with this question was to set it aside until he could give a reasonably satisfactory answer to a prior question: "What sort of thing does actually happen when ordinary people are asked 'How do you know?'"° That is, before tackling the difficult question of how we know the contents of the minds of others, Austin examines the way or ways in which ordinary competent speakers answer questions of the form "How do you know?" in unproblematic contexts.

Austin notes that questions of this kind can be answered in a variety of ways:

> Suppose I have said "There is a bittern at the bottom of the garden," and you ask "How do you know?" my reply may take very different forms.
>
> (a) I was brought up in the fens.
> (b) I heard it.
> (c) The keeper reported it.
> (d) By its booming.
> (e) From the booming.
> (f) Because it is booming.ᴾ

---

[15]The title is a pun on Jane Austen's novel *Sense and Sensibility*.

Austin notes that each of these responses provides a reason for accepting the identification of the bird as a bittern. He also notes that these responses concern different aspects of the situation. They can concern the expertise of the person giving the identification ("I was brought up in the fens"), the particular way that the identification was made ("I heard it"), the source of the information ("The keeper reported it"), the distinctive aspect of the bittern used in identifying it ("By its booming"), and so on. These are all ordinary ways of responding to the question "How do you know it's a bittern?" What sort of justification will be given depends on context—in particular, on the kind of challenge that has been made or might reasonably be made. This can be seen in the following contrasting dialogues:

I   A. How do you know it's a *bittern*?

      B. From its markings.

II   A. How do *you* know it's a bittern?

      B. I was brought up in the fens.

Austin's reflections on the *actual* ways we answer challenges to our knowledge claims show a number of important things. First, they remove what might be called a certain *false dignity* that philosophers often attach to the concept of knowledge. Knowledge claims are made in everyday life to achieve everyday purposes. They provide a way, for example, of assuring others that we have sufficient grounds for what we are saying and could produce them if challenged to do so. Furthermore, in common life, these *challenges* themselves are controlled by practical considerations. The question "How do you know?" is usually not asked unless there is some good reason for thinking that someone has made a claim without adequate backing. Furthermore, the reasons that a person gives when asked "How do you know?" are not expected to deal with every possibility, however remote. Austin puts it this way:

> (a) If you say "That's not enough," then you must have in mind some more or less definite lack. "To be a goldfinch, besides having a red head it must also have the characteristic eye-markings": or "How do you know it isn't a woodpecker? Woodpeckers have red heads too." If there is no definite lack, which you are at least prepared to specify on being pressed, then it's silly (outrageous) just to go on saying "That's not enough."
>
> (b) Enough is enough: it doesn't mean everything. Enough means enough to show that (within reason, and for the present intents and purposes) it "can't" be anything else, there is no room for an alternative, competing, description of it. It does *not* mean, for example, enough to show it isn't a *stuffed* goldfinch.�q

If it does turn out to be a stuffed goldfinch, then, of course, the person who said that it was a goldfinch did not know that it was one. One cannot know things that are false, though, of course, one may *think* that one knows something that is false.

Austin summarizes his account of the way we ordinarily use the expression "I know" in these words:

> (d) Whenever I say I know, I am always liable to be taken to claim that, in a certain sense appropriate to the kind of statement (and to present intents and purposes), I am able to *prove* it.[r]

Again, it is important to remember that Austin does not idealize the notion of a proof. A proof establishes the truth of something in the way appropriate to establishing the truth of that sort of thing. Again, proving a theorem in mathematics usually involves producing a demonstration; proving that a cup contains coffee, not tea, is usually done by tasting it.

At this point the reader might ask, reasonably enough, about the point of all this. Austin has described the way in which we actually use the verb "to know," noticing, among other things, that the rules governing its use are, on the one hand, more complicated and subtle than is commonly acknowledged by philosophers and, on the other hand, generally less stringent than what philosophers often demand. What, however, does this have to do with the philosopher's concern with the problem of knowledge? Characteristically, Austin had very little to say directly on this subject. Perhaps he thought that anyone with any wit would just see the relevance to philosophy, so there was no need to belabor the point. At various places, however, Austin provides indications of the conception of knowledge he is trying to combat. He rejects the idea that knowledge is, as we might say, a supermental state. That is, he rejects a conception of knowledge that we might describe in the following way:

> Human beings can have *cognitive* attitudes at various levels. They might *wonder* whether something is true. They may *believe* that it is true. They may be *certain* or *absolutely dead certain* that something is true. Finally, they can *know* that something is true. Knowledge differs from belief in that you can believe something without being certain of it. But knowledge differs from certainty as well, for one can be certain of something though, in fact, it is false. In contrast, if we know something, we cannot be wrong about it. Knowledge, on this view, is a state of mind that is truth-guaranteeing. The philosopher's task is to discover just which mental states possess this property.

Austin found this conception of knowledge wholly misconceived. To claim to know something was not to claim to be in some cognitively self-justifying mental state. It is, instead, a way of indicating that one can deliver the goods when asked to justify a particular claim.

> [Saying] "I know" . . . is *not* saying "I have performed a specially striking feat of cognition, superior, in the same scale as believing and being sure, even to being merely quite sure": for there *is* nothing in that scale superior to being quite sure.[s]

We can imagine levels of commitment going from having a *hunch,* through *believing,* up to being *absolutely dead certain,* with various gradations in between. We can, perhaps, say that all of these expressions *describe* mental states. The mistake, according to Austin, is to suppose that *knowing* is a mental state at the very top of this hierarchy. But putting knowing on the same scale with believing and being certain—even at the very top if it—is, according to Austin, a fundamental mistake. It involves associating the word "knowing," which is *not* (primarily, at least) a description of a mental state, with a set of terms ("believing," "being sure," etc.) that *are* primarily descriptive of mental states.[16]

Unfortunately, Austin combined his important ideas about knowledge with other important ideas about a class of utterances that he later labeled performatives or performative utterances in a way that led him into confusion. Performatives will be examined in detail later on, but, briefly, with a performative utterance the *saying* of something amounts to *doing* it. For example, if someone says "I promise to call you tomorrow," she thereby promises to call someone tomorrow. If someone says "I apologize for being late," she thereby apologizes for being late. Since the very saying constitutes the doing, both utterances are performative utterances. In contrast, if someone says "I own a BMW convertible," she does not thereby own a BMW convertible. In this case, just saying it does not make it so.[17]

Specifically, at the time that he wrote "Other Minds," Austin was struck by what he took to be important similarities in the function of the expressions "I know" and "I promise."

> When I say "I promise" . . . I have not merely announced my intention, but, by using this formula (performing this ritual), I have bound myself to others and stake my reputation, in a new way. [Similarly] when I say "I know," I *give others my word:* I *give others my authority for saying* that "S is P."†

Here, apparently without noticing it, Austin offers an account of knowledge claims different from and incompatible with the account given fourteen pages earlier in "Other Minds." There he said that to claim to know something was to say that one was able to prove it. Here, Austin associates knowledge claims with expressions of the form "I promise that. . . ."

Which view is more plausible? Surely the earlier view. For notice that the analogy between making a promise and making a knowledge claim breaks down at once. If I promise to do something and do not do it, it is still *true* that I promised.

---

[16] Many philosophers hold that knowing something involves believing it or perhaps being certain of it. If that is correct, then attributing knowledge to someone would involve attributing a mental state to her. Austin, I think, could accept this, adding only that the distinctive feature of a knowledge claim is its assessment of a person's grounds for believing what she does.

[17] This, as it stands, does not do justice to Austin's complex treatment of performatives, but it is good enough for our present purposes.

If, on the other hand, I claim to know something and it turns out to be false (or if I do not have adequate grounds for my claim), then it is *false* that I knew. In the normal case, saying "I promise" *constitutes* promising, whereas saying "I know" *does not constitute* knowing. Also, if a person says "I promise," it is out of place, except perhaps as a joke, to reply "No you don't," whereas such a response is often suitable for knowledge claims. And so on.

It is something of a mystery how Austin failed to see the force of these clear disanalogies between making a promise and making a knowledge claim. One possible explanation is that his philosophical imagination was captured by important new ideas and he simply overextended them. When he wrote "Other Minds," Austin already held that philosophers often go wrong by supposing that sentences—or at least indicative sentences—all function in the same way: to offer descriptions that state how things are. To suppose this is to commit what Austin called the *descriptive fallacy.* Performative utterances were initially important to Austin because they could be used to break the spell of the descriptive fallacy. Sentences beginning with "I warn," "I apologize," or "I define" are perfectly meaningful utterances that, according to Austin, are not descriptions. His enthusiasm for these new ideas lies in back of the following passage:

> To suppose that "I know" is a descriptive phrase, is only one example of the *descriptive fallacy,* so common in philosophy. Even if some language is now purely descriptive, language was not in origin so, and much of it is still not so. Utterance of obvious ritual phrases, in the appropriate circumstances, is not *describing* the action we are doing, but *doing* it ("I do").[u]

This passage had the unfortunate effect of obscuring Austin's important insights concerning the nature of knowledge claims. It is also embarrassing that one of Austin's first applications of his notion of a performative utterance was a misapplication. In fact, however, Austin's mistaken assimilation of knowledge claims to performatives had no lasting bad effects on his discussion of performatives and the speech-act theory that grew out of it.

But what about the problem of *other minds*—the supposed topic of Austin's essay? How are we able to know, for example, that another is angry when we have no access to that person's mind? Or to put the question somewhat differently: With another person, we can only examine the *symptoms* or the *signs* of anger, whereas the person herself actually feels the anger. What justifies the inference from the symptoms of anger, which we can observe, to the feeling of anger, which we cannot?

Austin refuses to take this question head-on because he thinks that it is misleadingly stated:

> In the first place, "symptoms" . . . is being used in a way different from ordinary usage, and one which proves to be misleading.[v]

In particular, according to Austin, we speak of symptoms or signs of something only when the thing is not present or not open to view. A rash may be a symptom of a disease, gathering clouds may be a sign of an impending storm, and so forth. However, talk about signs and symptoms is wholly out of place when the thing in question is right before us:

> When we talk of "signs of a storm," we mean signs of an impending storm, or a past storm, or a storm beyond the horizon: we do *not* mean a storm on top of us.[w]

In the same way, we can talk of traces of cheese when there are only a few crumbs left, but it is misleading to speak of traces of cheese when a large lump is sitting right before us. Austin makes a parallel point about the symptoms or signs of anger:

> "Symptoms" or "signs" of anger tend to mean signs of *rising* or *suppressed* anger. Once the man has exploded, we talk of something different—of an expression or manifestation or display of anger, of an exhibition of temper, and so forth. A twitch of the eyebrow, pallor, a tremor in the voice, all these may be symptoms of anger: but a violent tirade or a blow in the face are not, they are the acts in which the anger is vented.[x]

But granting the niceties of speech, is it not true that Austin's argument is flawed in an obvious way? With signs of storms and traces of cheese, the items themselves—the storms and the cheese—can come right before our eyes, and then, of course, talk about signs and traces will be out of place. A feeling of anger, however, is never right before us in the same way—open to view—unless it is our own anger we are concerned with. Austin himself seems to concede as much with his reference to "an expression or manifestation or display of anger." The only response to this criticism is to deny the sharp distinction between the feeling of anger and its behavioral manifestations. Austin attempts to do this in the following passage:

> It is then, clear, that more is involved in being, for example, angry than simply showing the symptoms and feeling the feeling. For there is also the display or manifestation. And it is to be noted that the feeling is related in a unique sort of way to the display. When we are angry, we have an impulse, felt and/or acted on, to do actions of particular kinds, and, unless we suppress the anger, we do actually proceed to do them. There is a peculiar and intimate relationship between the emotion and the natural manner of venting it, with which, having been angry ourselves, we are acquainted. The ways in which anger is normally manifested are *natural* to anger just as there are tones *naturally* expressive of various emotions (indignation, &c.). There is not normally taken to

be such a thing as "being angry" apart from any impulse, however vague, to vent the anger in the natural way.[y]

The key idea here is that there are natural ways of expressing emotions. People suffering pain, for example, do not usually smile and giggle. They not only do not do this, given what pain is like, it would be inappropriate (unnatural) for them to do so. It is because emotions have natural forms of expression (and also because they naturally arise in certain standard settings) that we can know that others are in pain, angry, jealous, and so on.

There is, Austin acknowledges, a problem that arises with knowledge claims about the mental states of others that does not arise, for example, in identifying a bird. A person can act as if she is angry when she is not—she can pretend to be angry and perhaps fool us. Austin's strategy for dealing with this problem is to treat it as a purely practical difficulty:

> There are (more or less roughly) established procedures for dealing with suspected cases of deception. . . . By these means we do very often establish (though we do not expect *always to* establish) that someone is acting. . . . These special cases where doubts arise and require resolving, are contrasted with the normal cases which hold the field *unless* there is some special suggestion that deceit, &c., is involved, and deceit, moreover, of an intelligible kind in the circumstances. . . . There is no suggestion that I *never* know what other people's emotions are, nor yet that in particular cases I might be wrong for no special reason or in no special way.[z]

Notice Austin's strategy: instead of directly confronting the abstract question "How can we ever know that another is not deceiving us about her feelings?" he asks us to reflect on circumstances where deceit is a matter of practical concern. In such contexts we can often (though, of course, not always) detect the deceit. Looked at in this way, the claim that we can never know (or never *really* know) that another is angry comes across as a plain falsehood.

A feeling can persist that Austin has really missed the point of *philosophers'* concerns with the problem of other minds. Philosophers are not worried about the *practical* problem concerning how we actually go about detecting deceit. Their question, we are inclined to say, goes deeper. What we really want to know is how we can have access to the feelings of others. Austin's strategy here, as elsewhere, is to try to convince us—or show us—that this philosophical problem is an illusion generated by insufficient attention to how we actually use words that ascribe feelings to others. He closes "Other Minds" with these words:

> [To] suppose that the question "How do I know that Tom is angry?" is meant to mean "How do I introspect Tom's feelings?" (because, as we know, that's the sort of thing that knowing is or ought to be), is simply barking our way up the wrong gum tree.[a]

AUSTIN AND THE PROBLEM OF PERCEPTION

The slim book *Sense and Sensibilia* was reconstructed largely from Austin's notes from lectures he gave on the problem of perception from 1947 until 1958. It provides a forceful example of Austin's use of the methods of ordinary-language philosophy—an examination of *what we should say when*—as a tool for combating philosophical confusion. It also provides an example of an ordinary-language philosopher targeting a specimen of earlier analytic philosophy for criticism.

Sense and Sensibilia is basically an examination of a single argument—the so-called argument from illusion—primarily (though not exclusively) as it was presented by A. J. Ayer in his *Foundations of Empirical Knowledge.*[18] According to Austin, the argument from illusion is intended to establish the following general doctrine:

> We never see or otherwise perceive (or "sense"), or anyhow we never *directly* perceive or sense, material objects (or material things), but only sense-data (our own ideas, impressions, sensa, sense-perceptions, percepts, &c.).[b]

The argument itself, as Austin describes it, has two parts:

> The argument from illusion is intended [first] to persuade us that, in certain exceptional, abnormal situations, what we perceive—directly anyway—is a sense-datum; but then comes the second stage, in which we are to be brought to agree that what we (directly) perceive is *always* a sense-datum, even in the normal, unexceptional case.[c]

The argument from illusion, which is intended to establish these conclusions, has appeared in a variety of forms throughout the history of philosophy, and remains a favorite topic in introductory philosophy courses. It is noted, for example, that if you poke your eye in the right sort of way, a tree in front of you will appear double. But surely by poking your eye you cannot produce two trees out of one. (As Joyce Kilmer put it, "Only God can make a tree.") Yet while poking your eye, you are aware of two distinct treelike entities. Since there is only one tree, at least one of these entities cannot be the tree itself. Here it is natural to suppose that at least one of these entities is a mental image of the tree. That is the first stage of the argument. The second stage of the argument is intended to convince us that we are not directly aware of the tree even when looking at it without poking at our eyes (or doing anything else peculiar). When you stop poking at your eye—unless you poked too hard—you immediately become aware of a single treelike entity. But all three treelike entities—the two that appear when the eye is poked and the one that appears when it is not poked—are said to be *perceptually indistinguishable*. That is, all these treelike entities seem to be on a par in how they appear. Since we have agreed that at least one of the pair of entities in the eye-poking case

[18] Macmillan, New York, 1940.

must be a mental image, the fact of indistinguishability is supposed to convince us that all of them are mental images. That is the second stage of the argument.

Austin does not attempt a simple knockdown refutation of arguments of this kind.

> My general opinion about this doctrine is that it is a typically *scholastic view*, attributable, first, to an obsession with a few particular words, the uses of which are over-simplified, not really understood or carefully studied or correctly described; and second, to an obsession with a few (and nearly always the same) half-studied "facts." . . . The fact is, as I shall try to make clear, that our ordinary words are much subtler in their uses, and mark many more distinctions, than philosophers have realized; and that the facts of perception, as discovered by, for instance, psychologists but also as noted by common mortals, are much more diverse and complicated than has been allowed for.[d]

Austin begins his investigation by noting that it is far from clear what the argument is supposed to show—or what its conclusion even means. According to A. J. Ayer, ordinary people believe that they are *directly aware* of *material objects,* whereas philosophers hold that we are not directly aware of material objects, but only directly aware of *sense data.* The first difficulty Austin finds is that the phrase "material object" is a philosopher's invention not found in common discourse and thus stands in need of definition, or at least explanation. But no such definition or explanation is forthcoming.

> We are given, as examples, "familiar objects"—chairs, tables, pictures, books, flowers, pens, cigarettes; the expression "material thing" is not further defined.[e]

But, as Austin puts it, the plain man does not think that the things he perceives all fall into this category of "moderate sized specimens of dry goods."[f] In daily life we speak about seeing such things as "rainbows, shadows, pictures on the screen of the cinema," and so on. Thus the identification of what the plain man thinks he perceives with material objects is wrong right from the start. Ordinary people do not have such a simpleminded view of the nature of the things they perceive. Simple people do not have simpleminded ontologies of the kind that philosophers often attribute to them. Austin sums up his complaint about the notion of a material object in these words:

> The trouble is that the expression "material thing" is functioning *already,* from the very beginning, simply as a foil for "sense-datum"; it is . . . never given any other role to play, and apart from this consideration it would surely never have occurred to anybody to try to represent as some single *kind of things* the things which the ordinary man says that he "perceives."[g]

That is, right from the start we are supposed to understand what is meant by a "material object" and by a "sense datum" and have at least an intuitive grasp of the difference between them, whereas, in fact, the meanings of these expressions are yet to be determined.

Furthermore, once this contrast between material objects and sense data has been introduced, it seems mandatory to ask how they are related, and then it can seem that there is a genuine problem here even if ordinary people do not recognize it. Suppose, to cite Austin's example, I look at a chair a few yards in front of me in broad daylight. Here the philosopher will ask whether, in such circumstances, we can *really* be certain that there is a chair before us. Some philosophers might say yes, and give reasons for saying this; other philosophers might disagree. In contrast, Austin tells us, "The plain man would regard doubt in such a case, not as far-fetched or over-refined, or somehow impractical, but as plain *nonsense;* he would say, quite correctly, 'Well, if that's not seeing a real chair then *I don't know what is.*'"[h] This is an important move in Austin's argument—not simply a rhetorical flourish. He seems to have something of the following sort in mind: Expressions gain their meaning through application in standard unproblematic cases where doubt (genuine doubt) has no place. There are, however, contexts in which the application of a term is genuinely problematic; for example, the light might be bad or the setting might be in some other way peculiar. Here expressions of doubt make sense. On the other side, expressions of certainty are used to exclude doubts, but when I see a chair before me in broad daylight, there is no doubt to be excluded. Austin is saying that to suppose that a doubt is even *intelligible* in such contexts is to misuse language and thus to create a problem where none exists.

This is not the only linguistic confusion Austin claims to find in the very formulation of the argument from illusion. Another, according to him, is the use of the seemingly innocent word "directly":

> Philosophers, it is said [by Ayer], "are not, for the most part, prepared to admit that such objects as pens or cigarettes are ever directly perceived." Now of course what brings us up short here is the word "directly"—a great favorite among philosophers, but actually one of the less conspicuous snakes in the linguistic grass. We have here, in fact, a typical case of a word, which already has a very special use, being gradually stretched, without caution or definition or any limit, until it becomes, first perhaps obscurely metaphorical, but ultimately meaningless.

Austin then adds:

> One can't abuse ordinary language without paying for it.[i]

This passage makes two claims. The first is that the word "directly" has a very special use; the second is that philosophers often fail to recognize this and thereby generate confusion. Here Austin introduces one of his favorite ideas—that of a *trouser word:*

> First of all, it is essential to realize that here the notion of perceiving *in*directly wears the trousers—"directly" takes whatever sense it has from the contrast with its opposite.[j]

For example, if I say that I did not get the news directly from her, I am indicating that the news came through some third party. If I say that I did not come directly home, I am indicating that I made a stop along the way. If I say that I did not look at her directly, I am indicating that I did not make eye contact. But to say a concert is being broadcast directly from a concert hall does not mean that the signal has not passed through relay stations; it simply means that the concert was not previously recorded. And so on. In each case it is the particular form of indirectness that gives the notion of directness its significance.

Now what, Austin asks, would it be like to *perceive* something directly? He gives some examples.

> We might, for example, contrast the man who saw the procession directly with the man who saw it *through a periscope;* or we might contrast the place from which you can watch the door directly with the place from which you can see it only *in the mirror.*[k]

So it is possible, then, to speak significantly about perceiving things indirectly. There are, that is, contexts where this makes sense. But, according to Austin, such unproblematic uses have the following feature:

> If we are to be seriously inclined to speak of something as being perceived indirectly, it seems that it has to be the kind of thing which we (sometimes at least) just perceive, or could perceive, or which—like the backs of our own heads—others could perceive. For otherwise we don't want to say that we perceive the thing *at all,* even indirectly.[l]

In contrast with this, many philosophers have held that we are *never* directly aware of such things as chairs and pens. In principle, they say, we can only be aware of them indirectly. This leads Austin to conclude that

> it is quite plain that the philosophers' use of "directly perceive," whatever it may be, is not the ordinary, or any familiar, use; for in *that* use it is not only false but simply absurd to say that such objects as pens or cigarettes are never perceived directly. But we are given no explanation or definition of this new use—on the contrary, it is glibly trotted out as if we were all quite familiar with it already.[m]

Here it is important to note a striking feature of this much of Austin's treatment of the argument from illusion: he has yet to say anything about the *reasons* philosophers give for the claim that we are never directly aware of material objects. He has, instead, challenged the very intelligibility of the issue in dispute—whether we are ever directly aware of material objects. He has not taken sides on this issue, nor will he.

Turning to the standard premises of the argument from illusion, Austin finds that they are as infected with linguistic confusion as is the conclusion. Recall that the first stage of the argument from illusion is intended to show that at least sometimes we are only indirectly aware of material objects, not directly aware of them. Here we can only consider one example of such an argument—the old favorite of the straight stick looking bent when it is partially immersed in water. Austin summarizes Ayer's rendition of this argument as follows:

> Refraction—the stick which normally "appears straight" but "looks bent" when seen in water. [Ayer] makes the "assumptions" (a) that the stick does not *really change its shape* when it is placed in water, and (b) that it *cannot be* both crooked and straight. He then concludes . . . that "at least one of the *visual appearances* of the stick is *delusive*." Nevertheless, even when "what we see is not the *real quality* of a *material thing*, it is supposed that we are still seeing something"—and this something is to be called a "sense-datum." A sense-datum is to be "the object of which we are *directly* aware, in perception, if it is not *part* of any *material thing*."[n]

The italics in this passage were introduced by Austin to mark what he takes to be misleading uses of language by Ayer.

Austin first notes the sly shift from the use of the word "illusion" to the use of the word "delusion." These, he remarks, are very different notions:

> The most important differences . . . are that the term "an illusion" . . . does not suggest that something totally unreal is *conjured up*. . . . whereas the term "delusion" *does* suggest something totally unreal, not really there at all.[o]

To cite one of Austin's favorite examples, in the theater it is possible to create the illusion of a headless woman walking across the stage by having her walk in front of a black background with a black sack over her head. (Presumably, this can be quite effective.) This is an illusion, but certainly not a delusion. The people in the audience see a woman walking across the stage; indeed, they see a woman with a black sack over her head walking across the stage even if they do not realize how the illusion is created. The headless woman is not something merely in the heads (or minds) of the audience. She is right up there in front of them.

But why should this shift from "illusion" to "delusion" make any difference? Austin explains as follows:

> The way in which the "argument from illusion" positively trades on not distinguishing illusions from delusions is, I think, this. So long as it

is being suggested that the cases paraded for our attention are cases of *illusion,* there is the implication (from the ordinary use of the word) that there really is something there that we perceive. But then, when these cases begin to be quietly called delusive, there comes in the very different suggestion of something being conjured up, something unreal or at any rate "immaterial."ᴾ

If Austin is right, this loose talk about delusions prepares the way for further loose talk. Still considering the bent stick, he asks:

What is wrong, what is even faintly surprising, in the idea of a stick's being straight but looking bent sometimes? Does anyone suppose that if something is straight, then it jolly well has to *look* straight at all times and in all circumstances? Obviously, no one seriously supposes this. So what mess are we supposed to get out of here, what is the difficulty? For of course it has to be suggested that there *is* a difficulty—a difficulty, furthermore, which calls for a pretty radical solution, the introduction of sense-data.�q

The argument from illusion, we noted, has a second stage. If we have been convinced, in the first stage, that sometimes at least we are not directly aware of material objects but of sense data instead, then the second stage is supposed to convince us that we are *never* directly aware of material objects. This is called the *indistinguishability argument.* To go back to our first example of the argument from illusion, it was claimed that my perceptions of a tree when I poke my eye (and hence see double) are qualitatively indistinguishable from my perception when I do not poke my eye. Since in the eye-poking case I am plainly aware of an image of a tree, this fact of indistinguishability should lead me to hold that I am only aware of an image when I am not poking my eye.

Austin makes quick work of the indistinguishability argument. He simply rejects the claim made by Ayer that "there is no intrinsic difference in kind between those of our perceptions that are veridical in their presentation and those that are delusive."ʳ Austin, of course, thinks that this statement is already packed with misleading expressions—or expressions being used in misleading ways—but, as he says:

Waiving as far as possible the numerous obscurities in and objections to this manner of speaking, let us ask whether what is being alleged here is actually true. Is it the case that "delusive and veridical experiences" are not "qualitatively different"? Well, at least it seems perfectly extraordinary to say so in this sweeping way. Consider a few examples. I may have the experience (dubbed "delusive" presumably) of dreaming that I am being presented to the Pope. Could it be seriously suggested that having this dream is "qualitatively indistinguishable" from *actually being* presented to the Pope? Quite obviously not. After all, we have the phrase "a dream-like quality"; some waking experience is said to have this dream-like quality, and some artists and writers occasionally try to impart it, usually with scant success, to their works. But of course, if the fact here alleged *were* a fact, the phrase would be perfectly meaningless, because applicable to everything.[s]

This argument seems to depend on a principle something like this: For an expression that assigns a quality to things to be meaningful, there must be things that lack this quality. Thus, if all experiences had a dreamlike quality, then saying that an experience was dreamlike would not distinguish it from any other experience, and that, Austin seems to be saying, would render the expression "dreamlike" meaningless. But it is far from obvious that if an expression applies to everything, then it is meaningless. Being identical with itself is a quality that everything possesses, but this does not render the expression "is identical with itself" meaningless. To cite a more concrete example, not being a pigeon weighing two tons is also a quality that everything possesses, but, again, this does not make the expression "is not a pigeon weighing two tons" meaningless. It may be possible to formulate Austin's principle in a way that avoids these difficulties. What is odd here is that Austin, with his keen eye for philosophical oversimplifications in the writings of others, failed to detect this oversimplification in his own writing.

In examining some further examples, Austin gets back on firmer ground by simply denying the factual claim of indistinguishability:

> It is simply not true to say that seeing a bright green after-image against a white wall is exactly like seeing a bright green patch actually on the wall; or that seeing a white wall through blue spectacles is exactly like seeing a blue wall; or that seeing pink rats in D.T.s is exactly like really seeing pink rats; or (once again) that seeing a stick refracted in water is exactly like seeing a bent stick. In all these cases we may *say* the same things ("It looks blue," "It looks bent," &c.), but this is no reason at all for denying the obvious fact that the "experiences" are *different*.[t]

Someone steeped in the traditional way of dealing with the problem of perception may think that this last passage—like many passages in *Sense and Sensibilia*—simply begs the question. Is Austin not simply assuming the very point at issue, namely, that we can always distinguish delusive from veridical perceptions? Austin does not think we can *always* do this. "There may be cases," he acknowledges, "in which 'delusive and veridical experiences' really are 'qualitatively indistinguishable.'"[u] For him it is also important to note that we often *do* distinguish them, usually with little difficulty. Sense-datum theorists, however, can work themselves into a position where they forget these ordinary facts or think they can ignore them. Perhaps they could ignore these facts if they had succeeded in giving the argument from illusion an acceptable formulation. That, however, is precisely the point that Austin is challenging.

Our discussion thus far has been misleading in the following way: it represents Ayer as a proponent of a traditional sense-datum theory. That is wrong. Ayer, as

Austin acknowledges, did *not* accept the argument from illusion in its traditional form. In particular, Ayer did not follow traditional sense-datum theorists in trying to use this argument to establish the thesis that we are never directly aware of material objects but only directly aware of sensa. This is hardly a thesis that could be established on empirical grounds and it is not a truth of logic, so, as a logical empiricist, Ayer must declare the claims of traditional sense-datum theorists meaningless.[19] Ayer attempts to avoid this result by claiming that the introduction of sense data is not a matter of empirical discovery, but rather a linguistic recommendation. Ayer presents what is sometimes called a linguistic version of a sense-datum theory.

First, Ayer claims that ordinary language already contains two senses of the word "perceive." Sometimes when we use the word "perceive," we are saying that the object perceived really does exist and really does have the feature we attribute to it. If I claim to see a man standing on the roof, then my claim is true only if there is a man standing on the roof.[20] On the other hand, according to Ayer, sometimes our perceptual claims carry no such implications:

> If, being subject to an illusion of double vision, I say that I am perceiving two pieces of paper, I need not be implying that there really are two pieces of paper there.[v]

Ayer then tells us that, in the presentation of his theory, he is using the term in this second way:

> I am using it here in such a way that to say of an object that it is perceived does not entail saying that it exists in any sense at all. And this is a perfectly correct and familiar usage of the word.[w]

Though Ayer does not put it this way, we might call this the *noncommittal* use of the word "perceive." *Sense data,* we can now say, are the objects of this noncommittal kind of perception.

Austin's response to Ayer's linguistic variant of the sense-datum approach is twofold. He first denies that in ordinary language we do use words such as "perceive," "see," and so forth in the noncommittal sense that Ayer suggests. Austin spends a great deal of time trying to show that Ayer has simply been misled by certain metaphorical and other nonstandard uses of perceptual terms. We do, for example, speak of a deranged person "seeing things," but this is clearly a vivid metaphorical use of the word "seeing." Double vision presents a more difficult case. If an experimenter asks me what I see when I poke my eye, I might naturally say "I see two trees." This hardly seems to be a metaphor. Austin deals with this case by telling us that it is important to say that

> double vision is a quite *exceptional* case, so that we may have to stretch our ordinary usage to accommodate it. . . . But the fact that an

[19] See Ch. 5.
[20] This is not quite right, but it is good enough for our present purposes.

exceptional situation may thus induce me to use words primarily appropriate for a different, normal situation is nothing like enough to establish that there are, in general, two different, normal ("correct and familiar") *senses* of the words I use.[x]

Readers can decide for themselves how persuasive Austin is on this matter. Austin does, after all, have a certain proprietary interest in keeping ordinary language on his side. It is important to remember, however, that even if a noncommittal sense of perceptual terms is "correct and familiar," we can still ask why this use is given prominence by Ayer. Austin's general answer is that this supposedly linguistic restatement of sense-datum theory is really nothing more than the old version dressed in more-respectable clothing. This new version of the theory, Austin thinks, is driven by the same mistakes that drove the older version. Once these mistakes are revealed, it too collapses.

It is not possible to go into all of the details of Austin's relentless examination of what he takes to be Ayer's misuse of language in developing—or, as Austin might say, imposing on himself—the problem of perception. It will, however, be useful to examine a maneuver that Austin was fond of using which, as we shall see, Paul Grice challenged.

Ayer, like many philosophers in the empiricist tradition, held that material-object statements can never be completely verified. The reason for this, put roughly, is that statements about material objects imply endlessly many observation statements, and however good our evidence up to now is, it can always be overturned by future observations. Austin describes this rather common philosophical view as an "extraordinary doctrine" and then dismisses it in these words:

> It is, of course, not true in general that statements about "material things," as such, *need to* be "verified." If, for instance, someone remarks in casual conversation, "As a matter of fact I live in Oxford," the other party to the conversation may, if he finds it worth doing, verify this assertion; but the *speaker,* of course, has no need to do this—he knows it to be true (or, if he is lying, false). Strictly speaking, indeed, it is not just that he has no *need* to verify his statement; the cause is rather that, since he already knows it to be true, nothing whatever that he might do could *count* as his "verifying" it. Nor need it be true that he is in this position by virtue of having verified his assertion at some previous stage; for of how many people really, who know quite well where they live, could it be said that they have at any time *verified that* they live there?[y]

At least this much is clear: It would certainly be odd—in some sense a misuse of language—to speak of someone verifying something she already knows. But what are we to make of this oddity, and what conclusions can be drawn from it?

Austin makes a similar point about what he takes to be the philosopher's misuse of the notion of evidence:

The situation in which I would properly be said to have *evidence* for the statement that some animal is a pig is that, for example, in which the beast itself is not actually on view, but I can see plenty of pig-like marks on the ground outside its retreat. If I find a few buckets of pig-food, that's a bit more evidence, and the noises and the smell may provide better evidence still. But if the animal then emerges and stands there plainly in view, there is no longer any question of collecting evidence; its coming into view doesn't provide me with more *evidence* that it's a pig, I can now just *see* that it is, the question is settled.[z]

Again Austin is right: it would be odd to speak about evidence when the pig is plainly in sight. But precisely what conclusion can be drawn from this oddity?

At the very close of *Sense and Sensibilia* Austin examines another standard view of empiricists, namely, that statements about material objects are somehow based on statements of immediate perception. Roughly, as that theory goes, we hold that there *is* a tiger before us because there seems (or appears) to be one there. According to empiricists, these weak claims about how things seem (look or appear) are the ultimate basis for the strong claim about how things are. Speaking of G. J. Warnock's version of this doctrine,[21] Austin remarks:

His statements of "immediate perception," so far from being that from which we *advance* to more ordinary statements, are actually arrived at . . . by *retreating from* more ordinary statements, by progressive hedging. (There's a tiger—there *seems* to be a tiger—it seems *to me* that there's a tiger—it seems to me *now* that there's a tiger—it seems to me now *as if there were* a tiger.) It seems extraordinarily perverse to represent as that on which ordinary statements are based a form of words which, *starting from* and moreover incorporating an ordinary statement, qualifies and hedges in various ways. You've got to get something on your plate before you can start messing it around. It is not . . . that we can stop hedging if there is a good case for coming right out with it; the fact is that we don't *begin* to hedge unless there is some special reason for doing so, something a bit strange and off-colour about the particular situation.[a]

Austin is correct here, too. It would certainly be peculiar, standing in front of a cage with a tiger in plain view, to say something like "It seems to me now as if there were a tiger there." But what are we to make of this oddity?

It is certainly correct, then, that sense-datum theorists (and other philosophers) often speak of verification and evidence in odd ways, and use hedging terms in contexts where they are inappropriate. Austin treats these departures

---

[21] Warnock introduced the ideas under consideration in *Berkeley* (Penguin Books, London, 1952).

from everyday use as serious mistakes—amounting sometimes to speaking nonsense. Grice, as we shall see, challenges Austin on just this point and, in the process, deals a serious blow to the methods of ordinary-language philosophy as practiced, at least, by Austin.

PERFORMATIVES AND SPEECH-ACT THEORY

Sense and Sensibilia is largely a negative work. Though along the way it contains important discussions of perceptual terms and related expressions, its main task was to undermine the problem of perception as represented primarily, though not exclusively, by A. J. Ayer. In fact, Austin had little interest in offering *direct* answers to perennial philosophical questions. For all that, Austin thought that philosophy has played an important role in the development of a scientific understanding of the world and should continue to do so. In one of the few passages where he allows himself poetic license, Austin puts it this way:

> In the history of human inquiry, philosophy has the place of the initial central sun, seminal and tumultuous: from time to time it throws off some portion of itself to take station as a science, a planet, cool and well regulated, progressing steadily towards a distant final state. This happened long ago at the birth of mathematics, and again at the birth of physics: only in the last century we have witnessed the same process once again, slow and at the time almost imperceptible, in the birth of the science of mathematical logic, through the joint labors of philosophers and mathematicians. Is it not possible that the next century may see the birth, through the joint labors of philosophers, grammarians, and numerous other students of language, of a true and comprehensive *science of language*? Then we shall have rid ourselves of one more part of philosophy (there will still be plenty left) in the only way we ever can get rid of philosophy, by kicking it upstairs.[b]

In this passage Austin speaks of the possibility of developing a *comprehensive science of language*. Notice, however, that he does not underestimate the magnitude of this task. Speaking cautiously, he tells us that it may be possible to do so in the "next century." It is not clear whether Austin is here referring to the twenty-first century or to the hundred years beginning in 1956, the year he presented the paper containing this passage; whichever, he was projecting a long and difficult enterprise.

Austin's major contribution to this projected comprehensive science of language was the development of the notion of performative utterances and from this the further development of what came to be known as speech-act theory. There are two published sources of Austin's views on performatives and speech acts: *How to Do Things with Words,* given as the William James Lectures at Harvard in 1955, and a less technical presentation of his ideas given on the British

Broadcasting Corporation's Third Programme in 1956 under the title "Performative Utterances." Perhaps because it is addressed to a general audience, Austin uncharacteristically begins "Performative Utterances" with some general comments about philosophy. They are worth quoting at some length.

> We have not got to go very far back in the history of philosophy to find philosophers assuming more or less as a matter of course that the sole business, the sole interesting business, of any utterance—that is, of anything we say—is to be true or at least false. Of course they had always known that there are other kinds of things which we say—things like imperatives, the expressions of wishes, and exclamations—some of which had even been classified by grammarians, though it wasn't perhaps too easy to tell always which was which. But still philosophers have assumed that the only things that they are interested in are utterances which report facts or which describe situations truly or falsely. In recent times this kind of approach has been questioned—in two stages, I think. First of all people began to say: "Well, if these things are true or false it ought to be possible to decide which they are, and if we can't decide which they are they aren't any good but are, in short, nonsense." And this new approach did a great deal of good; a great many things which probably are nonsense were found to be such. It is not the case, I think, that all kinds of nonsense have been adequately classified yet, and perhaps some things have been dismissed as nonsense which really are not; but still this movement, the verification movement, was, in its way, excellent.
>
> However, we then come to the second stage. After all, we set some limits to the amount of nonsense that we talk, or at least the amount of nonsense that we are prepared to admit we talk; and so people began to ask whether after all some of those things which, treated as statements, were in danger of being dismissed as nonsense did after all really set out to be statement at all. Mightn't they perhaps be intended not to report facts but to influence people in this way or that, or to let off steam in this way or that? Or perhaps at any rate some elements in these utterances performed such functions, or, for example, drew attention in some way (without actually reporting it) to some important feature of the circumstances in which the utterance was being made. On these lines people have now adopted a new slogan, the slogan of the "different uses of language." The old approach, the old statemental approach, is sometimes called even a fallacy, the descriptive fallacy.[c]

As we saw in Chapter 7, the positivists were inclined to write off vast portions of philosophy as meaningless or, somewhat differently, to treat many philosophical problems as pseudoproblems. Notice that Austin does not complain about this; indeed, he suggests that some kinds of nonsense—presumably some kinds of philosophical nonsense—remain to be classified. Austin's complaint against the positivists is that they went beyond the condemnation of philosophical nonsense to declare large portions of common discourse nonsense as well. He seems to be saying that what is needed now is a second stage in the development of linguistic philosophy, one that will correct the excesses of Logical Positivism. Philosophers have often put forward (supposed) truth-claims where there was no possibility of determining whether the claim was true or false. The positivists were right in rejecting such claims as meaningless. But under the sway of the descriptive fallacy, the positivists *misidentified* expressions of ordinary language as attempted statements, and again, because there was no way of determining whether they were true or false, mistakenly called them meaningless as well. In *How to Do Things with Words,* Austin makes the point this way:

> It has now been shown piecemeal, or at least made to look likely, that many traditional philosophical perplexities have arisen through a mistake—the mistake of taking as straightforward statements of fact utterances which are *either* (in interesting non-grammatical ways) nonsensical or *else* intended as something quite different.[d]

The positivists initiated what Austin calls "a great revolution in philosophy"[e] by unmasking the first mistake. Austin is largely concerned with unmasking mistakes of the second kind.

Performative utterances first make their appearance in Austin's writings as an antidote to the descriptive fallacy. They provide a rich and unquestionable source of expressions that look like statements, are not statements, but still are not meaningless. About these utterances, Austin tells us:

> All will have, as it happens, humdrum verbs in the first person singular present indicative active. Utterances can be found, satisfying these conditions, yet such that
> A. they do not "describe" or "report" or constate anything at all, are not "true or false"; and
> B. the uttering of the sentence is, or is a part of, the doing of an action, which again would not *normally* be described as saying something.[f]

Austin then gives examples of utterances that satisfy these criteria:

> "I name this ship the *Queen Elizabeth*"—as uttered when smashing the bottle against [its bow].
> "I give and bequeath my watch to my brother"—as occurring in a will.
> "I bet you sixpence it will rain tomorrow."[g]

With the preliminary isolation of performatives completed, Austin next considers the conditions under which a performative utterance can be *successfully* used. With performatives, though saying *can* amount to doing, uttering a performative does not *always* amount to doing—for a performative utterance to come off, the circumstances have to be right. A person cannot use the sentence "I resign from the National Rifle Association" to resign from the National Rifle Association if, for example, she is not a member of that organization. Only certain people are empowered to marry people by pronouncing them husband and wife. Not everyone can cast a vote in Congress. And so on.

The possibility of such failures, Austin saw, provides a means for gaining insight into the rules governing the use of various performatives. If we are asked, for example, what promising consists in, we will probably be hard put to know what to say. In contrast, if we examine those cases in which someone utters the sentence "I promise . . . ," yet fails to make a promise, the conditions for successful promising come to the surface.

> Besides the uttering of the words of the so-called performative, a good many other things have as a general rule to be right and to go right if we are to be said to have happily brought off our action. What these are we may hope to discover by looking at and classifying types of cases in which something *goes wrong* and the act—marrying, betting, bequeathing, christening, or what not—is therefore at least to some extent a failure: the utterance is then, we may say, not indeed false but in general *unhappy.* And for this reason we call the doctrine of *the things that can be and go wrong* on the occasion of such utterances, the doctrine of the *Infelicities.*[h]

Presumably as a result of his study of cases where things *go wrong* with performative utterances, Austin is able to specify "some at least of the things which are necessary for the smooth or 'happy' functioning of a performative":

(A. 1)   There must exist an accepted conventional procedure having a certain conventional effect, that procedure to include the uttering of certain words by certain persons in certain circumstances, and further,

(A. 2)   the particular persons and circumstances in a given case must be appropriate for the invocation of the particular procedure invoked.

(B. 1)   The procedure must be executed by all participants both correctly and

(B. 2)   completely.

(G. 1)   Where, as often, the procedure is designed for use by persons having certain thoughts or feelings, or for the inauguration of certain consequential conduct on the part of any participant, then a person participating in and so invoking the procedure must in fact have those thoughts or feelings, and the participants must intend so to conduct themselves, and further

(G. 2)   must actually so conduct themselves subsequently.[i]

For Austin's purposes, it is important to examine these rules in detail, noting, in particular, the various ways in which infelicities can arise through their violation. In this way, he thinks, we can come to appreciate the complexity and subtlety of our use of performatives. Here we can only sample this rather long and detailed discussion, noting clear examples of violations of each of these conditions for a happy (or felicitous) use of a performative.

(A.1) For a performative to come off (be happy), *it has to be done in the context of an appropriate conventional procedure.* "Consider 'I divorce you,' said to a wife by her husband in a Christian country, and both being Christians rather than Mohammedans."[j] Clearly this does not count as divorcing someone. (A.2) *The person and circumstances must be appropriate.* "Suppose, for example, I see a vessel on the stocks, walk up and smash the bottle hung at the stem, proclaim 'I name this ship *Mr. Stalin*' and for good measure kick away the chocks: but the trouble is, I was not the person chosen to name it. . . . We can all agree . . . that the ship was not thereby named."[k] (B.1) *The procedure must be executed by all participants correctly.* For example, in legal matters, it is often important to use the right forms. (B.2) *The procedure must be executed completely.* If I offer someone a bet, and he says nothing, then no bet has been made. Finally, there are what might be called sincerity conditions. (G.1) *Certain thoughts or feelings are expected.* If I say "I apologize," I am expected to feel sorry. (G.2) *Certain actions can be expected.* If I say that I promise to do something, then, obviously, I am supposed to do it. Notice that there is an important difference between the A and B rules and the G rules. With a violation of either an A or a B rule, the performative does not come off—it is void. With a violation of a G rule, however, the performative does come off, though I am subject to criticism. For example, if I promise to do something without any intention of doing it (a G.1 infelicity), then I have promised insincerely, but still, I *have* made a promise and can be criticized if I do not keep it.

This seems a good beginning. Hitherto unappreciated forms of language have been recognized and rules sketched for their employment. Then Austin notices various difficulties with his account of performatives. First, he acknowledges that his discussion has been largely limited to just one sort of performative: those with "verbs in the first person singular present indicative active." These, he tells us, are the "commonest type of explicit performative."[l] Austin does not spell out what he means by an explicit performative, but these remarks clearly suggest that explicit performatives do not have to be constructions with verbs in the first person singular present indicative active. An explicit performative, it seems, is any performative that clearly exhibits its performative character in its linguistic expression. On that interpretation all of the following count as explicit performatives, even though they do not conform to Austin's original paradigm:

(1)   You are hereby authorized to pay . . .
(2)   Passengers are warned to cross the track by the bridge only.
(3)   Notice is hereby given that trespassers will be prosecuted.[m]

So being in the first person and being in the active voice are not essential even for explicit performatives.

Things become more complicated when we leave the domain of explicit performatives. Consider examples of the following kind:

(a)   A referee might say "You're offside"—an apparently descriptive remark—to call someone offside.[n]

(b)   A farmer may put up a sign reading "Dangerous Bull," or perhaps just "Bull," as a warning.[o]

Reflecting on examples of this kind, Austin came to the conclusion that there was no grammatical way of distinguishing general performative utterances from nonperformative utterances.

There were, however, deeper reasons for Austin's uneasiness about his original distinction between performatives and statements. The idea of a performative (though not yet under that name) appears first in "Other Minds," where Austin used it to attack what he called the *descriptive fallacy.* In that context, and in others dealing with the descriptive fallacy, it served Austin's purposes to stress the differences between performatives and statements.

> Statements, we had it, were to be true or false; performative utterances on the other hand were to be felicitous and infelicitous. They [performatives] were the doing of something, whereas for all we said making statements was not doing something.[p]

But as Austin's interest shifted from criticizing other philosophers to giving a positive account of language, he was increasingly struck by the similarities between performatives and statements.

Starting with statements, Austin notes that they "are also liable to infelicity every bit as much as are performative utterances."[q] When I state something, I am supposed to believe what I say. If I do not, then I have been insincere—an instance of a G infelicity. More interestingly, a statement, like a performative, can fail to come off. Going back to a familiar example, if someone now said that the present king of France is wise, Austin would say (taking the same line adopted by Strawson) that she has failed to make a statement at all, because there is no present king of France to make a statement about. So the applicability of the felicitous/infelicitous contrast does not separate performatives from statements; it applies to both.

Looking in the other direction, truth does bear in important ways on performatives. Suppose I warn you that bubonic plague is sweeping Paris when bubonic plague is not sweeping Paris. In that case a matter of truth has a bearing on my warning, even if it seems wrong to call the utterance "Let me warn you that bubonic plague is sweeping Paris" false. Also, the following exchange is perfectly natural:

> *Referee:*   Offside.
>
> *Player:*   I was not.

Here the player is challenging the correctness of the referee's call, presumably concerning a matter of fact. Indeed, often the correctness of the use of a performative utterance does turn on a question of fact. So truth does have a bearing on performative utterances in essential ways.

Austin was so struck by the similarities between performatives and statements that he was led into a blunder concerning them.

> In fact in general we may remind ourselves that "I state that . . ." does not look so very different from "I warn you that . . ." or "I promise to. . . ." It makes clear surely that the act that we are performing is an act of stating, and so functions just like "I warn" or "I order." So isn't "I state that . . ." a performative utterance? But then one may feel that utterances beginning "I state that . . ." do have to be true or false, that they *are* statements.ʳ

The closing remark in this passage clearly seems to be a mistake.[22] It is certainly true that if someone utters the sentences "I state that Smith was in Toronto on the night of the murder," that person thereby states that Smith was in Toronto on the night of the murder. Furthermore, what that person thereby states will be either true or false. But from that it does not follow that the entire performative utterance "I state that Smith was in Toronto on the night of the murder" can properly be called true or false. Notice how odd it would be to respond to this utterance by saying "No, you don't state that."

But even if Austin's reasoning was flawed—at least in this one respect—it led him to an important insight, namely, that "stating something is performing an act just as much as giving an order or giving a warning," which, he tells us, "seems to mean that in its original form our distinction between the performative and the statement is considerably weakened, and indeed breaks down."ˢ

Instead of discouraging Austin, this discovery that his initial contrast between performatives was ill conceived led him to introduce a new classification of the things we do with words.

> It is time then to make a fresh start on the problem. We want to reconsider more generally the senses in which to say something may be to do something, or in saying something we do something (and also perhaps to consider the different case in which *by* saying something we do something). Perhaps some clarification and definition here may help us out of our tangle.ᵗ

---

[22] This cannot be written off as a mere slip, for he says the same thing, in almost the same words, in *How to Do Things with Words*, p. 91.

Austin's program now becomes complicated. It falls into two parts; it operates at two levels. (1) He first offers a very general account of what it is to *issue an utterance*. He suggests that there are at least three kinds of acts involved in issuing utterances. He calls them, respectively, *locutionary, illocutionary,* and *perlocutionary* acts. (2) Having sorted out these three components of linguistic acts, he concentrates almost exclusively on offering a systematic account of illocutionary acts.

(1) *The General Account.* Here we can only present a simplified version of Austin's explanation of the differences among *locutionary, illocutionary,* and *perlocutionary* acts. (a) Roughly, to perform a locutionary act is to say something meaningful in a particular language. Thus unless we are merely babbling, every time we say something we are performing a locutionary act. Usually, of course, we are trying to do more than produce utterances meaningful in the language we speak. Sometimes, however, that is all that we are doing—for example, in a language drill where we are trying to improve our pronunciation. Here it does not particularly matter what we are saying, only that we are saying it correctly. (b) As Austin has noted a number of times, the very same utterance can be used to do different things. For example, the imperative "Close the door!" can be used to make a request, give advice, issue a command, and so forth. Knowing what the sentence means does not settle the issue. This leads Austin to introduce the notion of an illocutionary act.

> To perform a locutionary act is in general, we may say, also and *eo ipso* to perform an *illocutionary* act, as I propose to call it. Thus in performing a locutionary act we shall also be performing such an act as:
>
> asking or answering a question,
> giving some information or an assurance or a warning,
> announcing a verdict or an intention,
> pronouncing sentence,
> making an appointment or an appeal or a criticism,
> making an identification or giving a description.[u]

An illocutionary act, Austin tells us, is what we do

> *in* saying something as opposed to performance of an act *of* saying something; I call the act performed an "illocution" and shall refer to the doctrine of the different types of function of language here in question as the doctrine of "illocutionary forces."[v]

(c) Finally, Austin introduces the notion of a perlocutionary act, which he describes rather loosely as follows: "Saying something will often, or even normally, produce certain consequential effects upon the feelings, thought, or actions of the audience. . . . We shall call the performance of an act of this kind the performance of a 'perlocutionary' act."[w] Austin offers the following example illustrating the differences among the three kinds of acts he has distinguished:

> Act (A) or Locution
>
> > He said to me "Shoot her!" meaning by "shoot" *shoot* and referring by "her" to *her.*
>
> Act (B) or Illocution
>
> > He urged (or advised, ordered, &c.) me to shoot her.
>
> Act (C) or Perlocution
>
> > He persuaded me to shoot her.[x]

(2) *Illocutionary Acts.* Having outlined his general position, Austin turns his attention to illocutionary acts. They deserve special attention because, according to Austin, an understanding of illocutionary acts or illocutionary forces provides the key to developing a systematic account of the various uses of language. It is at this point that the notion of an explicit performative is revived and put to serious work.

> We said long ago that we needed a list of "explicit performative verbs"; but in the light of the more general theory we now see that what we need is a list of *illocutionary forces* of an utterance. The old distinction, however, between *primary* and *explicit* will survive the sea-change from the performative/constative distinction to the theory of speech-acts quite successfully. For we have since seen reason to suppose that the sorts of test suggested for the explicit performative verbs ("to say . . . is to . . . ," &c.) will do, and in fact do better for sorting out those verbs which make explicit, as we shall now say, the illocutionary force of an utterance, or what illocutionary act it is that we are performing in issuing that utterance.[y]

We can call the test that Austin has in mind the *explicit-performative test.* Start with the following pattern:

> To say I . . . is to. . . .

Plug the same verb into the two openings in this pattern; for example:

> To say I promise is to promise.

If the result is a true statement (as it is in this case), then the verb is a performative verb indicative of a kind of illocutionary act. Since the verb "promise" passes this explicit-performative test, promising can be considered a kind of illocutionary act. It is important to see that not every verb passes this test. For example, to say "I swim (orate, yodel, smoke, climb mountains)" is not to swim (orate, yodel, smoke, climb mountains); hence none of these verbs is a performative verb, and none indicates a kind of illocutionary act.

Working his way through the dictionary with the explicit-performative test in hand, Austin thus had a method for discovering different—often unexpected—kinds of illocutionary acts. In fact, using this method, Austin turned up a surprisingly large number of performative verbs.

> Using . . . this simple test (with caution) . . . and going through the dictionary (a concise one should do) in a liberal spirit, we get a list of the order of the third power of 10.[23,z]

There may, of course, be illocutionary acts with no performative verbs corresponding to them, and there may be illocutionary acts mirrored by more than one performative verb, so Austin's test may miss some illocutionary acts and double-count others. Granting this, the explicit-performative test still provides a powerful tool for doing what Austin liked to call *fieldwork* concerning the various uses of language.

In the final chapter of *How to Do Things with Words*, Austin lists 188 performative verbs. He begins to classify them, putting them in five major categories. He also comments on the systematic relationships among these categories. Just to give a feel for his method, here is his treatment of performative verbs he calls commissives:

> The whole point of a commissive is to commit the speaker to a certain course of action. Examples are:

promise	covenant	contract
undertake	bind myself	give my word
am determined to	intend	declare my intention
mean to	plan	purpose
propose to	shall	contemplate
envisage	engage	swear
guarantee	pledge myself	bet
vow	agree	consent
dedicate myself to	declare for	side with
adopt	champion	embrace
espouse	oppose	favour[a]

[23] The suggested figure must be intended as a joke. As Austin notes, to say that a quantity is "of the order of the third power of 10" is to say that it ranges from 1,000 to 9,999. If Austin had gone through the dictionary—as he suggests he had—he could certainly have told us more exactly how many performative verbs he actually turned up. That there might be as many as, say, 5,000 seems totally implausible. In any case, Austin turned up a great many performative verbs—more than one might expect.

In the final chapter of *How to Do Things with Words,* Austin begins the work, or at least the spadework, for the development of a general account of language. He thought that the development of such a theory would demand a great deal of detailed work involving the cooperation of many. Unfortunately, his early death did not allow him to carry this project very far. But even if his own work was left incomplete, this aspect of his philosophy continues to exert an important influence on both philosophy and linguistics. The invention of speech-act theory will almost certainly be remembered as Austin's most enduring contribution to twentieth-century thought.

Paul Grice

Paul Grice[24] had an anomalous position in the ordinary-language philosophy movement: He was one of its most subtle practitioners, but at the same time he was a devastating critic of many of the standard moves made by other members of this group. It seemed to be his special calling to resurrect traditional philosophical positions that other ordinary-language philosophers thought were safely buried once and for all.

THE CAUSAL THEORY OF PERCEPTION

Grice's distinctive ideas made their first public appearance in 1961 with his essay "The Causal Theory of Perception."[25] The view that Grice defends in this work is similar to the sense-datum position adopted by A. J. Ayer in *The Foundations of Empirical Knowledge*—a work, as we saw, subjected to severe criticism in Austin's *Sense and Sensibilia*. Though Grice does not mention Austin by name, it is Austin's critique of sense-datum theories that is the obvious target of Grice's essay.

A causal theory of perception, as Grice understands the notion, is the view that "'I am perceiving M' [where M is a material object] is to be regarded as equivalent to 'I am having (or sensing) a sense-datum which is caused by M.'"[b]

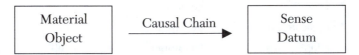

This view has two components that demand detailed development: (i) The nature of the causal relationship between the object M and the sense datum must be specified, and (ii) the notion of a sense datum itself must be explained.

[24] Paul Grice (1913–88) was educated at Oxford University, where he remained as a member of the faculty until 1967, when he was appointed a professor at the University of California at Berkeley.

[25] See p. 476 ff.

(i) Specifying the right sort of causal chain is an important task for a causal theory of perception, since not every causal chain leading from M to the sense datum will count as an instance of perceiving M. For example, if I view an image of an actor on a movie screen, there is a causal chain leading back from my sensing an image of the actor's face to the actor's face itself, yet this is not a case of my perceiving the actor's face. Though the causal chain exists, it does not seem *direct* enough to count as an instance of perceiving the object at the end of the causal chain. So, for the causal link to count as perceiving it has to be appropriately direct, but, as it turns out, it is by no means easy to specify just what the appropriate kind of directness amounts to. In "The Causal Theory of Perception," Grice makes no serious effort to deal with this difficult issue, contenting himself with citing common examples where we are said to perceive things because they stand in the right sort of relationship to our sense organs.

(ii) The central task of Grice's essay is to defend the legitimacy of introducing sense data as a technical notion for the analysis of perceptual judgments. Specifically, Grice defends the view that "the expression 'sense-datum' can (and should) be introduced as a technical term; its use would be explicitly defined by reference to such supposedly standard locutions as 'So-and-so looks f (e.g., blue) to me,' 'It looks (feels) to me as if there were a f so-and-so,' 'I seem to see a f' and so on."[c] Austin, as we saw, rejected theories of this kind by arguing that words such as "looks," "appears," and "seems" find employment in contexts where doubt—or at least some challenge—is appropriate. When used outside these contexts, they are misused and thus lose their meaning. Grice restates this (Austinian) objection this way:

> A general objection . . . might run as follows: When someone makes such a remark as "It looks red to me" a certain implication is carried. . . . It is implied either that the object referred to is known or believed by the speaker not to *be red, or* that it has been denied by someone else to be red, *or* that the speaker is doubtful whether it is red, *or* that someone else has expressed doubt whether it is red, *or* that the situation is such that, though no doubt has actually been expressed and no denial has actually been made, some person or other might feel inclined toward denial or doubt. . . . Let us refer to [this condition] as the *D-or-D* condition ("doubt or denial" condition). Now we may perhaps agree that there is liable to be something odd or even absurd about employing an "It looks to me" locution when the appropriate *D-or-D* condition is fairly obviously not fulfilled; there would be something at least prima facie odd about my saying "That looks red to me" (not as a joke) when I am confronted by a British pillar box in normal daylight at a range of a few feet. At this point my objector advances a twofold thesis, (*a*) that it is a feature of the use, perhaps of the meaning, of such locutions as "looks to me" that they should carry the implication that the *D-or-D* condition is fulfilled, and that if they were uttered by a speaker who did not suppose this condition was fulfilled he would be guilty of a misuse

of the locutions in question (unless of course he were intending to deceive his audience into thinking that the condition was fulfilled), (*b*) that in cases where the *D*-or-*D* condition is unfulfilled the utterance employing the "looks to me" locution, so far from being uninterestingly true, is neither true nor false. Thus armed, my objector now assails the latter-day sense-datum theorist.[d]

Notice that there are two forms that this criticism can take. The first criticism, (*a*), suggests that if the sentence "That looks red to me" is used in the absence of the *D*-or-*D* condition, then it is *meaningless.* The second criticism, (*b*), suggests that if this sentence is used in the absence of the *D*-or-*D* condition, then the utterance of the sentence will be *neither true nor false.* If either of these objections is correct, then sense-datum theories fail before they get off the ground, for utterances that are either meaningless or neither true nor false can hardly serve as a foundation for empirical knowledge.

To counter this argument, Grice suggests an alternative interpretation of the relationship between "That looks red to me" and the *D*-or-*D* condition:

> It is of course possible to take a different view of the linguistic phenomena outlined in my previous paragraph. One may contend that if I were to say "it looks red to me" in a situation in which the *D*-or-*D* condition is not fulfilled, what I say is (subject to certain qualifications) true, not "neuter"; while admitting that though true it might be very misleading and that its truth might be very boring and its misleadingness very important, one might still hold that its *suggestio falsi* is perfectly compatible with its literal truth.[e]

An example may help explain the difference between these alternative ways of dealing with the *D*-or-*D* condition. Standing in broad daylight in front of a fire engine, someone says things like this:

> This truck appears to be red.
> I have very good evidence that this is a red truck.
> It seems to me now that this is a red truck.
> This object has the look of something red.
> It looks to me to be red.

Unquestionably, given the context, all of these remarks would be odd, inappropriate, and, perhaps, misleading. On that point Austin and Grice would agree. The question is whether these remarks, however defective in these ways, may still be meaningful and, in fact, true. Grice says yes; Austin, though he is cautious, seems to say no. Who is correct?

We can try to settle this question at an intuitive level by trying to imagine what we would say if someone, standing in broad daylight in front of a bright red fire engine, actually said "It looks red to me." To that we would naturally say something like "What do you mean, it *looks* red to you? It obviously *is* red." To use a cautious way of speaking suggests that there is some good reason to be cautious, whereas, in the imagined case, there is none. This, then, is plainly an odd way of speaking—even a misuse of language—yet, when pressed, most people would acknowledge that what the person said makes sense and is even true, though perhaps so boringly true as not to be worth saying. If this is correct, it shows that someone can use an expression in a way that no ordinary person would—even use it in a way that is contrary to the way we ordinarily speak—but still be speaking meaningfully and, perhaps, still be speaking the truth. By making this rather simple point, Grice deprived Austin and other ordinary-language philosophers of one of their favorite tools of criticism. That we would not ordinarily say something, or find saying it very odd, by itself does not show that the utterance is either meaningless or lacking in a truth-value (i.e., neither true nor false).

Grice might have left his argument at this intuitive level, for even at that level it seems quite persuasive. That, however, was not Grice's style. His insight was that there are ways in which an utterance can be conversationally odd—even extremely conversationally odd—without being meaningless or lacking in a truth-value. To provide a basis for this claim, he set himself the task of giving a systematic account of the ways in which conversational oddity can arise. He sketched this theory in "The Causal Theory of Perception" and then gave it a fuller and more systematic statement in "Logic and Conversation." To avoid repetition, we will examine "Logic and Conversation" first, and then return to Grice's discussion of perception.

LOGIC AND CONVERSATION

Austin's "Other Minds" and Strawson's "On Referring" are classics of ordinary-language philosophy. Grice's "Logic and Conversation" was for years an underground classic. It was the first lecture in Grice's William James Lectures given at Harvard in 1967, but it did not appear in print until 1975.[26] During the interim, it was privately circulated and widely cited in the publications of other philosophers.

"Logic and Conversation" was an attempt to get clear about the difference between what is implied by what a person asserts and what is implied by a person's making an assertion. For example, suppose that Alan asserts that Bill Gates is very rich. What he has asserted logically implies that at least one person named Bill is very rich. Thus Alan could not make the following remark without contradicting himself:

> Bill Gates is very rich, but it is not the case that anyone named Bill is very rich.

In contrast, Alan's making the original assertion, that Bill Gates is very rich, also implies a number of things that are not implied by what he asserts. For example,

---

[26] A complete version of his William James Lectures, revised in 1987, appeared in *Studies in the Way of Words* the year after his death.

in saying that Bill Gates is very rich, Alan implies that he believes this. This comes out if we notice how odd it would be for Alan to say,

> Bill Gates is very rich but I do not believe it.

This is odd because generally we are not supposed to go around asserting things we do not believe to be true. Notice, however, though peculiar, this assertion could actually be true. It could be true that Bill Gates is very rich and also true that Alan does not believe it. What is odd is for Alan actually to *say* this. This leads to the distinction between what the *proposition* asserted implies and what the *making* of an assertion implies. These examples provide a rough idea of the difference between the *conventional* implications of *what is asserted* and the *conversational* implications of *asserting it*.

In "Logic and Conversation" Grice attempted to give a systematic account of this notion of conversational implication or, to use his phrase, conversational *implicatures*. His basic idea was that conversations (or conversational exchanges) are usually cooperative activities intended to achieve some shared goal. That is, when people speak to each other they are usually trying to achieve something—to exchange information, to coordinate their activities, and so on. Like other cooperative activities, they are more efficient when governed by mutually understood rules and procedures. Thus the most general rule governing conversational exchanges could be expressed in the single word "Cooperate!" More fully, Grice states this general principle this way:

> Make your conversational contribution such as is required, at the stage at which it occurs, by the accepted purpose or direction of the talk exchange in which you are engaged.[f]

Grice calls this the Cooperative Principle.[27]

Under this general principle, Grice ranges a number of maxims intended to give it more-specific contact:

> One may perhaps distinguish four categories under one or another of which will fall certain more specific maxims and submaxims, the following of which will, in general, yield results in accordance with the Cooperative Principle. . . . I call these categories Quantity, Quality, Relation, and Manner. The category of Quantity relates to the quantity of information to be provided, and under it fall the following maxims:
>
> 1.   Make your contribution as informative as is required (for the current purposes of the exchange).
> 2.   Do not make your contribution more informative than is required. . . .

---

[27] Of course, not all conversational exchanges are cooperative, but cooperative conversations provide the standard example.

Under the category of Quality falls a supermaxim—"Try to make your contribution one that is true"—and two more specific maxims:

1. Do not say what you believe to be false.
2. Do not say that for which you lack adequate evidence.

Under the category of Relation I place a single maxim, namely, "Be relevant." . . .

Finally, under the category of Manner, which I understand as relating not (like the previous categories) to what is said but, rather, to *how* what is said is to be said, I include the supermaxim—"Be perspicuous"—and various maxims such as:

1. Avoid obscurity of expression.
2. Avoid ambiguity.
3. Be brief (avoid unnecessary prolixity).
4. Be orderly.[g]

Having fleshed out the notion of the Cooperative Principle and the various maxims that fall under it, Grice tells us that he is "now in a position to characterize the notion of conversational implicature":

A man who, by (in, when) saying (making as if to say) that *p* has implicated that *q*, may be said to have conversationally implicated that *q*, provided that (1) he is to be presumed to be observing the conversational maxims, or at least the Cooperative Principle; (2) the supposition that he is aware that, or thinks that, *q* is required in order to make his saying or making as if to say *p* (or doing so in *those* terms) consistent with this presumption; and (3) the speaker thinks (and would expect the hearer to think that the speaker thinks) that it is within the competence of the hearer to work out, or grasp intuitively, that the supposition mentioned in (2) is required.[h]

An important feature of this account is that it relies on the *mutual recognition of intentions*—that is, we often intend to do something with the intention that others recognize our intention to do it. That sounds complicated, but it is a regular occurrence. For example, when we intentionally (rather than accidentally) signal for a turn when driving, we do this with the intention that anyone following us will take our signaling as intentional. Part of our intention is to make our intention clear. For obvious reasons, making our intentions mutually intelligible can facilitate cooperative activity.

Having sketched in a broad way how conversational implication depends on the Cooperative Principle and the maxims that fall under it, Grice presents a series of examples showing in detail how it works. Grice divides his examples into three broad groups: (A) those in which no maxim is violated, (B) those in which "a maxim is violated, but its violation can be explained by the supposition of a clash with another maxim," and (C) those in which the maxim is flouted. Here are some examples from each of these groups.

> Group A: [Where no maxim is violated]
> A is standing by an obviously immobilized car and is approached by B; the following exchange takes place:

> A: *I am out of petrol.*
> B: *There is a garage round the corner.*

> (Gloss: B would be infringing the maxim "Be relevant" unless he thinks, or thinks it possible, that the garage is open, and has petrol to sell; so he implicates that the garage is, or at least may be, open, etc.) . . .

> Group B: [Where a maxim is violated because of a clash with another maxim]
> A is planning with B an itinerary for a holiday in France. Both know that A wants to see his friend C, if to do so would not involve too great a prolongation of his journey:

> A: *Where does C live?*
> B: *Somewhere in the South of France.*

> (Gloss: There is no reason to suppose that B is opting out [i.e., refusing to be cooperative]; his answer is, as he well knows, less informative than is required to meet A's needs. This infringement of the first maxim of Quantity can be explained only by the supposition that B is aware that to be more informative would be to say something that infringed the second maxim of Quality, "Don't say what you lack adequate evidence for," so B implicates that he does not know in which town C lives.)[i]

Most of Grice's examples of conversational implicature fall into his third category. These implicatures arise through the flouting of conversational maxims, that is, through the intentional violation of one of the maxims, where there is no clash with other maxims, and furthermore with the intention that others recognize that we are intentionally violating the maxim. This may sound complicated, but it is the mechanism that underlies a great many common rhetorical devices. Here are some examples, with Grice's comments on them.

> (1a) A flouting of the first maxim of Quantity.
> A is writing a testimonial about a pupil who is a candidate for a philosophy job, and his letter reads as follows: "Dear Sir, Mr. X's command of English is excellent, and his attendance at tutorials has been regular. Yours, etc." (Gloss: A cannot be opting out, since if he wished to be uncooperative, why write at all? He cannot be unable, through ignorance, to say more, since the man is his pupil; moreover, he knows that more

information than this is wanted. He must, therefore, be wishing to impart information that he is reluctant to write down. This supposition is tenable only if he thinks Mr. X is no good at philosophy. This, then, is what he is implicating.) . . .

(2a) The first maxim of Quality is flouted.

Irony. X, with whom A has been on close terms until now, has betrayed a secret of A's to a business rival. A and his audience both know this. A says *X is a fine friend.* (Gloss: It is perfectly obvious to A and his audience that what A has said or has made as if to say is something he does not believe, and the audience knows that A knows that this is obvious to the audience. So, unless A's utterance is entirely pointless, A must be trying to get across some proposition other than the one he purports to be putting forward. This must be some obviously related proposition; the most obviously related proposition is the contradictory of the one he purports to be putting forward.) . . .

(3) The maxim of relevance is flouted.

[These] are perhaps rare, but the following seems to be a good candidate. At a genteel tea party, A says *Mrs. X is an old bag.* There is a moment of appalled silence, and then B says *The weather has been quite delightful this summer, hasn't it?* B has blatantly refused to make what he says relevant to A's preceding remark. He thereby implicates that A's remark should not be discussed and, perhaps more specifically, that A has committed a social gaffe.[j]

Grice goes into considerable detail in presenting such examples and commenting on them. One might wonder why. There are at least two reasons. First, the examination of conversational implication is intrinsically interesting, and its study soon takes on a life of its own. It provides the basis for giving a systematic account of the way much figurative language works and, in general, helps explain how so much information can be conveyed in relatively few words. For this reason, Grice's theory of conversational implicatures came to play an important part in the science of linguistics.

Second, there is a philosophical reason why Grice spends a great deal of time examining the various forms that conversational implications can take. Recall that the notion, though not yet the label, of conversational implicatures first appeared in "The Causal Theory of Perception," where Grice (against Austin) was arguing that the use of an expression can be odd or misleading and still, for all that, be both meaningful and true. Grice's point, to simplify, is that asserting something can be odd or misleading in what it conversationally implies, but still be meaningful and true in what it asserts. It would, however, seem altogether arbitrary if this distinction were introduced simply to defend a particular philosophical position from criticism. By exhibiting conversational implicatures as a widespread phenomenon capable of systematic explanation, Grice avoids this charge of arbitrariness. Yet an important question still remains: how, in a particular case, can we tell whether we are dealing with a conversational implication rather than a logical or conventional implication? Once the distinction is pointed out, it often seems obvious, for example, that we are dealing with a conversational rather than a logical implication, but it was uncharacteristic of Grice to argue at this intuitive level. He sought a systematic way of deciding in particular cases whether an implication was logical or conversational. He attempted to do this using the notions of *cancelability* and *detachability*. Since it is easier to understand and is all that is needed for the present discussion, we will consider only the test of cancelability.[28]

Grice describes cancelability in these words:

> [A] putative conversational implicature that *p* is explicitly cancelable if, to the form of words the utterance of which putatively implicates that *p*, it is admissible to add *but not p*, or *I do not mean to imply that p.*[k]

This provides a test for whether an implicature is conventional or not. Here, some examples using noncontroversial cases may help:

> Conventional Implication: Saying that Jones owns five cars conventionally implies that he owns more than one car.
>
> (This implication cannot be canceled; that is, one cannot say that Jones owns five cars but does not own more than one car. To say such a thing is to utter a contradiction—something obvious to anyone who knows the meaning of such words as "five" and "more than one.")
>
> Conversational Implication: Saying that Jones owns five cars can conversationally imply that he is rich.
>
> (This implication is cancelable. There is nothing wrong with the following remark: "Jones owns five cars, but that doesn't mean he's rich; they are all heaps that he cannot afford to have towed away." So the implicature, in being cancelable, cannot be a conventional implicature.)

Here is our test for deciding whether an implicature is conventional or conversational: If an implicature is cancelable, then it is not a conventional implicature and is likely to be a conversational implicature. That it is a conversational implicature can be established definitively by showing how it can be accounted for on the basis of conversational maxims.

PERCEPTION AGAIN

With all this machinery in place, we can now return to Grice's views on perception. Recall that there seemed to be two possible accounts of the relationship between a sentence of the form "It looks red to me" and the implication to what Grice called the Doubt or Denial Condition. Some philosophers held (or perhaps just took it for granted) that the Doubt or Denial Condition is part of the

[28] Detachability is discussed in *Studies in the Way of Words* on pp. 58, 229, 230, and 271.

conventional meaning of perceptual claims of this sort. Grice, in contrast, suggested that this condition is not conventionally implied by what the sentence means but is, instead, conversationally implied in the standard uses of such sentences. Once this distinction is clearly drawn, it has seemed to many that Grice is obviously correct. Though it is odd to say of a fire engine in plain view that it looks red to me, it is still true that it looks red to me, even if this suggests (implies) a doubt where there is none.

Grice, of course, gave some weight to this intuitive argument, but, as he knew, appeals to intuition have this disadvantage: If others do not share the intuition, then the argument has simply reached a standoff. Grice thought, however, that the notion of cancelability provided a decisive argument in favor of his position over his opponents. If the Doubt or Denial Condition is part of the conventional meaning of weak perceptual claims, then the inference from the weak perceptual claim to this condition cannot be taken back or canceled. But, according to Grice, this implication clearly is cancelable:

> It is surely clear that if I were now to say "Nothing is the case which would make it false for me to say that the palm of this hand looks pink to me, though I do not mean to imply that I or anyone else is or might be inclined to deny that, or doubt whether, it is pink," this would be a perfectly intelligible remark even though it might be thought both wordy and boring. Indeed, I am prepared actually to say it. . . . [Thus my opponent] must be wrong in thinking that this implication is not *cancelable*.[1]

Grice thought this argument was decisive in showing that the Doubt or Denial Condition was not a conventional implicature of weak perceptual judgments. This, together with his ability to derive the implication from general conversational rules, showed, he thought, that the implicature must be conversational.

Why is any of this important? The answer is that if Grice is correct, then one of the favorite arguments of ordinary-language philosophers has been undercut. It is not sufficient for rejecting a philosophical claim to point out that in ordinary discourse people do not speak as the philosopher speaks and if they did speak that way, others would consider it a misuse of language. As we saw earlier, Austin sometimes argued in just this way. The style of argument that Grice attacked could almost be called the characteristic move of ordinary-language philosophers.

INDICATIVE CONDITIONALS

Grice used the notion of conversational implicatures to defend a number of positions that had come under attack by other ordinary-language philosophers. As we have seen, he used this notion (yet unnamed) to defend a causal theory of perception against the kind of attacks that Austin had launched against it. He also set himself the task of defending formal logicians against the charge, made by ordinary-language philosophers and others, that their procedures distorted the meaning of the sentences they analyzed. Strawson, we saw, attacked Russell's theory of definite descriptions on just these grounds. Another favorite object of attack—and for that matter, ridicule—was the logician's standard treatment of indicative conditionals. Russell and many other logicians held that indicative conditionals—sentences of the form "If p, then q"—are to be declared *false* if "p" (the antecedent) is true and "q" (the consequent) is false, and declared *true* otherwise. This way of analyzing indicative conditionals can be represented by the following *truth table.*

p	q	If p, then q
T	T	T
T	F	F
F	T	T
F	F	T

The first two columns present all the ways in which "p" and "q" can be true and false. The third column indicates that "If p, then q" is only false in the second row, but true otherwise. To analyze indicative conditionals this way, it is said, is to treat them as *material conditionals.* Material conditionals were symbolized by Russell using the horseshoe sign: "$p \supset q$." By examining the truth table for material implication, it is easy to see that "$p \supset q$" is equivalent to "not-p or q." For example, the indicative conditional "If the value of the dollar increases, then the prices of foreign goods will fall," treated as a material conditional, is equivalent to "Either the value of the dollar will not increase or the prices of foreign goods will fall."

The second row of this truth table seems right, for we certainly wish to reject an indicative conditional where the antecedent is true and the consequent is false. But the other three rows seem highly problematic. Consider the first row. It tells us that an indicative conditional will be true if both its antecedent and its consequent are true, *but makes no demands beyond that.* So, given this definition, the following is a specimen of a true indicative conditional:

C1.   If 2 + 2 = 4, then George Washington came from Virginia.

This is obviously a peculiar remark, and we know exactly why it is peculiar: The antecedent and the consequent are completely unrelated—nothing ties them together. For this reason, it has seemed to many philosophers that the formal logician's account of indicative conditionals is wildly out of line with our common understanding of these constructions. Indeed, for many, the logician's treatment of indicative conditionals as material conditionals was a prime specimen of how the methods of symbolic logic distort rather than illuminate the meaning of what we commonly say.[29]

[29] It should be noted that many logicians also objected to treating indicative conditionals as material conditionals and attempted to produce logical analyses more in tune with our common way of using indicative conditionals.

Grice's treatment of this matter is extremely complicated, but his key move again relies on the notion of conversational implicature. Before turning specifically to Grice's treatment of indicative conditionals, we can first note that, in general, we do not connect sentences together that have nothing to do with each other. It is hard, for example, to imagine contexts in which people would make remarks of the following kind:

> 2 + 2 = 4 and George Washington came from Virginia.
> 2 + 2 = 4 or George Washington came from Virginia.

When we conjoin or disjoin sentences, we plainly *imply* that they have something to do with one another. This is reflected in Grice's maxim of relevance. These last two sentences are odd because they violate this maxim. Yet, if pressed, we would probably say that both sentences are true—stupid, but true. So the formula "odd, but still true" seems to work for them.

But the situation seems more difficult with the indicative conditional connecting unrelated propositions; for example:

> C1.   If 2 + 2 = 4, then George Washington came from Virginia.

If someone actually said this she might be met with the response: "What do you mean *if* 2 + 2 = 4? There's nothing *iffy* about that, and there is nothing *iffy* about George Washington coming from Virginia either. Not only that, two plus two equals four has *nothing to do with* the place where George Washington was born." These complaints are, of course, perfectly reasonable.

What is wrong with C1 becomes clear when we compare it with a conditional that is sensible:

> C2.   If the value of the dollar continues to fall against the yen, the price of Japanese imports will rise.

Why is C2, unlike C1, a sensible-sounding and perhaps useful statement? Let us suppose that right now we do not know whether the value of the dollar will continue to fall against the yen. What this indicative conditional seems to tell us is this: if it does, then we have adequate grounds for holding that the price of Japanese imports will rise. The central point of using a construction of the form "If p, then q" is to indicate that "p" (whose truth is now up in the air) may at some time provide the basis for establishing the truth of "q" (whose truth is also now up in the air). Clearly C1 will never play the role of establishing the truth of its consequent, for, first, the truth of the assertion that George Washington came from Virginia is *already* established, and second, if it were not established, 2 + 2 = 4 would give us no grounds for thinking it to be true.

It seems, then, that something crucial is missing in the treatment of indicative conditionals as material conditionals: the possibility that the conditional will, on some occasions, provide the basis for *inferring* the truth of the consequent from establishing the truth of the antecedent. Grice calls this feature of indicative conditionals the Indirectness Condition; why he calls it this, we will see in a moment. He describes it as follows:

> This condition has been variously formulated: "that p would, in the circumstances, be a good reason for q," "that q is inferable from p," "that there are non-truth-functional grounds for accepting p ⊃ q," are all versions of it.[m]

The question Grice poses is this: Is the Indirectness Condition part of the conventional meaning of indicative conditionals, or is it, rather, something conversationally implicated in the standard use of indicative conditionals? Those who adopt the first alternative Grice calls strong theorists. In opposition to the strong theorists, Grice adopts the second alternative. He argues for it as follows:

> To say that p ⊃ q is to say something logically weaker than to deny that p or assert that q, and thus less informative; to make a less informative rather than a more informative statement is to offend against the first maxim of Quantity, provided that the more informative statement, if made, would be of interest. . . . An infringement of the first maxim of Quantity . . . is most naturally explained by the supposition of a clash with the second maxim of Quality ("Have adequate evidence for what you say"), so it is natural to assume that the speaker regards himself as having evidence only for the less informative statement (that p ⊃ q)—that is, non-truth-functional evidence. So standardly he implicates that there is non-truth-functional evidence when he says that p ⊃ q; and there now seems to be no reason to reject the assumption that to say that p ⊃ q is the same as to say that if p then q, so far as concerns the presence of a generalized implicature of the Indirectness Condition.[n]

That is, if someone asserts that if p then q, that person is asserting no more than p ⊃ q (whose meaning is given in the truth table above). In doing so, however, this person conversationally implies that she is not in a position to assign definite truth-values to either p or q. Thus—and this is the crucial move—asserting that "if p, then q" conversationally implies the existence of some non-truth-functional ground for this claim.

To go back to our original specimen indicative conditionals, Grice would declare C1 true because both its antecedent and its consequent are true, and the truth-table definition declares all such indicative conditionals true. He would say, however, that C1 is unnatural (odd, misleading, etc.) because the use of an indicative conditional conversationally implies that its truth cannot be determined *directly* from the truth-values of the antecedent and consequent when, in fact, they can be. In contrast, there is nothing unnatural (odd, misleading, etc.) about C2. Anyone who uses this construction implies that the truth-values of the antecedent and consequent are still (at least somewhat) up in the air. Thus the truth of C2 can*not* be determined directly using the truth-table definition. C1 is odd and C2 is not because C1 does not satisfy the Indirectness Condition, whereas C2 does.

Though this seems to be a powerful argument, Grice, in fact, gives it only his qualified support:

> I think that this account is satisfactory so far as it goes, but it clearly does not go far enough, and further inquiry will, I suggest, bring to light a deeper reason for the existence of the generalized implicature under consideration.°

These deeper reasons are both subtle and complex, but they turn on an important difference between indicative conditionals on the one hand and both conjunctions and disjunctions on the other. Specifically, both conjunctions and disjunctions are commutable—that is, the order of their constituents can be reversed without changing their truth-value:

> "p and q" is logically equivalent to "q and p."
> "p or q" is logically equivalent to "q or p."

In contrast, "If p, then q" is not, in general, commutable:

> "If p, then q" is not equivalent to "If q, then p."

According to Grice, the noncommutability of indicative conditionals peculiarly suits them for a special role in our language: the construction of chains of reasoning. Given "If p, then q," establishing p allows me to infer that q. But I may also know that "If q, then r," and having gotten "q," I may now infer "r," and so on. Grice puts it this way:

> I take the noncommutative character of the conditional form as an indication that its special role lies in the presentation of cases in which a passage of thought, or inferential passage, is envisaged from antecedent to consequent, and possibly to a further consequent with respect to which the first consequent occupies the position of antecedent. . . . The conditional form can fulfill its role only insofar as the truth-value of the conditional itself can be recognized independently of the knowledge of the truth-values of the components of the conditional, that is to say, by virtue of strong connections between antecedents and consequents. A speaker, therefore, who nonconventionally implicates that he is using a condition to fulfill its special function will thereby implicate [though not assert] that a strong connection holds between antecedent and consequent.P

By showing, in detail, how the employment of a construction having the truth-table definition of material implication will, in normal circumstances, conversationally imply that a strong connection exists between the antecedent and the consequent, Grice has made a case for the plausibility of analyzing indicative conditionals as material implications. This, however, does not settle the matter, for we now have a choice between two accounts of indicative conditionals. The strong theorists—as Grice calls them—hold that the Indirectness Condition is part of the conventional meaning or semantic content of such constructions, whereas Grice holds that it is not part of their conventional meaning or semantic content, but something conversationally implicated in the standard use of these constructions. How can we decide which view is right? In a way that exactly parallels his earlier discussion of perception, Grice thought that this issue could be decided in his favor using the tests of detachability and cancelability.[30] Again, since it is easier to understand and it applies directly to the present issue, we will consider only the test of cancelability.

Just as he argued that the Doubt or Denial Condition is cancelable with weak perceptual judgments, he here argues that the Indirectness Condition is cancelable for indicative conditionals.

> To say "If Smith is in the library, he is working" would normally carry the implication of the Indirectness Condition; but I might say (opting out) "I know just where Smith is and what he is doing, but all I will tell you is that if he is in the library he is working." No one would be surprised if it turned out that my basis for saying this was that I had just looked in the library and found him working.[q]

Given this example as a model, it is easy enough to construct other cases where the implication of the Indirectness Condition is cancelable. This, according to Grice, shows that the implication cannot be conventional. The detailed derivation of this implicature from conversational rules seems to clinch the case that the implication is conversational.[31]

It seems that Grice has been able to do something that seemed quite impossible at the start: to show that $p \supset q$ (with its associated truth-table definition) provides an adequate account of the logic of indicative conditionals. He agrees with the strong theorists in thinking that an inferential link between the antecedent and the consequent is important for the employment of indicative conditionals, but he argues, with considerable plausibility, that this inferential link is not

---

[30] Grice discusses detachability and cancelability near the beginning of "Indicative Conditionals." It seems hard to understand the point of this discussion before Grice's own position is sketched out in some detail. For this reason we have reversed the order of presentation.

[31] It is important to see that Grice's arguments for treating an implicature as a conversational implicature must have two components. He must show that it is not conventional. The cancelability test is his favorite weapon for showing this. However, this by itself does not show that the implicature is conversational, for there may be kinds of implicatures that are neither conventional nor conversational. For this reason, in making the case that an implicature is conversational, it is essential for him to show how the implicature is grounded in conversational rules.

part of the conventional meaning of indicative conditionals but is, instead, something conversationally implied by their use in standard contexts.

There are, however, troubles with Grice's analysis that he recognized but never resolved. In particular, if indicative conditionals are analyzed as material conditionals, then the *denials* of indicative conditionals raise difficulties. Specifically, the denial of "$p \supset q$" is equivalent to "p and not q." For example, the denial of:

(C3)   If Jane comes to the party, so will Jim.

is:

(C4)   Jane will come to the party and Jim will not.

That, however, seems too strong. To reasonably deny (C3), I do not need to know definitely that Jane will come to the party and Jim will not; it might be sufficient to know, for example, that Jane often goes to parties that Jim does not attend. It seems that all I need to know reasonably to deny (C3) is that Jane *might* attend the party and Jim not. Grice made a number of attempts to deal with the problems raised by the denials of indicative conditionals, but in the end, none seemed satisfactory.

Problems with negation and related matters have led many logicians to reject Grice's attempt to analyze indicative conditionals as material conditionals. This, however, has not led them to reject Grice's distinction between what a sentence conventionally implies and what its use in particular contexts conversationally implies. In fact, alternative accounts of indicative conditionals rely on this distinction as well, but put it to different uses. This distinction is now firmly entrenched in the methodology of contemporary analytic philosophy. Its use has shed light on a wide range of philosophical topics. It has also been a powerful weapon in disposing of bad philosophical arguments, including, as we have seen, many that were produced by ordinary-language philosophers.[32]

[32] Grice's development of the theory of conversational implicatures and his use of this theory to shed light on a wide range of philosophical issues has proven his most lasting contribution. He did, however, pursue a number of other important philosophical projects; most notably, he attempted to produce a general account of meaning taking the psychological notion of an intention as central. Though this position has not survived criticism, it still contains insights of great importance. Grice's essays on meaning appear in part 2 of *Studies in the Way of Words*.

CHAPTER 13

Quine

Willard Van Orman Quine[1] had already established himself as one of America's leading logicians before he began writing on more-general philosophical topics. Over time he developed a full philosophical position of remarkable subtlety and complexity. Two essays can be viewed as the starting point of this philosophical development: "On What There Is" (1948) and "Two Dogmas of Empiricism" (1951).[a] These essays contain the seeds of many of his later thoughts; indeed, his later thoughts can often be viewed, in part at least, as carrying through insights first sketched in them. The situation is, however, complex, for while he expands certain of his ideas, he seems to retreat from others. As we shall see, in these two

---

[1]Willard Van Orman Quine (1908–) was born in Akron, Ohio, and was educated at Oberlin College and Harvard University. For more than four decades he was a leading figure in the Harvard philosophy department, where he became the Edgar Pierce Professor of Philosophy.

essays Quine was a pluralist in ontology, countenancing—indeed, encouraging—the development of alternative conceptual schemes. Later this commitment to pluralism was replaced by an almost unqualified commitment to a single ontological framework: physicalism. So Quine's views expanded in some ways and contracted in others, all of which makes his a complicated story to tell.

On What There Is

In "On What There Is," Quine asked "What is there?" and gave the startlingly simple answer "Everything."[b] Quine, of course, was not saying that everything that *could* exist *does* exist. He was offering the empty answer "There is what there is" as a preface to raising a different question: "[How can we determine] what ontology a given theory or form of discourse is committed to?"[c] The ontological commitments of a theory are the sorts of things—the kinds of existences—that the theory commits itself to.

Roughly, when we talk about things, we seem to commit ourselves to the existence of those things we are talking about. Usually if we talk about Eskimos, microscopes, and tulips, we commit ourselves to the existence of Eskimos, microscopes, and tulips. Ontological commitments are commitments to the existence of certain sorts of entities. To commit ourselves to the existence of something, we do not have to come right out and say that it exists. To commit ourselves to the existence of an individual entity, say, Steffi Graf, we do not have to say explicitly that Steffi Graf exists—in fact, that would be a peculiar remark to make. We commit ourselves to the existence of Steffi Graf simply by saying such things as "Steffi Graf won the U.S. Tennis Open."

Commitment to kinds of things (rather than to individual things) is a bit more complicated. Suppose I say that some tulips are red. In somewhat stilted language this could be stated as follows:

> There is at least one thing that is both a tulip and red.

This is a remark about objects or things in the world. More stilted yet, we might put this in the following way:

> (S) There exists at least one object in the world, x, such that x is a tulip and x is red.

In this sentence, the letter "x" functions as a variable, much as it functions as a variable in mathematics. The expression "There exists at least one x such that" is called a quantifier—in particular, an *existential* quantifier.[2] In sentence (S), this

---

[2] There are other quantifiers that mark ontological commitment as well, but the existential quantifier does this most transparently, and concentrating on it alone is adequate for our present purposes.

quantifier *governs* or *binds* the variables in the expression "x is a tulip and x is red." Notice that in isolation the expression "x is a tulip and x is red" is neither true nor false, since the letter "x," as a variable, does not refer to anything in particular. But if we combine this expression with—or *bind it by*—the existential quantifier, then we do get an expression that is either true or false, namely "There exists at least one x such that x is a tulip and x is red." Furthermore, those who accept this statement as true commit themselves to the existence of at least one thing that is a tulip and at least one thing that is red. Quine's general strategy, then, for deciding on the ontological commitments involved in a given theory is to translate the statements in the theory into sentences such as (S), where the relationship between quantifiers and bound variables is made explicit. This done, we can then apply Quine's criterion for determining the ontological commitment of a given theory.

> To be assumed as an entity is, purely and simply, to be reckoned as the value of a variable.[d]

There are, however, complications. As Russell noted early in this century in "On Denoting," the surface grammar of our language can sometimes suggest ontological commitments where there are none.[3] Consider, for example, the sentence "Round squares do not exist." Guided by the surface grammar alone, we seem to be referring to (or talking about) round squares, thereby committing ourselves to their existence, and then saying of them that they do not exist. We thus seem to be acknowledging the existence of something only to go on to deny its existence. Russell avoided this problem by translating "Round squares do not exist" (roughly) into "It is not the case that anything exists that is both round and square." In this way the offensive reference to round squares is eliminated and, thus, the need to suppose that they exist (in at least some sense) is avoided.

Quine's "On What There Is" is written fully in the spirit of Russell's "On Denoting." Quine's particular targets are sentences of the form "Pegasus does not exist," where we are dealing with a nonreferring *name* (such as "Pegasus") rather than with a nonreferring descriptive phrase (such as "round squares"). Quine extends Russell's analysis from descriptive phrases to proper names with breathtaking speed. He simply introduces the attribute "is-Pegasus" or "pegasizes" and then translates the claim that Pegasus does not exist into the claim that nothing pegasizes. In this way the apparent reference to a curious nonexistent entity is avoided.

So the application of Quine's criterion for ontological commitment is more complicated than it may at first have seemed. A theory or form of discourse is committed to the existence of the entities it quantifies over, provided there is no way within the theory of eliminating such references. Quine put the point this way:

---

[3] See pp. 180–87.

We may say, for example, that some dogs are white and not thereby commit ourselves to recognizing either doghood or whiteness as entities. "Some dogs are white" says that some things that are dogs are white; and, in order that this statement be true, the things over which the bound variable "something" ranges must include some white dogs, but need not include doghood or whiteness. On the other hand, when we say that some zoological species are cross-fertile we are committing ourselves to recognizing as entities the several species themselves, abstract though they are. We remain so committed at least until we devise some way of so paraphrasing the statement as to show that the seeming reference to species on the part of our bound variable was an avoidable manner of speaking.[e]

Thus a theory or form of discourse may have some apparent ontological commitments that can be analyzed away, yielding a reduced set of ontological commitments.

These last reflections raise a new possibility: perhaps the ontological commitments of a theory could be reduced to a smaller set of ontological commitments in a *variety* of ways. If that is correct, then Quine's test for the ontological commitment of a theory has lost its sharp edges. How are we to choose between these alternative reductions of particular theories? For that matter, even if we can settle on the ontological commitments of various theories, how do we choose among the rival theories? These reflections lead naturally to the question "How are we to adjudicate among rival ontologies?"[f] Quine is clear that *that* question cannot be answered by using his test for ontological commitment.

> How are we to adjudicate among rival ontologies? Certainly the answer is not provided by the semantical formula "To be is to be the value of a variable"; this formula serves rather, conversely, in testing the conformity of a given remark or doctrine to a prior ontological standard. We look to bound variables in connection with ontology not in order to know what there is, but in order to know what a given remark or doctrine, ours or someone else's, *says* there is; and this much is quite properly a problem involving language. But what there is is another question.[g]

How, then, are we to adjudicate between competing ontological commitments? At the close of "On What There Is" Quine recommends an open-minded, pluralistic answer to this question:

> The question what ontology actually to adopt still stands open, and the obvious counsel is tolerance and an experimental spirit. Let us by all means see how much of the physicalistic conceptual scheme can be reduced to a phenomenalistic one; still, physics also naturally demands pursuing, irreducible *in toto* though it be. Let us see how, or to what

degree, natural science may be rendered independent of platonistic mathematics; but let us also pursue mathematics and delve into its platonistic foundations.

From among the various conceptual schemes best suited to these various pursuits, one—the phenomenalistic—claims epistemological priority. Viewed from within the phenomenalistic conceptual scheme, the ontologies of physical objects and mathematical objects are myths. The quality of myth, however, is relative; relative, in this case, to the epistemological point of view. This point of view is one among various, corresponding to one among our various interests and purposes.[h]

As we shall see, in his later writings Quine no longer concedes epistemological priority to the phenomenalist conceptual scheme. Even so, he will continue to hold that a single theory or form of discourse can admit of a plurality of ontological interpretations without there being any evidential way of favoring one over all the rest. This leads to the notion of ontological relativity, which we will examine later.

Two Dogmas of Empiricism

The title of the famous essay "Two Dogmas of Empiricism" suggests that Quine is an opponent of empiricism, the doctrine that all knowledge—or at least all knowledge of synthetic propositions—must be based on experience. This reading is wrong. In this essay Quine attacks certain empiricists, in particular the logical empiricists, for not being empirical enough. He defends what he takes to be a more radical version of empiricism than that held by the logical empiricists.[4] He holds that the two dogmas he attacks have no place in a genuinely empiricist philosophy.

Quine describes the first dogma he will attack in these words:

> [The first dogma] is a belief in some fundamental cleavage between truths which are *analytic,* or grounded in meanings independently of matters of fact, and truths which are *synthetic,* or grounded in fact.[i]

But though it is clear that Quine will attack the analytic/synthetic distinction, it is possible to miss the central point of this attack. Quine is not simply arguing as follows: The analytic/synthetic distinction is so vague or so badly drawn that it is not possible to reach a consensus on how to apply the distinction. If that were his argument, he could be met with the decisive response that people, after being introduced to this distinction, generally do agree concerning which statements are analytic, which are synthetic, and which are hard to classify. Furthermore, the ex-

[4] See Ch. 7.

istence of this last group—those that are hard to classify—does not show that the contrast between analytic statements and synthetic statements breaks down. It is a feature of many contrasts, for example, tall/short, rich/poor, and so forth, that they admit of borderline cases. Provided that there are clear cases on both sides of these contrasts, and provided also that the borderline cases are not too numerous, the distinction between analytic statements and synthetic statements will be as serviceable as many other distinctions and should not be singled out for special criticism.[5]

Though some of Quine's remarks may invite this response, it actually misses the main point of what Quine is up to. He is not denying that this distinction might be drawn in such a way that people will apply it in a consistent and uniform manner; he is denying that it can be drawn in a way that will render it *philosophically* or *systematically* useful. The distinction will have no explanatory value, he argues, for it relies on notions that themselves stand equally in need of explanation. Consider the definition found in Kant that a statement is analytic if its denial is self-contradictory. About this, Quine remarks:

> But this definition has small explanatory value; for the notion of self-contradictories, in the quite broad sense needed for this definition of analyticity, stands in exactly the same need of clarification as does the notion of analyticity itself. The two notions are the two sides of a single dubious coin.[j]

It is the denial of *explanatory value* that lies at the heart of Quine's attack on this distinction.

Quine attempts to capture the gist of the traditional conception of analyticity using the following formulation:

> [A] statement is analytic when it is true by virtue of meanings and independently of fact.[6,k]

This formulation draws our attention to the concept of *meaning*. Meaning itself now stands in need of explanation. What are meanings? In an effort to get clear about this, Quine recalls a lesson taught by Frege.

> Meaning, let us remember, is not to be identified with naming. Frege's example of "Evening Star" and "Morning Star," and Russell's of "Scott" and "the author of *Waverley*," illustrate that terms can name the same thing but differ in meaning.[l]

[5] This is the response, broadly speaking, that Grice and Strawson made to Quine's attack on the analytic/synthetic distinction in their "In Defense of a Dogma," *Philosophical Review* 55 (1956): 141–58.

[6] It is far from clear, as Quine suggests, that this reformulation captures the Kantian notion of analyticity, but, broadly speaking, it does capture the notion of analyticity employed by the logical empiricists. In any case, it is the logical empiricists who are the primary target of Quine's strictures.

Having invoked Frege's distinction between meaning (*Sinn*) and reference (*Bedeutung*), Quine proceeds to employ it in a very un-Fregean way. For Frege, meaning (*Sinn*) was an abstract entity associated with a meaningful expression. Thus, for him, the expression "the ninth moon of Neptune" has two entities associated with it: (i) the meaning (*Sinn*) of the expression, and (ii) its reference, if any. The difference between the two is brought out by our ability to grasp the meaning (*Sinn*) of "the ninth moon of Neptune" without having any idea whether there is a ninth moon of Neptune. For Frege, a term's sense (*Sinn*) and reference (*Bedeutung*) are two sorts of entities. For Quine, in contrast, the distinction provides a justification for dropping talk about meanings as entities altogether.

> Once the theory of meaning is sharply separated from the theory of reference, it is a short step to recognizing as the primary business of the theory of meaning simply the synonymy of linguistic forms and the analyticity of statements; *meanings themselves, as obscure intermediary entities, may well be abandoned.*[m]

That is, instead of talking about meaning, we can discuss the notion of sameness of meaning—that is, synonymy.

Returning to the notion of analyticity, Quine distinguishes two ways in which a statement could be "true by virtue of meanings and independently of fact."

> Statements which are analytic by general philosophical acclaim are not, indeed, far to seek. They fall into two classes. Those in the first class, which may be called *logically true,* are typified by:
>
> (1)   No unmarried man is married.
>
> If we suppose a prior inventory of *logical* particles, comprising "no," "un-," "not," "if," "then," "and," etc., then in general a logical truth is a statement which is true and remains true under all reinterpretations of its components other than the logical particles.
>
> But there is also a second class of analytic statements, typified by:
>
> (2)   No bachelor is married.
>
> The characteristic of such a statement is that it can be turned into a logical truth by putting synonyms for synonyms.[n]

That is, we simply substitute the expression "unmarried man" for the expression "bachelor," and (2) is converted into (1).

Now, however, we have a new question: What is the criterion for counting two expressions synonymous? Here it is natural to brush the question aside by saying synonymy is simply a matter of definition. If you want to know whether two expressions are synonymous, look them up in a dictionary or, perhaps, in a thesaurus. Quine rejects this easy solution:

> But how do we find that "bachelor" is defined as "unmarried man"? Who defined it thus, and when? Are we to appeal to the nearest dictionary, and accept the lexicographer's formulation as law? Clearly this would be to put the cart before the horse. The lexicographer is an empirical scientist, whose business is the recording of antecedent facts; and if he glosses "bachelor" as "unmarried man" it is because of his belief that there is a relation of synonymy between those forms, implicit in general or preferred usage prior to his own work. The notion of synonymy presupposed here has still to be clarified, presumably in terms relating to linguistic behavior. Certainly the "definition" which is the lexicographer's report of an observed synonymy cannot be taken as the *ground of the synonymy.*°

Quine is not, of course, criticizing dictionary makers. Entries in dictionaries usually serve well enough to explain what particular words mean. His point is that we cannot cite dictionaries as *the ground of synonymy* because lexicographers, in writing dictionaries, take the notion of synonymy for granted.

What lexicographers seem to discover is that certain words or other expressions are interchangeable. This suggests the following definition or explanation of synonymy:

> The synonymy of two linguistic forms consists in their interchangeability in all contexts without change of truth value—interchangeability, in Leibniz's phrase, *salva veritate.*ᴾ

This may seem a reasonable suggestion, but there are some immediate problems with this suggestion. For example, the word "bachelor" is used in settings where "unmarried man" cannot be substituted for it without changing the truth-value of the whole sentence:

> Jane was awarded a bachelor of arts degree.
> Bachelor buttons [a flower] are very pretty.
> "Bachelor" has fewer than ten letters.

In the first two sentences, the word "bachelor" is being used in a sense different from the one we had in mind in our original example. In the third sentence, it is the word "bachelor," not a bachelor, that is being referred to. In all three cases, substitution *salva veritate* fails.

But even if we suppose, as Quine does, that we can deal with problems of this kind, deeper problems remain.[7] As Quine notes, two expressions might, in fact, have the very same extension—refer to the very same set of things—yet not be synonymous. For example, "creature with a heart" and "creature with a kidney" will refer to just the same things if all creatures with hearts have kidneys and,

---

[7] In what follows, Quine's argument has been simplified and reorganized.

conversely, all creatures with kidneys have hearts.�q That, of course, will not make the two expressions synonymous.

This leads to the suggestion that for two expressions to be synonymous their extensions must *necessarily* be the same. Trivially,

> Necessarily all and only bachelors are bachelors.

The suggested test for synonymy is interchangeability in this type of context. Substituting "unmarried men" for the second occurrence of "bachelors," we get:

> Necessarily all and only bachelors are unmarried men.

Since the substitution preserves the truth, we can now claim, using this test, that the expressions "bachelors" and "unmarried men" are synonymous expressions.

At this point, of course, our attention must shift to the notion of necessity. We can note first, though Quine does not here make this point explicitly, that not just any sort of necessity will do. The following statement is true:

> Necessarily all and only equilateral triangles are equiangular triangles.

Yet the expressions "equilateral triangle" and "equiangular triangle" are not synonymous. We are thus looking for the kind of necessity that guarantees the *synonymy* of expressions that are necessarily coextensive. The kind of necessity we are seeking, it seems, is just the sort of necessity possessed by *analytic* statements. This suggests the following test for synonymy:

> Two expressions "Ø" and "Ψ" are synonymous if and only if it is analytically necessary that all and only Øs are Ψs.

To retrace our steps: we began with the notion of analyticity, and tried to explain it using the notion of synonymy. Synonymy was explained using the notion of interchangeability, *salva veritate,* but the interchangeability had to be nonaccidental, so this led us to the notion of necessity. Finally, our attempt to get hold of the correct kind of necessity led us to the notion of analyticity. That, however, seems to put us right back where we started. Quine puts matters this way:

> The condition of interchangeability *salva veritate* varies in its force with variations in the richness of the language at hand. The above argument supposes we are working with a language rich enough to contain the adverb "necessarily," this adverb being construed as to yield truth when and only when applied to an analytic statement. But can we condone a language which contains such an adverb? Does the adverb really make sense? To suppose that it does is to suppose that we have already made satisfactory sense of "analytic." Then what are we so hard at work on right now?

> Our argument [i.e., the argument that Quine is rejecting] is not flatly
> circular, but something like it. It has the form, figuratively speaking, of
> a closed curve in space.[r]

The central point of Quine's argument is not simply that our attempts at a definition have led us in a circle, but, instead, that they have led us around a circle containing equally obscure notions. It is for this reason that Quine claims that the
distinction lacks explanatory power, and for this reason he rejects the idea that
this distinction has philosophical force.

We can now turn to the second dogma that Quine attacks. At the start of "Two
Dogmas of Empiricism," he describes it in these words:

> The [second] dogma is *reductionism:* the belief that each meaningful
> statement is equivalent to some logical construct upon terms which re-
> fer to immediate experience.[s]

For Quine, the two dogmas are closely related—indeed, he says that they are "at
root identical."[t] In any case, the discussion of the second dogma flows naturally
from the discussion of the first.

Before turning to Quine's presentation of the second dogma, it will help to
sketch—at least in broad outline—the type of view he is attacking. Suppose
we are presented with a full-blown scientific theory, say, Newtonian physics. It
seems plausible to view it as having two distinct components: a conceptual component and an empirical component. The conceptual component consists of a system of logically or semantically related concepts that provide the basic structure
of the theory. The conceptual component is the source of analytic truths. The empirical component concerns terms that are not defined within the system (*in-
trasystematically*), but rather with reference to experience. The addition of this
empirical component permits the system to have *extrasystematic* significance. This
approach can take various forms. In Wittgenstein's *Tractatus,* for example, the
deep underlying conceptual structure was immutable and held true of necessity.[8]
But in the *Tractatus* Wittgenstein also suggested that particular scientific theories
can employ different forms of conceptual organization:

> Newtonian mechanics, for example, imposes a unified form on the
> descriptions of the world. . . . [It] determines one form of description
> of the world by saying that all propositions used in the description of
> the world must be obtained in a given way from a given set of proposi-
> tions—the axioms of mechanics. It thus supplies the bricks for building
> the edifice of science, and it says, "Any building that you want to erect,
> whatever it may be, must somehow be constructed with these bricks
> and these alone."[u]

---

[8] See Ch. 6.

This passage suggests the possibility of alternative conceptual schemes—that is, alternative specifications of the basic categories that will be used in producing a theory of the world. Newtonian physics presents one such conceptual scheme, relativity theory another. Science, then, can advance in two ways: through making empirical discoveries within a particular framework, or through changing the framework itself. Rudolf Carnap called questions that arise within a particular framework *internal questions,* and those that arise concerning the framework as a whole external questions.[9] On a theory of this kind, then, the distinction between the conceptual and the empirical (hence, the analytic and the synthetic) is maintained, but in a sophisticated form. Whether a statement is analytic or synthetic can only be decided *within* the conceptual scheme in which it occurs. Thus sentences are not analytic or synthetic in isolation, for the same sentence can be analytic in one system, synthetic in another. We might say that the analytic/ synthetic distinction has been preserved, but only in a system-relativized way. This treatment of the analytic/synthetic distinction can be viewed in two ways: as a sophisticated (undogmatic) way of maintaining the distinction, or as a way of so weakening it that it is ready to be toppled altogether. Carnap took the first line, Quine the second.

Quine turns to the dogma of reductionism in a section of "Two Dogmas of Empiricism" entitled "The Verification Theory and Reductionism." "The verification theory of meaning," he tells us, "is that the meaning of a statement is the method of empirically confirming or infirming it. An analytic statement is that limiting case which is confirmed no matter what."[v] Furthermore, the verification theory of meaning seems to provide a way of determining synonymies:

> What the verification theory says is that statements are synonymous if and only if they are alike in point of method of empirical confirmation or infirmation.[w]

"So," Quine concludes, "if the verification theory can be accepted as an adequate account of statement synonymy, the notion of analyticity is saved after all."[x]

From the very start, the verification theory of meaning was beset with a large number of technical difficulties. In its early stages, an attempt was made to reduce all meaningful statements to statements about immediate experience. Such reductions were never achieved or even reasonably approximated. There were logical problems as well: What, for example, to make of a compound sentence that disjoins a meaningful statement with nonsense? Is the total sentence meaningful or meaningless? The status of the verifiability principle itself was questioned: Is it, by its own standards, meaningful or not? Problems of this kind and others eventually led to the abandonment of verificationism as a theory of meaning.[10]

Quine, however, in attacking the verification theory, does not insist on narrow points but asks, instead, a more global question:

[9] See pp. 260–62.
[10] See pp. 267–70.

Statement synonymy is said to be likeness of method of empirical confirmation or infirmation. Just what are these methods which are to be compared for likeness? What, in other words, is the nature of the relation between a statement and the experiences which contribute to or detract from its confirmation?[y]

As already noted, attempts to reduce meaningful statements to logical constructs made up of statements about immediate experience had failed, and the project of attempting to do so was abandoned. Yet, according to Quine, the memory has lingered on:

But the dogma of reductionism has, in a subtler and more tenuous form, continued to influence the thought of empiricists. The notion lingers that to each statement, or each synthetic statement, there is associated a unique range of possible sensory events such that the occurrence of any of them would add to the likelihood of truth of the statement, and that there is associated also another unique range of possible sensory events whose occurrence would detract from that likelihood. This notion is of course implicit in the verification theory of meaning.

The dogma of reductionism survives in the supposition that each statement, taken in isolation from its fellows, can admit of confirmation or infirmation at all. My countersuggestion . . . is that our statements about the external world face the tribunal of sense experience not individually but only as a corporate body.[z]

At this point, Quine thinks that the relationship between the two dogmas becomes clear:

The one dogma clearly supports the other in this way: as long as it is taken to be significant in general to speak of the confirmation and infirmation of a statement, it seems significant to speak also of a limiting kind of statement which is vacuously confirmed, *ipso facto,* come what may; and such a statement is analytic.

The two dogmas are, indeed, at root identical.[a]

We can now see why Quine rejects even the sophisticated theory that relativizes analyticity to particular systems. Even *within* a particular scientific system sentences cannot be sorted into the factual and the linguistic.

It is nonsense, and the root of much nonsense, to speak of a linguistic component and a factual component in the truth of any individual statement. Taken collectively, science has its double dependence upon language and experience; but this duality is not significantly traceable into the statements of science taken one by one. . . . The unit of empirical significance is the whole of science.[b]

This passage—particularly the last sentence—shows Quine's commitment to a strong version of holism. A word gets its significance from the role it plays in a sentence, but sentences, in their turn, gain their significance from the role they play in the total system of science.

In the closing section of "Two Dogmas," Quine introduces a theme that was to play an important role in the later development of his position: the *underdetermination* of our views about the world relative to the empirical evidence we possess. Expanding on the holistic standpoint, Quine puts it this way:

> Total science is like a field of force whose boundary conditions are experience. A conflict with experience at the periphery occasions readjustments in the interior of the field. Truth values have to be redistributed over some of our statements. . . . But the field is so underdetermined by its boundary conditions, experience, that there is much latitude of choice as to what statements to reevaluate in the light of any single contrary experience. No particular experiences are linked with any particular statements in the interior of the field, except indirectly through considerations of equilibrium affecting the field as a whole.[c]

Quine's thesis of underdetermination depends on two considerations. The first is a matter of logic. Consider the following argument:

(1) Either John committed the murder or Joan did.
(2) If Joan committed the murder, then she had a motive for doing so.
(3) Joan did not have a motive for doing so.

Therefore:

(4) John committed the murder.

The argument as it stands is valid—that is, *if* the premises are true, the conclusion must be true. Of course, noting that the argument is valid does not prove that John committed the murder, for one or more of the premises might be false. If we could establish that the premises were true, then, of course, we would have proved that John committed the murder.[11]

To relate this example to Quine's discussion, suppose that instead of establishing the truth of the premises, we somehow discover that the conclusion is false: John did not commit the murder. But if the premises of this argument were true, then the conclusion would have to be true as well, so at least one of these premises must be false.[12] If we were actually investigating this murder, we would have to

---

[11] Valid arguments with true premises are commonly said to be *sound*. An argument, if sound, guarantees the truth of its conclusion.

[12] It is a principle of logic that a valid argument with a false conclusion must have at least one false premise.

decide which premise or premises to challenge. Perhaps (1) is false. There may be other suspects we have not turned up. Perhaps (3) is false. Joan may have a secret motive unknown to us. The chances are, however, that we would not challenge (2) unless we absolutely had to. People rarely commit murders without a motive for doing so. Premise (2) then seems more secure—less subject to doubt—than the other two premises of the argument.

The second part of Quine's argument depends on the claim that "the total field is so underdetermined by its boundary conditions, experience, that there is much latitude of choice as to what statements to reevaluate in the light of any single contrary experience."[d] To see the force of this claim, suppose that, instead of dealing with a simple argument of the kind cited above, we are concerned with a very complex scientific theory, for example Newtonian physics or genetic theory. When evidence appears that is contrary to such a complex theoretical construction, adjustments have to be made, but, according to Quine, no particular adjustments are forced upon us by the contrary evidence.

> Any statement can be held true come what may, if we make drastic enough adjustments in the system. . . . Conversely, by the same token, no statement is immune to revision.[e]

How, then, do we decide what adjustments to make? Quine's answer is that we behave conservatively as long as we can. We "disturb the total system as little as possible."[f] But if contrary evidence keeps piling up and our ways of dealing with it become more and more arbitrary (or desperate), then a fundamental revision at or near the core of the system may be necessary. Quine suggests that there is no limit, in principle, about how deep such a revision might go.

> Revision even of the logical law of excluded middle has been proposed as a means of simplifying quantum mechanics; and what difference is there in principle between such a shift and the shift whereby Kepler superseded Ptolemy, or Einstein Newton, or Darwin Aristotle?[g]

Though we have a natural tendency to be conservative—to disturb our system as little as possible—under sufficient stress from contrary experience, we are sometimes forced to change our system in fundamental ways. When a roof has too many leaks, we stop patching and replace it.

Underlying these remarks about the revisability of conceptual schemes is a pragmatic—Quine calls it an empiricist—conception of conceptual schemes themselves:

> As an empiricist I continue to think of the conceptual scheme of science as a tool, ultimately, for predicting future experience in the light of past experience. Physical objects are conceptually imported into the situation as convenient intermediaries—not by definition in terms of

experience, but simply as irreducible posits comparable, epistemologically, to the gods of Homer. For my part I do, qua lay physicist, believe in physical objects and not in Homer's gods; and I consider it a scientific error to believe otherwise. But in point of epistemological footing the physical objects and the gods differ only in degree and not in kind. Both sorts of entities enter our conception only as cultural posits. The myth of physical objects is epistemologically superior to most in that it has proved more efficacious than other myths as a device for working a manageable structure into the flux of experience.

Positing does not stop with macroscopic physical objects. Objects at the atomic level are posited to make the laws of macroscopic objects, and ultimately the laws of experience, simpler and more manageable.[h]

This passage, and others like it, should be read with caution. On its surface it suggests an *anything-goes* attitude: "The ancient Greeks posited gods; ordinary people posit chairs and tables; modern physicists posit quarks. Take your choice." This is not Quine's position. He holds that the conceptual scheme of physical science has succeeded in organizing experience, making it predictable and sometimes controllable in ways that no other conceptual scheme has approximated. Abstractly, it did not have to turn out that way, but it did. For this reason, Quine is a physicalist—a commitment, as we shall see, that shapes the development of his ideas in fundamental ways.

Physicalism, the Single Option

A reader of "On What There Is" (1948) and "Two Dogmas of Empiricism" (1951) will reasonably come away with the impression of Quine as an openhanded pluralist encouraging a riot of competing conceptual schemes. Yet when we turn to Quine's central philosophical work, *Word and Object,* written nine years after "Two Dogmas of Empiricism," we find that the alternatives have been dramatically reduced—indeed, they have been reduced essentially to one: physicalism. Roughly, physicalism is the ontological thesis that what there is is what physicists say there is, and those things that are incompatible with what physicists say there is are not. Somewhat differently, for Quine, the only facts of the matter are physical facts of the matter.

Some readers of Quine were appalled by this contraction of options. Henryk Skolimowski put it this way:

> I remember the excitement with which Quine's *From a Logical Point of View*[13] was greeted in Warsaw in 1956. Quine was read and

---

[13][Where both "On What There Is" and "Two Dogmas of Empiricism" were reprinted and became generally known—AUTHORS.]

extensively discussed in Poland in the mid-1950s and was hailed as one of the world's leading philosophers.

In contrast, he tells us:

> *Word and Object,* and Quine's subsequent writings, seem to represent a retreat from commitment. There is no new development. Indeed one finds a retreat from the earlier bold pluralism of radical conventionalism and a retrenchment into monistic physicalism which verges on 19th-century scientism.[i]

Whatever we think of it, a change does seem to have taken place between Quine's early philosophical essays and his book *Word and Object.* The problem is to make sense of it.

In fact, despite his generous talk about alternative conceptual schemes, even in his early writings he seemed to take only three ontological stances seriously: phenomenalism, physicalism, and Platonism (at least in mathematics). By the time he wrote *Word and Object,* the fullest and most systematic presentation of his position, Quine had abandoned phenomenalism. The simplest explanation for this was that Quine came to the conclusion, as others did at about the same time, that the phenomenalist program had failed and that there was no serious possibility of reviving it. Quine's attitude toward Platonism was different. As a good empiricist, Quine had always taken it as his task to limit, if not completely eliminate, commitments to Platonic (or abstract) entities. This left physicalism as the primary ontology. He was thus faced with two tasks: first, to find ways that, as much as possible, avoided commitments to abstract (Platonic) entities, and second, to show how an austere physicalist language can serve as the basis for understanding how we comprehend the world about us.

THE PHYSICALIST'S AUSTERE PROGRAM

Phenomenalists were faced with the task of trying to show how statements about physical objects could be *reduced to,* or, if not that, could in some sense be shown to depend on, statements about sense data. These are, respectively, the reductionist (strong) version and the nonreductionist (weak) version of phenomenalism. Whether phenomenalism is pursued in its strong or weak form, it is committed in advance to employing very austere resources. The only things that the phenomenalist has at his or her disposal are simple statements about sense data together with various logical constructions made out of them. By the time Quine wrote *Word and Object,* he had rejected phenomenalism even in its weak or moderate form. Nonetheless, his research program continued to bear remarkable similarities to the program of the phenomenalists. For both Quine and the phenomenalists, one begins from an austere base of primary types of sentences and then attempts to build the edifice of knowledge in terms of them. The primary propositions for the phenomenalist were sense-data propositions; their primary task was to show how statements about physical objects could be grounded in them. The physicalist (roughly) starts out with propositions about physical objects as primary and then tries to show how other propositions, for example, propositions about the mental, can be grounded in them. Phenomenalism and physicalism move in opposite directions, but, even so, their methodologies are surprisingly similar. They each tell us that all we have to work with is *this,* and then go on to show what this base can sustain and what, given this base, must be rejected.

Quine's first limitation concerns what we might call *initial* evidence. The following is the opening passage of his late, summary work, *Pursuit of Truth:*

> From impacts on our sensory surfaces, we in our collective and cumulative creativity down the generations have projected our systematic theory of the world. Our system is proving successful in predicting subsequent sensory input. How have we done it?ʲ

As individuals, Quine tells us, our contact with the world is made through "impacts on our sensory surfaces." This, according to Quine, is our only mode of contact with the world. It is important to see that this is an assertion of physical fact. It is a statement about the actual mechanisms that get human beings in contact with the world around them. Here Quine separates himself from traditional empiricists, who used private experience as their starting point. He separates himself from traditional empiricists in another way as well. He starts right out talking about a public physical world without providing any justification for doing so, at least of the kind traditionally thought necessary. Quine sometimes writes as if he had never heard of the problem of the external world. For Quine, it is simply a well-established fact that our contact with the world is made through "impacts on our sensory surfaces." Quine has no patience—or perhaps has run out of patience—with all attempts to provide an external justification of the methods of science. For him, epistemology is an activity carried on from within the scientific perspective; it is not an attempt to justify the methods of science. This is part of what Quine has in mind when he speaks of epistemology naturalized.[14]

Although Quine begins by referring to impacts on sensory surfaces, he does not mean that we gain knowledge of the world around us through examining such surfaces. We do not, unless we are optometrists, spend our time examining retinas. We begin by examining the world around us, something, as science has shown us, we are able to do because we possess sensory organs. The world we examine contains other human beings who possess a language that they pass on to their offspring and charges. It is through observing the behavior of others—in particular, their verbal behavior in certain contexts—that we acquire a language. It is also through the use of language that we can formulate theories about the world. This raises two questions: How does our language get hooked up with the world, and

[14]For more on this, see his essay "Epistemology Naturalized," reprinted in *Ontological Relativity and Other Essays* (Columbia University Press, New York, 1969).

how do we acquire a language in the first place? Quine begins to answer both questions using the notion of an observation sentence, which he explains as follows:

> We were undertaking to examine the evidential support of science. That support, by whatever name, comes now to be seen as a relation of stimulation to scientific theory. Theory consists of sentences, or is couched in them; and logic connects sentences to sentences. What we need, then, as initial links in those connecting chains, are some sentences that are directly and firmly associated with our stimulations. Each should be associated affirmatively with some range of one's stimulations and negatively with some range. The sentence should command the subject's assent or dissent outright, on the occasion of a stimulation in the appropriate range, without further investigation and independently of what he may have been engaged in at the time. A further requirement is intersubjectivity: unlike a report of a feeling, the sentence must command the same verdict from all linguistically competent witnesses of the occasion.
>
> I call them *observation sentences*. Examples are "It's raining," "It's getting cold," "That's a rabbit." Unlike "Men are mortal," they are *occasion* sentences: true on some occasions, false on others. Sometimes it is raining, sometimes not. Briefly stated, then, an observation sentence is an occasion sentence on which speakers of the language can agree outright on witnessing the occasion.[k]

The dual role of observation sentences in both theory checking and language acquisition is celebrated in these passages:

> Observation sentences are thus the vehicle of scientific evidence, we might say—though without venturing a definition of "evidence" itself. But also they are the entering wedge in the learning of language. The infant's first acquisitions in cognitive language are rudimentary observation sentences, including "Mama," "Milk," and the like as one-word observation sentences. They become associated with stimulations by the conditioning of responses. Their direct association with concurrent stimulation is essential if the child is to acquire them without prior language, and the requirement of intersubjectivity is essential in order that he learn the expressions from other speakers on appropriately shared occasions.
>
> That observation sentences serve in both ways—as vehicles of scientific evidence and as entering wedges into language—is no cause for wonder. Observation sentences are the link between language, scientific or not, and the real world that language is all about.[l]

Of course, most of the sentences we utter are not observation sentences. First, an observation sentence is an occasion sentence, and many of our sentences, even those that rest on observation, are not occasion sentences. "Countries bordering the Mediterranean produce olive oil" is one example. Other sentences stand, at most, in only a remote relationship to observation sentences: truths of logic and mathematics, for example. Part of Quine's task is to provide an account of how such important nonobservation sentences are related to observation sentences.

Quine is also faced with a wide range of difficult conceptual issues. As prototypes of observation sentences, Quine offers "Lo, a pebble" and "Lo, blue." These would be suitable comments when our senses are stimulated by something that is a pebble and by something that is blue. These remarks, however, do not have to be about the same thing. We might be simultaneously confronted by a white pebble and a blue flower. We can make our first move in the direction of logical complexity by simply conjoining these two observation sentences, producing: "Lo, a pebble, and lo, blue."[m] This will be true just in case we are lo-ing something that is a pebble and also lo-ing something (not necessarily the same thing) that is blue. Often, however, we want to say something stronger than this: of an individual pebble, we want to say that *it* has a particular color. In other words, we want to say "This pebble is blue." This involves *predication,* which is a richer relation than mere conjunction. Quine explains the difference between conjunction and predication this way:

> The conjunction is fulfilled so long as the stimulation shows each of the component observation sentences to be fulfilled somewhere in the scene—thus a white pebble here, a blue flower over there. On the other hand the predication focuses the two fulfillments, requiring them to coincide or amply overlap. The [white] must encompass the pebble. It may also extend beyond; the construction is not symmetric.[n]

This development from simple observation sentences, to conjunctions of simple observation sentences, to observation sentences involving predication is the starting point for a long, complex program of providing a correct logical account of the rich system of conceptual structures found in everyday language and in the language of science and mathematics.

Extensionality

For a variety of interlocking reasons, Quine is committed to what is called extentionalism. In *Pursuit of Truth* he characterizes extensionality as

> the substitutivity of identity and more generally the interchangeability of all coextensive terms and clauses *salva veritate.*[o]

An example will help explain this principle. Suppose that Jane is an excellent chess player. Also suppose that she is the student body president. From this it follows that the student body president is an excellent chess player. Schematically, the argument can be represented as follows:

> a is F
> a = b
> b is F

This seems like a perfectly reasonable inference, for in saying that Jane is an excellent chess player, we are referring to a certain person and saying of her that she plays chess excellently. It really should not matter, so far as truth is concerned, how we go about referring to her. The assertion will be true provided that *that* person (call her "Jane" or call her "the president of the student body") is, in fact, an excellent chess player. The legitimacy of such substitutions seems, at first sight, to be wholly unproblematic. Yet consider the following example: John might believe that Jane is an excellent chess player, but not believe that the president of the student body is an excellent chess player, since he may not know or believe that Jane is the president of the student body. Contexts such as this, in which substitutivity fails in this way, Quine calls *opaque* contexts.

Opaque contexts arise in a variety of ways. As we have just seen, ascribing a belief to someone can produce an opaque context. More generally, opacity arises when we ascribe what has been called *propositional attitudes* to people. Quine gives some additional examples of propositional attitudes.

> In "perceives that *p*" and "believes that *p*" we have two among many idioms of *propositional attitude*. Others are "hopes that *p*," "regrets that *p*," "fears that *p*," "strives that *p*," "wonders whether *p*," and indeed "says that *p*."ᴾ

It is easy to find instances of opacity for sentences employing each of these constructions. Here are two other examples:

> John may hope that Jane plays excellent chess, but not hope that the president of the student body plays excellent chess (even though Jane is, in fact, the president of the student body).

Perhaps more strikingly:

> John may regret that Jane is the student body president, but not regret that Jane is Jane.

The use of such terms as "necessary" and "possible" (so-called modal terms) can also generate contexts in which failures of substitutivity seem to occur. Modal logics are logics concerned with such notions as necessity and possibility. It has been common in philosophy to treat certain propositions as necessary and others as nonnecessary. Intuitively, it is a necessary truth (it could *not* have been otherwise) that Jane is identical with Jane. It is not a necessary truth that Jane is the president of the student body (that *could* have been otherwise). But if we allow substitution of coreferential terms, we seem to be able to derive the second claim from the first:

> Jane is necessarily identical with Jane.
> Jane is (i.e., is identical with) the president of the student body.
> So Jane is necessarily the president of the student body.

Since we want to accept the first statement but not the third, it seems that we must disallow unrestricted substitution into modal contexts. Thus modal terms, like the ascription of propositional attitudes, generate opaque contexts.

Quine is suspicious of all contexts in which opacity arises. For him, they are guilty until proven innocent. He has a number of reasons for this. First, a claim such as "John regrets that Jane is president of the student body" seems to assert a relationship, not between John and some physical entity, but between John and a proposition. Propositions seem to be abstract entities, the very sort of entities that Quine, as a physicalist, attempts to minimize. Talk about necessities and possibilities also seems to introduce us into a spooky Platonic world. Second, extensional logics, namely logics in which there are no failures of substitution of the kind we are examining, have been rigorously developed, are well understood, and provide a powerful tool for philosophical analysis. Quine thought that nonextensional logics enjoyed none of these advantages.[15]

Of course, the ascription of beliefs, hopes, desires, and so on to human beings is a common and important practice in daily life. We also consider possibilities—things that do not actually exist, but could or might exist. In order to understand or anticipate how others will behave, it is often essential to know what they believe and what they desire. In order to make plans, we often consider the outcomes of various possible actions. Beliefs, desires (fears, hopes, etc.), and possibilities, even if they involve opacity, are not notions foisted on us by Platonist philosophers. They are important notions for everyday life. It would, then, strengthen Quine's position if he could, given his austere standards, provide an adequate way of explaining these notions within his empiricist-behaviorist-extensionalist-physicalist framework. Quine has, in fact, made some progress in analyzing some of these constructions. In general, however, he is deeply suspicious of both the mental and the modal. He is largely inclined to dismiss them rather than try to decipher them. His working principle seems to be this: given a type of discourse that is widely used and (seemingly) well understood, a good-faith effort should be made to show how it can be given a logical underpinning within the confines of the physicalist program. If this good-faith effort fails, this should be taken not as evidence that the physicalist program has failed, but instead as evidence that the discourse under discussion is not part of the symbolic system employed in "limning the true and ultimate structure of reality."q

---

[15] In recent years progress has been made in providing a systematic account of non-extensional logics, but Quine still remains largely unconvinced of the philosophical significance of such logics.

Translation and Indeterminacy

In the second chapter of *Word and Object,* Quine introduces the notion of *radical translation,* and goes on to draw some very strong conclusions concerning the *indeterminacy (or inscrutability) of reference* in particular and the *indeterminacy of translation* in general. There has, in fact, been considerable disagreement among writers on what Quine meant by these notions and how he related them to one another. Quine has sometimes complained that he has been misunderstood. Given the disagreements among writers on Quine and Quine's own complaints about being misunderstood, it is clear that this is a problematic aspect of his writings. Of the various commentators who have written on this subject, we will take Quine himself as the main guide, relying heavily on his late summary work, *Pursuit of Truth.*

In presenting the problem of radical translation, Quine imagines a linguist encountering a community whose language has hitherto been untranslated. These speakers speak no other language, and their language bears no obvious similarities to languages already understood. Our field linguist is thus faced with the task of producing a manual that will translate this language into his own language— and doing this from scratch. It is in this way that the linguist is faced with the task of *radical* translation. But why does Quine assign central importance to this particular linguistic activity, and, related to this, how, through examining it, can he draw fundamental conclusions about linguistic activities in general? Quine's remarkable answer is that each of us, as human beings, enters the world faced precisely with the task of radical translation. In *Pursuit of Truth* he puts it this way:

> Each of us learns his language by observing other people's verbal behavior and having his own faltering verbal behavior observed and reinforced or corrected by others. We depend strictly on overt behavior in observable situations. As long as our command of our language fits all external checkpoints, where our utterance or our reaction to someone's utterance can be appraised in the light of some shared situation, so long all is well. Our mental life between checkpoints is indifferent to our rating as a master of the language. There is nothing in linguistic meaning beyond what is to be gleaned from overt behavior in observable circumstances.[r]

So, for Quine, the radical translator's condition is the human condition—his capacities and limitations are our capacities and limitations.

The task of radical translations starts with entire sentences—it begins, as Quine puts it, *holophrastically.* Quine claims that radical translation would begin with the translation of occasion sentences in relatively clear contexts:

> The utterances first and most surely translated in such a case are ones keyed to present events that are conspicuous to the linguist and his informant. A rabbit scurries by, the native says "Gavagai," and the linguist

notes down the sentence "Rabbit" (or "Lo, a rabbit") as a tentative translation, subject to testing in further cases.[5]

The translation is tentative for, even at a commonsense level, it is easy to think of alternative translations: Perhaps "Gavagai" is the proper name of a particular pet rabbit; perhaps it is the term used to refer to any small animal; and so forth. In order to narrow the range of possible translations, the linguist will observe the use of the word "Gavagai" in various contexts. In this way some of the proposed translations will be confirmed and others disconfirmed. Through these procedures, the translator may gain strong inductive evidence that the sentence "Gavagai" and the sentence "Rabbit" have the same stimulus meaning. Establishing correlations of this kind between whole sentences in our language and sentences in the target language provides the "opening wedge" for the radical translator's enterprise.

Using this method of questioning "native sentences for assent and dissent under varying circumstances," the linguist could, according to Quine, translate observation sentences. Beyond this, he should be able to translate sentences that are built up out of observation sentences using words such as "and" and "or." Thus if the observation sentences "Gavagai" and "Bovar" get translated "Rabbit" and "Dog," then it will probably be reasonable to translate "Gavagai urgh Bovar" as "Rabbit and Dog" if the native speaker assents to this sentence just in those circumstances when both a rabbit and a dog are present. So far, at least, no serious indeterminacies have presented themselves.

Our discussion has, however, been limited in the following way: by treating sentences holophrastically we have not considered the internal structure of noncompound sentences. Taken holophrastically, the sentence "The cat is on the mat" would better be written "The-cat-is-on-the-mat," for, holophrastically, the symbol "cat" has no independent meaning. We enter the land of indeterminacy when the linguist moves from sentence meaning to word meaning. In order to discuss word meaning, the linguist must break down the total utterance into parts, and then try to find ways of translating these words into words in our language. Here Quine speaks of the linguist forming "analytic hypotheses."[†] For example, hearing the utterance "Gavagai," the linguist might speculate that it consists of two words, "Gava" and "Gai." This would be borne out if the linguist found these two sounds occurring in other utterances but not combined. Observing this, he might then try to decide which words in English best translate these two words in the native language. Quine's view is that there is an inherent indeterminacy in attempts to make such translations.

Quine argues for this point in a variety of ways. Most strikingly, he argues that this indeterminacy occurs even for sentences that seemingly contain only one word:

> Stimulus synonymy of the occasion sentences "Gavagai" and "Rabbit" does not even guarantee that "Gavagai" and "Rabbit" are coextensive terms, terms true of the same things.

> For, consider "Gavagai." Who knows but what the objects to which
> this term applies are not rabbits after all, but mere stages, or brief
> temporal segments, of rabbits? In either event the stimulus situations
> that prompt assent to "Gavagai" would be the same for "Rabbit." Or
> perhaps the objects to which "Gavagai" applies are all and sundry un-
> detached parts of rabbits; again the stimulus meaning would register no
> difference.[u]

In other words, the native speaker may assent to the observation sentence "Gavagai" in exactly the same situations in which we assent to the observation sentence "Rabbit," yet the native speaker may be referring to (what we would refer
to as) a batch of connected rabbit parts.

What is the point of introducing such highly artificial notions as rabbit stages
or undetached rabbit? Their possibility, according to Quine, establishes his thesis of Ontological Relativity—or as he earlier called it, Ontological Inscrutability.
Quine's point is that our ontological commitments—our commitments to what
sorts of objects actually exist—are not forced upon us by the observation statements we accept. Our observation statements, however rich, will always be compatible with a plurality of ontological commitments.

> What particular objects there may be is indifferent to the truth of
> observation sentences, indifferent to the support they lend to the
> theoretical sentences, indifferent to the success of the theory in its
> predictions.[v]

Using a cat named Tabitha as his example, Quine presents another striking example of ontological relativity using what he calls a *proxy function*. A proxy function starts with one object and then correlates it with a distinct different object.
Quine gives various examples of proxy functions, but his most elegant one involves Tabitha and what he calls her cosmic counterpart:

> We could reinterpret "Tabitha" as designating no longer the cat, but
> the whole cosmos minus the cat. . . . Reinterpreting the rest of our
> terms for bodies in corresponding fashion, we come out with an ontol-
> ogy interchangeable with our familiar one. As wholes they are empiri-
> cally indistinguishable. Bodies still continue, under each interpretation,
> to be distinct from their cosmic complements and from their singletons;
> they are distinguished in a relativistic way, by their roles relative to one
> another and to the rest of the ontology. Hence my watchword *ontolog-
> ical relativity*.[w]

Given this strong thesis of ontological relativity (or indeterminacy of reference), what is the point of talking about objects at all? For Quine, talk about objects involves *reification*: the introduction or the positing of enduring entities, as
it were, to hang our observations on:

> [I] see bodies materializing, ontologically speaking . . . as ideal nodes at the foci of intersecting observation sentences. Here, I suggest, is the root of reification.[x]

Again, observation sentences themselves do not determine which ideal nodes we introduce:

> [The] reification of bodies across time is beyond the reach of observation sentences. . . . Substantial reification is theoretical.[y]

For Quine, "ontology, like grammar, is part of our own contribution to our theory of the world."[z]

Of course, given our interests and our human makeup, certain reifications will seem more natural than others. It is hard, for example, to think of any reason for taking the cosmic complement of Tabitha as basic. It seems wholly "unnatural" as a way of organizing experience. About the only way we might use it is to take the cosmic complement of the cosmic complement of Tabitha in order to get kitty back again. Then, however, it would have been simpler to stay with Tabitha in the first place. Indeed, given the kind of creatures we are, we are naturally drawn to certain reifications, not others:

> Bodies were our primordial reifications, rooted in innate perceptual similarities. It would be gratuitous to swap them for proxies; the point was just that one could.[a]

We reify the entities we do because we are the sorts of creatures we are, doing the sorts of things we do. All this is reminiscent of the pragmatism found in "On What There Is" and "Two Dogmas of Empiricism."

Quine thinks that the discussion of proxy functions, among other things, puts the thesis of the indeterminacy of reference beyond serious dispute. However, he also argues for a stronger version of indeterminacy that is much less easy to understand, and hence assess. What we say here is controversial, but what Quine seems to have in mind is this:

(1) Indeterminacy of translation does not arise for observation sentences taken holophrastically—nor for conjunctions, disjunctions, etc., of observation sentences taken holophrastically.

(2) Indeterminacy of translation arises as soon as we treat sentences not holophrastically (or as compounds of holophrastic sentences), that is, as containing significant subholophrastic parts. It will always be the case that the evidence will equally support a variety of analytic hypotheses for the translation of these subholophrastic components.

Beyond this, Quine seems to be saying something like this:

(3)   Once we go beyond observation sentences (and compounds of them), indeterminacy of translation holds for sentences even when taken holophrastically.

It is, perhaps, unclear whether Quine always had this particular thesis in mind when he put forward his strongest version of the thesis of the indeterminacy of translation. (And the controversies that have arisen concerning just what he did mean suggest, perhaps, that his formulations of this thesis have not always been entirely clear.) In any case, whatever he may have said elsewhere, in *Pursuit of Truth* Quine is perfectly clear concerning what he had in mind in presenting a strong version of his indeterminacy thesis.

> Taken analytically, the indeterminacy of translation is trivial and indisputable. . . . It is an unsurprising reflection that divergent interpretations of words in a sentence can so offset one another as to sustain an identical translation of the sentence as a whole. It is what I have called inscrutability of reference; "indeterminacy of reference" would have been better. The serious and controversial thesis of indeterminacy of translation is not that; it is rather the holophrastic thesis, which is stronger. It declares for divergencies that remain unreconciled even at the level of the whole sentence, and are compensated for only by divergencies in the translations of other whole sentences.[b]

Abstractly, suppose we are presented with a system of sentences to be interpreted holophrastically: $S_1, S_2, \ldots S_n$. Quine's claim is that this system of sentences will not have a determinate translation, since alternative translations of each of these sentences can be compensated for by adjusting the translation of others.[16] It would, of course, be helpful if Quine could provide us with a clear illustration of this sort of indeterminacy. He candidly admits that this is probably not possible. He explains why in this rather obscure passage:

> The full or holophrastic indeterminacy of translation draws too broadly on a language to admit of factual illustration.[c]

Spelled out, Quine's strong thesis of the indeterminacy of translation is plainly another version of holism. In this way, it is reminiscent of the holism found in his early essays "On What There Is" and "Two Dogmas of Empiricism." The holism of these essays turned on the ability of scientific theories to be constructed in a variety of incompatible ways, all of which are adequate to the total set of evidence. This is possible because a theory can be adjusted to existing evidence in a variety of ways. At the close of *Pursuit of Truth,* Quine comments on the close parallel

---

[16] Echoing the first thesis listed above, Quine excludes certain observation sentences from this discussion: "Translation," he tells us, "does enjoy reasonable determinacy up through observation categoricals and into the logical connectives" (p. 53).

between his early notion of the empirical underdetermination of global science and the indeterminacy of translation in these words:

> In both cases the totality of possible evidence is insufficient to clinch the system uniquely. But the indeterminacy of translation is additional to the other. If we settle upon one of the empirically equivalent systems of the world, however arbitrarily, we still have within it the indeterminacy of translation.[d]

Pursuit of Truth closes with these words:

> What the indeterminacy of translation shows is that the notion of propositions as sentence meaning is untenable. What empirical underdetermination of global science shows is that there are various defensible ways of conceiving the world.[e]

It is not unreasonable to treat Quine's doctrine of the indeterminacy of translation as a radical extension of Quine's attack on word synonymy found in "Two Dogmas of Empiricism." The closing sentence echoes the pluralism of competing theories found in that essay as well—though the range of competing theories has now been sharply limited by Quine's commitment to physicalism.

Quine and Russell

As we noted at the beginning of this examination of Quine's philosophy, there are many close affinities between his position and that of Russell. They were not only both leading figures in the development of modern logic, they also both employed the methods of logic to deal with fundamental philosophical issues. In particular, they both employed logical analysis as a device for eliminating—as far as possible—unwanted abstract, or otherwise peculiar, entities. In this respect, Quine's "On What There Is" can, in a large part, be read as a continuation of the project launched by Russell in "On Denoting."[17]

But even if Russell and Quine often make a similar use of logical methods in dealing with ontological issues, their positions are profoundly opposed in other important respects. Most significantly, they have opposed views concerning meaning. Along with other classic analytic philosophers, Russell thought that it made sense to inquire into the meaning of a specific proposition. Propositions expressed in ordinary language may be vague or ambiguous, and their grammatical form may disguise their logical form, but, still, there was nothing wrong in asking what an individual proposition meant, and it was the business of the philosopher

[17] See pp. 180–87.

to answer just such questions. Logical atomism is the clearest example of philosophy operating under these assumptions.

Quine, in contrast, is wholly opposed to an atomistic conception of propositional meaning. The logical atomist believed that, down deep, determinate meanings can be found. The persistent theme in Quine's writings is *indeterminacy*—indeterminacy of reference, indeterminacy of translation, and so on. In place of the radical atomism found in the writings of Russell and the early Wittgenstein, Quine embraced an equally radical version of holism.

This is a remarkable development, for as we saw in Chapter 3, analytic philosophy arose, in part at least, in response to British Idealism (or Hegelianism), which dominated British philosophy at the beginning of the twentieth century. British Idealism had two sides: obviously it involved a commitment to idealism—the view that the universe is fundamentally spiritual, rather than material, in nature; but it also involved a commitment to the view that individual entities have no significance except in relation to the total system that contains them. Quine, of course, as a physicalist, would have no truck with idealism. He would also reject the British Idealist's version of holism because of its basis in Hegelian notions of logic. Quine's innovation was to combine holism—with its strong indeterminist implications—with austere commitments to an extensionalist logic and a physicalist ontology. Such a combination was undreamed of by analytic philosophers in the early part of the century.

CHAPTER 14

Derrida[a]

There is perhaps a deeper difference of opinion about Jacques Derrida[1] than about most contemporary philosophers. Consider, for instance, the following segment of Derridean text, which appears to be an answer of sorts to the question that many readers might want to ask, "To what does Derrida want to call attention by introducing the neologism *differance*?"

> This graphic difference (*a* instead of *e*), this marked difference between two apparently vocal notations, . . . remains purely graphic: it is read, or it is written, but it cannot be heard. It cannot be apprehended

[1] Jacques Derrida (1930–) was born in El Blair, Algiers, and was educated at the Ecole Normale Supérieure, Paris, and at Harvard University. From 1960 to 1964, he taught at the Sorbonne in Paris. Since 1965, he has been a professor of the History of Philosophy at the Ecole Normale Supérieure and has frequently held visiting appointments at American universities.

in speech, and . . . it also bypasses the order of apprehension in general.
It is offered by a mute mark, by a tacit monument, I would even say by
a pyramid, thinking not only of the form of the letter when it is printed
as a capital. But also of the text in Hegel's *Encyclopedia,* in which the
body of the sign is compared to the Egyptian Pyramid. The *a* of *differance,* then, is not heard; it remains silent, secret, and discreet as a
tomb.[b]

What is going on here? There will not only be differences of opinion about
what is going on—differences in interpretation, that Derrida himself would of
course welcome as confirmations of his thesis that all texts, including his own, can
be variously and endlessly deconstructed. There will also be radically different
opinions—which will probably be rather less welcome—about whether what is
going on is profoundly significant or merely fancy verbal footwork.

Neither party, I believe, can make a case that will have the least validity for
the other. Their underlying assumptions are so different that what is convincing
evidence for the one is either irrelevant or trivial for the other. In a word, the disagreement between Derrideans and anti-Derrideans is rooted in a deep difference in worldview and, like all such bipolarizations of opinion, nonterminating.[2]
This being the case, instead of contributing one more item to a series of inconclusive exchanges, I shall take a wholly different tack; I shall describe what I believe are the central features of Derrida's worldview. In particular, I hope to show,
first, that Derrida's worldview is unusual in being marked by an internal conflict,
and, second, that the tension generated by this conflict is responsible for those
features of his view on which opinion is most deeply divided.

These are the theses of this chapter. I shall support them by doing what I call
philosophical archaeology on *"Differance."* That is, I shall look below the surface[3]

---

[2] For an example of a nonterminating disagreement resulting from differences in worldviews, see p. 523.

[3] Derrideans may object at this point, even before I have well begun, that in introducing
the notion of differences in level I am casually taking for granted the distinction between surface and depth that Derrida has explicitly rejected, along with all other metaphysical dualities. Certainly there is much in this paper from which they will strongly
dissent, but the distinction I am proposing here is not metaphysical; it is no more than
the distinction between (1) what people say and (2) the unstated, and possibly unconscious, intentions that lead them to say what they say; and inasmuch as this is a distinction that Derrida himself constantly makes use of—for instance in his analysis, in *The
Truth in Painting,* of Meyer Shapiro's paper on *The Origin of the Work of Art*—I assume it is safe to make use of it in discussing one of Derrida's own papers.

Exception will also certainly be taken to what will be seen as my purloining of Derrida's term "deconstruction" to designate the kind of analysis I shall be doing. In reply,
two comments: First, given Derrida's view of reference (see pp. 515–17), he is not
justified in claiming even squatter's rights to any term, whatever that term may be. Second, there is an important (from my point of view) family resemblance between Derridean deconstruction and philosophical archaeology to which I want to call attention:
Philosophical archaeology *completes* the process of Derridean deconstruction by showing why Derrida assembled the bits and pieces of other texts that together form the text
of *"Differance"* in just the way he assembled them.

of this text to uncover the conflicted metaphysical expectations that Derrida brought to the problem he set out to discuss.

The practice of philosophical archaeology can be redescribed within the framework of Derridean deconstruction: Derrida himself, exploiting a metaphor of Claude Lévi-Strauss's, describes a text as bricolage, an assembly of bits and pieces derived from other texts, which in their turn are assemblages of bricolage derived from still other texts. To deconstruct a text one disassembles it back into the bits of bricolage of which it is composed. And these into other bits, indefinitely. But Derridean deconstruction stops there, or rather, it continues indefinitely at this, always textual, level.

Philosophical archaeology focuses, instead, on the pattern of interests that led the author of the text being deconstructed to assemble just these bits of bricolage and no others into just this arrangement and no other. For instance, if one deconstructs descriptions of U.S. interventions in Libya, Grenada, and Panama, one finds that the bricolage assembled by most Third World writers differs systematically from the bricolage assembled by most First World writers: the former contain bits of bricolage—"imperialism," for instance—that do not appear in the latter, and the latter contains bits—"terrorism," for instance—omitted from the former. And it is natural, having noted these differences, to read back from them to the very different underlying political beliefs and, what are perhaps more important, the deeper, inarticulate attitudes of the authors of those texts.

That political, religious, and ethnic interests affect the ways in which authors assemble bricolage; that it is possible to "read back" from the text to the interests and biases that have organized the bricolage in just this rather than any other way; that readers have their own interests and that these may be either very similar to or markedly different from the author's interests; that, finally, such similarities and dissimilarities account for some disagreements among readers with regard to the value and importance of a text—these are matters taken for granted by almost everybody, almost all the time. It would be hard to get through a single day without constantly trying to read back from what other people say to their interests and intentions, either conscious or unconscious.

But the interests to which most people read back are either fairly obvious psychological motivations (greed and vanity, for instance) or fairly glaring ethnic, racial, and religious biases, such as the political biases that were easily detected in Latin American and U.S. press releases on the intervention in Panama. Philosophical archaeology assumes, as a working hypothesis, that there are metaphysical biases as well and that they function in much the same way that ethnic and religious biases function—as Wittgensteinian lenses that bring into focus some features of the world while in effect filtering others out.

What are some of these metaphysical biases? Just as one can observe in the writing and discourse of some people an anti-Catholic bias, matched in the writings of others by a Catholic bias, so one can observe a contrast between on the one hand an underlying presupposition that the world is best understood from outside, contemplated at a distance, and on the other hand, a presupposition that it is best understood from inside and by becoming actively involved in it. And one can observe a contrast between an underlying presupposition that the world is a well-ordered cosmos and the presupposition that, so far from being a cosmos, it is a jumble, full of sound and fury, signifying nothing. Again, as a third example of contrasting metaphysical biases, there is the contrast between an expectation that the world is fundamentally unproblematic and easily decoded and an expectation that it is deep and that because it is deep it can easily be misread. Each person's experience tends, on the whole, to confirm that person's metaphysical expectations—because, as with paranoia, what would disconfirm the expectation is simply not noticed.

Thus metaphysical bias is for the most part self-confirming—but at the cost, I remark in passing, of generating nonterminating disagreement with those who, because they have a different set of metaphysical biases, encounter a different world. Nevertheless, there can be intrapersonal, as well as interpersonal, conflict. There are, that is, individuals some of whose own biases conflict. Because such conflicted biases lead to disconfirming, and so disturbing, experiences of the world, such individuals have to find ways of dealing with the conflict. Derrida's way, I shall suggest, is to dance.

What, then, are the conflicted metaphysical expectations that give the bricolage assembled into *"Differance"* the curious shape (curious, that is, when compared with traditional philosophical discourse) that is well represented in the passage cited at the start of this chapter?

I shall begin by saying what I take *"Differance"* to be "about"—a hazardous, not to say foolhardy, undertaking with respect to any paper by Derrida. I shall do this by locating *"Differance"* within the framework of more-familiar, but very different, approaches to the problem with which *"Differance"* is concerned. I shall then deconstruct Derrida's text by analyzing a number of phrases and words from his exposition—from the bricolage he has assembled—and reading back from Derrida's choice of just these, instead of other possible, bits of bricolage, to the metaphysical beliefs and attitudes that underlie these choices.

The topic discussed in *"Differance"* is, in the broadest sense, the topic that is the chief preoccupation of many contemporary philosophers: how to adjust to, how to live in, a world without foundations. This is an urgent problem for Derrida because of the solution he proposes for the problem of reference.

Though there has always been disagreement about what exactly words refer to, it has been commonly assumed, at least since Plato, that language is somehow related to an extratextual, nonlinguistic world, a world that is just whatever it is, independent of language. Though some philosophers have held that language is a veil that obscures, interferes with, one's access to that world, most have believed that, with practice and discipline, language can be improved, purified, so that it adequately reflects that world. Reference became a central, as distinct from a relatively peripheral, problem only when philosophers concluded that none of the "easy" solutions, in terms either of transcendental forms or, alternatively, sense data, was viable. In this situation, deeper divisions among philosophers have emerged. Anglo-American philosophers still commonly assume that words refer extratextually—they divide only on how, and how firmly, language is anchored to that nonlinguistic world.

These Anglo-American preoccupations are bypassed by Derrida, since in his view, *il n'y a pas d'hors texte*—there is nothing outside language. It does not follow, however, from the idea that nothing is outside language that everything is inside language. At least in Derrida's view this does not follow. For the kinds of disjunctions—for instance, if not inside, then outside—that have governed the thinking of Western philosophers since Plato and Aristotle, and which they one and all have regarded as outside language—are, according to Derrida, inside language. That is to say, we are inevitably embedded in language. And not only this. Much more radically, the concept of "we" (alternatively, the concept of "self" or "subject"), and the contrasting concept of "world," are themselves examples of this embeddedness, elements in what Derrida calls the "logocentric" conceptual scheme that, following Martin Heidegger, he assumes "we" have inherited from the Greeks of Plato's day. It does not follow, therefore, that logocentrism and its basic metaphysical categories are "inevitable"; on the contrary, the notion of "inevitability," as contrasted with "mere chance," is but another part of the baggage of logocentrism. Just as there once was, long ago, a transformation of a nonlogocentric language into a logocentric language, there may well occur some day a transformation of logocentrism—the language in which reference is a problem, the language in which "we" and "world" are fundamental organizing concepts—into "an entirely other language." If this happens it will be "a necessarily violent transformation."[4,c]

But whatever that language may be, it will still be *language;* philosophers will therefore be as far as ever from "presence," that is, from contact with a world unmediated by language. That is to say (1) language is inescapable and (2) "in language there are only differences *without positive terms.*"[d] What follows? I will first quote Derrida's answer and then try to deconstruct it into non-Derridean language.

> The first consequence to be drawn from this is that the signified concept is never present in and of itself, in a sufficient presence that would refer only to itself. . . . Every concept is inscribed in a chain or in a system within which it refers to the other, to other concepts, by means of a systematic play of differences. Such play, *differance,* is thus no longer simply a concept . . . [nor is it] simply a word, that is, what is generally

[4]Compare "The Ends of Man," a lecture Derrida presented in October 1968. Given the extraordinary impact that the student/worker strikes in May of that year had had on French intellectuals, and noting that Derrida dated this paper "May 12, 1968," it is not implausible to conclude that Derrida believed that the second of the two possible strategies he discussed at the end of the paper—"to decide to change terrain, in a discontinuous and disruptive fashion, by brutally placing oneself outside, and by affirming an absolute break and difference"—had already been launched.

represented as the calm, present, and self-referential unity of concept and phonic material.[e]

To say that "in language there are only differences" is, more or less, to say that all terms refer, and inevitably refer, only ambiguously. A term's referent, no matter how skillfully one tries to bound and confine it, is an indefinitely expanding open set.

The opening moves Derrida makes in *The Truth in Painting* illustrate this thesis.

> Someone, not me, comes and says the words: "I am interested in the idiom in painting." . . . You are not completely in the dark, but what does he mean exactly?
>
> Does he mean that he is interested in the idiom "in painting," in the idiom itself, for its own sake . . . but what is an idiom?
>
> That he is interested in the idiomatic expression itself? . . .
>
> That he is interested in . . . what pertains to the idiom, the idiomatic trait or style . . . in the domain of painting . . . ? . . .
>
> Which makes, if you count them well, at least four hypotheses; but each one divides again, is grafted and contaminated by all the others, and you would never be finished translating them.
>
> Nor will I.[f]

Thus it is only a dream of foundationists that there are rigid designators (to misappropriate a term of Saul Kripke's and, by doing so, to illustrate Derrida's thesis, inasmuch as I have just introduced a novel reference for "rigid designator," thereby demonstrating that "rigid designator" is not an unqualifiedly rigid designator).

Without pausing to evaluate Derrida's account of reference as open-ended, I shall ask what stance Derrida adopts, and what stance he recommends that others adopt, toward his discovery that language floats—his discovery that the terms in which metaphysicians since Plato have posed the questions they want to ask about the world—is it one? is it many? is it mind-dependent or mind-independent? and so on—do not refer to the world but only to other terms, in an ever-expanding circle of possible meanings.

Derrida's position seems to be this: We should cease looking for "the" meaning of a (any) term, for there is only a hole, an emptiness, where most people, including most scientists, expect to find a determinate meaning. This thesis, it is important to see, applies quite generally to all terms alike, as some deconstructivists have clearly recognized. For instance, Hillis Miller:

> The interpretation or solving of the puzzles of the textual web only adds more filaments to the web. One can never escape from the labyrinth because the activity of escaping makes more labyrinth. . . . Criticism is the production of more thread to embroider the texture or

> textile already there. This thread is like the filament of ink which flows from the pen of the writer, keeping him in the web but suspending him also over the chasm.[g]

On the whole, however, deconstructivists have understandably found it convenient to avoid facing up to this radically skeptical conclusion, and Derrida himself is careful to fix his entire attention on metaphysical terms and their alleged emptiness. But he does not conclude, as genuinely antifoundationist philosophers have done, that one ought to abandon metaphysics and turn one's attention to other matters. Rather, we should endlessly track the endless, and ever-expanding, circle of the referents of metaphysical terms. Alternatively put, we should continue metaphysical inquiry, but continue it as "play": We should follow "the play of *differance*" through and around the bits of bricolage that survive from earlier attempts by metaphysicians to provide determinate answers to the traditional foundationist questions about the world.

Since "play" is a bit of bricolage that occurs repeatedly in *"Differance,"* I will in my turn introduce a bit of bricolage—from "The Ends of Man," which is itself a bit of bricolage from *Zarathustra*. Friedrich Nietzsche, Derrida says, distinguished between the merely superior man and the overman.

> The first is abandoned to his distress in a last moment of pity. The latter . . . awakens and leaves without turning back to what he leaves behind him. He burns his text and erases the traces of his steps. His laughter will then burst out. . . . He will dance.[h]

On my reading of Nietzsche, overman's laughter and dance reflect Nietzsche's own joyful response to his discovery that, because reference is open-ended, the pursuit of determinate meanings is futile. Nietzsche and his overman were exhilarated, liberated, when they came to realize that texts refer only to texts, not to a world beyond all texts.

I shall support this reading of Nietzsche by two more bits of bricolage, one from "The Vision of the Loneliest" in *Zarathustra,* the other from "Homer's Conquest." In the former, Zarathustra sees a young shepherd, who is "writhing, gagging, in spasms, his face distorted, and a heavy black snake [hangs] out of his mouth." Zarathustra cries out to him, "Bite! Bite its head off! Bite!"

> The shepherd . . . bit with a good bite. Far away he spewed the head of the snake—and he jumped up. No longer shepherd, no longer human—one changed, radiant, *laughing!*

In the latter, this metaphor is unpacked. The black snake is the recognition that God is dead, that the world has no goal and no direction, that everything eternally returns. Overman is simply

> the truly exuberant, alive and world-affirming man who does not merely resign himself to and learn to get along with [this truth], but

who wants *everything as it was and is* back again, back forever and ever, insatiably calling *da capo,* not only to himself but to the whole spectacle and performance.

I have introduced these bits of bricolage here in order to bring out, by way of contrast, how very differently play functions in Derrida's own response to what he and Nietzsche both take to be the inevitable indeterminacy of reference. Where Nietzsche is liberated by this discovery and "burns his text" as being a useless encumbrance, Derrida not only preserves it but endlessly rereads it. Where Nietzsche "erases the traces of his steps," Derrida continuously tracks them.

Nietzsche and Derrida are both relativists; that they are follows, in the case of each of them, from the nature of language rendering rigid designation impossible. Nietzsche would agree with Derrida that the "Being" endlessly debated by the traditional metaphysicians is only a hole. But Nietzsche does not notice the hole; he laughs and dances because he has been liberated from metaphysics. Derrida has not been liberated; he is still very much a metaphysician, aware, therefore, of the hole; he dances around it—tracks the answers of earlier metaphysicians—in order to avoid looking into the emptiness where, as he believes, Being ought to be but where, as he is convinced, it is not.

In a word, Nietzsche is a happy relativist; that is why his laughter, as I read it, is joyous. Derrida is an unhappy relativist, a relativist *malgre lui,* who wishes things were different but who is persuaded that they cannot be. That is why Derridean wordplay, as I read it, is so very different from Nietzsche's. It is a form of therapy; it is designed to relieve people from the anxiety they feel whenever they attend to the idea that there is only a hole where rigid metaphysical designators ought to be. The therapy is in effect a dance around the hole—a dance intended to be so entertaining, so light and swift (the passage quoted at the beginning of this chapter is a good example of a Derridean dance), that both Derrida and his readers alike are quite distracted from any desire to have any philosophical question—for instance, the question of what is Derrida's theory of reference—definitively answered. In a word, the text of *"Differance"* does not tackle—does not try to solve, however indirectly, tangentially, or allusively—any philosophical problem; it illustrates how Derrida proposes that all philosophical problems be dealt with—by assembling the failed answers of earlier philosophers and then dancing around them.

Is Derrida a foundationist or an antifoundationist? If one reads the text of *"Differance"* at the surface level only, the answer is so obvious that it must seem silly to raise the question: he is a radical antifoundationist; that is the whole thrust of everything he says about the intrinsic indeterminacy of reference. However, if one looks below the surface—if one reads subtextually; if, in the language of this chapter, one does philosophical archaeology—things look very different.

Foundationist thinking has been dominated at least since Plato by an unconscious adoption of what I shall call the all-or-none rule, which excludes the possibility of there being anything, x, that is better than something else, y, unless there is something that is best, and excludes as well the possibility of any proposition being truer than any other proposition unless there is at least one proposition that is absolutely true.

The argument about measurement in *The Phaedo* has this all-or-none form: *either* there is an absolute criterion of equality *or* no comparative judgments of distance, size, or volume are possible; that being an absurd conclusion, it follows that there is an absolute criterion of equality. And it underlies the opening moves in *The Republic,* which sketch the overall strategy of the dialogue. The unstated assumption is the all-or-none rule: the only alternative to the use of force to control societies is rational persuasion, the possibility of which depends on the existence of forms. Since it is taken for granted that no one will opt for a society ruled by force, it follows that the forms exist.

Similarly with the Cartesians: *either* there is something (which turns out to be my own existence) that is indubitable *or* all is dubitable. So, too, with the Logical Positivists, who in other respects are unlikely bedfellows of the Platonists and Cartesians. Though sentences about the physical world are not anchored in the forms (which are dismissed as unverifiable) nor in self-evident rules (which are dismissed as tautologies), they *are* anchored—in protocol sentences that report unit sensory experiences—and just as firmly anchored as they are anchored for Platonists and Cartesians. That they might not be anchored was never seriously considered by the positivists, who, like other foundationists, assume, by the all-or-none rule, that the alternative to being securely anchored—too dreadful to contemplate—is to be hopelessly adrift on the sea of skepticism.

Philosophers whose thought does not move along these lines, who are antifoundationists, are rare indeed. David Hume, a professed "mitigated sceptic," is one of these exceptions, and an interesting one. For his "impressions," though they have a superficial family resemblance to the positivists' protocol sentences, function very differently. He did not use them to try to anchor the sciences; he was quite content if the sciences floated, because he thought of them as being "human," and having "a direct reference to action and society."[i]

I believe that, in these terms, Derrida is neither a foundationist nor yet an antifoundationist. He is conflicted, radically ambivalent about, the all-or-none rule. He alternates between adopting the "all," or foundationist, option and the "none," or unmitigated skeptical, option.

That this is the case with Derrida is perhaps not immediately obvious from the text of "*Differance.*" A clearer—indeed, a paradigmatic—example is the three-paper exchange with John Searle. It consists of (1) Derrida's "Signature Event Context," which is a criticism of an argument of J. L. Austin's; (2) Searle's "Reiterating the Difference: A Reply to Derrida," which argues that Derrida has misunderstood Austin; and (3) Derrida's "Limited Inc.," which is an attack on Searle.[j] There is an extraordinary contrast in style and in tone between (1) and (3): The former is serious; the latter is playful. In the former Derrida is embarked on the kind of cognitive inquiry that Searle is embarked on in (2), the kind of inquiry that Anglo-American philosophers commonly undertake. In (1) Derrida and in

(2) Searle, that is to say, both assume that philosophical terms designate sufficiently rigidly for a careful reader to ascertain what an author means, and in particular they assume that J. L. Austin's *How to Do Things with Words* refers to the events that Austin calls "speech acts." That being the case, the question is whether Austin got it wrong about speech acts, as Derrida maintains, or right, as Searle maintains. In (3) Derrida does not reply by undertaking to show that he is right about Austin being mistaken. On the contrary, reverting to his official position that all reference is open-ended—there is only a hole where Austin and Searle naïvely expect to find something referred to by "speech act"—he abandons the project, launched in (1), of discovering what speech acts are and takes to dancing around (2), starting out, for instance, by listing all the assumptions Searle had made when he copyrighted the manuscript of (2)—assumptions that may indeed be unwarranted in some ideal universe but that are quite irrelevant to the question debated in (1) and (2).

This confrontation between Derrida and Searle is typical of worldview disagreements. From Searle's point of view, Derrida changed the rules of the game as soon as he realized that by the rules they had adopted in (1) and (2) he had lost the game. Searle did not reply to (3) by dancing about Derrida's dance. If Searle did not want to answer (3) by dancing around it, he had no option save silence. But from Derrida's point of view, Searle's silence had a different interpretation: it demonstrated once again that philosophers cannot answer questions; they can only cite the unwarranted assumptions made by other philosophers in the course of seeking answers.

But I have introduced this exchange less to illustrate the nonterminating nature of worldview disagreements than to provide some guidelines for uncovering what is below the surface of *"Differance."* At various points in that essay Derrida ceases to dance; he becomes serious. That is, he shifts from the stance of (3) to the stance of (1). On these occasions he is either making cognitive claims that are at variance with his Saussurean view of reference as necessarily open-ended or he is expressing regret that the Saussurean position excludes the possibility of there being a "kingdom" of closed-ended reference. I focus on these points because I believe one can read back from them to fissures in Derrida's worldview. I hold—to anticipate the conclusion I am going to propose—that a subtextual reading of this bricolage shows that the therapy Derrida has proposed for coping in a world without foundations has not, even in his own case, been wholly successful.

Consider, as a start, these three bits of bricolage:

> "strange space" (p. 5)
> "bottomless chessboard" (p. 22)
> "irreparable loss" (p. 19)

The space discussed here is between "speech and writing"; the chessboard is the empirical world in which most people believe they conduct their extratextual traffic with nature and other men and women; the loss is the loss of "presence," that is, the failure to make contact with an unmediated, nonlinguistic reality.

But why "strange"? why "bottomless"? why "irreparable"? What does Derrida's choice of these adjectives suggest about his worldview? They reveal, I think, disappointed metaphysical expectations: it is only when one is expecting a familiar space and encounters an unusual one that one calls it "strange." And so, even more evidently, for "bottomless" and "irreparable." Since there is a close correlation between the level of one's expectation and the intensity of the disappointment one experiences if that expectation is defeated, a really radical reversal of expectations is reflected in these adjectives. It is not merely a matter of Derrida having been handed a partially filled glass when he expected one that was brimming full; it is rather a matter of his believing that, as he was bringing the glass to his lips, it wholly disappeared.

In a word, Derrida must at some time have had high metaphysical expectations—the usual expectations of the philosophical tradition, from the Platonists to the Cartesians and beyond—that firm foundations for metaphysical beliefs can be found. Moreover, in Derrida's text there is not merely disappointment that the world does not live up to his high expectations for it; there is also nostalgia for the lost world[5] that would have satisfied those expectations. Consider, for instance,

> Not only is there no kingdom of *differance,* but *differance* instigates the subversion of everything within us that desires a kingdom. Which makes it obviously threatening and infallibly dreaded by everything within us that desires a kingdom, the past or future presence of a kingdom.[k]

At a purely textual level what is being alluded to by "kingdom" is what is referred to by such expressions as "form of the good" in a Platonic vocabulary; by "self" in a Cartesian, and by "absolute" in a Hegelian vocabulary: the notion of a terminus, something toward which cognitive and moral inquiry is directed, and on which when it is reached, inquiry can end. Why then did Derrida prefer "kingdom" to these other terms? Because, read subtextually, "kingdom" has a connotation that "form of the good," "self," and "absolute" lack. "Kingdom" suggests, as those terms do not, that our cognitive security is, even at best, limited. Within the kingdom's walls all may be safe, but outside is insecurity; the barbarian, for all one knows, may be at the gate. And, this is the point, even the limited security that a kingdom would give is denied us. For there is no kingdom—no possibility of determinate reference. There is only *differance,* and *"differance* is not" (p. 21). Because *differance* is not, "the domination of beings"—that is to say, all that is— "shake[s] as a whole, . . . tremble[s] in entirety." The world, so far from having secure foundations, is seismically unstable.[6]

---

[5] It is possible not only to experience nostalgia for what has been lost—the prelogocentric language of the early Greeks; it is also possible to experience longing for the unknown future, the language hinted at in "The Ends of Man." And that Derrida did indeed experience this longing is suggested by his discussion of "Heideggerian hope" (see p. 526).

[6] Note the expressions "as a whole" and "in entirety." They reflect that influence on Derrida's thinking of the all-or-none rule: either all is firm or nothing is.

No wonder, then, that "everything within us that desires a kingdom" finds this situation "obviously threatening and infallibly dreaded" (p. 22). However inclusive or restricted Derrida's "us" may be, he has certainly included himself among these shaken people. That he has done so is evidence, I suggest, that he is a not entirely happy dancer. He is a dancer *faute de mieux,* a dancer who dances less because he delights in dancing than because he finds himself to be at the edge of the abyss of indefinite, infinitely expanding reference.

Support for this subtextual reading is to be found in still another bit of bricolage, this one an observation about names: "There will be no unique name, even if it were the name of Being" (p. 27). That there is no unique name is just a restatement of the already familiar, and thoroughly elaborated, proposition to the effect that in language "there are no positive terms" (p. 11), i.e., no terms that unambiguously refer. What is interesting is that when, as is the case here, he is thinking of the application of the doctrine of *differance* specifically to the term "Being"—the term that has been reserved by generations of philosophers since Plato as the name of the foundation of foundations—he feels called upon to add the warning, "we must think this thought without nostalgia." It is painful enough (this is the subtext of the bricolage of p. 11) to discover that the terms by which beings are thought to be named, whether in ordinary or in scientific discourse, so far from referring to extratextual horses, dogs, galaxies, and neurons, refer only to an indefinitely expanding textual abyss. But the shaking and trembling that this discovery causes is as nothing compared with the shaking and trembling experienced when one realizes that the term "Being" is itself unstable. Hence a warning is especially called for here: faced with the discovery that "Being" names nothing, that it is a "myth," "we" must resist nostalgia for the "lost native country of thought." Instead, we "must *affirm* this [discovery] with a certain laughter and a certain step of the dance" (p. 27).

Who is being warned here? As with the "us" of the passage on p. 22, the tone and the context certainly suggest that Derrida includes himself among those needing a warning. And, since one hardly issues warnings to those one believes are not prone to experiencing nostalgia, it is surely not unreasonable to conclude that the subtext here expresses Derrida's own nostalgia.

Possibly Derrideans will argue that Derrida himself does not experience nostalgia; his "we's" and "us's" are mere rhetorical ploys designed to suggest to the nostalgic that he shares their sentiment. Perhaps—if these were the only bits of bricolage available. But they are not. Hence, though the deconstruction of other Derridean texts is beyond the scope of this chapter, I will once again introduce a bit of bricolage from another text, because in it Derrida identifies himself quite explicitly and in a particularly revealing way with the sentiments that, I believe, also form the subtext of *"Differance."*

This bricolage is the conclusion of "Structure, Sign, and Play." He has just distinguished "two interpretations of interpretation" that are "irreducible," and "absolutely irreconcilable, even if, together, they share the field which we call the human sciences."[1] One of these modes of interpretation aims, and aims naïvely, at determinate reference; it "seeks to decipher, dreams of deciphering, a truth or an origin which is free from freeplay."[7,m] The second mode of interpretation has abandoned this dream because since the structures on which analysis terminates have a history and an origin, "the origin of a new structure [must be conceived] on the model of catastrophe—an overturning of nature in nature, a natural interruption of the natural sequence, a brushing aside *of* nature."[n] In other words, it recognizes that no terms, not even the scientific vocabulary of structuralism, are, or can be, rigid designators. This second mode of interpretation therefore "affirms freeplay and tries to pass beyond man and humanism."

What is Derrida's attitude toward this mode of interpretation? After noting that such terms as "gestation," "conception," and "labor" are appropriate for describing it, he comments:

> I employ these words, I admit, with a glance toward the business of childbearing—but also with a glance toward those who, in a company from which I do not exclude myself, turn their eyes away in the face of the as yet unnameable which is proclaiming itself and which can do so, as is necessary whenever a birth is in the offing, only under the species of the non-species, in the formless, mute, infant, and terrifying form of monstrosity.[o]

This company, in which Derrida explicitly includes himself—there is no possibly ambiguous "we" or "us" here—is the company that has also been instructed that it "must *affirm*" that the term "Being" names nothing. Taking these bits of bricolage together and noting that Derrida's italicization suggests resistance that has to be overcome, it seems not unreasonable to conclude that his attitude toward the absence of foundations is at the furthest extreme from what Derrida rightly calls "Nietzschean *affirmation*—the joyous affirmation of the freeplay of a world without truth, without origin, offered to an active interpretation.[p]

In such bits of bricolage as these one does not have to read subtextually to find the nostalgia; it is at the surface, recognized and acknowledged by Derrida himself. But with these overt expressions of nostalgia for foundationism as clues, one can find evidence of nostalgia below the surface at many other points—indeed, as I shall argue, wherever, as in the passages (p. 11 and p. 22) that I quoted earlier— the tone is serious, not playful as it is in those sentences about pyramids and tombs quoted at the start of this chapter. There, and often in *"Differance,"* he is in control; dancing, it seems, proves to be good therapy—he dances as gaily as ever Nietzsche did. But now and then the therapy fails; he becomes aware of the hole about which he is dancing and, overcome by a nostalgia for closure, for completeness, he ceases to dance and becomes in effect a traditional metaphysician seeking—and even finding!—answers to questions that, when he is in his usual,

---

[7] Derrida is thinking specifically of Lévi-Strauss at this point, but Jean Piaget would surely be another example. If so, we must add structuralism to Platonism, Cartesianism, and Logical Positivism as a fourth move by foundationists to anchor "the field of the human sciences."

antifoundationist stance, he holds to be unanswerable. This change in tone from playfulness to seriousness occurs at several other points in the essay—whenever (as I suggest) he allows himself to contemplate, head-on, the consequences for foundationism of the Saussurean view of language. At these points he discovers that the abyss is not quite empty: there is, after all, a *hors texte*.

Consider, for instance, one of the numerous mentions of "traces," that is, evidence in beings of the presence of Being. The problem of reference is once again raising its ugly head; restated in terms of "traces," it amounts to asking how one can find, within language, traces of what, because it is beyond language, anchors language. The difficulty, as Derrida sees, is that this seems to raise a question about origins, and since, from his point of view, the very notion of origin entails the notion of effect, has he not, he asks himself, committed himself to still another of those dialectically related pairs that are supposedly no more than features of the logocentric vocabulary we have all inherited? In short, as Derrida recognizes, the name "origin" no longer "suits" what he wants to talk about. How can he extricate himself from "the closure of this framework"? How can he extricate himself from this pair of interpretive concepts in which his thinking about presence is embedded? His answer is:

> I have attempted to indicate a way out . . . via the "trace," which is no more an effect than it has a cause, but which in and of itself, outside its text, is not sufficient to operate the necessary transgression.[q]

Here Derrida is no longer playful; he is serious. He is no longer dancing at the edge of the abyss; he is making two positive metaphysical claims: First, that there is, after all, evidence of there being something in the abyss; it has left a trace that marks its presence. Second, though there is enough of a trace to warrant a belief in an extralinguistic reality, it is, conveniently, not enough of a trace to undermine—to "transgress"—Derrida's fundamental thesis that, given the nature of language, there can be no determinate reference.

What is one to make of this claim? Though one can agree that "effect" may not be quite the right category under which to classify traces, it is surely the case that a trace, in order to be a trace, must be a mark, itself accessible, of something no longer accessible but once accessible. The trace may be faint; it may be fugitive; it may be ambiguous. But however ambiguous, however uncertain the reference, it must, if it is a trace, refer to *something*.

Derrida's position seems not unlike that of the woman who claimed her baby was too small to be illegitimate. One is inclined to reply that at the moment the baby becomes so tiny that it ceases to be illegitimate (at the point at which it ceases to be a "transgression"), just at that point it ceases to be a baby. *Mutatis mutandis* for traces.

Further, while Derrida's trace is obviously inside the text in which it occurs, is it a trace of something inside some other text, or is it a trace of "presence," that is, something outside all texts? If inside, the notion of trace is unproblematic, but useless for Derrida inasmuch as the trace is not a trace of what is extratextual, but only of another bit of textual bricolage. If outside, there is indeed the possibility that the text is a sign of what is beyond all texts, but only at the cost of another "transgression."

How might Derrida reply? Paul de Man has suggested to me (in a personal communication) that "trace" is to be understood in Lacanian terms as "an empty referent—there is not nor was there ever any actual content latent in the unconscious to which the trace refers . . . for Lacanians the signifier is the sign of a Lack." This seems to me a perspicuous reading of Derrida, but we have to distinguish the question of interpretation that Paul de Man is answering (What does Derrida mean by "trace"?) from the question that I am raising here: Does this notion of trace escape "the closure of the framework"?

It is clear, I think, that it does not. So far as Derrida adopts the orthodox reading of Freud he gives us an unproblematic notion of "trace," but one that it is not the "way out" that he sought, since the trace, so understood, is the marker of an earlier episode in the patient's life, which may be recovered by psychoanalysis, that is, something *hors texte*. So far, on the other hand, as he adopts a Lacanian reading, he explains one enigma by appeal to another enigma. I suspect that, if the notion of "trace" works for Derrida and the Derrideans it does so because of an unnoticed ambiguity between Lacanian and the orthodox interpretations of Freud; if one moves rapidly enough from one interpretation to the other, one avoids noticing the contradiction. It is doubtless easy for Derrida and the Derrideans not to notice contradictions because for them, of course, the law of contradiction is one more piece of logocentric baggage. Thus, later in *"Differance,"* he observes that "one can think without a contradiction, or at least without granting any pertinence to such a contradiction, what is perceptible and imperceptible in the trace. . . . Heidegger can therefore, in a contradiction without contradiction, consign, countersign, the sealing of the trace."[r]

This seems to amount to saying that one can both remember and at the same time forget that the trace is a trace. Whether this kind of "active forgetting" (as Derrida calls it) is a psychological possibility is one thing—given the spiritual exercises of the Jesuits and the "doublethink" described by George Orwell in *1984,* or given for that matter the amount of muddle-mindedness loose in the world— it would be naïve to rule out active forgetting as a procedure by which one can learn to believe conflicting propositions.

But to recognize this possibility does not eliminate the "pertinence" of the contradiction; it is merely to say that some individuals can learn to avoid thinking about the pertinence of a contradiction, that is, that doublethink is an alternative therapy for dealing with anxieties aroused by one's recognition that the world lacks foundations.

But the most striking venture into metaphysics occurs, not surprisingly, just after the warning against nostalgia, when, clearly, he is thinking of how very, very empty the abyss is:

> From the vantage of this affirmation foreign to all dialectics, the other side of nostalgia, what I will call Heideggerian *hope,* comes into

question. I am not unaware how shocking this word might seem here. Nevertheless I am venturing it, without excluding any of its implications.

These sentences introduce a long quotation from Heidegger, and the essay then concludes with the following comment:

> Such is the question: the alliance of speech and Being in the unique word, in the finally proper name. And such is the question in the simulated affirmation of *differance*. It bears (on) each member of this sentence: "Being/speaks/always and everywhere/throughout/language."[s]

There is nothing playful about this prose; Derrida is making a metaphysical claim—stating what he holds to be the case—about the world. What is the claim? That those who have just been warned against nostalgia, warned against regret for the loss of the kingdom, nevertheless have grounds for hope that there is a kingdom after all. And not only grounds for hope: there is evidence ("Being speaks") in every sentence uttered or written. Thus these comments on Heideggerian hope not only unsay the immediately preceding warning against nostalgia; they unsay the central thesis of *"Differance,"* namely, that there is no *hors texte.*

At the cost of digressing into one more Derridean text I shall point out still another, and quite remarkable, shift on the subject of the abyss. At the end of *"Differance,"* as we have just seen, Derrida slips into a Heideggerian view of the abyss. So far from the abyss being empty, Being speaks from it—speaks to all who will but "hearken" to its voice. Ten years later, in *The Truth in Painting,* he imposes on Heidegger a Derridean view of the abyss: it is quite empty. If there is anything clear about Heidegger it is that he held that Being speaks in paintings and other works of art (Heidegger's chief example was a painting of old shoes by Van Gogh) and, more generally in language, which, for Heidegger, as for Derrida, is an abyss. But for Heidegger, unlike Derrida, the abyss of language is not bottomless. For instance, as Heidegger wrote in the short paper "Language," if we fall into the abyss of language

> we do not go tumbling into emptiness. We fall upward, to a height. Its loftiness opens up a depth. The two span a realm in which we would like to become at home, so as to find a dwelling place for the life of man.[t]

Nothing, one would have thought, could be more explicit. Yet in *The Truth in Painting,* which purports to be an exposition of *The Origin of the Work of Art,* this Heideggerian abyss is emptied and brought into alignment with what may be called the official Derridean doctrine. So far from the depth opening up to a height, it is bottomless, and because it is bottomless one can save oneself from falling into the abyss only "by weaving and folding back the cloth to infinity"[8u]—that is, not by hearkening to the voice of Being, but by dancing, by

[8] It is interesting to note how closely Hillis Miller's metaphor echoes this passage.

tracking the indefinitely expanding network of always partial, always indeterminate references accumulated in other, earlier philosophical texts.

How does it come about that in the last pages of *"Differance"* Derrida makes a long move in the direction of Heidegger: the Derridean abyss is not quite empty, whereas in *The Truth in Painting*, Heidegger's abyss becomes Derridean, "bottomless" after all? I suggest that these shifts—of Derrida himself in the direction of Heidegger and then of Derrida's Heidegger in the direction of Derrida—reflect a marked ambivalence toward foundationism.

I have now cited a number of passages, in *"Differance"* and in related essays, in which Derrida shows himself to be enough of a foundationist to make metaphysical claims. These are just the points at which nostalgia is expressed (sometimes openly, sometimes covertly), as he comes to realize that, despite all his ingenuity, despite all his twistings and turnings, his Saussurean view of reference invalidates these claims. It follows, if this deconstruction of *"Differance"* is persuasive, that Derrida had by no means escaped from the "old debate full of metaphysical investments"[v]—at least not as late as 1978, when *The Truth in Painting* was published. As of that date and contrary to his claim that he had liberated himself from metaphysics, he was deeply in debt and unobtrusively making payments on account, in the hope, it would seem, of staving off a visit from the bailiff.

Was the debt subsequently paid off? One's answer to this question will in large measure turn on whether one believes there are two Derridas, an earlier Derrida and a later, quite different Derrida. That is an issue that has been much, and inconclusively, debated,[9] and I certainly do not propose to try to adjudicate it. Instead, since there is also a difference of opinion among Wittgensteinians about how much of a break there is between the *Tractatus* and the *Investigations,* and since Ludwig Wittgenstein's thought, as much as Derrida's, is driven by the need to cope with metaphysical anxiety, I shall conclude with a few remarks about the differences between their approaches.

When Derrida, instead of finding a kingdom of determinate references, discovered only an abyss at his feet, the therapy he undertook was linguistic, a dance around the abyss. The Wittgenstein of the *Tractatus* also experienced metaphysical anxieties, because, as he put it, he had discovered that "all that happens and is the case is accidental" (6.41). The strategy he proposed, like Derrida's, was linguistic. But it was not a dance around the gaping hole that marked the site of unanswerable metaphysical questions. It was an act of linguistic exorcism. He denied that metaphysical questions exist: "For [he assured himself] doubt can exist only where a question exists, a question only where an answer exists, and an answer only where something *can be said*" (6.51).

---

[9]There is a useful short discussion of this debate by Richard Rorty (in *Contingency, Irony and Solidarity* [Cambridge University Press, Cambridge, 1989], pp. 125ff.), who comes down firmly for a sharp discontinuity.

But recitation of this incantation, which was the most he was capable of in the *Tractatus*, apparently did not allay doubt; it proved necessary to *show*, not merely to *say*, that there are no metaphysical questions. For a time he therefore abandoned philosophical inquiry, and when he returned to it, it was in order to take up, one after another, traditional metaphysical puzzles, with the intention in each case of showing it to be the product of linguistic confusion. When a philosopher—Augustine, for instance—asks "What is time?" and is distressed because he cannot answer, the reason is that in this question language is spinning. The solution is to put language back into traction by employing it in the practical, getting-and-spending language games of everyday life ("What time does the flight leave?"), where use determines meaning. This he undertook to do in the *Investigations*. The therapy practiced there is still linguistic, but it is very different from Derrida's, being designed not (as with Derrida) to distract attention from an abyss, but to demonstrate that there is no abyss from which one must distract oneself.

That there is no abyss is doubtless something that must, for some uneasy minds, be demonstrated again and again, for language all too easily slips out of traction and begins spinning. But, whenever a Derridean abyss seems to yawn at one's feet, one can always dissipate it by putting language back into traction. The trouble with Derrida from Wittgenstein's point of view is that he never even tries to put language back into traction. His prescription—using metaphysical language, as he thinks, playfully—is no solution. For it is not playful; it is still metaphysical, still spinning. And as it spins, it generates a Derridean abyss even at the moment when, according to Derrida, it is supposed to be distracting us from it.

The contrast between these two approaches is instructive, and it is highly relevant to the "deep difference of opinion" about Derrida on which I remarked at the beginning of this chapter. Much of this difference turns on varying responses to Derrida's conflicted, on-again, off-again attitude toward the all-or-none rule. Most philosophers, as I have said, have not only taken this rule for granted; they have, almost all of them, opted for the "all" alternative. That is to say, almost all philosophical theory construction has been driven by a very low tolerance for cognitive and moral dissonance, by the need of the theorists for a universe in which they can feel comfortable, but a universe that they can contemplate at a distance, themselves uninvolved and uncommitted. It is evident, then, why foundationists would derogate *"Differance"*: it challenges their deepest beliefs and undermines their security.

But antifoundationist philosophers—those who, like Hume, Dewey, and Wittgenstein, reject the all-or-none rule—are as deeply offended by *"Differance"* as the foundationists, for they too take cognition seriously. It is just that, unlike Derrida and the foundationists, they hold serious cognitive and moral inquiry to be possible in a world without foundations. From their point of view, Derrida, like Wordsworth's pale rationalist, devotes himself to multiplying metaphysical distinctions, thereby justifying to himself his failure to tackle any real-life problems.

It is as if Derrida wants to be absolutely certain of eliminating every rat that happens to be roaming around the house before he starts to hunt any rat down.

Since, unlike the foundationists, he believes there to be an indefinitely large number of rat holes, none of which can be completely blocked, he spends his time pointing out how earlier rat-hunters failed to block holes completely. In contrast, the antifoundationists—John Dewey, for instance—are skeptical about the claim that there are unstoppable rat holes and still more skeptical that there is an indefinitely large number of them. "Wait and see" and "Time will tell" are their mottos: they propose to turn their attention to stopping rat holes only after they see rats escaping through them. Meanwhile they pursue every rat they encounter. That they do so follows from the fact that each of them, in his own way, regards the quest for certainty as a form of mental illness.

The pattern of worldview biases that leads to admiration for Derrida is quite different. People who share Derrida's nostalgia for the lost kingdom and his ambivalence toward foundationism—and I believe many do—will probably resonate with the passages in *"Differance"* on Heideggerian hope and on traces: Derrida will seem to them to offer a way out of relativism, skepticism, and pragmatism—a way of enjoying metaphysical cake without having actually to eat it.

Those who read the remarks on nostalgia differently from the way I read them, and who therefore miss the ambivalence that I detect, will view Derrida as having deployed weapons for as sweeping an attack on Western culture as has been contemplated since Nietzsche. For, viewed in this way, Derridean deconstruction does not merely mark the end of philosophy (an event few nonphilosophers would deeply regret). It also marks the end of the enterprise that has characterized the West since the Renaissance—inquiry into the nature of the *hors texte* world. Inasmuch as Derridean deconstruction is a broom that sweeps away beings as well as Being, it has a great appeal for all those critical of what they see as the "pretensions" of the natural and social sciences and of the economic, social, political, and literary establishments based on them.

Two, from many possible, examples: the women's movement and the humanities. It is understandable why Derridean deconstruction, as set out in *"Differance,"* would appeal to the more radical elements in the women's movement—at least until it occurred to them that the sword that they employ against phallocratic language can turn against the hand that is wielding it. Similarly, it is understandable why *"Differance"* would appeal to historians, literary critics, and other humanists whom it releases from what seems to them a will-o'-the-wisp pursuit of "the" meaning of some document or other.

In a word, responses to *"Differance"* are strongly affected by differential evaluations of the objectivity, neutrality, and seriousness that, for centuries, have been thought to be the appropriate attitudes to adopt in all cognitive enterprises, and more generally, by differential attitudes toward completion, closure, and risk taking. Since there are many—Westerners and non-Westerners—who are mounting attacks on the status quo, and as many others who want to defend it, it is not to be wondered at that opinion is bipolarized.[10]

[10] I am grateful to Steve Erickson, Paul Mann, and Arden Reed for detailed, helpful, and forbearing comments on successive drafts of this paper. (W.T.J.)

Notes

Chapter 1 / The World We Live In

a William Butler Yeats, "The Second Coming."
b Thomas Mann, *The Magic Mountain*, translated by H. T. Lowe-Porter (Secker and Warburg, London, 1928), p. 442.
c William Faulkner, "Old Man," in *The Portable Faulkner*, edited by M. Cowley (Viking, New York, 1954), pp. 568 and 578.
d Joyce Cary, *The Horse's Mouth* (M. Joseph, London, 1944), p. 295.
e Günter Grass, *The Tin Drum*, translated by Ralph Manheim (Crest, New York, 1964), pp. 565–66.
f Albert Camus, *The Myth of Sisyphus*, translated by Justin O'Brien (Vintage Books, New York, 1960), pp. 16 and 22.
g Jean-Paul Sartre, *The Reprieve*, translated by E. Sutton (Bantam Books, New York, 1960), p. 101.

h Fyodor Dostoyevsky, *Notes from Underground,* in *The Best Short Stories of Dostoyevsky,* translated by D. Magarshack (Modern Library, New York, n.d.), pp. 107 and 111.

i D. H. Lawrence, *Women in Love* (Modern Library, New York, 1922), pp. 17, 45, 36, and 143–44.

j Wallace Stevens, *The Collected Poems of Wallace Stevens* (Knopf, New York, 1955), p. 381.

k *Ibid.,* p. 373.

l T. S. Eliot, "East Coker," in *Four Quartets* (Harcourt Brace Jovanovich, New York, 1943), pp. 16–17.

m *Ibid.,* p. 13.

n Bertrand Russell, "What Is an Agonistic?" *Look Magazine* (1953), reprinted in *The Basic Writings of Bertrand Russell,* edited by R. E. Enger and L. E. Dennon (Simon and Schuster, New York, 1961), p. 582.

o Immanuel Kant, *Critique of Pure Reason,* translated by N. Kemp Smith (Macmillan, London, 1929), pp. xvi–xvii.

p *Ibid.,* p. xviii.

q William Wordsworth, *The Prelude,* Bk. II, ll. 252–60.

r Samuel Taylor Coleridge, *Biographical Literaria,* Ch. VIII.

s Quoted in Friedrich Nietzsche, "Schopenhauer as Educator," reprinted in *Existentialism from Dostoevsky to Sartre,* translated and edited by W. Kaufmann (Meridian Books, New York, 1956), p. 103.

t *Ibid.,* p. 102.

u Friedrich Nietzsche, *Beyond Good and Evil,* translated by M. Cowan (Regnery, Chicago, 1955), pp. 101, 3, 6, and 15.

v F. H. Bradley, *Appearance and Reality* (Clarendon Press, Oxford, 1930), p. 111, n. 1.

w *Ibid.,* p. 140.

Chapter 2 / Three Philosophies of Process: Bergson, Dewey, and Whitehead

a Henri Bergson, *An Introduction to Metaphysics,* translated by T. E. Hulme (Putnam, New York, 1912), pp. 1–19.

b *Ibid.,* pp. 21 and 39–40.

c Henri Bergson, *Creative Evolution,* translated by A. Mitchell (Henry Holt, New York, 1911), pp. 1–2 and 4–5.

d Bergson, *Introduction to Metaphysics,* pp. 55–56 and 62–64.

e Bergson, *Creative Evolution,* pp. 94–95.

f *Ibid.,* p. 127.

g *Ibid.,* pp. 126 and 98–99.

h *Ibid.,* pp. 109–11.

i *Ibid.,* pp. 131–32.

j *Ibid.,* p. 133.

k *Ibid.,* pp. 139 and 140–41.

l *Ibid.,* pp. 144–45.

m *Ibid.,* pp. 152–54.

n *Ibid.,* p. 160.

o *Ibid.,* pp. 165 and 153.

p Bergson, *Introduction to Metaphysics,* pp. 40–43.

q Bergson, *Creative Evolution,* pp. 136 and 176.

r Henri Bergson, *The Two Sources of Morality and Religion,* translated by R. Ashley Audra and C. Brereton (Henry Holt, New York, 1935), pp. 15–18.

s *Ibid.,* pp. 112, 5, and 121.
t *Ibid.,* pp. 59–60.
u *Ibid.,* p. 76.
v *Ibid.,* pp. 264–65, 257, 285, and 214–15.
w *Ibid.,* pp. 285, 287, and 289.
x *Ibid.,* pp. 300–301.
y Bergson, *Creative Evolution,* pp. 101–2 and 84.
z John Dewey, *Human Nature and Conduct* (Henry Holt, New York, 1922), pp. 42 and 15.
a *Ibid.,* pp. 95 and 155–57.
b John Dewey, *How We Think* (Heath, Boston, 1933), pp. 100–107.
c Dewey, *Human Nature and Conduct,* pp. 98–99 and 101.
d John Dewey, "Democracy and Educational Administration," *School and Society* (April 3, 1937), reprinted in *Intelligence in the Modern World,* edited by J. Ratner (Modern Library, New York, 1939), pp. 400–404.
e John Dewey, *The Quest for Certainty* (Minton, Balch, New York, 1929), pp. 3–24.
f John Dewey, *Experience and Nature* (Open Court, Chicago, 1929), pp. iii and 4a–I.
g *Ibid.,* pp. v and iv.
h *Ibid.,* pp. 318–20.
i *Ibid.,* pp. 182–83.
j *Ibid.,* p. 11.
k Dewey, *Quest for Certainty,* pp. 150–59.
l Dewey, *Experience and Nature,* p. 185.
m *Ibid.,* pp. 179 and 184–85.
n *Ibid.,* p. 319.
o *Ibid.,* pp. 6–8.
p Ludwig Wittgenstein, *Tractatus Logico-Philosophicus,* translated by D. F. Pears and B. F. McGuinness (Routledge and Kegan Paul, London; Humanities Press, New York; 1961), p. 25, 3.25.
q John Dewey, *Essays in Experimental Logic* (Dover, New York, 1953), pp. 37–38.
r *Ibid.,* pp. 39, 41, and 43.
s Dewey, *Experience and Nature,* p. 308.
t Dewey, *Essays in Experimental Logic,* p. 6.
u Dewey, *Experience and Nature,* p. 24, n. 1.
v *Ibid.,* p. 3a.
w *Ibid.,* pp. 321–22.
x *Ibid.,* pp. 161, 156, and 158.
y *Ibid.,* pp. ii–iii.
z *Ibid.,* pp. 2, 96, and 21.
a *Ibid.,* pp. iv–v.
b *Ibid.,* p. 394.
c *Ibid.,* pp. 395–96 and 403–4.
d *Ibid.,* p. 425.
e Dewey, *Quest for Certainty,* pp. 258–61.
f Dewey, *Experience and Nature,* p. 437.
g Alfred North Whitehead, "Autobiographical Notes," in *The Philosophy of Alfred North Whitehead,* edited by P. A. Schilpp (Northwestern University Press, Evanston, Ill., 1941), p. 5.
h Alfred North Whitehead, *Essays in Science and Philosophy* (Philosophical Library, New York, 1947), p. 14.
i Alfred North Whitehead, *Process and Reality* (Macmillan, New York, 1929), p. 15.
j Alfred North Whitehead, *Modes of Thought* (Macmillan, New York, 1938), pp. 233–34 and 237–38.

k   Alfred North Whitehead, *Science and the Modern World* (Macmillan, New York, 1925), p. 27.

l   Whitehead, *Modes of Thought,* p. 58.

m   Whitehead, *Process and Reality,* p. 30.

n   Whitehead, *Science and the Modern World,* pp. 29–41.

o   Whitehead, *Process and Reality,* pp. 7–12.

p   *Ibid.,* pp. 4–8.

q   *Ibid.,* pp. 11–14.

r   *Ibid.,* p. x.

s   *Ibid.,* pp. 21–22 and 25–26.

t   Whitehead, *Science and the Modern World,* pp. 71–74.

u   *Ibid.,* p. 24.

v   Alfred North Whitehead, *An Enquiry Concerning the Principles of Natural Knowledge* (Cambridge University Press, Cambridge, 1919), pp. 1–3.

w   *Ibid.,* p. 16.

x   Whitehead, *Science and the Modern World,* pp. 5–6.

y   Whitehead, *Principles of Natural Knowledge,* pp. 10–11.

z   Whitehead, *Science and the Modern World,* p. 80.

a   *Ibid.,* p. 127.

b   *Ibid.,* pp. 113–15.

c   *Ibid.,* p. 226.

d   Whitehead, *Principles of Natural Knowledge,* p. 13.

e   Whitehead, *Science and the Modern World,* pp. 52–55.

f   *Ibid.,* pp. 158–59 and 183.

g   *Ibid.,* pp. 189–90, and 191.

h   *Ibid.,* p. 150.

i   Whitehead, *Process and Reality,* p. 70.

j   Whitehead, *Science and the Modern World,* pp. 158, 126, and 227–29.

k   *Ibid.,* pp. 136–67.

l   *Ibid.,* pp. 250–57.

m   *Ibid.,* p. 228.

n   Alfred North Whitehead, "Mathematics and the Good," in *The Philosophy of Alfred North Whitehead,* pp. 674 and 677–78.

o   Alfred North Whitehead, "Immortality," in *The Philosophy of Alfred North Whitehead,* pp. 684 and 683–84.

p   Whitehead, *Science and the Modern World,* p. 275.

q   *Ibid.,* pp. 249–50.

r   *Ibid.,* pp. 266 and 264.

Chapter 3   /   Moore and the Revival of Realism

a   Thomas Hobbes, *Leviathan,* in *The English Works of Thomas Hobbes,* edited by W. Molesworth (Bohn, London, 1839), Vol. III, Pt. I, Ch. 4.

b   John Locke, *An Essay Concerning Human Understanding,* edited by A. C. Fraser (Clarendon Press, Oxford, 1894), Epistle to the Reader.

c   George Berkeley, *Principles of Human Knowledge,* edited by A. C. Fraser (Clarendon Press, Oxford, 1901), Introduction, §24.

d   G. E. Moore, "A Reply to My Critics," in *The Philosophy of G. E. Moore,* edited by P. A. Schilpp (Tudor, New York, 1952), pp. 675–76.

e   G. E. Moore, quoted in Morton White, "Memories of G. E. Moore," in *Studies in the Philosophy of G. E. Moore,* edited by E. D. Klemke (Quadrangle Books, Chicago, 1969), p. 294.

f John Maynard Keynes, *Two Memoirs: Dr. Melchior: A Defeated Enemy and My Early Beliefs* (Kelley, New York; Rupert Hart-Davis, London; 1949), pp. 84–86 and 88.

g G. E. Moore, *Some Main Problems of Philosophy* (Allen & Unwin, London; Macmillan, New York; 1953), p. 291.

h *Ibid.*, pp. 300–301.

i G. E. Moore, *Principia Ethica* (Cambridge University Press, Cambridge, 1929), p. vii.

j G. E. Moore, "An Autobiography," in *Philosophy of G. E. Moore*, p. 14.

k Moore, *Principia Ethica*, p. 222.

l C. H. Langford, "The Notion of Analysis in Moore's Philosophy," in *Philosophy of G. E. Moore*, p. 323.

m Moore, "A Reply to My Critics," p. 661.

n Moore, *Some Main Problems*, pp. 56 and 58.

o *Ibid.*, pp. 60–61.

p Moore, "A Reply to My Critics," p. 664.

q Moore, *Some Main Problems*, pp. 216–20 and 222.

r Keynes, *Two Memoirs*, p. 94.

s *Ibid.*, p. 86.

t G. E. Moore, *Philosophical Studies* (Harcourt Brace Jovanovich, New York; Kegan Paul, London; 1922), pp. 3 and 5.

u *Ibid.*, pp. 5–8.

v *Ibid.*, pp. 8–9.

w *Ibid.*, p. 10.

x *Ibid.*, pp. 13–14.

y *Ibid.*, p. 16.

z *Ibid.*, pp. 17–19.

a *Ibid.*, pp. 20 and 25.

b *Ibid.*, pp. 20–21 and 23–27.

c G. E. Moore, "The Subject Matter of Psychology," in *Proceedings of the Aristotelian Society*, New Series, Vol. X, p. 36.

d Bertrand Russell, "My Mental Development," in *The Philosophy of Bertrand Russell*, edited by P. A. Schilpp (Library of Living Philosophers, Evanston, Ill., 1946), p. 12.

e Moore, *Philosophical Studies*, pp. 190–92.

f *Ibid.*, pp. 195 and 196.

g Moore, *Some Main Problems*, p. 262.

h *Ibid.*, p. 264.

i *Ibid.*, p. 265.

j *Ibid.*, pp. 267–68.

k *Ibid.*, pp. 263 and 289–91.

l Moore, *Principia Ethica*, pp. vii–viii.

m *Ibid.*, pp. 22–23.

n *Ibid.*, pp. 148–49.

o *Ibid.*, pp. 152 and 155–56.

p *Ibid.*, p. 157.

q *Ibid.*, pp. 6 and 8.

r *Ibid.*, pp. 40–41.

s Moore, "A Reply to My Critics," p. 582.

t *Ibid.*, p. 591.

u *Ibid.*, pp. 8–9.

v *Ibid.*, p. 10.

w *Ibid.*, p. 13.

x *Ibid.*, p. 14.

y *Ibid.*, p. 16.

z   Moore, *Some Main Problems,* pp. 132 and 134–35.
a   Moore, *Philosophical Studies,* pp. 209–10.
b   G. E. Moore, *Philosophical Papers* (Macmillan, London, 1959), pp. 32–34.
c   *Ibid.,* p. 34.
d   *Ibid.,* pp. 35–36.
e   *Ibid.,* p. 36.
f   *Ibid.*
g   *Ibid.,* pp. 36–37.
h   *Ibid.,* p. 53.
i   *Ibid.,* p. 44.
j   *Ibid.*
k   *Ibid.*

Chapter 4 / Frege and the Revolution in Logic

a   Bertrand Russell, *Our Knowledge of the External World as a Field for Scientific Method in Philosophy* (Open Court, Chicago and London, 1915), pp. 38–39.
b   Gottlob Frege, *The Foundations of Arithmetic,* translated by J. L. Austin (Northwestern University Press, Evanston, Ill., 1968), p. 115[e].
c   *Ibid.,* p. 108[e].
d   *Ibid.,* pp. i[e]–ii[e] and iv[e]–v[e].
e   *Ibid.,* pp. v[e]–vii[e].
f   *Ibid.,* pp. iv[e].
g   *Ibid.,* pp. 32[e]–33[e].
h   *Ibid.,* p. viii[e].
i   Gottlob Frege, *Translations from the Philosophical Writings of Gottlob Frege,* edited by P. Geach and M. Black (Philosophical Library, New York, 1952), pp. 22–23.
j   Frege, *Foundations of Arithmetic,* p. 115[e].
k   *Ibid.,* p. 114[e].
l   Frege, *Translations from the Philosophical Writings,* pp. 2–3.
m *Ibid.,* pp. 23–25.
n   *Ibid.,* p. 25.
o   *Ibid.,* p. 22.
p   *Ibid.,* p. 25.
q   *Ibid.,* pp. 28–30.
r   *Ibid.,* pp. 31–32.
s   *Ibid.,* pp. 56–57.
t   *Ibid.,* p. 60.
u   *Ibid.,* pp. 62–63.
v   *Ibid.,* pp. 63 and 65.

Chapter 5 / Russell

a   Bertrand Russell, *My Philosophical Development, with an Appendix: Russell's Philosophy,* edited by A. Wood (Simon and Schuster, New York, 1959), p. 54.
b   Russell, "My Mental Development," pp. 11–12.
c   Bertrand Russell, "Logical Atomism," in *Contemporary British Philosophy,* edited by J. H. Muirhead (Macmillan, New York, 1924), p. 359.
d   Russell, "My Mental Development," p. 7.

e Russell, *My Philosophical Development,* p. 11.
f Bertrand Russell, *Portraits from Memory and Other Essays* (Simon and Schuster, New York, 1956), p. 54.
g *Ibid.*
h *Ibid.*
i *Ibid.,* p. 48.
j *Ibid.,* pp. 48–49.
k Russell, *My Philosophical Development,* pp. 63–64.
l *Ibid.,* pp. 12–13.
m *Ibid.,* p. 16.
n Russell, *Our Knowledge of the External World,* p. 33.
o *Ibid.,* pp. 57–58.
p *Ibid.,* p. 59.
q Bertrand Russell, *Introduction to Mathematical Philosophy* (Macmillan, New York, 1930), p. 4.
r *Ibid.,* p. 5.
s *Ibid.,* pp. 11 and 14–18.
t Bertrand Russell, "Mathematical Logic as Based on the Theory of Types," in *Logic and Knowledge: Essays, 1901–1950,* edited by C. Marsh (Allen & Unwin, London, 1956), pp. 59, 61–63, and 101.
u *Ibid.,* p. 102.
v Russell, "Logical Atomism," p. 371.
w Bertrand Russell, "On Denoting," in *Logic and Knowledge: Essays, 1901–1950,* pp. 41–42.
x *Ibid.,* p. 45.
y *Ibid.,* p. 43.
z *Ibid.,* p. 45.
a Russell, "My Mental Development," p. 13.
b Russell, "On Denoting," pp. 45–46.
c *Ibid.,* pp. 42–43.
d *Ibid.,* p. 51.
e *Ibid.,* pp. 52–53.
f *Ibid.,* p. 55.
g Russell, "Logical Atomism," p. 365.
h *Ibid.,* pp. 379–80.
i Bertrand Russell, *Mysticism and Logic* (Doubleday, New York, 1957), p. 94; Bertrand Russell, *Philosophy* (Norton, New York, 1927), p. 2.
j Russell, *Our Knowledge of the External World,* p. 49.
k *Ibid.,* p. 39, n. 1.
l *Ibid.,* p. 5.
m Bertrand Russell, "Philosophy in the Twentieth Century," in *Sceptical Essays* (Allen & Unwin, London, 1935), pp. 61–63.
n *Ibid.,* pp. 65–68.
o Russell, "Logical Atomism," p. 379.
p Russell, *Our Knowledge of the External World,* p. 4.
q Russell, "On Denoting," pp. 55–56.
r Bertrand Russell, *An Inquiry into Meaning and Truth* (Norton, New York, 1940), p. 23.
s Bertrand Russell, "On the Relations of Universals and Particulars," in *Logic and Knowledge: Essays, 1901–1950,* pp. 111–12.
t Russell, *Mysticism and Logic,* pp. 124–25.
u *Ibid.,* pp. 132–34.

v *Ibid.*, pp. 135–36.

w *Ibid.*, p. 124.

x *Ibid.*, p. 125.

y *Ibid.*, p. 134.

z Bertrand Russell, "The Philosophy of Logical Atomism," in *Logic and Knowledge: Essays, 1901–1950,* p. 274.

a Russell, *Mysticism and Logic,* pp. 138–39.

b Bertrand Russell, *The Analysis of Mind* (Allen & Unwin, London; Macmillan, New York; 1921), pp. 141–42.

c Russell, "Philosophy of Logical Atomism," pp. 277–79.

d Russell, *Inquiry into Meaning and Truth,* pp. 117 and 120–22.

e Russell, *My Philosophical Development,* pp. 16, 20, 22–23, and 25–27.

f Russell, *Our Knowledge of the External World,* p. 73.

g Russell, *My Philosophical Development,* p. 191.

h *Ibid.*, p. 207.

i *Ibid.*, p. 193.

j *Ibid.*, p. 190.

k *Ibid.*, p. 194.

l *Ibid.*, p. 205.

m Bertrand Russell, *Human Knowledge, Its Scope and Limits* (Simon and Schuster, New York, 1948), pp. 487–88.

n *Ibid.*, p. 489.

o *Ibid.*, pp. 490–91.

p *Ibid.*, pp. 491–92.

q *Ibid.*, p. 493.

r Russell, *My Philosophical Development,* p. 205.

s *Ibid.*, p. 204.

t Russell, *Human Knowledge,* pp. 495–96.

u *Ibid.*, p. 505.

v *Ibid.*, p. 507.

w Russell, *Inquiry into Meaning and Truth,* p. 15.

x Russell, "My Mental Development," and Bertrand Russell, "Reply to Critics," in *Philosophy of Bertrand Russell,* pp. 700, 716, and 719.

y Russell, *Philosophy,* p. 225.

z Bertrand Russell, *Religion and Science* (Thornton Butterworth, London, 1935), p. 175.

a *Ibid.*, pp. 230–31, 235–36, and 239–40.

b Bertrand Russell, *What I Believe* (Dutton, New York, 1925), pp. 1 and 16–17.

c Bertrand Russell, "Styles in Ethics," in *Our Changing Morality: A Symposium,* edited by Freda Kirchwey (Boni, New York, 1924), pp. 5–6 and 15–16.

d Russell, *Religion and Science,* pp. 233–35.

e Russell, *What I Believe,* pp. 20–21 and 24.

f Bertrand Russell, *Marriage and Morals* (Liveright, New York, 1929), pp. 291 and 293–94.

g Bertrand Russell, *Principles of Social Reconstruction* (Allen & Unwin, London, 1916), pp. 146, 163–65, and 167.

h *Ibid.*, pp. 119–22 and 134–35.

i Bertrand Russell, *The Impact of Science on Society* (Columbia University Press, New York, 1951), p. 59.

j Russell, *Religion and Science,* pp. 8, 144, and 7.

k Russell, *Impact of Science on Society,* p. 45.

l Bertrand Russell, "A Free Man's Worship," in *Mysticism and Logic,* p. 54.

m Russell, "My Mental Development," pp. 19–20.

Chapter 6 / *The* Tractatus

a Wittgenstein, *Tractatus Logico-Philosophicus*, p. 3.
b *Ibid.*, pp. 7, 11, and 13.
c *Ibid.*, pp. 25 and 59.
d *Ibid.*, p. 61.
e G. H. von Wright, "Biographical Sketch," in *Ludwig Wittgenstein: A Memoir*, by N. Malcolm (Oxford University Press, London, 1958), pp. 7–8.
f Wittgenstein, *Tractatus Logico-Philosophicus*, p. 16, 2.1 and 2.16.
g *Ibid.*, p. 17, 2.17.
h *Ibid.*, 2.21.
i *Ibid.*, pp. 15 and 17.
j *Ibid.*, p. 17.
k *Ibid.*, pp. 37 and 39.
l *Ibid.*, p. 73.
m *Ibid.*, p. 43.
n *Ibid.*, pp. 67–69.
o *Ibid.*, pp. 121 and 129.
p *Ibid.*, pp. 129 and 131.
q *Ibid.*, pp. 133, 6.2.
r *Ibid.*, pp. 133 and 135.
s *Ibid.*, p. 137, 6.3.
t *Ibid.*, p. 13, 2.062.
u *Ibid.*, pp. 19, 77, 79, and 143.
v *Ibid.*, p. 143.
w *Ibid.*, pp. 137, 139, and 141.
x *Ibid.*, p. 143.
y *Ibid.*, p. 19, 2.225.
z *Ibid.*, pp. 49 and 37.
a *Ibid.*, p. 51, 4.1212.
b *Ibid.*, p. 23, 3.221.
c *Ibid.*, p. 41, 4.022.
d *Ibid.*, pp. 51 and 17.
e *Ibid.*, "Introduction," p. xxii.
f *Ibid.*, p. 115, 5.6.
g *Ibid.*, p. 49.
h *Ibid.*, p. 151.
i *Ibid.*, 6.5222.
j *Ibid.*, pp. 145, 147, and 149.
k *Ibid.*, pp. 149 and 151.

Chapter 7 / *Logical Positivism*

a Moritz Schlick, "Positivism and Realism," translated by D. Rynin, in *Logical Positivism*, edited by A. J. Ayer (Free Press, New York, 1959), p. 86.
b *Ibid.*, pp. 86–88 and 106–7.
c Rudolf Carnap, *The Logical Syntax of Language* (Kegan Paul, Trench, Trubner, London, 1937), p. 320.
d Rudolf Carnap, *The Logical Structure of the World: Pseudoproblems in Philosophy*, translated by R. A. George (University of California Press, Berkeley and Los Angeles, 1967), pp. xvi–xvii.

e Rudolf Carnap, "Intellectual Autobiography," in *The Philosophy of Rudolf Carnap,* edited by P. Schilpp (Library of Living Philosophers, La Salle, Ill., 1965), pp. 25–28.
f Wittgenstein, *Tractatus Logico-Philosophicus,* p. x.
g *Ibid.,* pp. 25 and 23, 3.263 and 3.144.
h Schlick, "Positivism and Realism," p. 84.
i *Ibid.,* p. 93.
j *Ibid.,* pp. 93–94.
k Otto Neurath, "Protocol Sentences," translated by G. Schlick, in *Logical Positivism,* p. 202.
l *Ibid.,* p. 199.
m *Ibid.,* p. 202.
n *Ibid.,* pp. 199–200.
o *Ibid.,* p. 201.
p *Ibid.,* p. 203.
q Moritz Schlick, "The Foundation of Knowledge," translated by D. Rynin, in *Logical Positivism,* pp. 209–10, 213–14, and 216.
r *Ibid.,* p. 226.
s *Ibid.,* p. 225.
t *Ibid.,* p. 226.
u Rudolf Carnap, "Logical Foundations of the Unity of Science," in *International Encyclopedia of Unified Science,* edited by O. Neurath, R. Carnap, and C. Morris (University of Chicago Press, Chicago, 1955), pp. 49–52.
v *Ibid.,* pp. 56–57.
w *Ibid.,* p. 58.
x Carnap, *Logical Syntax of Language,* p. 321.
y *Ibid.,* pp. 51–52.
z *Ibid.,* p. 322.
a *Ibid.,* pp. 284–86.
b *Ibid.,* pp. 289–90.
c *Ibid.,* pp. 297–98.
d Rudolf Carnap, "Empiricism, Semantics, and Ontology," in *Meaning and Necessity: A Study in Semantics and Modal Logic* (University of Chicago Press, Chicago, 1956), p. 206.
e *Ibid.,* pp. 207–8.
f *Ibid.,* pp. 220–21.
g Carnap, *Logical Syntax of Language,* p. xv.
h A. J. Ayer, *Language, Truth, and Logic* (Dover, New York, n.d.), pp. 107–8.
i *Ibid.,* pp. 110–11.
j *Ibid.,* pp. 115–16.
k Rudolf Carnap, "The Elimination of Metaphysics," in *Logical Positivism,* pp. 78–80.
l Rudolf Carnap, *Testability and Meaning* (Graduate Philosophy Club, Yale University, New Haven, 1950), pp. 420–22 and 425.
m A. J. Ayer, "Editor's Introduction," in Carnap, *Logical Positivism,* pp. 15–16.

Chapter 8 / Husserl and the Phenomenological Tradition

a William Wordsworth, *The Prelude,* Bk. II, ll. 394–6.
b *Ibid.,* ll. 401–9.
c Quoted in H. Speigelberg, *The Phenomenological Movement* (Martinus Nijhoff, The Hague, 1965), p. 82.
d Edmund Husserl, *Ideas: General Introduction to Pure Phenomenology,* translated by

W. R. Boyce Gibson (Macmillan, New York, 1931), §19.

e   Edmund Husserl, *Cartesian Meditations,* translated by D. Cairns (Martinus Nijhoff, The Hague, 1960), §§9–10.

f   Edmund Husserl, "Philosophy as Rigorous Science," translated by Q. Lauer, in *Phenomenology and the Crisis of Philosophy* (Harper & Row, New York, 1965), pp. 81 and 77.

g   *Ibid.,* pp. 124–28.

h   Edmund Husserl, "Philosophy and the Crisis of European Man," translated by Q. Lauer, in *Phenomenology and the Crisis of Philosophy,* pp. 171 and 173.

i   *Ibid.,* p. 177.

j   *Ibid.,* p. 179.

k   *Ibid.,* p. 184.

l   *Ibid.,* pp. 184–86.

m   *Ibid.,* pp. 186–88.

n   Husserl, *Ideas,* §§27 and 30.

o   *Ibid.,* §§31–32.

p   *Ibid.,* §33.

q   *Ibid.,* §88.

r   *Ibid.,* §33.

s   Husserl, *Cartesian Meditations,* §§1–3 and 8.

t   *Ibid.,* §15.

u   *Ibid.,* §14.

v   *Ibid.,* §19.

w   *Ibid.,* §§5 and 24.

x   *Ibid.,* §§17–19.

y   *Ibid.,* §41.

z   R. B. MacLeod, "Phenomenology: A Challenge to Experimental Psychology," in *Behaviourism and Phenomenology,* edited by T. W. Wann (University of Chicago Press, Chicago, 1964), pp. 59–60.

Chapter 9   /   Heidegger

a   Martin Heidegger, "My Way to Phenomenology," in *On Time and Being,* translated by J. Stambaugh (Harper & Row, New York, 1972), p. 75.

b   *Ibid.,* p. 78.

c   *Ibid.,* p. 74.

d   Martin Heidegger, *Being and Time,* translated by J. Macquarrie and E. Robinson (Harper & Row, New York, 1962), pp. 59–62.

e   *Ibid.,* p. 19.

f   *Ibid.*

g   Martin Heidegger, *Existence and Being,* with an introduction by W. Brock (Vision, London, 1949), p. 380.

h   Heidegger, *Being and Time,* p. 17.

i   Martin Heidegger, "The Way Back into the Ground of Metaphysics," in *Existentialism from Dostoevsky to Sartre,* translated and edited b W. Kaufmann (Meridian Books, New York, 1957), pp. 208–12 and 220–21.

j   William Wordsworth, "Lines Composed a Few Miles above Tintern Abbey," ll. 94–99.

k   H. Speigelberg, *The Phenomenological Movement* (M. Nijhoff, The Hague, 1965), Vol. I, p. 292.

l   Heidegger, *Being and Time,* pp. 227 and 32–34.

m   *Ibid.,* p. 78.

n *Ibid.,* pp. 79–81.

o *Ibid.,* pp. 95 and 97–100.

p *Ibid.,* pp. 83–84.

q *Ibid.,* pp. 236–37.

r *Ibid.,* pp. 173–74.

s *Ibid.,* p. 86.

t *Ibid.,* pp. 98–99.

u *Ibid.,* pp. 128 and 129.

v *Ibid.,* pp. 87–89.

w *Ibid.,* pp. 184–85 and 189–90.

x *Ibid.,* p. 191.

y *Ibid.,* p. 235.

z *Ibid.,* pp. 82, 173–74, 271, and 321.

a *Ibid.,* pp. 228 and 231–32.

b *Ibid.,* p. 234.

c *Ibid.,* pp. 153–54 and 162.

d *Ibid.,* pp. 163–65.

e *Ibid.,* pp. 212–13.

f *Ibid.,* pp. 219–20 and 222.

g *Ibid.,* pp. 276–77.

h *Ibid.,* pp. 293–95.

i *Ibid.,* pp. 313–14 and 318–19.

j *Ibid.,* p. 91.

k *Ibid.,* p. 76.

l *Ibid.,* pp. 243–44.

m *Ibid.,* p. 323.

n *Ibid.,* p. 488.

o Martin Heidegger, "Time and Being," in *On Time and Being,* pp. 2–3.

p *Ibid.,* pp. 3–4.

q *Ibid.,* pp. 5–6.

r Heidegger, *Existence and Being,* pp. 328–29.

s Heidegger, "Time and Being," p. 7.

t *Ibid.,* pp. 13–14.

u *Ibid.,* pp. 24 and 2.

v Heidegger, *Existence and Being,* p. 299.

w *Ibid.,* p. 301.

x *Ibid.,* p. 303.

y *Ibid.,* p. 304.

z *Ibid.,* p. 305.

a *Ibid.,* p. 306.

b *Ibid.,* p. 314.

c Martin Heidegger, *On the Way to Language,* translated by P. D. Hertz (Harper & Row, New York, 1971), p. 199.

d *Ibid.,* p. 3.

e *Ibid.,* p. 4.

f *Ibid.,* p. 5.

g *Ibid.,* p. 26.

h *Ibid.,* p. 8.

i *Ibid.,* p. 22.

j *Ibid.,* p. 50.

k *Ibid.,* p. 26.

l *Ibid.,* pp. 50–53.

m Heidegger, "My Way to Phenomenology," p. 79.

Chapter 10 / Sartre

a   Jean-Paul Sartre, *Nausea,* translated by L. Alexander (New Directions, New York, 1959), pp. 16–17.
b   *Ibid.,* pp. 168–69.
c   *Ibid.,* pp. 22–23.
d   *Ibid.,* p. 130.
e   *Ibid.,* p. 227.
f   *Ibid.,* pp. 171–74.
g   David Hume, *A Treatise of Human Nature,* edited by L. A. Selby-Bigge (Clarendon Press, Oxford, 1896), Bk. I, Pt. IV, §VII.
h   Sartre, *Nausea,* p. 150.
i   *Ibid.,* p. 94.
j   *Ibid.,* pp. 116–17.
k   *Ibid.,* p. 166.
l   Sartre, *Reprieve,* pp. 280–87.
m   Jean-Paul Sartre, *Troubled Sleep,* translated by G. Hopkins (Bantam Books, New York, 1961), p. 200.
n   Jean-Paul Sartre, *The Transcendence of the Ego,* translated by F. Williams and R. Kirkpatrick (Farrar, Straus & Giroux, New York, 1957), p. 40.
o   *Ibid.,* pp. 43–44.
p   *Ibid.,* pp. 40–41.
q   *Ibid.,* pp. 44–45.
r   *Ibid.,* pp. 63–64.
s   *Ibid.,* p. 74.
t   *Ibid.,* pp. 94–96.
u   *Ibid.,* pp. 75–76.
v   *Ibid.,* pp. 86–87.
w   *Ibid.,* pp. 77–79.
x   *Ibid.,* p. 81.
y   *Ibid.,* p. 100.
z   *Ibid.,* pp. 99–100.
a   Jean-Paul Sartre, *Being and Nothingness,* translated by H. E. Barnes (Philosophical Library, New York, 1956), p. lxvi.
b   *Ibid.,* p. lxvii.
c   *Ibid.,* p. lxii.
d   *Ibid.,* p. lxvi.
e   *Ibid.*
f   *Ibid.,* p. 617.
g   *Ibid.,* p. lxiii.
h   *Ibid.,* p. 302.
i   *Ibid.,* p. 615.
j   *Ibid.,* pp. 476–79.
k   *Ibid.,* pp. 479–80.
l   *Ibid.,* p. 554.
m   Jean-Paul Sartre, *Existentialism,* translated by B. Frechtman (Philosophical Library, New York, 1947), pp. 20–21.
n   *Ibid.,* pp. 52–53.
o   Sartre, *Reprieve,* p. 101.
p   Sartre, *Nausea,* p. 234.
q   Jean-Paul Sartre, "Search for a Method," in *Critique of Dialectical Reason,* translated and with an introduction by H. E. Barnes (Vintage Books, New York, 1968), pp. 3–4 and 5–6.

r   *Ibid.*, p. 7.
s   *Ibid.*, p. 34.
t   Sartre, *Nausea*, p. 170.

Chapter 11   /   The Later Wittgenstein

a   Wittgenstein, *Tractatus Logico-Philosophicus*, 6.54.
b   Ludwig Wittgenstein, *Philosophical Investigations*, translated by G. E. M. Anscombe (Macmillan, New York, 1953), p. ix.
c   *Ibid.*, §§38 and 127.
d   *Ibid.*, §1.
e   *Ibid.*, §3.
f   *Ibid.*, §5.
g   *Ibid.*, §1.
h   *Ibid.*, §§2 and 6.
i   *Ibid.*, §§11–19, 23, 26–27, and 49.
j   St. Anselm, *Monologium*, translated by S. N. Deane (Open Court, Chicago, 1930), pp. 37–40.
k   Wittgenstein, *Philosophical Investigations*, §§65–67, 71, and 116.
l   *Ibid.*, §§68–69, 75–76, and 78–79.
m   *Ibid.*, §84.
n   *Ibid.*, §§87–88.
o   *Ibid.*, §47.
p   *Ibid.*, §§60 and 63.
q   *Ibid.*, §81.
r   *Ibid.*, §89.
s   *Ibid.*, §§89–91 and 97.
t   *Ibid.*, §101.
u   *Ibid.*, §§107–8.
v   *Ibid.*, §109.
w   *Ibid.*, §36.
x   *Ibid.*, §436.
y   *Ibid.*, §580.
z   *Ibid.*, §§305–8 and 154.
a   *Ibid.*, §383.
b   *Ibid.*, §607.
c   *Ibid.*, §§583–84.
d   *Ibid.*, §586.
e   *Ibid.*, §344.
f   *Ibid.*, §§627–28.
g   *Ibid.*, §246.
h   *Ibid.*, §293.
i   *Ibid.*, §268.
j   *Ibid.*, §115.
k   *Ibid.*, §114.
l   *Ibid.*, §103.
m   *Ibid.*, §111.
n   *Ibid.*, §19.
o   *Ibid.*, §309.
p   *Ibid.*, §241.
q   *Ibid.*, §226.

r   *Ibid.,* §116.
s   *Ibid.,* §118.

Chapter 12   /   Ordinary-Language Philosophy

a   Wittgenstein, *Tractatus Logico-Philosophicus,* 4.002.
b   Russell, *Introduction to Mathematical Philosophy,* p. 172.
c   J. L. Austin, *Philosophical Papers,* edited by J. O. Urmson and G. J. Warnock, 3d ed. (Oxford University Press, Oxford, 1979), p. 182.
d   *Ibid.,* p. 181.
e   *Ibid.,* pp. 233–34.
f   Wittgenstein, *Philosophical Investigations,* §109.
g   J. L. Austin, *Sense and Sensibilia,* edited by G. J. Warnock (Clarendon Press, Oxford, 1962), pp. 4–5.
h   Wittgenstein, *Philosophical Investigations,* §23.
i   Austin, *Philosophical Papers,* p. 234.
j   P. F. Strawson, *Logico-Linguistic Papers* (Methuen, London, 1971), pp. 6–8.
k   *Ibid.,* p. 9.
l   *Ibid.,* p. 12.
m   *Ibid.*
n   Bertrand Russell, "Mr. Strawson on Referring," *Mind* 66, no. 263 (1957): 387.
o   Austin, *Philosophical Papers,* p. 77.
p   *Ibid.,* p. 79.
q   *Ibid.,* p. 84.
r   *Ibid.,* p. 85.
s   *Ibid.,* p. 99.
t   *Ibid.*
u   *Ibid.,* p. 103.
v   *Ibid.,* p. 105.
w   *Ibid.,* p. 106.
x   *Ibid.,* p. 107.
y   *Ibid.,* pp. 108–9.
z   *Ibid.,* p. 112–13.
a   *Ibid.,* p. 116.
b   Austin, *Sense and Sensibilia,* p. 2.
c   *Ibid.,* p. 44.
d   *Ibid.,* p. 3.
e   *Ibid.,* p. 8.
f   *Ibid.*
g   *Ibid.*
h   *Ibid.,* p. 10.
i   *Ibid.,* p. 15.
j   *Ibid.*
k   *Ibid.*
l   *Ibid.,* p. 18.
m   *Ibid.,* p. 19.
n   *Ibid.,* p. 21.
o   *Ibid.,* p. 23.
p   *Ibid.,* p. 25.
q   *Ibid.,* p. 29.
r   *Ibid.,* p. 48.

s *Ibid.,* pp. 48–49.
t *Ibid.,* pp. 49–50.
u *Ibid.,* p. 52.
v Cited by Austin in *ibid.,* p. 85.
w Cited by Austin in *ibid.*
x *Ibid.,* pp. 90–91.
y *Ibid.,* pp. 117–18.
z *Ibid.,* p. 115.
a *Ibid.,* pp. 141–42.
b Austin, *Philosophical Papers,* p. 232.
c *Ibid.,* pp. 233–34.
d J. L. Austin, *How to Do Things with Words,* edited by J. O. Urmson and Marina Sbisa, 2d ed. (Harvard University Press, Cambridge, 1975), p. 3.
e Austin, *Philosophical Papers,* p. 234.
f Austin, *How to Do Things with Words,* p. 5.
g *Ibid.*
h *Ibid.,* p. 14.
i *Ibid.,* pp. 14–15.
j *Ibid.,* p. 27.
k *Ibid.,* p. 23.
l *Ibid.,* p. 56.
m *Ibid.,* p. 57.
n See *ibid.,* p. 58.
o See Austin, *Philosophical Papers,* p. 243.
p *Ibid.,* p. 247.
q *Ibid.,* p. 248.
r *Ibid.,* p. 247.
s *Ibid.,* p. 251.
t Austin, *How to Do Things with Words,* p. 91.
u *Ibid.,* pp. 98–99.
v *Ibid.,* pp. 99–100.
w *Ibid.,* p. 101.
x *Ibid.,* pp. 101–2.
y *Ibid.,* pp. 149–50.
z *Ibid.,* p. 150.
a *Ibid.,* pp. 157–58.
b Paul Grice, *Studies in the Way of Words* (Harvard University Press, Cambridge, 1989), p. 225.
c *Ibid.,* p. 87.
d *Ibid.,* p. 227.
e *Ibid.,* p. 228.
f *Ibid.,* p. 26.
g *Ibid.,* pp. 26–27.
h *Ibid.,* pp. 30–31.
i *Ibid.,* pp. 32–33.
j *Ibid.,* pp. 33–35.
k *Ibid.,* p. 44.
l *Ibid.,* p. 234.
m *Ibid.,* p. 58.
n *Ibid.,* pp. 61–62.
o *Ibid.,* p. 62.
p *Ibid.,* pp. 77–78.
q *Ibid.,* p. 59.

Chapter 13 / Quine

a   Both essays are reprinted in Willard Van Orman Quine, *From a Logical Point of View* (Harvard University Press, Cambridge, 1953).
b   *Ibid.,* p. 1.
c   *Ibid.,* p. 13.
d   *Ibid.*
e   *Ibid.*
f   *Ibid.,* p. 15.
g   *Ibid.,* pp. 15–16.
h   *Ibid.,* p. 19.
i   *Ibid.,* p. 20.
j   *Ibid.*
k   *Ibid.,* p. 21.
l   *Ibid.*
m   *Ibid.,* p. 22, emphasis added.
n   *Ibid.,* pp. 22–23.
o   *Ibid.,* p. 24, emphasis added.
p   *Ibid.,* p. 27.
q   *Ibid.,* p. 37.
r   *Ibid.,* pp. 29–30.
s   *Ibid.,* p. 20.
t   *Ibid.,* p. 41.
u   Wittgenstein, *Tractatus Logico-Philosophicus,* 6.341.
v   Quine, *From a Logical Point of View,* p. 37.
w   *Ibid.*
x   *Ibid.,* p. 38.
y   *Ibid.*
z   *Ibid.,* pp. 40–41.
a   *Ibid.,* p. 41.
b   *Ibid.,* p. 42.
c   *Ibid.,* pp. 42–43.
d   *Ibid.,* p. 42.
e   *Ibid.,* p. 43.
f   *Ibid.,* p. 44.
g   *Ibid.,* p. 43.
h   *Ibid.,* p. 44.
i   Quoted in Lewis Edward Hahn and Paul Arthur Schilpp, eds., *The Philosophy of W. V. Quine* (Open Court, La Salle, Ill., 1986), p. 473.
j   Willard Van Orman Quine, *Pursuit of Truth,* rev. ed. (Harvard University Press, Cambridge, 1992), p. 1.
k   *Ibid.,* pp. 2–3.
l   *Ibid.,* p. 5.
m   *Ibid.,* p. 4.
n   *Ibid.*
o   *Ibid.,* p. 72.
p   *Ibid.,* pp. 67–68.
q   Willard Van Orman Quine, *Word and Object* (MIT Press, Cambridge, 1960), pp. 221.
r   Quine, *Pursuit of Truth,* p. 38.
s   Quine, *Word and Object,* p. 29.
t   *Ibid.,* p. 68.
u   *Ibid.,* pp. 51–52.
v   Quine, *Pursuit of Truth,* p. 31.

w *Ibid.*, pp. 33–34.
x *Ibid.*, p. 24.
y *Ibid.*, p. 25.
z *Ibid.*, p. 36.
a *Ibid.*, p. 34.
b *Ibid.*, p. 50.
c *Ibid.*
d *Ibid.*, p. 101.
e *Ibid.*, p. 102.

Chapter 14 / Derrida

a With only minor changes, this chapter is a reprint of W. T. Jones, "Deconstructing Derrida: Below the Surface of *Differance*," *Metaphilosophy* 23, no. 3 (1992): 230–50.
b Jacques Derrida, *"Differance,"* in *Margins of Philosophy,* translated by Alan Bass (University of Chicago Press, Chicago, 1982), pp. 3–4.
c *Ibid.*, p. 25.
d *Ibid.*, p. 11.
e *Ibid.*
f Jacques Derrida, *The Truth in Painting,* translated by Geoff Bennington and Ian McLeod (University of Chicago Press, Chicago, 1987), pp. 1–2.
g J. Hillis Miller, "Stevens' Rock and Criticism as Cure, II," *Georgia Review* 30 (Summer 1976), p. 337.
h Jacques Derrida, "The Ends of Man," in *Margins of Philosophy,* pp. 135–36.
i David Hume, *An Enquiry Concerning Human Understanding,* sec. xii, part iii.
j Jacques Derrida, "Signature Event Context," *Glyph I;* John Searle, "Reiterating the Difference: A Reply to Derrida," *Glyph I;* Jacques Derrida, "Limited Inc.," *Glyph II.*
k Derrida, *"Differance,"* p. 22.
l Jacques Derrida, "Signature, Sign, and Play," in *The Structural Controversy,* edited by R. Macksey and E. Donato (Johns Hopkins University Press, Baltimore, 1972).
m *Ibid.*, p. 264.
n *Ibid.*, p. 263.
o *Ibid.*, p. 265.
p *Ibid.*, p. 264.
q Derrida, *"Differance,"* p. 12.
r *Ibid.*, pp. 24–25.
s *Ibid.*, p. 27.
t Martin Heidegger, "Language," in *Poetry, Language, Thought,* translated by A. Hofstadter (Harper & Row, New York, 1971), pp. 191–92.
u Derrida, *Truth in Painting,* p. 37.
v Derrida, *"Differance,"* p. 21.

Suggestions for Further Reading

The best course to pursue is to turn directly to the various great texts from which the selections in this volume have been drawn. Thus, instead of being content with the extracts given here, read more deeply in Moore's and Russell's writings, in Sartre's *Being and Nothingness,* and in Wittgenstein's *Philosophical Investigations.* Information concerning translations and editions will be found in the bibliographical notes. We have, for the most part, chosen books that present interpretations different from our own.

Beyond the masters themselves, here is a short list of books about them and their times that should help make their theories more intelligible.

BERGSON

H. W. Carr: *The Philosophy of Change* (London, 1914). The author had the "advantage of friendship and personal communication with M. Bergson himself."

J. Chevalier: *Henri Bergson,* translated by L. A. Clare (New York, 1928). Contains an account of the intellectual milieu in France in the second half of the nineteenth century, during which time Bergson's opinions were formed.

A. D. Lindsay: *The Philosophy of Bergson* (London, n.d.). Concentrates on Bergson's "critical rather than his constructive and positive work."

DEWEY

S. Hook (ed.): *John Dewey: Philosopher of Science and Freedom* (New York, 1950). Essays on various aspects of Dewey's thought and on his influence.

E. C. Moore: *American Pragmatism* (New York, 1961). A study of Peirce and James as well as of Dewey.

C. Morris: *The Pragmatic Movement in American Philosophy* (New York, 1970). "A work within American pragmatic philosophy, and not a book about it."

P. A. Schilpp (ed.): *The Philosophy of John Dewey* (New York, 1951). Contains a biography, a bibliography, critical essays by various writers on Dewey's logic, epistemology, psychology, and other topics, and Dewey's replies to these critics.

WHITEHEAD

W. A. Christian: *An Interpretation of Whitehead's Metaphysics* (New Haven, 1959). Attempts to meet "the need for something more advanced than the introductions and more comprehensive than the special studies" already available.

V. Lowe: *Understanding Whitehead* (Baltimore, 1962). "Meant to help people understand Whitehead's philosophy, no prior acquaintance with which is assumed."

I. LeClerc: *Whitehead's Metaphysics* (New York, 1958). Argues that "in developing the system which he elaborated in such detail in *Process and Reality"* Whitehead became involved in problems that were "specifically metaphysical, and not those which characterized his earlier investigations in the philosophy of natural science."

P. A. Schilpp (ed.): *The Philosophy of Alfred North Whitehead* (Evanston, Ill., 1941). Critical essays by a number of Whitehead's contemporaries, including Dewey; an autobiographical sketch; a bibliography.

THE ANALYTIC TRADITION

A. J. Ayer et al., with an introduction by G. Ryle: *The Revolution in Philosophy* (London, 1956). Short, popular lectures on Frege, Moore, Russell, Wittgenstein, and the Logical Positivists.

C. A. Mace (ed.): *British Philosophy in the Mid-Century* (London, 1957). The papers by Moore and Ayer and the long essay on C. D. Broad ("The Local Historical Background of Contemporary Cambridge Philosophy") are especially relevant to the topics discussed in this volume.

J. Passmore: *A Hundred Years of Philosophy* (London, 1957). Begins with Mill and ends with a "postscript" on existentialism; especially good on logic and epistemology in Britain, the topics on which it concentrates.

J. O. Urmson: *Philosophical Analysis* (Oxford, 1956). A survey of British philosophy between the world wars, beginning with logical atomism, passing on to Logical Positivism, and ending with the first signs of linguistic analysis.

G. J. Warnock: *English Philosophy since 1900* (Oxford, 1958). Aims at making "as clear as possible the general character of the philosophical landscape" and therefore concentrates on a few representative and influential figures—Moore, Russell, Wittgenstein, and the positivists.

MOORE

A. Ambrose and M. Lazerowitz (eds.): *G. E. Moore: Essays in Retrospect* (London, 1970). Nineteen essays, all written since 1958, that "examine various views to which Moore gave his attention and assess his claims and the central method he used to discover evidence for them."

A. J. Ayer: *Russell and Moore: The Analytical Heritage* (Cambridge, Mass., 1971). The author has developed his own "solutions to some of the problems which Russell and Moore raise."

E. D. Klemke (ed.): *Studies in the Philosophy of G. E. Moore* (Chicago, 1969). Essays on Moore's ethics, his ontology, and his methodology and epistemology, with an introduction by the editor on Moore's refutation of idealism, and with reminiscences of Moore by Morton White.

P. A. Schilpp (ed.): *The Philosophy of G. E. Moore* (New York, 1952). Critical essays by a number of Moore's contemporaries, a reply by Moore, and an autobiography.

A. R. White: *G. E. Moore: A Critical Exposition* (New York, 1969). In addition to chapters on the main features of Moore's theory there is a useful discussion of "the historical setting," including a brief "sketch of twentieth-century logical analysis."

FREGE

M. Dummett: *Frege: Philosophy of Language* (New York, 1973). An important but very difficult and detailed study, which "attempts not only an exposition, but also an evaluation."

R. Grossmann: *Reflections on Frege's Philosophy* (Evanston, Ill., 1969). Discusses a number of traditional ontological problems—among them the idealism-realism and the realism-nominalism issues—within the context of Frege's views.

J. D. B. Walker: *A Study of Frege* (Ithaca, N.Y., 1965). Begins with Frege's notion of a function and its linguistic analogue, the concept, and goes on to Frege's views on grammar and syntax and his general theories of meaning and truth.

RUSSELL

L. W. Aiken: *Bertrand Russell's Philosophy of Morals* (New York, 1963). Holds that Russell began as an intuitionist in ethics, moved on to noncognitivism, and "has come out at last for ethical naturalism."

E. R. Eames: *Bertrand Russell's Theory of Knowledge* (New York, 1969). "When the three central themes of Russell's epistemology, his analytic method, his empiricism, and his realism, are traced out, the continuity of Russell's thought becomes evident."

R. Jager: *The Development of Bertrand Russell's Philosophy* (London, 1972). Argues that Russell's philosophy "grew in a more or less logical way," passing through three phases, realist, atomist, and neutral monist.

E. D. Klemke (ed.): *Essays on Bertrand Russell* (Urbana, Ill., 1970). The essays in this volume cover three main topics: ontology, theories of reference and description, and philosophy of logic and mathematics.

D. F. Pears: *Bertrand Russell and the British Tradition in Philosophy* (New York, 1967). "The truest single thing that can be said about Russell's philosophy is that it stands in the direct line of descent from Hume's." Russell is "the philosopher who gave empiricism an adequate logical framework."

P. A. Schilpp (ed.): *The Philosophy of Bertrand Russell* (Evanston, Ill., 1946). Contains descriptive and critical essays, Russell's reply, an autobiographical sketch, and a bibliography.

THE PHENOMENOLOGICAL TRADITION

J. J. Kockelmans (ed.): *Phenomenology: The Philosophy of Edmund Husserl and Its Interpretation* (Garden City, N.Y., 1967). Includes discussions of Sartre, Heidegger, and Merleau-Ponty, as well as Husserl.

N. Lawrence and D. O'Connor (eds.): *Readings in Existential Phenomenology* (Englewood Cliffs, N.J., 1967). These twenty-two studies show the range of topics in psychology and the social sciences to which phenomenologists have applied their method.

M. Natanson (ed.): *Essays in Phenomenology* (The Hague, 1966). Among these studies are two short pieces by Sartre: "Official Portraits" and "Faces."

H. Speigelberg: *The Phenomenological Movement: A Historical Introduction* (The Hague, 1965). Discusses in detail the views of leading phenomenologists in Germany and France, with briefer accounts of the movement's developments elsewhere. Contains a glossary of phenomenological terms.

P. Thévenaz (trans. with an introduction by J. M. Edie): *What Is Phenomenology?* (Chicago, 1962). Attempts to "situate phenomenology in the history of Western philosophy"; contains essays on Husserl, Heidegger, Sartre, and Merleau-Ponty.

HUSSERL

R. O. Elveton (ed.): *The Phenomenology of Husserl* (Chicago, 1970). Six essays, originally written in German and translated for this volume, "provide a careful documentation of the major turning points in the development of Husserl's phenomenology."

M. Farber: *The Foundations of Phenomenology* (Cambridge, Mass., 1943). Portrays Husserl as "historically conditioned" but also as the "builder of a lasting scientific philosophy."

Q. Lauer: *Phenomenology: Its Genesis and Prospect* (New York, 1958). Examines "in detail the theoretical bases for phenomenology as such, as conceived and elaborated by Husserl."

D. M. Levin: *Reason and Evidence in Husserl's Phenomenology* (Evanston, Ill., 1970). Studies "Husserl's special theory of adequate and apodeictic evidence" in its relation to the rest of his system.

HEIDEGGER

J. J. Kockelmans (ed.): *On Heidegger and Language* (Evanston, Ill., 1972). Most of these papers presuppose readers who "already have a solid insight" into Heidegger's views.

J. L. Perotti: *Heidegger on the Divine* (Athens, Ohio, 1974). A "sympathetic reconstruction" of Heidegger's "thinking about God."

W. J. Richardson: *Heidegger: Through Phenomenology to Thought* (The Hague, 1974). A very long and detailed discussion of the three stages—"early," "reversal," and "later"—the author finds in Heidegger's thought. Includes a letter from Heidegger (1962) denying that any reversal occurred.

J. Sallis (ed.): *Heidegger and the Path of Thinking* (Pittsburgh, 1970). Each essay in this collection "seeks in its own way to come upon the path of thinking by way of an appropriation of Heidegger's work."

L. M. Vail: *Heidegger and Ontological Difference* (University Park, Pa., 1972). Discusses the difference, on Heidegger's view, between Being and beings.

SARTRE

W. Desan: *The Tragic Finale* (New York, 1960). "Concerned with Sartre the philosopher, pure and not-so-simple," and restricted "entirely to his phenomenological ontology as it appears principally in *Being and Nothingness.*"

R. Lafarge: *Jean-Paul Sartre* (Notre Dame, Ind., 1970). Despite "fundamental disagreement" with Sartre's metaphysics, the author attempts to describe his view "with the greatest objectivity."

A. Manser: *Sartre* (London, 1967). Holds that, "in spite of the exaggeration of which he is sometimes guilty, [a] hard core of philosophical argument" runs through all of Sartre's works.

J. H. McMahon: *Human Beings: The World of Jean-Paul Sartre* (Chicago, 1971). Discusses the problem of "living free" in the light of Sartre's literary works as well as his philosophical studies.

I. Murdoch: *Sartre: Romantic Rationalist* (New Haven, 1953). Approaches Sartre's philosophy primarily through the novels; maintains that "he has the style of the age."

J. F. Sheridan: *Sartre: The Radical Conversion* (Athens, Ohio, 1969). Undertakes to refute critics who maintain that "Sartre's later work is sharply inconsistent with his earlier efforts."

WITTGENSTEIN

A. Ambrose and M. Lazerowitz (eds.): *Ludwig Wittgenstein: Philosophy and Language* (London, 1972). The essays in this volume are "serious attempts to elucidate Wittgenstein's thought" on such topics as philosophy of mathematics, abstract entities, logical necessity, private language, psychoanalysis, and ethics.

I. M. Copi and R. W. Beard (eds.): *Essays on Wittgenstein's Tractatus* (New York, 1966). These "often conflicting accounts illuminate from quite different perspectives various difficult and obscure corners of the *Tractatus.*"

K. T. Fann: *Ludwig Wittgenstein: The Man and His Philosophy* (New York, 1967). Includes memoirs of Wittgenstein by friends as well as essays on *Philosophical Investigations.*

R. J. Fogelin: *Wittgenstein,* 2d ed. (London, 1987). Part 1 of this book presents a critical examination of Wittgenstein's *Tractatus.* Part 2 examines the *Philosophical Investigations* together with some topics in Wittgenstein's philosophy of mathematics and philosophy of psychology.

A. Kenny: *Wittgenstein* (Cambridge, Mass., 1973). Concentrates on Wittgenstein's philosophy of language and mind, "emphasizing the continuity of Wittgenstein's thought and tracing its evolution through the recently published and little studied works of his middle years."

D. F. Pears: *Ludwig Wittgenstein* (New York, 1970). "All his philosophy expresses his strong feeling that the great danger to which modern thought is exposed is domination by science, and the consequent distortion of the mind's view of itself."

G. Pitcher: *The Philosophy of Wittgenstein* (Englewood Cliffs, N.J., 1964). The focus of this book is about equally divided between the *Tractatus* and the *Investigations,* which are held to differ in fundamental ways.

D. Pole: *The Later Wittgenstein* (London, 1958). A short, well-balanced study.

E. Stenius: *Wittgenstein's Tractatus* (Oxford, 1960). A very useful, and very detailed, exposition of the main arguments of the *Tractatus,* with an interesting concluding chapter on Wittgenstein "as a Kantian philosopher."

ORDINARY-LANGUAGE PHILOSOPHY

E. Gellner: *Words and Things: An Examination of, and Attack on, Linguistic Philosophy* (London, 1959, revised 1968 and 1979). A lively and controversial attack on both Wittgenstein's later philosophy and the philosophy of ordinary language.

A. P. Martinich: *The Philosophy of Language,* 3d ed. (New York, 1995). This anthology contains many of the essays discussed in this chapter. It also contains brief, but useful, introductions to these essays.

G. Warnock: *J. L. Austin* (London, 1989). A sympathetic account of Austin's philosophy, written by a philosopher who worked closely with him.

QUINE

R. Gibson: *The Philosophy of W. V. Quine* (Tampa, 1982). A general discussion of Quine's philosophy, emphasizing Quine's strong commitment to naturalism.

C. Hookway: *Quine: Language, Experience, and Reality* (Cambridge, England, 1988). Another general discussion of Quine's position, particularly good in explaining the development of Quine's views in relation to logical empiricism.

W. V. Quine: *Pursuit of Truth,* rev. ed. (Cambridge, Mass., 1992). In this work Quine presents an elegant, clear, and short account of the main features of his own position. Except for some brief discussions toward the end of the book, this work is accessible to readers unfamiliar with formal logic.

DERRIDA

S. Cavell: *Philosophical Passages: Wittgenstein, Emerson, Austin, Derrida* (Oxford, 1995).

N. Garver: *Derrida and Wittgenstein* (Philadelphia, 1994.) Both books compare Derrida's philosophy with the writings of other philosophers examined in this volume.

Glossary

Short, dictionary-type definitions of philosophical terms are likely to be misleading, for philosophers use terms in many different ways and with little regard to common usage (on which, of course, dictionary definitions are based). Accordingly, many of the definitions given in this Glossary are accompanied by references to places in the text where the terms in question appear in a concrete context. For terms not defined in the Glossary, consult the Index; for fuller treatment of the terms defined here and of other philosophical terms, see *The Encyclopedia of Philosophy,* edited by P. Edwards (Free Press, New York, 1973). Also available are the *Dictionary of Philosophy,* edited by D. D. Runes (Littlefield, New York, 1960), and *Dictionary of Philosophy and Psychology,* edited by J. M. Baldwin (Macmillan, New York, 1925).

Absolute: A term used, in connection with the degrees-of-truth doctrine, to designate the most real thing of all. Also used, in connection with the doctrine that all finite things are parts of one infinite thing, to designate this all-inclusive whole. Hence that which is unconditioned and free from any limitations or qualifications.

Abstraction: The power of separating, in thought, one part of a complex from the other parts and attending to it separately. Thus to consider the color of an apple in isolation from the apple's other qualities would be to abstract this quality for attention.

Analysis: A variously used term. For Moore's use of "analysis," see pp. 95–105.

A priori: What is known independently of sense perception and for this reason held to be indubitable.

Attribute: See **Substance.**

Axiom: A proposition held to be self-evidently true and so neither requiring nor indeed capable of proof. Hence a first principle from which all proofs start. Those who deny the self-evident truth of axioms hold them to be simply postulates from which such and such theorems can be deduced. Thus, according to this view, the axioms of one deductive system may be deduced from another set of postulates in some other deductive system.

Category: Any very general, fundamental concept used for interpreting experience. See, for instance, Whitehead's "categorial scheme" (p. 79, n. 23).

Conceptualism: The view that universals are neither independently existing entities nor mere names, but are concepts formed in the mind. See **Nominalism, Realism,** and **Universal.**

Constructivism: The view that what we experience is not a world wholly independent of ourselves, but one to which the activity of mind contributes certain features. For a discussion of the nineteenth-century background, see pp. 8–14.

Contingent: That which may be and also may not be. Hence an event whose occurrence is not necessarily determined (see **Determinism**) by other events.

Conversational implicature: An expression introduced by Paul Grice in order to draw a distinction between what a sentence logically implies and what the utterance or use of a sentence suggests or indicates. For example, the proposition "There is a dog on the roof" logically implies that there is something on the roof. In contrast, if someone says "There is a dog on the roof," this conversationally implies—though does not logically imply—that the person believes this, has good reason for doing so, etc. Grice held that a great many philosophical errors have arisen from confusing logical and conversational implications. (See pp. 473–76.)

Cosmology: The study of the universal world process. Distinguished from ontology (see definition) chiefly in that, whereas the latter asks what reality *is*, cosmology asks how reality unfolds and develops in successive stages.

Deduction: A type of inference (see definition) that yields necessary conclusions. In deduction, one or more propositions (called "premises") being assumed, another proposition (the conclusion) is seen to be entailed or implied. It is usually held that in deduction the movement of thought is from premises of greater generality to a conclusion of lesser generality (from the premises "All men are mortal" and "All Greeks are men," we deduce that "All Greeks are mortal"), but the chief mark of deduction is the necessity with which the conclusion follows from the premises.

Determinism: The theory that denies contingency (see **Contingent**) and claims that everything that happens happens necessarily and in accordance with some regular pattern or law.

Discursive: The characteristic of human intelligence that limits it, in the main, to a step-by-step reasoning—from premises to conclusion, from this conclusion to another, and so on. Hence to be contrasted with the all-inclusive vision of the mystic, with the possible operation of a suprahuman intellect, and with the way in which, according to some writers, axioms (see **Axiom**) and other self-evident principles are comprehended by the mind.

Dualism: Any view that holds two ultimate and irreducible principles to be necessary to explain the world—as, for instance, mind and matter.

Empiricism: The view that holds sense perception to be the sole source of human knowledge.

Epistemology: From the Greek terms *episteme* (knowledge) and *logos* (theory, account). Hence the study of the origins, nature, and limitations of knowledge.

Essence: The that-about-a-thing-that-makes-it-what-it-is, in contrast to those properties that the thing may happen to possess but need not possess in order to be itself. Thus it is held (1) that we have to distinguish between those properties of Socrates that are "accidental" and so nonessential (for example, dying by hemlock) and those properties that are essential (for example, those traits of character and personality that made him the man he was). Further, it is held (2) that we have to distinguish between essence and existence (see definition): it is possible according to this view to define Socrates' essence exhaustively; yet when we have done so, the question still remains whether any such being exists. Holders of this view would maintain that there is only one object in which essence and existence are inseparable; this object is God. According to Dewey, we call "essential" whatever properties happen to interest us; hence the essence of anything varies in different contexts (see pp. 48–49). For Husserl's defense of essences, see pp. 292–303.

Existence: Actuality or factuality. Contrasted with essence (see definition). For Sartre's assertion of the primacy of existence over essence, see pp. 382–83. For Heidegger's view of existence, see pp. 319–31.

Experiment: A situation arranged to test a hypothesis. Contrasted with "mere" observation.

Extensionality vs. intensionality: (Note spelling). A context is extensional (or transparent) if expressions having the same reference can be substituted for one another without altering the reference (or the truth-value) of the total expression. A context is intensional (or opaque) if it is not extensional. For example, since "Cicero" and "Tully" name the same Roman citizen, and since it is true that Cicero spoke Greek, then it is also true that Tully spoke Greek. This shows that the context "X spoke Greek" is extensional. In contrast, someone might believe that Cicero spoke Greek but not believe that Tully spoke Greek because she does not believe that Cicero and Tully are the same person. This shows that the context "A believes that X spoke Greek" is intensional (or opaque). Sentences attributing propositional attitudes to people are a rich source of intensional context (see **propositional attitudes**). (See pp. 502–04.)

Free will: The doctrine of contingency (see **Contingent**) applied specifically to human behavior; the denial that our acts are completely determined (see **Determinism**). The question of free will is important because many philosophers hold that "ought" implies "can"—that moral judgments of approbation and disapprobation are meaningless unless the acts judged are free, that is, under the control of the agent, who, had he or she so chosen, might have done otherwise. The main problems connected with free will are (1) what meaning, if any, can be attached to the notion of a free choice and (2) how the possibility of being otherwise is compatible with either (a) belief in an omnipotent and omniscient Deity or (b) the doctrine of universal causal determinism. For Sartre's assertion of human beings' radical and total freedom, see pp. 376–78.

Hedonism: The view that pleasure is the good. *Ethical hedonism* holds either (1) that an individual's own pleasure is the sole end worth aiming at or (2) that other people's pleasure is to be taken into account. *Psychological hedonism* holds that, whatever one ought to aim at, one does in fact aim at pleasure.

Holism: A feature is holistic if a thing cannot possess it without participating in some larger whole or totality. To cite an obvious example, a person cannot be a team member without participating in a team. Philosophical holism emerges when a philosophically interesting characteristic is described as holistic. Quine, for example, held that no sentence is meaningful in isolation, and that it becomes meaningful only through its relationships with other sentences. Traditional defenders of a coherence theory of truth maintain a similar theory with respect to truth, namely, that the truth of a particular belief depends on its relationships to the total system of mutually supporting beliefs. (See pp. 495–96.)

Humanism: A variously used term. Employed (1) to describe the type of view that distinguishes human beings from animals on the ground that the former have certain moral obligations. Also used (2) to contrast a secular type of ethics with a religious ethics. Thus Plato's and Aristotle's ethics could be called "humanistic," in contrast with the ethics of Augustine, on the ground that they hold humans themselves, rather than God, to be the supreme value. Also used (3) to designate a particular historical movement, beginning in the fourteenth century, that emphasized the study of classical literature and the revival of classical ideals.

Idealism: In general, any view that holds reality to be mental or "spiritual" or mind-dependent. *Subjective idealism* emphasizes the ultimate reality of the knowing subject and may either admit the existence of a plurality of such subjects or deny the existence of all save one (in which case the view is called solipsism). *Objective idealism* denies that the distinction between subject and object, between knower and known, is ultimate and maintains that all finite knowers and their thoughts are included in an Absolute Thought. Twentieth-century philosophy is in many ways a series of reactions against Objective Idealism. (See **Constructivism** and, especially, pp. 8–14.)

Induction: A type of inference (see definition) in which (in contrast to deduction [see definition]) the movement of thought is from lesser to greater generality. Thus induction begins, not from premises, but from observed particulars (for example, the observation that A, B, and C all have the property x) and seeks to establish some generalization about them (for example, that all members of the class y, of which A, B, and C are members, have the property x). The main problem connected with induction is the difficulty of determining the conditions under which we are warranted in moving from an observed "some so-and-so's have such and such" to the unobserved "All so-and-so's probably have such and such."

Inference: The movement of thought by which we reach a conclusion from premises. Thus we speak of inductive and of deductive inference.

Intuition: Direct and immediate knowledge. To be contrasted with discursive (see definition) knowledge.

Judgment: The movement of thought by which, for example, we assert (or deny) some predicate of a subject, or, more generally, by which we connect two terms by some relation. Thus when we say "This rose is red" or "New York is east of Chicago," we judge. Following Kant, most philosophers distinguish between (1) *analytical judgments,* in which the predicate concept is contained in the subject concept, and (2) *synthetical judgments,* in which the predicate concept is not so contained; and also between (3) *a priori judgments,* which are universal and necessary, and (4) *a posteriori judgments,* which are not universal and necessary.

Materialism: The doctrine that reality is matter. Whereas idealism (see definition) holds that matter is "really" the thought of some mind or other, materialism holds that minds and all other apparently nonmaterial things are reducible to the complex motions of material particles.

Metaphysics: The study of the ultimate nature of reality, or, as some philosophers would say, the study of "being as such." To be contrasted, therefore, with physics, which studies the "being" of physical nature; with astronomy, which studies the "being" of the solar system; with biology, which studies the "being" of animate nature; and so on. By "being as such," these philosophers mean, not the special characteristics of special kinds of things (for example, living things), but the most general and pervasive characteristics of all things. For some criticisms of metaphysics using a variety of strategies against it, see pp. 44–47, 265–67, and 415–20.

Modal logic: Originally a discipline that studied the logical properties of sentences of the form "It is necessary that p" and "It is possible that p." Expressions such as "It is necessary that" and "It is possible that" are called modal operators. Techniques developed for these operators were later applied to a wide range of other operators, including epistemic operators ("It is known that") and deontic operators ("It ought to be that").

Mysticism: The view that reality is ineffable and transcendent; that it is known, therefore, by some special, nonrational means; that knowledge of it is incommunicable in any precise conceptual scheme; and that it is communicable, if at all, only in poetic imagery and metaphor. For Wittgenstein on "the mystical," see pp. 236–37; for Heidegger on "silence," see pp. 354–57.

Naturalism: A variously used term. (1) In one meaning, naturalism is a view that excludes any reference to supernatural principles and holds the world to be explicable in terms of scientifically verifiable concepts. In this meaning, naturalism is roughly equivalent to secularism and, like humanism (see definition), can be contrasted with a religiously oriented view like Kierkegaard's. (2) In another meaning, the emphasis is on the unity of behavior; any difference in kind between human beings and animals is denied, and human conduct and human institutions are held to be simply more complex instances of behavior patterns occurring among lower organisms. It was naturalism in this sense that Husserl and Heidegger criticized (see pp. 342–45 and 281–86).

Nominalism: The view that only particulars are real and that universals (see **Universal**) are but observable likenesses among the particulars of sense experience.

Nondemonstrative inference: See **Induction**.

Objective: To say that anything is "objective" is to say that it is real, that it has a public nature independent of us and of our judgments about it. Thus the question of whether or not values are objective turns on whether or not values are more than private preferences. If they are private preferences, our value judgments are subjective, and there is no more disputing about them than there is about judgments of taste: my good is what *I* prefer; yours is what *you* prefer. On the other hand, if values are objective, it follows that when we differ about them, at least one of us is mistaken.

Ontological argument: An argument for the existence of God, first formulated by St. Anselm. According to this argument, since perfection implies existence, God necessarily exists.

Ontology: From the Greek term *ontos* (being) and *logos* (theory, account). For many philosophers ontology is equivalent to metaphysics (see definition). For instance, to inquire about the "ontological status" of something, say, perception, is to ask whether the objects of perception are real or illusory, and, if real, what sort of reality they possess (for example, whether they are mind-dependent or whether they exist independently of minds), and so on. For the phenomenologists (see **Phenomenology**), however, ontology is the science of being as it is revealed in phenomenological observation, in contrast to metaphysics, which is concerned with things-in-themselves (see pp. 310–11 and 342–45).

Performative utterance: An expression introduced by J. L. Austin to refer to utterances that, in a certain sense, *do* something rather than merely *describe* something. For example, in a normal setting, in saying "I promise to meet you tomorrow" I perform the act of promising. Saying this constitutes the promising and does not simply describe it.

Phenomenalism: A type of view that, like idealism (see definition), holds that what we know is mind-dependent, but unlike idealism, holds that reality itself is not mind-dependent. Hence Kant's view that we do not know reality (that is, things-in-themselves) and that our knowledge is limited to the data of inner and outer sense (that is, the sensuous manifold organized by the categories and the forms of sensibility) is a type of phenomenalism.

Phenomenology: The name Husserl gave to his philosophical theory, which is characterized by a method of "bracketing" as a result of which the intentional acts and intentional objects within experience are brought into view (see pp. 458–68). Not to be confused with the much broader and looser term "phenomenalism" (see definition).

Physicalism: A modern descendent of materialism. It holds that physics describes the most basic underlying structure of the universe. Since modern physics has established an equivalence between matter and energy, the older term "materialism" now seems out of date and therefore has largely been abandoned.

Positivism: A term first introduced by Comte to describe his account of the nature of knowledge. Also used, more broadly, to characterize any view that rules out the possibility of metaphysical knowledge and that limits a priori truths to analytical statements. *Logical Positivism* (see Chapter 7), a movement derived from positivism in this broad sense, was chiefly characterized by its assertion of the Verifiability Principle (see definition).

Primary qualities: Those qualities thought to belong to bodies. To be distinguished from secondary qualities, which are held to be products of the interaction between our sense organs and the primary qualities of bodies.

Propositional attitude: A sentence expressing a propositional attitude indicates that a person stands in a mental relationship to the content of some proposition. For example, Columbus believed that the earth was round, hoped that the earth was round, wondered whether the earth was round, and so on. In each case, Columbus is said to stand in a specific mental relationship to the proposition that the earth is round. Though there has been a great deal of discussion of constructions expressing propositional attitudes, no consensus has emerged concerning how they should be understood.

Rationalism: (1) As contrasted with empiricism (see definition), rationalism means reliance on reason (that is, on deduction, on the criterion of logical consistency). (2) As contrasted with authoritarianism or mysticism (see definition), rationalism means reliance on our human powers.

Realism: (1) As contrasted with nominalism (see definition), realism holds that universals are real, and more real than the particulars of sense experience. (2) As contrasted with idealism (see definition), realism holds that the objects of our knowledge are not mind-dependent but are independently existing entities. (For Realism in this sense, see especially the discussion of Moore, Chapter 3). (3) As contrasted with Idealism in still another sense, realism is the point of view that interests itself in people and institutions as they are, rather than as they ought to be. In this sense, realism is almost equivalent to naturalism (see definition).

Relativism: The view that maintains our judgments to be relative to (that is, conditioned upon) certain factors such as cultural milieu or individual bias. Hence the view that we do not possess any absolute, objective (see definition) truth. The relativist need not hold that all judgments are relative; it is possible, for instance, to hold that the physical sciences yield absolute truth while maintaining that in other fields (for example, ethics and religion) there is no absolute truth.

Skepticism: The position that denies the possibility of knowledge. Here, as with relativism (see definition), it is possible either to have a total skepticism or to limit one's skepticism to certain fields.

Subjectivism: See **Constructivism, Objective, Relativism,** and **Skepticism.**

Substance: A variously used term. (1) In one meaning, substance is simply that which is real. Thus, because Aristotle held reality to consist of amalgams of matter and form, he called each such amalgam a "substance." (2) In another meaning, substance is about equivalent to essence (see definition). Also (3) substance is contrasted with attribute (or property, or quality) as that which *has* the attributes. Thus substance is the underlying (and unknown) ground in which properties are thought to inhere; it is that about which we are judging when we assert properties of a subject, for example, when we say, "The rose is red." Hence (4) substance is that which, unlike an attribute or property, exists in its own right and depends on nothing else.

Teleology: From the Greek terms *telos* (end, goal) and *logos* (theory, account). Hence the view that affirms the reality of purpose and holds the universe either to be consciously designed (as with the Christian doctrine of a providential God) or (as with Aristotle) to be the working out of partly conscious, partly unconscious purposes that are immanent in the developing organisms.

Universal: A universal is that which is predicable of many. Thus "man" is a universal because it is predicable of Washington, Jefferson, Hamilton, and all other individual men. The main problem about universals concerns their ontological status (see **Ontology**). Are they (1) separate entities distinct from the individuals of which they are predicable, (2) real but not separable, or (3) not real at all, but merely the names of likenesses shared by certain particulars? See **Nominalism** and **Realism.** For Wittgenstein's "dissolution" of the problem of universals, see pp. 401–04.

Verifiability principle: According to this principle, the meaning of a statement is the method of its verification. A statement that cannot be verified (for example, "God exists") is without cognitive meaning (see pp. 240–42 and 267–71).

Voluntarism: The theory that asserts the primacy of will over intellect as an explanatory principle of human behavior, of God's nature, and of the universe as a whole. For Sartre's version of voluntarism, see pp. 382–86.

Credits

Index

This is principally an index of proper names. Thus titles and principal topics of discussion are indexed under the authors. Topics that recur in the works of several philosophers are also indexed as main entries. Page numbers in *italics* refer to quotations; those in **boldface** refer to major discussions.